THREE BOOKS
IN ONE VOLUME

BEGINNING
OF THE END

FINAL DAWN
OVER JERUSALEM

DAY OF
DECEPTION

JOHN HAGEE

THOMAS NELSON PUBLISHERS®
Nashville

Published in Nashville, Tennessee, by Thomas Nelson, Inc.

The individual books in this omnibus edition were originally published by Thomas Nelson, Inc. as follows: *Beginning of the End,* Copyright © 1996 by John C. Hagee; *Day of Deception,* Copyright © 1997 by John C. Hagee; *Final Dawn Over Jerusalem,* Copyright © 1998 by John C. Hagee.

Unless otherwise noted, Scripture quotations are from THE NEW KING JAMES VERSION. Copyright © 1979, 1980, 1982, Thomas Nelson, Inc., Publishers.

Scripture quotations noted NASB are from the NEW AMERICAN STANDARD BIBLE®. © Copyright The Lockman Foundation 1960, 1962, 1963, 1968, 1971, 1972, 1973, 1975, 1977, 1995. Used by permission. (www.Lockman.org)

Scripture quotations noted NIV are taken from the HOLY BIBLE: NEW INTERNATIONAL VERSION®. Copyright © 1973, 1978, 1984 by International Bible Society. Used by permission of Zondervan Publishing House. All rights reserved.

Scripture quotations noted KJV are from THE KING JAMES VERSION of the Bible.

Library of Congress Control Number: 00-132917

ISBN 0-7852-6761-1

Printed in the United States of America

1 2 3 4 5 6 BVG 05 04 03 02 01 00

BEGINNING OF THE
END

The Assassination of
Yitzhak Rabin and the
Coming Antichrist

JOHN HAGEE

THOMAS NELSON PUBLISHERS®
Nashville

TO MY MOTHER AND FATHER,

Reverend Bythel Hagee and Vada Swick Hagee,
whose love of God's Word
has been the guiding force in my life.

Contents

Introduction

For hundreds and even thousands of years, Christians and Jews have been looking for their Messiah. To the Jewish people, the Messiah has yet to come. To Christians, He has already come and will come again.

I am writing this book because I want you to know that the coming of the Messiah is not a theory for scholars to debate. It is not a fable for the sophisticated to ignore. It is not a factoid for the fastidious to file. It is not a riddle for the obsessive to solve. It is instead the most important truth of our age—not merely to understand but to anticipate, embrace, and live out.

I believe this not only because of my unshakable confidence in what the Bible says about the future, but also because the events of these last months draw me inexorably to the conclusion that the Messiah is coming very soon. And no other event in recent history underscores this more than the assassination of one of the greatest men of our age—Yitzhak Rabin.

I'm writing this book to help you see how the events of recent days fit into God's accelerating prophetic timetable for the world, Israel, and you. But I want you to do more than just see the outline—I want you to grasp the outcome. I want this book to be a wake-up call to you that the prophesied events are fast approaching and will affect you!

With every tick of the clock, the prophecies of the Word of God come closer and closer to fruition. This is not just an intriguing coincidence—it is an irrefutable demonstration that God is in complete control over all of human history. God's will is going to be accomplished. His victory is going to be complete. As you're reading this book, I want you to ask yourself whether the God who controls history controls you? Have you yielded fully to His sovereignty? Or are you a speed bump God will roll over as He brings His Word to pass?

I'm also writing this book to help you understand that tomorrow might not be like today. This evening might not be like this morning. The next hour might not be like this hour. There is absolutely no guarantee that tomorrow will be like today, and I hope this book will make that fact very clear. There is a tomorrow that will usher in events that will completely change this planet and that will radically change your life and your future. This is not the time to put off doing what you know to be right. This is not the time to procrastinate. This is not the time for complacency. This is not the time to be lukewarm. This *is* the time to realize that one day time will be no more and the choices you have made in life will be irrevocably ratified for all eternity.

I'm writing this book with three distinct audiences in mind:

- *For Jews:* I am writing as a friend to set before you what God's Word says about the momentous choices Israel and the Jewish people face as you cope with the assassination of Yitzhak Rabin and the prospect and price of peace in the Middle East. I want to show you God's future for Israel and Jerusalem. And I want to share with you what the Word of God says about Messiah's past and His future.

- *For Christians:* I am writing to increase your confidence in God and His Word. What He has predicted will come to pass, and it is happening right before our very eyes. I am writing to bolster your courage—God not only provides, He protects: as we do His work, and from the wrath to come. Now more than ever we need to be strong and courageous—to attempt great things for God and to expect great things from God. The time is short.

- *For those who have missed the Rapture:* I am writing to the one who finds this book in the future time of Tribulation. You may be confused and terrified by the momentous events you are experiencing. You may be in hiding. Like so many other books, this book may be contraband. You may feel alone. You may be hungry, thirsty, homeless, and desperately ill. You may ache inside from grieving over the horrific human slaughter—not only in the world as a whole but also among *your* family and *your* friends. You may be tempted to believe the explanation for these events offered by the world leader—explanations that everyone around you seems to believe. Know this: the Word of God has predicted all of these events for centuries. And just as what you're now experiencing was foretold long ago, the Word of God also predicts that all enemies of the Messiah will be conclusively and completely destroyed soon. Read this book and you'll meet the real Messiah. Take heed to this book, then lift up your heads—your redemption draws near.

CHAPTER ONE

The Assassination

Yigal Amir, a young Jewish student who studied law and computers at Tel Aviv's Bar Ilan University, dressed himself carefully. Before leaving his room, he paused for a long moment to stare at his face in the mirror.

The date was Saturday, November 4, 1995—the night Israeli Prime Minister Yitzhak Rabin would attend a peace rally in Tel Aviv.

The large, soulful brown eyes blinked slowly. Twice before, at the Yad Vashem Holocaust Memorial, he had been close to the prime minister, but security had been too tight. The gun had stayed in his pocket, out of sight. But it was ever-ready, loaded with dumdum bullets specially made by Yigal's brother, Hagai. Hagai had hollowed out the noses of the nine-millimeter bullets, making them more lethal. It would only take one . . . when the time came. When the time was right.

He studied his reflection: his mother's eyes, a soft, curling beard like his father's.

Tonight, if God was good, an opportunity would show itself. No longer would Rabin be able to transfer Israeli lands to Palestinians. The damage he'd done in the West Bank and Gaza Strip was enough. Israel had a divine right to the land, and to give it away was an act of treason against Israel and an abomination to God.

Yigal gave his reflection a slow smile, then pulled his jacket over the T-shirt he was wearing and walked out into the street.

Two hours later, he walked through the crowd toward the prime minister's car. He exchanged pleasantries with a policeman who did not seem in the least suspicious. The security men were looking for Arab assassins; they did not appear to care about the knot of young Jewish men who huddled near the armored vehicle.

Amir loitered near the car, once even exchanging a quick smile with a bodyguard who must have taken him for a driver.

He ducked behind a large potted plant and pulled the gun from his pocket. Cold. Heavy in his hand. A good weapon for the defense of Israel and the will of God.

The crowd stirred, and Rabin walked toward Amir, his head bobbing as he spoke with a man to his left.

Yigal stretched out his arm and squeezed the trigger of the 9mm Beretta. Point blank range. Someone was shouting, "It's nothing! It's nothing!" and Yigal was amazed to realize the voice was his own.

Rabin and a wounded bodyguard collapsed into the car as strong hands seized Yigal's shoulders and arms. Someone wrenched the gun from his hands; other hands forced him to the ground, where he felt the asphalt against his cheek.

Screams. Shouts. Exhilaration.

"I acted alone on God's orders, and I have no regrets," he whispered, his breath stirring the dirt on the road. He whispered the line again, practicing. Soon he would tell the world why. For now, he was content to let the world discover what he'd done.

Yitzhak Rabin, the Warrior Statesman

The world reeled in shock and grief when the hand of hatred assassinated Prime Minister Rabin of Israel. It was not a kaffiyeh-wearing Arab terrorist who had committed this heinous crime. It was another Jew.

Yitzhak Rabin was a warrior statesman whose masterful organization of the Israeli Defense Forces in 1967 led to the absolute demolition of the enemies of Israel. He was an old soldier who could be very tough with the Palestinians; they knew he was a man of action.

Yet he was equally a man of peace. He was not a dreamy-eyed idealist reaching for the impossible peace accord between ancient enemies. He was a veteran statesman with nerves of steel, pursuing the treasure of peace so coveted by Israel.

The world mourned his passing. World leaders gathered around his coffin at Jerusalem's Mount Herzl cemetery.

Egypt's President Hosni Mubarak and King Hussein of Jordan paid tribute to the man who had led Israel against them in 1967.

Bill Clinton, George Bush, and Jimmy Carter were among those representing the United States; British Prime Minister John Major, German Chancellor Helmut Kohl, and French President Jacques Chirac also attended.

Representatives of six Arab states and the Palestinian Authority attended the funeral, most of whom were visiting the homeland of their ancient enemies for the first time. Reuters NewMedia reported, "The presence of officials from so many Arab states, and from Israel's former arch-enemy, the Palestine Liberation Organization, would have been unthinkable just three years ago when Rabin took office."[1]

Yasser Arafat, chairman of the Palestine Liberation Organization, watched the funeral on television and later visited Rabin's widow and offered his condolences. "I am hoping God will help us to continue our very difficult march and the peace process," he said.

Acting Israeli Prime Minister Shimon Peres said, "We are determined to continue the peace process."

And Leah Rabin, the assassinated leader's widow, told a crowd outside her home, "I think the cold-blooded murder of this man, who made such a gigantic contribution to the peace process, will shock many people and perhaps . . . be a turning point in the public conscience."[2] I believe her words will prove to be prophetic.

But the speaker who tugged on the world's heartstrings was Noa Ben-Artzi Philosof, Rabin's eighteen-year-old granddaughter. Choking back tears, she stood before a sea of television cameras and quietly asked the angels to protect him. "Great men have already eulogized you but no one has felt, like I have, the caress of your warm and soft hands, or your warm embrace which was reserved for us alone and your half-smile which always told me so much. That same smile is no more and froze with you," she said. "We love you, grandfather, forever."[3] The world listened and wept.

After returning from Rabin's funeral, Southern Baptist Convention President Jim Henry said, "This [assassination] will galvanize [world leaders] for the immediate future to press on with it. [Rabin's] death made people realize, in a sense, what peace costs. And they want to move on with it; they want to get something done. He was the cement, the glue in the process, and how that plays out in the long run will be interesting."[4]

Interesting? Very—I believe the instant that Yigal Amir pulled the trigger will stand as a defining moment in world history.

Memories of Rabin

I met Prime Minister Rabin on a number of occasions— when he was the prime minister and when he was not. Typically, most people who met him first noticed a certain shyness about him, but after several minutes of conversation his warmth and brilliance would reveal themselves.

Our first meeting was the most memorable. My wife, Diana, and I were at the Westin Hotel in Houston where Israel Bonds, a Jewish fund-raising group, was hosting a dinner intended to raise money for the state of Israel.

Cornerstone Church in San Antonio, where I serve as pastor, has been producing an event called "The Night to Honor Israel" since 1981, so we were invited to the Israel Bonds dinner, which was attended by the who's who of Houston's Jewish community.

Diana and I were thrilled to be part of the evening, so we flew from San Antonio to Houston and took a taxi to the Westin Hotel. We were early. Outside the banquet hall, Yitzhak Rabin was standing near the door with representatives of the Israel Bonds.

I was formally introduced to the future prime minister by Bob Abrams, the director of Israel Bonds. I extended my hand, and Rabin shook it warmly and asked me, "What is 'The Night to Honor Israel'?"

"It is an event inspired while I was praying at the Western Wall in Jerusalem in the spring of 1978," I answered. "It was my first time in Israel, and I felt a very special presence in the city of Jerusalem. Somehow, I felt Jerusalem was my spiritual home."

Rabin listened thoughtfully, so I went on. "As I prayed at the Wall, a Jewish man dressed in his prayer shawl and yarmulke was praying next to me, bowing and kissing his prayer book. As I watched him pray, I realized I knew very little about my Jewish roots as a Christian. From that moment I have felt divinely inspired to bring Christians and Jews together in a public arena to celebrate the things we have in common, to honor the nation of Israel, and to combat anti-Semitism."

Rabin cocked his head sideways, looked me straight in the eye for at least ten seconds without saying a word. *Is he going to answer me?* I wondered.

Finally he gave me that world famous half-smile and said, "That's good. Thank you, Pastor, for your help."

Diana and I entered the magnificent banquet hall and located our table. I have been to legions of banquets, but this was one of the most lavish I have ever attended. A two-tiered dais with about thirty people on each tier was situated at the front of the room: the movers and shakers of Houston.

My wife and I were the only Gentiles present.

After a kosher meal and delightful conversation, Yitzhak Rabin was introduced, and the statesman gave an update on conditions in Israel and the state of the American-Israeli relationship. He spoke very slowly in a deep, stentorian voice that captivated the audience. His analysis of world conditions was brilliant, and his points were well-reasoned.

After Rabin's speech, Billy Goldberg, chairman of the event, took the microphone. Billy is a bottom-line, cut-to-the-chase kind of guy. He announced that to save time, every table should select a spokesperson to announce the gifts to Israel Bonds that each individual would make.

At that moment I felt perspiration forming on my brow.

Then Billy Goldberg took my breath away by declaring that he was going to give $250,000. He pointed to one of his associates and said, "And he's going to give $250,000."

Thank you, God, that Billy doesn't know me!

Every person on the dais made their pledges—huge, unbelievable sums. Then the attention turned to the people on the main floor of the banquet hall. The smallest pledge made at the first two tables was $25,000—offered by a little Jewish lady, clutching her purse tightly.

Diana leaned over and whispered, "John, I think she has the money in her purse!"

I looked back at her and asked one of the most stupid questions of my adult life: "Did you bring the checkbook?"

She looked at me and laughed out loud. When she had regained her composure, she whispered, "What difference does that make?" she answered, smiling. "You can have every check in the book, but there's nothing in the bank." At that point our church was much smaller and our finances were tighter than the bark on a tree.

Panic time. We were at the third table and it was time to declare what we would give. I was looking around, thinking I could fake a heart attack and have Diana carry me out.

I told Diana we would find one thousand dollars somewhere, even if we had to go to the bank and borrow it. Meekly and in the most muffled voice I could manage, I told the captain of our table that Diana and I would be giving one thousand dollars.

He blinked, then said, "Would you mind repeating that?" And so, my face burning, I said it again: "A thousand dollars." It felt like so little; I wanted the floor to open up and just swallow me whole.

I was totally unprepared for what happened next. The captain of our table announced with thunderous delight to the entire banquet hall: "Reverend and Mrs. Hagee will be giving one thousand dollars."

The next moment was an eternity. Dead silence filled the banquet hall. I wanted to disappear, not knowing what they were thinking of us, but imagining all sorts of things . . . all of them negative.

At that moment Yitzhak Rabin's face shifted into a half-smile, and he began to clap, slowly, methodically, rhythmically. Startled, I looked up at him, then the entire room exploded into applause. The other guests rose to their feet, still clapping, and I grabbed Diana's hand and looked at the floor, my face as red as a ruby. A standing ovation for one thousand dollars?

What I had imagined as a small gift was appreciated in Rabin's eyes. Gratitude poured from my heart because he approved of two Gentiles who didn't have a lot to give but who were concerned for Israel.

I was never more embarrassed in all my life and never received more recognition for giving a thousand dollars. But I'll always be grateful to Yitzhak Rabin for a memory of warmth and kindness that I'll treasure for life.

Peace at Any Price

The shot that killed Yitzhak Rabin launched Bible prophecy onto the fast track. Why?

In order to understand the reasons behind the assassination, we must first understand Israel's recent history. Listen to Rabbi Eliezer Waldman as he explains how and why many Israelis were frustrated with the Declaration of Principles (also called the Oslo Accords) signed by Israel and the PLO at the White House in 1993: "Our government went behind the back of the people to meet secretly, against the law, with the PLO," he says. "It pushed through legislation which made profound and dangerous changes in Israeli policy, changes which clearly affected the security of the nation. With the barest majority of the government, and, very possibly, against the majority of the people, it agreed to give away vital parts of our homeland. And, what is most painful, they agreed to compromise on Jerusalem. It closed all avenues of protest and even excessively punished those who voiced opposition to such changes."[5]

Rabin's assassination came at a time when public opinion of the peace process in Israel was lukewarm at best. The 1995 Interim Agreement with the PLO stipulated that Israeli troops would withdraw from six major towns in the West Bank, turning them over to Palestinian self-rule after twenty-eight years of occupation. Early surveys showed that public opinion of the Oslo Accords was evenly divided between approval and disapproval, but a Dahaf poll released the week after Rabin's murder indicated that an astounding 74 percent of Israelis believed the government should continue implementing the Palestinian self-rule accord. And, while fall 1995 polls showed Labor leader Rabin trailing his rival, opposition Likud leader Binyamin Netanyahu, the Dahaf survey showed 54 percent would vote for Peres and the Labor party if the election were held then, and only 23 percent for Netanyahu.[6]

The bullets from Yigal Amir's gun shed the blood of a Nobel Peace Prize winner, who was proclaimed a martyr for peace within minutes of his death. His blood will now become the bonding force that will drive the nation of Israel and other leaders of the Middle East to new heights of unity to secure a legacy of peace for Yitzhak Rabin.

"There is nothing else that we can do . . . but to continue a great road paved by a great leader," acting Prime Minister Shimon Peres told reporters after an emergency cabinet meeting within hours of the assassination. "I asked myself if this happened to me, what would I want to happen later," Peres said. "I have one answer—to continue the path of peace."[7]

Jordan's King Hussein, who in 1994 ended forty-six years of hostility with Israel, stood at Rabin's funeral and proclaimed that he hoped to leave behind a legacy of peace when he died. "Standing here, I commit before you," he said, "before my people in Jordan, and before the world, to continue to do our utmost to ensure that we leave a similar legacy. When my time comes, I hope it will be like my grandfather's and like Yitzhak Rabin's."[8]

United States President Bill Clinton urged the Middle Eastern countries toward peace. "Your prime minister was a martyr for peace," he said. "Surely we must learn from his martyrdom. . . . Now it falls to all of us who love peace and all of us who loved him to carry on the struggle to which he gave life and for which he gave his life."[9]

In November 1994, I was touring Israel with three hundred American Zionists, a mixture of Jews and Gentiles who support Israel. After a long day of seeing the historical sites, I had gone to my hotel room. I was tired and nearly asleep, but I was brought wide awake by an unexpected knock at my door.

I looked through the peephole in the door and recognized a friend of mine who was an orthodox rabbi. He had three strangers with him, two men and a woman, but I trusted him. So I put on my robe, opened the door, and let them in.

"Can we talk to you?" they asked. After introducing themselves and telling me they were Israeli journalists, they said, "We want to tell you what's going on in Israel with regard to the peace process."

Each one of them gave a similar testimony, but one thing became very clear: any journalist who said anything negative about the peace process did so at the risk of his career. Such a journalist ceased to be invited to government press conferences. Not only were they taken "out of the loop" professionally, but the government of Israel was placing in ninety-day detention any individual who said or did anything to discredit the peace process publicly. They told me that the democratic process had been totally derailed in Israel. People were picked up at all hours of the night and day for questioning. Anyone who was in any way critical of the peace process was subject to governmental harassment.

That happened before the assassination and Rabin's martyrdom. Now that the mood of the people has gone into the euphoric dimension of "peace at any price," the situation will be even more intense to guarantee the success of the peace movement.

The journalists told me, "You are on national television in America, you speak to millions of people, and at some point we want you to let the American people know how the democratic process here is being scrubbed in a fanatical pursuit of peace. We want you to know how intensely the government is pressing this peace issue. The authorities are abandoning the democratic procedure for which Israel is so very well known. There are things being done in the name of peace that threaten the security of Israel, but if we write about those things, we will never be invited to another press conference and we could lose our jobs or go to jail."

What was once a political operation has blossomed into a national mandate, created by the blood of a martyr.

The Mountain Moves: Syria Is Willing to Negotiate

Israel had treaties with Egypt and Jordan prior to the Rabin assassination and had signed an accord with the PLO. But Syria, a dominant player in the Middle East, has never been able to come to terms with Israel because at the heart of the Syrian-Israeli dispute is the strategic Golan Heights. Israel captured this region from Syria in the 1967 Six-Day War and later annexed it.

The Golan Heights, a strategic plateau overlooking northern Israel and the southern Syrian plains, is critical both militarily and as a watershed (see map on page 12). The area is a towering plateau which measures about 480 square miles and is distinguished by two levels: the Lower Golan in the south, with altitudes between 600 and 1,900 feet, and the Upper Golan in the north, rising to altitudes of up to 3,000 feet above sea level. A number of hilltops reach as high as 4,400 feet.

This lofty platform is the perfect place from which to launch rockets to reach Jerusalem. Israel lies at the base of the Golan Heights. One guiding principle in warfare is to "take the high ground": whoever owns the Golan Heights could make all of Israel a killing field.

Never before has Israel even hinted that it might be willing to negotiate on issues regarding the Golan Heights, but now, in the words of Warren Christopher, United States Secretary of State, Israel and Syria will open a "new phase" of intensive and broad peace negotiations. Though two previous attempts to open talks on security issues collapsed in recent years, Christopher says there is a "new mood" in Israel since Rabin's assassination.[10]

Upon taking office on November 22, 1995, Peres said, "I would like to propose to the president of Syria that we each do our utmost to put an end to the era of wars in the Middle

East." He has declared that he is open to any form of negotiations with no preconditions. The *New York Times* reports that Israeli news reports speculate that Peres would be prepared to return virtually all of the Golan in exchange for firm security and a comprehensive Mideast peace.[11]

GOLAN HEIGHTS

(Aerial View)

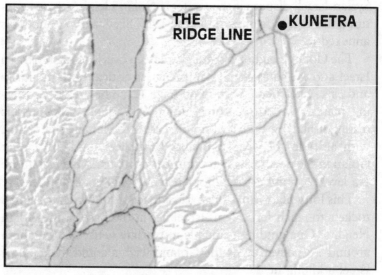

(Elevation View)

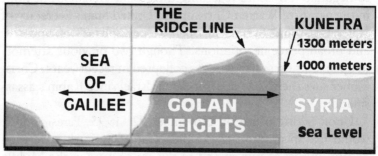

The Assassination's Prophetic Significance

In the surge of advocates for peace, voices of dissent will be shouted down or ignored. The peace process will cease to become a political action; it will become a spiritual mandate for a nation.

Based on the words of the prophets of Israel, I believe this peace process will lead to the most devastating war Israel has ever known. After that war, the longed-for Messiah will come. This book was written to reveal how the peace process will likely develop and the reasons for a war over the three-thousand-year-old city of Jerusalem.

Several years ago, someone asked me, "Dr. Hagee, your father was a prophecy scholar, and you have followed in his footsteps. Do you believe the Arabs will ever gain a sufficient foothold in Israel to birth a Palestinian state or gain control of a portion of the city of Jerusalem?"

Ten years ago, no one could imagine such a thing ever happening. Israel is the fourth-greatest military power on the face of the earth; they have defeated the combined Arab armies on several occasions. Israel is the dominant military force in the Middle East, and no one reasonably believes that the Arab nations could ever defeat them. But the prophecies of Scripture indicate the Arabs will gain a foothold in the Middle East sufficient enough to convince them they can defeat Israel in a war.

Think back with me to September 13, 1993. Israeli Prime Minister Rabin stood in the White House Rose Garden with Yasser Arafat. President Clinton stood between them, eager to announce that Rabin and Arafat had, the previous day, signed the Oslo Accords. At that signing, Rabin had declared that the land flowing with milk and honey should not become a land flowing with blood and tears.

Now on public display, the world watched and waited as the peace accord was announced. Would the warrior statesman who masterminded the 1967 war shake hands with Arafat the terrorist, the man who had engineered murderous attacks on buses, retirement homes, and orphanages? And would Arafat take the hand of his sworn enemy?

At a dramatic moment, Arafat extended his hand in friendship and Yitzhak Rabin shook it before the cameras of the world. Some saw it and wept. Others applauded. Others saw it as an act of treason against the state of Israel and began to call for the expulsion of Yitzhak Rabin as Prime Minister. Others watched and grimly decided that Rabin deserved to die.

Yigal Amir saw it and believed that Rabin was a traitor to the Jewish cause. "The entire nation did not pay attention to the fact that a Palestinian state was being created," Amir told an Israeli court after his arrest. "I did not try to stop the peace process because there is no such concept. . . . I was at the demonstration. It was fifty percent Arabs. What will you do when there are two million Arabs here? Will we give the state to the Arabs?"[12]

The question now being asked around the world and in the halls of Congress is: "Will this assassination slow down the peace process or speed it up?" We can find the answer in our own American history books.

In the months prior to John F. Kennedy's assassination, very little of his party's legislation passed in Congress. But after JFK's murder, when Lyndon Baines Johnson went to the White House, virtually everything Johnson urged forward in Kennedy's name sailed through both houses of Congress. Johnson himself was elected president in 1964 by the largest majority ever at that time.

Now Israel faces a similar situation. The nation is uniting; all Israel will now pursue peace with a passion that throws caution to the wind. To honor the life and memory of Yitzhak Rabin, Israel will pursue peace with dogged determination.

CHAPTER TWO

The Mind of
an Assassin

Yigal Amir, Rabin's murderer, is the second of eight children. His father works as a scribe who handwrites holy Scriptures, his mother, as a nursery school teacher. Yigal Amir had worked abroad as an envoy for an Israeli government agency. He had no police record. Nothing in his family life suggested that he might pick up a gun and murder his country's prime minister. Why did he do it?

Amir told a Jerusalem court that he was required to kill Rabin because the prime minister was handing over parts of the West Bank to Palestinians, a step Amir believed would lead to war and the loss of Jewish life. Therefore, said the assassin, Rabin was a would-be murderer, and under Jewish law intended to allow for self-defense, it is permissible to kill such a person. Outside Jewish Orthodoxy, nearly everyone disagrees with Amir's understanding of that law. Yet within Orthodoxy, a minority supports it.[1]

The Israeli government interrogated two rabbis who were suspected of authorizing, approving, or inspiring Yigal Amir. Authorities believe that the rabbis may have branded Rabin a traitor or *rodef*, the ancient term for a pursuer who is about to kill a Jew. Under Halacha, or Jewish law, it is permissible to kill a *rodef*.[2]

"That this centuries-old concept has emerged in the investigation underscores a deep schism between the religious Zionist view of Israel as a biblical homeland given to the Hebrews by God and a more secular vision of Israel as a modern, democratic state," says Storer Rowley, a writer for the *Chicago Tribune*.[3]

"There's a deep spiritual battle, a cultural war, going on as to what Jewish tradition is about," said Rabbi David Hartman, founder-director of the Shalom Hartman Institute for Judaic Studies in Jerusalem. "And the nature of this people and the future of Israel depends on how this battle is going to be fought."[4]

It is important to understand that although there are many groups of Jews in Israel, most can be divided into two categories. One category is composed of religious Jews who believe, among other things, that Israel has a holy deed to the land. The other group is made up of cultural or ethnic Jews who place no great importance on the religious beliefs of the Jewish people. This second group believes the destiny of the Israeli nation must be accomplished through the political process. They seek a young, modern, prosperous nation with an economy based on technology and tourism. Like so many others in the twentieth century, they place more faith in man than in the God of their fathers. And, having no firsthand experience with a pogrom or mass genocide, they are weary of war.

"For the generation of Israelis who can remember the 1948 war for independence, the idealized image of their Israel was the sun-bronzed kibbutznik with a shovel in one hand and a rifle in the other," says Tom Hundley, a writer for the *Chicago Tribune*. "For the generation who came of age after the 1967 Six-Day War that brought Israel the West Bank, the kibbutznik was replaced by the settler, Bible in one hand, rifle in the other."[5]

Sadly enough, Rabin's assassination may dissuade the second group of Jewish people from seeking to know more about their religious faith. According to Noam M. M. Neusner, a Jewish writer watching the American scene, Amir's murderous act "threatens to undermine a nascent movement in the mainstream American Jewish community toward religion. People now recognize that for Judaism to survive, it must matter more than ethnicity, politics and culture, which have predominated for 300 years. For the first time in their history, American Jews were turning to Judaism for guidance on issues beyond ritualistic nit-picking."[6]

Did Amir push that train off the tracks? Perhaps.

Modern Israel

In Tel Aviv today you can find restaurants offering shrimp, ham, and goose liver in cream sauce; not exactly kosher cuisine, since Jewish law forbids the eating of shellfish, pork, and organ meats. Today's Israeli citizen shops in Tel Aviv for Gucci, Gaultier, and Donna Karan. The economy is booming; per capita income is nearly $17,000—about the same as Britain's and more than double what it was in the seventies. A new Israeli-made soap opera features the opulent lifestyle of the fictional Linowitz family and their relentless pursuit of sex and money.[7]

"I would say the country is in great danger of losing its Jewish soul," Orthodox Rabbi David Hartman told *Newsweek*. "There is a great danger that Israel will be swept up by the MTV-Madonna culture."[8]

Political Jews are not looking for the coming of the Messiah. Menachem Begin, a former prime minister of Israel, was a devout Jew who read the Scripture every day, prayed regularly, quoted the Word of God in his speeches, and openly declared that Israel had a holy mandate to exist and to possess *Eretz Yisrael,* the Land of Israel. But Menachem Begin now belongs to the ages, and Israel's current leaders care more for political processes than for religious tenets and convictions.

Liberal Zionism, according to Zeev Sternhell, a professor of political science at Hebrew University, is "a recognition of the fact that Israel is more than a Jewish state, that it belongs also to the 20 percent of its citizens who are Arab. . . . What counts are the universal values, the Rights of Man, and not the particularist Jewish values of Judaism."⁹

The United States has been waging a similar struggle—have we wandered far from the Judeo-Christian ideals upon which we were founded and, if so, should we return? But our struggle has been somewhat diluted by the sheer size and diversity of our country. Israel is a smaller place, surrounded by hostile neighbors for most of its history; passions flare higher because the land at stake is more rare, more precious. When they tried to trade land for peace with Egypt in the seventies, then Prime Minister Golda Meir said, "Israel has no more land to give!"

Many religious Israelis are motivated by a biblical imperative to redeem the land of Israel for the Jews and usher in the coming Messiah. The leading rabbis from Israel and the Diaspora held a conference at the Ramada Renaissance Hotel in Jerusalem in November 1993. Among the resolutions approved at that meeting were the following declarations:

> The assembly restates the fact that the Jewish People are the only legitimate owners of the Land of Israel. This right to the land derives from the promise that God made to the nation's forefathers, and from the unbroken connection of our people to our land throughout the generations even after we were forcibly exiled from it. Through the power of this faith and this connection we returned to the land with the consent of the nations by the monumental decision of the U.N. We reconquered the historic heartland of the land during the Six Day War which was the revelation of Hashem's salvation of His people, a miracle witnessed by the whole world. [*Hashem* is Hebrew for "the name," the sacred four-letter name of God which is never spoken or written.]
>
> The assembly of Rabbis declares that according to the laws of the Torah it is forbidden to relinquish the political rights of sovereignty and national ownership over any part of historic Eretz Yisroel to another authority or people. All of the historic Eretz Yisroel which is now in our possession belongs to the

entire Jewish people past, present and future, and therefore no one in any generation can give away that to which he does not have title. Therefore any agreement to do so is null and void, obligates no one, has no legal or moral force whatsoever.

The assembly calls on the government to fulfill their pledge that no settlement will be dismantled. . . .

The assembly expresses its fear that the "agreement" will endanger the lives of all the inhabitants of Israel, and in particular the lives of those living in Judea, Samaria, and Gaza. The arming of an Arab police force made up of murderous terrorists will be a direct danger in and of itself. . . . Anyone who fails to act in order to prevent the execution of the "agreement" transgresses the sin of "Do not stand still while your neighbor's life is in danger."

We are extremely concerned over the present trend that aims to create a secular culture here which is to blend into "a new Middle East"—a trend which will lead to assimilation. We have a sacred obligation to strengthen and deepen our people's connection to the Torah and to Jewish tradition as passed down through the generations.

We support the continuation of protests, demonstrations, and strikes within the framework of the law. In addition, we encourage educating and informing the masses in order that they may realize the falseness of this "peace" . . .[10]

The above declarations were made two short years ago, but how times have changed!

Rabin's assassination has added fuel to an already hot fire.

The Sacred Title of Property

Who is right? Who owns the land of Israel? The answer is found in the Word of God and can be traced all the way back to Abraham. God sent an angel to tell Abraham that he would be the father of a great nation: "And behold, the word of the LORD came to him, saying . . . 'one who will come from your

19

own body shall be your heir.' Then He brought him outside and said, 'Look now toward heaven, and count the stars if you are able to number them.' And He said to him, 'So shall your descendants be'" (Gen. 15:4–5).

This was surprising news for Abraham, since his wife was already past menopause and had never borne a child. Abraham's wife thought to help God out a bit, and so she asked Abraham to go into the tent of her Egyptian maid, Hagar, and have a child with her—not an unusual practice in those days.

So Abraham slept with Hagar and Ishmael was conceived and born. Later, just as God had foretold, Abraham's wife did conceive and give birth to a miracle baby, Isaac. The people of Israel are descended from Isaac; the people of the Arab nations descended from Ishmael.

To whom does the land of Israel belong? The greatest political controversy of this century is rooted in this question. The Arabs say the land belongs to them, that they've lived in the land for centuries while the Jewish people were scattered across the globe. But the Jewish people claim that the land has belonged to them from the time of Abraham, when Jehovah God entered into a blood covenant with the "Father of all who believe," Abraham, conveying the Promised Land to the children of Abraham, Isaac, and Jacob forever (see Gen. 15:12–17).

If you've bought a house recently, you know that an abstract of title must trace ownership from the very first owner to the present owner, making sure that there is no lien or other claim on the property. Who was the original owner of the land we call Palestine? The answer is recorded many places in Scripture. In Psalm 24:1, we read "The earth is the LORD'S." In Psalm 89:11, "The heavens are Thine." In Leviticus 25:23, "The land moreover shall not be sold permanently, for the land is Mine."

Today in Israel, citizens can't own the land; instead they lease it from the government of Israel. If I'm a farmer, I can lease land for forty-nine years, and my son can lease it when my term is done. But neither of us can own it. The land is under the stewardship of the children of Israel, but it ultimately belongs to the Lord. Therefore, God alone can give the land away. When Prime Minister Rabin gave land for peace, religious Jews saw his actions as an attack upon God Himself.

"In the beginning God created the heavens and the earth," we read in Genesis 1:1. God is the Creator/Owner of the earth, and He has the power to confer the title upon whomever He will. In Genesis 12:1 we read that he did transfer title to Abraham, once called Abram: "Now the LORD had said to Abram: 'Get out of your country, from your family and from your father's house, to a land that I will show you.'"

After Abram went to the land God intended, God spoke again to him:

> And the LORD said to Abram, after Lot had separated from him: "Lift your eyes now and look from the place where you are—northward, southward, eastward, and westward; for all the land which you see I give to you and your descendants forever. And I will make your descendants as the dust of the earth; so that if a man could number the dust of the earth, then your descendants also could be numbered. Arise, walk in the land through its length and its width, for I give it to you." (Gen. 13:14–17)

Before Isaac's birth, Abraham asked God if Ishmael might have the royal land grant: "And Abraham said to God, 'Oh, that Ishmael might live before You!'" (Gen. 17:18). In answer, God said he would make Ishmael fruitful, the father of twelve rulers, and a great nation. But God's covenant would be established with Isaac, who was to come. So the title to the land passed from Abraham to Isaac, and eventually, to Jacob.

Isaac was the son of promise, the son of the true wife. Abraham also had six sons with Keturah, the wife he took after Sarah's death. Keturah bore him Zimran, Jokshan, Medan, Midian, Ishbak, and Shuah. These sons became the ancestors of a number of North Arabian peoples who say, "The land is ours! Abraham was our father, too!"

But Abraham made provision for those sons while he lived. "And Abraham gave all that he had to Isaac. But Abraham gave gifts to the sons of the concubines which Abraham had; and while he was still living he sent them eastward, away from Isaac his son, to the country of the east" (Gen. 25:5–6; see also 1 Chron. 1:32–33).

God reviewed and reaffirmed his intention to give the land to Isaac by speaking to him personally.

> Dwell in this land, and I will be with you and bless you; for to you and your descendants I give all these lands, and I will perform the oath which I swore to Abraham your father. And I will make your descendants multiply as the stars of heaven; I will give to your descendants all these lands; and in your seed all the nations of the earth shall be blessed; because Abraham obeyed My voice and kept My charge, My commandments, My statutes, and My laws. (Gen. 26:3–5)

At sixty years of age, Isaac, title holder to what we know as the Holy Land, discovered that his wife, Rebecca, was expecting. God performed a sonogram and told Rebecca the results: "And the LORD said to her: 'Two nations are in your womb, two peoples shall be separated from your body; one people shall be stronger than the other, and the older shall serve the younger'" (Gen. 25:23).

Jacob and Esau emerged from Rebecca's womb. But Esau, the older twin, did not inherit the title to the land because it passed to Jacob, to whom his father said, "May God Almighty bless you, and make you fruitful and multiply you, that you may be an assembly of peoples; and give you the blessing of Abraham, to you and your descendants with you, that you may inherit the land in which you are a stranger, which God gave to Abraham" (Gen. 28:3–4).

And God Himself confirmed Jacob's ownership of the title when Jacob met God in a dream of a stairway to the stars:

And behold, the LORD stood above it and said: "I am the LORD God of Abraham your father and the God of Isaac; the land on which you lie I will give to you and your descendants. Also your descendants shall be as the dust of the earth; you shall spread abroad to the west and the east, to the north and the south; and in you and in your seed all the families of the earth shall be blessed." (Gen. 28:13–14; see also Gen. 35:9–12)

And so the title remained with Jacob and his twelve sons. As Joseph, Jacob's beloved son, lay dying in Egypt, he reviewed the title's progression: "And Joseph said to his brethren, 'I am dying; but God will surely visit you, and bring you out of this land to the land of which He swore to Abraham, to Isaac, and to Jacob'" (Gen. 50:24).

How much land is contained within this royal land grant? God Himself has established Israel's boundaries: "On the same day the LORD made a covenant with Abram, saying: 'To your descendants I have given this land, from the river of Egypt to the great river, the River Euphrates'" (Gen. 15:18). The eastern boundary was the Euphrates River, the western boundary the Egyptian River, identified in Exodus 23:31 as the Red Sea. As the children of Israel crossed the Red Sea and left Egypt after the captivity, God said, "Every place on which the sole of your foot treads shall be yours: from the wilderness and Lebanon, from the river, the River Euphrates, even to the Western Sea [the Mediterranean], shall be your territory" (Deut. 11:24). The northern boundary is established in Ezekiel 48:1 as the city of Hamath; the southern boundary is established in Eze-kiel 48:28 as the city of Kadesh.

Given these boundaries found in holy Scripture, we discover that Israel will have far more land when Messiah comes than she presently does. Israel's boundaries, established time and time again in the Old Testament, will include all of present-day Israel, all of Lebanon, half of Syria, two-thirds of Jordan, all of Iraq, and the northern portion of Saudi Arabia.

An Ancient Rivalry

The competition that existed in Abraham's household still exists today. The conflict between Arabs and Jews does not involve the West Bank, Judea, or Samaria; it has little to do with the Golan Heights, even though that geographical area is critical to the nation's defense.

The conflict between Arabs and Jews goes deeper than disputes over land. It is theological. It is Judaism versus Islam. Islam's theology insists that Islam triumph over everything else—that's why when you visit an Arabic city, the Islamic prayer tower is the highest point in the city. A follower of Islam is called *Muslim,* a term referring to "one who submits"; the word *Islam* itself literally means "submission." The Arabs believe that while Jesus, Moses, David, and several other Hebrews were prophets, Muhammad was the greatest prophet. Though Muslims revere the Bible, including the Torah, the Psalms, and the Gospels, they hold that the *Al-Quran* (the Koran) is the absolute true word of God, revealed through the angel Jibraeel (Gabriel) to Muhammad. Muslims believe that Allah is God, that he has neither father nor mother, and that he has no sons.

The Muslim Imperative

Did you know that Islam is the fastest growing religion in the United States today?[11] Though most Muslims are peaceful and law-abiding, others have taken advantage of America's civil liberties and have established themselves as "research," "charitable" or "civil rights" institutions. Oliver B. Revell, a former senior FBI official in charge of counterterrorist and counterintelligence investigations, says these groups "are ultimately committed to waging holy war, both in the Middle East and the world at large against all of their opposition."[12]

Seif Ashmawi, an Egyptian-born American-based publisher, agrees. "The aim of these groups," he says, "is the same as their aim in the Middle East: to build and expand their radical religious-political empire and eliminate or discredit all their enemies."[13]

At national conventions sponsored by the Muslim Arab Youth Association (maya), anti-Israeli rhetoric can regularly be heard. At a maya conference held at a Hyatt hotel in Chicago during December 1994, Bassam al-Amoush, a member of the Islamic coalition in the Jordanian parliament, told a joke: "Somebody approached me at the mosque and asked me, 'If I see a Jew in the street, should I kill him?'" Al-Amoush painted on a dumbfounded expression. "'Don't ask me,' I said to him. 'After you kill him, come and tell me.'" The crowd roared with laughter, and al-Amoush continued. "'What do you want from me, a *fatwa* [a religious ruling]? Really, a good deed does not require one.'"[14]

Moments later, journalist Steven Emerson reports, the master of ceremonies held up a note he'd just been handed. "We have very good news," he told the crowd. "There was an attack on a bus in Jerusalem, perpetrated by a Palestinian policeman. Nineteen were wounded and three were killed." The crowd responded with shouts of "Allahu Akbar!"[15]

Why does such enmity exist between the Jews and the Arabs? Much of it probably springs from the ancient rivalry between Isaac and Ishmael. Most of it is due to the fact that the Arab Palestinians feel they have been displaced by Israel. They certainly have been defeated in battle, and for years a constant wariness and tension have existed between the two groups. Neither group trusts the other.

The Koran declares: "To those against whom war is made, permission is given [to defend themselves], because they are wronged and verily, Allah is Most Powerful to give them Victory—[they are] those who have been expelled from their homes in defiance of right—[for no cause] except that they say, 'Our Lord is Allah'" (22:39–40).

The Koran also permits fighting to defend the religion of Islam. "Fight in the cause of Allah against those who fight against you, but do not transgress limits. Lo! Allah loves not aggressors. . . . And fight them until persecution is no more, and religion is for Allah" (2:190).

The Arabs believe they have been persecuted by Israel. The Koran further advises, "If you fear treachery from any group, throw back [their treachery] to them, [so as to be] on equal terms" (8:58). The prophet Muhammad undertook a number of armed campaigns to remove treacherous people from power. He launched armed campaigns against several tribes, defeated them, and exiled them from the land.

According to the Koran, Allah further advises his followers to defend themselves through preemptive strikes: "Fighting is prescribed upon you, and you dislike it. But it may happen that you dislike a thing which is good for you, and it may happen that you love a thing which is bad for you. And Allah knows and you know not" (2:216). Muhammad said, "Strive [Jahidu] against the disbelievers with your hands and tongues" (Sahih Ibn Hibban #4708).

"And why should you not fight in the cause of Allah and of those who, being weak, are ill-treated [and oppressed]? Men, women, and children, whose cry is: 'Our Lord! Rescue us from this town, whose people are oppressors; and raise for us from You, one who will protect; and raise for us from You, one who will help'" (4:75).

Regardless of the stipulations of Islamic law, there are many Islamic radicals bent on the destruction of the Jewish people. The strategy of Islamic Jihad is as simple as it is satanic: "Kill so many Jews that they will eventually abandon Palestine."[16]

26

The late Imam Hasan al-Bana of the Islamic Resistance Movement, HAMAS, summed up their philosophy so well that it was included in their covenant: "Israel will exist and will continue to exist until Islam will obliterate it, just as it obliterated others before it."[17]

But Israel will not be defeated easily. Her people are saying, "God gave us a blood covenant to this land forever, and we're not going to give it up. Our forefathers marched into the gas chambers singing *Hatikvah* [the anthem which speaks of the hope within the heart of all Jews to be members of a free people in the land of Zion and Jerusalem], but we will not willingly be slaughtered again. We are going to defend ourselves to the death if we are encircled, and if this is another Masada, so be it. We're standing our ground until hell freezes over."

To the Muslims, Israel is as troublesome as a cornered copperhead. But mark this: if the Arabs do not eventually defeat Israel in combat, Muhammad lied, the Koran is in error, and Allah is not the true God. These are heretical ideas to the Muslim—absolutely unthinkable. The existence and survival of Israel flies in the face of Muslim theology. As long as Israel survives, their triumph-based theology cannot be affirmed. So, despite the peace treaties, the conflict is not done. Many Muslims will continue to fight Israel at every opportunity.

"Our objective is the destruction of Israel," Arafat once said. "There is to be no compromise and no moderation. No, we do not want peace. We want war and victory. Peace for us means the destruction of Israel and nothing else.[19] . . . We shall fight together as one Muslim nation under one flag. We are all zealots of the Muslim faith. We shall all stand together under the Muslim flag."[20]

Can a devoted follower of the Muslim faith change his mind? Apparently he did, for Arafat himself signed the Oslo Accords in the White House, then shook hands with Yitzhak Rabin as the world watched.

Muslims have also persecuted Christians with bloody fervor. In July 1995, the *Wall Street Journal* reported that "the rise of Islamic fundamentalism has effectively criminalized the practice of Christianity."[21] Under Islamic apostasy doctrines, writes Michael Horowitz, "Muslim converts to Christianity may be punished by death. Until recently, such doctrines were routinely ignored by Islamic governments, or interpreted liberally. But particularly in the case of Christian converts and evangelical Protestants, this is no longer true."[22]

Of course there are many Muslims who sincerely want peace, but the radical, extremist Muslims who think Yasser Arafat has compromised still intend to destroy Israel and Jerusalem. These are the people who believe that anyone who will not confess that Allah is God, that Muhammad is his prophet, and that the Koran is the perfect fulfillment of God's Word, should be put to death.

Israel's Present

Why did Yigal Amir kill Rabin? He did it because he is part of the two-faced Janus that is Israel. Janus was the Roman god of doors and gateways, of beginnings. Janus, for whom the month of January was named, was always pictured with two faces looking in opposite directions, one young and one old.

Israel is like Janus: one face belongs to religious Jews who believe the holy Scriptures are absolute truth, that Israel has a divine mandate to possess the land and to build in it. Yet part of the same body is the other face, the nonreligious Jews who believe political solutions only come through the peace process. Rabin was like Janus: to many he represented the hope that Israel would emerge from isolation, persecution, and bloodshed to find acceptance in the modern world community. To others, he embodied the threat that Israel would negotiate away the national identity they had gained by conquest, United Nations charter, and divine right.[23]

Leah Rabin, visiting New York with her husband's successor, Prime Minister Shimon Peres, told a huge gathering at Madison Square Garden that Israel should strive for unity. "We are undergoing a crisis. We need to change the climate of hatred and violence that brought about the assassination," she told the crowd exactly one month after her husband's death. "In his death he bequeathed to us peace; he bequeathed to us solidarity; he bequeathed Jewish unity."[24]

Peres echoed the sentiments of Rabin's widow. "Yitzhak Rabin never tried to please you," he told the crowd. "He tried to lead you. That was his obligation. We do recognize the right of the opposition to oppose us. We do recognize the right of the opposition to try to change the government. But we do expect the opposition, with us, to make our nation free and democratic, having many views and remaining together. We should also be united against violence, against murder, against curses. Let's argue, not hate."[25]

Although the cry for peace and unity is being proclaimed with new passion, it is not new. The last time I was in Israel I witnessed a demonstration unlike anything I have ever seen in the United States. A great throng of people, marching side by side, line after line, came down the street shouting, "Peace now! Peace now!" They made a thunderous noise; the walls of the building vibrated with the sound of their protest.

After seeing that, I began to think that perhaps we Americans don't know what true political activism is! Everybody in Israel is politically active and passionate about their beliefs. The generation that survived the Holocaust and came to Palestine was united because they faced a common enemy. In Israel's early years, during the wars of 1948 and 1967, it was "us against them," and Israel fought for its life and placed its destiny in Jewish hands. But now the children of those soldiers are adults, and they are saying, "Times are changing, what happened to you is past, and we want peace now. If land is the price for peace, so be it; just give peace a chance. If the Syrians want the Golan Heights, give them the Golan Heights."

And so Israel stands with a Janus face before the world: young people who want peace at any price resist older, more skeptical people. But, as any zoologist will tell you, a two-headed creature will not survive long; a house divided against itself cannot stand. Israel will unite and peace will prevail . . . when the country accepts the false man of peace who steps out onto the world's stage.

Israel's Future

Israel holds clear title to the land she possesses. She has never, for any reason, forfeited that title. God has told His people,

> My mercy I will keep for him forever, and My covenant shall stand firm with him. His seed also I will make to endure forever, and his throne as the days of heaven. If his sons forsake My law and do not walk in My judgments, if they break My statutes and do not keep My commandments, then I will punish their transgression with the rod, and their iniquity with stripes. Nevertheless My lovingkindness I will not utterly take from him, nor allow My faithfulness to fail. My covenant I will not break, nor alter the word that has gone out of My lips. (Ps. 89:28–34)

God told Abraham that the land would belong to his offspring forever; He reminded the psalmist that He will not violate His covenant or change His mind. God is not like men; His promises are secure and eternal. We can trust them, and we can trust the prophecies He gave to His prophets.

The prophet Ezekiel writes of a time when Israel will be a land of unwalled villages, a land of peaceful and unsuspecting people. An enemy army will look upon a land that is resettled ruins and populated by people gathered from the nations, rich in livestock and goods.

Someone else will look upon her, too . . . the Antichrist.

CHAPTER THREE

The Panorama
of Prophecy

Before we delve further into the rapidly-approaching end times, let me introduce or reacquaint you with some terms referring to events in the last days.

The *Rapture* is the literal, physical "snatching away" of those who have placed their faith in Jesus Christ. The Rapture could come at any moment, and it will occur without warning. Every single member of the corporate body of Christ, the genuine believers, will be taken alive to "meet him in the air" (1 Thess. 4:17). Those who have suffered physical death will be resurrected with incorruptible, supernatural bodies.

The *Antichrist,* whom we will later discuss at length, will be revealed shortly after the Rapture has occurred. He is the man who will establish a one-world government, a one-world religion, and a one-world economy. He is also known by other names, among them "the Beast," and "666."

The *Tribulation* is the seven-year period which follows the disappearance of the Church. The Bible says this time will be a literal hell on earth, replete with famine, natural disasters, epidemic sickness, war, and treachery.

At the close of the time of tribulation, life on earth as we know it will change dramatically. Israel's Messiah will come to earth as a reigning king to vanquish the enemy armies which have surrounded Israel. With him will come the heavenly armies, clothed in white. Satan and the Antichrist will be defeated, and Satan will be bound. The Messiah will establish an earthly kingdom of peace and righteousness which will last for one thousand years. People who have survived the Tribulation will sing, "Joy to the world, the Lord has come, let Earth receive her king!" This thousand-year reign of the Messiah is known as the *Millennium*.

Because God created man with a free will and wants man to freely choose to worship Him, after one thousand years Satan will be released. The Deceiver will be allowed to attempt to convince the people of the millennial world that he is worthy of worship. But once again God will step in with His heavenly armies and Satan's uprising will be defeated.

At that point, every person who has ever lived will stand before the throne of God at the event called the *Great White Throne Judgment*. There every man and woman, rich or poor, great or small, will be judged according to whether he or she accepted or rejected the King of Kings and Lord of Lords, Israel's Messiah, Jesus the Christ. Those who have accepted Him will enter into blessed eternity; those who have rejected Him will depart God's presence and join Satan in the eternal fires of hell. This present earth will be destroyed with a "great and fervent heat," and God will create a new heaven and a new earth in which we will dwell for eternity (see 2 Pet. 3:10–13).

Nebuchadnezzar's Dream

The second chapter of Daniel gives a glimpse of the end times. God sent Nebuchadnezzar, king of Babylon, a dream of an image that perfectly describes the empires that would rule the earth from the time of the Babylonian king until the end of the world.

A major obstacle facing those who tried to interpret Nebuchadnezzar's dream was the fact that he forgot it. He decreed that if his magicians, astrologers, and sorcerers could not reveal his dream and its meaning, they would be "cut into pieces" and their houses turned into "piles of rubble." Since the king's wise men had no choice but to produce or perish, the occult crowd began to massage their chicken bones and call upon their gods of darkness to reveal the king's forgotten dream.

No answers came. They went as a group before Nebuchadnezzar and said, "There is not a man on earth who can tell the king's matter; therefore no king, lord, or ruler has ever asked such things of any magician, astrologer, or Chaldean. It is a difficult thing that the king requests, and there is no other who can tell it to the king except the gods, whose dwelling is not with flesh" (vv. 10–11).

THE FOUR KINGDOMS

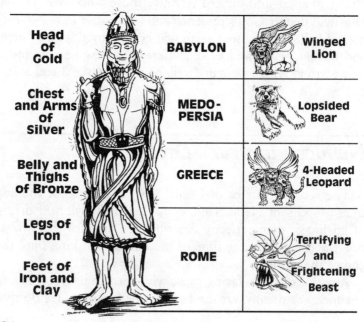

Head of Gold	BABYLON	Winged Lion
Chest and Arms of Silver	MEDO-PERSIA	Lopsided Bear
Belly and Thighs of Bronze	GREECE	4-Headed Leopard
Legs of Iron — Feet of Iron and Clay	ROME	Terrifying and Frightening Beast

Enter Daniel, a Jewish captive from Jerusalem, who served the living God of Abraham, Isaac, and Jacob. The Bible tells us that "the secret was revealed to Daniel in a night vision. So Daniel blessed the God of heaven" (v. 19).

In the presence of the mortified astrologers, magicians, and sorcerers, Daniel went before King Nebuchadnezzar and proclaimed,

> But there is a God in heaven who reveals secrets, and He has made known to King Nebuchadnezzar what will be in the latter days. Your dream, and the visions of your head upon your bed, were these: As for you, O king, thoughts came to your mind while on your bed, about what would come to pass after this; and He who reveals secrets has made known to you what will be. But as for me, this secret has not been revealed to me because I have more wisdom than anyone living, but for our sakes who make known the interpretation to the king, and that you may know the thoughts of your heart. (vv. 28–30)

Can't you just see those astrologers squirming? They had just proclaimed that God would not bother to speak to lowly men, and yet Daniel had a direct hot line to heaven!

Daniel paid them no attention, but went on proclaiming the things which were to come:

> You, O king, were watching; and behold, a great image! This great image, whose splendor was excellent, stood before you; and its form was awesome. This image's head was of fine gold, its chest and arms of silver, its belly and thighs of bronze, its legs of iron, its feet partly of iron and partly of clay. You watched while a stone was cut out without hands, which struck the image on its feet of iron and clay, and broke them in pieces. Then the iron, the clay, the bronze, the silver, and the gold were crushed together, and became like chaff from the summer threshing floors; the wind carried them away so that no trace of them was found. And the stone that struck the image became a great mountain and filled the whole earth. This is the dream. (vv. 31–36)

I'm sure Nebuchadnezzar was about to rise up off his throne as Daniel's words touched the chords of memory in his mind. Yes, he remembered the image, and yes, he knew it spoke of something dreadfully important! But what did it all mean? He did not interrupt as Daniel continued to speak.

Now we will tell the interpretation of it before the king. You, O king, are a king of kings. For the God of heaven has given you a kingdom, power, strength, and glory; and wherever the children of men dwell, or the beasts of the field and the birds of the heaven, He has given them into your hand, and has made you ruler over them all—you are this head of gold. But after you shall arise another kingdom inferior to yours; then another, a third kingdom of bronze, which shall rule over all the earth. And the fourth kingdom shall be as strong as iron, inasmuch as iron breaks in pieces and shatters everything; and like iron that crushes, that kingdom will break in pieces and crush all the others. Whereas you saw the feet and toes, partly of potter's clay and partly of iron, the kingdom shall be divided; yet the strength of the iron shall be in it, just as you saw the iron mixed with ceramic clay. And as the toes of the feet were partly of iron and partly of clay, so the kingdom shall be partly strong and partly fragile. As you saw iron mixed with ceramic clay, they will mingle with the seed of men; but they will not adhere to one another, just as iron does not mix with clay. And in the days of these kings the God of heaven will set up a kingdom which shall never be destroyed; and the kingdom shall not be left to other people; it shall break in pieces and consume all these kingdoms, and it shall stand forever. Inasmuch as you saw that the stone was cut out of the mountain without hands, and that it broke in pieces the iron, the bronze, the clay, the silver, and the gold—the great God has made known to the king what will come to pass after this. The dream is certain, and its interpretation is sure. (vv. 36–45)

History has proven Daniel's interpretation of Nebuchadnezzar's dream to be accurate. As Daniel prophesied, the empire which supplanted Nebuchadnezzar's head of gold was the

Medo-Persian, the breastplate of silver. The powerful Babylonians were displaced by Alexander the Great of Greece, the loins of brass. Alexander's empire fell to the Roman Empire, the strong and mighty domain which eventually divided into eastern and western empires.

You'll notice that as Daniel's eye traveled down the image, the strength of the metals progressed from soft (gold) to very hard (iron). This is a prophetic picture of the military strength of nations that would develop in years to come. Mankind has progressed from relatively weak weapons such as spears and cudgels to smart bombs, scud missiles, and thermonuclear devices that could leave Earth a spinning graveyard in space.

It is important to note that the strength of the iron kingdom seemed to be diluted over time. The lower the eye descends, the weaker the material becomes, until the feet are composed of iron and clay, two materials which simply will not blend with each other. The "partly strong and partly broken" kingdom of Rome did weaken as it aged, until it finally divided into ten toes, or ten kingdoms. Though several biblical commentators have made lists of the ten kingdoms, few writers agree as to which kingdoms or nations the ten toes actually represent. Prophecy scholar Dwight Pentecost says, "The ten kingdoms are to exist at one time, not through a period of several centuries, and all are to form one confederation. There is nothing in the past history of the kingdoms of Europe that answers to this."[1]

What are the two substances that will not mix? Scholar William Kelly suggests that the final form of power from the old Roman Empire will be a federation composed of autocracies and democracies, represented by iron and clay. In his view, iron represents nations ruled by a monarch; clay represents nations which adhere to a democratic or representative form of government.[2]

These ten toes, or empires, will be some sort of European federation. Today there are sixteen members of the European Union (formerly known as the European Common Market), fifteen members of the European Council, sixteen members of NATO, and thirty-three members of the Council of Europe. The Antichrist could spring from any of these groups. Just as the original six nations of the European Common Market grew to the sixteen member European Union, any of these groups could consolidate to ten.

The Bible revealed that a confederated union of ten nations will exist in the last days. These ten nations—some ruled by monarchs, some by democratic governments—could very well be the "ten toes" to be crushed by the stone cut without hands, Israel's Messiah. Nebuchadnezzar's image, representing the glorious and powerful kingdoms of the world, will be ground to powder and totally obliterated.

Daniel's Dream of Four Beasts

God wanted us to know the future, so He revealed to us the nations that would rule from Nebuchadnezzar through the terminal generation. Not only did he grant Nebuchadnezzar a vision of things to come, years later he repeated the same scenario with Daniel, this time using animals rather than metals. Why? Because animals have abilities and dispositions that vividly portray the profile and personality of coming kings and their kingdoms.

Listen to Daniel as he tells us about his dream in Daniel 7:

In the first year of Belshazzar king of Babylon, Daniel had a dream and visions of his head while on his bed. Then he wrote down the dream, telling the main facts.

Daniel spoke, saying, "I saw in my vision by night, and behold, the four winds of heaven were stirring up the Great Sea. And four great beasts came up from the sea, each different from the other. The first was like a lion, and had eagle's wings. I watched till its wings were plucked off; and it was lifted up from the earth and made to stand on two feet like a man, and a man's heart was given to it." (vv. 1–4)

In Daniel's dream we see the same parade of nations described in Nebuchadnezzar's vision, but with a different and disturbing twist.

During the reign of Belshazzar, Nebuchadnezzar's grandson, Daniel dreamed and saw four beasts rise up from the sea. The first beast was like a lion with the wings of an eagle: an exact representation of the Babylonian national symbol, a winged lion. Daniel had already seen the fulfillment of part of this vision. Nebuchadnezzar, who had risen to staggering heights of accomplishment, took pride in his success, but God struck him to the ground in a supernatural display of real power. Nebuchadnezzar lost his mind and actually ate grass like an ox for seven years, after which God restored his mind. He returned to his kingdom with "the heart of a man" and a new appreciation for the power of God.

But Babylon was doomed to failure. King Cyrus of Persia moved to capture the Babylonian empire in 539 B.C. and defeated Babylon's army on the Tigris River just south of modern-day Baghdad. The Babylonian Chronicle reports that the army of Cyrus entered Babylon without a battle.[3]

"And suddenly another beast, a second, like a bear. It was raised up on one side, and had three ribs in its mouth between its teeth. And they said thus to it: 'Arise, devour much flesh!'" (v. 5).

The second beast, a lopsided bear (because the Medes were more prominent than the Persians), represents the Medo-Persian Empire. The three ribs in the bear's mouth graphically illustrate the three prominent conquests of the empire: Lydia in 546 B.C., Babylon in 539 B.C., and Egypt in 525 B.C.[4]

"After this I looked, and there was another, like a leopard, which had on its back four wings of a bird. The beast also had four heads, and dominion was given to it" (v. 6).

The third beast, the leopard with four wings and four heads, represents Greece under Alexander the Great. The leopard is a swift animal, symbolizing the blinding speed with which Alexander's military juggernaut attacked its enemies.

What is the significance of the four heads? Through the telescope of history, their significance is clear. At age thirty-two, Alexander died in Babylon in 323 B.C. At his death, his four leading generals divided his kingdom: Ptolemy I took Israel and Egypt, Seleucus I reigned over Syria and Mesopotamia, Lysimachus chose to rule Thrace and Asia Minor, and Cassander took charge of Macedonia and Greece.

"After this I saw in the night visions, and behold, a fourth beast, dreadful and terrible, exceedingly strong. It had huge iron teeth; it was devouring, breaking in pieces, and trampling the residue with its feet. It was different from all the beasts that were before it, and it had ten horns" (v. 7).

The frightening fourth beast, more terrifying than its predecessors, represents the Roman Empire and the final form of Gentile power on the earth. The most important thing to notice about this horrifying beast is not its strength, its ferocity, or the fact that it has destroyed all the other beasts before it. The most important fact is that it has ten horns.

The ten horns of Daniel's dream correspond to the ten toes of Nebuchadnezzar's, and the horns represent ten kings or leaders who will lead nations that have risen from the fourth great world kingdom.

And while Daniel sat and thought about those ten leaders, another rose among them, a little one, who immediately uprooted or destroyed three of the ten. This horn had eyes like the eyes of a man and a mouth that spoke boastfully:

"I was considering the horns, and there was another horn, a little one, coming up among them, before whom three of the first horns were plucked out by the roots. And there, in this horn, were eyes like the eyes of a man, and a mouth speaking pompous words"(v. 8).

From among the ten kingdoms will arise one individual, the Antichrist, who will control the entire federation of nations.

Who is this "little horn"? And how can he wield enough power to control Europe, establish a worldwide religion, a worldwide economy, and a worldwide government? The answers to these questions can be found in God's Word, which we will discuss in coming chapters.

I watched till thrones were put in place, and the Ancient of Days was seated; His garment was white as snow, and the hair of His head was like pure wool. His throne was a fiery flame, its wheels a burning fire; a fiery stream issued and came forth from before Him. A thousand thousands ministered to Him; ten thousand times ten thousand stood before Him. The court was seated, and the books were opened.

I watched then because of the sound of the pompous words which the horn was speaking; I watched till the beast was slain, and its body destroyed and given to the burning flame. As for the rest of the beasts, they had their dominion taken away, yet their lives were prolonged for a season and a time.

I was watching in the night visions, and behold, One like the Son of Man, coming with the clouds of heaven! He came to the Ancient of Days, and they brought Him near before Him. Then to Him was given dominion and glory and a kingdom, that all peoples, nations, and languages should serve Him. His dominion is an everlasting dominion, which shall not pass away, and His kingdom the one which shall not be destroyed. . . .

This is the end of the account. As for me, Daniel, my thoughts greatly troubled me, and my countenance changed; but I kept the matter in my heart. (vv. 9–14, 28)

The Coming Victorious Messiah

Though Daniel's dream ended with the good news of the permanent reign of Christ, still he was troubled. Four great

41

kingdoms would arise, and from them a ten-kingdom confederation. From the confederation would come a pompous destroyer who would finally be destroyed by the Son of Man. The victory would be God's, but not before the world had suffered greatly.

Notice that Daniel saw one like the Son of Man coming to God, the Ancient of Days. To Him was given the everlasting kingdom that would not be destroyed. Before Him all people of all nations bowed. They served and worshiped the Son of Man, who is the Son of God.

Just as present-day Israel has two faces, so does its Messiah. He is both a suffering servant and a reigning king. He is both a gentle shepherd and a victorious warrior.

God often allows us to see the future in the past. Consider the story of Joseph, the beloved son of Jacob. He was betrayed by vengeful, jealous brothers who planned his death but eventually sold him into slavery in Egypt. He suffered among people who were not of his heritage, and after many years of slavery and imprisonment, he was elevated to the second highest position in the land. His brothers, driven by the gnawing pain of hunger, ventured into Egypt and stood before Joseph three times before he revealed his identity.

The Jewish people, sons of Abraham, have now returned to their land three times. The first time was when they returned from Egypt under the direction of Moses. The second time they returned from captivity with Nehemiah to rebuild the wall. In 1948, they reclaimed their ancestral title to the land for the third time. Now, after this third visitation, they will recognize their Brother when He reveals Himself.

Joseph told the sons of Jacob, "I am your brother who you rejected, but I have been exalted" (see Gen. 45). Zechariah says,

> And I will pour on the house of David and on the inhabitants of Jerusalem the Spirit of grace and supplication; then they will look on Me whom they pierced. Yes, they will mourn for Him

as one mourns for his only son, and grieve for Him as one grieves for a firstborn. In that day there shall be a great mourning in Jerusalem, like the mourning at Hadad Rimmon in the plain of Megiddo. (Zech. 12:10–11)

The first time Messiah came He was a baby in a manger, surrounded by donkeys and goats. The next time He comes He will be mounted on a milk-white stallion thundering through the clouds of heaven with the armies of heaven following Him. On His head will be many crowns, for He will come back to this earth as King of kings and Lord of lords.

The first time He came He was brought before Pilate; He was dragged before Herod. He was mocked, spit upon, and forced to wear a scarlet robe of mockery. The next time He comes, Pilate shall be brought before Him. Herod will be dragged before Him. Hitler will be hauled before Him, and that infamous hater of the Jewish people will bow before the King of the Jews and confess that He is Lord to the glory of God the Father.

The first time He came He was nailed to a bitterly rugged cross where He suffered and bled and died alone. The next time He comes He will put His foot on the Mount of Olives and it shall split in half. He will walk across the Kidron Valley and through the eastern gate and set His throne up on the temple mount, and from there He shall reign for one thousand years in the Millennium. Following that will be the Great White Throne Judgment, after which time shall cease and eternity will begin.

In the words of Daniel, "To Him will be given dominion and glory and a kingdom. People of all nations and languages will serve Him. His dominion will be an everlasting dominion which shall not pass away. And His kingdom is the one which shall not be destroyed."

CHAPTER FOUR

Can You Trust Prophecy?

Yes, you may be thinking, some biblical predictions have come true, but Bible prophecy is so vague it could never affect the decisions or conclusions I will make about the future. Wrong!

The eternal and almighty God, creator of Heaven and Earth, reigns over the past, present, and the future. Henry Ward Beecher said, "The Bible is God's chart for you to steer by, to keep you from the bottom of the sea, and to show you where the harbor is, and how to reach it without running on rocks and bars."

God has given us His Word in prophecy because He has always wanted His people to understand His actions. When God decided to destroy Sodom and Gomorrah, He decided to warn Abraham: "Shall I hide from Abraham what I am doing?" He asked (Gen. 18:17).

And while giving Abraham title to the land of Israel, God placed him in a deep sleep and said,

"Know certainly that your descendants will be strangers in a land that is not theirs, and will serve them, and they will afflict them four hundred years. And also the nation whom they serve I will judge; afterward they shall come out with great possessions. Now as for you, you shall go to your fathers in peace; you shall be buried at a good old age. But in the fourth generation they shall return here, for the iniquity of the Amorites is

not yet complete." . . . On the same day the LORD made a covenant with Abram, saying: "To your descendants I have given
this land, from the river of Egypt to the great river, the River
Euphrates." (Gen. 15:13–16, 18)

God displayed the entire panorama of future events concerning Abraham's descendants, and every word came to pass.
Prophecy, even a relatively short-term prophecy like the one
God gave Abraham, is important! I was at a gathering of
evangelical pastors several years ago in Houston and a well-
known preacher got up and said, "I do not study prophecy
and I do not teach prophecy because I don't understand it and
I don't think it's relevant for the twentieth century."

Friends, about one quarter of the Bible was prophetic when
it was written! Why would God choose to make a quarter of
His Word irrelevant or indecipherable? He didn't. He wants
us to understand the things to come. Bible prophecy proves
beyond any reasonable doubt that God knows and controls
the future. He's not sitting on the circle of the earth as a mere
observer, He is in charge!

Daniel Webster, writing in *Confession of Faith,* said, "I believe that the Bible is to be understood and received in the
plain and obvious meaning of its passages; since I cannot
persuade myself that a book intended for the instruction and
conversion of the whole world, should cover its true meaning
in such mystery and doubt, that none but critics and philosophers can discover it."[1]

If you doubt that the Word of God is accurate, consider the
prophecies concerning a city called Tyre. In Ezekiel 26, God
forecast the end of Tyre: many nations would come against it
(Ezekiel. 26:3); Babylon would be the first to attack it (v. 7);
Tyre's walls and towers would be broken down (vv. 4, 9); the
stones, timbers, and debris of the city would be thrown into
the sea (v. 12); its location would become a bare rock and a
place for fishermen to dry their nets (vv. 4–5, 14); and the city
of Tyre would never be rebuilt (v. 14).[2]

Tyre was no insignificant fishing village. It was a great city of Phoenicia and a prominent world capital for over two thousand years. Yet at the peak of its power, the prophet Ezekiel had the audacity to predict a violent future and ignominious end for the mighty city of Tyre. This downfall would come about because of the city's flagrant wickedness and arrogance, traits personified in its ruler, Ittobal II, who claimed to be God.[3]

History proved Ezekiel's words. Many nations did come against Tyre: first the Babylonians, then the Greeks, the Romans, the Muslims, and the Crusaders. After a thirteen-year siege, Nebuchadnezzar of Babylon broke down Tyre's walls and towers and massacred all of its inhabitants, except for those who escaped to an island fortress a half-mile out in the Mediterranean Sea. Centuries after Ezekiel had spoken, Alexander the Great conquered the island fortress of Tyre by building a causeway from Tyre's mainland to the island, using the millions of cubic feet of rubble left from the destroyed city. Thus Tyre was scraped bare as a kneecap, just as Ezekiel had predicted.[4]

And, astonishingly, Tyre has never been rebuilt. Despite its strategic and beautiful location, despite the fact that it contains the Springs of Reselain, which pump ten million gallons of fresh water daily, Tyre finally and irrevocably fell in A.D. 1291, never to be rebuilt. What covers those acres today? The drying nets of fishermen.[5]

In the last chapter of the book of Daniel there is an interesting prophecy: "Blessed is he who waits, and comes to the one thousand three hundred and thirty-five days" (Dan. 12:12).

What's the meaning of this verse? First, it's important to remember that prophecy often has both a primary literal fulfillment—in this case, of 1335 days, which will come to pass at the end of the age—and a secondary symbolic fulfillment, perhaps, in this case, years. (Consider Numbers 14:34: "According to the number of the days in which you spied out the land, forty days, God told the children of Israel, for each day you shall bear your guilt one year, namely forty years, and you shall know My rejection.") If it is possible for this verse to have a literal year-to-the-day fulfillment, then we have seen this verse come to pass in this century.

Let me explain. Islam began in A.D. 622. Shortly after this time, Jerusalem was taken by Muslims and occupied by them until A.D. 1917. In that year, Jerusalem was released by British General Edmund Henry Allenby, who rode into Jerusalem upon a white horse. About that time the British government proclaimed that the Jews would be permitted to return to their land. This proclamation, called the Balfour Declaration, was issued exactly thirteen hundred and thirty five years later according to the Islamic system of reckoning time. The coins of the Ottoman empire minted in that year bore the date "1335" on one side and "1917" on the other.

Daniel's prophecy may then mean that after 1335 years a time of blessedness would come to the land of Israel. Those who watched and waited would have the opportunity to enjoy great blessing. In 1917, many German Jews returned to Palestine. Many of those who passed up this opportunity remained in Germany and were unable to escape Hitler's genocide. Perhaps this is the blessing to which Daniel referred.

Messianic Prophecies

Recently a well-known preacher was on *Larry King Live*. King, who is Jewish, asked this nationally known pastor, "How do you know Jesus Christ was the Son of God?" The minister smiled and said, "I just have to accept that by faith."

Faith is important to God, for "without faith it is impossible to please Him" (Heb. 11:6), but our faith is not blind! Most of us find that the more we learn, the more our faith is assured by the facts. Many a seeker of God has begun to study the facts of Jesus' life and ministry and found Him more than worthy of complete and total faith. With a heart searching for truth, they have examined the facts, then proclaimed with heartfelt sincerity, "Jesus is Lord!"

God created our minds; He knows we are a people who want to understand. As a result, He has given us Bible prophecies that verify Jesus' claim to be the Messiah. Canon Liddon, a Bible scholar, says that there are 332 distinct predictions in the Old Testament which were literally fulfilled in Jesus Christ.[6] I have listed just eighty-eight of these which prove that Jesus Christ is the only man dead or alive who could possibly be the Messiah.

Many mainline Christian voices are now saying Jesus Christ is neither virgin-born nor the Messiah. Examine the evidence before you accept such a view.

My single purpose in writing this book is to prepare you for the future and the coming of the Antichrist. We have seen how accurate biblical prophecy is, and I can assure you that these events will come to pass. But just as the Antichrist is coming, you can be certain that the Messiah is also coming. Like the two faces of Janus which look forward and backward, these two beings represent completely opposite spiritual kingdoms. One wants to destroy you, the Other wants to give you life. One will bathe the world in blood, the Other will bring the golden era of peace.

Let me introduce you to Jesus Christ, a Jewish Rabbi who came to Earth the first time as a suffering Savior and will come again as a conquering king and the Prince of Peace. His personality, advent, and agenda are clearly revealed through the following eighty-eight major prophecies related by the Old Testament prophets. The fulfillment of God's Word is as sure as night following day, and just as every prophecy about Jesus' first coming has been literally fulfilled, every prophecy relating to his second coming and the events of the end times will also come to pass exactly as God has predicted.

Moses Profiles the Messiah

God hinted at the coming Messiah as early as the Garden of Eden when He predicted the coming and mission of the Messiah: "And I will put enmity between you and the woman, and between your seed [the Serpent, Satan] and her Seed [the Messiah, Jesus Christ]; He shall bruise your head [Satan's destruction], And you shall bruise His heel [Messiah's death and Resurrection]" (Gen. 3:15). Then God again hints at the mission of the Messiah to Abraham:

> Now the LORD had said to Abram: "Get out of your country, from your family and from your father's house, to a land that I will show you. I will make you a great nation; I will bless you and make your name great; and you shall be a blessing. I will bless those who bless you, and I will curse him who curses you; *and in you all the families of the earth shall be blessed.*" (Gen. 12:1–3, emphasis mine)

But it was Moses who gave us the first extended biblical description of the coming Messiah. In Deuteronomy 18:18–19, Moses brings to Israel the following promise from God: "I will raise up for them a Prophet like you from among their brethren, and will put My words in His mouth, and He shall speak to them all that I command Him. And it shall be that whoever will not hear My words, which He speaks in My name, I will require it of him."

In Acts 3:22–26, the apostle Peter explains how this prophecy of Moses applies to Jesus Christ of Nazareth as Israel's Messiah:

> For Moses truly said to the fathers, "The LORD your God will raise up for you a Prophet like me from your brethren. Him you shall hear in all things, whatever He says to you. And it shall be that every soul who will not hear that Prophet shall be utterly destroyed from among the people." Yes, and all the prophets, from Samuel and those who follow, as many as have spoken, have also foretold these days. You are sons of the prophets, and

of the covenant which God made with our fathers, saying to Abraham, "And in your seed all the families of the earth shall be blessed." To you first, God, having raised up His Servant Jesus, sent Him to bless you, in turning away every one of you from your iniquities.

Moses' words established three facts: First, God promised to send to Israel a particular prophet at a later time. The language Moses uses is singular throughout: "*a* Prophet . . . *His* mouth . . . *He* shall speak." These words cannot describe the later prophets in Israel as a whole. They referred to one special Prophet.

Second, this Prophet would have unique authority, above all others who had gone before Him, and if anyone in Israel refused to hearken to this Prophet, God would bring judgment upon that person.

Third, this Prophet would be like Moses in ways that would distinguish Him from all other prophets. A careful comparison of the lives of the two men reveals twenty-seven distinct parallels between the lives of Moses and Jesus.

1. **Both Moses and Jesus were born in a period when Israel was under foreign rule.**

   "Now there arose a new king over Egypt, who did not know Joseph. . . . Therefore they set taskmasters over them to afflict them with their burdens. And they built for Pharaoh supply cities, Pithom and Raamses" (Ex. 1:8, 11).

   "And it came to pass in those days that a decree went out from Caesar Augustus that all the world should be registered. This census first took place while Quirinius was governing Syria. So all went to be registered, everyone to his own city. Joseph also went up from Galilee, out of the city of Nazareth, into Judea, to the city of David, which is called Bethlehem, because he was of the house and lineage of David, to be registered with Mary, his betrothed wife, who was with child" (Luke 2:1–5).

2. **Cruel kings decided that both Moses and Jesus should be killed as infants.**

   "Then the king of Egypt spoke to the Hebrew midwives, of whom the name of one was Shiphrah and the name of the other Puah; and he said, 'When you do the duties of a midwife for the Hebrew women, and see them on the birthstools, if it is a son, then you shall kill him; but if it is a daughter, then she shall live.' But the midwives feared God, and did not do as the king of Egypt commanded them, but saved the male children alive" (Ex. 1:15–17).

   "Then Herod . . . was exceedingly angry; and he sent forth and put to death all the male children who were in Bethlehem and in all its districts, from two years old and under, according to the time which he had determined from the wise men" (Matt. 2:16).

3. **The faith of both Moses' and Jesus' parents saved their lives.**

   "So the woman [the mother of Moses] conceived and bore a son. And when she saw that he was a beautiful child, she hid him three months. But when she could no longer hide him, she took an ark of bulrushes for him, daubed it with asphalt and pitch, put the child in it, and laid it in the reeds by the river's bank. And his sister stood afar off, to know what would be done to him" (Ex. 2:2–4).

   "By faith Moses, when he was born, was hidden three months by his parents, because they saw he was a beautiful child; and they were not afraid of the king's command" (Heb. 11:23).

   "Now when they had departed, behold, an angel of the Lord appeared to Joseph in a dream, saying, 'Arise, take the young Child [Jesus] and His mother, flee to Egypt, and stay there until I bring you word; for Herod will seek the young Child to destroy Him.' When he arose, he took the young Child and His mother by night and departed for Egypt" (Matt. 2:13–14).

4. **Both Moses and Jesus found protection for a time with the people of Egypt.**

"And the child grew, and she brought him to Pharaoh's daughter, and he became her son. So she called his name Moses, saying, 'Because I drew him out of the water'" (Ex. 2:10).

"When he arose, he took the young Child [Jesus] and His mother by night and departed for Egypt, and was there until the death of Herod, that it might be fulfilled which was spoken by the Lord through the prophet, saying, 'Out of Egypt I called My Son'" (Matt. 2:14–15).

5. **Both Moses and Jesus displayed unusual wisdom and understanding.**

"And Moses was learned in all the wisdom of the Egyptians, and was mighty in words and deeds" (Acts 7:22).

"Now so it was that after three days they found Him [Jesus] in the temple, sitting in the midst of the teachers, both listening to them and asking them questions. And all who heard Him were astonished at His understanding and answers" (Luke 2:46–47).

6. **Both Moses' and Jesus' characters were marked by meekness and humility.**

"Now the man Moses was very humble, more than all men who were on the face of the earth" (Num. 12:3).

"[Jesus said,] 'Come to Me, all you who labor and are heavy laden, and I will give you rest. Take My yoke upon you and learn from Me, for I am gentle and lowly in heart, and you will find rest for your souls. For My yoke is easy and My burden is light'" (Matt. 11:28–30).

7. **Both Moses and Jesus were completely faithful to God.**

"My servant Moses . . . is faithful in all My house" (Num. 12:7).

"Therefore, holy brethren, partakers of the heavenly calling, consider the Apostle and High Priest of our confession, Christ Jesus, who was faithful to Him who appointed Him, as Moses also was faithful in all His house. For this One has been counted worthy of more glory than Moses, inasmuch as He who built the house has more honor than the house. For every house is built by someone, but He who built all things is God. And Moses indeed was faithful in all His house as a servant, for a testimony of those things which would be spoken afterward, but Christ as a Son over His own house, whose house we are if we hold fast the confidence and the rejoicing of the hope firm to the end" (Heb. 3:1-6).

8. **Both Moses and Jesus were rejected by Israel for a time.**

"And when [Moses] went out the second day, behold, two Hebrew men were fighting, and he said to the one who did the wrong, 'Why are you striking your companion?' Then he said [to Moses], 'Who made you a prince and a judge over us?'" (Ex. 2:13-14).

"Now when the people saw that Moses delayed coming down from the mountain, the people gathered together to Aaron, and said to him, 'Come, make us gods that shall go before us; for as for this Moses, the man who brought us up out of the land of Egypt, we do not know what has become of him'" (Ex. 32:1).

"The governor answered and said to them, 'Which of the two do you want me to release to you?' They said, 'Barabbas!' Pilate said to them, 'What then shall I do with Jesus who is called Christ?' They all said to him, 'Let Him be crucified!'" (Matt. 27:21-22).

9. **Both Moses and Jesus were criticized by their brothers and sisters.**

"Then Miriam and Aaron spoke against Moses because of the Ethiopian woman whom he had married; for he had married an Ethiopian woman" (Num. 12:1).

"For even His [Jesus'] brothers did not believe in Him" (John 7:5).

10. **Both Moses and Jesus were received by Gentiles after being rejected by Israel.**

"Moses fled [Egypt] and dwelt in the land of Midian. . . . Then Moses was content to live with the man [Reuel], and he gave Zipporah his daughter to Moses" (Ex. 2:15, 21).

"On the next Sabbath almost the whole city [Jerusalem] came together to hear the word of God. But when the Jews saw the multitudes, they were filled with envy; and contradicting and blaspheming, they opposed the things spoken by Paul. Then Paul and Barnabas grew bold and said, 'It was necessary that the word of God should be spoken to you first; but since you reject it, and judge yourselves unworthy of everlasting life, behold, we turn to the Gentiles. For so the Lord has commanded us: "I have set you as a light to the Gentiles, that you should be for salvation to the ends of the earth."' Now when the Gentiles heard this, they were glad and glorified the word of the Lord [Jesus]. And as many as had been appointed to eternal life believed" (Acts 13:44–48).

11. **Both Moses and Jesus prayed asking forgiveness for God's people.**

"Then Moses returned to the LORD and said, 'Oh, these people have committed a great sin, and have made for themselves a god of gold! Yet now, if You will forgive their sin—but if not, I pray, blot me out of Your book which You have written'" (Ex. 32:31–32).

"Then Jesus said [concerning those who were crucifying Him], 'Father, forgive them, for they do not know what they do'" (Luke 23:34).

12. **Both Moses and Jesus were willing to bear the punishment for God's people.**

"Then Moses returned to the LORD and said, 'Oh, these people have committed a great sin, and have made for themselves a god of gold! Yet now, if You will forgive their sin—but if not, I pray, blot me out of Your book which You have written'" (Ex. 32:31–32).

"For Christ also suffered once for sins, the just for the unjust, that He might bring us to God, being put to death in the flesh but made alive by the Spirit" (1 Pet. 3:18).

13. **Both Moses and Jesus endured a forty-day fast.**

"So he [Moses] was there with the LORD forty days and forty nights; he neither ate bread nor drank water. And He wrote on the tablets the words of the covenant, the Ten Commandments" (Ex. 34:28).

"And when He [Jesus] had fasted forty days and forty nights, afterward He was hungry" (Matt. 4:2).

14. **Both Moses and Jesus spoke with God face-to-face.**

"Not so with My servant Moses; He is faithful in all My house. I speak with him face to face, even plainly, and not in dark sayings; and he sees the form of the LORD" (Num. 12:7–8).

"But since then there has not arisen in Israel a prophet like Moses, whom the LORD knew face to face" (Deut. 34:10).

"No one has seen God at any time. The only begotten Son [Jesus], who is in the bosom of the Father, He has declared Him" (John 1:18).

15. **Both Moses and Jesus went up into a high mountain to have communion with God, taking some of their closest followers with them.**

"Then Moses went up [to Mount Sinai], also Aaron, Nadab, and Abihu, and seventy of the elders of Israel, and they saw the God of Israel. And there was under His feet as it were a paved work of sapphire stone, and it was like the very heavens in its clarity" (Ex. 24:9–10).

"Now after six days Jesus took Peter, James, and John his brother, led them up on a high mountain by themselves; . . . While he was still speaking, behold, a bright cloud overshadowed them; and suddenly a voice came out of the cloud, saying, 'This is My beloved Son, in whom I am well pleased. Hear Him!'" (Matt. 17:1, 5).

16. **After their mountaintop experiences, both Moses' and Jesus' faces shone with supernatural glory.**

"But whenever Moses went in before the LORD to speak with Him, he would take the veil off until he came out; and he would come out and speak to the children of Israel whatever he had been commanded. And whenever the children of Israel saw the face of Moses, that the skin of Moses' face shone, then Moses would put the veil on his face again, until he went in to speak with Him" (Ex. 34:34, 35).

"And He [Jesus] was transfigured before them. His face shone like the sun, and His clothes became as white as the light" (Matt. 17:2).

17. **God spoke audibly from heaven to both Moses and Jesus.**

"Moses spoke, and God answered him by voice. Then the LORD came down upon Mount Sinai, on the top of the mountain. And the LORD called Moses to the top of the mountain, and Moses went up" (Ex. 19:19–20).

"But Jesus answered them, saying, 'The hour has come that the Son of Man should be glorified. . . . Father, glorify Your name.' Then a voice came from heaven, saying, 'I have both glorified it and will glorify it again'" (John 12:23, 28).

18. **Both Moses' and Jesus' places of burial were attended by angels.**

"Yet Michael the archangel, in contending with the devil, when he disputed about the body of Moses, dared not bring against him a reviling accusation, but said, 'The Lord rebuke you!'" (Jude 9).

"And behold, there was a great earthquake; for an angel of the Lord descended from heaven, and came and rolled back the stone from the door, and sat on it. . . . But the angel answered and said to the women, 'Do not be afraid, for I know that you seek Jesus who was crucified. He is not here; for He is risen, as He said. Come, see the place where the Lord lay'" (Matt. 28:2, 5–6).

19. **Both Moses and Jesus appeared alive after their deaths.**

"And behold, Moses and Elijah appeared to them [Jesus, Peter, James, and John], talking with Him" (Matt. 17:3).

"Then, the same day at evening, being the first day of the week, when the doors were shut where the disciples were assembled, for fear of the Jews, Jesus [after his death, burial, and resurrection] came and stood in the midst, and said to them, 'Peace be with you.' When He had said this, He showed them His hands and His side. Then the disciples were glad when they saw the Lord" (John 20:19, 20).

20. **Both Moses and Jesus were teachers.**

[Moses is speaking] "Now, O Israel, listen to the statutes and the judgments which I teach you to observe, that you may live, and go in and possess the land which the LORD God of your fathers is giving you" (Deut. 4:1).

"There was a man of the Pharisees named Nicodemus, a ruler of the Jews. This man came to Jesus by night and said to Him, 'Rabbi, we know that You are a teacher come from God; for no one can do these signs that You do unless God is with him'" (John 3:1–2).

21. **Both Moses and Jesus were shepherds to God's people.**

"You led Your people like a flock by the hand of Moses and Aaron" (Ps. 77:20).

"[Jesus said,] 'I am the good shepherd. The good shepherd gives His life for the sheep. . . . My sheep hear My voice, and I know them, and they follow Me'" (John 10:11, 27).

22. **Both Moses and Jesus revealed God's name to his people.**

"Then Moses said to God, 'Indeed, when I come to the children of Israel and say to them, "The God of your fathers has sent me to you," and they say to me, "What is His name?" what shall I say to them?' And God said to Moses, 'I AM WHO I AM.' And He said, 'Thus you shall say to the children of Israel, "I AM has sent me to you"'" (Ex. 3:13–14).

"[Jesus prayed:] 'I have manifested Your name to the men whom You have given Me out of the world. They were Yours, You gave them to Me, and they have kept Your word. . . . Now I am no longer in the world, but these are in the world, and I come to You. Holy Father, keep through Your name those whom You have given Me, that they may be one as We are. While I was with them in the world, I kept them in Your name'" (John 17:6, 11–12).

23. **Through both Moses and Jesus God gave His people food from a supernatural source.**

"When the dew was gone, thin flakes like frost on the ground appeared on the desert floor. When the Israelites saw it, they said to each other, 'What is it?' For they did not know what it was. Moses said to them, 'It is the bread the LORD has given you to eat'" (Ex. 16:14–15 NIV).

"And [Jesus] directed the people to sit down on the grass. Taking the five loaves and the two fish and looking up to heaven, he gave thanks and broke the loaves. Then he gave them to the disciples, and the disciples gave them to the people. They all ate and were satisfied, and the disciples picked up twelve basketfuls of broken pieces that were left over. The number of those who ate was about five thousand men, besides women and children" (Matt. 14:19–21 NIV).

24. **Both Moses and Jesus brought deliverance to God's people.**

"The LORD said [to Moses], 'I have indeed seen the misery of my people in Egypt. I have heard them crying out because of their slave drivers, and I am concerned about their suffering. So I have come down to rescue them from the hand of the Egyptians and to bring them up out of that land into a good and spacious land, a land flowing with milk and honey. . . . So now, go. I am sending you to Pharaoh to bring my people the Israelites out of Egypt'" (Ex. 3:7–8, 10 NIV).

"The scroll of the prophet Isaiah was handed to [Jesus]. Unrolling it, he found the place where it is written: 'The Spirit of the Lord is on me, because he has anointed me to preach good news to the poor. He has sent me to proclaim freedom for the prisoners and recovery of sight for the blind, to release the oppressed, to proclaim the year of the Lord's favor.' . . . And he began by saying to them, 'Today this scripture is fulfilled in your hearing'" (Luke 4:17–19, 21 NIV).

25. **Both Moses and Jesus brought healing to God's people.**

"The soul of the people [Israel] became very discouraged on the way. And the people spoke against God and against Moses. . . . So the LORD sent fiery serpents among the people, and they bit the people; and many of the people of Israel died. Therefore the people came to Moses, and said, 'We have sinned, for we have spoken against the LORD and against you; pray to the LORD that He take away the serpents from us.' So Moses prayed for the people. Then the LORD said to Moses, 'Make a fiery serpent, and set it on a pole; and it shall be that everyone who is bitten, when he looks at it, shall live.' So Moses made a bronze serpent, and put it on a pole; and so it was, if a serpent had bitten anyone, when he looked at the bronze serpent, he lived" (Num. 21:4, 6–9).

"Jesus went throughout Galilee, teaching in their synagogues, preaching the good news of the kingdom, and healing every disease and sickness among the people" (Matt. 4:23 NIV).

"He himself [Jesus] bore our sins in his body on the tree, so that we might die to sins and live for righteousness; by his wounds you have been healed" (1 Pet. 2:24 NIV).

26. **Both Moses and Jesus worked great miracles.**

"Since then, no prophet has risen in Israel like Moses, whom the LORD knew face to face, who did all those miraculous signs and wonders the LORD sent him to do in Egypt—to Pharaoh and to all his officials and to his whole land. For no one has ever shown the mighty power or performed the awesome deeds that Moses did in the sight of all Israel" (Deut. 34:10–12 NIV).

"Men of Israel, listen to this: Jesus of Nazareth was a man accredited by God to you by miracles, wonders and signs, which God did among you through him, as you yourselves know" (Acts 2:22 NIV).

27. **Both Moses and Jesus established and sealed with blood a covenant between God and His people.**

"Then [Moses] took the Book of the Covenant and read it to the people. They responded, 'We will do everything the LORD has said; we will obey.' Moses then took the blood, sprinkled it on the people and said, 'This is the blood of the covenant that the LORD has made with you in accordance with all these words'" (Ex. 24:7–8 NIV).

"When Christ came as high priest of the good things . . . He entered the Most Holy Place once for all by His own blood, having obtained eternal redemption. The blood of goats and bulls and the ashes of a heifer sprinkled on those who are ceremonially unclean sanctify them so that they are outwardly clean. How much more, then, will the blood of Christ, who through the eternal

Spirit offered himself unblemished to God, cleanse our consciences from acts that lead to death. . . . For this reason Christ is the mediator of a new covenant" (Hebrews 9:11–15).

Not only does Scripture paint a vivid picture of Christ's similarity to Moses the Deliverer, but the prophets foretold his coming and ministry for thousands of years. The prophets spoke both of a suffering Messiah and a kingly, conquering Messiah, and all these prophecies below were fulfilled by Jesus Christ at His first appearance.

1. **The Messiah will be born of a woman.**

   Prophecy: When Adam and Eve sinned in the Garden of Eden, God the Father made this statement to Satan: "And I will put enmity between you [Satan] and the woman, and between your offspring and hers; he will crush your head [destroy you], and you will strike his heel [hurt him]" (Gen. 3:15 NIV).

   Fulfillment: "But when the time had fully come, God sent his Son, born of woman, born under law" (Gal. 4:4 NIV).

   The Messiah's first coming was from a mother's womb, as is the case with everyone who is born. What is interesting in the passages above is that the woman is emphasized, not the man. This is because Jesus was conceived not through the joining of a man and woman but by the power of the Holy Spirit overshadowing the virgin Mary (see Luke 1:35).

2. **The Messiah will be born of a virgin.**

   Prophecy: "Therefore the Lord Himself will give you a sign: Behold, a virgin will be with child and bear a son, and she will call His name Immanuel" (Is. 7:14 NASB).

   Fulfillment: "Now in the sixth month the angel Gabriel was sent by God to a city of Galilee named Nazareth, to a virgin betrothed to a man whose name was Joseph, of

61

the house of David. The virgin's name was Mary. . . . Then the angel said to her, 'Do not be afraid, Mary, for you have found favor with God. And behold, you will conceive in your womb and bring forth a Son, and shall call His name JESUS.' . . . Then Mary said to the angel, 'How can this be, since I do not know a man [that is, have not had sexual relations with a man]?' And the angel answered and said to her, 'The Holy Spirit will come upon you, and the power of the Highest will overshadow you; therefore, also, that Holy One who is to be born will be called the Son of God. . . . For with God nothing will be impossible.' Then Mary said, 'Behold the maidservant of the Lord! Let it be to me according to your word.' And the angel departed from her" (Luke 1:26–27, 30–31, 34–35, 37–38).

3. **The Messiah will be the Son of God.**

Prophecy: "I will surely tell of the decree of the LORD: He said to Me, 'Thou art My Son, today I have begotten Thee'" (Ps. 2:7 NASB).

Fulfillment: "And behold, a voice [God the Father's] out of the heavens, saying, 'This is My beloved Son, in whom I am well-pleased'" (Matt. 3:17 NASB).

"And the unclean spirits, whenever they saw Him, fell down before Him and cried out, saying, 'You are the Son of God'" (Mark 3:11).

Psalm 2:7 is a Royal Psalm, and in it the Messiah is proclaiming the affirmation of the Father about the Sonship of the Messiah.

4. **The Messiah will be the Seed of Abraham.**

Prophecy: "In your [Abraham's] seed all the nations of the earth shall be blessed, because you have obeyed My voice" (Gen. 22:18).

"Abraham will surely become a great and powerful nation, and all nations on earth will be blessed through him" (Gen. 12:3).

Fulfillment: "The book of the genealogy of Jesus Christ, the Son of David, the Son of Abraham" (Matt. 1:1).

"The promises were spoken to Abraham and to his seed. The Scripture does not say 'and to seeds,' meaning many people, but 'and to your seed,' meaning one person, who is Christ" (Gal. 3:16 NIV).

5. **The Messiah will be a Son of Isaac.**

Prophecy: "Then God said [to Abraham], 'Yes, but your wife Sarah will bear you a son, and you will call him Isaac. I will establish my covenant with him as an everlasting covenant for his descendants after him'" (Gen. 17:19 NIV).

Fulfillment: "Abraham was the father of Isaac, Isaac the father of Jacob, Jacob the father of Judah and his brothers . . . and Jacob the father of Joseph, the husband of Mary, of whom was born Jesus, who is called Christ" (Matt. 1:2, 16 NIV).

"Jesus, . . . the son of Isaac, . . ." (Luke 3:23, 34).

6. **The Messiah will be a son of Jacob.**

Prophecy: "I see him, but not now; I behold him, but not near; a star shall come forth from Jacob, and a scepter [ruler] shall rise from Israel, and shall crush through the forehead of Moab, and tear down all the sons of Sheth" (Num. 24:17 NASB).

Fulfillment: "Abraham was the father of Isaac, Isaac the father of Jacob, Jacob the father of Judah and his brothers . . . and Jacob the father of Joseph, the husband of Mary, of whom was born Jesus, who is called Christ" (Matt. 1:2, 16 NIV).

"Jesus, ... the son of Jacob, . . ." (Luke 3:23, 34).

7. **The Messiah will be from the tribe of Judah.**

Prophecy: "The scepter will not depart from Judah, nor the ruler's staff from between his feet, until he comes to whom it belongs and the obedience of the nations is his" (Gen. 49:10 NIV).

Fulfillment: "Judah begot Perez and Zerah by Tamar . . . and Jacob begot Joseph the husband of Mary, of whom was born Jesus who is called Christ" (Matt. 1:3, 16).

"Jesus, . . . the son of Judah, . . ." (Luke 3:23, 33).

"For it is evident that our Lord arose from Judah" (Heb. 7:14).

8. **The Messiah will be of the family line of Jesse.**

Prophecy: "Then a shoot will spring from the stem of Jesse, and a branch from his roots will bear fruit" (Is. 11:1 NASB).

Fulfillment: "And Jesse begot David the king . . . and Jacob begot Joseph the husband of Mary, of whom was born Jesus who is called Christ" (Matt. 1:6, 16).

"Jesus, . . . the son of Jesse, . . ." (Luke 3:23, 32).

The prophecy of Isaiah is figurative language, depicting Jesse as the stem of a tree, and the "shoot" which shall come as someone from his lineage. Isaiah predicted that one would come from Jesse's line and bear much fruit. Jesus Christ, who descended from the line of Jesse, has borne much spiritual fruit—more than anyone else in history. Those who trust Him as Savior are reborn in Him, becoming the children of God through the power of His name, and manifesting spiritual fruit through Him.

9. **The Messiah will be of the house of David.**

Prophecy: "For to us a child is born, to us a son is given, and the government will be on his shoulders. And he will be called Wonderful Counselor, Mighty God, Everlasting Father, Prince of Peace. Of the increase of his government and peace there will be no end. He will reign on David's throne and over his kingdom, establishing and upholding it with justice and righteousness from that time on and forever. The zeal of the LORD Almighty will accomplish this" (Is. 9:6–7 NIV).

Fulfillment: "David the king begot Solomon by her who had been the wife of Uriah . . . and Jacob begot Joseph the husband of Mary, of whom was born Jesus who is called Christ" (Matthew 1:6, 16).

"Jesus, . . . the son of David, . . ." (Luke 3:23, 31).

Jesus descended from the lineage of David, and in His future millennial kingdom He will uphold the world with righteousness and justice. One day He, as a son of David, will rule from the Temple Mount in Jerusalem, and His kingdom will last forever.

10. **The Messiah will be born at Bethlehem.**

Prophecy: "But as for you, Bethlehem Ephrathah, too little to be among the clans of Judah, from you One will go forth for Me to be ruler in Israel. His goings forth are from long ago, from the days of eternity" (Mic. 5:2 NASB).

Fulfillment: "Jesus was born in Bethlehem of Judea" (Matt. 2:1).

11. **A star will announce the birth of the Messiah.**

Prophecy: "I see him, but not now; I behold him, but not near; a star shall come forth from Jacob, and a scepter [ruler] shall rise from Israel, and shall crush through the forehead of Moab, and tear down all the sons of Sheth" (Num. 24:17 NASB).

Fulfillment: "Now after Jesus was born in Bethlehem of Judea in the days of Herod the king, behold, wise men from the East came to Jerusalem, saying, 'Where is He who has been born King of the Jews? For we have seen His star in the East and have come to worship Him'" (Matt. 2:1–2).

A Bible commentator notes, "Many feel the Magi's comments reflected a knowledge of Balaam's prophecy concerning the star that would come out of Jacob."[7]

12. Herod will kill the children.

Prophecy: "Thus says the LORD, 'A voice is heard in Ramah, lamentation and bitter weeping. Rachel is weeping for her children; she refuses to be comforted for her children, because they are no more'" (Jer. 31:15 NASB).

Fulfillment: "Then when Herod saw that he had been tricked by the magi, he became very enraged, and sent and slew all the male children who were in Bethlehem and in all its environs, from two years old and under, according to the time which he had ascertained from the magi" (Matt. 2:16 NASB).

Wise men came from the east and told Herod that a new king had been born, this one to rule the Jews. Politically, Herod could not afford another uprising in the lands he oversaw for Rome, and the title, King of the Jews, was at the moment his. So, not knowing the exact identity of the newborn King, he decreed that all babies two years old and younger should be slaughtered in the desperate hope that by doing so the infant King would be among those killed.

13. The Messiah has preexisted.

Prophecy: "But as for you, Bethlehem Ephrathah, too little to be among the clans of Judah, from you One will go forth for Me to be ruler in Israel. His goings forth are from long ago, from the days of eternity" (Mic. 5:2).

Fulfillment: "And He is [has existed prior to] before all things, and in Him all things consist" (Col. 1:17).

14. The Messiah shall be called "Lord."

Prophecy: "The LORD says to my Lord: 'Sit at My right hand, until I make Thine enemies a footstool for Thy feet" (Ps. 110:1 NASB).

Fulfillment: "Then Jesus answered and said, while He taught in the temple, 'How is it that the scribes say that the Christ is the Son of David? For David himself said by the Holy Spirit: "The LORD said to my Lord, 'Sit at My

right hand, till I make Your enemies Your footstool.'"
Therefore David himself calls Him "Lord"; how is He
then his Son?' And the common people heard Him gladly"
(Mark 12:35–37).

The Bible Knowledge Commentary examines David's
prophecy: "David heard a heavenly conversation between the
Lord *(Yahweh)* and David's Lord *('adonay),* that is, between
God the Father and the Messiah. The verb *says* is . . . a word
often used to depict an oracle or a revelation. In this oracle
Yahweh said that David's Lord, the Messiah, is seated at Yahweh's right hand (cf. v. 5), the place of authority, until the
consummation of the ages (cf. 2:8–9). At that time the Lord
will send David's Lord, [Jesus] the Messiah, to make His enemies subject to Him. A footstool pictures complete subjugation. With His scepter the Messiah will . . . rule over His
enemies."[8]

15. **The Messiah shall be called Immanuel (God with us).**
    Prophecy: "Therefore the Lord Himself will give you a
    sign: Behold, a virgin will be with child and bear a son,
    and she will call His name Immanuel" (Is. 7:14 NASB).

    Fulfillment: "'Behold, the virgin shall be with child,
    and bear a Son, and they shall call His name Immanuel,'
    which is translated, 'God with us.' Then Joseph, being
    aroused from sleep, did as the angel of the Lord com-
    manded him and took to him his wife, and did not know
    her till she had brought forth her firstborn Son. And he
    called His name Jesus" (Matt. 1:23–25).

16. **The Messiah shall be a prophet.**
    Prophecy: "I will raise up a prophet from among their
    countrymen like you, and I will put My words in his
    mouth, and he shall speak to them all that I command
    him" (Deut. 18:18 NASB).

Fulfillment: "And the multitudes were saying, 'This is the prophet Jesus, from Nazareth in Galilee'" (Matt. 21:11 NASB).

17. The Messiah shall be a priest.

Prophecy: "The LORD has sworn and will not change His mind, 'Thou art a priest forever according to the order of Melchizedek'" (Ps. 110:4 NASB).

Fulfillment: "Therefore, holy brethren, partakers of a heavenly calling, consider Jesus, the Apostle and High Priest of our confession" (Heb. 3:1 NASB).

"During the days of Jesus' life on earth, he offered up prayers and petitions with loud cries and tears to the one who could save him from death, and he was heard because of his reverent submission. Although he was a son, he learned obedience from what he suffered and, once made perfect, he became the source of eternal salvation for all who obey him and was designated by God to be high priest in the order of Melchizedek" (Heb. 5:7–10 NIV).

18. The Messiah shall be a judge.

Prophecy: "For the LORD is our Judge, the LORD is our Lawgiver, the LORD is our King; He will save us" (Is. 33:22).

Fulfillment: "I charge you therefore before God and the Lord Jesus Christ, who will judge the living and the dead at His appearing and His kingdom" (2 Tim. 4:1).

God the Father has given the role of Judge to Jesus Christ. On one day still to come, every man, woman, and child will stand before Jesus Christ the judge and acknowledge that He is Lord.

19. The Messiah shall be King.

Prophecy: "Of the increase of his government and peace there will be no end. He will reign on David's throne and over his kingdom, establishing and upholding it with justice and righteousness from that time on and forever.

The zeal of the Lord Almighty will accomplish this" (Is. 9:7 NIV).

Fulfillment: "'You are a king, then!' said Pilate. Jesus answered, 'You are right in saying I am a king. In fact, for this reason I was born, and for this I came into the world, to testify to the truth. Everyone on the side of truth listens to me'" (John 18:37 NIV).

20. **The Messiah shall be anointed by the Holy Spirit.**

Prophecy: "And the Spirit of the LORD will rest on Him, the spirit of wisdom and understanding, the spirit of counsel and strength, the spirit of knowledge and the fear of the LORD" (Is. 11:2 NASB).

Fulfillment: "And after being baptized, Jesus went up immediately from the water; and behold, the heavens were opened, and he saw the Spirit of God descending as a dove, and coming upon Him, and behold, a voice out of the heavens, saying, 'This is My beloved Son, in whom I am well-pleased'" (Matt. 3:16–17 NASB).

21. **The Messiah will have great zeal for God.**

Prophecy: "Because zeal for Your house has eaten me up, and the reproaches of those who reproach You have fallen on me" (Ps. 69:9).

Fulfillment: "Now the Passover of the Jews was at hand, and Jesus went up to Jerusalem. And He found in the temple those who sold oxen and sheep and doves, and the moneychangers doing business. When He had made a whip of cords, He drove them all out of the temple, with the sheep and the oxen, and poured out the changers' money and overturned the tables. And He said to those who sold doves, 'Take these things away! Do not make My Father's house a house of merchandise!' Then His disciples remembered that it was written, 'Zeal for Your house has eaten Me up'" (John 2:13–17).

22. The Messiah will be preceded by a messenger.

Prophecy: "A voice is calling, 'Clear the way for the LORD in the wilderness; make smooth in the desert a highway for our God'" (Is. 40:3 NASB).

Fulfillment: "In those days John the Baptist came preaching in the wilderness of Judea, and saying, 'Repent, for the kingdom of heaven is at hand!' For this is he who was spoken of by the prophet Isaiah, saying: 'The voice of one crying in the wilderness: "Prepare the way of the LORD; make His paths straight"'" (Matt. 3:1–3).

23. The Messiah will minister in Galilee.

Prophecy: "But there will be no more gloom for her who was in anguish; in earlier times He treated the land of Zebulun and the land of Naphtali with contempt, but later on He shall make it glorious, by the way of the sea, on the other side of Jordan, Galilee of the Gentiles" (Is. 9:1 NASB).

Fulfillment: "Now when Jesus heard that John had been put in prison, He departed to Galilee. And leaving Nazareth, He came and dwelt in Capernaum, which is by the sea, in the regions of Zebulun and Naphtali, that it might be fulfilled which was spoken by Isaiah the prophet, saying: 'The land of Zebulun and the land of Naphtali, by the way of the sea, beyond the Jordan, Galilee of the Gentiles: The people who sat in darkness have seen a great light, and upon those who sat in the region and shadow of death light has dawned.' From that time Jesus began to preach and to say, 'Repent, for the kingdom of heaven is at hand'" (Matt. 4:12–17).

The prophecy of Isaiah was "fulfilled when Jesus ministered in Capernaum— near the major highway from Egypt to Damascus, called 'the way of the sea.'"⁹

24. The Messiah's ministry will include miracles.

Prophecy: "Then the eyes of the blind will be opened, and the ears of the deaf will be unstopped. Then the lame will leap like a deer, and the tongue of the dumb will shout for joy" (Is. 35:5–6 NASB).

Fulfillment: "And Jesus was going about all the cities and the villages, teaching in their synagogues, and proclaiming the gospel of the kingdom, and healing every kind of disease and every kind of sickness" (Matt. 9:35 NASB).

25. **The Messiah will be a teacher of parables.**

Prophecy: "I [the prophet is speaking for the Messiah] will open my mouth in a parable; I will utter dark sayings of old" (Ps. 78:2).

"And He said, 'Go, and tell this people: "Keep on hearing, but do not understand; keep on seeing, but do not perceive." Make the heart of this people dull, and their ears heavy, and shut their eyes; lest they see with their eyes, and hear with their ears, and understand with their heart, and return and be healed'" (Is. 6:9–10).

Fulfillment: "All these things Jesus spoke to the multitude in parables; and without a parable He did not speak to them, that it might be fulfilled which was spoken by the prophet, saying: 'I will open My mouth in parables; I will utter things kept secret from the foundation of the world'" (Matt. 13:34–35).

"Then His disciples asked Him, saying, 'What does this parable mean?' And He said, 'To you it has been given to know the mysteries of the kingdom of God, but to the rest it is given in parables, that "Seeing they may not see, and hearing they may not understand"'" (Luke 8:9–10).

26. **The Messiah will enter the temple.**

Prophecy: "And the Lord, whom you seek, will suddenly come to His temple" (Mal. 3:1).

Fulfillment: "Then Jesus went out and departed from the temple, and His disciples came up to show Him the buildings of the temple. And Jesus said to them, 'Do you not see all these things? Assuredly, I say to you, not one stone shall be left here upon another, that shall not be thrown down'" (Matt. 24:1–2).

All Jews of Jesus' day entered the outer courts of the Temple, but this prophecy clearly indicates that Messiah would come when the Temple existed. The Temple at Jerusalem was destroyed in A.D. 70, so no would-be Messiah has been able to fulfill this prophecy since that date.

27. **The Messiah would enter Jerusalem on a donkey.**

Prophecy: "Rejoice greatly, O daughter of Zion! Shout in triumph, O daughter of Jerusalem! Behold, your king is coming to you; He is just and endowed with salvation, humble, and mounted on a donkey, even on a colt, the foal of a donkey" (Zech. 9:9 NASB).

Fulfillment: "Now when they drew near Jerusalem, and came to Bethphage, at the Mount of Olives, then Jesus sent two disciples, saying to them, 'Go into the village opposite you, and immediately you will find a donkey tied, and a colt with her. Loose them and bring them to Me. And if anyone says anything to you, you shall say, "The Lord has need of them," and immediately he will send them.' All this was done that it might be fulfilled which was spoken by the prophet, saying: 'Tell the daughter of Zion, "Behold, your King is coming to you, lowly, and sitting on a donkey, a colt, the foal of a donkey."' So the disciples went and did as Jesus commanded them. They brought the donkey and the colt, laid their clothes on them, and set Him on them" (Matt. 21:1–7).

28. **The Messiah will be a "stone of stumbling" to the Jews.**

Prophecy: "The stone which the builders rejected has become the chief cornerstone" (Ps. 118:22).

Fulfillment: "Therefore it is also contained in the Scripture, 'Behold, I lay in Zion a chief cornerstone, elect, precious, and he who believes on Him [Jesus] will by no means be put to shame.' Therefore, to you who believe,

He is precious; but to those who are disobedient, 'The stone which the builders rejected Has become the chief cornerstone,' and 'A stone of stumbling and a rock of offense'" (1 Pet. 2:6–8).

29. The Messiah will be a light to the Gentiles.

Prophecy: "I, the LORD, have called You in righteousness, and will hold Your hand; I will keep You and give You as a covenant to the people, as a light to the Gentiles, to open blind eyes, to bring out prisoners from the prison, those who sit in darkness from the prison house" (Is. 42:6–7).

Fulfillment: "The people who sat in darkness have seen a great light, and upon those who sat in the region and shadow of death light has dawned" (Matt. 4:16).

"A light [Jesus, the Messiah] to bring revelation to the Gentiles, and the glory of Your people Israel" (Luke 2:32).

The following prophecies from the Old Testament (numbers 30 through 58), were spoken by many different voices over a period of five hundred years, yet all of them were fulfilled in Jesus Christ during a single twenty-four hour period.

30. The Messiah will be betrayed by a friend.

Prophecy: "Even my close friend, in whom I trusted, who ate my bread, has lifted up his heel against me" (Ps. 41:9 NASB).

Fulfillment: "I [Jesus] do not speak concerning all of you. I know whom I have chosen; but that the Scripture may be fulfilled, 'He who eats bread with Me has lifted up his heel against Me.' Now I tell you before it comes, that when it does come to pass, you may believe that I am He. . . . Most assuredly, I say to you, one of you will betray Me" (John 13:18–19, 21).

"Judas Iscariot, who also betrayed Him" (Matt. 10:4).

Judas Iscariot, one of the trusted twelve disciples, ate the Passover dinner with Jesus the same night he betrayed Christ.

31. **The Messiah will be betrayed for thirty pieces of silver.**

    Prophecy: "And I said to them, 'If it is good in your sight, give me my wages; but if not, never mind!' So they weighed out thirty shekels of silver as my wages" (Zech. 11:12 NASB).

    Fulfillment: "Then one of the twelve, called Judas Iscariot, went to the chief priests and said, 'What are you willing to give me if I deliver Him [Jesus] to you?' And they counted out to him thirty pieces of silver. So from that time he sought opportunity to betray Him" (Matt. 26:14–16).

On the evening of the Passover dinner, Judas Iscariot, one of Jesus' twelve disciples, went to the chief priests and inquired if he might betray Jesus into their hands. As payment for his services, he was given thirty pieces of silver.

32. **The Messiah's "blood money" will be cast into God's house.**

    Prophecy: "So I took the thirty shekels of silver and threw them to the potter in the house of the LORD" (Zech. 11:13 NASB).

    Fulfillment: "And he [Judas] threw the pieces of silver into the sanctuary and departed (Matt. 27:5).

After betraying Jesus, Judas, overcome by remorse, threw the money back into the Temple and went outside and hanged himself.

33. **The price of betraying the Messiah will be given for a potter's field.**

    Prophecy: "So I took the thirty shekels of silver and threw them to the potter in the house of the LORD" (Zech. 11:13 NASB).

    Fulfillment: "And they [the chief priests and elders] counseled together and with the money [that had been thrown into the temple by Judas] bought the Potter's Field as a burial place for strangers" (Matt. 27:7 NASB).

The priests of the Temple, after hearing of Judas' end, decided to use the money to buy a field, where strangers were buried. It was known as the "potter's field."

34. The Messiah will be forsaken by his followers.

Prophecy: "Strike the Shepherd, and the sheep will be scattered" (Zech. 13:7).

Fulfillment: "Then Jesus said to them, 'All of you will be made to stumble because of Me this night, for it is written: "I will strike the Shepherd, and the sheep will be scattered."' . . . And they all forsook Him and fled" (Mark 14:27, 50).

The twelve disciples, who had followed Jesus faithfully for three years, fled into the night.

35. The Messiah will be accused by false witnesses.

Prophecy: "Malicious witnesses rise up; they ask me of things that I do not know" (Ps. 35:11 NASB).

Fulfillment: "Now the chief priests and the whole Council kept trying to obtain false testimony against Jesus, in order that they might put Him to death; and they did not find any, even though many false witnesses came forward" (Matt. 26:59–60 NASB).

The chief priests, trying to find fault with Jesus, bribed false witnesses to accuse Him of things He had no personal experience with—things He did not "know." Though, of course, He knew everything they would say and do.

36. The Messiah will be silent before his accusers.

Prophecy: "He was oppressed and He was afflicted, yet He did not open His mouth" (Is. 53:7 NASB).

Fulfillment: "And while He was being accused by the chief priests and elders, He answered nothing" (Matt. 27:12).

Throughout the litany of lies and false accusations, Jesus remained silent.

37. **The Messiah will be scourged and wounded.**

    Prophecy: "But He was pierced through for our transgressions, He was crushed for our iniquities; the chastening for our well-being fell upon Him, and by His scourging we are healed" (Is. 53:5 NASB).

    Fulfillment: "Then he released Barabbas to them; and when he had scourged Jesus, he delivered Him to be crucified" (Matt. 27:26).

38. **The Messiah will be smitten and spit upon.**

    Prophecy: "I gave My back to those who struck Me, and My cheeks to those who plucked out the beard; I did not cover My face from shame and spitting" (Is. 50:6).

    Fulfillment: "Then they spat in His face and beat Him with their fists; and others slapped Him" (Matt. 26:67 NASB).

39. **The Messiah will be mocked.**

    Prophecy: "All those who see Me ridicule Me; they shoot out the lip, they shake the head, saying, 'He trusted in the LORD, let Him rescue Him; let Him deliver Him, since He delights in Him!'" (Ps. 22:7–8).

    Fulfillment: "Then two robbers were crucified with Him, one on the right and another on the left. And those who passed by blasphemed Him, wagging their heads and saying, 'You who destroy the temple and build it in three days, save Yourself! If You are the Son of God, come down from the cross.' Likewise the chief priests also, mocking with the scribes and elders, said, 'He saved others; Himself He cannot save. If He is the King of Israel, let Him now come down from the cross, and we will believe Him. He trusted in God; let Him deliver Him now if He will have Him; for He said, "I am the Son of God."' Even the robbers who were crucified with Him reviled Him with the same thing" (Matt. 27:38–44).

40. **The Messiah will be weak; he will be an object of scorn.**

Prophecy: "My knees are weak from fasting; and my flesh has grown lean, without fatness. I also have become a reproach to them; when they see me, they wag their head" (Ps. 109:24–25 NASB).

Fulfillment: "And those who passed by blasphemed Him, wagging their heads and saying, 'Aha! You who destroy the temple and build it in three days, save Yourself, and come down from the cross!'" (Mark 15:29–30).

After a time without food, a beating, and intense interrogation, Jesus went out, carrying his cross, before a crowd of mocking, scornful onlookers.

41. **The Messiah's hands and feet will be pierced.**

Prophecy: "They pierced My hands and My feet (Ps. 22:16).

Fulfillment: "And when they came to the place called The Skull, there they crucified Him" (Luke 23:33 NASB).

It is interesting to note that this prediction of pierced hands and feet was made long before crucifixion was invented as a form of capital punishment. The psalmist wrote this prophecy over a thousand years before crucifixion was made common by the Romans, and the Jews never practiced crucifixion.

42. **The Messiah will be put to death alongside transgressors.**

Prophecy: "Because He poured out Himself to death, and was numbered with the transgressors" (Is. 53:12 NASB).

Fulfillment: "At that time two robbers were crucified with Him, one on the right and one on the left" (Matt. 27:38 NASB).

43. **The Messiah will intercede for his persecutors.**

Prophecy: "Yet He Himself bore the sin of many, and interceded for the transgressors" (Is. 53:12 NASB).

Fulfillment: "Father, forgive them [those who were crucifying them]; for they do not know what they are doing" (Luke 23:34 NASB).

44. The Messiah will be rejected by his own people.

Prophecy: "He was despised and forsaken of men, a man of sorrows, and acquainted with grief; and like one from whom men hide their face, He was despised, and we did not esteem him" (Is. 53:3 NASB).

Fulfillment: "Then Pilate, when he had called together the chief priests, the rulers, and the people, said to them, 'You have brought this Man to me, as one who misleads the people. And indeed, having examined Him in your presence, I have found no fault in this Man concerning those things of which you accuse Him; no, neither did Herod, for I sent you back to him; and indeed nothing deserving of death has been done by Him. I will therefore chastise Him and release Him' (for it was necessary for him to release one to them at the feast). And they all cried out at once, saying, 'Away with this Man, and release to us Barabbas. . . . Crucify Him [Jesus], crucify Him!' Then he said to them the third time, 'Why, what evil has He done? I have found no reason for death in Him. I will therefore chastise Him and let Him go.' But they were insistent, demanding with loud voices that He be crucified. And the voices of these men and of the chief priests prevailed. So Pilate gave sentence that it should be as they requested. And he released to them the one they requested, who for rebellion and murder had been thrown into prison; but he delivered Jesus to their will" (Luke 23:13–18, 21–25).

45. The Messiah will be hated without a cause.

Prophecy: "Those who hate me without a cause are more than the hairs of my head" (Ps. 69:4).

Fulfillment: "But this happened that the word might be fulfilled which is written in their law, 'They hated Me without a cause'" (John 15:25).

Even though Jesus had done nothing wrong, the crowd clamored for His death, and He was hated.

46. The Messiah's friends will stand afar off.

Prophecy: "My loved ones and my friends stand aloof from my plague, and my relatives stand afar off" (Ps. 38:11).

Fulfillment: "And all his acquaintances and the women who accompanied Him from Galilee, were standing at a distance [from the events of Jesus' death], seeing these things" (Luke 23:49 NASB).

47. People will shake their heads at the Messiah.

Prophecy: "I also have become a reproach to them; when they see me, they wag their head" (Ps. 109:25 NASB).

Fulfillment: "And those who were passing by were hurling abuse at Him, wagging their heads" (Matt. 27:39 NASB).

48. People will stare at the Messiah.

Prophecy: "They look, they stare at me" (Ps. 22:17 NASB).

Fulfillment: "And the people stood looking on" (Luke 23:35).

49. The Messiah's garments will be parted and lots cast for them.

Prophecy: "They divided My garments among them, and for My clothing they cast lots" (Ps. 22:18).

Fulfillment: "Then the soldiers, when they had crucified Jesus, took His garments and made four parts, to each soldier a part, and also the tunic. Now the tunic was without seam, woven from the top in one piece. They said therefore among themselves, 'Let us not tear it, but cast lots for it, whose it shall be,' that the Scripture might be fulfilled which says: 'They divided My garments among them, and for My clothing they cast lots.' Therefore the soldiers did these things" (John 19:23–24).

Which did they do, divide the garments or cast lots? This statement seems almost contradictory until you realize what happened at the cross. They ripped the outer garment, but paused when they picked up the tunic. It was a fine piece of work, all in one piece, and so they decided to cast lots for it.

50. The Messiah will suffer thirst.

Prophecy: "And for my thirst they gave me vinegar to drink" (Ps. 69:21).

Fulfillment: "After this, Jesus . . . said, 'I thirst!'" (John 19:28).

51. They will offer the Messiah gall and vinegar to drink.

Prophecy: "They also gave me gall for my food, and for my thirst they gave me vinegar to drink" (Ps. 69:21).

Fulfillment: "They gave Him sour wine mingled with gall to drink. But when He had tasted it, He would not drink" (Matt. 27:34).

Gall is a poisonous, bitter herb. A stupefying drink, made of wine mingled with gall, was offered to Jesus, but he would not drink it.

52. The Messiah will utter a forsaken cry.

Prophecy: "My God, my God, why hast Thou forsaken me?" (Ps. 22:1 NASB).

Fulfillment: "And about the ninth hour Jesus cried out with a loud voice, saying, 'Eli, Eli Lama Sabachthani' that is, 'My God, My God, why hast Thou forsaken Me?'" (Matt. 27:46 NASB).

53. **The Messiah will commit himself to God.**

Prophecy: "Into Thy hand I commit my spirit" (Ps. 31:5 NASB).

Fulfillment: "And Jesus, crying out with a loud voice, said, 'Father, into Thy hands I commit My spirit!'" (Luke 23:46 NASB).

54. **None of the Messiah's bones will be broken.**

Prophecy: "He guards all his bones; not one of them is broken" (Ps. 34:20).

"And all My bones are out of joint" (Ps. 22:14).

Fulfillment: "But coming to Jesus, when they saw that He was already dead, they did not break His legs" (John 19:33 NASB).

While hanging on the cross by the hands and feet, it is very likely that all a man's bones would separate from their joints. The Romans used to hasten death by breaking the legs of the crucified criminals, but when they reached Jesus, they saw that He was already dead.

55. **The Messiah's heart will literally break.**

Prophecy: "My heart is like wax; it has melted within me" (Ps. 22:14).

Fulfillment: "But one of the soldiers pierced His side with a spear, and immediately blood and water came out" (John 19:34).

The blood and water which came forth from his side is believed by some to be evidence that Jesus' heart had literally burst. The appearance of both blood and water indicate that he had been dead long enough for the blood to separate into its component elements.

56. **The Messiah's side will be pierced.**

Prophecy: "They will look on Me whom they pierced" (Zech. 12:10).

Fulfillment: "But one of the soldiers pierced His side with a spear" (John 19:34).

57. Darkness will cover the land from noon until three o'clock.

Prophecy: "'And it will come about in that day,' declares the Lord God, 'that I shall make the sun go down at noon and make the earth dark in broad daylight'" (Amos 8:9 NASB).

Fulfillment: "Now from the sixth hour [noon] darkness fell upon all the land until the ninth hour [three o'clock]" (Matt. 27:45 NASB).

58. The Messiah will be buried in a rich man's tomb.

Prophecy: "His grave was assigned with wicked men, yet He was with a rich man in His death" (Is. 53:9 NASB).

Fulfillment: "There came a rich man from Arimathea, named Joseph . . . and asked for the body of Jesus. . . . When Joseph had taken the body, he wrapped it in a clean linen cloth, and laid it in his new tomb" (Matt. 27:57–60).

In fulfilling these last three prophecies, Jesus reflects the supernatural nature of the Messiah.

59. The Messiah would rise from the dead.

Prophecy: "For Thou wilt not abandon my soul to Sheol; neither wilt Thou allow Thy Holy One to undergo decay" (Psalm 16:10).

Fulfillment: "You seek Jesus of Nazareth, who was crucified. He is risen!" (Mark 16:6).

60. The Messiah will ascend to heaven.

Prophecy: "Thou hast ascended on high" (Ps. 68:18 NASB).

Fulfillment: "He [Jesus] was lifted up while they were looking on, and a cloud received Him out of their sight" (Acts 1:9 NASB).

61. **The Messiah will be seated at the right hand of God.**

Prophecy: "The LORD says to my Lord: 'Sit at My right hand, until I make Thine enemies a footstool for thy feet'" (Ps. 110:1 NASB).

Fulfillment: "When He had made purification of sins, He sat down at the right hand of the Majesty on high" (Heb. 1:3 NASB).

The prophecies listed above could not have been purposely fulfilled by Jesus Christ unless he was God. How could a mere man control the place or time of his birth? Why would a self-serving false messiah want to fulfill the manner of Christ's death and burial?

Some skeptics claim that sheer coincidence accounts for these fulfilled prophecies. You might be able to find some men whose lives would agree with a few of the above prophecies, but Jesus Christ is the only person, living or dead, who could have fulfilled all eighty-eight! And these are only a handful of the Messianic predictions found in Scripture.

I've included this section on Messianic prophecy to illustrate one key point: just as every prophecy about Jesus' first coming has been literally fulfilled, every prophecy relating to his second coming and the events of the end times will also be fulfilled . . . exactly as God has predicted.

We have seen how Jesus fulfilled Scripture related to His first coming as a suffering servant—prepare yourself for what the Bible predicts about His second coming at the conclusion of the last generation!

CHAPTER FIVE

Are We the Terminal Generation?

About two years ago, *Time* magazine's cover read, "Thinking the unthinkable!" The story stated that mankind is at the brink of disaster in a world bristling with nuclear weapons. Harvard professor Bernard Lown lamented that mankind is doomed, locked into a race toward Armageddon.

In December 1995, keepers of the famous Doomsday Clock moved the hands three minutes closer to midnight. Leonard Rieser, chairman of the Bulletin of the Atomic Scientists, reset the clock at fourteen minutes before midnight, or "Doomsday." As they announced the move, Rieser and his associates told the press that, contrary to popular belief, the threat of nuclear apocalypse did not end with the Cold War.[1]

When Scripture tells us that heaven and earth will pass away, you can be sure that this world will definitely end. There will be a last baby born, a last marriage performed, a last kiss, a last song, a last hurrah. This world will not continue forever. The Second Law of Thermodynamics, otherwise known as the Law of Entropy, declares that all organized systems tend to disorder after time. Like all things, the earth, along with this physical universe, will wear out.

Ten Road Signs Confirming the End of the Age

When will the world end? And how? The Scriptures are not silent; God tells us when, how, and where the world as we know it will end: Armageddon.

Armageddon is the Hebrew word meaning "the mountain of Megiddo." The mountain of Megiddo lies east of Mount Carmel in the northern part of Israel. I've stood upon this mountain, and from its vantage point I could see a great extended plain stretching from the Mediterranean Sea eastward across the northern part of Israel.

Napoleon looked at the expanse of Armageddon and described it as the most natural battlefield on the face of the earth, for armies would be able to maneuver easily over its empty plains. On those plains, the Bible tells us, human blood will flow to the height of a horse's bridle for two hundred miles. There the false man of peace, the Antichrist, will join with his armies to fight the Son of God for supremacy.

We will discuss the who, when, and why of the battle at Armageddon later. First I want to show you ten signs which indicate that we're well on our way there.

1. The Knowledge Explosion

The first road sign pointing toward Armageddon is found in Daniel 12:4: "But you, Daniel, shut up the words, and seal the book until the time of the end; many shall run to and fro, and knowledge shall increase." The literal translation of this Scripture indicates that during the end time, or the terminal generation, an explosion of knowledge will occur.

Just such an explosion has occurred in the last century. From the Garden of Eden until A.D. 1900, men walked or rode horses just as King David and Julius Caesar did. In the span of a few years, however, mankind invented the automobile, the jet plane, and the space shuttle. You can fly from New York to Paris in three hours today. Just think of all the knowledge involved in developing these marvels of modern technology.

Our technology has increased exponentially. Technology, while not necessarily advancing knowledge in the average man or woman, has made fathomless depths of knowledge and information available to us at the press of a button. You can receive faxes in your car, take a message on your sky pager, and explore encyclopedias of vast knowledge small enough to fit in the palm of your hand. You can sit in the quiet of your own home and drown yourself in information from the Internet.

In the last two generations we have put men on the moon and redefined both death and life. Medical science has the ability to keep a corpse breathing for months on life support. Tiny babies weighing less than one pound can survive, and unborn babies can even undergo surgery while within the womb.

All this knowledge ought to be a good thing, but still we're on the road to Armageddon. Our knowledge has not produced utopia; instead it has created a generation of well-informed people who know more about rock stars than history. Our "enlightened" society seeks freedom and self-expression, but is actually enslaved by drugs, perversion, and occult practices.

We favor death for the innocent and mercy for the guilty. We tout the benefits of secular humanism, the worship of man's intellect, yet our enlightened, religion-free government finds itself impotent in the face of growing crime. Why? Because knowledge without God can only produce intellectual barbarians, smarter sinners. Hitler's Nazis threw Jewish children alive into the ovens. Many of them were educated men, some had Ph.D.s, but their education was accomplished without the acknowledgment or the knowledge of God.

We are the terminal generation, "always learning but never able to come to the knowledge of the truth" (2 Tim. 3:7) because we seek truth apart from God. You can't think your way to truth. You can't philosophize your way there. You can't think happy thoughts and find truth. The only way you will ever find eternal, ultimate truth, is by seeking and finding God.

If you reject truth, the only thing left to accept is a lie. America has rejected the truth of God's Word. We have rejected God Himself, and all we have left is the secular humanist lie. But Jesus said, "You shall know the truth, and the truth shall make you free" (John 8:32).

---

2. Plague in the Middle East

My father's generation could not understand several prophetic passages of Scripture. One such prophecy was Zechariah 14:12–15:

> And this shall be the plague with which the LORD will strike all the people who fought against Jerusalem: their flesh shall dissolve while they stand on their feet, their eyes shall dissolve in their sockets, and their tongues shall dissolve in their mouths. It shall come to pass in that day that a great panic from the LORD will be among them. Everyone will seize the hand of his neighbor, and raise his hand against his neighbor's hand; Judah also will fight at Jerusalem. And the wealth of all the surrounding nations shall be gathered together: gold, silver, and apparel in great abundance. Such also shall be the plague on the horse and the mule, on the camel and the donkey, and on all the cattle that will be in those camps. So shall this plague be.

Zechariah had a vision and didn't know how to describe what he saw, so he called the gruesome results a plague. The plague which could consume a man's flesh while he was still standing was as much a mystery to my father's generation as it was to Zechariah. But now we know about the Ebola virus and other deadly, swift diseases. Author Richard Preston describes an Ebola victim in his best-seller, *The Hot Zone:*

> They opened him up for an autopsy and found that his kidneys were destroyed and that his liver was dead. His liver had ceased functioning several days before he died. It was yellow, and parts of it had liquefied—it looked like the liver of a three-day-old cadaver. It was as if [the victim] had become a corpse before his death. Sloughing of the gut, in which the intestinal lining comes off, is another effect that is ordinarily seen in a corpse that is days old. . . . Everything had gone wrong inside this man, absolutely everything, any one of which could have been fatal: the clotting, the massive hemorrhages, the liver turned into pudding, the intestines full of blood.[2]

Preston states that an airborne strain of Ebola could emerge and circle around the world in about six weeks, like the flu, killing large numbers of people.[3] Of course, Ebola doesn't kill a man instantly as does the plague described in the Bible, but in the great influenza epidemic in 1918, people died within hours of first manifesting symptoms. Zechariah's plague could be another virus, one we have not yet seen. Despite our great increase of knowledge, we are not equipped to handle the hantavirus, Ebola, or the host of other "new" mutated viruses that could strike swiftly and severely. If new strains of these viruses were introduced through chemical or biological warfare, we could very well see a plague like the one Zechariah described.

Zechariah's plague could also be the logical result of massive radiation. A docudrama about Hiroshima presented a reenactment of the bombing that ended World War II. Watching the program, I saw flesh literally melting off the bones of the victims before the corpses could hit the ground. Suddenly I understood that Zechariah could have been describing nuclear warfare.

Consider this fact: every military weapon ever invented has been used. After we bombed Japan and ended the second World War, everyone became aware of the atomic bomb's immense power. An A-bomb can produce a temperature of 150 million degrees Fahrenheit in one millionth of a second. Under such conditions, a man's tongue and eyes can be consumed before his corpse can hit the ground.

But we've come a long way since the A-bomb. A one megaton nuclear blast, a firecracker compared to the massive H-bomb, creates a great noise (like the one described in 2 Peter 3:10), instantly atomizing everything within a two-mile radius. For the next eight miles, everything instantly catches fire. The land becomes a raging inferno, a literal hell on earth. Radiation breaks down at thirty-five miles and the earth is good for nothing for a hundred years.

Saddam Hussein, another enemy of Israel, is presently trying desperately to get a nuclear bomb put together to conquer the entire Middle East because he wants to be another Nebuchadnezzar. A U.S. Congressman recently sat in my office and said that many of the nuclear weapons produced by the former Soviet Union have disappeared—we assume that they have been sold to Israel's enemies. And don't forget chemical weapons.

According to a study of chemical weapons by Dr. Danny Shoham of the Begin-Sadat Center for Strategic Studies at Bar-Ilan University, Syria today is the strongest military power in the Arab world in the area of chemical weapons. The Syrians have produced thousands of chemical bombs as well as a well developed delivery capability including both attack planes and Scud-B missiles (100 to 200). Recently the Syrians began producing the longer range Scud-C and possibly the M9 missiles in cooperation with Iran, North Korea and China. Using these longer range missiles, the Syrians will be able to strike literally every point in Israel from any location in Syria.[4]

And even the Patriot missiles used in the Gulf War wouldn't afford much protection for Israel. "In point of fact, as far as Israel is concerned, American technology was a dismal failure during the Gulf War: the Patriot missiles failed to intercept even one Iraqi Scud and American technology failed to destroy or even keep track of the Scud missile sites."[5]

The coming military attack upon Israel will be ferocious and fast. "Let him who is on the housetop not go down to take anything out of his house," the Bible warns. "And let him who is in the field not go back to get his clothes" (Matt. 24:17, 18). Why? There will be *no time*.

Israel, of course, knows that she has enemies. Israel currently has the nuclear capacity to turn the sands of Baghdad into a molten sea of glass if Hussein ever attacks. If you're interested in further reading, I recommend *The Samson Option* by Seymour M. Hirsh (Random House), which describes in detail Israel's nuclear capability.

The *Sunday Times* of London once printed a story given to them by Mordecai Vanunu. Vanunu reported that Israel had two hundred nuclear bombs in addition to the neutron and the H-bomb. After this revelation, Vanunu was immediately arrested by the Mossad and sentenced to eighteen years in prison for a breach of security. His arrest confirmed that he was telling the truth. If he had been lying, the Mossad would have never bothered with him.[6]

Incidentally, we Americans often think that we're somehow protected from nuclear warfare. That is a misguided notion. During the Persian Gulf War, General Schwarzkopf asked President Bush for permission to explode an electromagnetic pulse device high in the heavens. Such a device would have instantly cut off all communication between Saddam Hussein and his troops. Bush did not give his permission, and the device has not yet been tested on the battlefield.[7]

Such a device, known to military strategists as an "electric blanket," sounds like something out of a James Bond movie, but it could easily be used against North America. A satellite carrying a nuclear warhead crossing over America at the height of 450 kilometers (279 miles) would explode, sending out an electronic pulse of enormous energy harmless to humans but fatal to our delicate electronic machines, which are designed to operate with minuscule amounts of energy. In one billionth of a second, all communication would be cut off. Transmissions to cars and trucks and machinery would grind to a halt as their electrical systems fried; radio and television stations would blink off the air. Planes would crash, missile systems would fail, the President and Commander-in-Chief would be unable to communicate with his military forces. Everything that relied on electricity would stop functioning. Military strategists have predicted that in the event of a nuclear war, this is how the enemy will terminate all electrical transmission. Vital to the success of any military system are the "three Cs": command, control, and communication. The "electric blanket" would wreak havoc among an enemy by eliminating all three.

And in addition to all of this, it may be only a matter of time before some terrorist abandons diesel fuel and fertilizer for a nuclear weapon smuggled from the shards of the Soviet Empire and blows up an entire city just to make a political statement.

Nuclear bombs and star wars weapons systems—other irrefutable signs that we are the terminal generation.

3. The Rebirth of Israel

I remember very clearly one day when I was eight years old—May 15, 1948. I was sitting at our kitchen table with my father, a quiet man with a brilliant mind. Dad loved books and he was a student of prophecy, but he didn't always do too well with people. He didn't talk much, but when he did speak, what he said was worth hearing.

Dad and I were quietly listening to the radio. Then the newscaster from the radio station made an announcement: "The United Nations has today announced that they have formally recognized the state of Israel."

My father put the book he was holding down on the table and said nothing for a long moment. I knew from the look in his eyes that he had been profoundly moved. Then he looked at me and said, "We have just heard the most important prophetic message that will ever be delivered until Jesus Christ returns to earth."

I've forgotten many episodes from my youth, but I never forgot that night or my father's words. He was right: biblical prophecy states that Israel must experience a rebirth before the coming of her Messiah.

The Bible also prophesies that a nation will be born in a day:

"Who has heard such a thing? Who has seen such things? Shall the earth be made to give birth in one day? Or shall a nation be born at once? For as soon as Zion was in labor, she gave birth to her children. Shall I bring to the time of birth, and not cause delivery?" says the LORD. "Shall I who cause delivery shut up the womb?" says your God. "Rejoice with Jerusalem, and be glad with her, all you who love her; rejoice for joy with her, all you who mourn for her." (Is. 66:8–10)

The disciples came to Jesus and asked him for the signs of the end of the age. "Tell us," they said, "when will these things be? And what will be the sign of Your coming, and of the end of the age?" (Matt. 24:3).

Jesus responded by saying, "Now learn this parable from the fig tree: When its branch has already become tender and puts forth leaves, you know that summer is near. So you also, when you see all these things, know that it is near—at the doors! Assuredly, I say to you, this generation will by no means pass away till all these things take place" (Matt. 24:32–34).

In Bible prophecy Israel is often pictured as a fig tree. Jesus says, "As soon as its twigs get tender and its leaves come out." His meaning is very clear: when Israel is a young tree, reborn and growing, putting forth leaves, it should be *obvious to all* that the end times are at hand.

Jesus said, "This generation will certainly not pass away until all these things have happened." The generation which sees the rebirth of Israel is the terminal generation.

4. *The Jews Will Return Home*

From A.D. 70, when the Romans attacked Jerusalem, destroyed the Temple, and set into motion a series of events which resulted in the Diaspora, the Jewish people have been scattered throughout the Mediterranean Basin, and from there throughout the entire world. They were not in control of their own destiny, nor did they dwell in a homeland of their own until May 15, 1948.

Jeremiah declared that the Jews must return to Israel before Messiah comes: "'Therefore, behold, the days are coming,' says the LORD, 'that they shall no longer say, "As the LORD lives who brought up the children of Israel from the land of Egypt," but, "As the LORD lives who brought up and led the descendants of the house of Israel from the north country and from all the countries where I had driven them." And they shall dwell in their own land'" (Jer. 23:7, 8).

The Jews from the north country (Russia) have returned to Israel by the tens of thousands, as have Jewish people from around the globe. We have seen them on CNN disembarking from planes in Tel Aviv. We have read it in every form of print media. They do live in their own land, just as Jeremiah predicted. Their return to their homeland is another sign of the terminal generation.

5. *Jerusalem No Longer Under Gentile Rule*

Biblical prophecy states that Jerusalem will not be under Gentile rule in the terminal generation, a situation which had existed from A.D. 70 until the Six Day War of 1967. Jesus Christ predicted that Jerusalem would be "trampled by the Gentiles until the times of the Gentiles are fulfilled" (Luke 21:24). David the psalmist predicted that the Lord would rebuild Zion and appear in his glory there (see Ps. 102:16).

That's why David wrote, "Pray for the peace of Jerusalem" (Ps. 122:6).

6. *International Instant Communication*

And I will give power to my two witnesses, and they will prophesy one thousand two hundred and sixty days, clothed in sackcloth. . . . When they finish their testimony, the beast that ascends out of the bottomless pit will make war against them, overcome them, and kill them. And their dead bodies will lie in the street of the great city which spiritually is called Sodom and Egypt, where also our Lord was crucified. Then those from the peoples, tribes, tongues, and nations will see their dead bodies three-and-a-half days, and not allow their dead bodies to be put into graves. And those who dwell on the earth will rejoice over them, make merry, and send gifts to one another, because these two prophets tormented those who dwell on the earth. (Rev. 11:3, 7–10)

The two witnesses, who many theologians believe to be Elijah and Enoch, will appear on the earth during the Tribulation. They wear the traditional clothing of mourning, and their mission will be to call men to repentance.

Prophecy states that the whole world will, at the same time, be able to see the two witnesses in the streets of Jerusalem. My father's generation could not explain that. How could the whole world see two dead men lying in the streets of Jerusalem at one time? It was a mystery.

Then came television, followed by international satellites, the Internet, and wireless communication. In this generation we can see any major news story happening anywhere on the globe within seconds of the event. Virtually the entire world has access to the same information as an event happens. World leaders communicate with each other via CNN, confident that owing to an antenna, a cable, or a satellite dish in some remote place, the other person is watching.

This was not possible in 1900!

This was not possible in 1960!

It is possible today . . . because this could be the terminal generation. The entire population living during the Tribulation will see the two witnesses slain in the streets of Jerusalem, will see the Antichrist, and will see the coming of Messiah.

---

7. Days of Deception

In Matthew 24, Jesus warned, "Take heed that no one deceives you" (v. 4). Bible prophecy declares that deception will be epidemic on the earth in the terminal generation: "Everyone will deceive his neighbor, and will not speak the truth; they have taught their tongue to speak lies; they weary themselves to commit iniquity" (Jer. 9:5).

Deception is going to be the cardinal indicator of the terminal generation, and though deception has always been with us, the coming Antichrist and his "PR man," called the "false prophet" by the apostle John, will elevate deception to an art form. Even the appellation of the Antichrist, "Man of Peace," is a lie.

But the world will be ready for him, eager and willing to believe anything. Why wouldn't it be? For generations we've been cutting our teeth and weakening our wills with lies. Secular humanism is deception, for it holds that man can usurp the role of God. The teaching of situational ethics, the philosophy that there is no absolute right or wrong, has produced a generation riddled with AIDS and abortion-induced guilt.

New Age theories and philosophies are nothing but deception. They are the same lie Satan told Eve: "And you shall be like God." The environmental gurus who teach that the earth is but the breast of "mother goddess" are doling out deception—some of America's finest young men are going out into the woods, ripping off their clothes, hugging a tree, and baying at the moon, trying to discover who they are. That's deception, because you can't find the Creator if you're worshiping the creation.

Satanism and teachings of the occult are nothing but deception. The apostate church, which has a form of godliness but denies the power of God, is peddling sheer deception because it has exchanged the truth of God for a lie (see 2 Tim. 3:5; Rom. 1:25). Such churches deliberately ignore the imminent coming of Christ, saying, "Where is the promise of His coming? For since the fathers fell asleep, all things continue as they were from the beginning of creation" (2 Pet. 3:4).

You can't find truth in the world's best-sellers! What God wants you to know about the future is written in His Book, not in *The Celestine Prophecy.* Run from those who tell lies, and turn your attention to God's truth, lest your senses become dull like others of the terminal generation and you can no longer discern what is true and what is not.

---

8. Famines and Pestilence

America has the ability to feed the world, yet we pay farmers not to grow certain crops lest they glut the market and drive prices down. And every night on television we see footage of starving children with bloated bellies, bulging eyes, and bare ribs. There are many hungry children even in the United States.

The Bible predicted that we would know famine. Jesus said that in the latter days "there will be famines, pestilences, and earthquakes in various places. All these are the beginning of sorrows" (Matt. 24:7, 8).

Another translation calls these signs "the beginning of birth pains" (NIV). Famine, pestilences, and earthquakes are the pains experienced at the birth of the terminal generation. When a woman begins to feel her first sharp pains, she knows the end of her pregnancy is near. The event she's been waiting and praying for is finally upon her.

The Jewish people know about these birth pangs. Hebrew eschatology, called *acharit ha-yamin,* describes the pre-Messianic era as one of great upheavals and wars, known as "the birth pangs of the Messiah," and Jewish suffering and exile.

The *Talmud* describes this era as the "footprints of the Messiah"—a time when arrogance will increase. The government will turn to heresy, and there will be no one to rebuke its wrongdoing. Young people will shame their elders, a person's own family will become his enemies.[8]

Pestilence—incurable disease—is another sign that we have reached the terminal generation. Many years ago I was preaching about pestilence and a man came up later and said, "Look, Pastor Hagee, I've got a bone to pick with you. You said pestilence is incurable disease, but medical science has the ability to control every sickness known to man."

I answered that the Bible said things would change. According to Joshua Lederberg, a Nobel laureate from Rockefeller University, many experts were absolutely confident in the 1960s that medical science had solved forever the problem of infectious diseases. But today, say the medical experts, disease is on the march, and the human race is not now ready to defend itself against what is really "an unending siege by pestilence."[9]

A few years ago we discovered AIDS, the Ebola virus, and antibiotic-resistant bacteria. None of these will be conquered easily. AIDS alone is a medical black hole that has touched the life of practically every American, and after more than a decade of intense research, still virtually everyone who gets it dies.

According to the most recent mortality study conducted by the U.S. Centers for Disease Control and Prevention, AIDS is now the leading cause of death for twenty-five to forty-four year olds and was ranked as the eighth leading cause of death overall for Americans in 1992. Scientists estimate that one million Americans—one in every 250 people—are infected with HIV.[10]

I believe the power of God can heal an AIDS victim, and that's the only real hope those victims have. The answer can't be found in condoms, "safe sex," or even research—the answer is found in obeying the moral laws of God!

AIDS, Ebola, and killer viruses are a trumpet blast from the throne of God to the spiritually deaf . . . *You are the terminal generation!*

9. *Earthquakes*

Earthquakes are another sign of the last days. Historians of the fifteenth century recorded 115 earthquakes in various places. Two hundred fifty-three earthquakes were recorded in the sixteenth century. There were 378 recorded earthquakes in the seventh century, 640 in the eighteenth, and 2,119 in the nineteenth.[11] Someone might try to explain this away by thinking that there are no more earthquakes today than in the past, and it's just that our ability to detect them has improved. But the number of earthquakes recorded has risen from 2,588 in 1983 to 4,084 in 1992.[12]

Now we are nearing the end of the twentieth century and bracing for the "big one" that is sure to come for Southern California. California is split by the San Andreas Fault while geologists probe the breast of mother earth for any clues that might predict when California might experience the "big one."

The Bible records at least thirty-three instances of God using earthquakes to communicate with the spiritually hard of hearing. The earth quaked at Mount Sinai when Moses received the Ten Commandments (see Ex. 19:18); God used an earthquake in Jerusalem at the crucifixion to split the veil of the temple from the top to the bottom (see Matt. 27:51). He used an earthquake at the resurrection to roll the stone from the borrowed tomb—not to let Jesus out, but to let others in (see Matt. 28:2). He used an earthquake to set Paul and Silas free from the jail at Philippi (see Acts 16:26). And He will announce the coming of Israel's Messiah with an earthquake: "And he said, 'The LORD roars from Zion, and utters His voice from Jerusalem; and the pastures of the shepherds mourn, and the top of Carmel withers'" (Amos 1:2). At the coming of the Messiah, the Dome of the Rock in Jerusalem (if it is still standing) will collapse and Mount of Olives will split in half.

The constant trembling of the earth is God's voice speaking through nature, reminding us that we are the terminal generation.

---

10. As in the Days of Noah . . .

But of that day and hour no one knows, not even the angels of heaven, but My Father only. But as the days of Noah were, so also will the coming of the Son of Man be. For as in the days before the flood, they were eating and drinking, marrying and giving in marriage, until the day that Noah entered the ark, and did not know until the flood came and took them all away, so also will the coming of the Son of Man be. (Matt. 24:36–39)

What characteristics marked the "days of Noah"? Genesis tells us that man's wickedness on the earth was very great and that "every intent of the thoughts of his heart was only evil continually" (Gen. 6:5).

If you open your morning paper at breakfast tomorrow, you're likely to lose your appetite. Murders, rapes, kidnapping, assault, child abuse, spouse abuse, parental abuse—these are common headlines for even small town newspapers. Men are thinking evil all the time. And just as the flood waters caught them unaware, so the end of the earth will catch these deceived sleepers. The Messiah will come, the thread of history will snap, and those who were unprepared will be caught up in the Tribulation which is to follow.

CHAPTER SIX

What Is the Rapture and When Will It Happen?

K nowing this first: that scoffers will come in the last days, walking according to their own lusts" (2 Pet. 3:3). The simple fact that we hear voices denying the certainty of a literal Rapture is, in and of itself, another sign that we are the terminal generation.

Listen to the writers of the Bible as they describe this incredible, soon-coming event: 1 Thessalonians 4:16–18 says, "For the Lord Himself will descend from heaven with a shout, with the voice of an archangel, and with the trumpet of God. And the dead in Christ [Christians who have died] will rise first. Then we who are alive and remain shall be caught up together with them in the clouds to meet the Lord in the air. And thus we shall always be with the Lord. Therefore comfort one another with these words."

Matthew 24:30 says, "Then the sign of the Son of Man will appear in heaven, and then all the tribes of the earth will mourn, and they will see the Son of Man coming on the clouds of heaven with power and great glory."

In Acts 1:11, after Jesus had ascended into heaven, an angel appeared and spoke to the stunned disciples: "'Men of Galilee, why do you stand gazing up into heaven?' the angel said. 'This same Jesus, who was taken up from you into heaven, will so come in like manner as you saw Him go into heaven.'"

"For as the lightning comes from the east and flashes to the west, so also will the coming of the Son of Man be" (Matt. 24:27).

Put these verses together and we have this picture: Jesus Christ, the Prince of Glory, will appear suddenly in the heavens, brilliantly, in a way that no one will be able to miss.

When I was attending graduate school at North Texas State University, I was in the library doing research for a term paper when a book dealing with weather patterns attracted my attention. I took the book off the shelf, dusted it off, and began to read. One section that dealt with storms caught my eye, and one specific line seemed to leap off the page: "When lightning flashes from the east to the west, you can be sure the storm is over."

When Jesus Christ, the Light of the World, appears in the heavens as lightning flashing from the east to the west, the storms of life will be over for the believer.

A Mystery

In 1 Corinthians 15:51–52, Paul writes, "Behold, I tell you a mystery: We shall not all sleep, but we shall all be changed—in a moment, in the twinkling of an eye, at the last trumpet. For the trumpet will sound, and the dead will be raised incorruptible, and we shall be changed."

Paul addressed this problem because the people of the New Testament Church were beginning to die—and they had fully expected Jesus Christ to come back to earth for them before any of them passed away. So Paul shares with them a "mystery," a term used in Scripture to denote something God has not previously chosen to share with men. They wanted to know what would happen after death. Would those who died have a part in the eternal kingdom to come?

Paul answered their questions by explaining the mystery of things to come. Believers who had died would not miss the

Savior's coming, Paul told them, but would come out of the grave at the sound of the trumpet to be raised incorruptible, with a new, supernatural, immortal body. Those who had not yet died a physical death would be caught up in the clouds to meet Jesus Christ. This mass ingathering of believers is commonly called the Rapture.

Now if you were to ask ordinary church members in America what they thought of the Rapture, far too many would look at you with puzzled expressions on their faces. Many have never heard the word mentioned from their pulpits and haven't the foggiest idea what the word means.

Many evangelical churches have preached the doctrine of the Rapture for years, but now even they are under attack for teaching that a literal gathering of the church will occur. More liberal theologians are even shouting in chorus, "There will never be a Rapture!"

But what does the Word of God say?

When and How Will Jesus Come for the Believers?

Jesus said, "But of that day and hour no one knows, not even the angels in heaven, nor the Son, but only the Father" (Mark 13:32). Despite the thousands of people who would like to predict the exact year, month, date, or hour of Christ's return, Jesus said no man knows. But God the Father knows when He will send Jesus to fetch His bride home, and when He gives the word, Jesus will leave the right hand of the Father and descend through the clouds to gather in His church.

Immediately following Jesus' appearing in the heavens, the trumpet of God will sound, announcing the appearance of royalty, for He is the Prince of Peace, the Lord of Glory, the King of Kings and the Lord of all Lords. The voice of the archangel will summon the dead from their graves and all over the earth the graves of those who have trusted Christ as their Messiah will explode as their occupants soar into the heavens to meet the Light of the World. Marble mausoleums will topple as the bodies of resurrected saints rise to meet the Lord. Cars will empty beside the interstate, their engines running, their drivers and occupants strangely missing. Supper dishes will steam in the homes of believers, food will boil on their stoves, but no one will remain to eat this earthly dinner, for all believers will be taking their places at the heavenly table for the marriage supper of the Lamb.

The next day, headlines of local, national, and international newspapers will scream, "MILLIONS MISSING WITH NO EXPLANATION." New Age devotees might explain the mass disappearance by insisting that a vast armada of UFOs have abducted millions of people.

TV stations will broadcast live from local neighborhoods and cemeteries, and their cameras will capture empty graves, ruptured mausoleums, silent homes, wrecked cars. They'll interview neighbors who dab their eyes with tissue and exclaim, "I was right here talking to Mr. Jones and suddenly he disappeared. Right in front of my eyes, I tell you. He was here— and then he vaporized! Like something out of *Star Trek,* but faster!"

Nightline will feature a panel of esteemed educators, philosophers, and clergymen who will attempt to explain what has happened. The token psychologist will declare that the world is experiencing unprecedented mass hysteria. The venerable theologian will jabber about "right-wing, Bible-thumping, politically incorrect hate-mongers" who believed an invalid and nonsensical theory about something called the Rapture.

Yet there is one person who will have an explanation for the Rapture that will satisfy many of those who are left behind—his name will be Antichrist.

Telephone lines around the world will jam as families try to check on their loved ones. And the churches of the world will be packed with weeping, hysterical people who see the truth too late and cry, "The Lord of Glory has come and we are left behind to go through the Tribulation and to face the coming Antichrist."

What is the Rapture? It is the literal ingathering of the Church as explained clearly in the Word of God. It's the only way to fly!

Signs of an Imminent Rapture

Jesus Christ, the Messiah for Jews and Gentiles alike, first came to earth nearly two thousand years ago. He will come to earth again when He sets foot on the Mount of Olives just outside Jerusalem, but He will appear briefly to gather his church before the Antichrist, or the "man of lawlessness" is revealed:

> Let no one deceive you by any means; for that Day will not come unless the falling away comes first, and the man of sin is revealed, the son of perdition, who opposes and exalts himself above all that is called God or that is worshiped, so that he sits as God in the temple of God, showing himself that he is God.
>
> Do you not remember that when I was still with you I told you these things? And now you know what is restraining, that he may be revealed in his own time. For the mystery of lawlessness is already at work; only He who now restrains will do so until He is taken out of the way. And then the lawless one will be revealed, whom the Lord will consume with the breath of His mouth and destroy with the brightness of His coming. The coming of the lawless one is according to the working of Satan, with all power, signs, and lying wonders, and with all unrighteous deception among those who perish, because they did not receive the love of the truth, that they might be saved. (2 Thess. 2:3–10)

According to Paul, author of the letters to the believers at Thessalonica, the Antichrist cannot be revealed until the One who holds back the power of sin and lawlessness is taken out of the way. The One who restrains sin is the Holy Spirit, the One who indwells every member of the sanctified Church, those who have trusted Jesus Christ as their Lord and Savior, the One who right now is continuously convicting the world of sin, righteousness, and judgment (see John 16:8–11).

How is the Holy Spirit removed from the earth? This will occur when those who have placed their faith and trust in Jesus Christ are snatched away. This momentous event, which will occur in "the twinkling of an eye," could happen at any time. No one knows the day or the hour. As they did when Noah was building the ark, people on earth will be conducting their daily affairs, eating and drinking, marrying and giving in marriage, buying and selling. And just as God set apart his chosen ones by placing Noah and his family into the ark for safekeeping, He will remove his set-apart Church from the seven years of tribulation to come.

The Importance of Understanding the Rapture

Some of you may be tempted to ask, "Pastor Hagee, what difference does it make? I'm not going to change the way I live whether the Rapture is coming or not."

Friend, the truth and implications of the Rapture are not take-it-or-leave-it teachings. The Bible says, "Watch therefore, and pray always that you may be counted worthy to escape all these things that will come to pass, and to stand before the Son of Man" (Luke 21:36), and "The end of all things is at hand; therefore be serious and watchful in your prayers" (1 Pet. 4:7). Also, in the parable of the five wise virgins and the five foolish virgins, Jesus urges us to be ready for the appearance of the bridegroom (see Matt. 25:1–13).

If you want to go with Him, you need to be watching for Him.

We need to be watching, praying, ever-ready for the appearance of Jesus Christ to gather those who believe in Him. We can't get too comfortable with the things of this world because, as the Scriptures say,

> [We] are a chosen people, a royal priesthood, a holy nation, a people belonging to God, that [we] may declare the praises of him who called [us] out of darkness into his wonderful light. Once [we] were not a people, but now [we] are the people of God; once [we] had not received mercy, but now [we] have received mercy. Dear friends, I urge you, *as aliens and strangers in the world, to abstain from sinful desires, which war against your soul.* Live such good lives among the pagans that, though they accuse you of doing wrong, they may see your good deeds and glorify God on the day he visits us. (1 Pet. 2:9–12 NIV, emphasis mine)

The Heavenly Wedding Reception

In the "twinkling of an eye" all the believers in Jesus the Messiah from throughout the church age will stand in the heavens. The bride of Christ, the Church, will gather there, ten thousand times ten thousand of us. God shall wipe away every tear. That, my fellow Christian, will be our heavenly reunion. We'll have supernatural, incorruptible bodies which will no longer know suffering, disease, or pain. I will stand before God's throne with my father, my mother, my grandparents, and hundreds of dear saints who went before me into Heaven. The saints of Christ will be wearing crowns and dazzling white robes of righteousness, for we are the bride, adorned for our wedding with Christ, our heavenly groom.

Through his grace, we His bride will stand before our Bridegroom Jesus and offer to Him our dowry, the things we have done in His name. These works do not buy our entrance into heaven, but we offer them in love, as gifts from a loving Church to a waiting Savior. And for our efforts, we may receive as many as six crowns:

- The crown for those who love His appearance (2 Tim. 4:8): "Finally, there is laid up for me the crown of righteousness, which the Lord, the righteous Judge, will give to me on that Day, and not to me only but also to all who have loved [earnestly longed for] His appearing."

- The crown for enduring trials (James 1:12): "Blessed is the man who endures temptation; for when he has been approved, he will receive the crown of life which the Lord has promised to those who love Him."

- The crown for those willing to feed the flock (1 Pet. 5:2–4): "Shepherd the flock of God which is among you, serving as overseers, not by compulsion but willingly, not for dishonest gain but eagerly; nor as being lords over those entrusted to you, but being examples to the flock; and when the Chief Shepherd appears, you will receive the crown of glory that does not fade away."

- The crown for those who are faithful unto death (Rev. 2:10): "Do not fear any of those things which you are about to suffer. Indeed, the devil is about to throw some of you into prison, that you may be tested, and you will have tribulation ten days. Be faithful until death, and I will give you the crown of life."

- The crown for those who win souls (1 Thess. 2:19): "For what is our hope, or joy, or crown of rejoicing? Is it not even you in the presence of our Lord Jesus Christ at His coming?"

- The crown for those who master the old nature (1 Cor. 9:24–25): "Do you not know that those who run in a race all run, but one receives the prize? Run in such a way that you may obtain it. And everyone who competes for the prize is temperate in all things. Now they do it to obtain a perishable crown, but we for an imperishable crown."

Once we have received our crowns, we will sit at the wedding feast prepared for the bride of Christ. The Church, the body of believers, is the bride without spot or wrinkle, the bride purchased with the blood of Jesus, the Lamb of God who died for us and in our place to pay the penalty for our sins. That dinner will be a glorious celebration, for the bride has been victorious over the powers and principalities of darkness. We, the members of His raptured Church, were the salt and light of the earth, the pure in heart, the peacemakers, the ones who endured persecution in Jesus' name.

If you listen closely, you can almost hear the orchestra of heaven beginning to play the wedding march.

Don't Be Fooled by a False Groom

Think about it! Anyone can stand on the Mount of Olives in Jerusalem and say, "I am Jesus." Anyone can wear a white robe. Anyone can claim to be the descendant of King David and have his followers crown him as the king of the new Israel on Jerusalem's temple mount. Anyone could place surgical scars in his hands and feet. There are warlocks and witch doctors on the earth right now who can call fire from heaven and perform miracles. You can turn on your television and watch "healers" do bloodless surgery with their fingernails. Remember this: a man with supernatural power is not necessarily from God. The devil has supernatural power, too, as do his demons.

How are you going to recognize the real Jesus? Jesus said, "Then if anyone says to you, 'Look, here is the Christ!' or 'There!' do not believe it" (Matt. 24:23). The world is full of false messiahs and false Christs, and during the Tribulation, God will send a powerful spirit of delusion:

> The coming of the lawless one [Antichrist] is according to the working of Satan, with all power, signs, and lying wonders, and with all unrighteous deception among those who perish, because they did not receive the love of the truth, that they might be saved. And for this reason God will send them strong delusion, that they should believe the lie, that they all may be condemned who did not believe the truth but had pleasure in unrighteousness. (2 Thess. 2:9–12)

In the eighties *USA Today* ran a full page ad that read, "Christ Is Now on the Earth." The *New York Times* carried a similar ad proclaiming, "Christ is Now Here." Those ads ran in the early eighties, and I threw them away after showing them on national television. Christ isn't on the earth in bodily form, for when He comes again, the entire world will know about it!

Once one of our church members told me, "Pastor Hagee, a lady told me she was driving in California and suddenly Jesus appeared in the car with her. What do you think?"

"I'll tell you what I think," I answered. "I don't believe it."

Jesus is not in California, New York, or Rome. He is seated at the right hand of God the Father, where He will stay until Gabriel blows the trumpet to call the dead in Christ from their dusty couches of slumber to mansions on high.

Let me ask again: How will you be able to tell the real Jesus from the false pretenders? Jesus knew and prophesied that many pretenders would come saying, "I am Christ." So God installed a fail-safe mechanism that is so staggering in supernatural power, so earth-shattering, that not even Satan himself could imitate it, much less duplicate it. That fail-safe method is the Rapture!

Satan has always tried to imitate whatever God does. In the Old Testament, Jannes and Jambres imitated Moses (see 2 Tim. 3:8 and Ex. 7:10–12). When Moses threw his rod down and it became a serpent, they threw their rods down and their rods became serpents too. But when Moses' snake consumed their snakes, Jehovah God was demonstrating that He will not be outwitted or overcome by Satan's imitations.

But still Satan tries to deceive. The Antichrist will seek to imitate and ultimately supplant Jesus Christ. In Revelation 6:2 we see that the Antichrist makes his appearance on the world stage riding a white horse:

> "And I looked, and behold, a white horse. He who sat on it had a bow; and a crown was given to him, and he went out conquering and to conquer." [The Antichrist makes this kind of glorious entrance because Jesus Christ comes to earth the second time on a white horse:] "Now I saw heaven opened, and behold, a white horse. And He who sat on him was called Faithful and True, and in righteousness He judges and makes war." (Rev. 19:11)

How will you know when the real Jesus comes to earth? He won't take out an ad in the *New York Times*. He won't speak through some theologian or some charismatic personality who stands on the Mount of Olives or Hollywood Boulevard in a white suit proclaiming that he is the king of the new Israel. He won't come through some warlock who calls down fire from heaven.

I'll know Jesus has reappeared when my glorified body sails through the heavens past the Milky Way into the presence of God. I'll know I'm with the real Jesus when I stand in His glorious presence with my brand new disease-proof, never-dying, fatigue-free body that looks better, feels better, and is better than Arnold Schwarzenegger's.

What Skeptics Say

Those who attack the doctrine of the Rapture are usually those who teach that the Bible is not to be taken literally. Some honor the Word of God in their hearts but nevertheless insist that what is important is the spiritual meaning of Bible passages, which often transcends (and sometimes conflicts with) the literal words themselves. But if you abandon the plain meaning of the text, how do you have any way of evaluating what the "spiritual meaning" is? And thus they face the possibility of giving Scripture a "private interpretation," which is explicitly warned against: "And so we have the prophetic word confirmed, which you do well to heed as a light that shines in a dark place, until the day dawns and the morning star rises in your hearts; knowing this first, that no prophecy of Scripture is of any private interpretation, for prophecy never came by the will of man, but holy men of God spoke as they were moved by the Holy Spirit" (2 Pet. 1:19–21).

Still others who have no more regard for the Word of God than for *Politically Correct Bedtime Stories* insist that whatever meaning the Scriptures have is allegorical at best. But if the Bible is only a collection of fables and allegories, it's a myth and not fit for human consumption—let alone consideration.

Why would God bother to give us a collection of allegories? There is no answer for this because He gave us no such book. The Bible I revere is a literal book from cover to cover, meant to be understood and acted on, not deciphered and dismissed. This is just like God, who, as Augustine somewhere said, "caught orators by fishermen—not fishermen by orators." Consider the following:

- Jesus was literally born of a virgin named Mary.

- He was literally born in Bethlehem.

- He literally healed people.

- He literally died on the cross.

- He literally was buried in a borrowed grave.

- He literally rose from the dead on the third day.

If those things are *literally* true, why shouldn't He *literally* come back to earth with power and great glory? Why shouldn't the Bible be literally true when it says that "every knee should bow . . . and that every tongue should confess that Jesus Christ is Lord, to the glory of God the Father" (Phil. 2:10–11)?

Why shouldn't I literally rise and meet Him in the air as will every believer who looks for His glorious appearing?

Why shouldn't I literally walk on streets of gold? Why shouldn't I literally wear a crown of life? Why shouldn't I literally live forever and forever? Why shouldn't there be a New Jerusalem? Why shouldn't those who are looking for Him literally walk through its gates shouting, "Glory!"?

Critics of the Rapture doctrine are quick to point out that the word *Rapture* does not appear in the Bible. That's absolutely true. The Bible does not contain the term *Trinity* either, but over and over it refers to the "oneness" of God and the "threeness" of God:

1 Corinthians 8:6: "There is but one God, the Father, from whom all things came and for whom we live" (NIV).

Ephesians 4:6: "One God and Father of all, who is above all, and through all, and in you all."

Matthew 28:19: "Go therefore and make disciples of all the nations, baptizing them in the name of the Father and of the Son and of the Holy Spirit."

John 14:26: "But the Helper, the Holy Spirit, whom the Father will send in My name, He will teach you all things, and bring to your remembrance all things that I said to you."

John 15:26: "But when the Helper comes, whom I shall send to you from the Father, the Spirit of truth who proceeds from the Father, He will testify of Me."

2 Corinthians 13:14: "The grace of the Lord Jesus Christ, and the love of God, and the communion of the Holy Spirit be with you all. Amen."

1 Peter 1:2: "According to the foreknowledge of God the Father, in sanctification of the Spirit, for obedience and sprinkling of the blood of Jesus Christ: Grace to you and peace be multiplied."

Though the term *Trinity* isn't in the Bible, the truth of God's three-in-one nature is. The same is true with the truth of the Rapture: the *term* itself isn't in Scripture but the *truth* most certainly is.

Other critics of the Rapture say, "The Rapture teaching is nothing but escapism. You people are trying to escape from the real world." Right now I'm living in the real world, and if I wanted to escape it, I could think of no better way than working and waiting for the coming of my Lord. But I'm thrilled that Jesus Christ is my Lord and Savior, heaven is my home, and that I'm not going to walk in the fires of an eternal hell. If that's escapism, so be it.

Let's face it, everyone wants to escape from something. Environmentalists want to escape from pollution. The people in peace movements want to escape from war. The Bible teaches us to prepare for our escape: "Watch therefore, and pray always that you may be counted worthy to escape all these things that will come to pass, and to stand before the Son of Man" (Luke 21:36).

God Will Rapture His Church to Allow Escape from Tribulation

What does the Rapture allow us to escape? The Tribulation to come. Walk with me through the pages of Revelation chapters six, eight, nine, and sixteen, and let me briefly describe the living hell you will escape by being part of the Rapture:

These are but a few of the things that will happen during the Tribulation:

- One-fourth of mankind will die (see Rev. 6:8), some because of war, some because of famine, and still others by the wild beasts of the earth. Whether by death that is swift and instant or death that is lingering and excruciating—25 percent of all people will die. Now the world's population in 1995 is 5,733,687,096, so a quarter of this is 1,433,421,774 or almost five and a half times the current population of the United States—can you imagine that? And remember that the population of the world is doubling every 39.5 years. So every day the number of people who will die becomes larger and larger.[1]

- One third of all vegetation will be burned up. All grass, every tree, everything green will be destroyed (see Rev. 8:7).

- The sun and the moon will be darkened as nature goes into revolt (see Rev. 8:12).

- The gates of hell will open and hordes of locusts, the size of horses, will come upon the earth. Those locusts will be allowed to sting men like scorpions and the pain will last for five months. The Bible says men will beg God to let them die but they will not die (see Rev. 9:3–6).

- There will be worldwide famine unlike anything the world has ever seen (see Rev. 18:8).

- There will be a world war so bloody that the blood of those killed in battle will flow for two hundred miles up to the bridle of a horse in the valley of Jezreel. This will be the Battle of Armageddon. During the Great Tribulation, one third of all the people on the earth will be killed (see Rev. 14:20).

- Every person on earth will be covered with great running, festering boils. Have you ever had one boil? Imagine being covered in them, not being able to walk, lie down, or sit without pain (see Rev. 16:2–11).

- The seven seas of the earth will be turned into blood. Every river, every stream will become as blood. Every basin in your home will run with hot and cold blood. This plague will produce mind-numbing thirst from which there will be no relief (see Rev. 8:8, 11:6).

- The sun will scorch the earth and men with fire. Major uncontrollable fires will break out all over the world, spontaneously destroying homes, vegetation, and livestock (see Rev. 16:8).

- Mighty men, kings, and men of power will gnaw their tongues in pain and crawl into caves and beg God to kill them (see Rev. 6:15).

- The earth will quake so severely that the islands of the sea will disappear. Puerto Rico and Hawaii will be covered with water. Every building, every wall will crumble. Millions will be trapped beneath the rubble with no one to come to their aid (see Rev. 16:18).

Now I ask you, do you want to escape the coming Tribulation? I do! And I am going to escape. When the archangel blows the trumpet and the dead in Christ rise immediately, those of us who are still alive when Jesus the Messiah returns will rise into the air in the twinkling of an eye to trade the coming hell on earth for the wonder and majesty of heaven. We will meet the real Jesus. He is the Lion of the tribe of Judah. He is the Lord of glory. He is the Light of the world, the Lamb of God, and the Lover of my soul.

The literal, physical appearance of Jesus Christ will come soon. And as soon as the Church is gone, the Antichrist, the son of Satan, will appear upon the stage of the world.

CHAPTER SEVEN

The Coming Antichrist

Jesus warned that the times of the Antichrist will be by far the worst the world has ever known. In his discourse to the disciples regarding "the tribulation of those days" as recorded in Matthew 24, Mark 13, Luke 21, and John 16, He foretold of a period of false messiahs, rumors of war, sorrow, betrayal, deceit, iniquity, persecution, and catastrophe. The end times would bring conditions so terrible that "unless those days were shortened, no flesh would be saved" (Matt. 24:22).

Who Is the Antichrist, the False Man of Peace?

The Antichrist will be a man who makes his debut upon the stage of world history with hypnotic charm and charisma. He will probably come from the European Union or a country or confederation that was once part of the Roman Empire, which stretched from Ireland to Egypt and included Turkey, Iran, and Iraq. In Daniel's vision, the "little horn" sprouted among the other ten, which we know are somehow ten divisions of the old Roman Empire. In his rise to power, the Antichrist will weave his hypnotic spell, first over one nation in the ten-kingdom federation, then over all ten. He will conquer three of the ten nations and then assume primacy over all of them; next he will turn his ravenous eyes toward the Apple of God's eye—Israel.

The Antichrist will be a man who has "paid his dues" in the military and the political sense, and many will willingly follow him. He will rule over those in his federation with absolute authority and will do as he pleases (see Dan. 11:36).

We also know that the Antichrist will enter the world stage with a reputation of being a powerful man of peace. Perhaps he will be a Nobel Peace Prize winner. He will defeat and merge three kingdoms—could they be Serbia, Bosnia, and Croatia? Certainly that would be a modern-day miracle. Anyone who could bring peace and unification to the centuries-old strife of that region would surely be known as the greatest man of peace in the modern era. Daniel 8:25 says that by peace he "shall destroy many." He will guarantee peace for Israel and the Middle East and sign a seven-year peace treaty, but will break that seven-year treaty in only three and one-half years (see Dan. 9:27). His peace is neither eternal nor true.

First John 2:18 boldly declares, "Little children, it is the last hour; and as you have heard that the Antichrist is coming, even now many antichrists have come, by which we know that it is the last hour." The Antichrist—capital A—is coming. Though many people throughout the years have been anti-Christ, there is coming a man who is the devil incarnate, the son of Satan, evil personified.

The Antichrist's three-point plan for world domination consists of a one-world economic system in which no one can buy nor sell without a mark sanctioned by the Antichrist's administration; a one-world government, now being called "The New World Order"; and a one-world religion that will eventually focus its worship on the Antichrist himself.

The One-World Economy

The Antichrist's economy will be a cashless society in which every financial transaction can be electronically monitored. John, author of the book of Revelation, described the situation: "He causes all, both small and great, rich and poor, free and slave, to receive a mark on their right hand or on their foreheads, and that no one may buy or sell except one who has the mark or the name of the beast, or the number of his name" (Rev. 13:16–17).

The cashless society may ostensibly be presented to the world as a way to control drug lords, tax evaders, and the like, and so it will be. It may be presented as a foolproof way to end theft or as the ultimate in convenience for the shopper who can go to the supermarket without even a wallet. He will simply have his hand or forehead scanned by an electronic device that reflects the amount of cash he has in the bank, makes the deduction for his purchase, and gives him a current balance.

This scenario doesn't sound nearly as far-fetched as it used to, does it? My bank today offers a debit card; even today I don't need money to go to the grocery store. Everything is scanned these days, from library cards to thumbprints, and it doesn't require a great leap of imagination to see how this cashless, computerized system of buying and selling will be placed into operation. A day is coming when you will not even be able to buy Rolaids without the proper approval, without having a mark upon your hand or forehead scanned.

The computer revolution has made this phenomenal accomplishment well within our grasp. We have become accustomed to being managed by government with numbers. Our children are routinely assigned Social Security numbers by the time they are two years old. Why not make things easier and cut down on the likelihood of fraud by invisibly tattooing a person's identification number or implanting a computer chip beneath the skin of their foreheads or hands?

Because I'm on television, people bring me all sorts of things. A scientist recently brought to my office a box marked "Top Secret." Inside that box was a sample of computer chips that could be implanted in a person's hand or forehead and could contain every fact the government would care to know about an individual. This type of microchip implantation has been done with race horses and other animals for years. Why couldn't it be done with humans?

American politicians are now talking about implementing a national identity card, ostensibly to cut down on illegal aliens. Our government is putting on a full-court press that will ultimately give them the power to control cash transactions.

We are not alone. The European Union is also considering a universal monetary system. *Time* magazine notes, "One month after the latest monetary crisis, Cabinet officers, legislators and bankers on both sides of the Atlantic are intensely debating a lengthening list of ideas" for developing "a global financial system."

The signs are all around us. Bank America has advertised the slogan, "The whole world welcomes world money." A Reader's Digest article entitled "Coming Soon: Electronic Money" claimed that millions of Americans are already receiving their wages and salaries electronically via direct bank deposits. We allow people to automatically draft our bank accounts for loan payments, insurance payments, and many other bills.

I believe the main reason the Antichrist will cause everyone to receive what is known as the "mark of the beast" is to control everyone and crush all who worship the God of Abraham, Isaac, and Jacob. If he cannot personally have the joy of controlling or killing them, he will have the satisfaction of knowing they will starve to death. Without his mark no one will be able to buy a loaf of bread or a drop of milk. They may not be able to buy homes or make rent payments. They may not be able to hold jobs.

The New World Order

Never in the world's history has one government completely ruled the world, but the false man of peace will "devour the whole earth" (Dan. 7:23). He will rule over them by their own consent and with absolute and total authority (see Dan. 11:36). His personality will be marked by great intelligence, persuasiveness, subtlety, and craft. His mouth "speaks pompous words" (Daniel 7:8), and he is a "master of intrigue" (Dan. 8:23 NIV). He will be the world's most prominent, powerful, and popular personality.

The Antichrist will set up a one-world government, a new world order. And believe me, there's nothing new about this new world order! Satan has been scheming to institute one ever since Nimrod proposed to build a mighty tower on the plains of Shinar. The purpose of what we know as the Tower of Babel was to defy God's authority on Earth—to cast God out and institute the government of man. While God commanded men to "Be fruitful and multiply, and fill the earth," (Gen. 9:1), the people had a different idea:

Now the whole earth had one language and one speech. And it came to pass, as they journeyed from the east, that they found a plain in the land of Shinar, and they dwelt there. . . . And they said, "Come, let us build ourselves a city, and a tower whose top is in the heavens; let us make a name for ourselves, lest we be scattered abroad over the face of the whole earth." (Genesis 11:1–2, 4)

God endured the builders' brashness for a limited time, then he scattered them across the earth.

After World War I, "the war to end all wars," President Woodrow Wilson crafted the League of Nations to uphold peace through a one-world government. Adolph Hitler told the German people he would bring a "new order" to Europe. He did, dragging Europe into the bowels of a living hell and turning the streets crimson with rivers of human blood.

The communists of the former Soviet Union pledged to institute a new world order and erected an atheistic empire that has now collapsed like a house of cards.[1] Now the United Nations wants to establish a new world order!

What does it mean? Brock Chisolm, Director of the United Nations World Health Organization, says, "To achieve world government, it is necessary to remove from the minds of men their individualism, loyalty to their families, national patriotism, and religion."

Destruction of Nationalism and Patriotism

Notice that in essence he called national patriotism and religion enemies of the new world order. Historically, it's interesting to note that George Washington, the father of our country, connected patriotism and religion. He said, "It is impossible to rightly govern the world without God and the Bible. Do not ever let anyone claim to be a true American patriot if they ever attempt to separate religion from politics."[2]

What has happened to American patriotism? I believe it has been slowly dying since the Korean War. That war was officially not our war at all, but a United Nations "police action." Our objective was not total victory; it was repelling the North Koreans without provoking the Chinese and Soviets. General Douglas MacArthur, who resigned at the request of President

Harry Truman, said, "In war, there is no substitute for victory."[3] History has proven MacArthur right.

The Vietnam War was a controlled war. We were not allowed to invade Hanoi. For years we were forbidden to attack the enemy in Laos. The result? America was portrayed to the world as a military loser, incompetent and impotent.

We were in the Gulf as part of the United Nations force by our own insistence; we are in Bosnia as part of NATO at the request of the UN by our own insistence. It is through these kinds of things that many are learning to think of themselves as citizens of the world first and citizens of America second, if at all. Quietly and with great subtlety, the road is being paved for the one-world government of the Antichrist.

Destruction of Evangelical Faith

Underneath the facade of popular peacemaker, the Antichrist will be evil incarnate. He will hate all things of God and will take pleasure in perverting God's intentions. He will rant and rave against God, publicly and privately; he will persecute Christians and Jews alike. He will reject all previous laws, particularly those based on Judeo-Christian values, and institute his own lawless system: "He will speak against the Most High and oppress his saints and try to change the set times and the laws" (Dan. 7:25 NIV).

Every single new world order, including the coming Antichrist's, has had one common trait: an attempt to cast God out of the affairs of men. Why?

As long as we believe the Word of God and are loyal to the kingdom of God, we represent a government within a government. We are pilgrims and strangers who worship another King and have another citizenship, and as such, we are a hindrance to the New World Order. When our government condones what God condemns, those who have trusted in

Him become the enemy. And so the Bible-believing Christians of America are labeled dangerous, "intolerant," and enemies of the state.

Or even freeloaders. A group of people in Colorado has been circulating petitions to place on the ballot an initiative that would call for churches and other nonprofit organizations to pay property tax on their land. But the resolution would not apply to all nonprofit groups. One man explained it this way: "The measure would exempt certain nonprofits, such as schools and charities, that perform necessary community duties. However, other tax-exempt groups, including religious organizations and fraternal lodges, have vast holdings of properties but pay nothing for fire and police protection or infrastructure, nor do they contribute to the public schools."[4] In other words, unlike some institutions that "perform necessary community duties," churches that perform such unimportant functions as preaching salvation, caring for the sick, clothing the naked, feeding the hungry, educating the ignorant, and setting the prisoner free are little more than parasites, and the church is nothing more than a Moose Lodge with a cross on it. This is what the Church of Jesus Christ looks like to those who, as a result of rejecting Jesus the Messiah, have become futile in their thoughts and foolish in their hearts (see Rom. 1:21).

Christian bashing is already an art form in the popular media. Christians are the only group in America that it is politically correct to hate, discriminate against, and lampoon. We are attacked through the law, through the media, through Hollywood, and through educational institutions that belittle the Word of God and traditional family values. When is the last time you saw a heroic, Bible-believing contemporary character on a television show? I can't think of a single instance of twentieth-century faith in God being portrayed as a positive thing. The few good examples of faithful TV characters I can recall are those from shows set in the pioneer days, and their faith is presented as a sentimental quality of the past.

No other group of people on the earth are so constantly maligned on prime-time television. Persistent portrayals of Christians and clergymen as lechers, murderers, and psychopaths betray the deep-seated hostility the media has toward Christianity and faith in God. Perhaps TBS mogul Ted Turner articulated the unverbalized values of his peers when he confided to the TV critic of the *Dallas Morning News:* "Christianity is religion for losers."[5] Imagine what would happen if he said this about Judaism or Islam!

And it goes on and on. National Public Radio commentator Andrei Codrescu described the return of Christ and Christian theology (in 1 Thess. 4:17) as "crap." According to a December 19, 1995, transcript of National Public Radio's *All Things Considered*, Codrescu said, "The evaporation of four million [people] who believe in this crap would leave the world in an instantly better place."[6] If Codrescu had said that about Muslims, he would join Salman Rushdie in perpetual hiding to avoid the *fatwa* that would be issued against him. If he had said it about Jews or blacks or homosexuals, he would have been banished from the airwaves forever. But here in America, not only can Codrescu say these things, he can also count on your tax dollars to subsidize his message of hate.

The Antichrist's one-world government will persecute all those who believe in God. This is not at all far-fetched; in fact the handwriting is already on the wall. The American Bar Association, the foremost legal fraternity in America, offered sessions on "How to sue the church through tort law" at its national 1993 convention in San Francisco. In Colorado it looks as if there will be a state law passed under the banner of "hate crimes." No one serious about glorifying God could harbor the cancer of hatred within his soul, but these hate crimes bills are more like a Trojan horse because, as written, they give the state the power to put people in jail for expressing what could be interpreted as their first amendment religious rights—among other things, these laws could be twisted to forbid speaking negatively about a person's "sexual preference."

For instance, if a rabbi or minister told his congregation that homosexuality is an abomination before God—which Scripture says it is—he could be fined and thrown in jail. As America slides deeper into the slime of secular humanism, I believe the law will eventually be interpreted in this way.

Consider the attack being made against religion in the public schools of America. When my son, Matthew, was in the third grade, his teacher asked the class to write a two-paragraph story about Christmas. Because his mother is Hispanic, Matthew chose to write about Christmas in Mexico. He described *Las Posadas*[7] and how the wise men went from house to house, searching for the Christ child.

His paper was rejected because he mentioned the name of Jesus in the second paragraph. Since baby Jesus was the object of the wise men's search, it was impossible to tell the story without including His name. But under the rationale that church and state must be separated, his paper was rejected.

Well, this father was at the school in short order. After a brisk conversation with the teacher and the principal and an absolute promise that a lawsuit would follow if that paper was not accepted, common sense suddenly prevailed. But unfortunately, this hostile environment toward Christianity continues to grow in far too many American public schools.

Recently a school principal in Jackson, Mississippi, allowed a student to read this prayer over the public address system: "Almighty God, we ask Your blessing on our teachers, our parents, and our nation. Amen."

The result? The principal was immediately put on probation and forced to call in by phone every hour and report his activities to authorities. Criminals on parole are treated better.

Today in most American public schools you can distribute condoms, teach lifeboat ethics, and affirm that it's normal for Heather to have "two [lesbian] mommies," but you can't read the Bible. What would John Quincy Adams have said in response to this? One of our nation's founding fathers, he declared, "So great is my veneration for the Bible that the earlier my children begin to read it, the more confident will be my hope that they will prove useful citizens for their country and respectable members of society. I have for many years made it a practice to read the Bible through once every year."[8] Today Quincy would be despised as a bigot and arrested as a lawbreaker, as would Abraham Lincoln for having the audacity to say, "I believe the Bible is the best gift God has given to man."[9]

And yet the Supreme Court has ruled that it is unconstitutional for the Ten Commandments to be posted on a classroom wall. Why? Because students might read them and the words might affect their moral character. Heaven help us, for in a generation marked by drive-by shootings, murder, rape, teenage suicides, drug abuse, homosexuality, pornography, and satanism, we certainly wouldn't want to affect moral character development! "Political correctness" is the new commandment foisted on all children.

What irony! Russia, formerly an atheistic state, is desperately trying to repair the moral wreckage brought upon its people by godlessness. Immediately after the collapse of the Soviet regime, the people were begging for Bibles, for copies of the Ten Commandments, for preachers and ministry groups to participate in their public school programs. Yet in America, one of the most "religious" countries on earth, we forbid those very things!

For thirty years the minds of our children have been vacuumed and sanitized. They have been taught political correctness. They know how to put a condom on a banana and why they should be sensitive to spotted owls and sucker fish. But CBS released a poll that stated that 75 percent of America's recent high school graduates can't name the last three presidents of the United States.

An educational commission said of the American public school system, "If a foreign power had done to our schools what we have done, we would consider it an act of war."

Believe me, friends, a new world order is coming and a new world orderer (the Antichrist), but this new world order is not going to be the utopia that politicians, professors, and pundits have predicted. It's going to be hell on earth, a time of severe tribulation and testing. And it will come from Satan's false messiah, the Antichrist, the so-called man of peace who will make Hitler look like a choirboy! He will set himself up as God—and people will believe in him by the millions.

The Antichrist's One World Religion

What is the Antichrist's chief desire? He is a false christ, and Christ is worthy of our worship and praise. Satan knows the prophecy that one day every knee will bow before Jesus Christ, but so great is his hatred toward God that he's determined to lash out at God by keeping as many people from salvation as possible. And who knows, maybe Satan even thinks he can defeat the Lord God somehow. During the Antichrist's limited time on earth, he wants to be worshiped. He will set up his image in Jerusalem and all who refuse to worship him will be murdered (see Rev. 13:15).

Jesus confirmed that Satan's messiah, the Antichrist, will demand worldwide worship. "'Therefore when you see the "abomination of desolation," spoken of by Daniel the prophet, standing in the holy place' (whoever reads, let him understand), 'then let those who are in Judea flee to the mountains'" (Matt. 24:15).

The Jewish temple will be rebuilt in Jerusalem. During the first half of his rule, the Antichrist will allow the Jewish people to resume making sacrifices in the temple. They will rejoice and many of them may even believe him to be their Messiah. But during the last three-and-a-half years of his reign, he will forbid the offering of sacrifices.

The last time I was in Israel, I was amazed to discover that a temple society there has already made all of the implements necessary for temple worship to be reinstated exactly as in the days of Moses. Every detail in every instrument and every fabric has been replicated as they prepare to make daily sacrifices in the temple again.

Daniel makes it clear that the continual burnt offering stops three-and-a-half years (1,290 days) before the end of the Tribulation. Why? The Antichrist will introduce idolatrous worship inside the holy temple and set himself up as God: "He will confirm a covenant with many for one 'seven,' [a term of seven years] but in the middle of that 'seven' he will put an end to sacrifice and offering. And one who causes desolation will place abominations on a wing of the temple until the end that is decreed is poured out on him" (Dan. 9:27 NIV).

"He opposes and exalts himself over everything that is called God or is worshiped, and even sets himself up in God's temple, proclaiming himself to be God" (2 Thess. 2:4 NIV). The Antichrist is not alone. In this perverted satanic trinity, Satan (the first person of this twisted trinity) supplies the power to the Antichrist (the second person), who in turn has a helper, the devilish "False Prophet," who works signs and wonders in the Antichrist's name (just as the Holy Spirit does in the Blessed Trinity): "And he [the False Prophet] deceives those who dwell on the earth by those signs which he was granted to do in the sight of the beast, telling those who dwell on the earth to make an image to the beast who was wounded by the sword and lived. He was granted power to give breath to the image of the beast, that the image of the beast should both speak and cause as many as would not worship the image of the beast to be killed" (Rev. 13:14–15). Through the False Prophet's demonic power, the image of the Antichrist is made to speak like a man.

The False Prophet is to the Antichrist what the Holy Spirit is to Jesus Christ. When the False Prophet causes this statue to speak, most will bow and worship on the spot.

The fact that the Antichrist will present himself to the world as God is verified in Daniel 11:36: "Then the king [Antichrist] shall do according to his own will: he shall exalt and magnify himself above every god, shall speak blasphemies against the God of gods, and shall prosper till the wrath has been accomplished; for what has been determined shall be done."

Israel has yet to endure her darkest night. I believe the peace process now under way will prove alas to be a Trojan horse. Instead of bringing the long-sought-for peace, it will bring the Antichrist and the most horrible war the Holy Land has ever known. The religious Jews of Israel are about to experience the most blasphemous campaign of all time to force them to abandon their faith when the Antichrist demands that they worship his image in the holy city of Jerusalem or else.

CHAPTER EIGHT

Conspiracies, Coalitions, and Catastrophes

A "man of peace" quite different from Yitzhak Rabin will soon step onto the world's stage. One of his foremost Bible names is "the son of perdition" (2 Thess. 2:3), which can also be translated as "chief son of Satan."

The Son of Satan

Time magazine, in its review of the movie *The Omen*, noted that this dark and disturbing movie "rests on the biblical prophecy about the return of the Prince of Darkness taken from *The Revelator* to fit certain events of our time—the creation of Israel and the Common Market [now known as the European Union.]"[1] The magazine article concluded that these are "times to believe in a reincarnated devil."

The Antichrist's origin, methods, agenda, and goal are clearly revealed in Bible prophecy. The Antichrist, or deceptive "man of peace," could very well be alive right now.

The Strategy of Satan

But in order to fully understand the agenda of the Antichrist, it is important to grasp the overall strategy of Satan. Satan's goal is to "be like the Most High" (Isa. 14:14). In fact, he wants to go beyond that and *dethrone* the Most High.

Somewhere in the early dawn of time, Satan, the most perfect being ever created, convinced one-third of the angels to join him in his reckless attempt to supplant God as the ruler of all. Decisively defeated, Satan has continued in open opposition to God, seeking wherever possible to lash out at God and to attempt to destroy, deceive, or discredit that which is important to Him.

We get a hint of this from the very name "antichrist." The prefix *anti-* in Greek has two meanings. The first is what we naturally think of in English: against. The second is in some ways far more interesting, for *anti-* also means "in place of." And both of these definitions apply in the case of the Antichrist: Satan and his unholy conspirators are both against God and seeking to take the place of God.

Certainly Satan and his demons know what the Word of God says about their ultimate doom, so why do they persist in this ultimately futile endeavor? There is no doubt that part of the answer could lie in the evil and spite that are the defining qualities of their character. It could also be because somehow Satan and his demons fancy that they can alter their destiny and actually dethrone God Almighty. After all, Satan's original sin was pride. Certainly evil is at the very core of Satan's motivation, but I believe the very events of the Tribulation demonstrate that Satan still believes he can ultimately succeed in taking God's place, and that is why Satan's works in the Tribulation so doggedly and yet so ineffectively attempt to imitate the worldwide rule of God in the Millennium.

With "the Restrainer" (the Holy Spirit at work on the earth through the Church) removed, Satan feels he has the best shot he has ever had in taking God's place. But what Satan has in the way of opportunity, he lacks in the realm of originality.

Just as the One God has existed for all eternity as Father, Son, and Holy Spirit, so Satan creates his own twisted trinity of Satan, the Antichrist, and the False Prophet.

But while the Father omnipotent rules from heaven on high, Satan is cast down from heaven and confined first to a bottomless pit and then to hell, the eternal lake of fire.

While Jesus offers eternal salvation to those who will trust Him, the Antichrist can only provide eternal damnation for those foolish enough to trust him. And while Jesus will rule a world of peace and prosperity during the thousand-year period known as the Millennium, the Antichrist will rule (if you can call it ruling) for a mere seven years—years which are characterized by unprecedented war, deprivation, and chaos.

While the Holy Spirit testifies of Jesus and provides comfort, joy, and strength to those who follow the Savior, the False Prophet testifies of the Antichrist and enforces allegiance to him through threats, deception, and naked aggression.

Satan knows that God is planning a thousand-year rule over the earth—one thousand years that will be characterized by one world religion, one world government, one world economy. So of course Satan tries to implement the same thing.

Satan seeks to impose one world religion, but instead "a great multitude that no one can count" rejects this religion and recognizes Jesus as their Messiah. And while Jesus offers eternal salvation to those who trust Him, the Antichrist can only promise temporal salvation (the ability to buy and sell) to those who deny Christ.

Satan seeks to impose a single world government, but instead the Antichrist seems to spend at least the second half of the Tribulation fighting off one challenge after another to his rule—only to have his one-world government of one thousand years cut short at seven.

Satan seeks worldwide compliance to his laws, but the best the Antichrist can do is to rush around attempting to quash one rebellion after another. And he will never fully succeed.

The Number of a Man: 666

John the Revelator writes, "Here is wisdom. Let him who has understanding calculate the number of the beast, for it is the number of a man [or, the number of man]: His number is 666" (Rev. 13:18). The meaning of the number "666" provides an ideal transition from looking at the satanic trinity as a whole to focusing on the second member of that Trinity, the Antichrist.

"The number of a man," according to Bible scholars, is six. Under the Law, man's labor was limited to six days, for God created man to rest on the seventh day. The seventh day is God's day, and seven is the number of divine completeness throughout the Scripture. Six falls short of seven, just as anything done by created beings falls short of the Creator's perfection.

The Antichrist's number of 666 could also represent the satanic trinity: Satan, the Antichrist, and the False Prophet who will lead the worldwide cult that worships the son of Satan. For just as six falls short of seven, we have seen that Satan falls short of being God the Father, the Antichrist falls short of being God the Son, and the False Prophet falls short of being God the Holy Spirit.

The number 666 could also be a reference to the worldwide idolatry attempted by Nebuchadnezzar when he erected a statue of himself and commanded all the world to worship it or face death (see Dan. 3). You might say that 666 was stamped upon the very image of Nebuchadnezzar since the image was 60 cubits high and 6 cubits wide (see v. 1).

Now remember, in Revelation 13 the focal point is the rise of a man, the Antichrist, and 666 is said to be "the number of a man." In light of this emphasis, there is another possible explanation of the cryptic name "666." I am speculating here, but certainly some of John's readers were familiar with the method of calculating a name by the use of numbers, a practice known to the Jews as *Geometria* (or *Gimetria*). The Greeks also practiced it, but not as seriously as the Jewish people.

This transition from number to letter or from letter to number was possible because most ancient languages did not have independent symbols for numbers as we do. Rather, the letters of the alphabet were also used to designate numbers in the way that Roman numerals use letters to designate numbers. It was a simple matter for members of the early church to convert a number into a name or a name into a number.

In Revelation 13:18 John made it possible for the world to identify the Antichrist. This cryptic puzzle is not intended to point a finger at some unknown person. It is, however, intended to confirm to the world someone already suspected as being the Antichrist. And in the idolatry of the end time, "the number of a man" is fully developed and the result is 666.

This information about how to identify the Antichrist is of no practical value to the Church since we will be watching from the balconies of heaven by the time he is revealed. But for those of you who are reading this book after the church has been taken in the Rapture, and for those of you who come to trust Christ during the Tribulation, you will have the ability to confirm which personality rising out of a European federation is the devil incarnate, the son of Satan.

During the late 1930s and early 1940s a flurry of pamphlets identified Adolf Hitler as the Antichrist. Others declared that Mussolini was the Antichrist because of his relationship to Rome. But no one who lives from the time of Pentecost until the Rapture of the church can possibly know who the Antichrist is because he will not make his appearance upon the world stage until the Church, indwelt by the Restrainer, the Holy Spirit, has been removed from the earth.

This so-called man of peace, this son of Satan, this false messiah, the Antichrist, is probably alive right now and may even know his predestined demonic assignment. And though we may not know who the Antichrist *is,* we certainly know in great detail what the Antichrist will *do.*

The Antichrist Described

In the thirteenth chapter of Revelation we find one of the most descriptive accounts of the Antichrist's activities. Here he is referred to as "the Beast," whose number is 666. In Daniel,

BEGINNING OF THE END

where he is described even more fully, you will recall that he is the "little horn" of chapter seven. He is also referred to as the "king of fierce features" of Daniel 8, the "prince who is to come" in chapter nine, and the "willful king" of chapter eleven.

As we have already shown, the son of Satan will be a counterfeit of the son of God. But we learn even more about the personality and plan of the Antichrist by understanding how completely opposite he is from Jesus, the true Son of God.

Christ came from heaven (John 6:38)	the Antichrist will come from hell (Rev. 11:7)
Christ came in His Father's name (John 5:43)	the Antichrist will come in his own name (John 5:43)
Christ humbled Himself (Phil. 2:8)	the Antichrist will exalt himself (2 Thess. 2:4)
Christ was despised and afflicted (Is. 53:3)	the Antichrist will be admired and lauded (Rev. 13:3, 4)
Christ came to do His Father's will (John 6:38)	the Antichrist will come to do his own will (Dan. 11:36)
Christ came to save (Luke 19:10)	the Antichrist will come to destroy (Dan. 8:24)
Christ is the Good Shepherd (John 10)	the Antichrist will be the Evil Shepherd (Zech. 11:16, 17)
Christ is the Truth (John 14:6)	the Antichrist will be "the lie" (2 Thess. 2:11)
Christ is the Mystery of Godliness, God manifested in the flesh (1 Tim. 3:16)	the Antichrist will be "The Mystery of Iniquity," Satan manifested in the flesh (2 Thess. 2:7–9), the living son of Satan

The Antichrist Comes to Power

The Antichrist will first take control of one nation in the federated block, which could come from the current European Union. At a moment of instability, which could be caused by war in Bosnia or some United Nations sanctioned action, he will take control of three nations within the federation.

John describes him in Revelation 13:1: "Then I stood on the sand of the sea. And I saw a beast rising up out of the sea, having seven heads and ten horns, and on his horns ten crowns, and on his heads a blasphemous name."

Notice that the beast rises from the sea—the sea, in prophetic symbolism, represents the Gentile world—and he wears ten crowns on seven heads. In other words, he has conquered three of ten nations and rules over them, wearing ten symbolic crowns.

Israel Entrusts Its Security to the Antichrist

Desperate for peace and ignorant of the Antichrist's true nature, Israel will soon sign a seven-year treaty of peace with the Antichrist. In fact, the signing of the treaty is the event that will inaugurate the seven-year Tribulation. In this treaty the Antichrist himself will guarantee Israel's security. "He [the Antichrist] will confirm a covenant with many for one 'seven.' In the middle of that 'seven' he will put an end to sacrifice and offering" (Dan. 9:27 NIV).

Now before reading on, just take a moment to think about what the Word of God says. If you've ever been to Israel, you'll note that their history of betrayal and persecution makes them extremely wary to entrust their safety to anyone other than themselves. In fact, this history is part of the great need for the Jewish people to have their own homeland—they can trust their government because their government is truly their own. You could even say that the nation of Israel is an incarnation of their desire as expressed in the solemn utterance "Never again." Never again a pogrom; never again a persecution; never again an exile; never again a holocaust. So just imagine what it would take for them to entrust their security to another. This gives you an idea both of the coming change of attitude in Israel and of the incredible power and credibility of the Antichrist.

In the months ahead, it is a distinct possibility—and as far as I'm concerned a probability—that Israel will relinquish all or part of the Golan Heights to Syria and then invite the United Nations or some other international force to occupy that region to guarantee their national security. That will be a defining moment in history because the nation of Israel has never relied upon anyone else for its national safety.

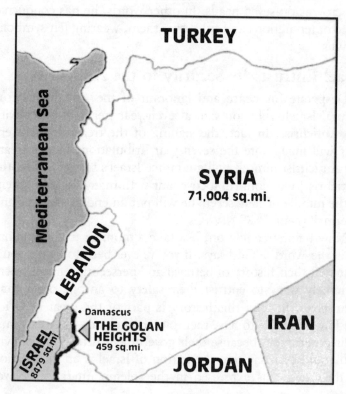

The Golan Heights, a strategic plateau overlooking northern Israel and the southern Syrian plains, is critical both militarily and as the principal source of water for the nation of Israel. The area is a towering plateau about twelve miles wide that measures about 480 square miles and is distinguished by two levels; the Lower Golan in the south, with altitudes between 600 and 1,900 feet, and the Upper Golan in the north, rising to altitudes of up to 3,000 feet above sea level. A number of hilltops reach as high as 4,400 feet.

The Israeli observation posts on the Golan Heights make it virtually impossible for Syria to launch a sneak attack against Israel, and weather conditions are such that satellite surveillance would be difficult and airborne surveillance extremely costly.

As a small country, Israel has no land that can be yielded to an attacker during the first blow of a military attack. Accordingly the IDF (Israel Defense Forces) have always relied heavily on preemptive strikes and rapid mobilization of reserves to resist hostile enemies massed on their borders. But this also means that it is an absolute necessity for Israel to have accurate and timely information to anticipate and preempt any military actions by their enemies.

And while it is true that the Syrians can reach any location in Israel from any location in Syria with their Scud-C missiles (whether the missiles carry conventional or chemical warheads), it is also true that the Golan Heights is laid out in such a way that a Syrian invasion can only come through two areas: the Tel Fars area and the Quneitra area. This explains why, when the Israelis were completely surprised by the Yom Kippur war and initially overrun by Egypt, a small force of heroic Israeli troops were able to hold at bay one thousand Syrian tanks until the reserves were able to reach the area. However, had the Israelis not had the Golan Heights, they would have had to repel an attack inside Israel in the heavily populated Hula Valley, the Jordan Valley, and the Galilee. The casualties would have been horrific.

Perhaps even more important on a day-to-day basis, the Golan Heights are rich in water resources, and these resources are in desperate demand in the desert that comprises so much of Israel and the Middle East. By contrast, Syria is rich in water resources and has regularly tried to dry out Israel by diverting the sources of the Jordan River.[2]

Since June 1974, as many as 1,250 troops of the United Nations Disengagement Observer Force have patrolled the area of separation between Israeli and Syrian forces. Obviously there aren't enough of them to prevent aggression because of their limited size and strength. Instead they are "trip wires"—like the allied forces were in West Berlin during the Cold War. Our forces could have been overwhelmed by the Communists, but to do so they would have had to take the lives of allied soldiers, and thus make *full* allied involvement in a *wider* war *inevitable*. So the UN troops are human shields and hostages, ensuring that the aggressor who harms them will face the wrath of the world community.[3] Nevertheless, right now it can be said that only in some small ways is the UN acting as a guarantor of peace for Israel. Yet far from entrusting their security to the UN, the IDF actively and vigorously maintains a defense of the Golan, and it maintains the fourth most powerful military force in the world.

Yet outrage at the assassination of Prime Minister Yitzhak Rabin will unite Israeli public opinion and galvanize their government to pursue peace with the Palestinians and Syrians. Just a few months ago, world leaders and theologians would have considered this utterly impossible, but it is happening now before our very eyes. Rabin believed in peace strongly enough to stake the final portion of his political career—and ultimately, his life—in pursuit of it.

According to experts in Israeli politics, before the Rabin assassination "the truism of Israel politics was: Peres was too eager to shake Arafat's hand, while Rabin was just reluctant enough to do it."[4] But now the world is eager for the Israelis to shake the Arabs' hands. Shimon Peres, often described as "the dovish foreign minister," was the chief negotiator with the Palestinians. He initiated the secret contacts in Oslo, Norway, that led to the 1993 Accord.

So despite Israel's history, the transition to a less defensive posture is already underway. When the time comes, so great will be the confidence and trust of the Israelis in the protection of the Antichrist that when they are attacked just before the three-and-a-half-year mark of the Tribulation, they will be described as "a land of unwalled villages . . . a peaceful people, who dwell safely, all of them dwelling without walls, and having neither bars nor gates" (Ez. 38:11). Now this is absolutely remarkable. If you've ever been to Israel, you know that security is their top priority—soldiers, machine guns, tanks, walls, and concertina wire are everywhere! It would be one thing if you found a prophetic reference to a tranquil nation like Costa Rica that is free of defenses, but it's something else altogether for a nation like Israel to surrender its national security to a foreign military force.

Perhaps it is because of the euphoria they will feel over the rebuilding of the Temple.

The Temple Is Rebuilt

One of the specifications of the agreement between Israel and the Antichrist will allow the religious Jews to rebuild the Temple and to initiate daily sacrifices. We know this because the Antichrist will stop sacrifices and offerings at the mid-point of the Tribulation, and sacrifices have to have been started again in order for the Antichrist to stop them. Another clue that the Temple will be rebuilt is that the Antichrist will take over the Temple, an event which also occurs at the midpoint of the Tribulation: "He [the Antichrist] opposes and exalts himself over everything that is called God or is worshiped, and even sets himself up in God's temple, proclaiming himself to be God" (2 Thess. 2:4). Again, a temple must have been built in order for the Antichrist to seize and defile it as he will.

Now the rebuilding of the Temple constitutes an enormous political and religious problem, for the place the Bible decrees for the location of the Temple is currently occupied by the Dome of the Rock.

The Dome of the Rock, located on the temple mount, or Mount Moriah, is the third holiest place in the world for Muslims. Listen to it described by The Islamic Association for Palestine:

"Glory be to Him Who did take His servant for a journey by night from the sacred (Haram) mosque to the farthest (Aqsa) mosque whose precincts We did bless, in order that We might show him some of Our signs: for He is the One Who hears and sees (all things)" (Qur'an 17:1). Al-Aqsa mosque is the third holiest place in Islam, the second house of worship on Earth, and was the first direction of prayer for Muslims. One prayer in Al-Aqsa mosque is equivalent to 500 times the prayers in any other mosque except for the Haram Mosque in Makka and the Prophet's (An-Nabawi) Mosque in Madina. In the journey to heaven, Prophet Muhammed (pbuh) prayed in Al-Aqsa mosque, leading all the prophets.[5]

If you doubt that the Jewish people would ever attempt something so audacious, you need to know that some Jewish people are *already* planning for it, working to make all the necessary preparations for the construction and operation of the *third* Temple (the first being Solomon's and the second being Herod's). One of the organizations working toward this end is called the Temple Foundation. Here is how they describe their work:

Today, at the Temple Institute in Jerusalem, Biblical prophecy is being fulfilled. Here, you can see something which has not been seen on the face of the earth for 2,000 years: In preparation for the Third Temple, the Temple Institute has created authentic Temple vessels and priestly garments according to Biblical specifications. This is an ongoing process, and to date over 60 sacred objects have been recreated from gold, silver and copper. These vessels are not models or replicas, but they are actually made according to all the complicated nuances and requirements of Biblical law. If the Holy Temple were to be rebuilt immediately, the Divine service could be resumed utilizing these vessels. . . .

In addition to its work on the recreation of Temple vessels, the Institute is conducting a number of related research projects. These include the importation of authentic Red Heifers to Israel, in preparation for the ritual purification detailed in Numbers 19. Other firsts include the identification and gathering together of all 11 ingredients of the incense offering, and the long and exhaustive research in identifying the stones of the High Priest's breastplate—the Urim and Thummim. There is even advanced work being done by technicians and architects, using sophisticated computer technology, to design actual blueprints for the Third Temple.[6]

Only the destruction of the great mosques in Mecca and Medina could have a more explosive effect on Muslims. And perhaps no greater blow (apart from the battles described in this chapter and the next) has ever been inflicted on them than what Israel will accomplish in the removal of the Dome of the Rock to build the third Temple. But even as an international force guarantees the security of Israel in their decision to rebuild the Temple, the Islamic nations will prepare for war. The "King of the North" will lead them toward Israel.

An Islamic Jihad Against Israel

In response to the destruction of the Dome of the Rock, the Islamic nations of Africa and the Middle East will form a Pan-Islamic Coalition to destroy Israel, eliminate the Jewish people, and destroy the third Temple. Of course the removal of the Dome of the Rock in and of itself will seem like reason enough for the Islamic nations of Africa and the Middle East to put aside their historic and multifaceted squabbles. Yet building this alliance will take time, and the Coalition will not strike until around the middle of the seven-year Tribulation. Yet I believe that Israel, while enjoying a time of relative peace, will nevertheless be continuously hounded by terrorist groups like HAMAS and the Islamic Jihad.

But we must also remember that militant Islam harbors so much hatred toward the Jewish people that it won't take much to work them into a frenzy to accomplish what they have longed for for years: "Six million descendants of monkeys [i.e., Jews] now rule all the nations of the world, but their day, too, will come. Allah, Kill them all, do not leave even one."[7]

The Scriptures describe this coming Coalition as a confederation of two great kings: the King of the South and the King of the North.

The King of the South, according to Ezekiel, will control the borders that were then known as Persia, Ethiopia, and Libya. Persia is modern-day Iran, the present incubator and disseminator of militant Islam. Libya here (literally "Put"), refers to the same general area that the modern terrorist state of Libya now occupies. Ethiopia may represent more than the one country that now bears its name. Its ancestry is traced to Cush, a grandson of Noah (see Genesis 10), whose descendants must have migrated southward into all parts of Africa.

Nothing could make more sense in the light of current events. The Islam of the Iranian fundamentalists is on the march in Africa, not only in north Africa but throughout the entire continent as well. Right now, there is an epic battle raging between Christianity and Islam for the hearts and souls of men and women in Africa. With the church removed from that continent, Islam will have an open road to prosyletize. And interestingly, The Islamic Association for Palestine reports:

- That the original 1947 recommendation to create a "Jewish State" in Palestine was approved, at the first vote, only by European, American, and Australian States . . . for every Asian State, and every African State (with the exception of the Union of South Africa) voted against it.

- That, when the vote was cast in plenary session on 29 November 1947, urgent American pressures (which a member of the Truman cabinet described as "bordering onto scandal") had succeeded in prevailing only upon one African country (Liberia) . . . which had special vulnerability to American pressures, to abandon their declared opposition.

- That Israel remained, ever since its inception, a total stranger in the emerging world of Afro-Asia; and that Israel has been refused admission to any inter-state conference of Asian, African, Afro-Asian, or Non-Aligned States ever held.[8]

Now if even half of those statements are true, it is clear that there will be no shortage of volunteers from Africa to take up arms against Israel (to say nothing of her enemies in the Middle East).

Also mentioned as conspiring with the Coalition of the Kings of the South and North are the nations of Sheba (modern Yemen), Dedan (a territory in Southern Edom, located today in southern Jordan), and Tarshish (which is traditionally identified as being on the coast of southern Spain or the Mediterranean island of Sardinia).

The other dread participant in this coming Jihad is the King of the North. Looking at the modern location of the names of the combatants mentioned in Ezekiel 38 and 39 and their location as shown on the map entitled "The Nations of Genesis 10," it becomes clear that they come from the general area of Turkey, Syria, Iraq, and at least some of the Islamic republics of the former (and I believe future) Soviet Union, if not from Russia herself.[9]

Don't count Russia out of this coming Jihad that will take place just before the halfway point of the Tribulation. In Ezekiel 38 and 39 there are tantalizing references to "Gog, of the land of Magog" (38:2) who "will come from [his] place out of the far north, [he] and many peoples [or nations] with [him], all of them riding on horses, a great company and a mighty army" (Ez. 38:15). And while no one knows the exact location of the land of Magog, going north from Israel will eventually land you in Russia. And even if it is later determined that the land of Magog is located in modern-day Turkey or the land bridge between the Black and Caspian Seas,[10] this does not rule out the possibility that these areas are conquered by Russia in the days immediately before the Rapture (which I believe we are living in) or immediately after.

Whatever the identity of "Gog, of the land of Magog," it is leading many nations in the war against Israel and the Jewish people. Interestingly enough, a substantial number of the na-

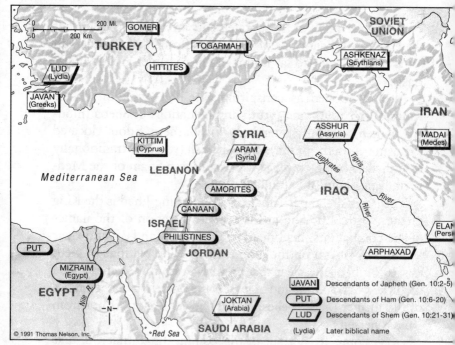

The Nations of Genesis 10

tions mentioned in Ezekiel 38 and 39 have been allied with Russia in recent times: "These include Iran ('Persia'), Sudan and northern Ethiopia ('Cush'), Libya ('Put'), and Turkey ('Meshesh,' 'Tubal,' 'Gomer,' and 'Beth Togarmah')."[11]

A Reborn Russia Conspires with Islam

You may be asking, "How could the Soviet Union ever be reborn?" or, "What interest would either Russia or a reborn Soviet Union have in cooperating in this military campaign against Israel and the temple in Jerusalem?" or for that matter, "Why would this Muslim Coalition have any interest in teaming up with Russia?" The answer is as close as today's newspaper.

Russia's Motivation

Now make no mistake, this alliance will be a marriage of convenience—not love. Each will have something that the other wants. For Russia, two things stand out.

Russia longs to be a superpower again. The empire the Soviets built during the time of Communist rule was a source of great pride to many. The humiliation of losing that empire combined with the impoverishment of their faltering economy have left the Russian people romantic about their past, bitter about their present, and skeptical about their future. It is in such a climate that dictatorship grows, and indeed you need look no further than the recent elections to the Russian Duma to find an indication of where Russia is headed. While the leading politicians of Russia are separated on many issues, Gennadi Zyuganov, the leader of the resurgent Communist Party; Vladimir Zhirinovsky, the deranged ultranationalist; and Aleksandr Lebed, the former general, are all looking at the future through the lens of their authoritarian and atheist past. They are relying on the resentment of the Russian people toward reform and the West to sweep them into office. And once in office, they must deliver.

As it now stands, the Russian constitution vests far more powers in the president than in the parliament. And because the top two vote-getters in the presidential election face a runoff with each other, the system greatly favors coalition governments. And indeed the process of forming coalitions to reverse the reforms of Gorbachev and Yeltsin has already begun.[12]

Russia has much natural wealth, but it is hard to access. Not only does Russia long to be a superpower again, she also needs money. Unfortunately for the world, when a nation combines poverty with ambition the result is almost always an effort to expand. For while Russia longs for the glory days, right now it has trouble even paying its armed forces. And although Russia is rich with oil reserves and other natural resources, those riches tend to be located in remote areas that are difficult to access. This problem is compounded by their rudimentary technology and their lack of hard currency to buy technology from the West. And after being defeated in Afghanistan and bloodied in Chechnya, Russia's nationalist leaders may believe that the country needs a military victory to increase their prestige and send a suitable message to the world—especially the West.

So to regain its empire, Russia needs money, military victory, and western technology—but on Russia's terms, not by going hat in hand to the West. What better way to achieve all three than by controlling the main source of the industrialized world's oil—the Persian Gulf? By controlling and selling Middle Eastern oil, Russia would be able to blackmail the industrialized nations into submission.

If the Islamic nations cede some control of their oil to Russia in return for her cooperation in the invasion, then the price will be right for her to join the Islamic nations in their campaign to destroy Israel and the temple.

What the Islamic Coalition Gains

What could the Islamic nations possibly get from Russia that would be worth allowing the Russians into their land and giving them control over their oil riches? I can think of at least four reasons.

The Islamic nations would greatly benefit from the strength of Russia's armed forces. Although they are much less powerful than they were during the Cold War, Russia's armed forces are vastly superior to those of any of the Muslim countries, and provide them with a formidable threat in both land, sea, air, and space. Furthermore, the Islamic countries will be only too aware of their inability to defeat Israel's military and the considerable military prowess of the Antichrist, who is guaranteeing the security of Israel.

Russia will be able to threaten to use its nuclear, biological, or chemical weapons, should either Israel or the West threaten to intervene or escalate the conflict by using such weapons. It has long been known that Israel possesses nuclear weapons, as I talked about in a previous chapter, and we can only assume that it has chemical and biological weapons as well to be able to respond to any attack or threat in kind.

Now it is unclear from Ezekiel 38:11 if Israel has retained its arsenal, but even if it has, the Russians can threaten to lob missiles loaded with nuclear, chemical, or biological warheads upon Israel from the relative safety of their borders in the far north, should Israel try to escalate the conflict.

But perhaps even more significant, Russia can threaten the Antichrist with its arsenal, should he try to fulfill his treaty obligations and come to the defense of Israel. And as enraged as the Muslims are about the rebuilding of the Temple and the very existence of Israel, ceding a measure of control over their oil might seem a reasonable price for ridding the world fully and finally of the Jewish State.

Many of the nations identified in Ezekiel 38 and 39 have been past allies of the Russians. Returning to a former alliance may give them a feeling of familiarity, security, and even control.

The Islamic nations may be mindful of Russia's experience in Afghanistan. Remember, as I said earlier, Islam is a religion of truimphalism. It believes that time and history are on its side. So even if eventually their alliance with Russia ruptures and they find themselves at war with her, they may very well believe that they will ultimately prevail over Russia, as was the case in the Afghanistan war.

Why Israel?

As I'm sure you can guess, there are two primary reasons to focus on the elimination of Israel: its religious importance and its strategic importance.

For the Islamic nations, the erection of the third temple on Mount Moriah and the elimination of their Dome of the Rock will be an affront so profound and disturbing that they simply must respond. To get an idea of the depth of their anger, if you're Jewish, imagine what you feel when you see a Nazi propaganda film and multiply that emotion by ten. If you're Christian, imagine what you feel when you hear that an exhibition of art featuring a crucifix submerged in a beaker of urine was paid for through the tax dollars provided to the National Endowment for the Arts; again, multiply that anger and indignation by ten. Even at that, your feeling will not compare with the depth of feeling the Muslims will have over the elimination of the Dome of the Rock and the construction of the third temple on its former site. This combined with their deep-seated hatred of the Jewish people will be more than enough to spur them to spend anything and sacrifice anything to eliminate the object of their abhorrence.

Of more importance to the Russians will be Israel's strategic importance. In order to control the oil of the Middle East, in order to dictate peace to the Antichrist on its own terms, Israel must be eliminated as a threat. By guaranteeing the peace of Israel, the Antichrist establishes a friendly outpost in the very heart of the Muslim world. Thus Israel becomes a forward station in the quest for empire. It will not escape the attention of the Russians that the Antichrist is every bit as determined as she is to build an empire and that some day their empires will clash. Nor will it escape the attention of the Muslims that the religion embraced and propagated by the Antichrist is vastly different from their own (though the religions of both will reject the Divine Trinity and the need of all people to trust Jesus Christ, the Son of God, as their Savior and Lord).

Although Israel has no oil, she is poised to control the export of oil from the Middle East. Because of her location and military strength—particularly her air force, if she retains it after entering into the covenant of peace with the Antichrist—she can disrupt the oil shipping routes in the Eastern Mediterranean, the Suez Canal, the Persian Gulf, and even the Strait of Hormuz. Thus Israel's air force and arsenal give her a trump card over the Muslims' expectation of triumph and the Russians' need to control the oil of the Middle East.

For all of these reasons and more, both the Russians and the Muslims will agree that Israel and the Jewish people must disappear from the Middle East. And just before the midpoint of the Tribulation, they seize their opportunity and attack.

The Battle for Israel and Jerusalem (Ezekiel 38 & 39)

Like so many things, what man intends for evil God intends for good, and this monumental battle between Israel and the coalition of Islam and Russia is no exception. For while this dread army believes that they have devised this battle of their own accord to serve their own ends, in fact it is God the Father who has brought them.

The Kings of the North and South Are Drawn into Battle

Ezekiel 38:4–6 declares:

> I will turn you around, put hooks into your jaws, and lead you out, with all your army, horses, and horsemen, all splendidly clothed, a great company with bucklers and shields, all of them handling swords. Persia, Ethiopia, and Libya are with them, all of them with shield and helmet; Gomer and all its troops; the house of Togarmah from the far north and all its troops—many people are with you.

And again we see the Lord orchestrating the battle in 38:16: "It will be in the latter days that *I* will bring you against My land" (emphasis added).

Instead the Kings of the North and the South only see Israel as "the land of those brought back from the sword and gathered from many people on the mountains of Israel, which had long been desolate; they were brought out of the nations, and now all of them dwell safely" (38:8). As a result of Israel's covenant of peace with the Antichrist and the coalition's own strategic preparations, Israel will appear to be more vulnerable than ever—a "land of unwalled villages . . . a peaceful people, who dwell safely, all of them dwelling without walls, and having neither bars nor gates . . . and against a people gathered from the nations, who have acquired livestock and goods, who dwell in the midst of the land" (38:11, 12).

As a result, the Coalition will "come from [its] place out of the far north, [it] and many peoples with [it], all of them riding on horses, a great company and a mighty army. [The coalition] will come up against My people Israel like a cloud, to cover the land" (38:15, 16).

And yet in spite of their strength and initial occupation of the land, the defeat of the Russian-Islamic coalition will be sudden, horrible, and complete.

The Kings of the North and South Are Defeated in Battle

The Kings of the North and South find an easy entry into the Promised Land. As they had hoped, the Antichrist makes no move whatsoever to fulfill his treaty obligations to Israel. And so with gratefulness to Allah (or Lenin), they are about to execute their plan of plunder and genocide. The vast majority will never know what hit them.

The battle is the Lord's. King David identified the source of Israel's military might: "He who keeps Israel shall neither slumber nor sleep" (Ps. 121:4). After watching the Jews of the Holocaust walk into the gas chambers, after seeing the "apple of His eye" thrown into the ovens and their ashes dumped by the tons into the rivers of Europe, after seeing the "land of milk and honey" run red with Jewish blood in five major wars for peace and freedom, God stands up and shouts to the nations of the world, "Enough! My fury shall come up in my face."

God shatters His silence.

> "'Surely in that day there shall be a great earthquake in the land of Israel, so that the fish of the sea, the birds of the heavens, the beasts of the field, all creeping things that creep on the earth, and all men who are on the face of the earth shall shake at My presence. The mountains shall be thrown down, the steep places shall fall, and every wall shall fall to the ground.' I will call for a sword against Gog throughout all My mountains," says the Lord GOD. "Every man's sword will be against his brother. And I will bring him to judgment with pestilence and bloodshed; I will rain down on him, on his troops, and on the many peoples who are with him, flooding rain, great

hailstones, fire, and brimstone. Thus I will magnify Myself and sanctify Myself, and I will be known in the eyes of many nations. Then they shall know that I am the LORD." (Ez. 38:19–23)

God unleashes His supernatural arsenal against Israel's enemies with lethal results. First, He shakes the earth with a mighty earthquake that will neutralize every tank and every foot soldier instantly. Some will doubtless be buried alive.

Second, God causes mass confusion to come upon every army coming against Israel. Every man turns his sword against his brother. This is exactly what God did when He commanded Gideon to blow the trumpets and break the pitchers. The Philistines became divinely confused and turned their swords on each other. Gideon won a great military victory without one casualty. God will do it again in defense of Israel.

This passage could be interpreted in two ways. First, the "fire and brimstone" may refer to Israel's release of nuclear weapons in a last-ditch attempt to prevent annihilation. The second interpretation is that this event is a repeat of Sodom and Gomorrah. God will blast Israel's enemies into oblivion by raining fire and brimstone from heaven. In either case the results are equally catastrophic.

The victory is complete. Ezekiel's graphic account in chapter 39 makes clear just how thorough and disastrous is the defeat of this Russian-Muslim coalition.

Ezekiel opens chapter 39 by stating: "I am against thee, O Gog." When what is left of the world living in the Tribulation looks at the millions of bloated bodies in the warm Israeli sun, this statement will go down in history as one of the greatest understatements of all time.

In this passage God does not tell us how many died, He tells us how many are left: only a "sixth part" (39:2 KJV). That means that the casualty rate for this battle will be 84 percent, unheard of in modern warfare.

The narrative of the aftermath of the war continues. Ezekiel says that the bloated bodies of the enemies of Israel will be a banquet for buzzards. The beasts of the field will have a feast unlike anything since dogs ate the body of Jezebel.

"You shall fall on the open field; for I have spoken," says the Lord GOD. "And I will send fire on Magog and on those who live in security in the coastlands. Then they shall know that I am the LORD. So I will make My holy name known in the midst of My people Israel, and I will not let them profane My holy name anymore. . . . It will come to pass in that day that I will give Gog a burial place there in Israel, the valley of those who pass by east of the sea; and it will obstruct travelers, because there they will bury Gog and all his multitude. Therefore they will call it the Valley of Hamon Gog. For seven months the house of Israel will be burying them, in order to cleanse the land. Indeed all the people of the land will be burying, and they will gain renown for it on the day that I am glorified," says the Lord GOD. "They will set apart men regularly employed, with the help of a search party, to pass through the land and bury those bodies remaining on the ground, in order to cleanse it. At the end of seven months they will make a search. The search party will pass through the land; and when anyone sees a man's bone, he shall set up a marker by it, till the buriers have buried it in the Valley of Hamon Gog. The name of the city will also be Hamonah. Thus they shall cleanse the land." (Ez. 39:5–7, 11–16)

The dead bodies of the invaders will be strewn in the fields and mountains of Israel, and the burial detail will take seven months and will involve all the people of Israel. Ezekiel hints very strongly that even tourists will be asked to look for stray bodies to mark the spot for burial details. *Hamon-Gog* is a Hebrew word for "the multitude of Gog," which is to become the name of this vast cemetery for the invaders of Israel.

"And as for you, son of man, thus says the Lord GOD, 'Speak to every sort of bird and to every beast of the field: "Assemble yourselves and come; gather together from all sides to my sacrificial meal which I am sacrificing for you, a great sacrificial meal on the mountains of Israel, that you may eat flesh and drink blood. You shall eat the flesh of the mighty, drink the blood of the princes of the earth, of rams and lambs, of goats and bulls, all of them fatlings of Bashan. You shall eat fat till you are full, and drink blood till you are drunk, at My sacrificial meal which I am sacrificing for you. You shall be filled at My table with horses and riders, with mighty men and with all the men of war," says the Lord GOD.'" (Ez. 39:17–20)

But not only is there tremendous carnage, the weapons left by these devastated forces provide fuel for Israel for seven years—in other words, beyond the Tribulation and into the Millennium:

"Then those who dwell in the cities of Israel will go out and set on fire and burn the weapons, both the shields and bucklers, the bows and arrows, the javelins and spears; and they will make fires with them for seven years. They will not take wood from the field nor cut down any from the forests, because they will make fires with the weapons; and they will plunder those who plundered them, and pillage those who pillaged them," says the Lord GOD. (Ezekiel 39:9–10)

Can you imagine burning weapons for seven years? I was in Israel during Operation Peace for Galilee led by General Ariel Sharon back in the eighties. I personally saw Israeli eighteen-wheel trucks bringing back the spoils of war in a convoy that stretched farther than my eye could see. The trucks, bumper-to-bumper coming out of Lebanon, were carrying maximum loads of war booty back to Israel. These were supplies that had been stored in Lebanon by the Soviet Union and were said to be enough to keep 500,000 men in combat for six months. As great as those spoils were, it was only a matter of days before the Israeli army collected and stored them. But Ezekiel describes a war so vast that it will take seven years to burn the weapons of war.

Israel will derive an unexpected benefit from this. Ezekiel says that the war booty from this massive invasion will provide Israel with fuel for seven years, and because of this the forest will be spared.

It has been my pleasure over the years to plant a tree each time I go to Israel. We have a "Night to Honor Israel" plot in an Israeli forest that we systematically add to each time we visit Israel. I'm glad to know that the invading armies will leave such a massive amount of firewood that "my" trees will survive the war!

The Nations Are Made to Understand Because of the Battle

Why does God allow the nations to make war upon Israel? There is only one answer: for the glory of God. Ezekiel makes it very clear that the world will know that God is God Almighty.

Ezekiel declares: "Thus I will magnify Myself and sanctify Myself, and I will be known in the eyes of many nations. Then they shall know that I am the LORD" (38:23).

The earth is full of so-called gods! Some claim Buddha, others Muhammad, some Satan, some gods of their own making, but who is the Almighty God? When the God of Abraham, Isaac, and Jacob finishes mopping up the enemies of Israel on the mountains of Israel (note that Jerusalem and the cities are saved), there will be no doubt that Jehovah God is the Almighty God.

"It will be in the latter days that I will bring you against My land, so that the nations may know Me, when I am hallowed in you, O Gog, before their eyes" (Ez. 38:16).

Truly the only way we can understand the significance of this incredible defeat is to accept it as an act of God, which is what Ezekiel said it is. It accomplishes the purpose of glorifying God before Israel and the world and, as we shall see, finally beginning the return of the much-chastened Israel to the God of Abraham, Isaac, and Jacob. Ezekiel wants the world to know that God supernaturally neutralizes the enemies of Israel and destroys them that His name might be glorified.

The Jewish People Begin to Turn

A second reason for this great display of God's power is to testify to His beloved Jewish people that He alone is their God. Through their miraculous deliverance the hearts of the Jewish people begin to soften again to the God of Abraham, Isaac, and Jacob:

> "So the house of Israel shall know that I am the LORD their God from that day forward. The Gentiles shall know that the house of Israel went into captivity for their iniquity; because they were unfaithful to Me, therefore I hid My face from them. I gave them into the hand of their enemies, and they all fell by the sword. According to their uncleanness and according to their transgressions I have dealt with them, and hidden My face from them.
>
> Therefore thus says the Lord GOD: Now I will bring back the captives of Jacob, and have mercy on the whole house of Israel; and I will be jealous for My holy name—after they have borne their shame, and all their unfaithfulness in which they were unfaithful to Me, when they dwelt safely in their own land and no one made them afraid. When I have brought them back from the peoples and gathered them out of their enemies' lands, and I am hallowed in them in the sight of many nations, then they shall know that I am the LORD their God, who sent them into captivity among the nations, but also brought them back to their land, and left none of them captive any longer. And I will not hide My face from them anymore; for I shall have poured out My Spirit on the house of Israel, says the Lord GOD." (Ez. 39:22–29)

Now please note very carefully that the Jewish people at this point have yet to accept Jesus as their Messiah. The Bible is very clear that this will happen at the end of the Tribulation, when the Jewish people who remain living "will look on Me whom they pierced. Yes, they will mourn for Him as one mourns for his only son, and grieve for Him as one grieves for a firstborn" (Zech. 12:10). That is the day, the Scripture declares, when "all Israel will be saved" (Rom. 11:26).

But because of this cataclysmic battle on the soil of the Holy Land, the nation of Israel will abandon its disastrous relationship with the Antichrist and begin turning toward the Most High God.

Now the question is, Where was the Antichrist? Didn't he guarantee the peace and safety of Israel? Yes he did . . .

CHAPTER NINE

Violence, Vengeance . . . Vindication

The events I am now about to describe will happen very quickly after the ultimately unsuccessful invasion of the Kings of the North and South. Some of these events will occur in a matter of days, others within a few months. But remember, from the time the Antichrist occupies Israel until his conclusive and cataclysmic defeat at the hands of the Messiah, only three-and-a-half years will elapse. It is during this period that the real forces driving the Antichrist become apparent. But before we document the Antichrist's short and steep slide into "the lake of fire burning with brimstone," don't lose track of his goals throughout the Tribulation:

- A one-world government

- A one-world religion

- A one-world economy

And pay very careful attention to his outcome. As the agent and incarnation of Satan on the earth, the Antichrist will accomplish in the Tribulation exactly what Satan has accomplished throughout history:

- He will lie

- He will rob

- He will kill
- He will destroy
- *He will fail*

And when any of us rejects God's authority in any area of our lives, the outcome is as certain as betting on yesterday's football game:

- We will be deceived
- We will be robbed
- We will be killed
- We will be destroyed
- We will not succeed

Today the media would have you believe that the worst thing that could happen to America would be for the so-called "ayatollahs of the Christian right" to set the moral agenda for this nation. Now about the only thing worse than having the "ayatollahs of the Christian right" set the moral agenda for our nation is *not* having them set the moral agenda. And while the exaltation of God in America has brought unparalleled blessings to our land, there is no greater example of what happens when Jehovah God is abandoned and then banished than the state of the world during the reign of the Antichrist— and there is no better time than right now to let the life-giving, devil-defeating, bondage-breaking presence of Jesus the Messiah reign in your heart, your family, and your community.

The Antichrist: Master of Politics

The Antichrist will sit out the Islamic-Russian war over Israel. Following in Satan's footsteps as "a liar and the father of lies," the Antichrist will break the covenant he has made with the nation of Israel first by failing to come to its aid, and then by taking the land of Israel and its temple for himself.

While the Antichrist's actions are contemptible, they are also very shrewd. Instead of coming to the aid of Israel and thus exposing his military to danger, the Antichrist instead will let the Kings of the North and the South expend their resources on their own campaign against Israel. Israel's defeat at the hands of other armies might make her easier for the Antichrist to occupy. On the other hand, should Israel put up a fight and damage either the King of the North or the King of the South, then these weakened rival kingdoms would be even more susceptible to subjugation by him. So goes the Antichrist's reasoning.

Of course the results of this strategy will exceed his wildest imagination. Not only are these invading nations weakened, but with casualty rates of 84 percent, their capacity to wage war or even defend themselves simply does not exist for the moment. And while the Antichrist may have had some reason to worry about his supply of Middle Eastern oil if the Russian-Islamic Coalition would have succeeded, the facts on the ground after the battle are that Africa and the entire Middle East will be his for the taking with hardly the effort it would have taken before their war with Israel. "Yes," the Antichrist thinks, "life *is* good! This is the right time for the other shoe to drop."

The Antichrist: Master of Religion

After the dramatic weakening of the Kings of the North and the South, the Antichrist decides the time is right to extend his influence and power by executing two of the most daring and reckless gambits ever attempted in human history. His first gambit is to abrogate his covenant with Israel.

The importance of Israel—really Jerusalem and its temple—makes sense only in the light of his second gambit: a lightning-swift coup d'état against the key power behind his rise to power—the planet-wide interlocking system of religion and commerce known (at least from God's perspective) as "BAB-YLON THE GREAT, THE MOTHER OF HARLOTS AND OF THE ABOMINATIONS OF THE EARTH" (Rev. 17:5). As you might imagine, being viewed by God as "Babylon" turns out not to be a good thing.

It is easy to develop the impression that the Antichrist rose to the center of the world's stage strictly by virtue of his military prowess. Now while his military prowess is indeed significant, never forget that he also grows in power by virtue of his ability to cunningly form alliances and just as cunningly break them when doing so is to his advantage.

The rise of the Antichrist is due in no small measure to the patronage he enjoys from this Babylonian system, described for us in Revelation chapters 17 and 18. Scholars disagree on the fine points of the exact meaning and timing of this passage, but there is much that is clear.

The system that John reveals as "Babylon the great" will be the dominant force in the world throughout the first half of the Tribulation. She will rule over the nations of the world as well as over the Antichrist and his European federation, which is signified in the book of Revelation by Babylon sitting on top of first the nations and then specifically the Antichrist and his federation (Rev. 17:1–3). Her influence over the world stems from her complete dominance of two major areas: religion and commerce.

As a religious system, it is *powerful*—dominating the earth (17:1); *perverted*—not only glorifying a false god, but sanctioning wicked living (17:2–4); *persecuting*—"I saw the woman, drunk with the blood of the saints and with the blood of the martyrs of Jesus" (17:6).

I believe that the way is already being paved for this world-wide religious system through the spread of New Age religious beliefs. By this I don't mean people who sleep under pyramids, pray to Gaia, wear custom crystals, hug trees, and listen to John Denver music. I mean the growing convergence of religion and morality around a few central beliefs:

- Every practice must be permitted, for we must not judge anyone.*

- Every belief must be respected, for we must not be bigoted toward anyone.*

- Every form of expression must be allowed, for we must not censor anyone.*

Now the asterisks above are significant because they highlight an important exception to each of these principles. In the Babylonian system, and to some extent even now, each of these statements will end with the words "anyone except Christians." It will be perfectly acceptable to judge Christians, to be prejudiced toward Christians, and to censor Christians. In fact, the world will commend these actions. Thus you can see even today that the stage is being set for people to come together based on their hatred of Christians—which is why during the Tribulation this whorish religion called Babylon will be able to kill Christians by the thousands and advance perversion, yet still be regarded as the quintessential guardian of faith and morality. In at least the first half of the Tribulation, political correctness will be god, and Babylon this religion's high priestess.

The commercial aspects of the Babylonian system are set forth in Revelation 18. Bible scholars disagree about whether Babylon will operate commercially before its subjugation by the Antichrist, or if her commerce will begin after the Antichrist takes her over, specifically when the False Prophet makes buying and selling possible only for those who have "the mark of the Beast."

In any event, this commercial system will be a source of vast wealth for the kings and merchants who choose to make a pact with Babylon:

"For all the nations have drunk of the wine of the wrath of her fornication, the kings of the earth have committed fornication with her, and the merchants of the earth have become rich through the abundance of her luxury." . . . "The kings of the earth who committed fornication and lived luxuriously with her will weep and lament for her, when they see the smoke of her burning" . . . "And the merchants of the earth will weep and mourn over her, for no one buys their merchandise anymore." (Rev. 18:3, 9, 11)

As a religious system, Babylon will dominate the spiritual life of the people on earth; as a commercial system, it will determine the prosperity of the merchants and governments on earth. Therefore, it is the most powerful force on earth— a direct obstacle to the Antichrist's schemes to be the central figure in the religion, economy, and government of the earth. Babylon must go—and it happens so swiftly that those watching are dumbfounded, both at the speed of its demise and the consequent obliteration of their source of riches (see Rev. 18:19).

At the level that the Antichrist is aware of, he accumulates the power he needs to eliminate the Babylonian system through a conspiracy with

"ten kings who have received no kingdom as yet, but they receive authority for one hour as kings with the beast. These are of one mind, and they will give their power and authority to the beast. . . . And the ten horns which you saw on the beast, these will hate the harlot, make her desolate and naked, eat her flesh and burn her with fire." (Rev. 17:12–13, 16)

But what the Antichrist does not realize is that God has sovereignly moved to give him the ability to overthrow the Babylonian system—and that soon it will be the Antichrist's turn to experience a judgment that is swift, total, and dreadful: "For God has put it into their hearts to fulfill His purpose, to be of one mind, and to give their kingdom to the beast, until the words of God are fulfilled" (Rev. 17:17).

Once the Antichrist has eliminated Babylon, he will move with alacrity to fill the void with his own system. His first step is to provide a replacement worldwide religion. This is when the temple in Jerusalem becomes important—and this is when his treaty with Israel is cast aside. "Then he shall confirm a covenant with many for one week; but in the middle of the week he shall bring an end to sacrifice and offering. And on the wing of abominations shall be one who makes desolate, even until the consummation, which is determined, is poured out on the desolate" (Dan. 9:27).

The Antichrist not only ignores his own treaty with Israel, he seizes Jerusalem's temple to serve as the focal point of the new religion that will bring the world together, the new trinity that the world will bow before, and the new commercial force that will have a stranglehold on the commerce and communication of the world. This religion is nothing less than the worship of Satan, who is pictured in Revelation as the dragon; worship of Satan's visible manifestation on earth, the Antichrist; and worship of the Antichrist's chief assistant on earth, the False Prophet (see 2 Thess. 2:3, 4). The temple's use for sacrifices and the observance of holy days will be immediately outlawed (see Dan. 7:25).

These two audacious gambits—the overthrow of Babylon along with the seizing of the temple in Jerusalem make the Antichrist the center of world attention. But he has reached too far.

The Antichrist: Master of Miscalculation

The Bible is clear: "Pride goes before destruction, and a haughty spirit before a fall" (Prov. 16:18). The greatest human example of this immutable fact will be the Antichrist. From the very beginning, Satan has overestimated his abilities and overreached his boundaries—and the Antichrist follows in the

Evil One's dubious footsteps. After the destruction of the Babylonian system and the seizing of the temple, the Antichrist no doubt will think that accomplishing his objectives will all be downhill from here—coasting to worldwide dominion. And he's right in a way. From here it *is* all downhill—straight to the pit.

By seizing the temple and destroying the Babylonian system, the Antichrist succeeds not in eliminating his enemies but in enraging them and increasing their number. The location of the temple is still the same—smack-dab on the third most holy spot in Islam. So now the Muslims will transfer their hatred and desire for revenge from the Jews to the Antichrist.

But most importantly, the Antichrist's actions will enrage the Jewish people, sparking white-hot fury in the very core of their being by the most appalling of insults to the true God and the temple set apart to the holiness of His name. They will be already disgusted by the Antichrist's failure to honor his treaty with them by coming to their aid when the Kings of the North and South invade. Israel's heart will be already beginning to soften toward the Most High God because of His miraculous intervention to defeat the Kings of the North and South. Now motivated by a combination of fury and zeal, they will turn to their history for guidance and resort to the same measures they took in the times of the Maccabees, but instead of merely waging guerrilla war, they will attempt to assassinate the Antichrist—and they will succeed.

His Descent to Hades

Lulled into a sense of complacency by both his arrogance and the ease of his victories, the Antichrist's security breaks down. An assassin will exploit the opportunity and strike a lethal blow to the head of the Antichrist, a wound so grievous that those attending to him might as well take him directly to the coroner, bypassing the hospital and the EMTs altogether—the Antichrist is dead (see Rev. 13:3). I believe that upon death he will descend directly into Hades or Sheol—the hellish holding tank where those who have rejected the Messiah wait for their ultimate and irreversible consignment to the eternal lake of fire. I believe this is at least part of the reason why the Antichrist is depicted in the book of Revelation as being he who ascends from the Abyss to prevaricate and plunder.

Satan's Offer

Just as Satan took Jesus up into a mountain, showing Him all the kingdoms of the world and offering them as a reward, I believe that Satan may take the Antichrist into the depths of the Abyss and offer him the kingdoms of the world. And while Jesus refused to bow down to Satan, the Antichrist will gladly bow to Satan and worship him. In return for this worship, Satan reanimates the Antichrist, infusing him to the very core of his being with wickedness, rage, and ruthlessness: "Now the beast which I saw was like a leopard, his feet were like the feet of a bear, and his mouth like the mouth of a lion. The dragon gave him his power, his throne, and great authority" (Rev. 13:2).

When the Antichrist ascends from Sheol, his mortal wound miraculously healed, he will fully unveil his worldwide religion. And from this foundation, he will then implement the worldwide system of commerce that becomes the leverage he uses to force the nations of the world to submit to his political control. But first he will capture the imagination and confidence of the world through his miraculous recovery:

> I saw a beast rising up out of the sea, having seven heads and ten horns, and on his horns ten crowns, and on his heads a blasphemous name. . . . The dragon gave him his power, his throne, and great authority. And I saw one of his heads as if it had been mortally wounded, and his deadly wound was healed. And all the world marveled and followed the beast. So they worshiped the dragon who gave authority to the beast; and they worshiped the beast, saying, "Who is like the beast? Who is able to make war with him?" (Rev. 13:1–4)

To the satanically blinded world of the Tribulation, the Antichrist's healing will look exactly like the death and resurrection of Jesus Christ—except in this instance they will see it happen with their own eyes on CNN.

The World's Awe

The Antichrist will capitalize on the world's amazement to point the world to worship not only him, but also the ultimate source of his power—Satan himself. "So they worshiped the dragon [Satan] who gave authority to the beast; and they worshiped the beast" (Rev. 13:4).

Satan is the source of the Antichrist's power, but the Antichrist will delegate this power to a nefarious man designated in Scripture as the "False Prophet." While the Antichrist "was given a mouth to utter proud words and blasphemies" (Rev. 17:5 NIV), the False Prophet will work tirelessly to either persuade or intimidate the world into submission to the Antichrist.

At first appearing as gentle and harmless as a lamb, the False Prophet's mission of persuasion, persecution, and propaganda will reveal his real nature to be the very same as Satan's and the Antichrist's (see Rev. 13:11). But while the Antichrist comes from "the sea," a designation for the Gentile nations, the False Prophet comes from the "the earth," a designation for Israel. Forcing some to worship the Antichrist, he also will convince many others, chiefly relying on the ability given him to perform "great signs, so that he even makes fire come down from heaven on the earth in the sight of men. And he deceives those who dwell on the earth by those signs which he was granted to do in the sight of the beast" (Rev. 13:13–14). Because of the miracles he performs and because he is Jewish, some may believe that the coming attempt to eliminate the Jewish people is in fact a divinely sanctioned fulfillment of Jewish teaching—so great will be the spirit of deception during the Tribulation.

Chief among the seemingly miraculous abilities given to the False Prophet is his construction in the temple of an image of the Beast:

> And he [the False Prophet] deceives those who dwell on the earth by those signs which he was granted to do in the sight of the beast, telling those who dwell on the earth to make an image to the beast who was wounded by the sword and lived. He was granted power to give breath to the image of the beast, that the image of the beast should both speak and cause as many as would not worship the image of the beast to be killed. (Rev. 13:14–15)

In other words, this statue—"Terminator 3," if you please—has the ability to discover those who will not worship the satanic trinity and destroy them. Actually, the Scriptures have already given a name to this statue: "the abomination which causes desolation."

Because of the supernatural life-and-death power of this image, it is only a short hop to accomplish another goal of the Antichrist's mission—control of the world's economy: "He [the False Prophet] causes all, both small and great, rich and poor, free and slave, to receive a mark on their right hand or on their foreheads, and that no one may buy or sell except one who has the mark or the name of the beast, or the number of his name" (Rev. 13:16–17). Some people will be persuaded by the False Prophet; some will be eliminated by the False Prophet; some will be intimidated by the False Prophet—but all with the exception of the elect will participate in the system (see Rev. 13:8).

As a result of his mortal wound and his miraculous recovery, the Antichrist, renowned before his assassination as a "man of peace," now becomes the veritable incarnation of Satan. He is the greatest monster the world has ever seen. You could say he's mad as hell at the Jewish people. And his hatred is shared by Satan himself.

Satan: Father of Miscalculation

At the midpoint of the Tribulation, the Antichrist makes his play to control the earth. Simultaneously, Satan makes his play to control heaven. But while the Antichrist appears to be successful at first, Satan's all-out war against the archangel Michael for control of heaven results not only in a stunning defeat, but in banishment from heaven as well:

> "And war broke out in heaven: Michael and his angels fought with the dragon [Satan]; and the dragon and his angels [demons] fought, but they did not prevail, nor was a place found for them in heaven any longer. So the great dragon was cast out, that serpent of old, called the Devil and Satan, who deceives the whole world; he was cast to the earth, and his angels were cast out with him." (Rev. 12:7–9)

Not powerful enough to prevail in heaven, Satan lashes out on the earth against everything God holds dear:

> "Therefore rejoice, O heavens, and you who dwell in them! Woe to the inhabitants of the earth and the sea! For the devil has come down to you, having great wrath, because he knows that he has a short time." Now when the dragon saw that he had been cast to the earth, he persecuted the woman [Israel] who gave birth to the male Child. . . . And the dragon was enraged with the woman, and he went to make war with the rest of her offspring, who keep the commandments of God and have the testimony of Jesus Christ. (Rev. 12:12–13, 17)

Vengeance Against Jews and Christians

With Satan and his angels cast down to earth to join forces with the Antichrist and the False Prophet, the powers of hell will be unfurled on the earth as never before in human history. The objects of their wrath will be the physical seed of Abraham (the Jewish people), and the spiritual seed of Abraham, "[those] who keep the commandments of God and have the testimony of Jesus Christ"—in other words, those who come to know Jesus as their Messiah during the Tribulation.

Satan will target Jews and Christians because attacking them is the only way he can retaliate against God. Unable to prevail against God militarily, Satan will seek revenge against Him by targeting the Jewish people, the apple of God's eye, for extermination. The Antichrist will be similarly motivated, seeking revenge against the Jews who attempted to snuff out his life. All of this will happen at about the same time that the image of the Antichrist is erected in the temple. God's warning to the seed of Abraham in that day is clear—and urgent.

> [Jesus said,] "Therefore when you see the 'abomination of desolation,' spoken of by Daniel the prophet, standing in the holy place" (whoever reads, let him understand), "then let those who are in Judea flee to the mountains. Let him who is on the housetop not go down to take anything out of his house. And let him who is in the field not go back to get his clothes. But woe to those who are pregnant and to those who are nursing babies in those days! And pray that your flight may not be in winter or on the Sabbath. For then there will be great tribulation, such as has not been since the beginning of the world until this time, no, nor ever shall be. And unless those days were shortened, no flesh would be saved; but for the elect's sake those days will be shortened." (Matt. 24:15–22)

God will prepare a special place of refuge for His people in the desert. Those who follow the words of Jesus and flee to the desert will be taken care of by God throughout the last half of the Tribulation (see Rev. 12:6).

The desert area of divine protection is identified as Edom, Moab, and Ammon—modern-day Jordan (see Dan. 11:41). Undoubtedly Jordan presently enjoys a more cordial relationship with Israel than any other Arab nation. Interestingly, although the south of Jordan (Edom) will be part of the first Islamic-Russian invasion of the Holy Land, all of Jordan will be spared from the epic battles of the last half of the Tribulation that lead up to the Battle of Armageddon.

Some Christians and Jews who are unable to flee to the Jordanian wilderness will be sheltered from the genocide by caring individuals (see Matt. 25:31–46). Others will be captured and put to death, and these saints will receive a special blessing from God for their courageous devotion to Him in the midst of horrific persecution and torture (see Rev. 14:13).

This time of persecution will last three-and-a-half years, for Daniel 7:21–22, 25 reveals what will happen to the "saints," or the children of Israel during that time:

> As I watched, this horn [the Antichrist] was waging war against the saints [the Jews] and defeating them, until the Ancient of Days came and pronounced judgment in favor of the saints of the Most High, and the time came when they possessed the kingdom [the end of the tribulation period]. . . . He [the Antichrist] will speak against the Most High and oppress his saints and try to change the set times and the laws. The saints will be handed over to him for a time, times, and half a time [the last three and a half years of the Tribulation]. (NIV)

Vindication: The Battle of Armageddon

Just as God removed Satan from the hallowed halls of heaven, He now will begin to dislodge him and his influence from the earth. We often think of the Battle of Armageddon as a short battle that occurs at the end of the Tribulation, but this is only part of the picture. Actually the Battle of Armageddon is a desperate three-and-a-half year campaign by the Antichrist to fend off challenge after challenge to his world rule, culminating in the battle on the plains of Armageddon—the greatest battle ever fought, the most decisive victory ever achieved, and the greatest defeat ever suffered.

There are many reasons why the reign of the satanic trinity will be contentious and short-lived, not the least of which is the curse of God upon their efforts. It is important to realize that the satanic trinity will not dominate the world because of its *power* but instead because of God's *permission*. The Tribulation will last exactly as long as God ordained it to. Satan, the Antichrist, and the False Prophet will stir up exactly as much trouble as God allows them to, and they will experience exactly as much difficulty and frustration as God intends.

Yet there are also three possible reasons from a human point of view why so many are opposed to the rule of the Dragon, the Beast, and the False Prophet. One explanation is the continuing concern of the Muslim world over the desecration of Mount Moriah (the former location of the Dome of the Rock). Another would be that the Antichrist is simply too powerful and too untrustworthy to be allowed to continue to grow in power without a fight. But the explanation that makes the most sense to me is that the nations of the world simply do not want the Antichrist to control Middle Eastern oil, and they will do whatever they can to pry his hands off of it. Now these three reasons could all be true, but I believe the last reason will be the most significant one. So it is in this context that the campaign leading to Armageddon will be set in motion.

The Battle Joined

At the time of the end the king of the South shall attack him [the Antichrist]; and the king of the North shall come against him like a whirlwind, with chariots, horsemen, and with many ships; and he [Antichrist] shall enter the countries, overwhelm them, and pass through. He shall also enter the Glorious Land, and many countries shall be overthrown; but these shall escape from his hand: Edom, Moab, and the prominent people of Ammon. He shall stretch out his hand against the countries, and the land of Egypt shall not escape. He shall have power over the treasures of gold and silver, and over all the precious things of Egypt; also the Libyans and Ethiopians shall follow at his heels. But news from the east and the north shall trouble him; therefore he shall go out with great fury to destroy and annihilate many. And he shall plant the tents of his palace between the seas and the glorious holy mountain [Jerusalem]; yet he shall come to his end, and no one will help him. (Dan. 11:40–45)

This is not the first time we have seen the Kings of the North and the South. This time, as before, they represent a resurgent Russian Empire conspiring with a Pan-Islamic Confederation to cleanse Jerusalem and seize control of the oil of the Middle East. Though savaged in battle when they attack Israel, these kings will draw on their vast resources of men and materiel to field a viable fighting force once again—but this time they will have even more help, for fighting beside them this time will be the kings of the East. And this new enemy will disturb the Antichrist very much.

The advancing army of the kings of the East is 200 million strong, marching right through the supernaturally dried bed of the Euphrates River to the very center of the Antichrist's empire. Given these facts, describing the Antichrist as "troubled" is probably a bit of an understatement. Nevertheless, the Antichrist will still take solace in the fact that he has defeated the Kings of the North and South before, and while they may have an extra ally in the form of a confederation of the kings of the East, the Antichrist has three additional allies of his own now as well—Satan; the False Prophet, with his ability to call down fire from heaven; and the image of the Beast, which has the power to destroy those who refuse to obey the Antichrist. So if it's a fight these kings want, it's a fight they'll get.

Why will the "kings from the East," move toward Israel? There are a number of possibilities. First, don't forget how strong Islam is in the East. While the Kings of the North and the South seem to come from Africa, the Middle East, and

Russia, there are many millions of Muslims zealous for their faith living in Afghanistan, Pakistan, India, Malaysia, and Indonesia. Though not part of the first fight to reclaim the holy site of Mount Moriah, they will be no less outraged by its desecration. And perhaps this time Islam will bring all that it has at its disposal to dislodge the blasphemy of the Antichrist from Jerusalem, destroy the third temple, and reconstruct the Dome of the Rock.

Of course the 200 million men could come from the thoroughly secularized and massively populated nation of China, who could also have its own designs on Middle Eastern oil. Japan, secularized, prosperous, and completely dependent on oil imports for the functioning of its economy could certainly play a leadership role in this coming confederation of kings. In any case, I believe that the quest to control Middle Eastern oil is the most likely scenario to drive the kings of the East to the Holy Land. But to control the oil of the Middle East, they must first depose the Antichrist—which means marching on his headquarters in Jerusalem. The Bible itself does not tell us why the "kings of the East" move to confront the Antichrist, only that they will do so.

After hearing the news about the advancing eastern army, the Antichrist will advance from the territory of the twice-defeated King of the South to Armageddon—a natural battlefield—to face the onslaught from the North and East.

Yet as the armies of the world converge upon Armageddon on a massive collision course, suddenly their objective will change. Instead of contending with each other, they will unite to fight the armies of the Messiah that descend from heaven to the storied fields of Armageddon.

The Victory Won

I do not know what will turn these enemy armies into allies united in their commitment to resist the return of the Messiah. Perhaps the Antichrist will remind these armies of what happened to the Kings of the North and the South when they intervened in Israel before. Perhaps the False Prophet will have prophesied this event, predicting a far different outcome than will actually be the case. Whatever the reason, the would-be enemies will be united in their resistance to the Messiah, and united in the destruction they will soon experience.

Armies Defeated. The Second Coming of Jesus Christ to the fields of Armageddon is at once a towering event of human history and the most staggering defeat that any army has ever endured. No one can improve on John's majestic description of this event in Revelation 19:

I saw heaven standing open and there before me was a white horse, whose rider is called Faithful and True. With justice he judges and makes war. His eyes are like blazing fire, and on his head are many crowns. He has a name written on him that no one but he himself knows. He is dressed in a robe dipped in blood, and his name is the Word of God. The armies of heaven were following him, riding on white horses and dressed in fine linen, white and clean. Out of his mouth comes a sharp sword with which to strike down the nations. "He will rule them with an iron scepter." He treads the winepress of the fury of the wrath of God Almighty. On his robe and on his thigh he has this name written: KING OF KINGS AND LORD OF LORDS.

And I saw an angel standing in the sun, who cried in a loud voice to all the birds flying in midair, "Come, gather together for the great supper of God, so that you may eat the flesh of kings, generals, and mighty men, of horses and their riders, and the flesh of all people, free and slave, small and great."

Then I saw the beast [the Antichrist] and the kings of the earth and their armies gathered together to make war against the rider on the horse and his army [Jesus, his angels, and the saints raptured to heaven at the very beginning of the Tribulation.]. But the beast was captured, and with him the false prophet who had performed the miraculous signs on his behalf. With these signs he had deluded those who had received the mark of the beast and worshiped his image. The two of them were thrown alive into the fiery lake of burning sulfur. The rest of them were killed with the sword that came out of the mouth of the rider on the horse, and all the birds gorged themselves on their flesh. (vv. 11–21 NIV)

John writes that Christ had a name "written on him that no one but he himself knows." As a Jew, John remembers that God appeared to Abraham, Isaac, and Jacob by the name of God Almighty, *El Shaddai*. But He did not reveal Himself to them by the name of Jehovah *(Yahweh)* (see Exodus 6:3). The patriarchs knew God as the Almighty One, but they had no concept of Him as an intimate friend and master—the One who delights to walk with His children "in the cool of the day." But Christ's robe, dipped in His spotless blood shed on the cross, is His prayer shawl, and upon this shawl is written KING OF KINGS AND LORD OF LORDS.

John wrote that Christ's name was written on His thigh. You may be wondering how anything could be written on a man's thigh and be visible to passersby. As the corners of His prayer shawl rest on his thighs, the name of Jehovah God will be spelled out on each of the shawl's four corners with the unique coils and knots of the *tzitzit,* which is Hebrew for "fringes." Thus on his robe and on his prayer shawl He wears the name "Lord."

The prophet Zechariah adds to the description of this longed-for day, when those martyred for their testimony are vindicated as God lays waste His foes:

A day of the LORD is coming . . . I will gather all the nations to Jerusalem to fight against it; the city will be captured, the houses ransacked, and the women raped. Half of the city will go into exile, but the rest of the people will not be taken from the city.

Then the LORD will go out and fight against those nations, as he fights in the day of battle. On that day his feet will stand on the Mount of Olives, east of Jerusalem, and the Mount of Olives will be split in two from east to west, forming a great valley, with half of the mountain moving north and half moving south. You will flee by my mountain valley, for it will extend to Azel. . . . Then the LORD my God will come, and all the holy ones with him.

On that day there will be no light, no cold or frost. It will be a unique day, without daytime or nighttime—a day known to the Lord. When evening comes, there will be light.

On that day living water will flow out from Jerusalem, half to the eastern sea [the Dead Sea] and half to the western sea [the Mediterranean], in summer and in winter.

The LORD will be king over the whole earth. On that day there will be one LORD, and his name the only name.

The whole land, from Geba to Rimmon, south of Jerusalem, will become like the Arabah [wilderness, or desert]. But Jerusalem will be raised up and remain in its place, from the Benjamin Gate to the site of the First Gate, to the Corner Gate, and from the Tower of Hananel to the royal winepresses. It will be inhabited; never again will it be destroyed. Jerusalem will be secure.

This is the plague with which the LORD will strike all the nations that fought against Jerusalem: Their flesh will rot while they are still standing on their feet, their eyes will rot in their sockets, and their tongues will rot in their mouths. (14:1–12 NIV)

The battle over Jerusalem is part of the battle of Armageddon, a confrontation so encompassing that soldiers will cover the land like locusts, from the plains of Megiddo north of Palestine, through the valley of Jehoshaphat near Jerusalem, and on down to the land of Edom to the south and east of Jerusalem.

Revelation 14:20 declares that the blood from this battle will rise "up to the horses' bridles" for a distance of 1600 furlongs, approximately two hundred miles. And if you measure from the northern part of Palestine to the southern boundaries described in this prophecy, you'll discover that the distance is approximately two hundred miles.[1]

Armageddon, the world's most natural battlefield, will be bathed in blood. The Bible has predicted it, down to the length of the battlefield. Mark my words, this battle of unsurpassed carnage is not a fable, it is a fact—and every tick of the clock brings us closer to it.

The crowning event of this battle occurs when the Antichrist, who believes he can defeat God Almighty, will gather his forces to face a heavenly army led by the Messiah Himself. He will be done with shaking his fist in the face of God; his boastful, deceitful tongue will be silenced forever. The Scripture tells us, "But the beast was captured, and with him the false prophet who had performed the miraculous signs on his behalf. With these signs he had deluded those who had received the mark of the beast and worshiped his image. The two of them were thrown alive into the fiery lake of burning sulfur" (Rev. 19:20 NIV). The victory is the Lord's!

Israel Protected. Not only will the armies of the world be defeated, but the Jewish people—the object of God's loyal covenant love—will be protected.

One of the most commonly ignored biblical truths is this: what a nation or an individual does to the nation of Israel is what God repays to them. God couldn't have been more clear: "I will bless those who bless you, and I will curse him who curses you" (Gen. 12:3).

The Antichrist will track down, torment, and attempt to annihilate Israel; in return, God will track down, torment, and annihilate him from the face of the earth. The true Messiah will come, bringing the armies of heaven with him, and the Antichrist and his forces will be demolished.

If you doubt this principle from the Word of God, consider this: Once I was standing at Checkpoint Charlie at the divide separating West and East Berlin. I had been invited to Germany to speak to the United States military and was taking a few hours to look around. Our West German guide asked me,

"Pastor Hagee, why do you think God permitted the communists to build a wall around us?"

The answer came to me instantly because the day before I had visited Dachau. "Because your parents built a wall around the Jews in Dachau and Auschwitz," I answered. "Just look at this wall. It's twelve feet high, just like the one at Dachau. It's electrified at the bottom, just like the one at Dachau. It has machine gun towers down the middle, just like the one at Dachau. It has killer dogs roaming in between the inner and outer walls, just like the one at Dachau. Everything your parents did to the Jewish people, son, the communists are doing to you."

You'll find this principle illustrated from the Scriptures in the story of the Passover: Pharaoh instructed the midwives of Egypt to kill male Jewish children. When Israel left Egypt, God killed the firstborn child in every Egyptian family (see Exodus 1:15–16; 4:22; and 11:5).

The Reconciliation Complete

Ah, my friend, I want you to know that I expect Him to appear twice in the days ahead: the first time only for an instant to protect the Church, His Bride, from the wrath of the Tribulation by removing her from the earth before it begins. But He will also appear on earth a second time as well. Jesus Christ will step down from heaven and place his foot on the Mount of Olives. He will win the battle for Jerusalem and Israel. In the aftermath of this battle, His people will finally understand who He really is and what He has come to offer them. The hearts of the Jewish people—warmed toward God because of His intervention to defeat the Russian-Islamic coalition, will now turn fully to their true God: "And I will pour on the house of David and on the inhabitants of Jerusalem the Spirit of grace and supplication; then they will look on Me whom they pierced. Yes, they will mourn for Him as one mourns for his only son, and grieve for Him as one grieves for a firstborn" (Zech. 12:10). And in that moment, the blindness of the Jewish people toward their Messiah will be taken away and they will be saved:

> For I do not desire, brethren, that you should be ignorant of this mystery, lest you should be wise in your own opinion, that blindness in part has happened to Israel until the fullness of the Gentiles has come in. And so all Israel will be saved, as it is written: "The Deliverer will come out of Zion, and He will turn away ungodliness from Jacob; for this is My covenant with them, when I take away their sins." Concerning the gospel they are enemies for your sake, but concerning the election they are beloved for the sake of the fathers. For the gifts and the calling of God are irrevocable. For as you were once disobedient to God, yet have now obtained mercy through their disobedience, even so these also have now been disobedient, that through the mercy shown you they also may obtain mercy. For God has committed them all to disobedience, that He might have mercy on all. Oh, the depth of the riches both of the wisdom and knowledge of God! How unsearchable are His judgments and His ways past finding out! "For who has known the mind of the LORD? Or who has become His counselor?" "Or who has first given to Him and it shall be repaid to him?" For of Him and through Him and to Him are all things, to whom be glory forever. Amen. (Rom. 11:25–36)

Jerusalem's Rebirth

Of whom was Zechariah speaking when he wrote,

> "'Sing and rejoice, O daughter of Zion! For behold, I am coming and I will dwell in your midst,' says the LORD. 'Many nations shall be joined to the LORD in that day, and they shall become My people. And I will dwell in your midst. Then you will know that the LORD of hosts has sent Me to you. And the LORD will take possession of Judah as His inheritance in the Holy Land, and will again choose Jerusalem'" (2:10–12)

The apostle Paul wrote "here we do not have an enduring city, but we are looking for the city that is to come" (Heb.

13:14 NIV). Jerusalem has existed for at least three thousand years; she is holy to Jews, Christians, and Muslims. Throughout history, she has been targeted for conquest many times, and by many nations: Babylon in 586 B.C., Rome in 63 B.C., the Muslims in A.D. 637, the Crusaders in A.D. 1099, and the Muslims again in A.D. 1187. During the Arab-Israeli Wars (pre-1967), the city was divided; the Old City was retained by Jordan and the New City became the capital of Israel. But in the 1967 Six-Day War, Israel captured the Old City and formally annexed it as her own.

But what does Jerusalem's future hold? The Bible has much to say about David's City of God: "On that day living water will flow out from Jerusalem, half to the eastern sea [the Dead Sea] and half to the western sea [the Mediterranean], in summer and in winter" (Zech. 14:8 NIV). The lifeless Dead Sea will live for the first time since Creation, connecting through Jerusalem to the Mediterranean.

"The LORD will be king over the whole earth. On that day there will be one LORD, and his name the only name" (Zech. 14:9 NIV). Jerusalem will be the capital city from which Jesus Christ will reign over the entire earth.

"The whole land, from Geba to Rimmon, south of Jerusalem, will become like the Arabah. But Jerusalem will be raised up and remain in its place, from the Benjamin Gate to the site of the First Gate, to the Corner Gate, and from the Tower of Hananel to the royal winepresses. It will be inhabited; never again will it be destroyed. Jerusalem will be secure" (Zech. 14:10, 11 NIV). The environs around Jerusalem will be transformed into a broad, low valley, like the Arabah. This will both make Jerusalem stand out and make the surrounding areas more fertile.[2]

The New Jerusalem

The true Messiah, Jesus Christ, upon His return from Heaven and victory over the satanic trinity, will rule from Jerusalem in the Millennium—the thousand-year reign of God upon the earth. For the first time in centuries, Jerusalem will not fear her enemies. And after the Millennium, when Satan and his followers have been eternally banished to the lake of fire, God will destroy this present world. He will then present us with a new heaven and a new earth, to which a New Jerusalem will descend.

> Then I saw a new heaven and a new earth, for the first heaven and the first earth had passed away, and there was no longer any sea. I saw the Holy City, the new Jerusalem, coming down out of heaven from God, prepared as a bride beautifully dressed for her husband. And I heard a loud voice saying, "Now the dwelling of God is with men, and he will live with them. They will be his people, and God himself will be with them and be their God. He will wipe every tear from their eyes. There will be no more death or mourning or crying or pain, for the old order of things has passed away." . . .
>
> One of the seven angels who had the seven bowls full of the seven last plagues came and said to me, "Come, I will show you the bride, the wife of the Lamb." And he carried me away in the Spirit to a mountain great and high, and showed me the Holy City, Jerusalem, coming down out of heaven from God. It shone with the glory of God, and its brilliance was like that of a very precious jewel, like a jasper, clear as crystal. It had a great, high wall with twelve gates, and with twelve angels at the gates. On the gates were written the names of the twelve tribes of Israel. There were three gates on the east, three on the north, three on the south and three on the west. The wall of the city had twelve foundations, and on them were the names of the twelve apostles of the Lamb.
>
> The angel who talked with me had a measuring rod of gold to measure the city, its gates and its wall. The city was laid out like a square, as long as it was wide. He measured the city with the rod and found it to be 12,000 stadia [about 1400 miles] in length, and as wide and high as it is long. He measured its wall and it was 144 cubits [about 200 feet] thick, by man's measurement, which the angel was using. The wall was made of jasper, and the city of pure gold, as pure as glass. The foundations of

the city walls were decorated with every kind of precious stone. The first foundation was jasper, the second sapphire, the third chalcedony, the fourth emerald, the fifth sardonyx, the sixth carnelian, the seventh chrysolite, the eighth beryl, the ninth topaz, the tenth chrysoprase, the eleventh jacinth, and the twelfth amethyst. The twelve gates were twelve pearls, each gate made of a single pearl. The street of the city was of pure gold, like transparent glass.

I did not see a temple in the city, because the Lord God Almighty and the Lamb are its temple. The city does not need the sun or the moon to shine on it, for the glory of God gives it light, and the Lamb is its lamp. The nations will walk by its light, and the kings of the earth will bring their splendor into it. On no day will its gates ever be shut, for there will be no night there. The glory and honor of the nations will be brought into it. Nothing impure will ever enter it, nor will anyone who does what is shameful or deceitful, but only those whose names are written in the Lamb's book of life.

The angel showed me the river of the water of life, as clear as crystal, flowing from the throne of God and of the Lamb down the middle of the great street of the city. On each side of the river stood the tree of life, bearing twelve crops of fruit, yielding its fruit every month. And the leaves of the tree are for the healing of the nations. No longer will there be any curse. The throne of God and of the Lamb will be in the city, and his servants will serve him. They will see his face, and his name will be on their foreheads. There will be no more night. They will not need the light of a lamp or the light of the sun, for the Lord God will give them light. And they will reign for ever and ever. (Rev. 21:1–4, 9–26; 22:1–5 NIV)

What a glorious picture! Jerusalem, which has endured so much suffering, will be magnificently redeemed! The Bible tells us that by faith Abraham looked forward to the New Jerusalem of eternity, "the city which has foundations, whose builder and maker is God" (Heb. 11:10). Many of the Old Testament saints longed for the New Jerusalem, "therefore God is not ashamed to be called their God, for he has prepared a city for them" (Heb. 11:16).

Soon and Very Soon

As I write this, my heart is warmed by the realization that Jerusalem, the united capital of the Jewish homeland, is celebrating her three thousandth anniversary in 1996. I'm planning to visit that beloved city during her celebration, but as I walk down those cobbled roads I know my thoughts will turn from the sights before me to things that happened centuries ago—and things sure to take place in the not-too-distant future.

When I stand outside Jerusalem, I will remember what Jesus said when the Pharisees tried to keep Him away from the city, warning Him darkly of plots to assassinate Him: "Jesus told them, . . . I will drive out demons and heal people today and tomorrow, and on the third day I will reach my goal" (Luke 13:32 NIV). That is a prophetic statement as well as a historic one. The psalmist wrote that a thousand years in God's sight are like a day that has just gone by, as a mere watch in the night (see Ps. 90:4).

A thousand years is as a day. Today and tomorrow—two days. Two thousand years. The power of the Gospel has covered the earth, and on the third day the Messiah will be glorified in his thousand-year reign on earth, the Millennium. We are coming to the end of the second day. And the third day is forming just below the horizon; it will dawn with the appearing of Messiah, *Mashiach,* the Anointed One who will be sent by God to inaugurate the final redemption at the end of days.

What then shall we do?

As the Apostle Peter wrote: "And so we have the prophetic word confirmed, which you do well to heed as a light that shines in a dark place, until the day dawns and the morning star rises in your hearts; knowing this first, that no prophecy of Scripture is of any private interpretation, for prophecy never came by the will of man, but holy men of God spoke as they were moved by the Holy Spirit" (2 Pet. 1:19–21).

Peter testified in this passage that the accounts of the life, miracles, ministry, death, and resurrection of Jesus Christ are not the product of cunning fables. Peter and the other disciples saw Jesus. They touched him, ate with him, talked to him— they even saw him ascend into heaven. They were *eyewitnesses* of his majesty. And so Peter says "we have the prophetic word *confirmed*." Peter himself, a Jewish man well-acquainted with the writings of the prophets, saw how the Lord Jesus fulfilled the prophecies of the Old Testament. And he was convinced that just as Jesus fulfilled the prophecies concerning His first coming, so too would Jesus fulfill the prophecies of the times yet to come.

My friends, if you remember nothing else about this book, please grasp with your head and your heart this overpowering truth from the Word of God—we are the terminal generation. We are the ones who need to prepare today for our ever after. Like no other generation, we are the ones who cannot take for granted tomorrow. We must not put off until tomorrow spiritual decisions and spiritual actions which can be done today.

If you are a believer in Jesus the Messiah, lift up your head and rejoice, for your redemption is drawing near. Too many Christians are living as if they're going to be here forever. To them the words of Jesus shine like a warning beacon: "And this gospel of the kingdom will be preached in all the world as a witness to all the nations, and then the end will come" (Matt. 24:14).

If you have yet to trust Jesus Christ as Messiah, the signs of the times should compel you to recognize that the hand of God is moving in the city of Jerusalem and in the nation of Israel. Messiah is soon to come. If you listen closely, you can hear the footsteps of Messiah walking through the clouds of heaven. You can hear the thundering hoofbeats of the four horsemen of the Apocalypse as even now they pick up speed, racing to their rendezvous with destiny on the fields of Armageddon.

If this book outlives my time on earth, and I honestly believe it will, let me assure you that it is not too late to recognize Jesus Christ as the Son of God, the promised Messiah. He is truly King of Kings and Lord of Lords; and He wants to bring you life abundant on earth and life eternal in the world to come. He extends to you the opportunity to escape the coming time of trial.

Like the two-faced Janus of old, Israel will soon see the advent of two Messiahs: one false, one true.

Which one will you choose?

Notes

Chapter 1

1. Reuters NewMedia, "Arab Leaders Flock to Rabin Funeral," 6 November 1995.

2. Reuters NewMedia, "Israel Lays Rabin to Rest," 6 November 1995.

3. Ibid.

4. Michael Chute, "Jim Henry Attends Rabin Funeral; Says World 'Galvanized' for Peace," Baptist Press. [no date given]

5. Rabbi Eliezer Waldman, Rosh Yeshiva, Yeshivat Kiryat Arba, "Analysis of a Tragedy: From the Pain Must Come Renewed Dedication Toward Rebuilding Jewish Life with Unconditional Love for our Fellow Jew," November 1995. Also, a survey conducted by Gallup Israel during May 22–28 on behalf of the Israel/Palestine Center for Research and Information revealed the following on Israeli attitudes toward Jerusalem:

- Less than ⅔ (65%) of the Israeli Jewish adult public voiced full support for exclusive Israeli sovereignty over all of Jerusalem.
- Only 8% of the Israeli Jewish adult public believe that the Palestinians will accept the solution of exclusive Israeli sovereignty over all of Jerusalem.
- 28% of the Israeli Jewish adult public is ready to accept the solution of divided sovereignty whereby Israel will have sovereignty over all of West Jerusalem and the Jewish neighborhoods in East Jerusalem, while the Palestinians will have sovereignty over the Arab parts of East Jerusalem.

- 25% of the Israeli Jewish adult public believe that the Palestinians will accept the option of Israeli sovereignty over all of West Jerusalem and the Jewish neighborhoods in East Jerusalem, while the Palestinians will have sovereignty over the Arab parts of East Jerusalem.
- 56% of the Israeli Jewish adult public believe that the Palestinians will only settle for exclusive Palestinian sovereignty over East Jerusalem on the basis of the June 4, 1967 lines.
- 3% of the Israeli Jewish adult public support joint Israeli-Palestinian undivided sovereignty over all of Jerusalem.
- 3% of the Israeli Jewish adult public support the internationalization of the city under the United Nations.

6. Tom Hundley and Storer H. Rowley, "Israelis Again Rally for Peace," *Chicago Tribune,* 13 November 1995.

7. Reuters NewMedia, "Stunned Israel to Continue Rabin's Peace Policy," 5 November 1995.

8. Reuters NewMedia, "Jordan's King Invokes Martyrdom," 6 November 1995.

9. Reuters NewMedia, "Clinton Urges Israelis to Follow Rabin Path," 6 November 1995.

10. Serge Schmemann, *New York Times* News Service, 18 December 1995. It is nevertheless important to recognize that as of December 1995, most Israelis are not in favor of surrendering the Golan Heights—regardless of how much the current Israeli government is willing to deal. Here's what the polls reveal:

Do you believe that the President of Syria wants to reach a true peace with Israel?

Yes 46%

No 48%

No reply 6%

Are you for or against full withdrawal from the Golan in return for full peace with Syria and appropriate security arrangements?

For 42%

Against 55%

No reply 3%

The Dahaf Institute survey was carried out for "Yediot Ahronot" on Tuesday and Wednesday 12–13 December and covered 503 who are a representative sample of the adult population in the country. The standard error is + / − 4 percent. (Published in "Yediot Ahronot" on December 15, 1995.)

Are you for or against withdrawal from the Golan Heights in return for a full peace agreement with Syria, on the terms of the agreements which were signed with Egypt and Jordan?

For 35%

Against 46%

Don't know 12%

Refuse to reply 7%

The "Mutagim" survey was carried out for "Maariv" on Wednesday, December 13, and covered a sample of 536 interviewees from the adult Jewish population in the country. The standard error is + / − 4.5 percent. (Published in "Maariv" December 15, 1995.)

11. Ibid.

12. Reuters NewMedia, "Israeli Student Confesses to Killing Rabin," 6 November 1995.

Chapter 2

1. Noam M. M. Neusner, "Saving Faith," *The Tampa Tribune,* 10 December 1995.

2. Storer H. Rowley, "Probe Divides Israel's Self-Image," *Chicago Tribune,* 28 November 1995.

3. Ibid.

4. Quoted in Rowley, "Israel's Self-Image."

5. Tom Hundley, "Beyond Rabin: Life in Israel Has Been Changing for Years," *Chicago Tribune,* 12 November 1995.

6. Neusner, "Saving Faith."

7. Hundley, "Beyond Rabin."

8. Jerry Adler and Jeffrey Bartholet, "Souls at War," *Newsweek,* 20 November 1995, 59.

9. Quoted in Adler and Bartholet, "Souls at War," 59.

10. Union of Rabbis for Eretz Yisrael, "Leading Rabbis from Israel and the Diaspora Held a Conference at the Ramada Renaissance Hotel, Jerusalem, on the 27th Day of Heshvan 5754," *Jerusalem One,* 11 November 1993.

11. Steven Emerson, "A Look Inside the Radical Islamist Network," *The New Republic,* 12 June 1995.

12. Quoted in Emerson, "The Radical Islamist Network."

13. Ibid.

14. Ibid.

15. Ibid.

16. Ibrahim Sarbal, leader of the Islamic Jihad Movement in Palestine—al Aqsa Brigades. Quote is provided by the Anti-Defamation League of B'nai B'rith.

17. Quote is provided by the Anti-Defamation League of B'nai B'rith.

18. Amos Oz, "Israelis Will Not Stand for Fanaticism," *Newsweek,* 20 November 1995.

19. Esquiu, Buenos Aires, 21 March 1971.

20. Speech given in Teheran, Associated Press, 19 February 1979.

21. Michael Horowitz, "New Intolerance Between Crescent and Cross," *Wall Street Journal,* 5 July 1995.

22. Ibid.

23. Marty Croll, "Israel Asks: Where Is Peace?" *Baptist Press.*

24. "Israelis Appeal for Unity," *The Tampa Tribune,* 11 December 1995.

25. Ibid.

Chapter 3

1. J. Dwight Pentecost, *Things to Come* (Grand Rapids, MI: Zondervan, 1958), 320.

2. William Kelly, *Notes on Daniel* (New York: Loizeaux Brothers), 50.

3. Charles H. Dyer and Angela Elwell Hunt, *The Rise of Babylon* (Wheaton, IL: Tyndale, 1991), 116.

4. Ibid., 107.

Chapter 4

1. Frank S. Mead, ed., *The Encyclopedia of Religious Quotations* (Old Tappan, NJ: Revell, 1965), 34.

2. Hank Hanegraaff, "Fulfilled Prophecy As an Apologetic," *Christian Research Journal* (Fall 1989):7.

3. Ibid.

4. Ibid.

5. Ibid.

6. Floyd Hamilton, *The Basis of Christian Faith* (New York: Harper and Row, 1964), 160.

7. John F. Walvoord and Roy B. Zuck, eds., *The Bible Knowledge Commentary, New Testament Edition* (Wheaton, IL: Victor Books, 1983), 21.

8. John F. Walvoord and Roy B. Zuck, eds., *The Bible Knowledge Commentary, Old Testament Edition* (Wheaton, IL: Victor Books, 1985), 873.

9. Footnote for Isaiah 9:1, *The NIV Study Bible, 10th Anniversary Edition* (Grand Rapids, MI: Zondervan, 1995), 1023.

Chapter 5

1. "Doomsday Clock Reset," *Tampa Tribune,* 9 December 1995.

2. Richard Preston, *The Hot Zone* (New York: Random House, 1994), 20.

3. Ibid., 46.

4. Dr. Aaron Lerner, Associate, Independent Media Review and Analysis, "Golan Facts and Myths."

5. Ibid.

6. John Wesley White, *Thinking the Unthinkable* (Orlando: Creation House, 1992), 35.

7. Ibid.

8. Alan Unterman, *Dictionary of Jewish Lore and Legend* (New York: Thames and Hudson, 1991), 72.

9. "Experts Warn of Threat Posed by Reinvigorated Diseases," *AIDS Weekly Plus,* 7 August 1995, 13–14.

10. "Living Longer with AIDS: The True Cost," *AIDS Weekly Plus,* 31 July 1995, 31.

11. Gordon Lindsay, *Forty Signs of the Soon Coming of Christ* (Dallas: Christ for the Nations, 1969), 20.

12. U.S. Geological Survey National Earthquake Information Center, "Frequency of Occurrence of Earthquakes." They note, "As more and more seismographs are installed in the world, more earthquakes can be and have been located. However, the number of large earthquakes (magnitude 6.0 or greater) have stayed relatively constant. Note, in fact, that the last decade has produced substantially fewer large earthquakes than show in the long-term averages." Nevertheless,

it is true that the Bible predicts that earthquakes *will* increase in the last days, and the number of earthquakes measured has increased 1.58 times between 1983 and 1992.

Chapter 6

1. Population statistics from *The 1995 CIA World Fact Book*.

Chapter 7

1. To be sure, as the people of formerly communist countries face the hardships involved in modernizing their economy, they long for aspects of their former life. And so communists (usually reborn as free-market capitalists) are sometimes elected to political office. Memory is like that: the people remember the days when they could afford food and rent—and they forget that while the necessities were affordable, they couldn't buy anything because the shelves of their stores were bare and that they waited for years and years before an apartment became available for rent.

2. Quoted in Henry H. Halley, *Halley's Bible Handbook* (Grand Rapids, MI: Zondervan, 1962), 18.

3. Douglas MacArthur, Address to a Joint Meeting of Congress, 19 April 1951.

4. "What Rights Are Being Trounced Upon Here?" *Rocky Mountain News,* 9 December 1995.

5. Quoted in Don Feder, *Pagan America* (Lafayette, LA: Huntington House, 1993), 134.

6. Quoted in a press release from the Christian Coalition on December 22, 1995. It goes on to say, in part, "After Christian Coalition contacted NPR executive producer Ellen Weiss, Weiss admitted that Codrescu's commentary 'crossed the line.' When Christian Coalition pressed NPR to make a public apology, Weiss initially declined, but contacted Christian Coalition late yesterday evening and said an apology may be forthcoming on today's broadcast [and in fact 30 seconds were devoted to an apology on December 22]. No punitive action is planned against Codrescu. NPR declined to allow Christian Coalition Executive Director Ralph Reed two minutes of air time on 'All Things Considered' to offer an opposing view. . . . 'This is one more example of religious bigotry subsidized with tax dollars,' said Ralph Reed. 'We have long passed the time for full privatization of

National Public Radio. These attacks on people of faith must end.'"
And they will—when Messiah comes.

7. *Las Posadas* is the Mexican version of the search for the Christ child.

8. Quoted in Halley, *Halley's Bible Handbook,* 19.

9. Ibid., 18.

Chapter 8

1. Quoted in John Wesley White, *The Coming World Dictator* (Minneapolis: Bethany Fellowship, 1981), 21.

2. Much of this information comes from the Golan Heights Information Server on the World Wide Web. For more information, or to help, contact:

The Golan Residents Committee (GRC)
P.O. Box 67
Qazrin 12900, Israel
E-mail: golan-r@golan.org.il
Mailing list: golan-h@golan.org.il
Telephone: (+ 972)-6-962966/77
Fax: (+ 972)-6-962429
Web: http://www.golan.org.il/

3. The United Nations Disengagement Force is headquartered in Damascus, Syria. Currently about 1,031 troops, assisted by the military observers of UNTSO's Observer Group Golan, patrol the area of separation. The force has suffered thirty-seven fatalities in the course of its mission. See the U.N. Web page for more information (http://www.CAM.ORG/~sac/SACIS).

4. "World Waits to See If Peace Process Will Survive," *The Orlando Sentinel,* 5 November 1995.

5. For more information about the Islamic Association for Palestine, access their Web page at http://www.io.org/~iap/.

6. Chaim Richman, "What Is the Temple Institute?" To find out more about the work of the Temple Institute, Jerusalem, and the Temple, send an email message at crlight@netvision.net.il, or fax: Rabbi Chaim Richman, 972-2-860-453.

7. Imam Sheik Ahmad Ibrahim, HAMAS leader, in a sermon at the Palestine Mosque in Gaza. Quote is provided by the Anti-Defamation League of the B'nai B'rith.

8. The Islamic Association for Palestine, "Did You Know?: Basic Facts about the Palestine Problem," as found on their Web site at http://www.io.org/~iap/.

9. Walvoord and Zuck, *The Bible Knowledge Commentary, Old Testament Edition,* 1299–1300.

10. Note that renowned evangelical scholar Edwin Yamauchi suspects that Magog is located in Turkey, while Charles Dyer believes that the far north "probably" encompasses "the land bridge between the Black and Caspian Seas."

11. Walvoord and Zuck, *The Bible Knowledge Commentary, Old Testament Edition,* 1300.

12. *New York Times,* 31 December 1995, Editorial Section.

Chapter 9

1. J. Dwight Pentecost, *Prophecy for Today* (Grand Rapids, MI: Zondervan, 1961), 142.

2. Walvoord and Zuck, *The Bible Knowledge Commentary, Old Testament Edition,* 1571.

FINAL DAWN

DAWN

OVER JERUSALEM

JOHN HAGEE

THOMAS NELSON PUBLISHERS®

Nashville

Lovingly dedicated to my children:
Tish, Christopher, Christina, Matthew, and Sandra

CONTENTS

CONTENTS

FOREWORD

The English statesman and author Benjamin Disraeli once said, "The view of Jerusalem is the history of the world; it is more, it is the history of earth and of heaven."[1]

I'd like to amend Disraeli's astute comment—in a view of Jerusalem we uncover more than the *history* of the world; we also discover the *forecast*. In Jerusalem we can find the key to the future of the universe and the hope of all mankind. One day in the not-too-distant future a king will come, the promised Messiah. Then Jew and Gentile alike will see Him walk upon the streets of Jerusalem. Together we will shout for joy as we look upon the King of kings, and the Lord of lords.

The Messiah for whose coming we yearn will establish a kingdom of lasting peace—how fitting that His capital will be Jerusalem, whose very name means "city of peace." As the nations of the world cry out for peace, the winds of war are gathering over the ancient city of Jerusalem. The sun—the God-ordained timekeeper that has faithfully risen and set over that beloved site since time began—will descend behind the Holy City's walls one last time. And in the morning, when that final day dawns over Jerusalem, the King of kings will establish His kingdom. The Chosen People, the Seed of Abraham, will welcome their Messiah, and He will be the Lamp of the City and the Light of the World.

I have a deep and abiding love for Jerusalem. I made my first visit to that Holy City in April 1979, when as a goy tourist preacher I walked through those ancient streets and marveled at the beauty of the city and the spirit of its people. I could not write about the war and desolation to come without a broken heart unless I had the confidence to also write about the victorious final chapter in Jerusalem's history. Darkness will come, and it will be the darkest night in Israel's history. But with the morning come great joy and the final dawn.

Jerusalem will greet its Messiah. At the dawning of that day, the Messiah will rule the world with truth and grace. He will make the nations prove the glories of His righteousness and the wonders of His love.

Come with me as we explore this Holy City and the chosen people of God who stand to inherit it. If we are to understand *why* God will do what He is planning to do in the future, we must understand *the people* through whom He has chosen to work.

The dawning of Jerusalem's glory is not far away.

PART I

THE
PEOPLE
OF
JERUSALEM

CHAPTER 1

JERUSALEM, CITY OF PEACE

June 7, 1981, began like any quiet Sunday in Washington, D.C. A hot afternoon sun flooded the Rose Garden behind the White House and lit the white pillars of that stately residence. Nothing seemed amiss; President and Mrs. Reagan were away at Camp David for a restful weekend retreat.

But in his office, National Security Adviser Richard V. Allen was trying to stifle his panic as he telephoned the president. An aide answered the phone at Camp David and told Allen that the president had just boarded the helicopter for the return trip to Washington. "Get him off the chopper," Allen said bluntly. "It's imperative that I speak to him at once."

"You've got to be kidding. The chopper's already revved up—"

"Get him off."

Moments later the president took the phone. As helicopter blades whirred and chopped in the background, Allen explained that the Israelis had just taken out a nuclear reactor in Iraq. "They used American F-16s, sir. We sold those seventy-five F-16s with the stipulation that they be used only for defensive purposes."

"What do you know about it?" asked the president.

"Nothing, sir. I'm waiting for a report."

"Why do you suppose they did it?"

Allen mulled the question for a moment. "Well, sir . . . boys will be boys."[1]

Objective: Osirak

At 4:40 P.M. Israeli time, a secret squadron had left underground bunkers at Israel's Etzion air base in the Sinai. The formation of flyers crossed the Gulf of Aqaba and flew over Jordan. Taking advantage of blind spots in the Arab radar system, the fourteen aircraft stayed close to the ground. To deceive any radio intervention, each pilot spoke flawless Arabic.

Back in Jerusalem, Israeli cabinet members were assembling at Menachem Begin's private residence in the Rehavya suburbs. Each official had been summoned by private invitation, and each stepped into the reception area only to discover himself among a group of confused and curious colleagues. The officials were soon shocked to hear that they were part of a clandestine meeting.

At 5:15 P.M. Begin emerged from his private office with astounding news. The prime minister, casually dressed in shirtsleeves, calmly announced, "Several of our planes are now on their way to their target in Iraq. I hope our boys will be able to complete their mission successfully and return to base."[2]

As the sun set over Baghdad, six F-15 camouflaged interceptors fell into a protective formation above eight F-16s carrying 2,000-pound bombs. The timing had been carefully orchestrated to minimize the possibility of injuring

Iraqi civilians at the reactor site. At the agreed-upon time, the Israeli jets dropped out of the sky, blasting the nuclear reactor station at Osirak.

When the lead plane released the first salvo, video-guided "smart" bombs blew holes in the concrete barriers around the reactors. No one would find the remains of the homing device that ensured that the missiles went straight to their target. The device had been hidden in a briefcase planted earlier by an agent of the Israeli secret service, Mossad. After the first explosions, the roof of the reactor collapsed, sending hundreds of tons of concrete and steel crashing to earth. Within moments, the Iraqis' $260 million nuclear-research reactor and all of its technical equipment became a smoking rubble. Saddam Hussein's ability to build an atomic bomb was crushed for the moment.

Two Israeli F-16s made a final pass to photograph the destruction. Complete desolation was confirmed, with one civilian casualty. With their mission accomplished, the squadron began the fifty-minute return flight home.

In Jerusalem, the stunned cabinet members assembled at Begin's residence gained their composure and debated how they should respond if one of their planes was shot down. Shortly before 7:00 P.M., a phone call reported the safe return of every plane. The jubilant assembly applauded and celebrated. Within a few moments, Begin lifted the phone and telephoned the U.S. ambassador to Israel to explain the raid.

Ambassador Samuel Lewis's reply to the news that American-supplied jets had just struck Iraq? "You don't say."

Not every reaction was so laconic. TASS, the Soviet news agency, immediately labeled the raid an "act of gangsterism" and accused the United States of complicity. Egypt's former prime minister warned that the time was approaching to take action against Israel. Arab League Secretary General Chedli Klibi demanded U.N. sanctions against Israel.

On Monday morning, leading figures in the Reagan administration met to assess the situation. Vice President George Bush and Chief of Staff Jim Baker urged significant sanctions against Israel. Secretary of Defense Caspar Weinberger wanted to cancel further F-16 sales. President Reagan was personally pleased with the Israelis, believing that their willingness to use force was the most effective path to peace. In the end, however, the White House released a terse, harsh statement criticizing the action, condemning the attack, and threatening punitive response. The State Department said the surprise raid "cannot but seriously add to the already tense situation in the area."

Menachem Begin answered immediately. "The Iraqis were preparing atomic bombs to drop on the children of Israel," he told the world. "Haven't you heard of one and a half million little Jewish children who were thrown into the gas chambers?" He did not hesitate to employ passionate rhetoric. "Another Holocaust would have happened in the history of the Jewish people. Never again, never again. Tell your friends, tell anybody you meet, we shall defend our people with all the means at our disposal."

Despite Begin's eloquent defense of his actions, a cartel of nations pressed for retribution. After six days of debate at the United Nations, Ambassador Jeane J. Kirkpatrick voted against America's staunch friend Israel, saying, "The means Israel chose to quiet its fears have hurt, not helped, the peace and security of the area." Ambassador Kirkpatrick joined fifteen other members of the U.N. Security Council and condemned the Israeli raid. An Arab diplomat analyzed the vote by saying, "The United States saved face in the Middle East. The Iraqis won a moral victory."[3]

In the days that followed, the Begin government published several previously classified facts. Over thirteen feet beneath the demolished reactor, the Iraqis maintained a secret installation for use in developing an atomic weapon. The Iraqis had also stockpiled 200 tons of natural uranium called *yellowcake,* the deadly powder used to create plutonium. Tiny Israel knew it could not survive a first-strike nuclear attack. Every military base would be gone in one blast. Anticipatory self-defense was the only intelligent option for survival.

In subsequent weeks, newspapers across the world blasted Israel in column after column of bitter denunciation. The American Congress held special hearings and suspended further sales of F-16s to Israel. While popular at home, Menachem Begin became a pariah in the eyes of the world. His description of Saddam Hussein as an evil ruler was universally rejected.

Saddam Hussein Unveiled

A decade later, the sons and daughters of American citizens joined with troops from across the world to stop Hussein's sudden, devastating attack on Kuwait. With his sophisticated Iraqi army, Hussein destroyed oil wells and crushed the small country's meager military resources. Hussein, the "victim" of the Osirak raid, had acquired a new image as the madman of the Middle East. The nations in the Security Council who had so vehemently condemned the Israeli attack found themselves forced to change their opinions about Middle East aggressors. Menachem Begin now appeared to be a prophet.

Americans were slow to realize the full ramifications of that hot, quiet afternoon in June 1981. If Israel had not destroyed Hussein's atomic bomb factory, thousands of America's finest and best would have been slaughtered in a nuclear holocaust in the desert.

The secret raid at sundown had saved the world from an Armageddon appointment.

I remember reading the screaming headlines of the *New York Times*: ISRAELI JETS DESTROY IRAQ ATOMIC REACTOR—ATTACK CONDEMNED BY U.S. AND ARAB NATIONS. The gripping account of Israel's preemptive strike on Hussein's atomic reactor was also front-page news in San Antonio. I read the articles with a grim expression, knowing that Hussein's frantic attempts to develop weapons of mass destruction were for only one diabolical end—Iraq intended to blow Jerusalem off the map.

Excellent, I thought as I read. *Israel struck first, just like you'd shoot a coiled rattlesnake on the front porch. You wouldn't wait to see if the serpent was bluffing.*

Israel knows that the Hitlers, Stalins, Ayatollah Khomeinis, Husseins, and other lunatics of the world must be taken seriously. The Israeli Defense Force (IDF) action upon Osirak was simple and logical. If more countries took evil as seriously as Israel, the Hitlers of history would not have the opportunity to accumulate enough power to drag the world into a bloodbath.

I turned to the editorial page of the San Antonio paper, expecting to find an enthusiastic endorsement of Israel, but I was shocked. Our best ally in that volatile part of the globe was the target of several scathing attacks. My local newspaper condemned Israel as being as aggressive as Libya. I was deeply disturbed about my local paper's position. I sought out other national newspapers and discovered more of the same. The American media was in a feeding frenzy, and the State of Israel was the only item on the menu.

From deep within my soul, a trumpet sounded. I knew I could not stand idly by and let this moment, this unjust criticism, pass unchallenged. I reminded myself of a familiar Edmund Burke quote: "The only thing necessary for the triumph of evil is for good men to do nothing."

A Cradle-Roll Zionist

My support for the State of Israel began at our family altar. For fifty years, my father was a minister of the gospel and a Bible scholar. Many evenings our family gathered around the dining table as my father taught us from the Bible that the Jewish people were "the apple of God's eye." He taught the members of his congregation that the nation of Israel is God's prophetic timepiece for the ages. He taught that Jerusalem, the city of God, would be the focal point of the world from this moment until the coming of the Messiah.

During the darkest days of World War II, Dad kept reminding his congregants that they would see the day when the State of Israel would be reborn "in a day." On May 15, 1948, we were in our kitchen listening to the radio when the greatest political miracle of the twentieth century became a reality. Our family sat mesmerized as my father's teachings passed from prophecy into history. The birth of the State of Israel confirmed the accuracy of Bible prophecy and was God's notary seal on my father's ministry.

In April 1979 I took my first trip to Israel. I walked in the steps of Christ from His birth in Bethlehem, His baptism in the Jordan, His betrayal by Judas in Gethsemane, and His brilliant resurrection at the Garden Tomb. I sailed across the Sea of Galilee, the same sea my Savior traversed in the midst of a raging storm to calm His terrified disciples. I stood at the rocky crest of Calvary and marveled at the miracle of redemption.

Though I was tremendously excited about my pilgrimage, nothing prepared me for the beauty of the land and the spirit of the people. The accomplishments of Jewish sweat, blood, tears, and genius had changed the desert into a garden, poverty into prosperity, a forsaken wilderness into a wonderland.

Barren mountains had become forests of green. Malaria-infested swamps had disappeared to make way for groves of eucalyptus trees. A dispossessed people had turned a damaged land into everything promised by the prophet Isaiah.

Struggling through unbearable obstacles at incalculable personal cost, doctors, lawyers, professors, merchants, and musicians speaking more than sixty languages abandoned their European heritages and prosperous lifestyles to reconstitute the nation promised to Abraham. With the blood of King David flowing in their veins, these pioneers came back once again to banish the local Goliaths. With not much more firepower than David's slingshot, they faced Arabs armed to the teeth by the British. Not giving an inch, the dispossessed became the masters of what had been Palestine.

This land, promised to Abraham, Isaac, and Jacob, was theirs forever through the unconditional and unbreakable blood covenant expressed in Genesis: "On the same day the LORD made a covenant with Abram, saying: 'To your descendants I have given this land, from the river of Egypt to the great river, the River Euphrates—the Kenites, the Kenezzites, the Kadmonites, the Hittites, the Perizzites, the Rephaim, the Amorites, the Canaanites, the Girgashites, and the Jebusites'" (Gen. 15:18–21).

The courageous enthusiasm of these sons and daughters of Gideon gave birth to modern Israel and magnetically invited their still-wandering relatives to return. The spirit of Theodor Herzl, Chaim Weizmann, Golda Meir, Moshe Dayan, and Menachem Begin surged across the fruited coastal plains and sent my imagination soaring to the heights of Mount Hermon.

I loved the spirit of these people. Since statehood, they have consistently been America's only true friends in the Middle East.

A Time to Act

But while the Iraqi reactor at Osirak smoldered in ruins, many American friends of Israel were ominously quiet. As the American press blasted Israel with scathing denunciations and threats of political reprisal, I felt it was time to stand and speak up. It was time to do something, but what? Instantly a concept exploded in my mind. Why not have a massive public demonstration of support for Israel? Americans are quick to demonstrate for things we are *against,* why not demonstrate for causes we *support*? We would call it "A Night to Honor Israel."

The morning this idea came to me, my wife, Diana, and I sat at the breakfast table, and I shared the concept with her. I reached for pad and pen to put a few thoughts on paper. Maybe other clergy would stand with me, I told Diana. I would send at least 150 letters to other clergymen across San Antonio, inviting them to join me in a public statement and display of support for Israel. We would hold a press conference to announce our intention to convene A Night to Honor Israel. Within a few minutes, everything fell into place . . . on paper.

I had mistakenly thought that most clergymen in San Antonio would be happy to join me, but only one pastor, Dr. Buckner Fanning of Trinity Baptist Church, answered my letter favorably. I soon discovered that anti-Semitism was alive and well in the church that had been founded by a Rabbi who taught "love thy neighbor as thyself."

Strange, isn't it, that we tend to forget that Jesus was Jewish? Too many Christians believe that Jesus was the son of Mr. and Mrs. Christ, that He was born in Bethlehem, and that He later called twelve nice, blond, blue-eyed disciples to help Him found the church.

In any case, I found myself planning a gala night without much support. I soon found my life threatened.

With Dr. Fanning, the pastor who agreed to join me, and two local rabbis, I organized a press conference to announce the upcoming event. We made our statements, the photographers snapped our pictures, and then the fireworks started. Within an hour after the newspapers hit the stand the next morning, someone called a death threat in to my church. "Tell that preacher he'll be dead by Friday!" the caller said.

I take death threats seriously, so I contacted our chief of security and was told to immediately discontinue all my routine activities. "Do not go to the office the same way every day," he told me. "Use a different car, study in a different place, cancel your social engagements, and buy and wear a bulletproof vest." You can be sure I did as I was told.

I had begun to think the threat wasn't serious until the windows of my car were shot out while the vehicle was parked in front of my home. Tension mounted as the date for A Night to Honor Israel drew near.

On September 10, 1981, the Lila Cockrell Theater for the Performing Arts was filled to capacity with friends who wished to honor Israel. All of the San Antonio rabbis were in attendance, as well as myself and the lone Baptist pastor who had joined with me. The rabbis and Buckner Fanning stood with me on the platform as the Cornerstone Church sanctuary choir and orchestra played and sang Hebrew songs in Hebrew (well, *Southern* Hebrew). I smiled and listened to the music, glancing over the crowd, looking for any unusual movements. I was extremely tense, but the evening progressed smoothly.

What we wanted to demonstrate that night wasn't simply support, but love. Love isn't what you say—it's what you *do*. It wasn't enough to express support for Israel and the Jewish people of the world; we knew we had to do something tangible to demonstrate our love. We decided prior to this night to take an offering for Hadassah Hospital in Jerusalem, a medical facility that treats both Jews and Arabs.

After the choir sang so beautifully "Jerusalem of Gold," "Y'Varech'Cha," and other songs, I walked to the lectern and delivered a speech unlike any I had ever given in decades of ministry. "Israel and the Jews have heard the voices of their enemies for centuries," I began. "They have endured untold hardship and persecution, but we are here tonight to say it's time for them to hear the voices of their friends, loud and clear. It's time for courage and conviction to replace cowardice and complacency."

I told them of my pilgrimage to Jerusalem and how I felt a very special presence in that Holy City, the city of God. As I stood on the cobblestone streets of the Old City, I knew I had found my spiritual home.

Next, I addressed the issue of the Israeli air raid on the nuclear reactor at Osirak. "We are here tonight to loudly say that we are not appalled by Israel's defending itself in a climate of war. Rather, we applaud Israel for its courage and determination to give no quarter to terrorists in the Middle East."

I pressed even harder on an issue that is the lifeblood of America's economy—oil. "Sooner or later, the present oil glut will be used up and foreign governments will demand we make a choice," I said. "They will tell us, 'Stop supporting Israel or you'll buy no more oil from the Persian Gulf states!'" I paused and looked over the crowd. "I hope and pray when that day arrives, millions of Americans will stand up and tell the oil monarchs to keep their oil. We'd rather ride bicycles and support the State of Israel!"

The audience was stunned. I don't know what they were expecting me to say, but they obviously weren't expecting that kind of support.

I went on to quote the words of Pastor Martin Neimoller, whose voice from the Nazi era reminded us of the importance of speaking up for right and becoming involved: "When Hitler attacked the Jews, I was not a Jew; therefore, I was not concerned. And when Hitler attacked the Catholics, I was not a Catholic, and, therefore, I was not concerned. And when Hitler attacked the unions and the industrialists, I was not a member of the unions, and I was not concerned. Then Hitler attacked me and the Protestant church—and there was nobody left to be concerned."[4]

I closed my speech by reviewing the blessings the Jewish people have brought to America in the fields of education, finance, medicine, music, science, and philanthropy. I also praised the 500,000 Jewish soldiers who served the United States with valor in World War II.

"It is not possible for a man to truthfully say, 'I am a Christian,' and not love the Jewish people," I concluded.

As soon as my speech had ended, we took an offering for Hadassah Hospital.

I presented a four-foot cardboard check for $10,000 to the local president of Hadassah. As I announced the amount of the check to the crowd and to those who would later watch on national television, tears began to flow down the cheeks of the woman to whom I was presenting the gift. A moment later, her tears turned into audible sobs; in an instant, the thousands of people in that auditorium melded together. I scanned the audience and saw some of the most influential citizens of San Antonio openly weeping. I shall always cherish that memory.

Terrorism in San Antonio

After presenting the check, I introduced Rabbi Scheinberg to give the benediction. As he began to pray, an aide slipped to my side and pressed a message into my hand—someone had called a bomb threat into the *San Antonio Express-News* newspaper. Terrorists threatened to blow up the auditorium at 9:30 P.M. My watch said 9:27.

As the rabbi's last words left his mouth, I leaped for the microphone. "I hate to end this lovely evening on a negative note," I said, "but security has informed me that in two minutes a bomb is supposed to explode in this building. Please leave quickly."

Most of the Christians ran for the doors with shock and terror evident on their faces. To my surprise, most of the Jews flipped their hands in traditional Hebrew fashion as if to say, "We've been through this a thousand times. We're not being intimidated by screwballs." Most of my congregation scurried for shelter as I watched. The resolve of the

Jewish community profoundly impressed me. They leisurely greeted their friends, finished their conversations, and took their leave.

Security guards rushed Diana and me out the back door with Zion Evrony, the consul general of Israel. As we were driving back to his hotel, a thunderbolt of righteous anger shot through my soul. "I'm not going to let a Nazi mentality terrorize me into silence and submission," I told Consul General Evrony. "If they want a fight, we'll give them more than they bargained for. If A Night to Honor Israel made them mad, let's see their response to our repeating the event throughout the length and breadth of America."

That night I knew we had to take A Night to Honor Israel across the nation. We would take the choir, the orchestra, and whoever would go to America's great metropolitan centers. My intention was to stand against anti-Semitism in the church and in the bloodstream of America until the vipers that made the threatening phone calls slithered back into the sewer.

We took A Night to Honor Israel to Houston, Austin, Dallas, Fort Worth, Phoenix, Los Angeles, and Tulsa, where goose-stepping skinheads marched down the street in front of the auditorium in full Nazi uniform, screaming, "Seig Heil" while carrying signs that read, WHO PAYS JOHN HAGEE?

One of the highlights of my life was taking A Night to Honor Israel to Jerusalem. Transporting a 200-voice choir with full orchestra was expensive, but our people believed in this effort. Some sold the furniture out of their homes, and others sold their second cars to raise money for the trip. After months of fund-raising, we had the necessary finances. We boarded an El Al jet, and on wings of eagles sailed toward the Promised Land.

When our choir and orchestra performed at Tel Noff, Ayellet Hasahar, and the Jewish Theater in Jerusalem, the performance was electrifying. I could feel the brush of angels' wings and the very presence of God.

What began as a onetime event has now become an annual celebration at Cornerstone Church. Each year in the month of May we televise via satellite "A Night to Honor Israel" from the sanctuary of Cornerstone Church to our national television audience. Sixteen years have passed since September 10, 1981, but the issues are no less pressing today. The personal threats haven't subsided, and the message hasn't been restrained. Verbalized suspicion from both Christians and Jews has never ceased. We don't honor Israel and the Jewish people for applause or approval; we do it because we have a biblical mandate to bless God's people.

Why is the world so quick to turn against Israel? Why has Christianity persecuted the Jews for 2,000 years? How logical is it for Christians to praise dead Jews of the past—Abraham, Isaac, Jacob, David, Jesus, and Paul—while cursing the Jewish people of the present?

The attacks against Israel, against Jerusalem, and eventually against the Jews themselves will escalate toward Jerusalem's darkest hour. The present peace process will prove to be the womb of war. As the fanatical attacks on Jerusalem increase, we must let the world know that if a line has to be drawn, it will be drawn around Christians as well as Jews. We are united and indivisible.

Israel, you are not alone.

CHAPTER 2

HE WHO
BLESSES ISRAEL . . .

Israel and its Holy City, Jerusalem, hold the keys to the future. What happens in the Jewish state affects what God is doing with the rest of the world, so the better we understand Israel, the more comprehensive will be our grasp of things to come.

Using a favorite Hebrew figure of speech, Zechariah described Israel as "the apple of God's eye." "For thus says the LORD of hosts," the prophet wrote, "'He sent Me after glory, to the nations which plunder you; for he who touches you touches the apple of His eye'" (Zech. 2:8).

In biological terms, the "apple" is the pupil, or center, of the eye. This is the most sensitive part of the human body. God is saying through the prophet Zechariah, "When you touch Israel, you have touched the most sensitive part of My being. When you attack Israel or the Jewish people, you are sticking your finger in the center of My eye. Do it and see what happens!" Anyone who harms the Jewish people with malice aforethought will experience the instant wrath of God.

Israel's Birthright

God watches over Israel as a protective parent hovers over an only child. In order to understand how those who bless Israel will themselves be blessed, we need to comprehend these four principles:

1. *The nation of Israel was created by a sovereign act of God.* All other nations were created by an act of war or a declaration of men, but Israel was intentionally created by God so that He would have a physical place of inheritance on the earth (Isa. 19:25).

   By what right? By the right of ownership. God created the earth (Gen. 1:1), and it is His to give to whomever He chooses (Ex. 19:5). He chose to give a specific part of the earth to Abraham, Isaac, Jacob, and their descendants, and He sealed His agreement in a blood covenant that He has sworn to uphold forever (Gen. 15:18–21).

2. *God established Israel's national geographic boundaries.* The exact borders of Israel are detailed in Scripture just as our heavenly Father dictated them. The divine Surveyor drove the original stakes into Judean soil and decreed that no one should ever change these property lines. The real estate contract and land covenants were signed in blood and stand to this very hour. Jews have the absolute right as mandated by God to the land of Israel and, more specifically, to the city of Jerusalem.

3. *Israel has a Spy in the sky.* The psalmist wrote that "He who keeps Israel / Shall neither slumber nor sleep" (Ps. 121:4). No nation in the world can match the defensive force guarding the State of Israel. The archangel Michael has a special assignment to guard Israel (see Dan. 10:13, 21; 12:1; Rev. 12:7), and his supernatural power is far greater than all the military muscle of every

army on earth. The Lord stands watch in the darkest night with an eye trained on the nation of Israel and, more specifically, Jerusalem. Those who fight with Israel fight with Him.

4. *Prosperity or punishment depends on how we treat Israel.* In the moment that God covenanted with Abraham, the Almighty gave him an awesome promise: "I will bless those who bless you, / And I will curse him who curses you; / And in you all the families of the earth shall be blessed" (Gen. 12:3). No pronouncement of Scripture is clearer or more decisive. God smiles on the friends of the descendants of Abraham, and they enjoy heavenly favor.

In contrast, God will answer every act of anti-Semitism with harsh and final judgment. This fourth principle is critical for every citizen of the United States of America. No matter how clever our economic policies or how comprehensive our military preparation, the most significant action our nation can take is our compassionate support of the State of Israel. The quickest and most effective way to be on God's side is to stand with the State of Israel and the Jewish people in their hour of need.

A Guideline for Greatness

God blesses the man or nation that blesses Israel or the Jewish people. This principle is demonstrated in the story of Jacob and Laban in Genesis 29–31. Jacob had agreed to work seven years for Laban on the condition that he be given the hand of beautiful Rachel in marriage. Laban deceived Jacob and gave him his homely daughter, Leah, instead, and Jacob was forced to work another seven years for Rachel's hand.

While Jacob worked for Laban, God greatly blessed the deceptive Gentile. When Jacob asked Laban's permission to leave after fourteen years of service, Laban replied, "Please stay, if I have found favor in your eyes, for I have learned by experience that the LORD has blessed me for your sake" (Gen. 30:27). God blessed Laban, a Gentile, through Jacob.

The story of Joseph is another good illustration of how God blesses Gentiles who bless the Jews. Joseph was a Jewish teenager sold into the land of Egypt by his jealous brothers. In time, with his God-given wisdom, Joseph rose from the penitentiary to the pinnacle of power, becoming prime minister of all Egypt. Through a series of dreams, God revealed to Joseph that seven years of plenty would be followed by seven years of worldwide famine. Pharaoh rewarded Joseph's discernment by placing his signet ring on Joseph's hand and a gold chain about his neck. Pharaoh made Joseph, a Jewish slave, the second most powerful man on earth.

Joseph prepared Egypt for the devastating famine by storing grain during the seven years of abundance. When the seven years of famine came, Egypt was at the apex of its power, literally controlling the world's economy through food.

How did this happen? One Jewish man with supernatural revelation literally saved the Gentile world from starvation. God blesses the Gentiles through the Jewish people.

Jesus Himself said, "Salvation is of the Jews" (John 4:22). He was alluding to the Jewish contribution to Christianity, for without Jews, there would be no Christianity. The prophets, the patriarchs, the apostles, the men who wrote the Bible (with the exception of Luke, who was probably Greek), Mary, Joseph, and Jesus—all were Jewish.

In the seventh chapter of Luke, we read of a Roman centurion who had heard of Jesus Christ, the healing Rabbi. He wanted Jesus to come to his house to pray for a sick servant, but it was forbidden for a righteous Jew to enter a Gentile's house. The centurion asked the Jewish elders how he could get Jesus to come and pray for his servant.

What logic did the Jewish elders use to persuade Jesus to help the centurion? They said, "He loves our nation, and has built us a synagogue" (Luke 7:5). This centurion had blessed Israel and the Jewish people with a practical act of kindness, so Jesus prayed for the centurion's servant, who was healed.

In the tenth chapter of Acts, the Bible declares that Cornelius, a Roman centurion who lived in Caesarea, gave alms to the Jewish people and was of good reputation among all the nation of the Jews. Cornelius was a righteous man who benefited from the principle of blessing the Jews. What was his most extraordinary blessing?

God gave the apostle Peter a vision of a prayer shawl held by its four corners descending from heaven. All manner of four-footed beasts and wild beasts and creeping things and fowls of the air moved inside this shawl. This vision signified the religious barrier forbidding Jews from associating with unclean Gentiles in spiritual matters. Understanding God's message, Peter went at once to Cornelius's house, preached the gospel, and those in the house were saved and filled with the Spirit.

"While Peter was still speaking these words, the Holy Spirit fell upon all those who heard the word. And those of the circumcision who believed were astonished, as many as came with Peter, because the gift of the Holy Spirit had been poured out on the Gentiles also. For they heard them speak with tongues and magnify God" (Acts 10:44–46).

What made this possible? A Roman centurion—a Gentile—blessed the Jewish people, and God opened the windows of heaven and poured upon him and his house a blessing he could not contain.

American History and Jewish Blessing

Jewish influence has permeated all corners of the globe and every page of history, including American history. Jews were very involved in Columbus's expedition to find the New World. Levi Ben Gershon, a Jew, invented the sea quadrant, used for navigation. Jewish cartographers drew most of the sea charts of the age. And centuries before Columbus, Jews had disproved the notion that the world was flat. In the *Zohar,* 200 years before Columbus, Moses de Leon, a Jew, stated that the earth revolves like a ball and is covered by daylight on one side and darkness on the other.[1]

Jewish influence extended far beyond the discovery of America. During a particularly dark time of the American Revolution, George Washington and the Continental Army were freezing and starving in the snows of Valley Forge. Without food, arms, or ammunition, it seemed that the fledgling nation was doomed to die. But Haym Salomon, a Jewish banker from Philadelphia, arranged for the Jews of the thirteen colonies to respond with financial aid that turned the tide of the war and enabled General Washington to defeat the British. Salomon believed that until Jerusalem would once again welcome the children of Israel, America could be the Promised Land for the Jews.[2]

"It can be documented," writes David Allen Lewis, "that Salomon gave his personal fortune, and in addition raised huge sums of money through business transactions, buying financial papers and leverage accounts on various European and American markets. He could have made himself rich and left a fine estate for his lovely wife and children. He died sick and penniless at the age of 45. . . . He had given all he had, and now his body lies in a lonely, unmarked, forgotten grave in Philadelphia."[3]

No one is certain exactly how much money Haym Salomon loaned to our infant country, but reports range from $600,000 to $800,000. If we assume the loan amount was $700,000, compounded quarterly at 7 percent interest over a period of 222 years, conservative estimates indicate that the United States owes *over $2.5 trillion* to Haym Salomon's heirs. America's foreign aid to Israel doesn't come close to paying our debt to the Jewish people.

Washington was so appreciative of the Jewish contribution to the birth of America that he instructed the engravers of the American one-dollar bill to engrave a tribute to the Jewish people over the head of the bald eagle. If you look carefully, above the eagle's head you'll see the Star of David surrounded by the brilliant light of the Shekinah glory that dwelled above the Mercy Seat in the Holy of Holies in the Jewish tabernacle.[4]

If you turn your one-dollar bill upside down and place your thumb over the eagle's head, the shield becomes the menorah, or the seven golden candlesticks of Israel. Placing your thumb completely over the shield leaves the tail of nine feathers that represent the flames of the Hanukkah Menorah.

But the symbolism doesn't stop there. To the Israelites, the number thirteen was a significant number. Including the Levites, there were thirteen tribes of Israel. Thirteen is also the age at which a boy or girl reaches adulthood. Now look on the one-dollar bill—there are thirteen leaves in the olive branch in the right talon of the eagle, thirteen arrows in the left talon, thirteen stripes on the shield, thirteen stars in the cloud representing the thirteen colonies. Every American who carries a single dollar bill holds a constant reminder that in Israel, "all the nations of the earth shall be blessed."

John Adams, another of our country's founding fathers, respected the Jews. In a letter to his friend F. A. Van der Kemp, he wrote:

> In spite of . . . Voltaire [an ardent anti-Semite], I will insist that the Hebrews have done more to civilize men than any other nation. If I were an atheist and believed in blind eternal fate, I should still believe that fate had ordained the Jews to be the most essential instrument for civilizing the nations. . . . I should believe that chance had ordered the Jews to preserve and to propagate to all mankind the doctrine of a supreme, intelligent, wise, almighty sovereign of the universe, which I believe to be the great essential principle of all morality, and consequently of all civilization.[5]

Pro-Jewish Voices

Sir Winston Churchill

Sir Winston Leonard Spencer Churchill, beloved British statesman, soldier, and author, certainly seemed to enjoy the blessing of God upon his life. He was not only intelligent, but intuitive, and was among the first to publicly issue warnings about the threat of Nazi Germany. Unfortunately, his warnings were not heeded.

In 1940, seven months after the outbreak of World War II, Churchill became Britain's prime minister. His stirring speeches, his energy, and his refusal to placate Hitler were crucial to bolstering the British troops and ensuring that country's resistance to the enemy. In June 1941, after the Germans invaded Russia, Churchill went on British radio and scathingly remarked that when Hitler entered his newly conquered territory, "All his usual formalities of perfidy were observed with scrupulous technique."[6]

Churchill was knighted in 1953, and in that same year was also awarded the Nobel Prize in literature for his writing.[7]

Why did God bless Winston Churchill? I believe it was, in part, because Churchill loved the apple of God's eye, the Jews.

As early as 1908, a full forty years before the State of Israel was established, Churchill expressed his "full sympathy with the historical aspirations of the Jews" to restore "a center of racial and political integrity" in Palestine.[8]

In June 1954 Churchill told a group of American journalists, "I am a Zionist, let me make that clear. I was one of the original ones after the Balfour Declaration and I have worked faithfully for it. I think it is a most wonderful thing that this community should have established itself so effectively, turning the desert into fertile gardens and thriving townships and should have afforded refuge to millions of their co-religionists who suffered so fearfully under Hitler, and not only under Hitler, persecution. I think it is a wonderful thing." He opposed the White Paper Policies that limited the number of Jews who could enter Britain during Hitler's reign of terror, and on the fate of Jerusalem, Churchill had one terse comment—"You ought to let the Jews have Jerusalem; it is they who made it famous."[9]

Chaim Weizmann

During World War I, when the prospect of an Allied victory was dim and freedom in the Western world hung by a thread, the British navy ran short of gunpowder. The First Lord of the Admiralty, Sir Winston Churchill, contacted a brilliant Jewish chemist, Chaim Weizmann, for help. Churchill asked Weizmann if he could produce 30,000 tons of synthetic acetone so the British could manufacture cordite gunpowder. Harnessing his genius and setting his energies to the task, Weizmann produced the synthetic acetone, thus assuring British superiority on the high seas.

When asked what he wanted for his services to England and the Allies, Weizmann replied, "There is only one thing I want—a national homeland for my people." On November 2, 1917, British Foreign Secretary Arthur J. Balfour issued the Balfour Declaration, promising the Jews of the world a homeland. The declaration stated that the British government favored "the establishment in Palestine of a national home for the Jewish people and will use their best endeavours to facilitate the achievement of that object, it being clearly understood that nothing shall be done which may prejudice the civil and religious rights of existing non-Jewish communities in Palestine."[10]

Weizmann saw his dream come true, and in 1948 he was named the first president of Israel. The free world owes a tremendous debt of gratitude to him.

Theodore Roosevelt

Theodore Roosevelt, America's original Rough Rider, had a wry sense of humor, and never was it better displayed than on one occasion when he dealt with an anti-Semite. Roosevelt was police commissioner of New York City in

1895, and an anti-Semitic preacher from Berlin came to New York to preach a crusade against the Jews. "Many of the New York Jews were much excited and asked me to prevent him from speaking and not to give him police protection," Roosevelt wrote in his autobiography. "This, I told them, was impossible; and if possible would have been undesirable because it would have made him a martyr. The proper thing to do was to make him ridiculous.

"Accordingly I detailed for his protection a [Jewish] sergeant and a score or two of [Jewish] policemen. He made his harangue against the Jews under the active protection of some forty policemen, every one of them a Jew."[11]

Albert Einstein

When the Axis powers plunged the world into World War II, again it was the Seed of Abraham to whom God chose to reveal the secrets of the universe. Albert Einstein, an American theoretical physicist, was born a German Jew; he was later recognized as one of the greatest physicists of all time. In 1914 he became titular professor of physics and director of theoretical physics at the Kaiser Wilhelm Institute in Berlin. But under Hitler's anti-Semitic policies, in 1934 the Nazi government confiscated his property and revoked his German citizenship. In 1940 Einstein became an American citizen, holding a post at the Institute for Advanced Study in Princeton from 1933 until his death.

Einstein, the genius who gave the world the formula $E=mc^2$, was well acquainted with anti-Semitism. "If my theory of relativity is proven correct," he said, thinking of his heritage, "Germany will claim me as a German and France will declare that I am a citizen of the world. Should my theory prove untrue, France will say that I am a German and Germany will declare that I am a Jew."[12]

In 1939, when approached by his friend Szilard about new research into atomic power, Einstein sent the following message to President Franklin Delano Roosevelt, urging him to investigate the possible use of atomic energy in bombs:

> Some recent work by E. Fermi and L. Szilard which has been communicated to me in manuscript leads me to expect that the element uranium may be turned into a new and important source of energy in the near future. Certain aspects of the situation which has arisen seem to call for watchfulness and, if necessary, quick action on the part of the Administration. . . . In the course of the last four months it has been made almost certain . . . that it may become possible to set up a nuclear chain reaction in a large mass of uranium, by which vast amounts of power and large quantities of radium-like elements would be generated. . . . This new phenomenon would lead also to the construction of bombs.[13]

Though as an ardent pacifist Einstein was opposed to the use of the atomic bomb, it was as a result of his work that President Harry Truman decided to use the A-bomb. Knowing that the Japanese military leaders were prepared to fight a conventional war to the last man, Truman felt he had no other choice. His decision saved thousands of American lives and brought a halt to World War II.

Other Pro-Jewish Voices

As virulent and prevalent as anti-Semitism is, people throughout history have been willing to take a stand for the Jewish people. Who can forget the example of Corrie ten Boom and her family, who risked their own lives hiding Jews in their homes in Holland? Corrie and her family were sent to the Nazi concentration camps for hiding

Jewish refugees. Her father and sister literally starved to death in the camps. Corrie was released by clerical error and allowed to return to her home in Holland. A tree now grows in her honor in the Avenue of the Righteous Gentiles, just outside the Yad Vashem Centre in Jerusalem.

In 1894, when French intelligence learned that a French soldier had sold military secrets to Germany, Captain Alfred Dreyfus, a Jew, was immediately accused of being the spy. A military tribunal sentenced him to life imprisonment on Devil's Island though all the evidence pointed to the guilt of another soldier, Colonel Marie-Charles-Ferdinand-Walsin Esterhazy.

Fortunately, a few valiant souls would not allow such unfairness to go unchallenged. Émile Zola, a novelist, refused to let the case die. He wrote, "May all my words perish if Dreyfus is not innocent. . . . I did not want my country to remain in lies and injustice. One day, France will thank me for having helped to save its honor."[14]

France did. Despite relentless opposition from the French army, government officials, and the Catholic church, Dreyfus's case was reopened and the man exonerated—twelve years after his arrest.[15]

Changing Attitudes

"After centuries of intolerance, flecked with murder and crude social bigotry," writes David Aikman, "increasing numbers of Christians in recent years have been owning up to the Church's historical role in anti-Semitism. And they have, quite rightly, been repenting of it."[16]

Aikman, a correspondent with *Time* magazine, has noticed that recently many Christians have begun to experience a love for the Jewish people.

At the same time, enamored with Israel and the possibility that the "last days" might be just around the corner, increasing numbers of Christians began to see Jews in general—not just Israelis—no longer as "Christ killers" but as a people chosen by God and beloved by Him no less today than in Old Testament times. Not all Jews have been comfortable with this rather striking change in Christian perceptions of them—from "enemy" to "instrument" of God's purpose, so to speak. After all, some must wonder, if theology was the reason for the original antipathy of Christians toward them, and theology has now given birth to admiration, what happens if theology shifts once again?[17]

Anti-Semitism is sin, and sin damns the soul!
Pope John XXIII, who died in 1963, delivered the most open apology the Jews have ever received from the Catholic church. Shortly before his death, he published this prayer:

> We realize now that many, many centuries of blindness have dimmed our eyes, so that we no longer see the beauty of Thy Chosen People and no longer recognize in their faces the features of our first-born brother. We realize that our brows are branded with the mark of Cain. Centuries long has Abel lain in blood and tears, because we have forgotten Thy love. Forgive us the curse which we unjustly laid on the name of the Jews. Forgive us, that with our curse, we crucified Thee a second time.[18]

Jewish Blessings for All Mankind

There is no denying that mankind has been blessed by the Jewish people. Casimir Funk discovered vitamins;

Abraham Jacobi, founder of American pediatrics, invented the laryngoscope. Jonas Salk developed the polio vaccine. The American Medical Association was founded by a Jewish ophthalmologist, Isaac Hayes. Joseph Goldberger laid the foundation for the science of nutrition, while Simon Baruch was the first physician to identify and successfully complete an appendectomy.[19]

One Jewish man, Emile Berliner, invented the microphone and the gramophone. Other Jews invented calculators, synthetic rubber, and petroleum.

How many times have you enjoyed the works of Jewish people and not even realized it? Consider the many Jews who enrich our lives through entertainment and news: Douglas Fairbanks, Cary Grant, Kirk Douglas, Paul Newman, Shelley Winters, James Caan, George Segal, Goldie Hawn, Dustin Hoffman, Peter Sellers, Debra Winger, Lauren Bacall, John Houseman, Madeline Kahn, Barbra Streisand, Danny Kaye, Edward G. Robinson, Tony Curtis, Rod Steiger, Tony Randall, Jack Klugman, Hal Linden, Peter Falk, Ed Asner, Lorne Greene, George Burns, Gracie Allen, David Janssen, Jack Benny, Michael Landon, Linda Lavin, Ted Koppel, Howard Cosell, Barbara Walters, Mike Wallace, Larry King, and Ann Landers. These people are a living testimony that "in thee shall all the nations of the earth be blessed."

The world has been blessed by God's people, and it is time for us to bless the Jews. We can begin by praying for the nation of Israel and supporting their right to hold Jerusalem in peace. "Pray for the peace of Jerusalem," wrote the psalmist, "May they prosper who love you" (Ps. 122:6). God clearly promises to bless the man, the church, or the nation that blesses the State of Israel or the Jewish people.

From the time of Joseph in Egypt to Einstein in America, God has placed Jewish people at the major intersections of history to bless the world. And I've got news for you—God isn't finished. The people of Israel and their Holy City will soon fill the major role in a coming world drama.

CHAPTER 3

HE WHO
CURSES ISRAEL . . .

The man or nation that lifts a voice or hand against Israel invites the wrath of God. The second half of God's promise to Abraham includes the words, "And I will curse him who curses you" (Gen. 12:3).

History will validate this truth: What you do or attempt to do to the Jewish people, God will do to you.

Egypt

Consider Egypt. This fertile black land produced a wealth that was the envy of the world. The Egyptians built pyramids we study and admire to this day, but the pharaoh of the Exodus enslaved and burdened the children of Abraham, drowning their sons and attempting to crush their spirits with hard labor.

God sent Moses as a deliverer. As the Hebrews crossed the Red Sea, God drowned the sons of the Egyptians en masse as they pursued the Jews. In the end, Pharaoh's mighty army was consumed by God's wrath as He drowned them in the Red Sea. Pharaoh himself was soon found floating faceup, grotesquely bloated in the heat of Egypt's sun, his sightless eyes staring at God, whom he could not see and would never know. His arrogant query, "Who is the Lord, that I should obey Him?" received a divine response. In one hour, the most powerful man on earth was reduced to fish food!

Exactly what Egypt did to Israel, God did to Egypt.

Amalekites

Consider the Amalekites. As the children of Israel came out of the wilderness, the people of Amalek fought with Israel in a place called Rephidim (Ex. 17:8). Their objective was to utterly destroy Israel. God responded with rage. He said to Moses, "Write this for a memorial in the book and recount it in the hearing of Joshua, that I will utterly blot out the remembrance of Amalek from under heaven. And Moses built an altar and called its name, The-LORD-Is-My-Banner; for he said, 'Because the LORD has sworn: the LORD will have war with Amalek from generation to generation'" (Ex. 17:14–16).

What happened to the Amalekites? Seven hundred years later, when Saul was king of Israel, God sent Samuel to the king with this message: "Thus says the LORD of hosts: 'I will punish Amalek for what he did to Israel, how he ambushed him on the way when he came up from Egypt. Now go and attack Amalek, and utterly destroy all that they have, and do not spare them. But kill both man and woman, infant and nursing child, ox and sheep, camel and donkey'" (1 Sam. 15:2–3). Exactly what the Amalekites tried to do to Israel, God did to the Amalekites.

Haman

Consider Haman, the Old Testament Hitler who, in the book of Esther, devised a plan to exterminate the Jews of Persia. At that point in history, most of the Jews of the world were living under Persian control. Haman's success would have produced a holocaust that would have prevented the Word of God from being written by Jewish authors *and* Jesus Christ from being born. Haman planned to hang Mordecai, the Jew he hated most. But Haman and his sons were hanged on the very gallows he had designed for the Seed of Abraham. Exactly what Haman planned for the Jews, God did to Haman.

Spain

Consider Spain. In the midst of its so-called Golden Era, Spain was a world power in the fourteenth century. More than 850,000 Jews lived in that country, and they were valuable members of society who made great contributions. But in 1492, as Queen Isabella sought to purify the aristocracy, the Spanish crown issued an Edict of Expulsion. All Jews who were willing to convert could remain in Spain, all others were forced, upon pain of death, to leave immediately.

The Seed of Abraham left Spain at the same time Columbus sailed across the Atlantic and discovered the New World that would become another haven for the Jews. Spain slipped into the graveyard of human history as its Golden Era ended. Spain learned what Egypt and the Amalekites had learned.

John Phillips states that "not until the coming of Hitler did the Jews suffer such widespread persecution as they did in Spain. The decline and fall of the Spanish Empire can be dated from the time that Spain expelled all its Jews."[1]

England

Consider England. England has vacillated in its treatment of the Jews. At one time every Jew in England, regardless of age or sex, was imprisoned, and all Jewish wealth was confiscated. Another time they were expelled from England and not allowed to return for 400 years.

In more recent history, consider the British publication of the infamous White Paper Policy that barred the Jews of the Holocaust from entering Israel. By force the British captured Jews who had gone to Israel to escape Hitler and the Nazi death camps. After capturing them, the British sent them back to Europe to die.

With limited arms and an indefatigable spirit, the Jews of Palestine vigorously fought the British to prevent the certain death of fellow Jews. The Irgun, a Jewish resistance group brilliantly led by Menachem Begin, fought the British in battles that led to a stalemate.

In 1947 Great Britain's ambassador to the United Nations voted against Israel becoming a state. When Israel achieved statehood despite the British veto, British officers led the Arab armies in an all-out military attack, trying to exterminate the State of Israel at its birth.

Depending on its treatment of the Jews, the influence and prestige of Great Britain have waxed and waned. The kingdom that once boasted the "sun would never set on its dominions" is now a very small kingdom indeed.

Adolf Hitler

Consider Adolf Hitler. As a spiritual leader in the Roman Catholic Church, Hitler made the following outrageous statements about the Jews:

- "In the heart of every Jew flows a traitor's blood."
- "A Jewish child over the age of seven can be baptized against its parents' will."
- "No Christian may be in the service of a Jew."
- "No Christian woman may nurse a Jewish infant; this would appear to the Church an outrage; it means bringing the devil into contact with the Holy Ghost." (In Hitler's view, of course, the devil was the Jewish infant.)
- "A Christian may not eat with a Jew."
- "Even in a prayer the Jew must be referred to as 'perfidious.'"
- "A Jew may not be a soldier; he may only be a clothes dealer, a ragman, a peddler, or a money lender."[2]

I'm sure you don't need me to remind you of Hitler's evil. Over six million innocent Jews perished at his hands, and what was his end? He shot himself and ordered his fanatical followers to burn his body in order to prevent the Russians from mocking him as Mussolini was mocked after death.

Hitler closed his eyes in death and stepped into eternity to meet a Rabbi named Jesus of Nazareth as his final judge. "I will curse him who curses you. . . ."

Stalin and the Jews

In his book *Exploring the World of the Jew*, John Phillips recounts the fascinating story of Russia's Joseph Stalin and the Jews. When Stalin came to power, he never forgot that his greatest rival had been Leon Trotsky, a Jew born Lev Davidovich Bronstein. During Stalin's reign of terror, no prominent Jew was ever safe from persecution.

In early 1953 Stalin's secret police arrested nine "terrorist doctors," six of whom were Jewish, and charged them with plotting to murder Soviet leaders. The plot was a total fabrication, but Stalin laid careful plans to use this ridiculous story to proceed with his goals for the extermination of all Russian Jews.

Stalin read a statement to the assembled politburo outlining his plan of extermination. The Russian doctors would be tried, then hanged in Moscow. This would be followed by three days of "spontaneous rioting" against the Jews. The government would then step in and separate the Jews from the Russian people and ship the Jews to Siberia. Two-thirds of the captives, however, would never arrive—the "angry Russian people" would kill them along the way. The third who did arrive would die swiftly in slave labor camps.

Stalin's proposal was met with stunned silence. His plans proceeded, and the nine doctors were only days away from their execution when Stalin suffered a stroke on March 5.

On April 3, *Pravda* announced that the nine doctors had been declared "not guilty" and released. I have to agree with John Phillips's statement about this situation: "There is sometimes a grim appropriateness about the timing of God."[3] God watches over the apple of His eye.

Contemporary Evidence of God's Justice

Adolf Hitler systematically murdered six million Jews because good men did nothing and said nothing in the day of trouble.

In 1985, when I stood at Checkpoint Charlie and looked at the Berlin Wall, the young German woman the military had assigned as my personal guide asked, "Pastor Hagee, why did God allow the Communists to build a wall around the German people?"

My answer jolted her out of her shoes. "God allowed the Communists to build a wall around the Germans because your parents built a wall around the Jews," I told her. "What you do to the Jewish people, God will do to you."

As she gasped in surprise, I pointed to the fence dividing East and West Berlin. "Look at that fence," I said. "It's the same height as the fence at Dachau. It's electrified just like the fence at Dachau. It has guard towers in the center with attack dogs trained to rip out your throat—just like Dachau. God has done to you what you did to the Jews!"

Why should America support Israel? Because the blessing of God depends upon it. We do not have to agree with every political position Israel takes, but if we, as a nation, make Israel's life grievous by design, we will face the wrath of God.

The Jews' Divine Preservation

Mark Twain wrote the following in September 1898:

> If the statistics are right, the Jews constitute but one percent of the human race. It suggests a nebulous dim

puff of star dust lost in the blaze of the Milky Way. Properly the Jew ought hardly to be heard of; but he is heard of. He is as prominent on the planet as any other people, and his commercial importance is extravagantly out of proportion to the smallness of his bulk. His contributions to the world's list of great names in literature, science, art, music, finance, medicine, and abstruse learning are also away out of proportion to the weakness of his numbers. . . . The Egyptian, the Babylonian, and the Persian rose, filled the planet with sound and splendor, then faded to dreamstuff and passed away; the Greek and the Roman followed, and made a fast noise, and they are gone; other peoples have sprung up and held their torch high for a time, but it burned out, and they sit in twilight now, or have vanished. The Jew saw them all, beat them all, and is now what he always was, exhibiting no decadence, no infirmities of age, no weakening of his parts, no slowing of his energies, no dulling of his alert and aggressive mind. All things are mortal but the Jew; all other forces pass, but he remains. What is the secret of his immortality?[4]

I can explain the secret in just seven words: Israel is the apple of God's eye!

Where are the ancient civilizations today? Gone with the wind. They are little more than historical footnotes recognized by scholars and librarians. Where are the Jews? They flourish in Israel and around the globe. Why? Because He that keeps Israel never slumbers or sleeps. He keeps watch over His beloved ones.

The Battle for Jerusalem

The battle for Israel is now on the agenda of the National Council of Churches. In my office I have a copy of a one-page ad placed in the *New York Times* by the NCC.[5] In the name of peace, the ad calls for a "shared Jerusalem."

A shared Jerusalem? Never! A "shared Jerusalem" means control of the Holy City would be wrested away from the Jewish people and given, at least in part, to the Palestine Liberation Organization. I say "never," not because I dislike Arab people or Palestinians, but because the Word of God says it is God's will for Jerusalem to be under the exclusive control of the Jewish people until Messiah comes. According to Genesis chapters 12, 13, 15, 17, 26, and 28, only the Jewish people have a legitimate claim to the city. That's not my viewpoint, that's God's opinion! God doesn't care what the United Nations thinks or what the NCC believes. He gave Jerusalem to the nation of Israel, and it is theirs.

As Christian friends of Israel, we must urge the United States government to continue its unshakable support for the State of Israel and the Jewish people as the only legitimate heirs to the city of Jerusalem. Isaiah 62:6–7 urges us: "You who make mention of the LORD, do not keep silent, / And give Him no rest till He establishes / And till He makes Jerusalem a praise in the earth."

If we can learn anything from the example of those who cursed Israel, it is this: If America turns its back in Israel's hour of need, Israel will survive—but America will not. God could crush this nation economically by sending a depression that will make the crash of 1929 look like a walk in the park.

If we want to experience the unlimited favor of God, if we want to experience an explosion of prosperity, if we want a fresh outpouring of the Holy Spirit, we must bless Israel and oppose those who would curse the apple of God's eye.

CHAPTER 4

THE CRUCIFIXION OF THE JEWS

Of all the bigotries that savage the human temper there is none so stupid as [anti-Semitism]. In the sight of these fanatics, Jews . . . can do nothing right.

If they are rich, they are birds of prey. If they are poor, they are vermin.

If they are in favor of war, that is because they want to exploit the bloody feuds of Gentiles to their own profit. If they are anxious for peace they are either instinctive cowards or traitors.

If they give generously—and there are no more liberal givers than the Jews—they are doing it for some selfish purpose of their own. If they don't give, then what would one expect of a Jew?[1]

—David Lloyd George, British prime minister

The Jewish people have been persecuted throughout history. They were enslaved in Egypt, deported by the Assyrians, attacked by Nebuchadnezzar, nearly purged by Haman, and oppressed by Roman rule. The crucifixion of the Jews began with the pulpit propaganda of the early church fathers: Eusebius of Caesarea, Cyril, Chrysostom, Augustine, Origen, Justin, and Jerome. These men carried out an orchestrated and enormous campaign against the Jews, portraying them as "killers of Christ, plague carriers, demons, children of the devil, bloodthirsty pagans who are as deceitful as Judas was relentless."

The church fathers spelled the traitor's name as *Jewdas*. As Pope Gelasius I (A.D. 492–96) philosophized: "In the Bible the whole is often named after the part; as Judas was called a devil and the devil's workman, he gives his name to the whole race."[2]

How can we forget that Jesus was a Jew? That the apostles were Jewish? In condemning "the whole race," the church fathers condemned the apostles and the Savior they worshiped!

Desiderius Erasmus, an ordained Roman Catholic priest and one of the leading figures of the Renaissance, once stated, "If to hate Jews is to be a good Christian, we are all good Christians."[3]

Sometimes the Jews were hated for no good reason. One particular story about the Roman emperor Hadrian illustrates the depth of his hatred for the Jews. It is said that a Jew passed in front of Hadrian and greeted him. The emperor asked, "Who are you?"

The man answered, "I am a Jew."

"How dare a Jew pass in front of Hadrian and greet him?" the emperor roared. "Off with his head!"

Moments later, another Jew, who had not seen this exchange, passed in front of the emperor and did *not* greet him. Hadrian called out and asked, "Who are you?"

The man answered, "I am a Jew."

"How dare a Jew pass in front of Hadrian without giving a greeting?" he stormed. "Off with his head!"

Hadrian's senators said, "We don't understand your actions. How can you put to death the man who greeted you as well as the man who did not greet you?"

Hadrian scornfully replied: "Do you dare to advise me how I am to deal with those I hate?"[4]

The Jewish people were portrayed by the church fathers as bloodthirsty torturers of the Savior, pitiless killers, traitors who sold their souls for thirty pieces of silver, money changers who desecrated the temple, and more cruel than beasts because they demanded that the legs of the dying Christ be broken. In short, early church fathers taught that Jews were sons of the devil.

The church's earliest historian, Eusebius of Caesarea, declared his intention in *Church History* "to recount the misfortunes which immediately came upon the whole Jewish nation in consequence of their plots against the Savior."[5]

Eusebius only set the stage for his contemporaries. Saint Gregory of Nyssa mounted his pulpit ranting about the Jews:

> Slayers of the Lord, murderers of the prophets, adversaries of God, haters of God, men who show contempt for the law, foes of grace, enemies of their fathers' faith, advocates of the devil, brood of vipers, slanderers, scoffers, men whose minds are in darkness, leaven of the Pharisees, assembly of demons, sinners, wicked men, stoners and haters of righteousness.[6]

The Golden Mouth

The venom of Christian hatred for the Jews reached its crescendo with the coming of Saint John Chrysostom (A.D.

345–407), known as the "bishop with the golden mouth."
One of the first to describe the Jews as "killers of Christ,"
for centuries Chrysostom's anti-Semitic venom was considered classic Roman church reading.

"How can Christians," he wrote, "dare have the slight-
est converse with Jews, the most miserable of all men?"[7]
He went on to write:

> The Jews are the most worthless of all men. They are
> lecherous, greedy, rapacious. They are perfidious mur-
> derers of Christ. They worship the devil, their religion is
> a sickness. The Jews are the odious assassins of Christ
> and for killing God there is no expiation possible, no
> indulgence or pardon. Christians may never cease
> vengeance, and the Jew must live in servitude forever.
> God always hated the Jews. It is incumbent upon all
> Christians to hate the Jews.[8]

Chrysostom wrote that the Jewish synagogue was a "theater and a house of prostitution," a "cavern of brigands," a
"repair of wild beasts," and "the domicile of the devil."[9] This
Christian wrote that he hated the Jews because of their "odi-
ous assassination of Christ."[10] For this, he said, "there is no
expiation possible, no indulgence, no pardon. . . . God hates
the Jews and always hated the Jews. . . . I hate the Jews also
because they outrage the law."[11]

The natural progression for popular hatred is action.
Religious belief fosters deep feeling, and deep feeling demands
that action be taken to support that basic belief. Christian
action toward the Jews exploded with a demonic violence
beyond comprehension.

At Easter, when the Christian clergy would inflame
the passions of the faithful with the vengeful message that
the Jews killed Christ, the congregants would race out of

the church toward the Jewish quarter with clubs and beat Jews to death for what they did to Jesus on the cross.[12]

In some churches it became an annual custom at Easter to drag a Jew into the church and slap him on the face before the altar. Malcolm Hay explains:

> This ceremony was sometimes carried out with excessive vigor; on one occasion, recounts a monkish chronicler (without, however, expressing any disapproval), a distinguished nobleman who was taking part as chief celebrant "knocked out the eyes and the brains of the perfidious one (disbelieving Jew), who fell dead on the spot . . . his brethren from the synagogue took the body out of the Church and buried it."[13]

The torrent of hate continued in medieval times.

The Crusades

While some knights undoubtedly fit the romantic and popular notion of a chivalrous warrior on a holy pilgrimage to fight for a godly cause, most Christians are unaware of the tragic truth. The crusaders were, in fact, seasoned soldiers operating under a blanket of papal protection known as the indulgence. In issuing a call for the First Crusade, the Council of Clermont and Pope Urban summarized the benefits for a potential participant. The action the crusaders were about to undertake, they wrote, would be a penance so inclusive that it would pay back to God not only the debts of punishment owed for some past sins, but would also "pay for" sins recently committed.[14] In other words, the crusaders could kill, maim, rape, and steal from the Jews with impunity—and God would turn a blind eye to their sins. Any potential crusader who had been excommunicated from the church would be welcomed back into the fold with full forgiveness.

Not only were the crusaders promised forgiveness of *sin,* they also were promised the forgiveness of *debt.* Any man who answered the call of the Crusade could consider all of his financial debts to any Jewish creditor canceled. As a bonus, Christian crusaders were permitted to rob the Jews on the journey to and from Jerusalem.

During the First Crusade to the Holy Land, the crusading armies left a trail of Jewish blood across Europe. Within a three-month period, 12,000 Jews were slaughtered in Germany as the crusaders screamed, "The Jews have killed our Savior. They must convert or be killed."

Some Jewish communities were given the opportunity to save their lives by meeting the crusaders' demands for gold and silver. Those who could not meet the ransom demands were butchered "by the will of God." Others ran to the synagogue for sanctuary, locked the doors, said a final prayer, and then killed their wives and children quickly, lest the cross-carrying crusaders torture and butcher them. The fathers committed suicide to preserve the sanctity of the name of Jehovah God.

Not all the crusaders went to the Holy Land. Pope Urban II actively urged Catalan nobles who had taken the sign of the cross to fulfill their vows in Spain. In return for aiding the Church of Tarragona, they were given indulgences and promised the forgiveness of sin.[15]

Christians throughout Europe were armed and given an official holy pardon to kill, loot, and destroy anyone they considered an infidel. Immediately, appalling violence was unleashed against the Jews of northern France and the Rhineland, a region along the Rhine River in western Germany. Many of these crusaders, poor warriors who could not afford to mount a campaign to the Holy Land, were exceedingly brutal, vicious, and ferocious.[16] These were not genteel knights schooled in honor and chivalry. These were hungry, brutal, vengeful men intent upon rape and murder.

In the Rhineland city of Worms—a town between Mannheim and Mainz—lies an ancient Jewish cemetery. Some of the graves date from the eleventh century and three days in May 1096 when 800 Jews were massacred by crusaders setting out for the Promised Land.[17]

Crusaders under the command of Count Emich of Leiningren, a leading noble from Swabia, pulled the Jews from their houses, dragged them through the streets, and gave them the option of conversion or death. "Count Emich's fervor as a crusader was in no doubt, but it was hysterical and ignorant," writes Malcolm Billings. "He claimed to have a cross miraculously branded on his flesh, and some of his followers later marched behind a remarkable goose that was supposed to have been imbued with the Holy Spirit."[18]

Emich began to attack Jews near Speyer before he arrived at Worms, and 1,000 Jews fell victim to his campaign of terror in the town of Mainz. "It was not just a spontaneous outburst of greed and hooliganism by a leaderless collection of peasants," writes Billings. "That comforting thought is now dismissed by historians who believe that many nobles and experienced captains from Swabia, the Low Countries, France and England, who had joined Emich's crusade, encouraged the mobs."[19]

Arguing that the Jews were the race responsible for Christ's crucifixion, the nobles demonstrated how the clergy's call to free "Christ's inheritance," or Jerusalem, became distorted in the minds of listeners. One count, a man called Dithmar, reportedly said he would not leave Germany until he had killed a Jew. "The road to the Holy Land," reports Billings, "ran through what Jews later came to describe as the first Holocaust."[20]

As Godfrey of Bouillon took Jerusalem in the summer of 1099, he and his men spent their first week slaughtering Jews. When more than 900 Jewish women and children ran to their synagogue for safety, the crusaders set it ablaze. As the screams for mercy mingled with the roaring inferno, the crusaders marched around the synagogue singing "Christ, we adore Thee."[21] After taking Communion, the men who carried the cross into Jerusalem heartily devoted the day to exterminating Jewish men, women, and children—killing more than 10,000.[22] In a search for loot and treasure, Christian soldiers killed every man, woman, and child they met. When Raymond of Aguilers walked through the city, he saw "piles of heads, hands and feet . . . in the houses and streets, and indeed there was a running to and fro of men and knights over the corpses."[23]

Unbelievable? Yes, but even more, unconscionable! No wonder the word *crusade* has the power to nauseate some Jews.

Turn to the pages of Sir Walter Scott's great classic *Ivanhoe*. The story's plot is rife with expressions of hate and barbarism as the Christian Knights Templar prepare to burn a Jewish woman at the stake—another example of the prejudice against Jews during medieval times.

In 1208 Pope Innocent III wrote, "The Jews, against whom the blood of Jesus calls out . . . must remain vagabonds upon the earth, until their faces be covered with shame and they seek the name of Jesus Christ the Lord."[24]

And G. K. Chesterton, a twentieth-century Catholic author whose works are used in parochial schools, once expressed his regret that "the Crusaders who slaughtered

Jewish men, women and children could not be canonized [named as saints]."[25]

The Fourth Lateran Council

In November 1215, in response to the call of Pope Innocent III, the Fourth Lateran Council met in Rome. More than 1,000 delegates met in stormy sessions to determine what the official relationship between Christians and Jews should be. The official Christian policy, issued in a formal declaration, supported the conduct of the Roman church for centuries to come.

Concerned that Christians and Jews would intermingle, the Fourth Lateran Council decreed that all Jews must wear a "Jewish badge." Also, "That the crime of such a sinful mixture shall no longer find evasion or cover under pretext of error, we order that the Jews of both sexes, in all Christian lands and at all times, shall be publicly differentiated from the rest of the population by the quality of their garment, especially since this is ordained by Moses."[26]

The reference to Moses refers to the fact that Moses instructed the men of Israel to make prayer shawls (Num. 15:37–41) to be worn by adult men. Jesus Christ wore a prayer shawl from His thirteenth birthday until the day of His crucifixion. Taking this instruction completely out of context, the church fathers used Moses' instruction to force all Jews of both sexes to dress distinctively. When Hitler came to power, he used this long-established policy to force the Jews to wear a yellow Star of David, marking them for abuse and execution.

The Fourth Lateran Council also decreed that Jews could not hold public office. Following the spirit of this edict, on April 7, 1933, the Third Reich passed a law titled "Law for the Restoration of the Professional Civil Service." This lofty-sounding piece of legislation was the legal instrument through which the Nazis dismissed every Jew in Germany working at a civil service job. Overnight, thousands of Jews found themselves without jobs.

Finally, the Fourth Lateran Council ruled that Jews must tithe to the Roman church. Ten percent of any Jew's income was to be paid to the church because the Jews were now owners of lands that had previously belonged to Christians. The edict states: "And under the threat of the same penalty [social and economic boycott] we decree that Jews should be compelled to make good the tithes and dues owed to the Churches which the Churches have been accustomed to receive from the houses and other possessions of the Christians before they came into possession of the Jews, regardless of the circumstances, so that the Church be preserved against loss."[27]

Forcing Jews to tithe was nothing short of extortion, but the church could not afford a loss of revenue. The church was far from finished with the Jews. The church officially endorsed the ghetto system in 1555, in which Jews had to live apart from Christians. Under Pope Clement VIII, the persecution of Jews became a fixed part of papal policy.[28]

The Spanish Inquisition

In 1235 the Council of Arles had introduced a yellow circular patch that Jews were required to wear, and in 1391 massacres of Jews had occurred throughout Spain. Thousands of Jews converted to Christianity in order to avoid massacre, yet the Spaniards remained suspicious of these *conversos*. These people were hated by the Jews for being traitors to Judaism and despised by the church. All attempts to separate the new converts from Judaism via legislation, ghettoization, or education were fruitless.

The Spanish Inquisition struck the Jews like a bolt of lightning out of a blue sky. Queen Isabella and her husband, Ferdinand, were faced with three pressing problems: a political desire to achieve religious conformity in Spain, the failure of pressure to force Jews and Muslims to convert to Christianity, and a profound fear that insincere converts would somehow contaminate the Christian faith.[29] In other words, the Spaniards were afraid of the Jews—particularly since many Jews had intermarried with Spaniards and achieved considerable financial power and social status.

In 1474 Isabella ascended to the throne of Castile, and in 1479 Ferdinand succeeded to that of Aragon. In order to unite these two kingdoms and reassert the predominance of the aristocracy, Isabella and Ferdinand appealed to Pope Sixtus IV to establish an Inquisitor General. Fray Tomás de Torquemada was appointed, and the Inquisition was revived.

The king and queen gave the Jewish population of Spain exactly four months to decide whether they wanted to leave the country or to remain and convert to Christianity. Between 165,000 and 400,000 Jews left Spain before the end of July, many of them abandoning their businesses and paying exorbitant taxes to port officials as they departed. Despite the threat of persecution, as many as 50,000 Jews decided to remain in Spain.[30]

Those who remained faced a nightmare. Under the fanatical leadership of de Torquemada, treatment of the Jews reached levels of torture the world would not see again until Hitler's sadistic Nazi SS Corps blossomed into its fullest level of madness. In the effort to determine who was truly a loyal Christian and who was not, Jewish children were choked to death in the presence of their parents. Women's naked breasts were seared with hot irons to make them betray their husbands. The bodies of men were stretched on the rack where they were pulled in half, forcing them through excruciating pain to denounce their wives and children as false converts.

Published manuals of the Inquisition listed hints on how to spot a "backsliding Jew." Recorded along with these so-called insights were instructions on how to extend and intensify the suffering of the Jewish subject by flame, garrote, rack, whip, and needle. This cruelty, performed in the name of Christ, reached a pinnacle of expertise that left Reinhard Heydrich and Adolf Eichmann little to add for the Third Reich.

Historian Dagobert Runes notes:

> Neither illness nor pregnancy could spare a woman from the bit of the Inquisition instruments wielded by the protectors of the loving Christ. Since all the property of the convicted fell to the Inquisition corporation, to be shared equally by their majesties, there was an added incentive to intensify the Inquisition. Denouncers were well rewarded, and a person denounced was a person indicted and convicted, since no living creature could withstand the refined methods of punishment the clerics had devised. Every single part of the human anatomy had been carefully studied and experimented upon to find those most sensitive to pain.[31]

The Inquisition and its horror continued for years. As late as 1568, a Spanish woman was arrested on the grounds of not eating pork and changing her linen on Saturday. On the testimony of her neighbors, she was arrested and tortured, accused of being Jewish.[32]

The Spanish Inquisition gave birth to the phrase *limpieza de sangre,* meaning "purity of blood." The purity of blood and racial background were major considerations in the trial of an accused Jew. Because the Spaniards were intent upon purifying their aristocracy, those who could not prove that they were of pure Christian descent for at least three generations were doomed to unspeakable torture and death.

Hitler's blood-purity rule, which demanded that Germans prove they had no Jewish ancestors in the three previous generations, was clearly formulated from the example of the church 500 years before Hitler came to power.

Prejudice in the Reformation

"The worst evil genius of Germany," wrote Dean Inge, "is not Hitler, or Bismarck, or Frederick the Great, but Martin Luther." Luther's hatred for the Jews "was intensified by his intellectual vanity and the vigor of his faith, which, like that of many others before and since his time, was united to an equally unshakable conviction that anyone who did not agree with him was an obstinate enemy of the Holy Spirit who deliberately closed his eyes to the truth."[33]

Luther—who at one time wrote of the Jews, "We are aliens and in-laws, they are blood relatives, cousins, and brothers of our Lord"[34]—changed his views when the children of Israel did not convert to his reformed Christianity and join his assault on the Roman church. Luther said of the Jews, "All the blood kindred of Christ burn in Hell, and they are rightly served, even according to their own words they spoke to Pilate."[35]

Moreover, "The only Bible you have any right to," he told the Jews, "is that concealed beneath the sow's tail; the letters that drop from it you are free to eat and drink."[36] What a crude insult to the people of God!

The most vicious, hateful statements Luther ever wrote are found in his tract "On the Jews and Their Lies." In this work he wrote, "Know this, Christian, you have no greater enemy than the Jew." His tract called for the enslavement of the Jews because they were children of the devil and should never touch a Christian's hand. Luther demanded that their synagogues be burned to the ground, their books destroyed, their homes laid waste, their cash and treasure of silver and gold be taken from them, their rabbis be forbidden to teach, and "their tongues be cut out from their throats." He also advised that "young and strong Jews and Jewesses be given the flail, the ax, the hoe, the spade, the distaff, and spindle, and let them earn their bread by the sweat of their noses as is enjoined upon Adam's children. We ought to drive the lazy bones out of our system. . . ."[37]

"If, however," Luther continued, "we are afraid that they might harm us personally, or our wives, children, servants, cattle, etc., then let us apply the same cleverness [expulsion] as the other nations, such as France, Spain, Bohemia, etc., and settle with them for that which they have extorted from us, and after having divided up fairly let us drive them out of the country for all time.

"To sum up, dear princes and nobles who have Jews in your domains, if this advice of mine does not suit you, then find a better one so that you and we may all be free from this insufferable devilish burden—the Jews."[38]

Two days after writing this, Martin Luther died.

When the Nazis placed the Jews in ghetto stables and camps, they were following Luther's precepts. When they burned Jewish synagogues, homes, and schools, they carried out Luther's will. When the Germans robbed the Jews of their possessions, they did Luther's bidding. When the Germans reduced the Jews to concentration camp slavery, they followed Luther's teaching.

Adolf Hitler loved Luther's theology. His Nazi murder machine showed "a proper appreciation of the continuity of their history when they declared that the first large-scale Nazi program, in November, 1938, was a pious operation performed in honor of the anniversary of Luther's birthday."[39]

Twentieth-Century Persecution

Adolf Hitler publicly praised the later teachings of Martin Luther and carried out Luther's recommended attack against the Jews. With the teachings of the early church fathers to support him, Hitler set his plan for genocide into motion. The unwillingness of other countries to offer refuge to Jews convinced Hitler that he had international support for his crusade and that he was doing a good thing.

Roy Eckert has demonstrated how the Nazis prepared the German people for extermination of the Jews by exploiting the crucifixion theme with its corollary of unending divine judgment. The labeling of Jews as "Christ-Killers" motivated the German people to be silent and turn their backs while the Nazis marched Abraham's descendants toward mass extermination camps and finally into the ovens.

In 1942 officials in the Russian army examined Kerch, one of the largest Nazi extermination pits. One of their officers filed this report:

> It was discovered that this trench, one kilometer in length, four meters wide, and two meters deep, was filled to overflowing with bodies of women, children, old men, and boys and girls in their teens. Near the

trench were frozen pools of blood. Children's caps, toys, ribbons, torn off buttons, gloves, milk bottles, and rubber comforters, small shoes, galoshes, together with torn off hands and feet, and other parts of human bodies, were lying nearby. Everything was spattered with blood and brains.[40]

How could this madness happen in one of the most civilized and cultured nations on earth? How could such crimes be justified in the minds of German Christians? These heinous acts were excused with the oft-repeated phrase, "the Jews are the Christ-killers!"

The world's finest scholars have chronicled Hitler's atrocities toward the Jews. There is no purpose in retracing his bloody steps, but I want you to see that church policy shaped the policy of the Third Reich. When Hitler signed the Concordant with the Roman Church, he said, "I am only continuing the work of the Catholic Church."[41]

Let's examine the historical record.

ROMAN CHURCH POLICY	NAZI POLICY
1. Prohibition of intermarriage and of sexual intercourse between Christians and Jews, Synod of Elvira, A.D. 306.	1. Law for the Protection of German Blood and Honor, September 15, 1935.
2. Jews and Christians not permitted to eat together, Synod of Elvira, A.D. 306.	2. Jews barred from dining cars, December 30, 1939.
3. Jews not allowed to hold public office, Synod of Clermont, A.D. 535. Also Fourth Lateran Council, 1215.	3. Law for the Restoration of the Professional Civil Service, April 7, 1933, by which Jews were expelled from office and civil service jobs.

4. Jews not allowed to employ Christian servants or possess Christian slaves, Third Synod of Orleans, A.D. 538.

5. Jews not permitted to show themselves in the streets during Passion Week, Third Synod of Orleans, A.D. 538.

6. Burning of the Talmud and other books, Twelfth Synod of Toledo, A.D. 681.

7. Christians not permitted to patronize Jewish doctors, Trulanic Synod, A.D. 692.

8. Jews obligated to pay taxes for support of the church to the same extent as Christians, Fourth Lateran Council, 1215.

9. Jews not permitted to be plaintiffs or witnesses against Christians in the courts, Third Lateran Council, 1179.

10. Jews not permitted to withhold inheritance from descendants who had accepted Christianity, Third Lateran Council, 1179.

11. Jews must wear a distinctive badge, Fourth Lateran Council, 1215.

12. Construction of new synagogues prohibited, Council of Oxford, 1222.

---

4. Law for the Protection of German Blood and Honor, September 15, 1935, forbade Germans from hiring Jews.

5. Decree authorizing local authorities to bar Jews from the streets on certain days (Nazi holidays), December 3, 1938.

6. Nazi book burnings in Germany.

7. Decree of July 25, 1938, forbidding Germans from patronizing Jewish doctors.

8. Jews to pay a special tax in lieu of donations for Party purposes imposed on Nazis, December 24, 1940.

9. Jews not permitted to institute civil suits.

10. Decree empowering the Justice Ministry to void wills offending the "sound judgment of the people," July 31, 1938.

11. Decree forcing all Jews to wear the yellow Star of David, September 1, 1941.

12. Destruction of synagogues in entire Reich, November 10, 1938. The Jews refer to this night as *Kristalnacht*.

13. Christians not permitted to attend Jewish ceremonies, Synod of Vienna, 1267.

13. Friendly relations with Jews prohibited, October 24, 1941.

14. Jews forced to live in ghettos away from Christians, Synod of Breslau, 1267.

14. Jews forced to live in ghettos, order of Heydrich, September 21, 1939.

15. Jews not permitted to obtain academic degrees, Council of Basel, 1434.

15. All Jews expelled from schools and universities throughout the Third Reich with the Law Against Overcrowding of German Schools and Universities, April 25, 1933.

16. Mass extermination of the Jews in the Crusades. Fourth Lateran Council called upon secular powers to "exterminate all heretics," 1215. The Inquisition burned Jews at the stake while confiscating their property, 1478.

16. Hitler's Final Solution called for the systematic slaughter of every Jew in Europe. He took their homes, their jobs, their possessions (even the gold fillings in their teeth), and finally, their lives. His justification? "It's the will of God and the work of the Church."

The Holocaust did not begin with Hitler lining up the Jews outside the gas chambers. It began with religious leaders sowing the seeds of hatred toward Jews within their congregations. "I am convinced," wrote Pierre van Passen, "that Hitler neither could nor would have done to the Jewish people what he has done . . . if we had not actively prepared the way for him by our own unfriendly attitude to the Jews, by our selfishness and by the anti-Semitic teaching in our churches and schools."[42]

At the Nuremberg trials for major war criminals, a German general was asked how one of the world's most advanced societies could systematically murder six million people. He answered, "I am of the opinion that when for years, for decades, the doctrine is preached that Jews are not even human, such an outcome is inevitable."[43]

Hitler's Testimony

Most Christians have difficulty understanding why Jewish people think of Adolf Hitler as a Christian. Most Jews think Hitler was a Christian for the same reason the Southern Baptists think Billy Graham is a Christian. Billy Graham attended and graduated from a Christian school. He gives dynamic public testimony that he is a Christian in good standing with the Southern Baptist Convention. When he preaches, he quotes the Bible and announces that he is called of God to carry out His mission. Billy Graham's life and ministry verify that he is a man of God.

By no means am I meaning to equate Adolf Hitler with Billy Graham, but consider this: Adolf Hitler attended a Christian school under the tutelage of Padre Bernard Groner. Hitler told a friend that as a small boy he most wanted to become a priest. After he had written *Mein Kampf* (*My Battle*), a text of his political and personal philosophy (including his desire to exterminate the Jews), he gave public testimony that "I am now as before a Catholic and will always remain so."[44]

In December 1941 he gave his testimony when he announced his decision to implement the Final Solution after the bombing of Pearl Harbor. He ordered that the "killings should be done as humanely as possible." This was in line with his conviction that he was observing God's injunction to cleanse the world of vermin. He carried within him the Catholic teaching that Jews were Christ-killers. The mass extermination, therefore, could be carried out without a twinge of conscience, because he was merely acting as the avenging hand of God.[45]

The Jewish people believe Hitler was a Christian because the princes of the church scrambled to secure his favor. "Hitler knows how to guide the ship," announced Monsignor Ludwig Kaas. "Even before he was Chancellor, I met him frequently and was greatly impressed by his clear thinking, by his way of facing realities while upholding his ideals, which are noble. . . . It matters little who rules so long as order is maintained."[46]

The Vatican was so appreciative of being recognized as a full partner in his efforts that it asked God to bless the Reich. On a more practical level, it ordered German bishops to swear allegiance to the Nationalist Socialist regime. The oath concluded with these significant words: "In the performance of my spiritual office and in my solicitude for the welfare and interest of the German Reich, I will endeavor to avoid all detrimental acts that might endanger it."[47]

Perhaps the Jewish people consider Hitler a Christian because the Roman Catholic church honored Hitler on his fiftieth birthday. Special masses were celebrated in every German church "to implore God's blessing upon the Führer and the people." The pope also sent his congratulations.[48]

During World War II, the church bells of Europe rang for Hitler's birthday and his military victories. His picture hung in every Roman Catholic school in the Third Reich. When an assassination attempt on Hitler's demonized life failed, the pope sent a letter stating that God had spared his life. The Catholic press throughout the Reich piously declared that it "was the miraculous working of Providence which had protected the Führer."[49] Cardinal Innitzer of

Vienna pledged his loyalty to the Third Reich and asked Austrians to join Hitler in his "holy cause."

When Hitler's war machine crushed the brave but ill-prepared Polish army, Nazi newspapers carried a photo of the debris with a Scripture quoted beneath: "The Lord defeated them with horse, horsemen, and chariot."[50] When Hitler gave speeches in public, he was anointed with a supernatural demonic spirit in which he quoted sacred Scripture to justify his messianic mission to purge Germany and Europe of the Jews "once and for all." His mesmerizing voice thundered over the heads of his electrified audience as he proclaimed, "I'm doing the will of God."

After more than forty years following the Allies' liberation of the Jews from Auschwitz, not one word of official condemnation or excommunication concerning Hitler has been expressed by the Vatican. Why? Because six million people were murdered by baptized Christians in good standing with the church.

During our generation, one-third of the Jews of Europe were choked to death on Zyklon-B gas. On July 20, 1933, as Hitler signed the Concordant of Collaboration with the Vatican, he said, "I am only continuing the work of the Catholic Church, to isolate the Jews and fight their influence." Hitler later described the Concordant as an "unrestricted acceptance of National Socialism by the Vatican."

The bishops of Austria and Germany blessed the swastika flags of the Third Reich and pledged their loyalty "voluntarily and without duress." The Vicar of Christ looked out his window from the Vatican and watched the Nazis drag helpless women and innocent Jewish children from their homes, and load them like cattle into trucks for transport to a death of horror in the extermination camps.

What happened to those Jewish children? Read these reports from the Nuremberg trials:

> They killed them with their parents, in groups and alone. They killed them in children's homes and hospitals, burying them alive and in graves, throwing them into flames, stabbing them with bayonets, poisoning them, conducting experiments upon them, extracting their blood for the use of the German army, throwing them into prison and Gestapo torture chambers and concentration camps where the children died from hunger, torture, and epidemic diseases.[51]

> Very frequently women would hide their children under their clothes, but of course when we found them we would send the children in to be exterminated.[52]

> Mothers in the throes of childbirth shared cars with those infected with tuberculosis or venereal disease. Babies, when born, were hurled out of these cars' windows.[53]

> At that time, when the greatest number of Jews were exterminated in the gas chambers, an order was issued that the children were to be thrown into the crematory ovens, or into the crematory ditches, without previous asphyxiation with gas. . . . The children were thrown in alive; their cries could be heard all over the camp.[54]

If Jesus and his family, all Jews, had lived in Berlin, Germany, in 1940, they would have been prodded into cattle cars at bayonet point and shipped to Auschwitz.

Arriving at Auschwitz, they would have been ushered into a gas chamber en masse to scratch and claw at the walls in terror as they frantically gasped for breath. The gas chamber was camouflaged as a shower—an ordinary room, but fitted with airtight doors and windows, into which gas piping had been laid. The compressed-gas containers and the regulating equipment were located outside and operated by the Nazi doctors on duty.

Jesus Christ, along with Mary, Joseph, James, and John, would have been led into the gas chambers on the pretext that they needed a shower after their long train ride from Berlin to Auschwitz. They would have slowly choked to death on the gas for fifteen long minutes, still standing grotesquely erect because they were packed too tightly to fall. In dying, their bodies would have been covered with sweat and urine. Their legs would have been smeared with feces. This Nazi Final Solution would have been carried out by men whose leaders told them, "This is the will of God."

After death, the teeth of Jesus and His family would have been broken out with pliers or hammers in a search for gold fillings, their hair cut off to make mattresses, their flesh skinned for Nazi lamp shades. Their remains would have been thrown into an oven and cremated, the stench belching out through massive smokestacks that covered the countryside.

That night, the skies of Auschwitz would glow red with the ashes of dead Jews, the family of our Lord. Those ashes were often used to make soap or fertilizer for the Third Reich. Think of it! Fertilizing your roses with the ashes of the Virgin Mary, soaping your body with the remains of the apostle John, sleeping on a mattress of human hair provided by the apostle Peter.

But Hitler and his cronies couldn't see the Jews as the family of Jesus Christ. According to Hitler, Jesus was the first Jew hater. "Christ was the greatest early fighter in the battle against the world enemy, the Jews," Hitler ranted.[55]

Hitler knew that when his goose-stepping killers knelt to pray in Saint Matthew's Cathedral, they must not see Saint

Matthew as Jewish. How could they possibly leave the sanctuary of worship and then savagely machine-gun Jews in an open ditch? How could they kneel at the statue of the Virgin Mary holding the Christ child in her arms and then mercilessly slaughter one and a half million Jewish babies?

The mystery is solved by Hitler's own words. In 1927, when he dictated *Mein Kampf* to his aide, he ended his work by saying, "The great masses of the people . . . will more easily fall victims to a great lie than to a small one."[56]

Russian Anti-Semitism

The Russian word *pogrom*, which pertains to the massacre of a helpless people, passed into the international lexicon after the devastation of the Jews in the Ukraine in 1903. The Russian nation has been persecuting Jews since the time of the czars. In the span of time between the two world wars, the entire Jewish population of the Russian Western War Zone—including the old, sick, and children—were forcibly evacuated into the interior of the country on twelve hours' notice.

In August 1924 *Dawn* magazine reported:

> Wholesale slaughter and burials alive, rape and torture, became not merely commonplace but the order of the day. There were pogroms that lasted a week; and in several cases the systematic and diabolic torture and outrage and carnage were continued for a month. In many populous Jewish communities there were no Jewish survivors left to bury the dead, and thousands of Jewish wounded and killed were eaten by dogs and pigs; in others the Synagogues were turned into charnel houses by the pitiless butchery of those who sought refuge in them. If we add to the figures quoted above the number of those indirect victims who in consequence of the robbery

and destruction that accompanied these massacres were swept away by famine, disease, exposure and all manner of privations—the death total will be very near half a million human beings.[57]

Twenty years later, Hermann Grabe was an eyewitness to what happened at Dulmo, a city in the Ukraine. On October 5, 1942, Grabe went to his office in Dulmo and was told by his foreman that all the Jews in the neighborhood were being exterminated. Approximately 1,500 were being shot each day in massive ditches.

Grabe and his foreman drove to the execution ditches. As they arrived, Nazi SS troops with dogs and whips were driving Jews off packed trucks and toward the trenches. Grabe described the scene this way:

> The Jews were ordered to strip. They were told to put down their clothes in tidy order, boots and shoes, top clothing and underclothing. Already there were great piles of this clothing and a heap of eight hundred to a thousand pairs of boots and shoes. The people undressed. The mothers undressed their little children, without screaming or weeping. They had reached a point of human suffering where tears no longer flow and all hope has been abandoned. They stood around in family groups, kissed each other, said farewells, and waited. They were waiting for a signal from the SS man with a whip, who was standing by the pit. They stood there waiting for a quarter of an hour, waiting for their turn to come, while on the other side of the earthen mound, now that the shots were no longer heard, the dead and the dying were being packed into the pit. . . .
>
> I heard no complaints, no appeal for mercy. I watched a family of about eight persons, a man and a woman both about fifty, with their grown-up children, about twenty to twenty-four. An old woman with snow-white

hair was holding a little baby in her arms, singing to it and tickling it. The baby was cooing with delight. The couple were looking at each other with tears in their eyes. The father was holding the hand of a boy about ten years old and speaking to him softly; the boy was fighting his tears.[58]

These Jewish people were marched into the execution ditch and shot in the back of the head in the usual Nazi fashion, under orders from a man who claimed to follow the Christ of the Cross.

The Cross of Oppression

What do you think of when you see a cross? I'm reminded of the joy of redemption. I think of the Resurrection, of my beloved Lord, of hope, of eternal life. The cross, to me, is a life-affirming symbol.

But during the time of Christ, Jesus was one of between 50,000 and 100,000 Jews crucified as anti-Roman rebels in the first century. Historian Hyam Maccoby, speaking of the persecution the Jews experienced under the ancient Romans, wrote: "The cross became as much a symbol of Roman oppression as nowadays the gas chamber is a symbol of German Nazi oppression. . . . Associating the guilt of the cross with the Jews rather than the Romans is comparable to branding the Jewish victims . . . with the guilt of using gas chambers instead of suffering from them."[59]

When Christians see a cross, they think of redemption and forgiveness. When a Jew sees a cross, he sees an electric chair. For him and his people, a cross has been a symbol of death for centuries.

A Russian theologian, Nikolay Berdyayev, wrote: "Perhaps the saddest thing to admit is that those who have rejected the Cross have to carry it, while those who welcomed it are as often engaged in crucifying others."[60]

We must examine the lies from ancient times and expose them to the light of truth. It is time for Christian people to cast off the vicious legacy of the past and make sure our people no longer carry hateful tales in their memories or pass them on to the next generation.

Malicious Myths About Jewish People

It's said that if you tell a lie long enough, sooner or later people will begin to believe it. Though the number-one myth about the Jewish people is that the Jews killed Jesus, other fantastic tales have abounded throughout history. Some undoubtedly sprang into being through ignorance and fear; others were malicious rumors spread in order to drive Jews away and confiscate their property.

Economic Persecution

Greed is a driving force behind much of the persecution of the Jews. Perhaps Mark Twain said it best. In the September 1898 issue of *Harper's* magazine, Twain wrote:

> I feel convinced that the Crucifixion has not much to do with the world's attitude toward the Jew; that the reasons for it are much older than that. . . . I am convinced that in Russia, Austria and Germany nine-tenths of the hostility to the Jew comes from the average Christian's inability to compete successfully with the average Jew in business.

What motivates many of those who persecute the Jews? The love of money. Greed. Jealousy for a blessing given to them by God through Abraham: "I will bless you . . . and in you all the families of the earth shall be blessed" (Gen. 12:2–3).

In the Middle Ages, for instance, many Jews were involved in banking. In 1247 Pope Innocent III wrote that Christians should pay their debts: "Although the said Jews make honest loans of their money to these Christians, the latter, in order to drain from them all their wealth . . . refuse to repay their money to them."[61]

In his letter, the pope actually complimented Jewish honesty and admitted that Christians were trying to rob them. In fact, the practice went much farther than a simple refusal to repay. Often people would borrow money from a Jew, then when the loan fell due, they would appeal to the civil or ecclesiastical authorities on the grounds that the transaction was illegal or the rate unduly exorbitant. If the appeal failed, the debtors would then circulate rumors, organize riots, knock the creditor on the head, or resort to threats and intimidation.

How many times have you heard this or a similar expression: "He tried to jew me down on the price"? I'm not certain why Jews have been characterized as having a particular lust for money when history teaches that Gentiles hungered for Jewish money! Christian body snatchers of the thirteenth century rifled through Jewish cemeteries and exhumed corpses for the purpose of extorting money from the survivors.[62] On some occasions the bones of wealthy Jews were dug up, put on trial, and pronounced guilty of heresy in what amounted to little more than a monstrous act of extortion.

Pope Gregory X had to rebuke his flock for a similar situation. Certain Christian fathers whose children had died hid the children's bodies on Jewish properties, then proceeded to extort money from the Jews by threatening to accuse them of having murdered the children to obtain blood for the Passover ceremony.[63]

The Blood-of-Christian-Children Lie

Let me tell you about a malicious myth that was far from harmless. This story began during medieval times, and it survives to this present day. Unfortunately, it has been the cause of heartbreak, endless pain, and many terrible and tragic deaths.

This story, originally concocted by a monk named Theobald, was first put into writing by Thomas of Monmouth, an English monk of the Order of Saint Benedict. Thomas heard the story of a young boy named William, who had been found dead in the woods outside the town of Norwich. Some months later, Thomas of Monmouth accused Jews of killing the boy. He said they had enticed the boy into a house, tortured him, and crucified him.

Thomas's tale did not meet with the approval of his superiors, but it caught the imagination of the populace, who used it as an excuse for attacking the so-called enemies of Christ. While Jews were tortured until they "confessed," an actual cult arose to honor Blessed William, the first child martyr. The business of venerating the child proved profitable.

Thomas's story spread like an aggressive cancer. This lie about human sacrifice influenced the king of France, Philip Augustus, who in 1182 drove the Jews out of his country because he believed they were sacrificing Christian children.

On March 26, 1247, a little girl, two years old, was found dead in a ditch outside the French town of Valréas. A rumor quickly spread that the child had been abducted by Jews and that her blood had been used in their religious ceremonies—the Passover ritual was especially suspect.

Three Jews were arrested for the child's murder. They were tortured until they confessed, then they were put to death. Many other Jews in the district were rounded up, tortured, and burned at the stake. Pope Innocent was savvy enough to recognize the motivation behind this mass murder, and he sent envoys who condemned "the cruelty of Christians who, covetous of their possessions, thirsting for their blood, despoil, torture, and kill all Jews without legal judgment."[64]

Little Saint Hugh of Lincoln

In 1255 when a boy named Hugh of Lincoln disappeared, another version of the story began to circulate. In this adaptation of William's tale, Hugh was stolen by Jews and shut up in a room for the purpose of being crucified. The boy was subjected to diverse tortures, beaten until blood flowed, and crowned with thorns. His captors crucified him and pierced his heart with a lance. After the boy expired, they took his body from the cross and disemboweled it.

Meanwhile, in Lincoln, a search team found the boy's body in a well. There was no evidence, no mark, to indicate the boy had been murdered. Yet ninety-six Jews of Lincoln were taken to London, where eighteen of the richest and most powerful were hanged.

Young Hugh, promoted to the rank of martyr, was venerated for generations as Little Saint Hugh of Lincoln. A church was dedicated to his memory, and his tomb became a famous resort for pilgrims who came to worship and pray for miracles. Chaucer even mentioned the gruesome story in his fictional *Canterbury Tales*. In "The Prioress's Tale," Chaucer has his prioress state that because a young Christian boy constantly sang hymns to the Virgin, "from thence forth the Jews conspired this innocent out of this world to chase" (spelling modernized). The Jews of her story capture this innocent Christian boy, cut his throat, and cast him into a pit. The boy dies, but not before being rescued and pledging his loyalty to the Virgin, this despite having his "throat cut to the neck bone."[65] Chaucer ends his story with a reference to "young Hugh of Lincoln, slain also with cursed Jews."

Although Little Saint Hugh was revered for generations, the entire story was what we would now call an urban legend. There was no evidence that the boy had been killed by anyone, and yet every time a young child turned up missing, Jews were routinely hauled out and put to death for "confessions" under torture.

This outrageous slander was also cited as one reason why Ferdinand and Isabella chose to drive the Jews out of Spain in 1492. The story had grown by this time, and the storytellers spoke of a child named Richard who had been crucified by the Jews, William of Norwich, Little Saint Hugh, and another child named Robert.

The myths and calumnies continue to persist. Tomáš Masaryk, the first president of Czechoslovakia, wrote:

> In the fifties of the last [nineteenth] century every Slovak child in the vicinity of Goding was nurtured in an atmosphere of anti-Semitism; in school, church and society at large. Mother would forbid us to go near the Lechners because, as she said, Jews were using the blood of Christian children. I would therefore make a wide turn to avoid passing their house; and so did all my schoolmates. . . . The superstition of Christian blood

used for Passover cakes had become so much part and parcel of my existence that whenever I chanced to come near a Jew—I wouldn't do it on purpose—I would look at his fingers to see if blood were there. . . . Would that I may unmake all that anti-Semitism caused me to do in my childhood days.[66]

In 1936, 700 years after Pope Innocent's decree condemning the lie about ritual murder, a German newspaper, *Der Stürmer*, published illustrations showing Jews sucking the blood of innocent children.[67] Is it any wonder that Nazi propaganda in Germany issued periodic warnings for families to keep their children especially close at Passover time?

Oh, you may be thinking, *no rational person today would believe such things!* I beg to disagree! Samuel Macy, a thirty-three-year-old Harvard librarian, decided in 1996 to track hate groups on the Internet. As he surfed the Web, he discovered that so-called Christian identity groups in the United States are keeping the rumors alive. Their Web pages say that Jews are the product of a union between Eve and Satan, and they also report that Jews kill Christians and use their blood to make matzo.[68] How are they different from Chaucer's prioress, who said, "Our first foe, the serpent Satan . . . hath in Jews' hearts his wasp's nest"?[69]

Those who spread rumors about the Jews and lay the blame for Christ's death at the feet of the Jewish nation have made a grave mistake. But since the formation of the nation of Israel, the Jews have suffered at the hands of tyrants, so-called Christian emperors, crusaders, self-anointed and self-serving theologians, and everyday misinformed Christians. Constant historic expressions of anti-Semitism have spawned every imaginable theological and philosophical rebuttal to the rights of Jewish people to their land, their Holy City, and their place in God's eternal plan.

As late as 1770, Voltaire, the French Enlightenment's most prominent intellectual, wrote, "Jewish priests have always sacrificed human victims with their sacred hands." He went on to add that though the Jews were the "most abominable people in the world . . . nevertheless, they should not be burned at the stake."[70]

Modern anti-Semitism lives!

For 2,000 years Christian theology has been twisted into a lie that is the cornerstone of anti-Semitism. Singing hymns of love and claiming to act as the defenders of God, the faithful have stepped over the tortured bodies of ten million Jews whom anti-Semites have labeled "the Christ-killers!"

They are wrong, my friend. Read on.

CHAPTER 5

WHO REALLY
KILLED CHRIST?

Attempting to shed some light on the staggering accounts of the Jews' persecution, Dr. James Parker
wrote, "In our own day . . . more than six million deliberate murders are the consequences of the teachings about
Jews for which the Christian Church is ultimately responsible . . . which has its ultimate resting place in the teaching of the New Testament itself."[1]

The most deadly New Testament myth is the rumor that
the Jews killed Jesus! What can we find in the New Testament to support this supposition? Absolutely nothing!

If this were a criminal investigation and we set out to
discover who *really* killed Christ, we'd consider an eyewitness account the most reliable sort of testimony. Let's look
at the biblical text closely. What do the eyewitness accounts
of Matthew, Mark, Luke, and John actually say about
Christ's crucifixion?

The Jewish writers of the Gospels took special care to
record the fact that the Jewish people, their *own* people,
were not only not responsible, but were for the most part

unaware of the events that led up to the apprehension, trial, and condemnation of Jesus Christ.

Matthew's Testimony

In the most Jewish of all the Gospels, Matthew states that the Jews, as a people, had nothing to do with the political conspiracy against Jesus. He exposes the true conspirators in chapter 26 of his book: "Then the chief priests, the scribes, and the elders of the people assembled at the palace of the high priest, who was called Caiaphas, and plotted to take Jesus by trickery and kill Him" (v. 3–4).

Two very important points are clear:

1. There was a crucifixion plot.
2. The high priest, Caiaphas, carried out the intrigue, and he in no way represented the Jewish people. He was politically appointed by Herod Antipas, who was himself directly appointed by Rome. The Jewish people hated Herod and the high priest because they were political pawns in the hands of the pagan Romans.

Herod the Great, father of Herod Antipas, rose to power through the tyrannical intervention of Roman military rule forty years before Christ was born. Rome's Mark Anthony joined military forces with Herod the Great in an attack on the city of Jerusalem. After five months, Jerusalem fell, and Mark Anthony appointed Herod as its Roman supervisor. Herod was a paranoid dictator who murdered several members of his own family. He was a notoriously jealous and insanely insecure ruler, and it was in character for him to order the slaughter of all baby boys under two years old when he feared a report by wise men from the East that a "King of the Jews" had been born (see Matt. 2:1–12).

After rising to power, Herod the Great promptly ordered forty-five members of the Jewish Sanhedrin murdered in order to gain absolute dictatorial control and to silence the Jewish voice in government. During the reigns of Herod the Great and Herod Antipas, his son, the Sanhedrin was nothing more than a pawn of the state. Herod held absolute power by the will of Rome, not by the vote of the Jewish people.

Herod also appointed the high priest, Caiaphas, leader of the Calvary conspiracy, to carry out Rome's will. Caiaphas was an illegitimate priest, not selected by the Jewish people. During the Great Revolt of A.D. 66–70, Josephus records that religious Jews burned down the high priest's house because he was a corrupt puppet of Rome.

Into this shady political setting came a Rabbi called Jesus of Nazareth. Because the Jews were looking for a deliverer to lead a revolt and break the oppressive chains of Rome, Jesus' popularity spread like lightning. Anyone who could feed 5,000 people from one boy's lunch could feed an army to defeat Rome! Anyone who could heal and raise people from the dead could heal wounded soldiers and raise dead troops back to life. The people saw Jesus as their military answer to conquer mighty Rome. Rome saw Jesus as an insurrectionist too threatening to allow to live.

Seen in this light, Jesus was a serious political threat to Herod Antipas and to his stooge, Caiaphas. Consequently, they entered into a politically motivated plot to have Jesus killed Roman style—by crucifixion. Jewish law allowed execution by stoning only. Had the Jews killed Jesus, He would have been stoned, not crucified.

The Leaders Feared a Riot

When Caiaphas met with his political pawns to consider how best to kill Jesus of Nazareth, the Scriptures state that they decided to arrest Jesus in a secretive way so they wouldn't cause a riot among the Jewish people present in the city: "[They] plotted to take Jesus by trickery and kill Him. But they said, 'Not during the feast, lest there be an uproar among the people'" (Matt. 26:4–5).

If the Jews were behind the crucifixion plot, why would they fear a riot? A riot requires the spontaneous uprising among the general population. But the high priest knew that the majority of the Jewish people supported Jesus and would spontaneously erupt in anger if He were arrested. News of a riot would travel to Rome. Herod would be politically embarrassed, and the high priest would be instantly displaced from his lucrative and powerful position.

Matthew contributes more evidence that the leaders of this plot feared the Jewish people: "But when they sought to lay hands on Him, they feared the multitudes, because they took Him for a prophet" (21:46).

Certainly some Jews were displeased with Jesus' leadership and teaching. The School of Hillel, a group of Jewish religious rabbis, was furious because Jesus endorsed their opponent Shammai's teaching on divorce. No one had to urge Hillel's followers to scream for the crucifixion of Jesus. They numbered fewer than a few hundred, but they were more than glad to betray Him or anyone else who rejected their doctrine. Some things never change.

Even after Jesus' death, the enemies of Jesus weren't finished with their plotting. Big problems developed for the local theologians when He rose from the dead on the third day. The conspirators had a lot of explaining to do. Once again, Caiaphas's moral corruption manifested itself. He paid large bribes to the guards watching the tomb and told them to lie about what had happened.

Let the eyewitness account of Matthew speak for the record: "When they [the chief priests] had assembled with the elders and consulted together, they gave a large sum of money to the soldiers, saying, 'Tell them, "His disciples came at night and stole Him away while we slept." And if this comes to the governor's ears, we will appease him and make you secure'" (28:12–14).

Note five important points:

1. The chief priests were conspirators.
2. The chief priests were guilty of offering Roman soldiers a bribe, a criminal act punishable by death.
3. The chief priests were liars who paid other people to lie.
4. The guards at the tomb could have been put to death for sleeping at their post, but the chief priests were so totally confident of their political connections that they assured the guards they could appease the governor and keep the guards out of trouble.
5. Because the chief priests' political connections to Rome were common knowledge, the guards were not afraid to accept the bribe and become part of the plot.

The actions of a single man, Caiaphas, and of his conspiring cronies hardly constitute the actions of an entire nation.

Mark and Luke Agree

Luke and Mark join Matthew in contributing evidence that these political prostitutes did not represent the Jewish people (italics mine).

And the scribes and chief priests heard it and sought how they might destroy Him; for they feared Him, *because all the people* were astonished at His teaching (Mark 11:18).

And they sought to lay hands on Him, but *feared the multitude,* for they knew He had spoken the parable against them. So they left Him and went away (Mark 12:12).

And the chief priests and the scribes sought how they might take Him by trickery and put Him to death. But they said, "Not during the feast, lest there be an *uproar of the people*" (Mark 14:1–2).

And He [Jesus] was teaching daily in the temple. But the chief priests, the scribes, and the leaders of the people sought to destroy Him, and were unable to do anything; for *all the people were very attentive to hear Him* (Luke 19:47–48).

And the chief priests and the scribes that very hour sought to lay hands on Him, but *they feared the people*—for they knew He had spoken this parable against them (Luke 20:19).

And the chief priests and the scribes sought how they might kill Him, for they *feared the people* (Luke 22:2).

Jesus Himself identified His killers before His death (italics mine): "Then He took the twelve aside and said to them, 'Behold, we are going up to Jerusalem, and all things that are written by the prophets concerning the Son of Man will be accomplished. For He will be delivered *to the Gentiles* and will be mocked and insulted and spit upon. And they will scourge Him and kill Him. And the third day He will rise again'" (Luke 18:31–33).

The biblical text is perfectly clear. Jesus was crucified by Rome as a political insurrectionist. He was a threat to Herod's authority. He was a threat to the high priest. The men of Herod's inner circle produced the Calvary conspiracy. His death had nothing to do with the Jewish people as a race, nation, or civilization.

Consider the historical facts: At the time Jesus began His ministry, three out of four Jews did not live in Israel. Nine out of ten Jews during that time lived outside Jerusalem. At most, only a few hundred irate Pharisees could have possibly participated in or supported the high priest's Calvary plot.

What About the Mob at Pilate's Mansion?

Ah, yes, how many times have we heard "proof-text" Christians rattle on about the mob who screamed, "Let Him be crucified!" and "His blood be on us and on our children" (Matt. 27:23, 25). Surely *this* Scripture proves that all Jewish people are forever guilty of the blood of Jesus Christ.

The scriptural and historical fact is that the political puppet, Caiaphas, gathered and controlled that crowd. Remember, this was an orchestrated plot, not a spontaneous expression of the people. The chief priests were frightened of an honest crowd. Matthew, the eyewitness, tells us that "the chief priests and elders persuaded the multitudes that they should ask for Barabbas and destroy Jesus" (27:20).

How did they persuade the crowd? It didn't take much. These were the Pharisees who were as mad as a nest of hornets poked with a stick. Jesus had called them "whitewashed tombs" (Matt. 23:27) and told them that casual divorce was against God's plan. They were angry, and they took their opportunity to be rid of the One causing them trouble.

You may have noticed that I didn't include any passages from John when I mentioned the eyewitness accounts of the crucifixion. That's because John's Gospel requires a different examination.

The Jews of John's Gospel

For centuries preachers in Christian pulpits read the thirty-two references to Jews in John's Gospel and concluded that all Jews are bloodthirsty torturers, pitiless killers, and money-hungry temple desecrators. Christian pulpiteers pounded their pulpits and shouted a message of hatred. They quoted verses like John 5:16 ("For this reason the Jews persecuted Jesus, and sought to kill Him, because He had done these things on the Sabbath") and John 7:1 ("After these things Jesus walked in Galilee; for He did not want to walk in Judea, because the Jews sought to kill Him").

Were *All* the Jews Guilty?

For 1,500 years, the guilt of a handful of Jews who hated Jesus has been spread with a broad brush to include all Jewish people. For centuries, Christian leaders have used the above verses, and others like them, to justify anti-Semitism.

Saint John Chrysostom, he of the golden mouth, wrote, "The Jews . . . erred not ignorantly but with full knowledge."[2] Several hundred years later, just prior to the Second Crusade, Saint Bernard of Clairvaux agreed with Chrysostom's theology. Bernard wrote: "The Jews were all guilty; they acted with deliberate malice; that their guilt was shared by the whole Jewish people, for all time, and that they, and their children's children to the last generation, were condemned to live in slavery as the servants of Christian princes."[3]

Despite the passage of 700 years, Bernard echoed Chrysostom's malice. Eight hundred years after Bernard wrote his diatribe, we see that many historical figures, including Adolf Hitler, echoed Bernard's thoughts.

The Scripture says that the Jews hated Jesus, so who were these "Jews" in John's Gospel?

Let's compare the styles of Matthew and John in the reporting of a similar incident. In Matthew 12 we read the story of the man with a withered hand. Matthew says that when Jesus healed the man on the Sabbath, "The *Pharisees* went out and plotted against Him, how they might destroy Him" (v. 14, italics mine).

John, however, in reporting a similar incident, does not use the phrase *the Pharisees*, but uses the phrase *the Jews*: "The Jews therefore said to him who was cured, 'It is the Sabbath; it is not lawful for you to carry your bed.' . . . The man departed and told the Jews that it was Jesus who had made him well. For this reason the Jews persecuted Jesus, and sought to kill Him" (5:10, 15–16).

In a careful study of Scripture, you will see that "the Jews" of John 5 are "the Pharisees" of Matthew 12—the same fellows who were constantly trying to trap Jesus in a doctrinal error.

In his account of the healing of the man blind from birth (John 9:1–15), John describes the interrogation forced upon the man by the Pharisees. When the Pharisees were not satisfied with the man's response, they went to his parents. The parents admitted their son had indeed been healed, but indicated they did not know how he had been healed. John says they avoided answering because "they feared the Jews, for the Jews had agreed already that if anyone confessed that He was Christ, he would be put out of the synagogue" (9:22).

An observant study of the Bible makes it perfectly clear that "the Pharisees" of John 9:15 are "the Jews" who had intimidated the blind man's parents. But anti-Semitic leaders gladly read these passages of Scripture and assume that by writing "the Jews," John intended to accuse an entire race of people.

Who Are the Pharisees?

Scholars estimate that there were about one million Jews in Israel at the time of Christ. Of that one million, the Pharisees numbered a little more than 6,000.[4] The Pharisees, therefore, represented *less than 1 percent* of the Jewish population of Israel.

Furthermore, the Pharisees were divided into three schools of thought. One school was led by the famous Hillel, who wandered from Babylonia to Jerusalem and joined a house of study. In time, he was recognized as one of the foremost teachers of the Pharisees. Hillel served as a patriarch in Israel from 10 B.C. until A.D. 10. He fostered a systematic, liberal, relatively lenient interpretation of Scripture, and his students ruled Jewish life for more than 400 years.

A second school of thought among the Pharisees arose under the leadership of Shammai. Shammai and Hillel could agree on virtually nothing. They constantly debated right and wrong on practically every issue.

A third school of thought was formed by the Essenes, an ascetic Jewish sect whose members lived in the Judean desert. John the Baptist could have easily belonged to this community, as could have Jesus Christ. It is very possible that in the silent years of His life, between the ages of eighteen and thirty, Jesus studied Torah at Qumran, where the Dead Sea Scrolls were discovered in 1947. Qumran is only a short distance from the Jordan River, where Jesus was baptized by John. It is entirely conceivable that Jesus studied from the Dead Sea Scrolls now on display in Israel at the Shrine of the Book.

Regardless of membership in a sect, the Pharisees were set apart from the common people. The word *Pharisee* comes from the word *Perushim,* which means to be separated. These religious separatists held themselves aloof from all other Jews and from other Pharisees who did not agree with their doctrinal teaching. They were extremely careful in matters of ritual purity and refused to touch a menstruating woman, a woman who had just given birth, a corpse, a dead reptile, a leper, or anything else that smacked of being unclean.

The Pharisees believed that they alone were the rightful teachers and interpreters of the oral law. They believed in the resurrection of the dead, in angels, and in God's guidance of human events.

All three groups of Pharisees were powerful and influential. Chaim Potok wrote:

> It is an error to see these Pharisees as gentle old men with flowing white beards; see them rather as passionate followers of scribal teachings adept with sword and spear as well as with text of the law, quite willing to kill for the sake of their God. We are talking of a time when men easily took up the sword for what they held dear. The Pharisees killed for God rather than for plunder. It is to be doubted if those who fell by Pharisee swords were thereby consoled.[5]

During the time of Jesus, doctrinal disputes still raged between the followers of Hillel and Shammai concerning the law of divorce. Shammai taught that a man could not divorce his wife for just any trivial cause, but could get a divorce for fornication. (Biblically, fornication included adultery, homosexuality, bestiality, and lewdness.) For Jews, the scriptural right to divorce also included the right to remarry. This position was accepted without question throughout Israel.

Hillel was an extremist, teaching that a man could divorce his wife "for every cause." According to Hillel, a husband could divorce his wife for talking too loudly, for talking too much, for failing to prepare kosher meals, for seasoning food carelessly, for going into the street with loose or uncombed hair. A husband could divorce his wife if he found a more beautiful wife, or for any other reason.

The followers of Hillel were constantly trying to lure Jesus into this raging doctrinal dispute, and the story of how they approached Him is recorded in Matthew 19:3: "The Pharisees also came to Him, testing Him, and saying to Him, 'Is it lawful for a man to divorce his wife for just any reason?'"

Jesus knew His life was on the line. If He disagreed with those sword-carrying legalists, they would try to kill Him.

Jesus searched their hearts, looked them in the eye, and gave this answer: "Moses, because of the hardness of your hearts, permitted you to divorce your wives, but from the beginning it was not so. And I say to you, whoever divorces his wife, except for sexual immorality, and marries another, commits adultery; and whoever marries her who is divorced commits adultery" (Matt. 19:8–9).

With the utterance of those words, the fight was on! From that moment Jesus was seen as a living devil to the Pharisees who followed Hillel. They plotted to have Him killed. These were "the Jews" that Jesus said were of their "father the devil." These are "the Jews" that interrogated the parents of the blind man until they shook with fear. These are "the Jews" from whom Jesus' disciples were hiding behind closed doors. These are "the Jews" that Christians have used for 2,000 years to condone religious hatred, rape, murder, and execution.

But we can't assume that all the Pharisees opposed Jesus. Many Pharisees were friends of Jesus. They loved Him, He ate with them, and they tried to save His life.

Jesus' Pharisee Friends

In John's Gospel we read of Nicodemus, who went to Jesus "by night." Entirely too much criticism has been heaped upon Nicodemus for going to Jesus after dark as if he were sneaking around. Nothing could be farther from the truth. Nicodemus was a ruler of the Pharisees and was in the courts all day. The only logical time to see Jesus was after sundown.

Nicodemus did not hesitate to confess, "Rabbi, we know that You are a teacher come from God; for no one can do these signs that You do unless God is with him" (3:2).

Nicodemus admired and stood in awe of Jesus. He thought enough of Jesus to seek His opinions; he thought enough of Jesus to later bring 100 pounds of valuable myrrh and aloes to help with the burial of Jesus' body (19:39).

Nicodemus was not the only Pharisee to befriend Jesus. Though we do not have the names of others, we know that Jesus ate with Pharisees (Luke 7:37), an act that brought Him sharp criticism. In biblical times, you did not break bread with a man unless a bond of mutual esteem and respect existed between the two of you. In fact, betraying a man or speaking ill of him after eating with him was the ultimate act of disloyalty. It was unthinkable to eat with someone and then entrap him. King David once lamented: "Even my own familiar friend in whom I trusted, / Who ate my bread, / Has lifted up his heel against me" (Psalm 41:9).

Obviously, many Pharisees dined with Jesus and would not have done so without intending to support Him to the death.

What About Judas?

Because Judas betrayed Jesus as they were eating the Last Supper together, the name *Judas* has become the universal synonym for "traitor." So wasn't at least this specific Jew to blame for Jesus' death?

No. Judas was not an ethnic Jew. The church fathers who have called him "Jew-das" were in error.

Jesus chose twelve disciples. Only ten were necessary for a Jewish *minyan*, the minimum number required before religious services could be conducted. Ten of Christ's disciples were ethnic and religious Jews. Judas Iscariot and Simon the Canaanite were not ethnic Jews, but religious proselytes.

"Iscariot" was not Judas's last name. *Ish-Kirot* means he was a foreigner, an alien to the ethnic family of Israel. *Ish* means "man" and *Kirot* means he was a citizen of Kir or Kirot. Kirot was a Jewish city in southern Judea. In southern Moab across the Dead Sea, another Kir or Kirot existed. If Judas had been from the Kirot in Judea, his name would have been Judas Mi-Kirot, as Mary from Migdol was called Mary Magdalene. Since Judas was a foreigner, his name was Ish-Kirot.

In the Calvary plot, Judas the foreigner and Herod the Idumaean Jew (another foreigner) had common interest in the death of Christ. Some scholars believe that Judas was Herod's spy in the ministry of Jesus Christ from day one.

Why did Judas ask for thirty pieces of silver out of the nonnegotiable shekels of the temple treasury? As a devout Jew, he could not have spent the money. As devout Jews, the temple officials could not give Judas the money. Yet they did. The collusion suggests a long-standing connection between Judas, Herod, and Herod's politically appointed high priest, Caiaphas.

Herod and the Pharisees

Further scriptural evidence that many Pharisees supported Jesus is found in Luke 13:31: "On that very day some Pharisees came, saying to Him, 'Get out and depart from here, for Herod wants to kill You.'"

These Pharisees came to warn Jesus that Herod was angry and would kill Him just as he executed John the Baptist. Everyone in Israel knew Herod was a cold-blooded murderer—he had killed nine of his ten wives. If the Pharisees had wanted Jesus dead, warning Him was the last thing they would have done. Instead, they came to alert Jesus in an effort to save His life.

John's Gospel further demonstrates how the Pharisees were divided over Christ's ministry. The situation becomes clear in the story of Jesus healing the blind man by mixing clay with saliva.

Why did Jesus spit on the ground? Because Jews of the first century believed there was healing power in the spittle of the firstborn male of every family. By His action, Jesus was testifying to all that He was the firstborn of the Father, the only begotten Son of God.

"Therefore some of the Pharisees said, 'This Man is not from God, because He does not keep the Sabbath.' Others said, 'How can a man who is a sinner do such signs?' And there was a division among them" (9:16).

Nothing in Scripture indicates a unified Jewish front to oppose Jesus. On the contrary, many Pharisees confessed that He was a Man sent from God. They followed Him to the crest of Calvary.

So Why Are the Jews Blamed for the Crucifixion?

Anti-Semitism is a demonic spirit from the bowels of hell. I believe it is designed to torment the Jewish people for bringing the torch of truth, the Word of God, and the Light of the World into a void of spiritual darkness. Hate is a cancer on the intellect and pollutes the mind. Violence flames from the embers of malice like fire flashes from intense heat. No ethnic group knows this better than the Seed of Abraham.

The Jews are blamed for so many things, often without logical reasons, for the same reason that a successful businessman or a handsome youth is hated and envied by his peers. The nation of Israel is blessed; it has been chosen by God.

"For you are a holy people to the LORD your God," Moses wrote concerning Israel, "and the LORD has chosen you to be a people for Himself, a special treasure above all the peoples who are on the face of the earth" (Deut. 14:2).

Why did God choose the nation of Israel for His own? The answer to this question is bound up in God's purpose for Israel. When God promised Abraham that he would become the father of a great nation, He also promised that He would bless all peoples through that nation.

Israel was to be a channel of blessing as well as a recipient. Even their miraculous deliverance from Egypt was partially designed to show other nations that Israel's God was the only true God. Isaiah further prophesied that the Messiah would bring salvation to the Gentiles (Isa. 49:6). The life, ministry, and death of Jesus Christ all came through Israel as God's chosen channel of blessing.

The Jews have been tested, and they know how to exhibit courage. The test of *courage* arises when we are in the minority. The test of *tolerance* arises when we are in the majority. Jesus taught, "You shall love your neighbor as yourself" (Matt. 22:39). It is not possible for a person to say "I am a Christian" and not love the Jewish people.

So—Who Is to Blame?

Should we reserve our anger and hatred, then, for *certain* Pharisees and one politically controlled high priest? No, for in the last breath of His earthly life, Jesus forgave even those who plotted against Him, saying, "Father, forgive them, for they do not know what they do" (Luke 23:34). If God has forgiven that handful of Jews who participated in the Calvary conspiracy to crucify Christ, why can't Christians?

Who is responsible for the death of Jesus Christ? The simple answer, my friend, is that we are. Though we may not have been present during those clandestine meetings when the Calvary conspiracy was launched, and though we did not bargain for the Savior's life or surrender Him for a bag of silver, it was your need, and my need, that led the Savior to Calvary.

Jesus' life wasn't taken from Him—He willingly surrendered it. Jesus told His followers, "As the Father knows Me, even so I know the Father; and I lay down My life for the sheep. . . . Therefore My Father loves Me, because I lay down My life that I may take it again. *No one takes it from Me, but I lay it down of Myself.* I have power to lay it down, and I have power to take it again" (John 10:15, 17–18, italics mine).

Why should we care for the people of Jerusalem? Because Jesus said, "Assuredly, I say to you, inasmuch as you did it to one of the least of these My brethren, you did it to Me" (Matt. 25:40). Jesus' reference to "My brethren" was a reference to the Jewish people, not some Christian denomination. In Scripture, Jesus referred to Gentiles as "dogs" (Matt. 15:26–27), not as "My brethren."

Paul paints a bleak portrait of the spiritual position of Gentiles prior to the Cross when he wrote, "At that time you were without Christ, being aliens from the commonwealth of Israel and strangers from the covenants of promise, having no hope and without God in the world" (Eph. 2:12). But through salvation in Christ, we are given the opportunity to be adopted into the family of God. "But as many as received Him," wrote the apostle John, "to them He gave the right to become children of God, to those who believe in His name: who were born, not of blood, nor of the will of the flesh, nor of the will of man, but of God" (John 1:12–13).

In the same way a tangerine branch is grafted onto an orange tree to bear fruit, the Gentiles of the world were grafted into the blessings of Abraham through the blood atonement of a Rabbi, Jesus of Nazareth.

As a Gentile, I was guaranteed death, but Jesus, a Rabbi, went to the cross and gave me eternal life.

As a Gentile, I was guaranteed sickness, but by the stripes on the back of a Rabbi, I am healed.

As a Gentile, I was guaranteed depression, despair, and death, but a Rabbi gave His life that I might have joy unspeakable and peace that surpasses understanding. I have substituted garments of praise for the spirit of heaviness. I have acquired eternal life.

As a Gentile, I was an alien, an outcast far outside the commonwealth of Israel. Jesus grafted me into the royal family of God, and now all the blessings of Abraham are mine.

As a Gentile, I was guaranteed rejection, but through Jesus, God the Father adopted me and made me a joint heir with Christ.

All He had, I got; all I had, He took.

I took His wealth; He took my poverty.

I took His forgiveness; He took my sin and shame.

I took His love and acceptance; He took my rejection.

I took His healing; He took my sickness.

I took His power; He took my fear and weakness.

Jesus Christ paid a debt He did not owe, and I owed a debt I could not pay. At Calvary a Rabbi extended His nail-pierced hand to every Gentile who was cut off, without God, and without hope. He grafted us into the blessings of Abraham. Calvary was not caused by the Jews. It was pre-destined by God "from the foundation of the world" for us (Rev. 13:8).

Hallelujah for the Cross.

CHAPTER 6

HAS GOD REJECTED THE JEWS?

As I examined the onslaught of hate historically vented toward Israel and the Jews, I wondered what prompted these Christian attacks. Why would theologians in the first millennium, during medieval times, and in this century unleash such persistent and violent assaults? Aside from the malicious myths we've already discussed, some idea, proposition, or declaration had to have begun this avalanche of hate. As I searched, it didn't take long to find and identify the poisoned spring—replacement theology.

This heresy of hatred is being taught in Sunday schools to impressionable young minds. A generation of American children is growing up believing that heartless Jews captured and crucified the only begotten Son of God. Anti-Semitism is again being proclaimed by bellicose clerics as a Christian virtue. These preachers claim they are "defending the faith" and "fighting the devil" when they attack the Jews.

Adolf Hitler felt the same way. He said, "I am acting in accordance with the will of the Almighty Creator: by defending myself against the Jew, I am fighting for the work of the Lord."[1]

Most evangelicals believe the Jews rejected Jesus as Messiah and therefore qualify for God's eternal judgment. Replacement theologians write, "The covenant with Israel was broken because she would not accept Jesus Christ whom God sent."[2]

In the first century, theological anti-Semitism began teaching that "the church is the new Israel." Gentile converts resented the priority of the Jewish people in God's economy. A spirit of arrogance and pride causes this theology of hate to still flourish today. The concept appeals to the ego.

Hitler sold this idea to the German people, screaming to his enraptured audience, "We are the true people of God." On the other side of the globe, the Japanese called themselves the "sons of heaven." Of course, every American knows they are both wrong because God loves *us* best. Surely He's sitting on His throne waving the Stars and Stripes.

I'm kidding. You can see how foolish the God-loves-us-best concept is. But listen to the message coming from so many pulpits of America's 192 flavors of Christianity. The theme is very clear: "God loves my denomination best." Although narcissistic theology is a cancer of the soul, replacement theology is music to the ego.

The biblical truth is that our Father in heaven loves us all. He is not the enemy of my enemies. God is not even the enemy of His foes, for the Bible teaches to "love your enemies." It's a shocking thought, but God even loves the people who are in a different denomination.

As soon as we adopt the ego-gratifying idea that we are the only people of God, we are delighted to turn on the Jews because the Bible plainly identifies them as the "chosen people." We can't both be "the only people of God."

Replacement theology is not a new revelation; it's an old heresy. In his *Epistles,* Ignatius of Antioch, a Christian martyr who died in the first century, presented the church as "the new Israel." He also portrayed the prophets and heroes of Israel as "Christians before their time" and not part of the Jewish religion. Interestingly enough, this early church scholar had no trouble portraying Balaam, Absalom, and Judas as real Jews.

Replacement theologians must use the allegorical method of interpreting Scripture to support this position. This method, which was first taught in Alexandria and is based on the Platonic doctrine of ideas, spiritualizes the biblical text and purports to plumb hidden spiritual significance, yet it completely avoids the historical and literal meaning. Using the allegorical method of biblical interpretation, you can create a theology that says anything you want it to say. It's not truth; it's completely without biblical foundation. It's God's Word twisted to tell a lie.

Any group teaching that the church is the new Israel must use the allegorical method to justify their position. It is not possible to examine the literal statements of the Bible and conclude that God is finished with Israel and that the church has taken its place. Scripture plainly indicates that the church and national Israel exist side by side and that neither replaces the other—not yesterday, not today, not tomorrow.

Paul emphatically answers once and for all the question when he writes, "Has God cast away His people? Certainly not! . . . God has not cast away His people whom

He foreknew" (Rom. 11:1–2). This thought is so important that Paul addresses it a second time in the same chapter, saying, "Have they [Israel] stumbled that they should fall? Certainly not! But through their fall, to provoke them to jealousy, salvation has come to the Gentiles" (v. 11).

Did the Jews Reject Jesus as Messiah?

Did the Jews of Jesus' day reject Him as Messiah? Let's examine the biblical record.

Some Jewish sages taught that there are two aspects of the same Messiah in Scripture—a suffering Messiah (the Lamb of God) and a reigning Messiah (the Lion of Judah). In the biblical text, it is clear that this is the same Messiah making two different appearances.

Oppressed by Rome, the Jews of Jesus' day were only looking for the reigning Messiah. The crucified Nazarene didn't fit their idea of a triumphant Messiah. This blindness to the true identity of the Messiah was sent from God to the Jewish people (Deut. 29:4; Isa. 6:9; Jer. 5:21; Ezek. 12:2; Matt. 13:14–15; and John 12:40) and has not been lifted to this date.

Why? Because if the Jewish people had accepted the suffering Messiah, every Gentile would have been forever lost. Paul confirms this by saying, "Through their fall . . . salvation has come to the Gentiles" (Rom. 11:11).

The failure to see the suffering Jesus as the true Messiah was God's sovereign plan from the dawning of eternity so the Gentiles might have the opportunity of redemption. Paul says that "God has committed them all to disobedience, that He might have mercy on all" (Rom. 11:32).

God's Will for Jesus

Anyone who reads the Bible knows that no man or nation can change God's sovereign will. That is also true about the life of Jesus Christ. What was God's sovereign will for His life?

The Holy Spirit spoke through Simeon in the Gospel of Luke:

> So he [Simeon] came by the Spirit into the temple.
> And when the parents brought in the Child Jesus, to do
> for Him according to the custom of the law, he took
> Him up in his arms and blessed God and said:
> "Lord, now You are letting Your servant depart in
> peace,
> According to Your word;
> For my eyes have seen Your salvation
> Which You have prepared before the face of all
> peoples,
> A light to bring *revelation to the Gentiles*,
> And the glory of Your people Israel" (2:27–32, italics
> mine).

God the Holy Spirit announced through a Jewish prophet, Simeon, that the sovereign purpose for Jesus' life was to be a "light to the Gentiles." (See also Isa. 42:6.)

This was a shocking revelation because the Jews considered the Gentiles unclean. Gentiles were "aliens from the commonwealth of Israel and strangers from the covenants of promise, having no hope and without God in the world" (Eph. 2:12).

The disciples' prejudice against the "unclean" polytheistic Gentiles was so strong that it took a divine rebuke from the angel of the Lord to get Peter to share the gospel with Gentiles in the home of Cornelius (Acts 10:19–20). That's why Jesus commanded His disciples to "preach the gospel to every creature" (Mark 16:15). Gentiles were considered creatures.

John the Baptist Speaks

As Jesus came to the Jordan River to be baptized, John the Baptist told his listeners, "Behold! The Lamb of God who takes away the sin of the world!" (John 1:29). Every listening Jew understood the symbolism behind John's words. There was only one thing to do with a young, male lamb—kill it. John was stating that the primary purpose for Jesus' life was the Cross, not a crown. He spoke of Jesus' death, not of His diadem.

John the Revelator joins the parade of witnesses by describing Jesus as "the Lamb slain from the foundation of the world" (Rev. 13:8). From the dawning of time, God intended for Jesus to die. Had Jesus permitted Himself to become the Jews' reigning Messiah, He would have missed God's sovereign will for His life.

The Crisis Theory

Replacement theologians have created a crisis theory that's the catch-22 of the New Testament. The theory goes like this: God had Plan A and Plan B for the life of Jesus Christ. Plan A was for Jesus to be Messiah of Israel. Plan B was the Cross of Calvary. Since the Jews rejected Jesus as Messiah, God had no choice but to go to Plan B, the crucifixion.

That idea is utter rubbish. First, a sovereign and almighty God is not subject to the whims and choices of man. Second, the biblical text plainly indicates that God's plan, *from the beginning*, was for Jesus to die.

100

Jesus knew God's plan for His life. When Jesus spoke to Nicodemus, He said, "And as Moses lifted up the serpent in the wilderness, even so must the Son of Man be lifted up, that whoever believes in Him should not perish but have eternal life" (John 3:14–15). This was a clear reference to His coming death on the cross.

When Mary of Bethany anointed Jesus' feet, He said, "She has come beforehand to anoint My body for burial" (Mark 14:8). Jesus told His disciples, "Thus it is written, and thus it was necessary for the Christ to suffer and to rise from the dead the third day" (Luke 24:46). The biblical text makes it clear that God's will was for Jesus to die on the cross, and Jesus carried out that assignment with joy.

Since Jesus was so clear about the purpose of His life, why didn't the Jews accept Him as Messiah? Consider this:

- If it was God's will for Jesus to die from the beginning,
- and if it was Jesus' intention to be obedient unto death,
- if there is not one verse of Scripture in the New Testament that says Jesus came to be the *reigning* Messiah, and
- if Jesus refused by His words and actions to claim His throne as Messiah, then *the Jews cannot be blamed for rejecting what was never offered.*

Give Us a Sign!

The Jews demanded to know if Jesus was the Messiah, and yet He steadfastly refused to answer their demands. Consider biblical history. The Jews were accustomed to their leaders demonstrating their call from God with supernatural signs. When God called Moses to go into Egypt and lead millions of Hebrew slaves out of bondage, God gave

Moses four signs with which to convince the Israelites that he was the one chosen to lead them.

The first sign God gave Moses was the miracle of the shepherd's rod that became a snake. This sign convinced Moses as well as the people. Any nagging doubts Moses might have held vanished when he saw that serpent wriggling on the ground.

The next two signs were the affliction and healing of leprosy. God told Moses to put his hand in his bosom. He did, and it instantly became white with leprosy. God ordered Moses to put his hand in his bosom a second time, and when he pulled it out, his hand was restored "like his other flesh" (Ex. 4:7).

God continued His instructions to Moses by saying, "Then it will be, if they do not believe you, nor heed the message of the first sign, that they may believe the message of the latter sign. And it shall be, if they do not believe even these two signs, or listen to your voice, that you shall take water from the river and pour it on the dry land. The water which you take from the river will become blood on the dry land" (Ex. 4:8–9).

With these four signs, Moses convinced the children of Israel that he was God's anointed leader.

If God intended Jesus to be the Messiah of Israel, why didn't He authorize Jesus to use supernatural signs to prove He was God's Anointed One? Knowing of Moses' signs to Israel, the Jews asked for a supernatural sign to indicate that Jesus was the Anointed One.

"An evil and adulterous generation seeks after a sign," Jesus said, rebuking them, "and no sign will be given to it except the sign of the prophet Jonah. For as Jonah was three days and three nights in the belly of the great fish, so will the Son of Man be three days and three nights in the heart of the earth" (Matt. 12:39–40).

Jesus refused to give a sign. He compared Himself only to the prophet Jonah, who carried God's message of repentance to the Gentiles at Nineveh. Jesus was saying, "I have come to carry a message from God to the Gentiles, and just as Jonah was in the whale's belly for three days and three nights, I will be in My grave for three days and three nights."

Jesus also invoked Jonah's name when He gave Peter a special commission to the Gentiles. He told Peter, "Blessed are you, Simon Bar-Jonah" (Matt. 16:17). *Bar-Jonah* means "son of Jonah." Jesus wasn't referring to Simon's father, whose name was Jonah, but to the prophet Jonah who reluctantly carried God's message to the Gentiles at Nineveh. Peter was the Jewish messenger who would, as a "Jonah," carry the gospel message to the Gentiles in the house of Cornelius.

The Jews were not the only people to ask for a sign. When Jesus went on trial for His life, Herod Antipas was "exceedingly glad; for he had desired for a long time to see Him, because he had heard many things about Him, and he hoped to see some miracle done by Him" (Luke 23:8). If Jesus had wanted to install Himself as the reigning Messiah of Israel, it would have been a simple matter for Him to work signs and wonders before this king. But Jesus refused to produce a sign for Herod because it was not the Father's will. Jesus' repeated response to the Jewish people who urged Him to be their Messiah was "My kingdom is not of this world" (John 18:36).

"Tell No Man"

If Jesus wanted to be the reigning Messiah, why did He repeatedly tell His disciples and followers to "tell no man" about His supernatural accomplishments? Think about it. If He were trying to gain national attention to rally public support for the overthrow of Rome, He would not go around the country admonishing people to keep quiet.

He would have conducted Himself like any other politician, taking advantage of any and all opportunities for public exposure. The point of the political game is to *create public awareness of your cause,* to let people know who you are and what you propose to do.

But what did Jesus do?

On sixty-four occasions in the four Gospels, Jesus threw a wet blanket over His popularity, instructing those who were excited about His being Messiah to "tell no man." The people *wanted* Him to be their triumphant Messiah, but He absolutely refused.

When Jesus healed the leper, He instructed the man, "See that you tell no one; but go your way" (Matt. 8:4). When He raised Jairus's daughter from the dead, He charged the parents of the dead girl to tell no one what had happened (Luke 8:56). When He opened deaf ears, He commanded the people watching to tell no one (Mark 7:36). When He healed the blind man at Bethsaida by spitting on his eyes, He ordered him, saying, "Neither go into the town, nor tell anyone in the town" (Mark 8:26). When Jesus healed two blind men at once, He sternly warned them, "See that no one knows it" (Matt. 9:30).

When impetuous Peter could stand the mystery no longer, he blurted out, "You are the Christ" (Mark 8:29). In other words, he was saying, "You are the Anointed One; You are the Messiah that will lead the Jews in their revolt against Rome!"

Jesus commanded His disciples "that they should tell no one about Him" (Mark 8:30).

At the Transfiguration, Peter, James, and John heard Moses and Elijah talking to Jesus. They trembled as the voice of God spoke from a great cloud, saying, "This is My beloved Son. Hear Him!" And as they came down the mountain, Jesus commanded "that they should tell no one the things they had seen, till the Son of Man had risen from the dead" (Mark 9:7, 9).

Why did Jesus constantly command those who were excited about His supernatural power to "tell no man" prematurely? Because He did not come to be the reigning Messiah!

There were many Jews who would have followed Jesus when He fed 5,000 with two biscuits and five sardines! There were others who would have gladly pledged their lives when He raised Lazarus from the dead. But He performed these miracles to minister to the needs of the people, not to prove He was the Messiah.

The multiplied thousands who followed Jesus did not surrender the idea that He would be their reigning Messiah until they saw Him hanging from a Roman cross. Even after His resurrection and His repeated denials that He would not be the Messiah they expected, His disciples were still clinging to the last thread of hope that He would now smash Rome. "Lord," they asked Him, "will You at this time restore the kingdom to Israel?" (Acts 1:6).

The Jews who followed Jesus wanted Him to be their reigning Messiah, but He flatly refused.

The Jewish Mother

The mother of disciples James and John had her own ideas about Jesus' role as Messiah. Right up until the shadow of His cross fell across the bloody sands of Calvary, she tried to get Jesus to agree to place her two sons at His right and left hands when He established His kingdom (Matt. 20:20–23). She was not thinking about the suffering Messiah or a Roman cross; she wanted positions of influence and power for her sons in an earthly political kingdom. When Jesus defeated Rome as the reigning Jewish Messiah, she wanted her sons in positions of prominence.

What was Jesus' response? He looked at her and said, "You do not know what you ask" (Matt. 20:22). "The Son of Man did not come to be served, but to serve, and to give His life a ransom for many" (Matt. 20:28).

The Disciples on the Emmaus Road

The two disciples on the road to Emmaus (a settlement located seven miles outside Jerusalem) wanted Jesus to be the reigning Messiah. As they walked, Jesus Himself joined them on the road, but they did not recognize Him.

Jesus asked, "What kind of conversation is this that you have with one another as you walk and are sad?" (Luke 24:17).

The one named Cleopas answered, "Are You the only stranger in Jerusalem, and have You not known the things which happened there in these days?" (Luke 24:18).

Jesus answered, "What things?" (Luke 24:19).

"The things concerning Jesus of Nazareth," they answered, "who was a Prophet mighty in deed and word before God and all the people. . . . The chief priests and our rulers delivered Him to be condemned to death, and crucified Him. *But we were hoping that it was He who was going to redeem Israel*" (Luke 24:19–21, italics mine).

Those two disciples on the road to Emmaus had not rejected Jesus as Messiah—their hopes were dashed! It was not until Jesus entered their house for fellowship that they recognized Him. When He sat at their table, lifting His hands to bless and break the bread, they saw His nail-scarred hands and recognized Jesus. Instantly, He disappeared! He refused to be their reigning Messiah, choosing instead to be the Savior of the world.

Jesus Declines the Cup

As Jesus celebrated His last Passover with His disciples, He rejected, for the final time, the Messiahship of Israel.

Let me explain: It has been my privilege to join the Orthodox Synagogue in San Antonio in the celebration of Passover with Rabbi Arnold Scheinberg. Four cups of wine are served at the Passover with a meal that symbolizes the tears and suffering of the Hebrew slaves in Egypt.

- The first cup is the cup of Remembrance.
- The second cup is the cup of Redemption.
- The third cup is the cup of Salvation.
- The fourth cup is the cup of Messiah.

When Jesus and His disciples came to the final cup during their celebration of the Passover, Jesus *refused to drink* from the Messiah's cup. Instead He took it, gave thanks, and told His disciples, "Take this and divide it among yourselves; for I say to you, I will not drink of the fruit of the vine until the kingdom of God comes" (Luke 22:17–18).

In refusing to drink from the cup, Jesus rejected to the last detail the role of Messiah in word or deed. The Jews did not reject Jesus as Messiah; Jesus rejected the Jewish desire for Him to be their reigning Messiah. He was the Lamb of God. He had come to die, but even at that point the disciples were not ready to see the truth.

Two Israels

The scriptural portraits of two Messiahs—one suffering, one reigning—depict Jesus Christ as He came and as He will come. In a similar manner, Scripture describes and defines two Israels: One is a physical Israel, with an indigenous people, a capital city called Jerusalem, and geographic borders plainly defined in Scripture. Yet there is also a spiritual Israel, with a spiritual people and a spiritual New Jerusalem. Spiritual Israel, the church, may enjoy the blessings of physical Israel, but it does not replace physical Israel in God's plan for the ages.

This distinction is clearly stated in Isaiah 40:1: "'Comfort, yes, comfort My people!' / Says your God." Take a close look at the formal English. Who is being addressed? It is obvious that one group is being comforted and another is offering comfort.

Logic tells us we cannot be comforting and comforted at the same time. The people being comforted in this verse are "My people," or the Jewish people. The next verse makes this plain: "Speak comfort to Jerusalem, and cry out to her, / That her warfare is ended, / That her iniquity is pardoned" (Isa. 40:2).

The people doing the comforting are spiritual Israel, the church.

The Bible concept of two Israels, one physical and the other spiritual, is validated by God's revelation to Abraham concerning his seed. God showed Abraham his spiritual seed in Genesis 22:17: "Blessing I will bless you, and multiplying I will multiply your descendants as the stars of the heaven and as the sand which is on the seashore."

God mentions two separate and distinct elements: stars of the heaven and sand of the seashore.

The "stars of the heaven" represent the church, or spiritual Israel. Stars, as light, rule the darkness, which is the commission of the church. Jesus said, "You are the light of the world" (Matt. 5:14). Jesus is called "the Bright and Morning Star" (Rev. 22:16). Daniel 12:3 tells us that "Those who are wise shall shine / Like the brightness of the firmament, / And those who turn many to righteousness / Like the stars forever and ever." A star gave guidance and led wise men to the house in Bethlehem where Jesus was.

Stars are heavenly, not earthly. They represent the church, spiritual Israel.

The "sand of the seashore," on the other hand, is earthly and represents an earthly kingdom with a literal Jerusalem as the capital city.

Both stars and sand exist at the same time, and neither ever replaces the other. Just so, the nation of Israel and spiritual Israel, the church, exist at the same time and do not replace each other. In Revelation 7:4–8, physical Israel is alive and well, represented by twelve tribes and 144,000 who were sealed by God to preach the gospel during the Great Tribulation.

In 1948 Israel was reborn, and the Seed of Abraham returned to the Promised Land to become one of the world's most dynamic nations. Replaced? Never. Revived? Yes!

According to John the Revelator, Israel is still thriving during the Tribulation when the church is in heaven. John wrote: "And I heard the number of those who were sealed. One hundred and forty-four thousand of all the tribes of the children of Israel were sealed" (Rev. 7:4).

The two Israels will merge together on the day when the Messiah literally enters the physical city of Jerusalem. The prophet Zechariah describes the coming of the Messiah: "And I will pour on the house of David and on the inhabitants of

Jerusalem the Spirit of grace and supplication," wrote the prophet, "then they will look on Me whom they pierced. Yes, they will mourn for Him as one mourns for his only son, and grieve for Him as one grieves for a firstborn" (12:10).

Unless we grasp the concept of two Israels peacefully coexisting and never replacing each other, we will fall into the false doctrine of past centuries. The tragedy is that our ignorance ultimately injures Israel and the Jewish people and invites the wrath of God upon us and our descendants.

Boycott Israel?

American replacement theologians are preaching, "If Christians will quit supporting Israel and economically boycott the Christ-rejecting Jews, the Jews will accept Jesus Christ."[3]

An economic boycott of national Israel is not going to hasten the day Jews convert and become spiritual Israel. This anti-Semitic logic defies and ignores both history and the Bible.

The Jews were economically attacked by crusaders who murdered, raped, and robbed them in the name of God. They didn't accept Christ after that tragedy. The Jews of the Spanish Inquisition were tortured and terrorized as the church extorted their wealth. They did not become Christians, even when they were forced to surrender their children to be raised by Gentile neighbors because they were under death sentences from the church.

Economically, Adolf Hitler brought the Jews to their knees by forbidding them to have jobs. He destroyed their places of business in the infamous Night of Broken Glass, and then fined them billions of deutsche marks to repair the damage his Nazi hoodlums had inflicted. They did not become Christians even when he systematically slaughtered six million of them. As Jews walked to the gas chamber they sang "Hatkivah," not "Amazing Grace."

The Bible says:

- "And so all Israel will be saved" (Rom. 11:26).
- Israel will welcome the Messiah (see Zech. 12:10).
- Israel will come to repentance (see Rom. 11:27).

When will Israel welcome its Messiah? Look at Romans 11:25: "For I do not desire, brethren," Paul writes, "that you should be ignorant of this mystery, lest you should be wise in your own opinion, that blindness in part has happened to Israel until the fullness of the Gentiles has come in." The word translated *fullness* is the Greek word *pleroma*. The word refers not to a numerical capacity, but to a sense of *completeness*.

"The completion of the mission to the Gentiles will result in, or lead to, Israel's 'fullness' or 'completion' (Rom. 11:12), her 'acceptance' (Rom. 11:15)," write scholars Walter C. Kaiser Jr., Peter H. Davids, F. F. Bruce, and Manfred T. Brauch in *Hard Sayings of the Bible*. "Paul proclaims this future realization of God's intention as 'a mystery' (Rom. 11:25). . . . The most instructive parallel to this text—which envisions the grafting of both Gentile and Jew into the same olive tree—is Ephesians 3:3–6, where Paul says that the content of the 'mystery of Christ' is the inclusion of the Gentiles as fellow heirs of the promise with Jews in the new community of Christ's body."[4]

Bible scholars agree that Paul's statement that "all Israel will be saved" means Israel "as a whole," not every single individual. Just as the phrase "the fullness of the Gentiles" (Rom. 11:25) does not mean every single Gentile will accept

Jesus as Messiah, even so not every single child of Israel will place his or her faith in the Christ. But when the "fullness of the Gentiles" has come, that is, when the Gentiles' time of grace is completed, then God will remove their blindness (Rom. 11:10) to the identity of Messiah and "all Israel will be saved" (Rom. 11:26).

"What is also clear from the whole thrust of the discussion in Romans 9–11," write the aforementioned scholars, "is that God's purposes for the salvation of Israel will be realized in no other way and by no other means than through the preaching of the gospel and the response of faith."[5]

By faithfully sharing the gospel, you may lead a Jewish friend to Christ, but the idea that the Jews of the world are going to convert and storm the doors of Christian churches is a delusion born of ignorance. After 2,000 years of a loveless, anti-Semitic Christianity that has saturated the soil of the earth with Jewish blood, the Jews are not about to convert en masse.

Those who target Jews for conversion quoting Romans 1:16 ("For I am not ashamed of the gospel of Christ, for it is the power of God to salvation for everyone who believes, for the Jew first and also for the Greek") twist the Scripture. The subject of Romans 1:16 is *the gospel*. Paul's words "to the Jew first," do not refer to priority. His words are a statement of *sequence*, not *preference*. The gospel came to the Jewish people first (see Rom. 3:2), and then to the Gentiles. God is not a respecter of persons.

Where is the Christianity that says, "Love your neighbor as you love yourself"? Where is the Christianity that says, "Love suffers long and is kind; love does not envy"? Where are the Christians who practice "Love one another as I have loved you"? Where is the Christianity, born of the blood of Jesus of Nazareth, who said, "Inasmuch as you have done it unto the least of these *My brethren* [the Jews], you have done it unto Me"?

Jews and Judaism have not lost their credibility; but all too often a loveless Christianity has abandoned the law of love only to become sounding brass and clanging cymbals. Until the Lord's return, why should any Jew want to follow a Messiah whose followers feel compelled to hate, murder, rob, and rape while they brazenly proclaim, "We are the singular people of God"?

If Replaced, Why Reborn?

For 1,800 years, the church fathers ranted that the church is the new Israel. To prove that God had turned His back on the Jews, they pointed to the wandering, tormented Jews of the Diaspora, saying, "If God is with them, why has this homelessness befallen them?"

They forget that for the most part European Jews were living in states controlled by the Church of Rome. They were existing without rights, without property, without legal redress, and without human dignity. The medieval church created its own self-fulfilling prophecy.

Replacement theologians ignore a fundamental fact in the biblical text. When God removes or destroys something, you never hear from it again. Like Sodom and Gomorrah, which were so thoroughly destroyed that archaeologists can't even find the ashes of those cities, it is twice dead, plucked up by the roots and cast over the wall to be burned and forever forgotten. If the church fathers were correct and Israel were indeed replaced, she should have vanished like snow in the desert sun. By all rights, she should have disappeared. But she didn't.

On May 15, 1948, a theological earthquake leveled replacement theology when the State of Israel was reborn after 2,000 years of wandering. From the four corners of the earth, the Seed of Abraham returned to the land of their fathers. They arose from their Gentile "graves" (Ezek. 37:12) speaking sixty different languages, and they founded a nation that has become a superpower in forty years. Far from passing away, the State of Israel is building, growing, inventing, and developing. The desert is indeed blooming like a rose, just as Isaiah the prophet promised (35:1).

You can't avoid the central issue. If God was finished with the Jews and Israel, if they were really a cast-off relic of the past without divine purpose or destiny, why did He allow the State to be miraculously renewed? If replaced, why reborn?

The resurrection of God's chosen people is living prophetic proof that Israel has not been replaced. They were reborn in a day (Isa. 66:8) to form the State of Israel that shall endure until the coming of Messiah.

If Israel as a nation had not been reborn, if the Jews had not returned to the land, if the cities of Israel had not been rebuilt, if Judea and Samaria (the West Bank) had not been occupied, if the trees the Turks cut down had not been replanted, if the agricultural accomplishments of Israel had not been miraculous, there would be a valid reason to doubt that the Word of God is true. However, in light of the above-mentioned miracles, none can doubt the absolute accuracy of the prophetic Scriptures concerning the rebirth and restoration of the Jewish state.

Listen to God's Word as His prophets declare His intention for the Jews to inhabit Israel. Isaiah wrote:

> Fear not, for I am with you;
> I will bring your descendants from the east,
> And gather you from the west;
> I will say to the north, "Give them up!"

And to the south, "Do not keep them back!"
Bring My sons from afar,
And My daughters from the ends of the earth (43:5–6).

And the ransomed of the LORD shall return,
And come to Zion with singing,
With everlasting joy on their heads.
They shall obtain joy and gladness,
And sorrow and sighing shall flee away (35:10).

And they shall rebuild the old ruins,
They shall raise up the former desolations,
And they shall repair the ruined cities,
The desolations of many generations (61:4).

Who confirms the word of His servant,
And performs the counsel of His messengers;
Who says to Jerusalem, "You shall be inhabited,"
To the cities of Judah, "You shall be built,"
And I will raise up her waste places (44:26).

Ezekiel speaks:

"As I live," says the Lord GOD, "surely with a mighty
hand, with an outstretched arm, and with fury poured
out, I will rule over you. I will bring you out from the
peoples and gather you out of the countries where you
are scattered, with a mighty hand, with an outstretched
arm, and with fury poured out. . . . For on My holy
mountain, on the mountain height of Israel," says the
Lord GOD, "there all the house of Israel, all of them in
the land, shall serve Me; there I will accept them, and
there I will require your offerings and the firstfruits of
your sacrifices, together with all your holy things. I will
accept you as a sweet aroma when I bring you out from
the peoples and gather you out of the countries where
you have been scattered; and I will be hallowed in you

before the Gentiles. Then you shall know that I am the LORD, when I bring you into the land of Israel, into the country for which I raised My hand in an oath to give to your fathers" (20:33–34, 40–42).

"And they shall no longer be a prey for the nations, nor shall beasts of the land devour them; but they shall dwell safely, and no one shall make them afraid. I will raise up for them a garden of renown, and they shall no longer be consumed with hunger in the land, nor bear the shame of the Gentiles anymore. Thus they shall know that I, the LORD their God, am with them, and they, the house of Israel, are My people," says the Lord GOD (34:28–30).

Therefore say, "Thus says the Lord GOD: 'I will gather you from the peoples, assemble you from the countries where you have been scattered, and I will give you the land of Israel.' And they will go there, and they will take away all its detestable things and all its abominations from there. Then I will give them one heart, and I will put a new spirit within them" (11:17–19).

Jeremiah speaks:

Behold, I will bring back the captivity of Jacob's tents,
And have mercy on his dwelling places;
The city shall be built upon its own mound,
And the palace shall remain according to its own plan (30:18).

Hear the word of the LORD, O nations,
And declare it in the isles afar off, and say,
"He who scattered Israel will gather him,
And keep him as a shepherd does his flock."
For the LORD has redeemed Jacob,
And ransomed him from the hand of one stronger than he.
Therefore they shall come and sing in the height of Zion,

Streaming to the goodness of the LORD—
For wheat and new wine and oil,
For the young of the flock and the herd;
Their souls shall be like a well-watered garden,
And they shall sorrow no more at all (31:10–12).

> "For behold, the days are coming," says the LORD,
> "that I will bring back from captivity My people Israel
> and Judah," says the LORD. "And I will cause them to
> return to the land that I gave to their fathers, and they
> shall possess it. . . .
> "Therefore do not fear, O My servant Jacob,"
>   says the LORD,
> "Nor be dismayed, O Israel;
> For behold, I will save you from afar,
> And your seed from the land of their captivity.
> Jacob shall return, have rest and be quiet,
> And no one shall make him afraid.
> For I am with you," says the LORD, "to save you;
> Though I make a full end of all nations where I
>   have scattered you" (30:3, 10–11).

David speaks:

When the LORD brought back the captivity of Zion,
We were like those who dream.
Then our mouth was filled with laughter,
And our tongue with singing.
Then they said among the nations,
"The LORD has done great things for them" (Ps. 126:1–2).

Oh, give thanks to the LORD, for He is good!
For His mercy endures forever.
Let the redeemed of the LORD say so,
Whom He has redeemed from the hand of the enemy,
And gathered out of the lands,

From the east and from the west,
From the north and from the south (Ps. 107:1–3).

Zechariah testifies of things to come:

> So the angel who spoke with me said to me, "Pro-
> claim, saying, 'Thus says the LORD of hosts:
> "I am zealous for Jerusalem
> And for Zion with great zeal.
> I am exceedingly angry with the nations at ease;
> For I was a little angry,
> And they helped—but with evil intent."
> 'Therefore thus says the LORD:
> "I am returning to Jerusalem with mercy;
> My house shall be built in it," says the LORD of
> hosts,
> "And a surveyor's line shall be stretched out over
> Jerusalem."'
> Again proclaim, saying, 'Thus says the LORD of
> hosts:
> "My cities shall again spread out through prosperity;
> The LORD will again comfort Zion,
> And will again choose Jerusalem"'" (1:14–17).

The Old Testament prophets are clear and united in
their opinions—replacement theology is completely wrong,
misguided, deceived, ill conceived, and incorrect. The Jews
have not been replaced, for they will return to Jerusalem,
the city of God, and the God of Abraham, Isaac, and Jacob
will be their God.

Jesus Did Not Support
Replacement Theology

Jesus was the greatest teacher of the ages. He gave us
three chapters (Matt. 24, Mark 13, and Luke 21) that are
prophetic and present the chronological events of the future

from His time until His second coming. In Matthew 24:3, His disciples asked Jesus three questions:

1. *When shall these things be?* This question referred to the destruction of the temple. Jesus answered in Luke 21:20, "When you see Jerusalem surrounded by armies, then know that its desolation is near." This prediction was fulfilled in A.D. 70 when the Roman general Titus destroyed Jerusalem.
2. *And what will be the sign of Your coming?*
3. *And of the end of the age?* In spite of the "kingdom now" theology (whose adherents believe the church will be so victorious that we will usher in the millennial age), this world is coming to an end. In Galatians 1:4, Paul wrote that Christ "gave Himself for our sins, that He might *deliver us* from this present evil age, according to the will of our God and Father" (italics mine).

There is not a single hint in one of these passages supporting replacement theology. Paul did not mention the demise of the Jewish nation, nor did Jesus.

Let's look at Matthew 24:15–18, where Jesus described the great period of tribulation that will come upon the earth. This verse assumes that Israel is living in its homeland and in control of the city of Jerusalem. "Therefore," said Jesus, "when you see the 'abomination of desolation,' spoken of by Daniel the prophet, standing in the holy place . . . then let those who are in Judea flee to the mountains. Let him who is on the housetop not go down to take anything out of his house. And let him who is in the field not go back to get his clothes."

The "holy place" Jesus mentioned is the temple in Jerusalem. The Jews are in control of the temple at this time right before the Tribulation. How could they control the temple without being in control of Jerusalem? How could they be in control of Jerusalem if they were replaced?

"Let those who are in Judea flee to the mountains," Jesus said. Judea is what the media now call the West Bank. Jesus' statement assumes that in the last days the Jews would be living on the West Bank. In the next several verses, Jesus describes a general evacuation of the population in and around Jerusalem because of a pending military attack.

When this military attack comes, warned Jesus, don't go to Jerusalem for safety. You will have only a few minutes to save your life. Flee to the mountains outside Jerusalem as a matter of civil defense. Jesus continues, "Let him who is on the housetop not go down to take anything out of his house. And let him who is in the field not go back to get his clothes."

The rooftops in Jerusalem, both now and in Jesus' time, are flat. People store things on the roof and sometimes even sleep there. There is usually an outside stairway leading to the ground. When this attack comes, Jesus warned, don't worry about saving anything in the house, just run for your life. And if you are in the fields, laboring in your work clothes, don't run back to the house to change.

Jesus continues: "But woe to those who are pregnant and to those who are nursing babies in those days! And pray that your flight may not be in winter or on the Sabbath. For then there will be great tribulation, such as has not been since the beginning of the world until this time, no, nor ever shall be" (Matt. 24:19–21).

Why woe to those who are pregnant and with nursing babies? Why pray that your escape be not in winter or on the Sabbath? Because an escape would be much more difficult. This verse again indicates that the religious Jews are in control of an Israeli government where the laws of the Sabbath are being strictly enforced.

I don't know if you've had the opportunity to travel in Israel on the Sabbath, but I can assure you that everything shuts down on Saturday. There is no transportation. Even the elevators in the hotels and high-rise apartments stop on every floor automatically. If an Arab missile with a nuclear warhead or poison gas struck Jerusalem on the Sabbath, the attack would result in mass destruction.

Jesus confirms that the Jews are back in Israel in Matthew 24:22 when He says, "And unless those days were shortened, no flesh would be saved; but for the elect's sake those days will be shortened."

"The elect" are the Jewish people. If Jesus and the prophets were convinced that Israel would return to the land, and if they were certain Israel had not been cast aside or replaced in the economy of God, how is it that America's replacement theologians have come up with a different idea? Did it spring from narcissism? Anti-Semitism?

Replacement Theology Is Idolatry

Replacement theology violates the Ten Commandments. First Samuel 15:23 tells us, "For rebellion is as the sin of witchcraft, / And stubbornness is as iniquity and idolatry."

This verse says two things: (1) Rebellion equals witchcraft and (2) stubbornness equals idolatry. Who is a stubborn person? People who refuse to change their ideas even when they are in direct conflict with God's Word are the worst kind of stubborn. These people idolize their opinions and are soon in open rebellion against the will and Word of God.

Christians would never dream of allowing their pastor to preach with a statue of Buddha draped around his neck— that's open idolatry. But they think nothing of permitting their pastor, whose stubborn personal opinions about Israel are exactly opposite the Word of God, to lead them into dangerous deception.

Has the church replaced Israel? Not in the opinion of Jesus and the prophets of Israel. The canon of Scripture and modern history are witnesses to the fact that Israel has been reborn and will endure forever.

From the dark days of Jewish persecution in Germany, a legend has survived. According to the story, a pastor, acting on Nazi orders, looked out upon his congregation and told them, "All of you who had Jewish fathers will leave and not return."

A few worshipers rose and slipped out of the sanctuary. The pastor then said, "All of you who had Jewish mothers must go and not return."

Again, a few worshipers arose and departed. Suddenly those who remained in their pews turned pale and began to tremble with fear. The figure of Christ on the cross above the altar loosed itself and left the church.

Think about it. If Jesus Christ came to your church this Sunday morning, would the ushers let Him enter the front door? He would appear small and slender, with penetrating dark eyes, a swarthy complexion, and prominent Semitic features. He would have earlocks, hair uncut at the corners, and full beard. His shoulders would be draped with a tallit, or prayer shawl.

If Jesus identified Himself to your congregation as a Rabbi who befriended prostitutes and socialized with tax collectors and people with AIDS, would He be welcomed? If He confessed that He was hated by the government and traveled with twelve unemployed men with full beards and shoulder-length hair, could they find a seat in your pews?

If your deacons asked Him about His doctrinal positions and He responded, "I believe in baptism by immersion, casting out demons, and healing the sick," would they let Him stand behind your pulpit?

If He commanded your wealthiest church members to sell all they had to give to the poor, if He entered your beautiful church gym and turned over the bingo tables shouting, "My house shall be called a house of prayer," would you call the police?

The simple truth is this: After 2,000 years of anti-Semitic teaching and preaching, we have lost sight of the Jewishness of our Hebrew Savior. But He was born to Jewish parents, His ancestors were Jewish, He was raised in the Jewish tradition, He lived and worshiped as a Jew, He died as a Jew, and He will return as a Jew. When you kneel tonight to pray, the One who hears you is a Rabbi named Jesus of Nazareth.

PART II

THE
PROPHECIES
OF
JERUSALEM

CHAPTER 7

JERUSALEM THE GOLDEN

There is Israel, for us at least. What no other generation had, we have. We have Israel in spite of all the dangers, the threats and the wars, we have Israel. We can go to Jerusalem. Generations and generations could not and we can.

—Elie Wiesel, Romanian-born American writer[1]

We have discussed the *people* of Jerusalem—a nation that wandered homeless for thousands of years, a nation persecuted without valid cause even in the name of Christ. We've seen how God's divine principle of blessing and cursing Israel has been graphically demonstrated in the lives of individuals and political powers. We've learned that Israel has not been replaced or removed from God's covenant and plan. Now we will see how *prophecies* regarding the Seed of Abraham will affect the future of all men and every nation on earth.

127

Focal Point of the Past and Future: Jerusalem

Medieval mapmakers (quite rightfully, in my opinion) placed beautiful Jerusalem at the center of the world. They understood what Bible scholars have known for years—Jerusalem is the center of the universe, the focal point of things to come and things in the past.

The ancient city of Jerusalem is the heart and soul of the nation of Israel. While other cities around the world are known for their commerce, their size, their wealth, or their outstanding architecture, Jerusalem ascends to the pinnacle of world prominence with accolades that can be given to no other city on earth. Jerusalem is the chosen city of God:

> I [God] have chosen Jerusalem, that My name may be there. . . . For now I have chosen and sanctified this house [the temple], that My name may be there forever; and My eyes and My heart will be there perpetually. . . . In this house and in Jerusalem, which I have chosen out of all the tribes of Israel, I will put My name forever (2 Chron. 6:6; 7:16; 33:7).

Jerusalem is a small city by many standards. With a population of just over a half million, it is certainly not the most populous city in the world. And yet it dominates headlines of newspapers and is known as the Holy City to Muslims, Christians, and Jews.

History of the Holy City

Jerusalem, whose very dust is adored in Scripture, was first settled by Canaanites in the twentieth century B.C. Though only a little larger than twelve acres in size, the city was naturally well defended and had at its base one of the most abundant springs in the area. By about 1,000 years before Christ, Jerusalem was inhabited by Jebusites, a group of people related to the Hittites of the Old Testament.

By the time David was anointed king of Israel in the last decade of the eleventh century B.C., the nation of Israel needed a strong central capital. David searched for a location among the tribes, and in 1004 B.C. he conquered a Jebusite city and made it his capital.

David's passion for the Holy City is evident as that poet and warrior statesman of Israel wrote,

> If I forget you, O Jerusalem,
> Let my right hand forget its skill!
> If I do not remember you,
> Let my tongue cling to the roof of my mouth—
> If I do not exalt Jerusalem
> Above my chief joy (Ps. 137:5–6).

As you may recall, David was a musician. With his right hand he played the harp and sang the songs of Israel with such power that the demons of King Saul were silenced. If David's tongue were frozen to the roof of his mouth and his right hand could no longer play, his life as a musician would be over.

David's message was simple. If he were to forget Jerusalem, his life would have no meaning. If Jerusalem was not the source of his deepest joy, he felt there was no need to exist. He saw Jerusalem as the Holy City, the place God and God's people called home.

In Jerusalem, David's son Solomon built his magnificent and ornate temple.

In Jerusalem, Jeremiah and Isaiah uttered thoughts that molded the spiritual foundations of half the human race.

In Jerusalem, Jesus Christ of Nazareth wept on the Mount of Olives hours before His crucifixion. "O Jerusalem, Jerusalem," He prayed, "the one who kills the prophets and stones those who are sent to her! How often I wanted to gather your children together, as a hen gathers her chicks under her wings, but you were not willing!" (Matt. 23:37).

In A.D. 70 Titus sent his troops into Jerusalem and slaughtered the Jews until their blood literally streamed down the streets. The Romans completely sacked the city and destroyed most of the second temple, which had been completed only six years before. The Romans continued the slaughter of the Jews of Jerusalem. In A.D. 135 a Jewish Diaspora began as Hadrian, a second-century Roman emperor, barred Jews from Jerusalem and had survivors of the massacre dispersed across the Roman Empire. Many fleeing Jews escaped to Mediterranean ports only to be sold into slavery.

The crusaders, marching under the sign of the cross, stormed into Jerusalem in 1099. Again the streets of the city ran with blood as the crusaders slaughtered over 40,000 people and set fire to mosques and synagogues. As screams for mercy rose from the lips of tortured Jews inside their synagogues, the crusaders lustily sang hymns of praise to God.

Jerusalem means "city of peace," but it has known more war, more bloodshed, more tears, and more terror than any other city on earth. It has been conquered and reconquered thirty-eight times by Babylonians, Greeks, Romans, crusaders, and Ottomans, yet it stands united and indivisible.

Only the mighty hand of God could have preserved Jerusalem from its birth under King David until the stunning moment in the 1967 Six-Day War when Jewish soldiers broke through the Jordanian front and prayed together at the Western Wall. After almost 2,000 years, the ancient city of Jerusalem once again was restored into Jewish hands through a supernatural victory of the Israeli army.

But Jerusalem is the city that symbolizes God's power to protect His people:

> Those who trust in the LORD
> Are like Mount Zion,
> Which cannot be moved, but abides forever.
> As the mountains surround Jerusalem,
> So the LORD surrounds His people
> From this time forth and forever (Ps. 125:1–2).

God will preserve Jerusalem. It is *His* Holy City.

Jerusalem Today

What's happening in Jerusalem today? Jerusalem the Golden is caught in a supernatural crossfire. Trading land for peace will not bring peace. Making Jerusalem an international city under the pope will not bring peace. Giving Yasser Arafat and the PLO part of Jerusalem to establish a Palestinian city will not bring peace.

The enemies of Israel and of the Jewish people will not be satisfied until they control Jerusalem. Christians and Jews, let us stand united and indivisible on this issue: There can be no compromise regarding the city of Jerusalem, not now, not ever. We are racing toward the end of time, and Israel lies in the eye of the storm.

My newspaper's morning headlines recently screamed THIRTY-ONE PALESTINIANS SHOT AS HEBRON RIOTS RAGE. Jerusalem radio news programs frequently warn that terrorists may strike soon. The front page of the *Jerusalem Post*'s international edition declares, ISRAELI PRIME MINISTER REJECTS

MAKE-BELIEVE PEACE. As I write this, Islamic suicide bombers have just invaded the peaceful Mahaneh Yehuda market, leaving 16 dead and 176 innocent people wounded.

In recent days on the streets of Tel Aviv, a HAMAS (Islamic Resistance Movement) suicide bomber killed twenty-two and wounded nearly four dozen. The bomb he carried was so powerful that it shredded a bus. Bits of human hair and flesh had to be scraped off nearby walls.

Bloody street battles are fought weekly in West Bank cities. Stark images of mourners picking up rocks after a funeral and charging Israeli soldiers leap from the pages of *Time* and *Newsweek*. Rubber bullets and flying rocks in Ramallah are a testimonial that men cry "Peace, peace," but there is no peace. Anyone who thinks peace is coming to the city of Jerusalem and the Middle East is living in a world of illusion.

What is the meaning behind these signs of the times? The end of the world as we know it is drawing near. And although the action is now in Israel, the future and destiny of the entire planet hang in the balance.

God has made it possible to know the future through Bible prophecy. My years of studying the writings of the ancient Bible prophets have given me a panoramic view, not only of what is ahead, but how it will all unfold. The guidelines for tomorrow are available to us today.

God Remembers

God's megaphones came in human form. He chose righteous men to preach His message and proclaim prophecy. Zechariah was such a man. Born of priestly lineage, Zechariah lived during one of the most significant periods of upheaval in the saga of Israel. Struggling exiles returning from Babylon rebuilt the blackened ruins of

Jerusalem and the temple. Zechariah knew God was getting ready to do a great thing; however, in writing to encourage the weary laborers, he also left us with vital clues to understand God's everlasting plan.

Zekar-yah, the prophet's name in Hebrew, means "God remembers." In fact, Zechariah's theme is that Israel will be blessed precisely because God remembers the covenants and agreements He made with the patriarchs. No one was better equipped to explore the mind of God than this walking symbol of the faithful memory of Almighty God.

Zechariah wasn't surprised when he got the message about the future. Another prophet had already described what lay ahead for Israel. Isaiah foresaw the coming fall and conquest of the Hebrews by Babylonian hordes. Isaiah gave Zechariah his first inkling of an astonishing divine surprise awaiting Jerusalem and the Jews.

Through Isaiah, God promised the complete restoration of Jerusalem. He wrote, "I have set watchmen on your walls, O Jerusalem; / They shall never hold their peace day or night. / You who make mention of the LORD, do not keep silent, / And give Him no rest till He establishes / And till He makes Jerusalem a praise in the earth" (62:6–7).

The future of the Holy City is the centerpiece of God's blueprint for history. God will reorder, restore, redouble, redistribute, reclaim, remove, renovate, recycle, recommit, and redeem until Jerusalem has become the crowning gem of all the cities on earth.

Why You Should Study Prophecy

How can you sift the truth from the nonsense when you pick up a newspaper and read about Israel? You must pay careful attention to what God has already said about the future of Jerusalem and Israel. Prophecy is the divine security system to alert us ahead of time. Let me give you four reasons to study what God said centuries ago through His prophets:

1. *Prophecy reveals the purposes of God.* God wants the world to know what's coming. The heavenly Father desires to reveal Himself and His motives. God's way comes through God's Word. Holy Scripture is His vehicle for communication. When the wickedness of Sodom and Gomorrah reached intolerable proportions, God went first to Abraham and told him He was going to destroy the cities of Sodom and Gomorrah (Gen. 18). This was a revelation of the purpose of God through predictive prophecy.

In Genesis 18:17–18 we read, "And the LORD said, 'Shall I hide from Abraham what I am doing, since Abraham shall surely become a great and mighty nation, and all the nations of the earth shall be blessed in him?'" God divulged the future to Abraham. Otherwise Abraham might have asked himself, "Why did God do that? What was God's purpose in the destruction of every person in those two cities?"

God revealed His purpose to Abraham so that when the destruction took place Abraham would understand that God was holy and that He would not tolerate the sins of Sodom and Gomorrah.

As we study prophecy we understand the economic and political events in Europe that will bring the Antichrist to power; we understand Russia and its desire to once again become a military superpower by conquering Israel; we understand the global rush for a one-world currency, religion, and government. Prophecy reveals the purposes of God and demonstrates beyond any doubt that God knows the end from the beginning and that He is orchestrating the events on earth to fulfill His exact purposes.

2. *Prophecy demonstrates God's ability to know the future.* Powerful generals and clever politicians think they have the power and capacity to wield total authority and create empires, yet God is the One who raises up and puts down whom He chooses. Nations rise and fall by His design. Well before earthly coronations, the Almighty chooses who sits on the throne of each individual nation.

The second chapter of the book of Daniel contains one of the most remarkable visions God ever gave to humanity. Nebuchadnezzar thought of himself as the absolute emperor of the world, but God sent the king a particularly worrisome dream. Nebuchadnezzar dreamed of a great image made of gold, silver, bronze, and iron, with clay feet. In his dream, a massive boulder suddenly smashed into the statue, turning it into a mountain of rubble that filled the entire earth.

Nebuchadnezzar was troubled. In his heart of hearts he knew a force far greater than himself was the true power behind his throne. The king longed to understand the meaning of his dreadful dream, but when he awoke, only the troubled feelings remained—he had completely forgotten the details.

Daniel, who was in service to the Babylonian king, seized this opportunity to tell the king that God alone can reveal such mysteries because He alone knows the future. Daniel's inspired interpretation revealed the dream and completely explained each element of it.

The statue's golden head represented Nebuchadnezzar, and the other elements represented other kingdoms that would soon follow his. The Medes and the

Persians, symbolized by the image's breastplate of silver, were waiting in the wings. Their kingdoms were displaced by Alexander the Great of Greece, the statue's loins of brass. Alexander's kingdom fell to the Roman Empire, the strong and mighty domain, which eventually divided into Eastern and Western empires.

Daniel noted that the lower his inner eye descended over the image, the weaker the materials became. The statue's feet were composed of iron and clay, two materials that will not blend with each other. The "partly strong and partly broken" kingdom of Rome did weaken as it aged, until it finally divided into ten toes, or ten kingdoms.

Those ten toes, or kingdoms, will be some sort of European federation in the last days, and from this ten-member confederacy a "man of peace" will rise to take the world stage. He will be a masterful orator, and with his genius he will lead the world to a superficial, temporary prosperity.

He is the Antichrist. He will make Hitler look like a choirboy. He will sign a seven-year peace treaty with Israel and break it after three and a half years. At that time he will set himself up to be worshiped in the city of Jerusalem. He will want Jerusalem for his holy city, and he will try to exterminate every Jew in Israel.

But Nebuchadnezzar's dream did not end with the ten toes. The Babylonian king saw a rock "cut without hands" demolish the great image, and that indestructible stone was Jesus Christ. At His second coming, the world's Messiah will crush His adversaries and establish His Millennial Kingdom, the 1,000-year reign of Christ.

As he interpreted, Daniel reminded the king of the dream and revealed its hidden mystery. The king was astonished and cried out in awe, "Truly your God is the God of gods, the Lord of kings, and a revealer of secrets, since you could reveal this secret"(Dan. 2:47). Nebuchadnezzar had just become a believer in Bible prophecy. The king understood that God knows.

3. *Prophecy is absolutely accurate.* The apostle Peter read the writings of Zechariah, Isaiah, Daniel, and the other prophets. He had been an eyewitness to their fulfillment in the coming of Jesus Christ. Reflecting on the astonishing accuracy of the prophets, he wrote this summation:

> We have the prophetic word confirmed, which you do well to heed as a light that shines in a dark place, until the day dawns and the morning star rises in your hearts; knowing this first, that no prophecy of Scripture is of any private interpretation, for prophecy never came by the will of man, but holy men of God spoke as they were moved by the Holy Spirit (2 Peter 1:19–21).

Peter wanted every Christian to know that Jehovah not only speaks, but is 100 percent correct in what He says. While Peter had been an eyewitness to Jesus' ministry and resurrection, he knew prophecy was even more accurate than an eyewitness account. The human eye and ear are never completely trustworthy because distortions can creep in. But when God speaks, the communication is totally and completely perfect. You can bet your eternal soul on the accuracy of Bible prophecy.

4. *Prophecy validates the authority of God's Word.* Cults delight in making strange and esoteric statements. Although they love to tickle people's ears with fanciful ideas, they are strangely silent about the future. The Bible, however, is filled with specifics about tomorrow.

Consider the absolute accuracy concerning the life of Christ:

- The time of Jesus' birth is described in Daniel 9.
- The fact of Jesus' virgin birth is detailed in Isaiah 7:14.
- The place of Jesus' birth is forecast in Micah 5:2.
- The technicalities of His death are depicted in Psalm 22 and Isaiah 53.
- The Resurrection is prophesied in Psalm 16:10.

This is only a partial listing; I could list over six dozen references to prophecies about the Messiah that were fulfilled in Jesus Christ. In fact, the odds of those prophecies pointing to anyone other than Jesus are staggering.

One mathematician put his pencil to the problem and derived an extraordinary conclusion. The odds of all the Bible prophecies coming true in the life of one person—Jesus—are one in 87 followed by 93 zeroes!

CHAPTER 8

WINDS OF WAR OVER JERUSALEM

Think back with me, if you will, to September 13, 1993. Israeli prime minister Yitzhak Rabin stood in the White House Rose Garden with Yasser Arafat. President Bill Clinton stood between these two men, eager to announce that Rabin and Arafat had, the previous day, signed the West Bank accord. At that signing, Rabin declared that the land flowing with milk and honey should not become a land flowing with blood and tears. In a speech delivered only a few days before, Rabin had said, "We, the soldiers who have returned from battles stained with blood; we who have seen our relatives and friends killed before our eyes; we who have attended their funerals and cannot look in the eyes of their parents; we who have come from a land where parents bury their children; we who have fought against you, the Palestinians—we say to you today, in a loud and a clear voice: enough of blood and tears. Enough."

That was a desperate and sincere cry from the soul of a warrior, but two years later, in Jerusalem, Rabin was assassinated. Blood and tears flowed again, and the leaders of the world stood at his graveside and mourned the man who had tried to bring peace to his country and failed.

Why will there be no peace in that troubled part of the world? Because an ancient rivalry exists, one that goes back all the way to Abraham.

To honor Abraham for his faith and obedience, God dispatched an angel to tell Abraham that he would be the father of a great nation: "And behold, the word of the LORD came to him, saying, . . . 'One who will come from your own body shall be your heir.' Then He brought him outside and said, 'Look now toward heaven, and count the stars if you are able to number them.' And He said to him, 'So shall your descendants be'" (Gen. 15:4–5).

Abraham was more than a little surprised at this revelation because his wife was already postmenopausal and had never borne a child. Sarah, Abraham's wife, trying to help God out a bit, asked Abraham to visit the tent of her Egyptian maid, Hagar, and have a child with her—not an unusual practice in those days. Abraham said, "Sounds like God's will to me, Sarah. 'Bye."

So Abraham slept with Hagar, and Ishmael was born. Later, just as God had foretold, Sarah did conceive and gave birth to a miracle baby, Isaac, the son of laughter. The people of Israel, the Jews, are descended from Isaac; the Arabs are descended from Ishmael.

God did honor Ishmael—He promised that Ishmael would be fruitful, the father of twelve rulers, and a great nation. But in His sovereignty, God established His covenant with Isaac, the child of promise. The title to the Promised Land of Israel passed from Abraham to Isaac and then to Jacob.

You can imagine that there was more than a little competition in Abraham's household. That rivalry still exists today, but on a larger scale. The conflict between Arabs and Jews goes deeper than disputes over the lands of Palestine. It is theological. It is Judaism versus Islam. Islam's theology insists that Islam triumph over everything else—that's why when you visit an Arabic city, the Islamic prayer tower is the highest point in the city.

The Muslims believe that while Jesus, Moses, David, and several other Hebrews were prophets, Muhammad was the greatest prophet. Though Muslims revere the Bible, including the Torah, the Psalms, and the Gospels, they hold that the *Al-Quran* (the Koran) is the absolute true word of God, revealed through the angel Jibraeel (Gabriel) to Muhammad. Muslims believe that Allah is God, that he has neither father nor mother, and that he has no sons.

Understand this: No matter what the Arabs say about peace, their religion demands that they defeat the Jews. Islam proclaims a theology of "triumphantism." Simply translated, Muslims believe that it is the will of God for Islam to rule the world.

Islamic law stipulates that to fulfill Muhammad's task, every "infidel domain" must be considered a territory of war. According to Moris Farhi, author of *The Last of Days,* Muslims believe there can be no peace with the Jew or the Christian or any other non-Islamic people, and that if peace must be made, only a truce is permissible—and that "for a maximum of ten years as an expedient to hone our swords, whet our blood, and strengthen our will."[1] Muhammad made physical violence an invisible yet integral part of that faith.

The point is this: The fundamentalist Muslims must destroy the Jews and rule Israel, or Muhammad is a false prophet and the Koran is not true. Such a thought is inconceivable. For that reason, the fundamentalist Muslims must attack Israel and the Jews in order to be loyal to their prophet. The strategy of Islamic Jihad is as simple as it is satanic: "Kill so many Jews that they will eventually abandon Palestine."[2]

The late imam Hasan al-Banna of the Islamic Resistance Movement, HAMAS, summed up their philosophy so well that his statement was included in their covenant: "Israel will exist and will continue to exist until Islam will obliterate it, just as it obliterated others before it."[3]

History of the Current Conflict

Let me briefly give you a concise history of the contemporary Israeli-Arab conflict. On May 14, 1948, the United Nations recognized the State of Israel. After 2,000 years, the Jews of the world had a homeland. The *next day*, five Arab armies attacked Israel. They attacked Israel full force, trying to murder the Zionist state in the birth canal.

But He who keeps Israel neither slumbers nor sleeps. God Almighty came to Israel's defense. Their survival was a divine miracle.

From this war of 1948 was born the "Palestinian refugee problem," which the media have used to brainwash the Western world for the past fifty years. This "refugee problem" was created, sustained, and manipulated by Arab leaders against their own people to portray the Jews of Israel as heartless. It proved to be effective.

In her book *From Time Immemorial,* historian Joan Peters charts in painstaking detail, with irrefutable documentation, that just before the war of 1948 began, Arab leaders told the Palestinians to leave their homes. "As soon as we drive the Jews into the sea," they promised, "you can return."[4]

To the Arabs' shock and surprise, they lost the war. And soon an estimated 600,000 Palestinian refugees asked Jordan, Iran, Iraq, and Syria to let them immigrate.

But the Arab states would not let them immigrate, even though they had plenty of land and money. Even though they shared a common language, religion, and culture with these refugees, permission to immigrate was denied. Why? Because the refugees had become a lightning rod for the world media to attack Israel. "See how heartless the Jewish people are?" moaned the newspapers and reporters. "See how unreasonable Israel is? Look at those poor Arabs without homes!"

Few people know that the Israeli government, along with the United Nations, put up $150 million to resettle any Arab families who wanted to return to their homes. But those who did return were shot by the Palestine Liberation Organization. "The PLO, through intimidation and murder, has largely silenced moderate Arabs who might negotiate a peaceful resolution of the conflict."[5] That's the PLO, led by Yasser Arafat, the same man who shook Rabin's hand and promised to bring peace to Israel.

Since 1948 five brutal wars have been fought in Israel. A river of blood has been shed over control of Judea and Samaria (the West Bank), control of the Golan Heights, and control over the Holy City, Jerusalem.

The peace accord signed in 1993 will last only until Syria obtains control of the Golan Heights. From there an army can easily infiltrate the West Bank to attack Jerusalem in the ultimate holy war. What happened in the Rose Garden in 1993 was the first major birth pang of World War III. The peace process leads Israel down the road to disaster.

Here's the sequence of what will happen in the days of Jerusalem's impending darkness: Until the 1993 peace accord, we had no idea how the Arabs could possibly gain a military position strong enough to attack Israel. Now we know— it was given to them in a peace treaty. The Scud missiles Saddam Hussein launched from Iraq could next be launched from the Golan Heights. Or the attack could come from the Mediterranean Sea via missiles launched from Russian submarines sold to wealthy Arab nations. A U.S. congressman sat in my office and told me, "Pastor Hagee, when the Soviet Union collapsed, some of their nuclear weapons disappeared, and no one knows where they are!"

"For when they say, 'Peace and safety!' then sudden destruction comes upon them, as labor pains upon a pregnant woman" (1 Thess. 5:3). The prophet Ezekiel saw a vast Arab coalition of nations coming against Israel (Ezek. 38—39). These armies will cover the land like a cloud. But God says that His fury "will show in My face. For in My jealousy and in the fire of My wrath I have spoken" (Ezek. 38:18–19). God will be enraged. He gave the Promised Land to Abraham, Isaac, Jacob, and their seed forever by blood covenant, and His fury will be poured out on all who try to take it from them.

Russia Will Rebound from Its Current Malaise

Make no mistake, a reborn Russia seeking to again become a military superpower will in the near future lead a massive pan-Islamic military expedition in an attempt to conquer Israel. The prophet Ezekiel paints the portrait of the coming battle with shocking clarity. Just before the return of Jesus Christ, world powers will be divided into four great sectors:

1. The king of the North, or Russia. Moscow is directly north of Jerusalem.
2. The king of the South, which consists of Egypt and the nations south of Israel.
3. The king of the West, represented by the federated states of Europe that are now coming together under the European Union.
4. The king of the East, which is represented by the Asiatic powers lying to the east of the Euphrates River.

You may be asking, "How could the Soviet Union ever be reborn?" or "What interest would either Russia or a reborn Soviet Union have in cooperating with a military campaign against Israel?"

Russia longs to be a military superpower again. Many Russians were very proud of the empire the Soviets built during the time of Communist rule. The humiliation of losing that empire, combined with the impoverishment of its faltering economy, has left the Russian people feeling nostalgic about their past, bitter about their present, and skeptical about their future. Dictators grow in such a climate, and the winds of war sweep a nation toward military conflict.

Russia must have an unlimited supply of oil to become a military superpower. Although Russia is rich with oil reserves and other natural resources, those resources tend to be located in remote areas that are difficult to access. Therefore, it must gain control of the main source of the industrialized world's oil—the Persian Gulf.

When the Islamic nations, which constantly call for holy war to annihilate Israel, join forces with Russia, they will greatly benefit from the strength of Russia's armed forces. Russia will say to the Islamic nations, "You want Jerusalem and the temple mount as a holy site. We want the Persian Gulf oil. Let's join forces to rule the world!" Watch as in the future Russia becomes extremely congenial to all Islamic states.

What will be the result? A massive pan-Islamic military force led by Russia's command will come against Israel "like a cloud, to cover the land" (Ezek. 38:16).

A Global Confrontation

Let's read how the prophet describes the conflict to come against Jerusalem and Israel:

> Now the word of the LORD came to me, saying, "Son of man, set your face against Gog, of the land of Magog, the prince of Rosh, Meshech, and Tubal, and prophesy against him, and say, 'Thus says the Lord GOD: "Behold, I am against you, O Gog, the prince of Rosh, Meshech, and Tubal. I will turn you around, put hooks into your jaws, and lead you out, with all your army, horses, and horsemen, all splendidly clothed, a great company with bucklers and shields, all of them handling swords. Persia, Ethiopia, and Libya are with them, all of them with shield and helmet; Gomer and all its troops; the house of Togarmah from the far north and all its troops—many people are with you. Prepare yourself and be ready, you and all your companies that are gathered about you; and be a guard for them. After many days you will be visited. In the latter years you will come into the land of those brought back from the sword and gathered from many people on the mountains of Israel, which had long been desolate; they were brought out of the nations, and now all of them dwell safely. You will ascend, coming like a storm, covering the land like a cloud, you and all your troops and many

peoples with you." 'Thus says the Lord GOD: "On that day it shall come to pass that thoughts will arise in your mind, and you will make an evil plan: You will say, 'I will go up against a land of unwalled villages; I will go to a peaceful people, who dwell safely, all of them dwelling without walls, and having neither bars nor gates'—to take plunder and to take booty, to stretch out your hand against the waste places that are again inhabited, and against a people gathered from the nations, who have acquired livestock and goods, who dwell in the midst of the land. . . .

"Therefore, son of man, prophesy and say to Gog, 'Thus says the Lord GOD: "On that day when My people Israel dwell safely, will you not know it? Then you will come from your place out of the far north, you and many peoples with you, all of them riding on horses, a great company and a mighty army. You will come up against My people Israel like a cloud, to cover the land. It will be in the latter days that I will bring you against My land, so that the nations may know Me, when I am hallowed in you, O Gog, before their eyes" (Ezek. 38:1–12, 14–16).

Ezekiel makes it absolutely clear that God is talking about an attack upon Israel by its enemies. The leader of the attack is Gog, and his kingdom is Magog. *Magog* is referred to as one of the sons of Japheth in Genesis 10:2 and in 1 Chronicles 1:5. Ethnologists tell us that after the Flood, the Japhethites migrated from Asia Minor to the north, beyond the Caspian and Black Seas.

The only land north of this area is Russia!

God is specifically speaking of "the prince of Rosh, Meshech, and Tubal." Many people believe "Rosh" is related to the modern word *Russia* and that "Meshech" and "Tubal," respectively, are variations of the spelling of *Moscow* and *Tobolsk*, an area in the Ural section of Russia.

The names *Russia* or *Soviet Union* do not appear in Scripture, but this detailed description of the invader of Israel clearly fits Russia. Today, the former Soviet Union has split up into separate states—and five of them are controlled by Islamic fundamentalists. One of those states has most of the nuclear missile firepower of the former Soviet Union.

With this mighty army will come other invaders: Persia, Ethiopia, Libya, Gomer, and Togarmah. I believe when Ezekiel speaks of Persia, Ethiopia, and Libya, he is speaking of the same Iranian states that are now constantly calling for holy war to exterminate Israel. Gomer and Togarmah refer to the region now occupied by the nation of Turkey.

The Vigilant Guardian of Israel

If God created Israel by His spoken word, has sworn to defend Israel, and has chosen Jerusalem as His habitation on earth, then will He not fight against those who come against the apple of His eye?

Zechariah wrote:

Behold, the day of the LORD is coming,
And your spoil will be divided in your midst.
For I will gather all the nations to battle against Jerusalem;
The city shall be taken,
The houses rifled,
And the women ravished.
Half of the city shall go into captivity,
But the remnant of the people shall not be cut off
   from the city.
Then the LORD will go forth
And fight against those nations,
As He fights in the day of battle. (14:1–3).

148

In the latter days, just prior to the Second Coming, the nations of the world will gather to fight against Jerusalem, and God will defend His habitation on earth.

Zechariah records, "And this shall be the plague with which the LORD will strike all the people who fought against Jerusalem: Their flesh shall dissolve while they stand on their feet, / Their eyes shall dissolve in their sockets, / And their tongues shall dissolve in their mouths" (14:12).

I believe this is Zechariah's description of a nuclear blast, which can generate 150 million degrees Fahrenheit in one-millionth of a second. That's how your tongue and your eyes can dissolve in their sockets before your corpse hits the ground. God will allow the use of nuclear weapons in this great battle against Israel, but then He will step into the fray.

When the invading army comes to cover the land "like a cloud," God says, "My fury will show in My face" (Ezek. 38:18). God Himself, the Guardian of Israel who never slumbers or sleeps, will stand up and fight from the balconies of heaven to aid the Seed of Abraham.

First, He will send a mighty earthquake so devastating it will shake the mountains and the seas, and every wall shall fall to the ground (Ezek. 38:19, 20).

Second, God will send massive confusion to the multinational fighting force, and "every man's sword will be against his brother" (Ezek. 38:21).

Third, God will open fire with His divine artillery and rain down on Israel's offenders "great hailstones, fire, and brimstone" (Ezek. 38:22).

The battle casualties will be staggering. Five out of six enemy troops that attack Israel in this Russian-led pan-Islamic force will die. It will take seven months to bury the dead (Ezek. 39:12). It will take seven years to burn the implements of war (Ezek. 39:9).

Why does God slaughter the armies that invade Israel? Ezekiel gives the answer: "So I will make My holy name known in the midst of My people Israel, and I will not let them profane My holy name anymore. Then the nations shall know that I am the LORD, the Holy One in Israel. . . . So the house of Israel shall know that I am the LORD their God from that day forward" (Ezek. 39:7, 22).

Israel is the only nation created by a sovereign act of God, and He has sworn by His holiness to defend Jerusalem, His Holy City. If God created and defends Israel, those nations that fight against it fight against God.

But how short man's memory is. Soon after Russia moves against Israel, the Antichrist will walk purposefully into a political vacuum to become a worldwide dictator. Jerusalem will watch that man walk onto the stage of world history as a man of peace only to become Hitler incarnate.

Israel's False Messiah — the Antichrist

And in the latter time of their kingdom,
When the transgressors have reached their fullness,
A king shall arise,
Having fierce features,
Who understands sinister schemes (Dan. 8:23).

The Antichrist is a real, physical human being. Though some have hypothesized that the Antichrist, or Beast, will be a system or a computer, the Bible leaves us no doubt that he is a *person*.

In Matthew 24 Jesus said there would be many antichrists, or "false christs," who would come. But there is one unique, anointed of hell, brilliant, charismatic, articulate world leader who will arise at the dawn of the Tribulation and baptize the world in a river of blood. The Bible calls him the "son of perdition" (2 Thess. 2:3), which translates to "the chief son of Satan."

I believe that just as God waited for the fullness of time before He sent His Son to be born of a virgin, the people of the earth are awaiting the appearance of the Antichrist. Look around. Jesus had John the Baptist to shout, "Prepare the way of the LORD!" (Matt. 3:3) and we have many who are preparing the world for the advent of Antichrist.

Recently my daughter Christina, a junior at Oral Roberts University, burst into my bedroom and said, "Dad, you've got to see this." She flipped the TV channel to CNN's coverage of Marilyn Manson, a man who professes to be a high priest in the church of Satan. The lyrics of his songs encourage rape, incest, body mutilation, murder, and Satan worship. He hates capitalism and believes fascism is America's hope for the future.

Is he successful? Very. His recordings hit "triple platinum" status as soon as they are released (that's over three million copies sold), and thousands of American young people jam stadiums and arenas for his concerts. Manson and his deceived legions are begging for Satan's messiah to rule the world. They will get their wish.

The organized church in America has become anti-Christ, or "against Christ." Consider:

- The church that denies the Bible to be the inspired, inerrant Word of God is anti-Christ. Jesus said, "I am the way, the truth, and the life" (John 14:6). John's Gospel states "Your word is truth" (17:17) and "In the beginning was the Word, and the Word was with God, and the Word was God. . . . And the Word became flesh and dwelt among us, and we beheld His glory, the glory as of the only begotten of the Father, full of grace and truth" (1:1, 14). If Jesus is *truth*, and the Word is *truth*, to deny truth is indeed anti-Christ!

- The church that ordains homosexuals is anti-Christ. If you believe that God approves of homosexuality, reconsider His urban renewal program for Sodom and Gomorrah.
- The church that denies the virgin birth is anti-Christ.
- The church that has "a form of godliness but [denies] its power" (2 Tim. 3:5) is anti-Christ.
- The church that denies that Jesus Christ is Lord is anti-Christ!

Forty years ago most people laughed at the concept of a human Antichrist. They're no longer laughing. Thousands of high school and college students in America today proudly wear the number 666 on their clothes and schoolbooks and have it tattooed on their bodies.

The practice and study of satanism have exploded in America. Our youth are taking oaths of allegiance to Satan and his coming messiah, the Antichrist. Rock music groups have adopted his name, and their concerts resemble nothing so much as a demonic worship service.

Wake up, America! The songs we're singing, the books we're reading, the movies we're watching are glorifying the Prince of Darkness and his coming Antichrist.

The Time of His Appearing

After Russia and its Arab allies are defeated, the Antichrist, Satan's messiah, will step out onto the world stage. The earth is prepared for him, the time is nearly upon us. I believe he could be alive right now. And just as Jesus knew He was God's Son, sent into the world to redeem men, I believe the Antichrist knows he is Satan's emissary, sent into the world to destroy as many human lives as possible.

Jesus warned that the times of the Antichrist will be by far the worst the world has ever known. In His discourse to the disciples regarding "the tribulation of those days" as recorded in Matthew 24, Mark 13, Luke 21, and John 16, He foretold a period of false messiahs, wars, rumors of wars, sorrow, deception, iniquity, persecution, and world-wide catastrophe. The end times would be so terrible, Jesus said, that "unless those days were shortened, no flesh would be saved" (Matt. 24:22).

An Impostor of Peace

This false messiah will present himself to the world as a man of peace. Perhaps he will be a Nobel Peace Prize winner. At the beginning of his allotted time, he will defeat and merge three kingdoms, demonstrating his power to influence and lead men. Daniel 8:25 says that by cunning he "shall destroy many." To illustrate his diplomacy and desire for peace, he will make a seven-year treaty with Israel, but he will break this agreement after only three and one-half years.

The Antichrist will be a man with hypnotic charm and charisma. Interestingly enough, historians record that when Hitler was in power, men were afraid to look into his hypnotic eyes. The Antichrist will have awesome demonic power to control world leaders with his hypnotic gaze and the force of his personality.

The Antichrist will come from the federated states of Europe, the revived Roman Empire. In his rise to power, he will be the leader of one nation in the ten-kingdom federation, then he will conquer three of the ten nations and become the Beast of Revelation 13:1, "having seven heads and ten horns, and on his horns ten crowns, and on his heads a blasphemous name." He will instantly assume dictatorial authority over nations, turning his ravenous gaze toward the apple of God's eye—Israel.

The Antichrist will use military force to gain and maintain world supremacy. Daniel wrote, "But in their place he shall honor a god of fortresses" (Dan. 11:38). Though he comes as a man of peace, he will bathe the world in blood before he gets to Armageddon where blood will flow to the depth of a horse's bridle for a distance of 200 miles (Rev. 14:20).

Initially, the Antichrist will bring world prosperity. The prophet wrote, "Through his cunning / He shall cause deceit to prosper under his rule" (Dan. 8:25). This suggests that there might be a worldwide economic collapse, and the man of sin, the Son of Perdition, the Chief Son of Satan, will seduce the world with the promise of prosperity.

One Money, One Religion, One Ruler

The Antichrist's three-point plan for world domination consists of a one-world currency, a one-world religion, and a one-world government now being called the New World Order.

His economy will be a cashless society in which every financial transaction can be electronically monitored. No one will be able to buy or sell without a mark sanctioned by the Antichrist's administration. Therefore, the Antichrist will force every person on earth to receive a mark in the right hand or the forehead. Without this mark, you will not be able to legally buy groceries or hold a job. Revelation 13:16–17 tells us, "He causes all, both small and great, rich and poor, free and slave, to receive a mark on their right hand or on their foreheads, and that no one may buy or sell except one who has the mark or the name of the beast, or the number of his name."

Technology has made it possible for every person on earth today to be electronically monitored. With the implantation of a small computer chip, painlessly installed and virtually invisible to the naked eye, where you go and what you buy can be monitored by the Global Positioning System. The GPS involves a small, handheld device that bounces a signal to a satellite and back to indicate a monitored individual's exact position. It is accurate to within ten feet and is presently used in jet aircraft, naval vessels, and criminal monitors.

We're already scanning our pets. Responsible dog and cat owners are urged to microchip their animals. One tiny computer chip, no bigger than a grain of rice, is injected between the animal's shoulder blades. It's invisible and virtually undetectable, until someone swipes a scanner over the spot where the chip lies. Suddenly the animal's identification number comes up on the scanner, and from that number whoever needs information has access to the pet owner's address, phone number, veterinarian, and any other pertinent information. It's amazing, but it's nothing compared to the program the Antichrist will implement.

Satan has been scheming to institute a new world order since Nimrod proposed to build a mighty tower on the plains of Shinar—the Tower of Babel. During Christ's temptation, Satan offered Jesus a new world order if He would bow down and worship him. After World War I, the "war to end all wars," President Woodrow Wilson helped found the League of Nations to uphold peace through a one-world government. Adolf Hitler told the German people he would bring a "new order" to Europe.

Sound familiar? The Antichrist will institute a one-world government far more successful than any that have gone before him. There will be no national borders in his world; the nations will be ruled by international law imposed upon them by international leaders. Communication? Easy on the World Wide Web. Authority? Supported by an international peacekeeping force, instituted by a world court. The elements are already in place; the world looks only for a leader, a new Caesar.

Idolatry in Jerusalem

The Antichrist will have an evil counterpart, the False Prophet. Together they will perform miracles, and the world will marvel. The world looks for miracles today in the same way some of the scribes and Pharisees of Jesus' day asked that He give them a sign to prove His divinity.

Miracles are not a sign of God's approval. But men are easily deceived, and they will see the signs and wonders performed by the False Prophet, and they will believe that the Antichrist is divine.

In an attempt to stop Jesus Christ, the rightful Heir, from reclaiming His throne in Jerusalem, the Antichrist will establish his capital, his home, and his headquarters in God's Holy City. There he will set himself up as God, commanding the world to worship him. Those who do not worship him will be executed. Some theologians believe he will be homosexual, for Daniel 11:37 tells us, "He shall regard neither the God of his fathers *nor the desire of women,* nor regard any god; for he shall exalt himself above them all" (italics mine).

156

Jesus told His disciples that the Antichrist would demand worldwide worship. Matthew 24:15–16 records His warning: "'Therefore when you see the "abomination of desolation," spoken of by Daniel the prophet, standing in the holy place' (whoever reads, let him understand), 'then let those who are in Judea flee to the mountains.'"

The prophet Daniel wrote, "Then the king [Antichrist] shall do according to his own will: he shall exalt and magnify himself above every god, shall speak blasphemies against the God of gods, and shall prosper till the wrath has been accomplished; for what has been determined shall be done" (11:36).

John the Revelator explained it further: "Here is wisdom. Let him who has understanding calculate the number of the beast, for it is the number of a man: His number is 666" (Rev. 13:18). In the Bible, 6 is the number of sin. The number of the Antichrist is 666, meaning he is part of a threefold demonic trinity consisting of Satan, the Antichrist, and the False Prophet, who will work signs and wonders in the Antichrist's name to deceive the nations of the world. Many of them will believe that the Antichrist is God.

Why does the Antichrist demand to be worshiped? From the beginning, before Genesis 1:1, Satan has had a compulsion to be worshiped. Isaiah exposes Satan's sinister motives, saying:

How you are fallen from heaven,
O Lucifer, son of the morning!
How you are cut down to the ground,
You who weakened the nations!
For you have said in your heart:
"I will ascend into heaven,
I will exalt my throne above the stars of God;
I will also sit on the mount of the congregation

On the farthest sides of the north;
I will ascend above the heights of the clouds,
I will be like the Most High" (14:12–14).

Lucifer lusted for worship before the gates of Eden were open. This demonic compulsion drove Satan to tempt Jesus in the wilderness, saying, "All these things [the kingdoms of the world] I will give You if You will fall down and worship me" (Matt. 4:9). Satan's messengers now invite the world to worship the Prince of Darkness via music and moral rebellion against God.

During his reign on earth, the Antichrist will be the object of an assassination attempt. John says, "I saw one of his heads as if it had been mortally wounded, and his deadly wound was healed. And all the world marveled and followed the beast (Rev. 13:3). The Antichrist will be shot in the head and will miraculously recover, emulating the death and resurrection of Jesus Christ.

John records the prophecy of what will happen next: "And he [the False Prophet] deceives those who dwell on the earth by those signs which he was granted to do in the sight of the beast [the Antichrist], telling those who dwell on the earth to make an image to the beast who was wounded by the sword and lived. He was granted power to give breath to the image of the beast, that the image of the beast should both speak and cause as many as would not worship the image of the beast to be killed" (Rev. 13:14–15).

But the Antichrist will go too far. Revelation 13:6 tells us, "He opened his mouth in blasphemy against God, to blaspheme His name, His tabernacle, and those who dwell in heaven." As the Antichrist, Satan's messiah, stands on the plains of Megiddo, marshaling his massive army for the Battle of Armageddon, he will look into heaven at the angels who had the opportunity to follow him in his first rebellion against God. He will look at Christ, to whom Satan offered the kingdoms of the world. He will look up at the raptured believers who stand with their Lord, and he will say, "Look, all of you. Look where you would be if you had followed me. You would be rulers of the earth. I *forbid* God to send His Son to earth to reign. I am God here. I rule and reign in this city. Jerusalem is MINE!"

The Antichrist's End

Unlike Jesus Christ, whose throne will know no end, the Antichrist's days will be numbered. While God readies the armies of heaven, the nations of earth will rise against the Antichrist:

> At the time of the end the king of the South shall attack him; and the king of the North shall come against him like a whirlwind, with chariots, horsemen, and with many ships; and he [Antichrist] shall enter the countries, overwhelm them, and pass through. He shall also enter the Glorious Land, and many countries shall be overthrown. . . . But news from the east and the north shall trouble him; therefore he shall go out with great fury to destroy and annihilate many. And he shall plant the tents of his palace between the seas and the glorious holy mountain [Jerusalem]; yet he shall come to his end, and no one will help him (Dan. 11:40–41, 44–45).

We have met these kings of the North and South before. This time, as before, they represent a renewed Russian Empire conspiring with a pan-Islamic confederation to cleanse Jerusalem and seize control of the Middle East oil fields. The Antichrist has defeated these kings before, and he subdues them again. He is probably not too worried about their threat until he learns of the 200-million-warrior army (Rev. 9:16) advancing toward him from the east.

After hearing about the advancing eastern army, the Antichrist will advance from the territory of the twice-defeated king of the South to Armageddon, a natural battlefield, to face the armies from the North and the East.

And God, who has borne all the blasphemies He can bear, will say, "Son, take the armies of heaven—the angels, the Old Testament saints, the church—and return to earth as the King of kings and Lord of lords. Go and make Your enemies Your footstool. Go and rule the earth with a rod of iron. Go and sit upon the throne of Your father, King David."

Then will come the final invasion, not from the north, south, east, or west, but from heaven. It is the invasion described in Revelation 19, the attack led by Jesus Christ, the Lamb of God, the Lion of Judah, and the Lord of Glory!

Mounted upon a white horse, the King of kings will descend onto the battlefield at Armageddon. As He comes, His eyes are like blazing fire, and the armies of heaven follow Him on white horses. Out of the Messiah's mouth comes a sharp two-edged sword, the Word of God with which He created the world out of chaos, raised Lazarus from the dead, and rebuked the unruly wind and waves on the Sea of Galilee. His spoken word will crush His enemies in milliseconds.

Then shall the armies of the Antichrist and the kings of the earth gather to wage war against the Lion of Judah, who is mounted on His milk-white stallion and followed by His army wearing crowns and dazzling robes of white. I will be in that army, for it is composed of those who were raptured with the church and the loyal angels of God!

In Revelation 19:12, John wrote that Jesus had a name "written that no one knew except Himself." As a Jew, John knew that God appeared to Abraham, Isaac, and Jacob by the name of God Almighty, *El Shaddai*. But God did not reveal Himself to them by the name of Jehovah (*Yahweh*). The patriarchs knew God as the Almighty One, but they had no concept of Him as an intimate friend and Master, the One who delights to walk with His children "in the cool of the day" (Gen. 3:8) as God walked with Adam in the Garden of Eden.

Christ's robe, dipped in His innocent blood that was shed on the cross, is His prayer shawl. The *tsitsit* of His shawl in Hebrew spells "Jehovah God Is One," meaning He is the King of kings and Lord of lords.

"Then the beast [Antichrist] was captured, and with him the false prophet who worked signs in his presence, . . . These two were cast alive into the lake of fire burning with brimstone" (Rev. 19:20). The Antichrist who invaded Jerusalem, who murdered and killed righteous Jews who would not worship him, is cast alive and forever into the lake of fire. Hallelujah to the Holy One of Israel who shall rule and reign forever from Jerusalem. Of His kingdom there shall be no end.

CHAPTER 9

GLIMPSES OF THE FUTURE

The future is in the past.

Why is it so important for America to lock arms with the nation of Israel? The reasons are revealed in the biblical history of the Jewish people. America's fate depends upon our treatment of the nation of Israel. Look at the boneyard of human history. Examine the testimony of nations that had the opportunity to bless Israel but chose to curse Israel instead. Without exception, they experienced the judgment of God, sank into oblivion, and became historical footnotes in the annals of time. Their prosperity became poverty, their power replaced by international pity.

What About Tomorrow?

If you're concerned about prophecy for the future, the following pages will contain the most important clues you will find anywhere in the world. You could spend a lifetime researching libraries that will yield nothing more profitable than understanding the biblical basis of prophecy.

To know the future, you must master what the Bible tells you about the past. Everything God will do, He has done before.

In the movie *Back to the Future,* Marty McFly's DeLorean time machine fascinated millions of viewers. We applauded as Marty shot back through time in a matter of seconds. While some of us are intrigued to revisit our childhoods or investigate our ancestors, nothing the human imagination can conjure is equal to what God has already prepared to equip His people to read the future. Bible prophecy lifts the veil off tomorrow and shines the spotlight on what is to come.

Jesus and Joseph

If we study Joseph, the Old Testament champion who saved his father, his brothers, and his people from starvation, we can discover the hidden story of the Messiah. Theology calls this the principle of types and shadows. By studying one situation, life, or prophecy, we can glean truths and more deeply understand another situation.

Joseph enacted the future of Jesus Christ nearly 2,000 years before Jesus was born! Consider the startling similarities between the Hebrew ruler of Egypt and the Jewish Messiah.

- The names *Jesus* and *Joseph* come from the Hebrew root word for *salvation,* and each man was the means of saving grace to his people. God sent Joseph from his father's house to a strange land in order for his family to be fed in a time of drought and thirst, providing bread for the very brothers who betrayed him. God dispatched Jesus from the right hand of the Father to the earth as the "bread of life" (John 6:48) and "living water" (John 4:10).

- Joseph's brothers rejected and betrayed him. His siblings sold him into the hands of his enemies, and Jacob's favorite son became a slave. Jesus was betrayed by Judas, by Peter, by Thomas. The Bible tells us, "He came to His own, and His own did not receive Him" (John 1:11).

- Joseph's brothers sold him for twenty shekels of silver (Gen. 37:28), the common price of a slave. Judas sold Christ to the Pharisees for thirty pieces of silver (Matt. 26:15), the usual price of a slave.

- Joseph was falsely accused of rape by Potiphar's wife. Her lies sent him to prison (Gen. 39:19–20). Similarly, the Pharisees lied about Jesus' teaching, condemning Him to death. Because of false accusations, Jesus descended to the ultimate pit . . . death.

But there's more! Through an act of God, Joseph was released from prison and promoted to the palace where he sat at Pharaoh's right hand. Free of death's ultimate confinement and bondage, Jesus arose and ascended to the right hand of God the Father. At every point, Joseph walked the exact path Jesus trod generations later.

Read the Exodus story carefully and you'll discover that Joseph's brothers traveled to Egypt *three times* before the man who had worn the coat of many colors dropped his disguise. When Pharaoh's vizier dropped the masquerade and revealed himself, he said, "I am Joseph, your brother." His brothers wept openly and bitterly.

How does that aspect of Joseph's life translate to Jesus? The connection has to do with the land of Israel.

The first time the Jews entered the land under Joshua's leadership. After the Exile, the Hebrews entered the land a second time with Nehemiah in order to rebuild the walls of Jerusalem and reestablish the nation.

In 1948 the Jews entered Israel for the third time when the United Nations recognized their statehood. As foreseen by the prophet Isaiah, a nation was born in a day (66:8).

Just as Joseph revealed his identity to his brothers on their third visit, the last return of Israel in 1948 prepared the way for the revelation of the Messiah. As we examine the past, we know that immediately before us lies the moment when the people of Israel will discover the identity of Messiah. On the third visit, He will reveal Himself.

And, like Joseph's brothers, the children of Israel will weep openly and with bitter tears. Zechariah said, "They will look on Me [Jesus] whom they pierced. Yes, they will mourn for Him as one mourns for his only son, and grieve for Him as one grieves for a firstborn" (12:10).

When you understand Bible prophecy, you have the capacity to accurately anticipate the future. Biblical stories are a theology of hidden eschatology. Yesterday is a dramatic foreshadowing of the essence of tomorrow. Everything God will do, He has already done.

Joseph was a type, or foreshadow, of the Messiah. His shadow fell across the approaching centuries, leaving significant basic clues so others would recognize the Messiah when He came.

Seven Billboards Advertising Tomorrow

The prophetic principles of types and shadows are dramatically demonstrated in the seven great feasts of Israel. These annual events reveal a secret treasure of special insights to guide your decisions today.

The contemporary clues we need to understand the future are interwoven throughout Leviticus 23. The chapter begins with this directive to Moses: "Speak to the children of Israel, and say to them: 'The feasts of the LORD, which you shall proclaim to be holy convocations, these are My feasts" (v. 2).

The Lord Himself established seven occasions of worship to guide Israel through the centuries until the Messiah comes. Christians often falsely assume these feasts are exclusively Jewish occasions. But the Bible makes it clear these days belong *to the Lord*. These feasts of the Lord are established for divine purposes, and everyone has a right to draw near.

Just as seven days finish a weekly cycle, seven festival occasions complete the work of God on earth. Each holiday was and is a trail marker pointing to the future. The seven feasts are:

1. The Feast of Passover
2. The Feast of Unleavened Bread
3. The Feast of Firstfruits
4. The Feast of Pentecost
5. The Feast of Trumpets (Rosh Hashanah)
6. The Feast of Atonement (Yom Kippur)
7. The Feast of Tabernacles (Sukkot)

Every year, observant Jews fulfill the cycle of remembrances and find renewed peace of mind. Once we've completed the same spiritual journey, we can understand why God rested after the sixth day of creation. God was not tired; He rested to teach us a divine principle. After the sixth day He rested, and, after the sixth feast the world will enter into 1,000 years of perfect peace and rest called the Millennium.

Each of the feasts of Israel points to and describes what lies ahead.

Stepping-Stones to Splendor

Through His festivals, God gave us a dress rehearsal of what is ahead. The Hebrew word for feast, *mo'ed,* means "a set or appointed time." Of very similar meaning is *mikrah,* indicating "a rehearsal or recital." Each feast, like a dress rehearsal, offers a significant picture of the future. The combined seven feasts are a divine blueprint of what lies ahead for Jerusalem, Israel, and the rest of the world.

As we follow each holiday through the year, we are walking on God's pathway from here to eternity. While we cannot know "the day or the hour" of Jesus Christ's return to earth, we can reflect on the possible month for both the Rapture and the Second Coming. The date lies in the accumulative meaning of the seven feasts.

Remember the basic principle: Everything God will do, He has already done.

Through these seven events, God revealed His 7,000-year plan for humanity. The Bible says, "But, beloved, do not forget this one thing, that with the Lord one day is as a thousand years, and a thousand years as one day" (2 Peter 3:8). Every festival day represents one of God's millennial moments, and each feast is an indicator of a segment of heaven's special way to measure time.

When 6,000 years pass and the Sukkot moment has come, Jesus' 1,000-year reign will begin. We can forget the frustration we experienced every time we turned on the television and watched the evening news. We'll trade in the condom culture and politically correct madhouse for paradise. This AIDS-infected, abortion-loving, pornography-addicted, secular-humanist sewer will disappear as Jesus Christ redeems the entire creation.

The Two Appearances

How do we start calculating time on God's stopwatch? Israel's feasts occur during two different seasons, reflecting the two different appearances of Jesus Christ on the earth.

The first time He came as a suffering Savior. In the coming age, He will return as King of kings and Lord of lords.

The first time He came, He was dragged before Herod and Pilate. The next time He comes, Herod and Pilate will bow before Him, for "at the name of Jesus every knee should bow, of those in heaven, and of those on earth, and of those under the earth, and that every tongue should confess that Jesus Christ is Lord, to the glory of God the Father" (Phil. 2:10–11).

The first time He came, He was considered an insurrectionist too dangerous to live, and so He was crucified on a Roman cross. The next time He comes, He will sit on the throne of His father, King David (Luke 1:32), and of His kingdom there shall be no end.

The spring season has seen the suffering Savior. The fall season awaits the coming of the King of glory who will rule the earth with "a rod of iron."

The first four festivals take us from the beginning of spring to the gathering of the barley harvest. Passover, Unleavened Bread, Firstfruits, and Pentecost mark the passing of winter and the coming of summer.

The first of three fall festivals begins at the end of the wheat harvest. The Feasts of Trumpets, Atonement, and Tabernacles remind the Jews that winter is ahead.

The two sets of holidays also coincide with the two annual seasons of rain. Spring brings the former rain; the latter rain comes in the fall. The prophet Hosea knew the seasons and rain cycles were "insider information" pertaining to what lay ahead. He wrote, "He will come to us like the rain, / Like the latter and former rain to the earth" (6:3).

These holidays predict Jesus' coming by foreshadowing a chain of events leading up to His return!

Let's start with the feasts that occur in the season of the former rain and see what we can discover.

The First Festival: The Feast of Passover

On the tenth day of A'bib (March or April on the English calendar), preparation for the annual Passover observance begins. The Lord demanded, "This month shall be your beginning of months; it shall be the first month of the year to you. Speak to all the congregation of Israel, saying: 'On the tenth of this month every man shall take for himself a lamb, according to the house of his father, a lamb for a household'" (Ex. 12:2–3).

For four days a one-year-old male lamb without blemish was tied close to the house so the family would know and remember the lamb like a beloved pet. At 3:00 in the afternoon, the father of the house laid his hand upon the head of the lamb and cut its throat. Then he applied the blood of innocence to the sides of the door and smeared it on the doorposts. The house was literally sealed with blood.

The family not only remembered but reenacted the death angel's fearsome journey through Egypt. The firstborn sons of the Egyptians died, but the houses of Israel were spared. Where there was lamb's blood, the angel passed over. If the door was not sealed with the animal's blood, the firstborn child would die that night.

On this extraordinary evening, Israel learned the meaning of redemption by blood. As is true today, the father was the spiritual leader of the house. If the father failed in his spiritual duty, death came to his children. When the faith of contemporary fathers falters, children still die spiritually, and often physically.

How did Passover signal the shape of the future? Jesus fulfilled the meaning of the Passover ritual. The moment John the Baptist saw Jesus, he exclaimed, "Behold! The Lamb of God who takes away the sin of the world!" (John 1:29). Jesus was God's male lamb, without spot or blemish.

Even Pilate cried out, "I find no fault in Him" (John 19:6). And just as the Passover lamb was put on public display, Jesus stood before Israel in the temple and was examined by the Pharisees. He was God's final offering to end the reign of sin and death over humanity.

Death Dies

On the fourteenth day of A'bib, A.D. 33, at the third hour (9:00 A.M.), Israel's high priest tied the lamb to the altar for sacrifice. At that exact moment outside the city walls of Jerusalem, Jesus, the Lamb of God, was nailed to the cross. For six hours both the lamb and Jesus awaited death. Finally, at the ninth hour (3:00 P.M.), the high priest ascended the altar in the temple and sacrificed the lamb. His words thundered out over the city of Jerusalem, "It is finished!"

On Calvary's stark mountain, God the Father, the final High Priest of all creation, placed His holy hand on the head of His only begotten Son, allowing the total sin of the world to descend upon Jesus. Barely able to lift His blood-spattered face toward heaven, Jesus shouted in triumph, "It is finished!" (John 19:30).

The past was the guide to the future. The Passover forever declared that God saves His people through the shedding of blood.

My friend, we, too, are redeemed by blood, but not by the blood of goats and bullocks. We are saved by the precious blood that flows from Immanuel's veins. Not the blood that streamed from the altar when Solomon slaughtered 22,000 animals while dedicating the temple. We are cleansed from all sin by the blood Christ offered once and for all on the cross. We are not saved by the blood of infants slain by Herod to prevent the coming of Christ, but through the blood that makes every demon in hell tremble with fear.

Passover is Israel's great celebration of freedom. It is a matter of historical fact that the Hebrews were owned by Pharaoh, not by Egypt. The unyielding tyrant cared nothing for God or man. His foolish arrogance hung around his neck like a millstone, finally sending him to his death in the depths of the Red Sea. When Pharaoh drowned, his death canceled his control over the slaves. His ownership of the Jews ended instantly and permanently.

Every year when Passover comes, God reminds His people that He is the only one who can set them free. You and I were slaves to sin and Satan. We lived in chains and in bondage to fear. When Jesus Christ became our Passover Lamb, He ended the reign of death in our lives. The Lamb of God shouted from the cross, "It is finished!" At that moment, we were liberated from death, hell, and the grave; we were liberated from the guilt of the past and the fear of tomorrow. Satan is forever a defeated foe. "Therefore if the Son makes you free, you shall be free indeed" (John 8:36).

God's prophetic stopwatch started running on the night of Passover, A.D. 33. As the hands sweep past the numbers of each hour of the day, His people know they can look to the future without fear or apprehension. We have assurance of what cannot yet be measured.

You can no longer be defeated by yesterday. There is no need for you to be afraid of tomorrow. God does not say, "I am the great I WAS." Nor does He say, "I am the great I WILL BE." You can live in joy and victory *today* for God declares, "I AM the great I AM" (see Ex. 3:14). He's the God of the present.

Passover was the first prophetic sign of what was to come. Its meaning was fulfilled at Calvary. One epoch lies behind us, but six yet remain.

The Second Festival: The Feast of Unleavened Bread

On the fifteenth day of A'bib, the night after the week-long Passover festival begins, the Feast of Unleavened Bread is observed. Jews eat roasted lamb, bitter herbs, and unleavened bread. In Jesus' day, the people ate the sacrificial lamb that had been killed the day before.

This Passover meal, called the seder, is itself a picture of the death and resurrection of Christ. In the middle of the ritual, a piece of matzo (unleavened bread that is striped and pierced in the baking process) is broken into three pieces. The second piece, the *Afikomen,* is wrapped in white linen and hidden away for a little while, then found amid great rejoicing.

What an incredible picture and prediction of how Jesus Christ, the Bread of Life, would be wounded with the stripes of a whip, pierced with a sword, wrapped in linen, and hidden away in a borrowed tomb. On the night Jesus was betrayed, He ate the Last Supper (so called because it was the last meal in which leavened bread could be eaten before the festival) with His disciples and told them that the bread was His body that was to be broken for them.

Just as the matzo at the Feast of Unleavened Bread is without leaven, Jesus was without sin. His body was hidden away for three days, but then He rose and reappeared on the earth amid great rejoicing.

Before the feast can begin, the house must be cleansed of all leaven. Leaven, or yeast, makes the bread rise, and a practicing Jewish family will literally sweep the house clean to make certain there is no leaven on the premises. (Israel's kosher army will actually "sell" all of its warehouses, granaries, government food supplies, military cooking and eating equipment to a non-Jewish employee until after Passover.[1])

The heavenly Father decreed that any Jew eating leavened bread during this period should be cut off from the people (Ex. 12:15). Why was His judgment so strong? Because in the Bible, leaven is the type, or metaphor, for sin. Leaven represents the pride and arrogance that lead men to feel they have no need of God. Jesus said, "Take heed and beware of the leaven of the Pharisees and the Sadducees" (Matt. 16:6), and Paul added, "Your glorying is not good. Do you not know that a little leaven leavens the whole lump?" (1 Cor. 5:6).

The message of this feast? God has zero tolerance for sin.

Just like yeast, sin puffs us up. The Bible warns that our sins will always find us out, and the wages of sin is death. The Scriptures speak plainly about sin, for we are not only held responsible for our sinful acts, but we will be held accountable for the good deeds we neglected to do. "Therefore,"

James wrote, "to him who knows to do good and does not do it, to him it is sin" (4:17).

America, wake up. The Feast of Unleavened Bread warns us of an important eternal fact—no one can escape God's measuring stick. Nonobservant Jews were "cut off," or killed, for disobedience. We are no different. Tragically, too many Americans have forgotten that God hasn't changed His mind about the seriousness of sin.

During the past forty years secular humanism has stripped any sense of absolute right and wrong from American minds. Our children now live by "lifeboat" ethics. With the Ten Commandments exiled from our classrooms by the Supreme Court, and the ACLU seeking freedom *from* religion, our students no longer believe in sin. Liars are excused as being "extroverted" or "imaginative." Adultery is now "free love." Through the National Endowment for the Arts, our government feels free to use our tax money to pay artists to depict Jesus on a cross in a glass of urine. Why not? Nothing is sacred anymore in America.

Four thousand babies are murdered every day in America's abortion mills. Partial-birth abortion, a thoroughly repugnant practice, is more common than the experts would have you believe. The spreading culture of death spews blood and gore into our living rooms as week after week television offers an unending buffet of murder and mayhem.

To make matters worse, our political leaders are marching at the front of the parade leading to the moral abyss. The Clinton administration sells a night in the Lincoln bedroom to the highest bidder while China puts on a full-court press to subvert America's democratic process. In the halls of Congress, legislators peddle influence like souvenirs. Shame has no meaning!

How can a politician have sky-high approval ratings while swimming in one major scandal after another? He can't, unless there is no standard of righteousness, no concept of sin, no notion of honor, no understanding of integrity. Without these things, the country quickly sinks into the darkness of moral blindness. No one is listening to the Bible's warning that "righteousness exalts a nation, / But sin is a reproach to any people" (Prov. 14:34).

What's gone wrong in America? The church is certainly part of the problem. We're the embarrassment. The "greasy grace" preached from pulpits across this land set the stage for our brain-dead morality. People wink at sin and transgress with smiles on their faces. The self-satisfied settle back and smugly salve their consciences with a quick quip: "I'm covered by grace."

Let me tell you something, dear friend—greasy grace only forgives the sin. God's grace forgives the *sinner*. If you want to be truly forgiven and a new creation, go to God, not to those who will tell you that "slipping up" is only natural and to be expected. Quit trying to analyze your sin and just confess it.

Let me remind you of the eternal facts: Grace was never intended to be a license to sin. Extending forgiveness to anyone without demanding change in their conduct makes the grace of God an accomplice to evil. To the woman caught in adultery, Jesus said, "Go and sin no more." He expected her to change. He still expects transformation. Friends, pay attention to the Feast of Unleavened Bread. God has zero tolerance for sin.

God would have spared Sodom and Gomorrah if He could have found just ten righteous people within those walls. But because of the total moral collapse, He annihilated the entire society. Do you think God is going to make an exception for America? The eyes of God are studying our society this very moment. If the day comes when He can't find enough people to retard the moral and spiritual rot, God will crush this nation as well.

America's best national defense policy does not lie in producing more stealth bombers, manufacturing more condoms, propounding more sex education, or providing more clean needles for drug addicts. Our only hope lies in a revival of the righteousness of God to sweep this nation. America will either have a revival of righteousness or rebellion in the streets.

The Third Festival: The Feast of Firstfruits

On the sixteenth day of A'bib, immediately after the Feast of Unleavened Bread, the Feast of Firstfruits commemorates the day Israel went down into the depths of the Red Sea and came out the other side alive. The children of Israel marched into a watery grave and God raised them on the other bank a nation of free people. Little did they know they were also demonstrating how God would bring salvation to the entire world!

The Feast of Firstfruits is a foreshadowing of the work of both Good Friday and Easter, a type of the death and resurrection of Jesus Christ. Paul wrote, "But now Christ is risen from the dead, and has become the firstfruits of those who have fallen asleep [the dead]" (1 Cor. 15:20).

Jesus explored the chambers of death. He arose on the third day and announced, "I am the resurrection and the life. He who believes in Me, though he may die, he shall live. And whoever lives and believes in Me shall never die" (John 11:25–26). There is no spiritual death for the believer. Though his body may die, his spirit lives on with Christ.

Just as Israel marched out of the jaws of death (the Red Sea) to stand on solid ground, Jesus Christ arose the victor over death, hell, and the grave. Just as Jesus predicted, He arose the mighty conqueror over powers and principalities. Rome could not convict Him, the Cross could not conquer Him, and the grave could not contain Him. He is alive this very moment at the right hand of God, awaiting the hour of His second coming when kings, queens, presidents, and prime ministers shall bow at His feet and confess that He is Lord, to the glory of God the Father.

The Fourth Festival:
The Feast of Pentecost

On the second day of Si'van (May or June on the English calendar), exactly fifty days after the Feast of Firstfruits, the commemoration of the giving of the Law begins. Following the Exodus and the Hebrews' miraculous escape from the Red Sea where Israel traveled until they reached the foothills of Mount Sinai, God instructed Moses to have the people purify themselves. At the end of their forty-seven-day journey, they purified themselves for three days, resulting in a total of fifty days, hence the word *pentecost*. Fearfully and faithfully they approached Mount Sinai, the great mountain of God, to receive the Ten Commandments.

As Moses went up to speak with God, the ground shook and a mighty rushing wind roared over the desert plain. Fire glowed on the mountaintop. According to Jewish tradition, when God spoke to Moses, He not only spoke in Hebrew, but in every known tongue on earth. But something more happened in this story.

The stage was set for the future and God's mission to reach the entire Gentile world. Prophecy was written into the plot. God was doing exactly what He was going to do fifty days after the resurrection of Jesus Christ!

Keeping the story of the Hebrews at Sinai in mind, let's look at the story of Pentecost found in the book of Acts. Every aspect of that first Pentecost was duplicated as 120 faithful followers of Jesus gathered in the Upper Room, the site of Jesus' last supper. Ten people, a minyan, was the number required by Jewish law to have a kosher prayer meeting. Ten representatives for the twelve tribes of Israel (totaling 120) huddled together, trying to understand why Jesus had commanded them to "tarry in the city of Jerusalem until you are endued with power from on high" (Luke 24:49). As they prayed together, they joined together in one mind, one heart, and one spirit. Suddenly Moses' experience on Mount Sinai was duplicated again.

A rushing mighty wind filled the Upper Room. Tongues of fire rested on their heads just as fire rested on the crest of Mount Sinai. Days earlier Jesus had promised His followers, "But you shall receive power when the Holy Spirit has come upon you" (Acts 1:8).

Empowerment came in awesome ways. Just as God spoke on Mount Sinai in every known language, even so the disciples spoke in every known language in the Upper Room. The fire about Mount Sinai foreshadowed the coming power of Pentecost.

Paul proclaimed, "For the kingdom of God is not in word but in power" (1 Cor. 4:20). The gospel of the empty tomb is a story of power. Let no one mistake the message. There is power in His name, power in His gospel, power in His blood, and power in His church. If the apostles wanted to sing a contemporary hymn in the Upper Room, they couldn't have chosen a better one than "All hail the power of Jesus' name! Let angels prostrate fall; bring forth the royal diadem, and crown Him Lord of all!"

The purpose of Pentecostal power is evangelism. "But you shall receive power when the Holy Spirit has come upon you; and you shall be witnesses to Me" (Acts 1:8). The top priority of every Christian is to be a soul winner, and Solomon assured us that "he who wins souls is wise" (Prov. 11:30). The first evidence of supernatural power is soul winning. Without that, Christians are trees without fruit, wells without water, and clouds without rain.

Don't Miss the Dress Rehearsal

The feasts of the "former rain," consisting of Passover, Unleavened Bread, Firstfruits, and Pentecost, are acts one, two, three, and four in God's last-minute preparations for the divine drama of the Second Coming. The prophetic counterparts to these feasts are behind us, their roles fulfilled.

The hands on God's clock are swiftly moving. As the first four feasts predicted what is now past, so the next festivals help us calculate what lies ahead.

The Fifth Festival: The Feast of Trumpets (Rosh Hashanah)

Rosh Hashanah, the first day of the Jewish civil year, begins on the first of the seventh month, Tis'ri—September or October on the English calendar. According to Jewish custom, this is the date on which God created Adam, the first man. This is also called the Day of Judgment, when God sits on His throne and determines the destiny of each individual in the year ahead. In order to show trust in God's compassion, Jews dress in their best for this festival, usually in white, to signify purity, and celebrate the day with joy.[2]

Rosh Hashanah, the Feast of Trumpets, fulfills the Lord's command to Moses: "Speak to the children of Israel, saying: 'In the seventh month, on the first day of the month, you shall have a sabbath-rest, a memorial of blowing of trumpets, a holy convocation" (Lev. 23:24).

The "blowing of trumpets" refers to the shofar, the ram's horn that is blown exactly 100 times during the Rosh Hashanah service. Moses Maimonides, a Jewish scholar, explains the rationale behind the trumpet blowing:

> Although the sounding of the shofar on Rosh Hashanah is [observed because it is] a decree of the Torah, still it has a deep meaning, as if saying: "Wake up from your deep sleep, you who are fast asleep . . . search your deeds and repent; remember your Creator."[3]

While the first four festivals occur in close proximity, an entire season passes before the fall commemoration of trumpets begins. (See page 181—"The Jewish Calendar.")

This long period represents the dispensation of grace we now live in. Of all the feasts, this is the only time span in prophecy that cannot be exactly determined. The incalculable period is the one we're living in, the period of time where we wait for the angels to blow God's great trumpet that will call the Bride of Christ to her mansions on high.

The trumpets of God are the most important signal the world can possibly receive. Rosh Hashanah is a type of the Rapture of the church, a time that is drawing very near.

What is the Rapture? In 1 Corinthians 15:51–52, Paul wrote, "Behold, I tell you a mystery: We shall not all sleep, but we shall all be changed—in a moment, in the twinkling of an eye, at the last trumpet. For the trumpet will sound, and the dead will be raised incorruptible, and we shall be changed."

The Jewish Calendar

Month	Day	Festivals	Meaning of Word	English Months
1. A'bib	10th	Selection of Passover Lamb	Green Ears	March/ April
	14th	Passover		
	15th-21st	Unleavened Bread		
	16th	Firstfruits		
2, I'Jar			Brightness	April/ May
3. Si'van	6th	Pentecost		May/ June
4. Tam'muz				June/ July
5. Ab			Fruitful	July/ August
6. E'lul			Good for Nothing	August/ September
7. Tis'ri	1st	Trumpets	Flowing Rivers	September/ October
	10th	Day of Atonement (Yom Kippur)		
	15th-21st	Feast of Tabernacles (Sukkot)		
8. Mar-chesh'van			Rain	October/ November
9. Chis'leu				November/ December
10. Te'beth				December/ January
11. She'bat				January/ February
12. A'dar			Fire	February/ March

Paul explained the mystery of the Rapture, the next event on God's prophetic calendar. At the sound of God's trumpet, believers who have died will come out of the grave to be raised incorruptible, with new, supernatural, immortal bodies. Those who have not yet died a physical death will be caught up in the clouds to meet Jesus Christ. This mass ingathering of believers, the Bride of Christ, is commonly called the Rapture.

In explaining His return, Jesus left us with a paradox. On one hand, He said, "But of that day and hour no one knows, not even the angels of heaven, but My Father only" (Matt. 24:36). On the other hand, we *can* know that He "is near—at the doors!" (Matt. 24:33).

How can we know that He is near? A clue is found in Matthew 24:38–39: "For as in the days before the flood, they were eating and drinking, marrying and giving in marriage, until the day that Noah entered the ark, and did not know until the flood came and took them all away, so also will the coming of the Son of Man be."

Noah lived in a situation very similar to ours. God had issued a warning, a call to repentance, and He had told Noah to prepare and be ready. Noah obeyed. Even though he didn't know the exact time the Flood would come, He knew it was near, even at the door, because God put him, his family, and the animals on the boat and personally closed the door. Noah didn't know the exact moment the rains would fall and the fountains of the deep would be opened, but he knew without any doubt that the time was near.

We know, from signs of Bible prophecy such as those detailed in my book *Beginning of the End,* that the end is near. Without a doubt, we are the terminal generation.

When will the Rapture of the church take place? I believe it may happen at the Feast of Trumpets.

The Mystery of the Last Trumpet

Great confusion exists in Christian circles over the meaning of the Feast of Trumpets. Sincere people have missed the real meaning of Paul's instruction about the Rapture when he wrote, "We shall all be changed—in a moment, in the twinkling of an eye, at the last trumpet" (1 Cor. 15:51–52).

Some theologians reason that if there is a "last trump" there has to be a series of trumpets. The only series of trumpets mentioned in the New Testament is described in Revelation 8—9, so these theologians surmise that the church will go through the Great Tribulation. (Note: I have put together a series of studies featured in the *John Hagee Prophecy Bible* that explain in great detail why Christians will not go through any part of the Tribulation.)

If Gentile theologians are to get on track, they must understand the Jewish roots of our faith. The answer lies in what happened in the ancient Jewish wedding ceremony. Follow closely the nuptial chain of events:

In a traditional ancient ceremony, the hopeful bridegroom went to the home of his potential bride carrying three things: his best financial offering, a betrothal contract, and a skin of wine. If the father was impressed and accepted the bridegroom's offering, he called the daughter for her response. If things were acceptable to her, the bride-to-be drank the wine, and immediately a trumpet sounded to announce their betrothal.

During the following year of betrothal, the couple could not see each other alone, and a chaperone always accompanied them wherever they went. During this year, the bridegroom went to his father's house to prepare a place, a *chupah,* or honeymoon bed.

No engraved invitations were sent out for the wedding. If people preparing the calendar wanted to reserve a day for the celebration, they had a problem. When the young bridegroom was asked for the date of his wedding, he could only reply, "No man knows except my father." Why? Because he could not go get his bride until the father approved of his son's preparation.

The bride, therefore, had to be in a state of constant readiness lest the bridegroom's arrival catch her by surprise. Often she kept a light burning in the window and an extra jar of oil on hand, lest the bridegroom come in the night and find her unprepared.

When the groom's father decided everything was in place and released his son to go fetch his bride, a second trumpet was blown. This trumpet, to announce the groom's coming, was called the "last trump." Thus announced, the bridegroom took the marriage contract to present to the father of his intended bride. He claimed her as his bride and took her from her father's house to his father's house. His father would be waiting to receive the couple, and then the groom's father would take the hand of the bride and place it in the hand of his son. At that moment, she became his wife. That act was called the *presentation*.

After the presentation, the bridegroom would bring his bride to the place he had gone to prepare. There he would introduce her to all the society of his friends who had heard the trumpet and come to celebrate the marriage at the marriage feast. In 2 Corinthians 11:2, Paul wrote to the church, "For I am jealous for you with godly jealousy. For I have betrothed you to one husband, that I may present you as a chaste virgin to Christ."

What a powerful picture of what God has prepared for us. We are the betrothed bride of Christ, purchased at Calvary with His precious blood. Paul said, "For you were bought at a price" (1 Cor. 6:20). The Almighty Father looked down from heaven and accepted the price of our redemption. We, the bride, accepted the Groom and the evidence of His love for us.

In this interim, as we wait between Pentecost and Trumpets, Jesus Christ, our Bridegroom, returned to His Father's house to prepare everything for our arrival. Before He departed this earth, Jesus said, "In My Father's house are many mansions; if it were not so, I would have told you. I go to prepare a place for you. And if I go and prepare a place for you, I will come again and receive you to Myself; that where I am, there you may be also" (John 14:2–3).

How do we accept the proposal of Christ? Just like the bride, each time we take the Communion cup and drink the wine, we proclaim our wedding vows to our beloved Lord. We demonstrate that we love only Him, that we are loyal to Him, and that we are waiting for Him. Like the eager bride, we keep our lamps burning and strive to be ready, for we don't know when He might come.

Our Bridegroom *will* soon come for us. Make no mistake, we must wait with our ears attuned to hear the last trumpet sound.

We're not going into or through the Tribulation. We're going home, to the city where there will be no death, no parting, no sorrow, no sickness. We're going to the city where the Lamb is the Light, to the city where roses never fade, to the city inhabited by Abraham, Isaac, Jacob, and King Jesus.

The primary function of the Feast of Trumpets is to ask us one question: Are we prepared for the summons that will come when the world least expects it? Just as the blast of the shofar awakens the Jews and urges them to search their deeds and remember their Creator, the blast of the Lord's trumpet will awaken us to the realization that the Bridegroom has come.

Are you ready?

The Judgment Seat of Christ and the Bridegroom's Wedding Reception

What happens after the bridegroom takes his bride home? She must stand before him and await his appraisal. If she is wise, she has prepared a trunk with her wedding clothes, and she will adorn herself in beautiful garments that she has prepared because of her love for her bridegroom.

In biblical times the marriage feast was a celebration to honor not the bride, as is our custom, but the bridegroom. All the guests who assembled at the marriage banquet were expected to compose poems and sing songs to honor him as they appreciated the beauty and grace of his bride.

The Blessed Bridegroom has been presented with a bride, and now He is coming to display the bride to all His friends, not that they might honor the bride, but that they might honor the Bridegroom because of the bride's beauty. Jesus will be honored, not because of what we are, but because of what He has made us. Paul referred to this analogy in Ephesians when he wrote that Christ gave Himself for the church so that "He might present her to Himself a glorious church, not having spot or wrinkle or any such thing, but that she should be holy and without blemish" (5:27).

We're not holy by nature. We're not holy by practice. But the bride is the Father's love gift to the Son to honor the Son for His obedience to the Father's will. When Jesus, the Bridegroom, is presented with His bride, He will say, "She is beautiful, without spot or wrinkle." He will rejoice to lead her to the marriage banquet.

Imagine this, if you will: The bridegroom takes the bride into his chamber, looks her in the eye, and says, "Now I will take you in to meet all my friends. They will want to praise you, to exclaim over your beauty. So look into your hope chest and pull out those garments you have prepared for our marriage feast." What would you do if you looked into your hope chest and found nothing? Or perhaps you found only slipshod, poorly prepared garments? You would be embarrassed before your loving bridegroom, his father, and the assembled witnesses.

Soon after the Rapture, we Christians will stand before the Judgment Seat (sometimes called the "Bema Seat") of Christ. While Jesus took the full weight of God's judgment of sin for us, we must still stand before God for a final review of our faithfulness. As the nations of the world rise and fall because of their morality, our personal decisions and actions are creating evidence for the coming judgment on us. We will either receive crowns and commendation or reproof and reprimand. Our garments will either be designed to glorify our Bridegroom, or they will appear as filthy rags. The issue won't be salvation, because this judgment takes place in heaven with the redeemed. The qualities under examination will be our character and faithfulness.

In 1 Corinthians 3:11–15, Paul wrote:

> For no other foundation can anyone lay than that which is laid, which is Jesus Christ. Now if anyone builds on this foundation with gold, silver, precious stones, wood, hay, straw, each one's work will become clear; for the Day will declare it, because it will be revealed by fire; and the fire will test each one's work, of what sort it is. If anyone's work which he has built on it endures, he will receive a reward. If anyone's work is burned, he will suffer loss; but he himself will be saved, yet so as through fire.

On display at the Bema Seat will be five great crowns for the loyal and trustworthy servants of Christ who were faithful until death. To steadfast believers tested by prison and persecution even to the point of death, God will give a Crown of Life (Rev. 2:10). A never-fading, never-tarnishing diadem awaits the self-sacrificing pastor-shepherds of the flock (1 Peter 5:2–4). Everyone who ran life's race with patient endurance and perseverance will receive a Crown of Righteousness (2 Tim. 4:8). Evangelists and soul winners can eagerly anticipate receiving the Crown of Rejoicing (1 Thess. 2:19–20). Finally, all who overcome will be handed a wonderful Victor's Crown (1 Cor. 9:25).

Which crown will you wear?

Will you take your Bridegroom's arm with the scent of smoke upon you? Or will you join Him, dressed in white, with a glowing crown upon your head? John warns all believers, "Hold fast what you have, that no one may take your crown" (Rev. 3:11). Run the race to win!

The Sixth Festival: The Feast of Atonement (Yom Kippur)

On the tenth day of Tis'ri (September or October), the day of Yom Kippur, Israel comes together in worship, self-examination, reflection, and repentance. This is the most sacred day of the Jewish year. In ancient times it was the only occasion when the high priest entered the Holy of Holies, and a scapegoat bearing the sins of Israel was sent off to Azazel in the wilderness (Lev. 16:10).[4] On this day, righteous Jews must come to grips with their lives.

Daniel knew how extremely significant this feast would be in God's plan for the future. In Daniel 9:24, the prophet recorded the significance of the sixth feast:

> Seventy weeks are determined
> For your people and for your holy city [Jerusalem],
> To finish the transgression,
> To make an end of sins,
> To make reconciliation for iniquity [Yom Kippur],
> To bring in everlasting righteousness,
> To seal up vision and prophecy,
> And to anoint the Most Holy [Jesus Christ].

Just as the Crucifixion corresponded to the fulfillment of Passover down to the last detail, the Scripture points to the incredible promise of what will happen on this day, the Second Coming of Jesus Christ. Which Yom Kippur? No one knows "the day or the hour," but we know His coming is near, even at the door.

The second coming of Jesus Christ—and I'm not talking about the Rapture, where Jesus appears in the clouds without touching the earth—should occur 2,520 days, or seven prophetic years of 360 days, after the day Israel signs a seven-year peace accord with the Antichrist. The treaty signing will come after this extraordinary man emerges as the predominant leader of the European Union or a country or confederation that was once part of the Roman Empire. He will be the Beast described in Revelation 13:1, the creature who rises from the sea with "seven heads and ten horns, and on his horns ten crowns, and on his heads a blasphemous name." Ten crowns with seven heads of state indicate that three nations of his confederation have fallen under his control.

Although Israel will consider this thoroughly evil man to be the messiah, he will be Hitler reborn. His reign of evil influence will end, however, when Jesus Christ, Messiah, comes to destroy him. He will fulfill the intent of Yom Kippur, the day of reconciliation between people and God and His chosen people.

Yom Kippur's Meaning for the Church

The true bride of Christ will be gone by the time the Antichrist appears, but Yom Kippur reminds us that the church should be preaching repentance just before the Rapture. The last word Jesus Christ gave to the church was not the Great Commission. His last word to the church was *repent*.

In the first chapters of Revelation, Christ gave John the Revelator a message for seven churches of Asia. Five out of those seven churches were told to repent. I believe every detail in Scripture has a divine purpose. If five out of seven churches in Asia needed to repent, I believe five out of seven churches and five out of seven believers in America need to repent.

Repentance is the key to revival in America. We will either have national repentance and revival or revolution in the streets.

The Seventh Festival: The Feast of Tabernacles (Sukkot)

The Feast of Tabernacles, or Sukkot, is held by divine decree (Lev. 23:39) on the fifteenth through twenty-first days of Tis'ri, which falls in September or October. Sukkot begins after the ingathering of the harvest, and is the happiest of the biblical festivals. It celebrates God's bounty in nature and God's protection, symbolized by the fragile booths in which the Israelites dwelled in the wilderness. According to Jewish tradition, Sukkot is also a festival involving Gentiles, and seventy bullocks were offered up in the temple for the seventy nations of the world (all they knew existed in that time). In the messianic age, the Jews believe, all nations will come up to Jerusalem to celebrate Sukkot as an affirmation of faith in God's guidance of the world.[5]

As seven is the number of fulfillment and completion, this festival ushers in God's rest and points to the 1,000-year Millennium, the reign of Christ.

The Feast of Tabernacles is also called the Feast of Lights. The ancient custom in Israel during the festival was to place four great candelabra in the midst of the temple. Their large bowls were full of oil, and their wicks were made of holy garments the priests had worn during the preceding year. Everyone in Jerusalem could see the light.[6] How fitting that Jesus stood in the midst of the people and proclaimed, "I am the light of the world" (John 9:5).

We find our identity in Jesus Christ. He demonstrated who we are and what we are to be doing. The Bible urges us, "Let your light so shine before men, that they may see your good works and glorify your Father in heaven" (Matt. 5:16). Light reveals, exposes, and finally conquers darkness. We are to be the light in a dark world, just as Christ was.

Hear this! There can be no peaceful coexistence between light and darkness. "What communion has light with darkness?" asks the apostle Paul (2 Cor. 6:14). The time has come for the church of Jesus Christ to stop complaining about the darkness and turn on its light!

Don't whine. *Shine!*

Victory doesn't come without a fight. There is no sunrise without a night. There is no purchase without a cost. There is no crown without a cross. Don't curse the darkness, turn on the light.

Joy Unspeakable

The Feast of Tabernacles is also called "the season of our joy." I believe Jesus was born during the time of Sukkot. He was not born in December, for Luke 2:8 records that at the time of Jesus' birth there were "shepherds living out in the fields, keeping watch over their flock by night." From biblical times to the present, shepherds in Israel leave the cold of the open fields and pen their sheep up at night beginning in the month of October. Due to the nighttime cold, there were no shepherds in any fields in December. It was customary, however, to send flocks out after Passover, and they would remain in the fields until the first rain or frost in October. Jesus' birth, then, had to occur sometime between Passover and early October. I believe He was born during the season of Sukkot, the season of joy!

The angels gathered on the first Christmas morning and announced, "Do not be afraid, for behold, I bring you good tidings of great joy which will be to all people" (Luke 2:10). They knew the King of kings had come into the world. In the same way, the Feast of Sukkot celebrates the coming time when Jesus Christ will rule over the entire earth.

Zechariah prophesied that the Messiah would be God's greatest gift to the earth. "And the LORD shall be King over all the earth," he wrote, "In that day it shall be— / 'The LORD is one,' / And His name one" (14:9). The Messiah's coming will bring joy to the nations.

Jesus Christ is our joy. As we await His second coming when He will rule over the entire world, we rejoice in the power of the name that is above every name. One of the given names of Jesus, *Immanuel,* means "God with us." He is the wonderful Counselor, the mighty God, the everlasting Father, and Prince of Peace. Our Savior and Deliverer is also our Friend and Comforter. He gives us joy today that the world will know tomorrow. In His presence is the fullness of joy.

CHAPTER 10

THE FINAL DAWN OVER JERUSALEM

Nearly 250 years ago, the English writer Isaac Watts wrote a hymn based upon Psalm 98. Although we traditionally sing his song at Christmas, the lyrics are really about the Millennial reign of Christ:

> Joy to the world! The Lord is come;
> Let earth receive her king;
> Let every heart prepare Him room,
> And heaven and nature sing.
>
> Joy to the earth! The Savior reigns;
> Let men their songs employ;
> While fields and floods, rocks, hills and plains,
> Repeat the sounding joy.
>
> No more let sins and sorrows grow,
> Nor thorns infest the ground;
> He comes to make His blessings flow
> Far as the curse is found.
>
> He rules the world with truth and grace,
> And makes the nations prove

The glories of His righteousness,
And wonders of His love.[1]

Jerusalem, that blessed city, will be the capital of Jesus Christ when He rules in the Millennium, the 1,000-year reign of God upon the earth. For the first time in centuries, Jerusalem will rest securely, not fearing its enemies.

What Is the Millennial Kingdom?

Scripture has much to say about the Millennium. It is known in Scripture as "the world to come" (Heb. 2:5), "the kingdom of heaven" (Matt. 5:10), "the kingdom of God" (Mark 1:14), "the last day" (John 6:40), and "the regeneration" (Matt. 19:28). Jesus told His disciples, "Assuredly I say to you, that in the regeneration, when the Son of Man sits on the throne of His glory, you who have followed Me will also sit on twelve thrones, judging the twelve tribes of Israel" (Matt. 19:28).

The Millennium was foreshadowed in the Old Testament by the Sabbath, a time of rest. A rest was to be observed after six workdays, six workweeks, six work months, and six work years. In God's eternal plan, the earth will rest after 6,000 years as well, as He ushers in the Millennial Kingdom of the Messiah.

During the Millennium, the geography of Israel will be changed. Israel will be greatly enlarged and the desert will become a fertile plain. For the first time Israel will possess all the land promised to Abraham in Genesis 15:18–21. A miraculous river will flow east to west from the Mount of Olives into both the Mediterranean and the Dead Sea. But it will be "dead" no longer!

Listen to how Zechariah described it:

And in that day His feet will stand on the Mount of Olives,
Which faces Jerusalem on the east.
And the Mount of Olives shall be split in two,
From east to west,
Making a very large valley;
Half of the mountain shall move toward the north
And half of it toward the south.
Then you shall flee through My mountain valley. . . .
And in that day it shall be
That living waters shall flow from Jerusalem,
Half of them toward the eastern sea
And half of them toward the western sea;
In both summer and winter it shall occur. . . .

All the land shall be turned into a plain from Geba to Rimmon south of Jerusalem. Jerusalem shall be raised up and inhabited in her place from Benjamin's Gate to the place of the First Gate and the Corner Gate, and from the Tower of Hananel to the king's winepresses.

The people shall dwell in it;
And no longer shall there be utter destruction,
But Jerusalem shall be safely inhabited. . . .

And it shall come to pass that everyone who is left of all the nations which came against Jerusalem shall go up from year to year to worship the King, the LORD of hosts, and to keep the Feast of Tabernacles (14:4–5, 8, 10–11, 16).

Jerusalem, the apple of God's eye, will become the joy of the world. The city will become the international worship center, and people from all over the world will make pilgrimages to worship in the holy temple. Kings, queens, princes, and presidents shall come to the Holy City so "that at the name of Jesus every knee should bow, of those in heaven . . . and that every tongue should confess that Jesus Christ is Lord, to the glory of God the Father" (Phil. 2:10–11).

The prophet Micah wrote of the Millennial Kingdom, and the poetry of his verse has inspired many a public building (including the United Nations Building) to be inscribed with a portion of his words. But Micah wasn't writing about the United Nations, he was writing about God's Millennial capital, Jerusalem:

> Now it shall come to pass in the latter days
> That the mountain of the LORD's house
> Shall be established on the top of the mountains,
> And shall be exalted above the hills;
> And peoples shall flow to it.
> Many nations shall come and say,
> "Come, and let us go up to the mountain of the LORD,
> To the house of the God of Jacob;
> He will teach us His ways,
> And we shall walk in His paths."
> For out of Zion the law shall go forth,
> And the word of the LORD from Jerusalem.
> He shall judge between many peoples,
> And rebuke strong nations afar off;
> They shall beat their swords into plowshares,
> And their spears into pruning hooks;
> Nation shall not lift up sword against nation,
> Neither shall they learn war anymore (4:1–3).

The Holy City, now six miles in circumference, will occupy an elevated site and will be named *Jehovah-Shammah,* meaning "the Lord is there" (Ezek. 48:35) and *Jehovah Tsidkenu,* meaning "the Lord our righteousness":

> In those days Judah will be saved,
> And Jerusalem will dwell safely.
> And this is the name by which she will be called:
> THE LORD OUR RIGHTEOUSNESS (Jer. 33:16).

Millennial Judgment

After the Tribulation, the first thing God will do in the Millennial Kingdom is gather the nations of the earth and judge them for the manner in which they treated the nation of Israel. With the sound of the archangel and the blast of the trumpet, Jesus Christ is going to descend again to the Mount of Olives. The sides of the mountain will split in half, Jesus will walk across the Kidron Valley to enter the temple mount through the golden gate. At that moment, the Lion of Judah will assemble the divine tribunal and begin calling the nations to the bar of justice to answer for their abuse or blessing of the Jewish people and the State of Israel.

The arrogant and mighty men of war will grovel in the dust. The proud will beg for pity. Tyrants who showed Israel no mercy will plead for compassion. Generals and field marshals will attempt to hide behind lame excuses. The world will watch as God humbles and humiliates emperors, kings, and kingdoms. This is the judgment of nations.

Haman and his seven sons will march before the Lamb's bench for justice. During the days of the Babylonian exile, this treacherous demagogue sought to annihilate the Jewish people. Only the skillful intervention of Esther saved them. Even though the plot backfired and Haman was hanged, his trial will not be finished until God exposes him before the assembly of nations and angels escort him into the lake of fire.

Waiting in the wings will be Adolf Hitler, Heinrich Himmler, and every gestapo officer who worked in a Nazi death camp. Joseph Stalin and Nikita Khrushchev will stand behind them. When the holy gavel pounds on the Carpenter's bench, Hitler will bow in the presence of the Rabbi from Nazareth and plead for his very existence.

Nazi soldiers will have to explain how they could weep before statues of the Virgin Mary, who was Jewish, on Sunday and throw her descendants into gas chambers on Monday.

The Vichy government of France that cooperated with the monstrous Nazi death machine will cry out in sorrow because they betrayed the Jewish people. Lenin will rush forward, and Joseph Stalin will answer for decades of Russian anti-Semitism.

God does not forget. He will remember the six million Jews slaughtered in the Holocaust, one by one, to the creators of the Auschwitz ovens. Stripe for stripe, wound for wound, a complete accounting will continue until God has rectified every crime committed against His people. In a single stroke, He will mete out mercy and judgment.

The British Empire will be called to the judgment bar for their White Paper Policies during World War II and before. As Hitler was killing 25,000 people a day, multitudes of Jews tried to escape. Yet the British White Paper Policy allowed only 5,000 Jews a year to immigrate to Israel. Israel, under control of the British, returned helpless Jews to Hitler's death camps. The British captured Jews sneaking into Israel in leaky ships. The British closed the gates of mercy on Jews trying to escape. Almighty God will remember their actions on this judgment day.

The Great White Throne Judgment

But individuals will be judged as well as nations. The Great White Throne Judgment, where sinners stand in the presence of a holy God, is one of the most awesome revelations given to man in the Word of God. In Revelation 20:11, John wrote, "Then I saw a great white throne and

Him who sat on it, from whose face the earth and the heaven fled away. And there was found no place for them."

The judgment at the Great White Throne takes place after the Millennial reign is completed. It is held in an intermediate place, somewhere between heaven and earth. It could not take place on the earth, for the earth will be under renovation. It could not occur in heaven because sinners would never be permitted in the presence of a holy God.

There are two resurrections—the resurrection of the just, and the resurrection of the unjust. The resurrection of the just takes place in three phases. The first phase was at Calvary when men came out of their graves and were seen in the city of Jerusalem (Matt. 27:52–53). The second phase will be at the Rapture of the church. The third phase will be in the middle of the Tribulation, where martyred saints are taken into heaven.

All men, both righteous and unrighteous, will experience a resurrection day. In John 5:27–29, Jesus says that the Father "has given Him authority to execute judgment also, because He is the Son of Man. Do not marvel at this; for the hour is coming in which all who are in the graves will hear His voice and come forth—those who have done good, to the resurrection of life, and those who have done evil, to the resurrection of condemnation."

In Revelation 20:12, John continues to describe the Great White Throne Judgment, saying, "And I saw the dead, small and great, standing before God, and books were opened. And another book was opened, which is the Book of Life. And the dead were judged according to their works, by the things which were written in the books."

Notice that God has two sets of books. The first book, the Book of Life, contains the name of every person who accepted Jesus Christ while he or she was on the earth. When the wicked dead approach the Great White Throne, God will first look for their names in the Book of Life. Obviously, they will not be there.

Then He will open the books that are His written records of every word, thought, and deed of the wicked dead. The result? "And anyone not found written in the Book of Life was cast into the lake of fire" (Rev. 20:15).

In which judgment will you appear? Will you stand before the Judgment Seat of Christ where the works of believers are tried by fire, or the Great White Throne Judgment for those who have rejected Jesus Christ? The choice is yours.

The New Jerusalem: God's Golden, Glorious City

After the Millennium, when Satan and his followers have been eternally banished to the lake of fire, God will renovate this present world. He will then present us with a new heaven and a new earth, to which a *New Jerusalem* will descend from heaven. The apostle John described it in the closing chapters of the Revelation:

> Now I saw a new heaven and a new earth, for the first heaven and the first earth had passed away. Also there was no more sea. Then I, John, saw the holy city, New Jerusalem, coming down out of heaven from God, prepared as a bride adorned for her husband. And I heard a loud voice from heaven saying, "Behold, the tabernacle of God is with men, and He will dwell with them, and they shall be His people. God Himself will be with them and be their God.

"And God will wipe away every tear from their eyes; there shall be no more death, nor sorrow, nor crying. There shall be no more pain, for the former things have passed away." . . .

Then one of the seven angels who had the seven bowls filled with the seven last plagues came to me and talked with me, saying, "Come, I will show you the bride, the Lamb's wife." And he carried me away in the Spirit to a great and high mountain, and showed me the great city, the holy Jerusalem, descending out of heaven from God, having the glory of God. Her light was like a most precious stone, like a jasper stone, clear as crystal. Also she had a great and high wall with twelve gates, and twelve angels at the gates, and names written on them, which are the names of the twelve tribes of the children of Israel: three gates on the east, three gates on the north, three gates on the south, and three gates on the west. Now the wall of the city had twelve foundations, and on them were the names of the twelve apostles of the Lamb. And he who talked with me had a gold reed to measure the city, its gates, and its wall. The city is laid out as a square; its length is as great as its breadth. And he measured the city with the reed: twelve thousand furlongs [about 1,400 miles]. Its length, breadth, and height are equal. Then he measured its wall: one hundred and forty-four cubits [about 200 feet], according to the measure of a man, that is, of an angel. The construction of its wall was of jasper; and the city was pure gold, like clear glass. The foundations of the wall of the city were adorned with all kinds of precious stones: the first foundation was jasper, the second sapphire, the third chalcedony, the fourth emerald, the fifth sardonyx, the sixth sardius, the seventh chrysolite, the eighth beryl, the ninth topaz, the tenth chrysoprase, the eleventh jacinth, and the twelfth amethyst. The twelve gates were twelve pearls: each individual gate was of one pearl. And the street of the city was pure gold, like transparent glass.

But I saw no temple in it, for the Lord God Almighty and the Lamb are its temple. The city had no need of the sun or of the moon to shine in it, for the glory of God illuminated it. The Lamb is its light. And the nations of those who are saved shall walk in its light, and the kings of the earth bring their glory and honor into it. Its gates shall not be shut at all by day (there shall be no night there). And they shall bring the glory and the honor of the nations into it. But there shall by no means enter it anything that defiles, or causes an abomination or a lie, but only those who are written in the Lamb's Book of Life.

And he showed me a pure river of water of life, clear as crystal, proceeding from the throne of God and of the Lamb. In the middle of its street, and on either side of the river, was the tree of life, which bore twelve fruits, each tree yielding its fruit every month. The leaves of the tree were for the healing of the nations. And there shall be no more curse, but the throne of God and of the Lamb shall be in it, and His servants shall serve Him. They shall see His face, and His name shall be on their foreheads. There shall be no night there: They need no lamp nor light of the sun, for the Lord God gives them light. And they shall reign forever and ever (21:1–4, 9–27; 22:1–5).

Who will live in this Holy City? The holy angels, Christians who have placed their faith and trust in Christ, and redeemed Israel. Although the New Jerusalem is a wedding present from the Bridegroom to His bride, Israel is invited to dwell within these beautiful walls.[2]

In Hebrews 11, the roll call of faith, the author testifies of Jewish saints who placed their faith in God and obeyed His commands. They are invited to dwell in His heavenly city: "But now they desire a better, that is, a heavenly country. Therefore God is not ashamed to be called their God, for He has prepared a city for them" (v. 16).

Perhaps the most crucial occupant of heaven and the Holy City is Jesus Christ. He is the source, the strength, and the center of heaven.[3] By what right does He rule and reign over this Holy City?

Let's look back to the Abrahamic covenant. God promised Abraham, "I will make you exceedingly fruitful; and I will make nations of you, and kings shall come from you" (Gen. 17:6). God revealed how He planned to eventually rule over all the earth—through a king of His own appointment.

In Genesis 49 Jacob the patriarch called his twelve sons around his bed to give them a final blessing and to speak a prophetic word over each of them. His word over Judah is especially interesting:

> Judah, you are he whom your brothers shall praise;
> Your hand shall be on the neck of your enemies;
> Your father's children shall bow down before you. . . .
> The scepter shall not depart from Judah,
> Nor a lawgiver from between his feet,
> Until Shiloh comes (vv. 8, 10).

The word *Shiloh* may be rendered "He whose right it is to rule." Jacob thus prophesied that a king would come out of Judah's lineage who had the right to expect to be king.

In 2 Samuel 7:16, God made another promise, this one to King David: "And your house and your kingdom shall be established forever before you. Your throne shall be established forever." There are three important words in this verse:

house, kingdom, and *throne.* "Your house" is the descendants of David who would sit on his throne. "Your kingdom" is the kingdom of Israel. "Your throne" is his royal authority, the right to rule as God's representative. Twice in this one verse God told David that his dynasty, kingdom, and throne would last forever.

The last time I visited Jerusalem, I stood at the Shrine of the Book and stared for a long moment at the Dead Sea Scrolls. An overpowering feeling descended upon me—*those scrolls may have been touched and read by our blessed Lord.* It is one thing to think of Christ as a historical figure, a remote Savior who died 2,000 years ago and now sits at the right hand of the Father. It is quite another thing to walk the streets where He walked, to see items and objects that He might have held in His hands.

He was a man, but more than that, He is the King who will reign over Jerusalem forever. The throne of Jerusalem is His birthright.

The Gospel of Matthew opens with God breaking a silence of more than 400 years. Matthew gave Israel the message of the coming King by opening with a genealogy of Jesus Christ, "the Son of David, the Son of Abraham." If Jesus Christ is the son of Abraham, He is the Promised One through which all families of the earth should be blessed (Gen. 12:3). If Jesus Christ is the Son of David, He is the One who has the right to rule. He is Shiloh!

The angel of the Lord appeared to the Virgin Mary and said, "Do not be afraid, Mary, for you have found favor with God. And behold, you will conceive in your womb and bring forth a Son, and shall call His name JESUS. He will be great, and will be called the Son of the Highest; and the Lord God will give Him the throne of His father David. And He will reign over the house of

Jacob forever, and of His kingdom there will be no end" (Luke 1:30–33).

Jesus Christ was born, lived as a Jewish rabbi, and was crucified on a Roman cross. When Jesus ascended into heaven, God the Father said to Him,

Sit at My right hand,
Till I make Your enemies Your footstool (Matt. 22:44).

God is now preparing the nations for the last days. Jerusalem, who has suffered so much, stands on the brink of the greatest darkness it has ever known, but it will break forth into glorious light.

The nations of the world will gather in the Valley of Jehoshaphat for the Battle of Armageddon, when the nations meet the Son of God coming in the clouds of glory followed by His angels and the church triumphant.

John describes the sight, saying, "Now I saw heaven opened, and behold, a white horse. . . . [Messiah's] eyes were like a flame of fire, and on His head were many crowns" (Rev. 19:11–12). Why many crowns? Because He is "KING OF KINGS AND LORD OF LORDS" (Rev. 19:16). He is Shiloh, whose right to rule is given and guaranteed by God Almighty. He is the Son of David, and of His kingdom there shall be no end.

The citizens of Jerusalem, that ancient city that has seen so much suffering, will surrender streets that have flowed with blood for streets of pure gold. The desert sun will yield to the light of the Lamb, and the hatred of warring nations to the peace of God. The protective walls of Jerusalem, which were built and rebuilt with much toil and struggle, will be replaced by walls designed solely for beauty and glory. The Tree of Life, not seen or enjoyed since Eden, will grow in the center of the city. Nations will no longer look upon Jerusalem with jealousy or resentment but will look to it for the light of God's glory.

O Jerusalem, city of God, whose very dust and stones are loved by the faithful! The winds of war are fast approaching and bringing deep darkness. But by divine decree, the darkness will surrender to a beautiful and eternal dawn over Jerusalem.

On that final dawn over Jerusalem, when the Lamb who is the Light shall take His throne, there will be no more tears, no more pain, no more darkness.

Hallelujah! Joy to the world!

Notes

FOREWORD

1. Benjamin Disraeli, *Tancred,* bk. 3, ch. 4, *The Columbia Dictionary of Quotations,* licensed from Columbia University Press. Copyright © 1993, 1995 by Columbia University Press.

CHAPTER ONE

1. Seymour M. Hersh, *The Samson Option* (New York: Random House, 1991), p. 8.
2. "Attack—and Fallout," *Time,* June 22, 1981.
3. "A Vote Against Israel," *Newsweek,* June 19, 1981.
4. *The Congressional Record,* October 14, 1968, p. 31636.

CHAPTER TWO

1. John Phillips, *Exploring the World of the Jew* (Chicago: Moody Press, 1988), p. 128.
2. David Allen Lewis, *Israel and the USA, Restoring the Lost Pages of American History: The Story of Haym Salomon, Forgotten Patriot* (Springfield, MO: Menorah Press, 1993), pp. 3–10.
3. David Allen Lewis, *op. cit.,* p. 10.
4. Vendyl Jones, *Will the Real Jesus Please Stand?* (Tyler, TX: Priority Publishing, Institute of Judaic-Christian Research, 1983), pp. 220–28).
5. John Adams quoted in Rabbi Joseph Telushkin's *Jewish Wisdom* (New York: William Morrow and Company, 1994), p. 498.
6. *The Columbia Dictionary of Quotations* is licensed from Columbia University Press. Copyright © 1993, 1995 by Columbia University Press. All rights reserved.
7. *The Concise Columbia Encyclopedia* is licensed from Columbia University Press. Copyright © 1995 by Columbia University Press. All rights reserved.
8. Dr. Yoav Tenembaum, "The Last Romantic Zionist Gentile," © January 1996, *Jewish Post of New York Online.*
9. Dr. Yoav Tenembaum, *op. cit.*
10. *The People's Chronology* is licensed from Henry Holt and Company, Inc. Copyright © 1995, 1996 by James Trager. All rights reserved.
11. Theodore Roosevelt quoted in Rabbi Joseph Telushkin's *Jewish Wisdom, op. cit.,* p. 499.
12. Albert Einstein quoted in the *New York Times,* February 16, 1930.
13. *The People's Chronology* is licensed from Henry Holt and Company, Inc. Copyright © 1995, 1996 by James Trager. All rights reserved.

14. Emile Zola, *L'Aurore,* February 22, 1898, quoted in Rabbi Joseph Telushkin's *Jewish Wisdom, op. cit.,* p. 496.
15. Rabbi Joseph Telushkin, *op. cit.,* p. 498.
16. David Aikman, "For the Love of Israel," © 1996, Strang Communications.
17. David Aikman, *op. cit.*
18. Pope John XXIII quoted in Rabbi Joseph Telushkin's *Jewish Wisdom, op. cit.,* p. 469.
19. John Phillips, *op. cit.,* p. 129.

CHAPTER THREE
1. John Phillips, *op. cit.,* p. 111.
2. Dagobert Runes, *The War Against the Jew* (New York: Philosophical Library, 1968), p. 114.
3. John Phillips, *op. cit.,* pp. 115–16.
4. Mark Twain, *Harper's* magazine, September 1898.
5. *The New York Times,* December 21, 1996, p. A5.

CHAPTER FOUR
1. David Lloyd George quoted in Rabbi Joseph Telushkin's *Jewish Wisdom, op. cit.,* pp. 499–500.
2. Dagobert Runes, *op. cit.,* p. 106.
3. Malcolm Hay, *The Roots of Christian Anti-Semitism* (USA: Anti-Defamation League of B'nai B'rith and Alice Ivy Hay, 1981), p. 20.
4. Story of Hadrian contained in Lamentations Rabbah 3:9, quoted in Rabbi Joseph Telushkin's *Jewish Wisdom, op. cit.,* p. 463.
5. Malcolm Hay, *op. cit.,* p. 24.
6. Malcolm Hay, *op. cit.,* p. 26.
7. Chrysostom, Homily 4:1.
8. Malcolm Hay, *op. cit.,* p. 42.
9. Chrysostom, Homily 6:5 and 1:6.
10. Chrysostom, Homily 6:4.
11. Chrysostom, Homily 6:2, 6:4, 1:7, and 6:6.
12. Malcolm Hay, *op. cit.,* pp. 36–37.
13. Malcolm Hay, *op. cit.,* p. 37.
14. Jonathan Riley-Smith, ed., *The Oxford Illustrated History of the Crusades* (New York: Oxford University Press, 1995), p. 81.
15. Jonathan Riley-Smith, *op. cit.,* p. 39.
16. Jonathan Riley-Smith, *op. cit.,* p. 34.
17. Malcolm Billings, *The Cross & the Crescent: A History of the Crusades* (New York: Sterling Publishing Co., Inc., 1990), p. 15.
18. Malcolm Billings, *op. cit.,* p. 15.

19. Malcolm Billings, *op. cit.,* p. 16.

20. Malcolm Billings, *op. cit.,* p. 17.

21. Dagobert Runes, *op. cit.,* p. 37.

22. Malcolm Hay, *op. cit.,* p. 37.

23. Malcolm Billings, *op.cit.,* p. 66.

24. Rabbi Joseph Telushkin, *Jewish Wisdom, op. cit.,* p. 467.

25. Dagobert Runes, *op. cit.,* p. 34.

26. *Encyclopedia Judaica* (Jerusalem: Keter Publishing House, 1978), vol. 10, p. 114, and vol. 4, p. 64.

27. Malcolm Hay, *op. cit.,* p.37ff.

28. John Phillips, *op. cit.,* p. 113.

29. Edward Burman, *The Inquisition, Hammer of Heresy* (New York: Dorset Press, 1984), p. 135.

30. Edward Burman, *op. cit.,* p. 138.

31. Dagobert Runes, *op. cit.,* p. 87.

32. Edward Burman, *op. cit.,* p. 148.

33. Malcolm Hay, *op. cit.,* p. 160.

34. John Phillips, *op. cit.,* p. 112.

35. Malcolm Hay, *op. cit.,* p. 167.

36. Malcolm Hay, *op. cit.,* p. 167.

37. *Encyclopaedia Judaica,* vol. 11 (Jerusalem: Keter Publishing House Jerusalem Ltd., 1971), pp. 584–85.

38. *Encyclopedia Judaica,* vol. 3, *op. cit.,* p. 103.

39. Malcolm Hay, *op. cit.,* p. 169.

40. Malcolm Hay, *op. cit.,* p. 8.

41. Dagobert Runes, *op. cit.,* p. 114.

42. Malcolm Hay, *op. cit.,* p. 11.

43. Malcolm Hay, *op. cit.,* p. 3.

44. John Toland, *Adolf Hitler* (New York: Doubleday & Company, 1978), p. 326.

45. John Toland, *op. cit.,* p. 803.

46. John Toland, *op. cit.,* p. 331.

47. John Toland, *op. cit.,* p. 331.

48. John Toland, *op. cit.,* p. 617.

49. John Toland, *op. cit.,* p. 687.

50. John Toland, *op. cit.,* p. 287.

51. Nuremberg War Trials Staff, *Trial of the Major War Criminals, Before the International Military Tribunal: Nuremberg 14 November 1945– 1 October 1946,* vol. I, (Buffalo, NY: William S. Hein & Co., 1996), p. 50.

52. Nuremberg War Trials Staff, *op. cit.,* p. 251.

53. Nuremberg War Trials Staff, *op. cit.,* p. 439.

54. Nuremberg War Trials Staff, *op. cit.,*pp. 318–19.

55. John Toland, *Hitler, the Pictorial Documentary of His Life* (New York: Doubleday & Company), p. 287.

56. *The People's Chronology* is licensed from Henry Holt and Company, Inc. Copyright © 1995, 1996 by James Trager. All rights reserved.

57. D. M. Panton, "The Jew God's Dial," *Dawn*, August 15, 1924, pp. 197–201.

58. Malcolm Hay, *op. cit.*, p. 9.

59. Hyam Maccoby quoted in Rabbi Joseph Telushkin's *Jewish Wisdom, op. cit.*, p. 468.

60. Nikolay Berdyayev quoted in Rabbi Joseph Telushkin's *Jewish Wisdom, op. cit.*, p. 469.

61. Malcolm Hay, *op. cit.*, p. 116.

62. Malcolm Hay, *op. cit.*, p. 120.

63. Malcolm Hay, *op. cit.*, p. 121.

64. Malcolm Hay, *op. cit.*, p. 117.

65. Geoffrey Chaucer, *The Works of Geoffrey Chaucer*, ed. by F. N. Robinson (Boston: Houghton Mifflin Company, 1957), pp. 162–64.

66. Tomáš Masaryk quoted in Rabbi Joseph Telushkin's *Jewish Wisdom, op. cit.*, p. 497.

67. Malcolm Hay, *op. cit.*, p. 138.

68. Jeff Stein, "Hate on the Net," *Charlotte Observer*, August 24, 1997, pp. C1, 4C.

69. Geoffrey Chaucer, *op. cit.*, p. 162 (spelling modernized).

70. Voltaire's quote from his *Dictionnaire Philosophique* quoted in Rabbi Joseph Teluskin's *Jewish Wisdom, op. cit.*, p. 471.

CHAPTER FIVE

1. Malcolm Hay, *op. cit.*, p. 11.

2. Malcolm Hay, *op. cit.*, p. 20.

3. Malcolm Hay, *op. cit.*, p. 20.

4. Chaim Potok, *Wanderings* (New York: Fawcett Crest, 1978), p. 263.

5. Chaim Potok, *op. cit.*, p. 265.

CHAPTER SIX

1. Lucy Dawidowicz, *The War Against the Jews* (New York: Bantam Books, 1975), p. 27.

2. Malcolm Hay, *op. cit.*, p. 24.

3. Earl Paulk, *To Whom Is God Betrothed?* (Atlanta, GA: K-Dimension Publishers, 1985), p. 40.

4. Walter C. Kaiser Jr., Peter H. Davids, F. F. Bruce, and Manfred T. Brauch, *Hard Sayings of the Bible* (Downers Grove, IL: InterVarsity Press, 1996), pp. 569–70.

5. Kaiser, Davids, Bruce, and Brauch, *op. cit.,* p. 570.

CHAPTER SEVEN

1. Elie Wiesel quoted in *Writers at Work,* 8th ser., ed. George Plimpton, 1988.

CHAPTER EIGHT

1. Moris Farhi, *The Last of Days* (New York: Kensington Publishing Corporation, 1983), p. 201.

2. Ibrahim Sarbal, leader of the Islamic Jihad Movement in Palestine— al Aqsa Brigades. Quote is provided by the Anti-Defamation League of B'nai B'rith.

3. Quote provided by the Anti-Defamation League of B'nai B'rith.

4. Joan Peters, *From Time Immemorial* (New York: Harper and Row Publishers, 1984), pp. 391–412.

5. Mitchell G. Bard and Joel Himelfarh, *Near East Report Myths and Facts* (Washington, D.C.: 1992), p. 308.

CHAPTER NINE

1. David C. Gross, *How to Be Jewish* (New York: Hippocrene Books, 1991), p. 145.

2. Alan Unterman, *Dictionary of Jewish Lore and Legend* (London: Thames and Hudson, Ltd., 1991), p. 168.

3. Rabbi Joseph Telushkin, *Jewish Wisdom, op. cit.,* p. 387.

4. Alan Unterman, *op. cit.,* p. 208.

5. Alan Unterman, *op. cit.,* pp. 191–92.

6. Ralph Gower, *The New Manners and Customs of Bible Times* (Chicago: Moody Press, 1987), p. 358.

CHAPTER TEN

1. Isaac Watts, "Joy to the World," *The Baptist Hymnal* (Nashville: Convention Press, 1991), No. 87.

2. H. L. Willmington, *The King Is Coming* (Wheaton, IL: Tyndale House, 1988), p. 300.

3. Willmington, *op. cit.,* p. 301.

Kwawei Luxking Is Here, II. Paulist Public ... of Minka I J.
Braud, Illuvi ...o... ...r of the Bible Dur..., ... ng It s New York
... ..., 1996, pp. 464-70.
5. Kaare Davik, Name and Imah ..., p. 179.

CHAPTER ELEVEN
1. Eliz Wiesel quoted ...ra ... at the ...banch ... ... of ... long...Impre...
...on, 1988.

CHAPTER EIGHT
1. Merle Fain...Th... at y .... ed-k Fairground Publishing
Corporation, 1988, pp. 205.
2. Ibrahim ..., leader of the Islamic Jihad Movement in Palestine,
and Aqsa brigades. Quote is provided ... Sermon...-below ... the League
...see Ibid. ...id.
3. Quote provided by the Anti-Defamation League, of Brai...ith, T.
John Perkin, ..., Long Time Overcoming (New York, Harper and Row
Publishers, 1994), pp. 2.
5. Mitchell G. Bard and Joel Himmelfarb, Myth Fact Key to Myths and
Facts (Washington D.C., 1992), p. 208.

CHAPTER NINE
1. David G. ...oer, Faces of ... York in New York (New York, Penguin Books
1994), p. 145.
2. Alan Unterman, Dictionary of Judaism Lore and Legend (London,
Thames and Hudson, 1991), p. 164.
3. ...edd Ibraph Inhibition report by Wehds ...on. p...h, ... SRR.
4. Alan Unterman, op. cit., p. 214.
5. Alan Unterman, op. cit. pp. 191-92.
6. Ralph Gut..., The Wars, Origins and Casualties of Eight Types
of Religion (Amsterdam Press, 1983) pp. 5-31.

CHAPTER TEN
1. Bacs Wit..., Sanctions to the World (C. ... of Diplomatic Washington,
Conversation Press, 1981), pp. 8-9.
2. Eliza Wilburgton, The King & Country (Washington, Hale Unedale
House, 1959), pp. 300.
3. Wilburgton, ob. cit., p. 276.

Day of Deception

Separating
Truth from
Falsehood
in These
Last Days

JOHN HAGEE

THOMAS NELSON PUBLISHERS®
Nashville

Dedication

"He who gives a book gives more than cloth, paper, ink—more than leather, parchment, and words. He reveals a foreword of his thoughts, a dedication of his friendship, a page of his presence, a chapter of himself, and an index of his love."

—Unknown

To my wife, Diana Hagee

Contents

CONTENTS

Deception in Government

Chapter One

Witchcraft in the White House

He was a weak-willed, vacillating, Milquetoast figure who stood for nothing but his own self-interest. His positions changed depending on who stood before him. And usually the one who stood before him was his wife, who manipulated him and the government.

She was a highly motivated, politically directed feminist who knew how to use her position for personal gain. There was no doubt about it. She was the brains of the duo and as hard as nails. Her ambition was never satisfied.

Their greed was finally exposed to the nation through a mismanaged, fraudulent real estate deal. Her fingerprints were on the incriminating government documents. At least one man died because he knew too much. But even then, she was so feared that no one dared ask too many questions.

Sound familiar? Their names were Ahab and Jezebel. They ruled as King and Queen of Israel 2,800 years ago. They wove such a web of witchcraft that the whole nation became corrupt. Government officials lied about one another. People were falsely charged and sentenced. Justice was perverted. Some were executed![1]

Only a few men of God had the courage to speak up about government persecution of the godly, and they were living in caves, living on bread and water smuggled to them by fellow believers. The prophet Elijah, the only one to publicly challenge Ahab and Jezebel, was so discouraged he begged God to take his life.[2]

You have probably noticed the uncanny parallel between the ancient story of Ahab and Jezebel and America's own melodrama playing out in the White House of Bill and Hillary Clinton. Like Ahab and Jezebel before them, Bill and Hillary are trying to live down their association with a fraudulent real estate deal. Fourteen people have already been convicted or pled guilty in court. Four prominent White House staffers have resigned.[3]

As this book goes to press *USA Today* reports: "The White House expects a new round of Whitewater indictments by the end of February (1997) including some present or former staffers."[4] Whitewater special prosecutor Kenneth Starr is presently taking testimony from James McDougal. White House Counsel Jane Sherburne's on-the-record acknowledgment that indictments are expected is the first by a top White House aide.

Adding to White House woes is the mysterious death of the president's attorney and Hillary Clinton's close friend Vince Foster in Fort Marcy Park. Official police reports showed there were no fingerprints found on the gun that lay by his side.[5]

The newsrooms and pulpits of America should be in an uproar, but the newsrooms share the philosophy of today's Ahab and Jezebel. And the pulpits have been frightened into submission as government agencies have finally begun the long-anticipated pulling of tax-exempt status from anyone they view as "the enemy."[6]

Talking to the Dead

Jezebel, the daughter of Ethbaal, King of the Sidonians, brought witchcraft to Israel, lending the prestige of the palace to encourage the worship of Baal. Male and female prostitutes were used in the bizarre, satanic rites that accompanied this complex but seductive form of idolatry. And in a modern age, Hillary Clinton has brought witchcraft into the White House, lending her name and influence to medium and so-called psychic spiritualist Jean Houston.

Hillary and Jean have met together on numerous occasions in numerous places including several meetings in the private quarters of the White House.[7] Houston claims to have a mystical link with the ancient Greek goddess Athena. The remarkable relationship between Jean and Hillary received national publicity when the news leaked that Jean Houston was leading Hillary Rodham Clinton into "imaginary conversations" with the dead, while the president of the United States sat by looking on approvingly. Allegedly, the first lady spoke with Mahatma Gandhi and her earlier predecessor in the White House, former first lady Eleanor Roosevelt, dead since 1962. According to the story, Eleanor encouraged Hillary to keep doing what she was doing.[8]

Of course, today's New Age apologists have repackaged the goods. They have taken the ancient arts and practices of divination and the occult and recast them in a whole new modern language. They talk about "white witches" who use their power for the good of mankind. They refer to mediums as "spiritual guides" and refer to necromancy as a "mental exercise." Jean Houston, the first lady's New Age "spiritual guide," has experimented with LSD, eaten magical Chinese worms, and swum with the dolphins, but today she is cloaked in respectability.[9]

The Bible is very clear. Deuteronomy 18:10–11 says, "There shall not be found among you anyone . . . who practices witchcraft, or a soothsayer, or one who interprets omens, or a sorcerer, or one who conjures spells, or a medium, or a spiritist, or one who calls up the dead."

Clinton Women

Meanwhile President Clinton continues to be plagued by a different kind of witchcraft. New details of the president's extramarital affairs keep tumbling out of the closet. The press and public are almost immune. Gennifer Flowers's original story as Clinton's mistress includes hundred of pages of dates, times, and places confirmed by former Arkansas state troopers who served as Clinton security men and who have risked their careers and futures by speaking out. And yet, on the television program, *60 Minutes*, Clinton denied having an affair with Gennifer Flowers.[10]

In 1996, after being ridiculed and smeared by the press, Flowers released tape recordings of conversations she had with the president of the United States in which he called her "Darling" and "Baby" and bragged about his prowess at oral sex.[11] The media and the nation virtually ignored it.

During the 1992 presidential campaign more "Clinton women" started surfacing and journalists, egged on by Clinton political rivals, were in the hunt. A Clinton staffer, Betsey Wright, warned that there were going to be more "bimbo eruptions."[12]

Paula Jones woke up one morning after the campaign to see her own incident with Bill Clinton on the front pages. According to testimony, Jones was a young, former Arkansas state employee who had been invited up to the governor's suite. She later told a girlfriend that Clinton had closed the door, dropped his pants, and asked her to perform a sex act. Paula ran from the room, trembling and fearful. When the stories of "Clinton's women" started making another cycle in the press, a girlfriend told a journalist about Paula Jones. It was in the papers the next day.

Before Paula Jones could muster an explanation, she found herself on the front page of the nation's newspapers. One former White House aide described it as a "vicious campaign to destroy her credibility."[13] She hadn't yet said a word. By the end of the week, every private and secret deed of her life was broadcast to the world. Eventually, Paula Jones hired an attorney, hoping to stop the onslaught. The attorney promptly filed suit against the president.

Meanwhile, Bill Clinton's legal advisors have used every

trick in the book to keep the Paula Jones suit from coming to court. It has been successfully stalled for years. One device has been the use of the Soldiers and Sailors Civil Relief Act of 1940. This unique law, passed on the eve of America's entry into World War II, states that civil claims against military personnel can be put off while they are on active duty. Bill Clinton, famous as a draft dodger and protester during the Vietnam War, now claimed that as president he was Commander in Chief and thus exempt from Paula Jones's suit.[14]

Now other information reveals that notorious San Francisco private investigator Jack Palladino was paid at least $93,000 by the Clinton-for-President campaign to help counter stories of marital indiscretion.[15] Since the Gennifer Flowers incident, Bill Clinton has been careful not to deny the many accusations that he has been unfaithful to his wife, Hillary. And yet, the pulpits of America are silent.

Exposing the Darkness

You may ask, "But doesn't the Bible also tell us to pray for those who are in authority above us? How can you be so disrespectful to our leaders?" Yes. The admonition in 1 Timothy 2:2 is very clear. As Americans we should pray for our president, for our governor, and for our representatives. We should pray for those who are in authority no matter who they are or what their political views may be. Whether they are pro-abortion or pro-life, whether they favor allowing schoolchildren the right to start their day with a silent prayer or whether they don't. But the Bible does not tell us to turn a deaf ear to evil and corruption. In 1 Peter 2:13–16, we are told how to respect those in authority over us. But in the same paragraph it instructs us to live as free men "yet not using liberty as a cloak for vice."

The Bible says in Ephesians 5:11 to expose the "works of darkness." And it warns the powerful who think they can prey on the helpless and innocent that every secret sin will be exposed.[16] The Lord Himself promised to be the defender of the orphan and widow. The Bible admits that for a time, evil will prosper. But Jesus warned that whatever is whispered in secret shall be shouted from the housetop. Yes, we have a responsibility to pray for those in authority. But we have an equal responsibility to challenge corruption, defend the innocent, denounce witchcraft, and shine a light into the darkness of these latter days.

I am sometimes asked, "What right do you have to challenge government leaders?" John the Baptist boldly and publicly denounced King Herod for taking his brother's wife. It cost John the Baptist his life.[17] Jesus Himself had not yet met Herod when he publicly called him "that fox."[18]

Proverbs 28:4 says, "Those who forsake the law praise the wicked, / But such as keep the law contend with them." There are only two positions. Either we are praising the wicked who have abandoned God's laws or we are contending with them.

King David wrote, "You who love the LORD, hate evil!"[19]

Jesus said, "He who is not with Me is against Me, and he who does not gather with Me scatters abroad."[20]

James writes, "Whoever therefore wants to be a friend of the world makes himself an enemy of God."[21]

God's position is very clear. You are either wheat or tares, sheep or goats, light or darkness, saved or lost.

Jeremiah was all alone in boldly denouncing the policies of King Zedekiah whom he had never met. Even the religious leaders told him, "You are a troublemaker. You are disrespectful to authority. Your words are unfair." Yet Israel was deceived, even though it was heading for destruction and the signs were there for anyone to see. Jeremiah was ridiculed and harassed. He was called the "weeping prophet" because he so despaired over the unpopular message he had to deliver. Eventually, Jeremiah was thrown into a deep pit of miry clay where he was left to die in his own human waste—but God brought him out.

Policy or Morality?

Some say to me, "Well, you're biased because you're pro-life and the president is pro-choice. This is just about abortion, an issue of policy on which honorable people disagree." They are wrong on both counts. I am not biased. I am living in a "day of deception" and hold high the torch of truth in America's darkest hour. When public policy is immoral it *should* be challenged, regardless of who is in office. In my opinion, the liberal media slander any who dare raise their voices, saying they practice the "politics of hatred." It is never hatred to speak the truth. Compromise at the expense of principle is cowardice.

Dietrich Bonhoeffer stood up to Hitler in 1933, publishing a tract denouncing anti-Semitism, the de-Christianization of the school system, the new concentration camps, the legal non-accountability of the Gestapo, and the manipulation of the Reichstag elections.[22] Bonhoeffer's fellow churchmen denounced him. The Lutheran Council publicly disassociated themselves from the tract.[23] "What's wrong with Hitler?" everyone asked. "Wasn't British Prime Minister Winston Churchill saying that he 'hoped Great Britain would have a man like Hitler in time of peril?'[24] After only two years employment is restored. Our new autobahns are the wonder of the world. The new People's Car (Volkswagen) will soon make the automobile affordable to the masses. You, sir, are a troublemaker." Except for a handful of outspoken preachers, the German church was deceived.

Christians sat on their hands when the decree came down to allow abortions and "mercy killings" in hospitals. After all, the abortions were sometimes medically necessary and the mercy killings were only for mental patients who were suffering anyway. These were all "issues on which honorable people disagree." And no one raised an alarm when the word was finally given to terminate the handicapped and the invalid, including children, a great many of whom were hanged.

In 1937, when Nazi law made it illegal for churches to take collections, make proclamations, or circulate newsletters, members of Bonhoeffer's own evangelical Confessing Church implored him to stay quiet. Later that year the government arrested 807 pastors and leading laymen in the denomination. They even blamed the preacher. "After all, he was asking for it. The Bible says to live in peace."[25]

And so those evangelical pastors sat helplessly in concentration camps when the time came for the local Jewish baker, or doctor, or neighbors, or their children's school friends to start disappearing to the so-called resettlement camps in the East where they were actually being murdered. And the fact is they probably wouldn't have done anything about it anyway, even if they had been free. They had been deceived.

On April 9, 1945, near the end of the war, Dietrich Bonhoeffer was taken from his colleagues at the Buchenwald concentration camp and hanged by the Nazi government he had publicly denounced for years. Two days later American soldiers liberated Buchenwald. Christians who knowingly sat on their hands while Jews went to the gas chambers were as guilty as the government leaders who made the decisions.[26]

But Elijah, the prophet, boldly stood up to Ahab and Jezebel, the powerful Bill and Hillary Clinton of ancient Israel. Ephesians 5 says, "Let no one deceive you with empty words . . . And have no fellowship with the unfruitful works of darkness, but rather expose them. For it is shameful even to speak of those things which are done by them in secret. But all things that are exposed are made manifest by the light, for whatever makes manifest is light."[27]

WITCHCRAFT IN THE WHITE HOUSE

Nervous? It gets worse. We're only getting started. This book is not for the fainthearted! Truth is often violated by falsehood but can be equally outraged by silence.

Madison Guaranty Savings and Loan

The media are fond of confusing the public on the whole byzantine Whitewater controversy. If the public can't understand it, they certainly won't be able to make a judgment. But some aspects of the scandal are so clear that even the media can't obfuscate. Madison Guaranty, a savings and loan of Little Rock, Arkansas, was owned by Bill and Hillary's close personal friends, James and Susan McDougal. A Senate counsel has referred to Madison Guaranty as "a thoroughly corrupt, criminal and fraudulent enterprise."[28] The McDougals and the Clintons were also co-owners of the now-infamous Whitewater land development.

Now, stay with me. Let's take one more small step. The McDougals' Madison Guaranty Savings and Loan conducted a lot of business with Capital Management Services, Inc., owned by a certain judge David Hale, at the time another friend of Bill and Hillary. Allegedly, money went back and forth between the two companies to confuse any federal regulators who might later come snooping around.

When the Whitewater development started losing money, Bill and Hillary reportedly started putting the pressure on their partners, the McDougals, to take care of it. After all, Clinton was the governor, he didn't have any money. How was he supposed to make payments on the land? One can hear Bill Clinton complain, "The whole idea was for the project to make money, lots of money. The McDougals said it would turn a profit. They should take care of it."

Today former judge David Hale says that then-Governor Bill Clinton pressured him into fraudulently soliciting a

$300,000 government loan through Capital Services, Inc.[29] The money was then allegedly passed on to Susan McDougal, Clinton's Whitewater partner.[30] Presumably, Clinton could have boasted to the McDougals, "Now, I did my part. You take care of the rest."

Still with me? Prosecutors now are charging two Arkansas bankers, Herby Branscum Jr. and Robert Hill, with directly funneling bank funds back into Governor Clinton's 1990 reelection campaign. The indictment is not short of detail. Among other things, it charges that on December 14, 1990, in the governor's office, one of the bankers personally handed Clinton a $7,000 contribution for the campaign he had already won. One month later, Clinton named Branscum to the State Highway Commission.[31]

Meanwhile, investigators learned that Hillary Rodham Clinton, then an attorney at the Rose Law Firm in Little Rock, Arkansas, was, in fact, the lead counsel assigned to Madison Guaranty Savings and Loan. It is not a pretty picture. If testimony is true, her husband was pushing on one end, trying to get his friend to scam the government out of some money, while on the other end his wife was providing the legal advice.

The Clintons denied everything. No, they hadn't tried to pressure David Hale or the McDougals into doing the wrong thing, and it hadn't even been proven in court that any crime had been committed in the first place. Hillary even denied she was the lead attorney for Madison Guaranty, which would seem to be an easy thing to resolve. Either she was or she wasn't, and the billing records at the Rose Law firm would tell the tale one way or the other. And what difference did it make anyway if no one had done any of the things that were charged? When the White House was accused of covering up and pressuring witnesses to be silent, they responded sarcastically, "How can you have a cover-up without a crime?" The servile press dutifully picked up the drumbeat.

Out in the Open

Then a remarkable story began filtering out of Little Rock, Arkansas. A young law clerk at the Rose Law Firm said that he and others had been given orders to start shredding documents. The special prosecutor's office immediately issued a subpoena for the billing records, making it a federal crime to destroy them. For the next two years, investigators searched through the files in the Rose Law Firm in Little Rock, Arkansas, but they searched in vain.

In a 1994 White House press conference, Hillary Rodham Clinton made it very clear. "Over the past several years, we have made a very deliberate effort to try to obtain documents, and every document that we have obtained has been turned over to special counsel, no matter where it came from."[32] It wasn't her problem.

In January 1996, it suddenly became her problem after all. A member of her own personal staff admitted under oath that she had actually seen the famous billing records on a table in the upstairs, private living quarters of the White House. She wasn't going to lie and go to jail for the first lady. Very few staffers or citizens ever see the private quarters of the White House. No one has access without the president or first lady's invitation; it is their home. At night, the president and his family are literally locked in. To no one's surprise, investigators found Hillary's fingerprints all over the documents. And to no one's surprise, they clearly showed her major role as the lead attorney for Madison Guaranty during those years of "corrupt, criminal and fraudulent enterprise." There were personal notations on the document in the handwriting of White House Counsel Vince Foster,[33] the man later found dead in Fort Marcy Park.

By the summer of 1996, the Clintons could no longer sneer about "a cover-up without a crime." More than nine individuals had pleaded guilty to various crimes, spiraling out of Whitewater and its related scandals. Five others were found guilty by a jury of their peers, including judge David Hale and both James and Susan McDougal. There was now no question about whether the deed had been done. And there was no question that the crimes had benefited the Clintons' campaign and the Whitewater projects. The question was, who was lying, Bill and Hillary or everybody else?

That summer the fallout started hitting the White House as well. Bernard Nussbaum, Clinton's new counsel, resigned under pressure. He had blocked the FBI from searching Vince Foster's White House office after Foster's body was found in a public park.[34] Clinton friend Robert Altman, Deputy Treasury Secretary, was accused of misleading Congress, and later of improperly contacting government investigations looking into Madison Guaranty. He resigned as well, dragging two other treasury officials with him.[35] One was Treasury Chief of Staff Josh Steiner, who apparently wrote some things damaging to the Clintons in his personal diary. When it was discovered, Steiner stonewalled, making the incredible claim that he was lying to himself in his own diary.[36]

"Well," you say, "the president didn't get rich off of Whitewater. What's the big deal?" This is exactly the White House line. In the fall of 1993, Hillary Rodham Clinton continually complained publicly, "I'm bewildered that a losing investment . . . is still a topic of inquiry." But it is a disingenuous argument indeed. The point is that Whitewater could have cost them a small fortune in mounting debt but government loans, fraudulently obtained, saved them. Some of the people who were sent to prison for these crimes have spoken out, openly contradicting the Clintons' version of events, but there is no one to hear them and no one who cares. To paraphrase a famous saying of the Big Apple, "only the little people go to jail."

Since the White House is always reminding the public

that Whitewater was a money-losing investment, get out your flashlight, and let's take a look at a scam that didn't lose money. The story you are about to read has never been in print. How did I get it? It walked through my door. Sometimes, when a person takes a stand, other people will get enough courage to come in and whisper their stories in secret. Now, let's shout it from the housetop.

Witchcraft on the Commodities Market

One of the more bizarre tales to come tumbling out of the Whitewater closet was how Hillary Rodham Clinton parlayed an initial investment of $1,000 into $100,000 in only one year of trading on the commodities market. The public was obviously skeptical. One critic observed sarcastically, "Put the woman in charge of investing our United States savings bonds. Maybe she can generate that kind of interest for all of us. We could wipe out the national debt in three years."[37]

For a while reporters simply explained that she probably had an adviser, a seasoned, professional commodities trader, someone who made the recommendations. But then the commodities experts started weighing in on the talk shows. "No, not possible," they said. "No expert has ever been that successful with that many diverse transactions. It defies mathematical probability. Such a person would be a billionaire; he would not be a Little Rock broker." The famous Clinton research team, who answers every negative charge with a fax the next day, was uncharacteristically silent. Not one public relations genius or "spinmeister" in the country could come up with a credible explanation for the hapless Clinton White House. Couldn't be done. And yet Hillary Rodham Clinton wouldn't even admit that she had been advised by anybody. "I relied on the *Wall Street Journal*," she said.[38]

The obvious question was, why did her magical run last only a year? If she was that good at commodities trading, why didn't she keep it up? Maybe she wouldn't have repeated the phenomenal year of 99,000 percent, but she might at least make a paltry 20 percent. Even that would be four times the rate of inflation. Not a bad return. Why let the money sit?

The following story came to me from the comptroller of a Fortune 500 company whose close friend ended up as a senior executive with Tyson Foods of Arkansas. The two friends met from time to time, each representing his own company's interests. According to my source, Tyson began to "play games." The comptroller of the Fortune 500 company told his friend that, as far as he was concerned, one of Tyson's proposals amounted to outright extortion. He couldn't advise his company to go along. When he threatened to blow the whistle, he was given a hard civics lesson, Arkansas style. "You don't understand how this state works," he was told. "We have most of the judges down here in our pocket. The young attorney general [Bill Clinton] is our man and he's going to be the next governor." When he persisted anyway, his case eventually ended up in an Arkansas court, where the Tyson Company won, just as his friend had predicted. The young attorney general was now the governor.

The Fortune 500 comptroller was stunned. "Could this really be happening in the United States?" Over lunch his friend from Tyson consoled him and told the story of how they had gotten their hooks into Arkansas judges and politicians. "But the governor?" the comptroller protested. "The governor?"

"Oh, that was easy," his friend confided. "Have you ever played the commodities market? It's a pretty volatile business. You can win or lose a lot in a short amount of time. A few years ago several of us pooled our investments with a common commodities broker. He spread the money around, making a variety of investments. The young attorney general's wife threw her money into the same pot.

When it was over and we had sold out, we would decide who had their money in which investment. If it was a loser, one of us would take it. If it was a winner, we would say that it had been the investment of the attorney general's wife. Then, we'd buy another round of commodities and do the whole thing all over again. Week after week. Everybody got a good laugh out of it. Of course, frequently we lost money, but even then we were winning because the attorney general's wife was getting rich, which was the whole idea."

There it is. The best explanation you'll ever get on how to turn $1,000 into $100,000 in one year. You pick your stock *after* it goes up. Can't lose.

Travelgate Tells the Story

Proverbs 14:31 says, "He who oppresses the poor reproaches his Maker." God carefully watches how the powerful treat the weak. Nothing provides a more revealing insight into a man or woman's character.

According to published reports, the Clintons had their eye on the White House travel department even before the inauguration.[39] Bill and Hillary's famous Hollywood friend Harry Thomason, part-owner of a travel consulting firm who had worked for the Clinton campaign, wrote a series of memorandums on how the White House travel department could be reorganized. He knew the travel industry and knew who should get those contracts. Soon after the election Thomason's firm had tried to muscle in on the White House travel business but had been rightly rebuffed. It was an obvious conflict of interest.[40]

Hillary was reportedly furious. The de facto president liked Thomason's ideas and, anyway, she wanted her own people running things. Why couldn't they just sweep out the current staff and bring in some loyalists? In fact, Thomason started the process, appointing one of the president's young Arkansas cousins to an open slot. But there was a problem.

The White House travel office was doing just fine, thank you. It was one of the most popular and smoothest running pieces in the whole White House machine. Its workers had been there for years, serving presidents from both parties. But that was the problem. These were not political appointees who came and went with each administration. Billy Dale, who directed the office, had served John F. Kennedy, Lyndon Johnson, Richard Nixon, Gerald Ford, Jimmy Carter, Ronald Reagan, and George Bush.[41] These people had tenure. Legally, as government employees, they could not be fired without a reason.

First the White House leaked stories charging that the travel staff was disloyal—still committed to George Bush—hoping to get some sympathetic words from their friends in the press. When that didn't work, they started accusing the office of incompetence. But that didn't resonate either. The grumpy, supersensitive, supercritical White House press corps had nothing but praise for the White House employees. They knew them. They knew their work better than the newcomers, Bill and Hillary. Since John F. Kennedy, no other president had found them disloyal or incompetent. What was the problem?

Now, the president was really frustrated. Our modern-day Jezebel steps in. Her words were probably similar to that ancient queen's: "You're the king. Why are you sitting there so depressed? You want Naboth's vineyard? Take it! No, better yet. Stay right where you are. Let me get it for you."

According to the notes of White House Chief of Staff Mack McLarty on May 16, three days before the firings, Hillary started putting on the pressure.[42] A later memo from White House staffer Lorraine Voles says, "Hillary wants these people fired. Mack wouldn't do it."[43]

Now, why not? Weren't these people disloyal? Weren't they incompetent? Mack McLarty, Bill and Hillary's very own chief of staff, knew that the travel office people were innocent and that it was wrong to use the White House travel office as a payoff for relatives and Arkansas friends.

When McLarty wouldn't do the dirty deed, Hillary Clinton apparently conspired with close friend and president's counsel Vince Foster. According to a memorandum written by David Watkins, White House director of administration, "Foster regularly informed me that the first lady was concerned and desired action—the action desired was the firing of the travel office staff." Watkins, himself a friend of Bill and Hillary, was writing the memorandum to McLarty, explaining after the fact what had happened. "We knew that there would be hell to pay . . . we failed to take swift and decisive action in conformity with the first lady's wishes."[44]

According to FBI interviews and White House documents, "In the days before White House travel office workers were fired, Hillary Rodham Clinton pressed top presidential aides, including the chief of staff, to get the employees 'out of there.'"[45]

Watkins's own notes on a meeting with Hillary quote her as saying, "We need these people out. We need our people in."

When nothing worked, Hillary took a page from the story of Jezebel in the book of 2 Kings. Jezebel had arranged for the local authorities to falsely charge Naboth with a long list of crimes. He was brought to "justice" by his peers and, with the influence and power of the palace, found guilty. In the story of Bill and Hillary, a White House lawyer, William Kennedy, called in the FBI, ordering them to investigate the travel office and telling them that the whole issue was being "followed at the highest levels of the White House."

Meanwhile, pressured by Hillary, David Watkins arranged for an outside auditing firm to investigate the office. A quick observation from the firm noted that the office lacked a sense of "financial control consciousness."

That was good enough for Watkins. After all, the FBI was investigating them! The seven travel office employees were summoned to his office and immediately fired. Do not pass go. Do not collect your $200. When they returned to their desks to clean out any personal materials, their replacements, including Clinton cronies from Arkansas, had already taken their places. The stunned workers were hustled outside of the building and into the back of a van. Billy Dale, the man who had served eight presidents, counting Clinton, sat on the wheel hub. They were driven outside the gates, taken to the Ellipse in front of the Washington Memorial, and ordered to get out. Now, pay attention kids, that's how you take Naboth's vineyard!

Then the White House launched into high gear, bombarding the press with negative stories charging that the former travel office employees were guilty of embezzlement and all sorts of misdeeds. Billy Dale, who had served his country for a lifetime, was squashed like a bug. Jezebel wanted that vineyard.

Dale spent his life savings defending himself in court. The FBI, under pressure from the White House to find something, pored over every piece of paper Billy Dale had ever written or signed. When his daughter returned home from her honeymoon, the FBI was there to ask her how she paid for it. In Psalm 12:5 the Bible declares, "'For the oppression of the poor, for the sighing of the needy, / Now I will arise,' says the LORD; / 'I will set him in the safety for which he yearns.'" Clinton's justice department prosecuted Billy Dale, but in the end, after spending everything he had to defend himself, he was still found innocent by a jury of his peers.[46]

When Morality Doesn't Matter

"Well," you say, "what do the Clintons say about all of this? There are two sides to everything." And the answer is, they deny it all. Hillary denies that she was the lead Rose Law Firm attorney for Madison Guaranty, even while her own billing records show the opposite. She denies she recruited them as a client, contradicting testimony from Madison Guaranty executives Gary Bunch and John Latham and her own colleagues from the Rose Law Firm, attorneys Richard Massey and Ronald Clark.

She denies that she had anything to do with the travel office firings or that she even knew there was a travel office, in spite of dozens of memos from her own staff, including notes from the replacements brought in from Arkansas. She says she can't remember the David Watkins memos. The exasperated, distinguished columnist William Safire called the first lady a "congenital liar."

The president denies that he knew anything about any of the firings until it was all over, but documents obtained by the Associated Press show that he knew about the firings before they happened and that the very week of the firings he met twice with Hollywood producer and White House travel office reorganizer Harry Thomason.[47] But mostly the Clintons can't remember. Columnist Doug Bandow says that "the first lady, family friends, and administration officials have responded to various investigators' inquiries with 'I don't recall' nearly 1,000 times."[48]

"Well," you say, "what difference should that make to a preacher? So they lie. Lots of politicians lie. So they hurt innocent people. Lots of politicians hurt innocent people. So they steal or take a little bit for themselves. Lots of politicians steal; in fact, everybody steals. What does that have to do with preaching the gospel that Jesus saves? Quit trying to run the country. Stick to your pulpit. Leave those things to Rush Limbaugh. Do your job."

And the answer is this. Most of the Bible is written by heads of state or to heads of state. The Pentateuch, the first five books of the Bible, was written by Moses, the leader of Israel. The books of Joshua and Judges are the biographies of national leaders. Both books of Samuel, the two books of the Kings, and the two books of the Chronicles are all accounts of the public history of the Israelite nation and how God worked through the good and evil rulers of its government. Many of the Psalms were written by King David. His son King Solomon wrote three more books of the Bible: Ecclesiastes, the Song of Solomon, and Proverbs. The major and minor prophets wrote to the nation or to the leader of the nation, and their writings all involved public policy and its relationship to God's law. Revelation is written about the "judgment of the nations." Godly men and women cannot ignore the events of their nation. They will some day be held accountable for what they said or did not say in the face of evil. If godly men and women would stand up in the marketplaces and the pulpits of America and speak the truth fearlessly, exposing darkness, calling evil by its name, America wouldn't need Rush Limbaugh.

The Bible gives a very clear warning in 1 Corinthians 6:9–11, saying that neither the greedy, nor adulterers, nor the sexually immoral, nor swindlers will ever inherit the kingdom of God. And once more it begins its warning with those words, "Do not be deceived."

"Well," you say, "there are crimes worse than these. Ahab and Jezebel were murderers. Maybe Bill and Hillary were greedy and insensitive to the little guy in Travelgate. Is that a crime? And maybe the president's personal life has been immoral. But then, so are a lot of other people's lives. Let's forgive and forget. Granted, that witchcraft business may be playing with fire. It could possibly get dangerous, and we probably wouldn't know it until it was too late. But you can't really believe that a modern, educated woman like Hillary Rodham Clinton could be influenced by some ancient mumbo jumbo, do you? The Madison Guaranty Savings and Loan may very well have been a criminal enterprise, but that was back when Clinton was governor. Cut some slack."

This is America's great tragedy. She is deceived. She acknowledges evil and is not concerned. Remarkable polls made public in 1996 showed that most Americans didn't trust their president and public officials and, at the same time, most Americans didn't care that they were untrustworthy. Jeremiah the prophet saw the same thing happen just before Israel's terrible judgment at the hands of Babylon. He wrote about the nation's "casual harlotry."[49] David wrote about a time when "the wicked prowl on every side, / When vileness is exalted among the sons of men."[50]

Make no mistake about it, don't be deceived; morality matters to God. John writes in the book of Revelation that God will exclude "sorcerers and sexually immoral and murderers and idolaters, and whoever loves and practices a lie."[51]

Revelation 21:6–8 establishes God's standard, "I will give of the fountain of the water of life freely to him who thirsts. He who overcomes shall inherit all things, and I will be his God and he shall be My son. But the cowardly, unbelieving, abominable, murderers, sexually immoral, sorcerers, idolaters, and all liars shall have their part in the lake which burns with fire and brimstone, which is the second death."

"Well," you say, "at least nobody got killed in Whitewater."

Read on.

Chapter Two

Who Killed
Vince Foster?

They were like three peas in a pod: Webster Hubbell, Vince Foster, and Hillary Clinton. They made up the litigation department of the Rose Law Firm in Little Rock, Arkansas. Foster and Clinton had offices next to each other. Hubbell was across the hall. Other lawyers and clients often got confused. The trio was always in one another's offices or holding conferences together in the hallway.

Vince Foster and Hillary Clinton were especially close. They had lunch together almost every day. Friends say one would start a sentence and the other could finish it.[1] On special occasions, when the families of the firm got together and the men were off to the golf courses, Vince and Hillary always stayed behind to "talk." Inevitably, the gossip around town suggested that they were having an affair.[2] If nothing else, when stories of Bill's womanizing would get to Hillary, Vince was a shoulder to cry on.

When Bill Clinton became president of the United States, Webster Hubbell and Vince Foster moved to Washington, D.C., to become associate attorney general and deputy White House counsel respectively. The trio was intact.

Vince Foster was now working close by in the west wing of the White House. When Hillary Rodham Clinton wanted something done, she could count on Foster. He handled her blind trust and other personal legal matters.[3] She went to him with her new plans for the White House travel office. It was one of his colleagues, a White House attorney, who finally ordered the FBI to investigate Billy Dale and his people. When after two years the potentially incriminating billing records from the Rose Law Firm mysteriously surfaced in the private quarters of the White House, records further drawing Hillary into the whole Whitewater vortex, no one was surprised to see Vince Foster's handwritten notes along the margins. If anybody knew the secrets of Bill and Hillary Clinton, this man did. He was more than a lawyer who could claim confidentiality. He was a friend who could be trusted to keep a secret.

And yet, from July 20, 1993, when Vincent Foster's body was found in Fort Marcy Park, the White House of Bill and Hillary Clinton has seemed to block every legitimate attempt to solve the hundreds of attendant mysteries. Instead of leading the charge, raising a public cry to get to the bottom of what happened, calling for public support to help locate the people seen near the body and to solve the inconsistencies with the gun and the reported neck wound, they have seemingly rushed to have the whole affair buried with the body. I believe they have even used all their influence with media to hush the whole affair. Relatives and White House staffers have been told they don't have to talk to police. Curiously, it appears to me that the only person still patiently trying to put the pieces together is the independent prosecutor, Kenneth Starr, the same man who was assigned by a bipartisan Congress to pursue the crimes of Whitewater.

When Cain killed Abel, the Bible says Abel's blood cried out to God from the ground, demanding justice. Likewise, the facts surrounding the death of Vince Foster cry out to God demanding answers. Foster, who was the highest public official to die of mysterious circumstances since the assassination of John Kennedy, is not alive to tell us any-thing, but the evidence speaks with troubling clarity.

Fort Marcy Park

Ironically, the first record of any knowledge of Vincent Foster's death comes from police officers in Arkansas who, in sworn depositions, say they were informed at 6 P.M. EST. One of them immediately passed the report on to the Arkansas governor's wife. Likewise, the initial report of Chelsea's nanny, who was the same person who informed the Arkansas police, claims that the White House knew of the death at 6 P.M. Everyone else there, including the president and first lady, would deny they had any knowledge until almost three hours later.[4]

The person who found Vincent Foster's body is identi-fied in FBI reports as C.W. or "confidential witness." He was, of course, very curious. It isn't every day that you take a walk in the park and find a corpse. He told FBI investi-gators that without touching the body he examined Foster very carefully. He was within eighteen inches of Foster's face. The head was laid back, looking straight up. There were no bloodstains on his face, but it was very clear he had been shot through the mouth. Both of Foster's hands were lying palms up, with the thumbs pointed away from the body. There was no gun. C.W. is emphatic about that. He saw the hands. There was no gun.[5]

When the FBI later interviewed C.W., they let him know just how serious the investigation was. This was the presi-dent's lawyer. He was, perhaps, the first lady's closest friend. There would be a lot of media attention. He would have to give a sworn statement. He could get in very seri-ous trouble if he misrepresented any fact. C.W. said he understood. He had answered every question carefully and accurately, and he would continue to do so.

C.W. testified in his sworn deposition that the vegetation under Foster's feet and on the path had obviously been trampled. He saw a half-empty wine cooler bottle near the body. As he raced back to the parking lot looking for help, the confidential witness saw a white Nissan parked in the lot. Inside was a half-full package of wine cooler bottles similar to the one beside the body. There was also a brief-case and a suit jacket that matched Foster's dress pants.

The second person to approach the scene was park police officer Kevin Fornshill. Contradicting C.W., he would later tell a reporter from the CBS show *60 Minutes* that the vegetation near the body was undisturbed. But in his repeated statements to the Senate Whitewater Committee, as well as to the FBI, Fornshill also emphatically stated there was no gun.

Within short succession police and paramedics began arriving. By then there was mass confusion with people coming and going. George Gonzalez, lead paramedic and the first medical person to examine the body, was suspicious. He later told the Congressional Committee on Government Operations that it is "odd to have the body laid out like it was. I wouldn't expect the hand or body in the position found, the hands perfectly at the side."[6] One paramedic listed the death as a homicide on his report.[7]

The police now found a gun in Vince Foster's right hand. There was blood on his cheek. There was no wine cooler bottle. Had C.W. been mistaken? Had officer Fornshill been wrong? Or had someone tampered with the crime scene, placing a gun in Foster's hand?

There was no question that Foster had been shot though the mouth. But police were confronted with a conundrum. The gun was a .38 Colt. It should have blown off the back of his skull. There were no skull bone fragments, brain matter, or splattered blood nearby. Nor could anyone find the bullet. And how did Foster get there? There were no car keys: not in his pocket, not in his car. Nor had anyone yet found a suicide note. But that might be at his home or in his office.

Then there was a problem with the car. The white Nissan was no longer in the parking lot. But Vince Foster did not own a white Nissan. He owned a gray Honda that was found in the parking lot, parked on the other end. C.W. later told the FBI that he had not walked to that end of the lot but that he was very observant, mindful that this was a crime scene. But he had seen the white Nissan. He had looked through the windows and seen the wine coolers, the briefcase, and the matching jacket. The police found none of those things in Foster's gray Honda. Nor did they find his car keys.

Fairfax County EMS technician Richard Arthur noticed a small caliber bullet hole in Foster's neck. It was on his right side, halfway between the ear and the tip of the chin. Later, George Gonzalez, lead paramedic on the scene, told investigators he also remembered a second bullet wound.[8]

Dr. Donald Haut, the Fairfax County medical examiner, arrived at the scene some time later. By then the body had been rolled over. According to his FBI report, Haut described a "small" amount of blood behind Foster's head. The blood was matted and clotted, not liquid. Corey Ashford, one of the medical technicians who helped carry the body away, reported to the FBI that there was no blood on the ground.[9]

Dr. Haut described the exit hole in Foster's head as very small.[10] John Rolla, the lead investigator for the park police, was early on the scene. He, too, reported a "small" exit wound. Both testimonies would later cause confusion. A bullet from a .38 caliber weapon would not make a "small" wound. Was another gun actually used? Haut would change his mind later and say that the wound couldn't have been small. Yet both conclusions were first impressions of two separate professionals, each made without discussing it with the other.

The White House Reacts

Later that night, lead park investigator John Rolla visited Vince Foster's house to break the news to Foster's wife,

Lisa. Webster Hubbell and David Watkins arrived at the same time. Rolla asked Lisa if her husband had been upset or depressed.

"No," she said, "he was very happy." And then she asked if her husband had shot himself through the mouth. Webster Hubbell told Lisa that she did not have to talk to police, and everyone clammed up. Testimony was over.

President Clinton and his entourage arrived at the home soon after. If police investigator Rolla ventured a question, Clinton glared back at him.[11] The investigator finally left. He would drive to the morgue to take a more thorough look at the body. Lisa Foster would not be available to talk to police again for ten crucial days.

Park police investigators now telephoned the White House, asking to take a look in Vince Foster's office. Foster's boss, White House Counsel Bernard Nussbaum, said no. Later, the FBI made a similar request when they were finally brought into the case. They were also turned down. Meanwhile, within the first twenty-four hours, Vince Foster's pager and all of his personal effects were returned to the White House before investigators could catalog or examine them. The computer in his office was exchanged for another. Months later an old computer with the same serial number as Foster's would show up in the White House computer repair shop. The hard drive had been destroyed.[12]

Denied access to the victim's family, his office, his computer, and his official papers, including his scheduling book, park police then asked that Foster's White House office be sealed. According to the *Congressional Record* and testimony from Secret Service agents assigned to White House security, for the next twelve hours, late into the night, Clinton officials searched Vince Foster's office, taking Whitewater and other related documents out with them. Bernard Nussbaum, presidential assistant Patsy Thomasson, and Hillary Clinton's own chief of staff, Margaret Williams, conducted the search.

Then even stranger things began to happen. The car keys suddenly showed up. They were found in Foster's front pocket when the body arrived at the morgue, a pocket the police had already searched.

Even more troubling, lab reports came back showing no fingerprints on the gun. Later at FBI laboratories, the gun was taken apart piece by piece. The extensive research even revealed fingerprints made at the factory where the gun was manufactured years before, but still no fingerprints on the outside of the weapon. Had Foster put a bullet in his head and then wiped the pistol clean before taking it back into his hand?

The autopsy was performed by Dr. James Beyer, a coroner with a history of mistaking homicide for suicide. In 1989 he ruled that a Timothy Easley had stabbed himself in the chest. He didn't notice trauma to the young man's hand, a wound consistent with defensive action. An outside expert took on the case and Easley's girlfriend admitted to the murder.[13]

In 1991, in a case similar to that of Vince Foster, Beyer had ruled that a Mr. Thomas Burkett had killed himself with a gunshot wound to the mouth. The family had their doubts. The body was eventually exhumed and a second coroner discovered a broken jaw, a disfigured ear, and other evidence indicating a struggle. However, after an eighteen-month investigation the FBI still concluded that the death was a suicide.[14]

Nevertheless, that night, even before park investigator Rolla was able to take a close look at the body, it was officially announced that Vincent Foster had committed suicide.

The following morning the White House announced that the FBI would not be called into the case. It would be pursued by the park police. Investigator Rolla, who had never conducted a homicide investigation in his life, would have to plod on. The FBI was stunned. One agent remarked on the irony that the FBI had been called in to get rid of the travel office but weren't needed to follow through on the mysterious death of the number three man in the White House.[15]

That week, routine police work was prompting even more questions. The Saudi Arabian ambassador to the United States lived across the street from Fort Marcy Park. His security guards were on duty very close to the actual scene of the crime, but no one heard any shots. Vince Foster's shoes were clean. There were no grass stains or dirt or pieces of vegetation even though he had walked seven hundred yards to the second cannon in the park. There were carpet fibers or blond hair on Foster's clothing. Had the body been rolled up in a carpet and carried into the park? Had Foster been killed elsewhere? We may never know. Fibers and hairs on Foster's clothing and body would never be matched with fibers or hairs from his automobile.

Then a new witness surfaced. Patrick Knowlton had been in Fort Marcy Park just one hour before C.W. discovered the body. When he pulled into the parking lot there were only two other cars. Vince Foster's gray Honda was not one of them. Knowlton quickly noticed a man sitting in one of the cars. As Knowlton got out of the car the man gave him a menacing stare and then opened his own car door. Knowlton walked in the opposite direction, away from the man and away from the path that led to the future scene of the crime only minutes away. The man stared after Knowlton and then got back into his car. A statement prepared by the witness and his attorney says the strange man's actions were consistent with a lookout, "as if his purpose was to prevent any passersby from venturing into the area of the park where Vincent Foster's corpse was found one hour later."[16]

A Deepening Mystery

Great curiosity now attended the fact that there was no suicide note. But just as the keys would suddenly and conveniently appear to reassure skeptics, so the note showed up six days after the death. While the note did not suggest suicide it did talk about the anguish that Foster was experiencing in his work relating to Travelgate and Whitewater. Even though the note was not conclusive one way or the other, the way it surfaced did not reassure doubters. How had a note in his briefcase been missed in the first place? Why was it showing up now, days later? No one was surprised when it was learned that there were no fingerprints on the note. There was, however, a palm print. It was never matched with Foster's.

In July 1995, White House lawyer Miriam Nemetz wrote a memo quoting White House Chief of Staff Mack McLarty as saying that Hillary Rodham Clinton had favored delay in making the note public. "McLarty said that the first lady was very upset and believed the matter required further thought and that the president should not yet be told. They should have a coherent position and should have decided what to do before they told the president."[17]

In October 1995, three handwriting experts ruled that the so-called suicide note found six days after Foster's death was a forgery. Sponsored by Strategic Investment, Reginald Alton, a fellow emeritus of St. Edmund Hall, Oxford; Vincent Scalice, a former New York City police detective; and Ronald Rice, a professional handwriting analyst with eighteen years of forensic experience, all came to the same conclusion. Twelve samples of Foster's handwriting were compared to the note found in his briefcase. Each concurred that Foster couldn't have written the note. Foster, for example wrote the letter *b* with a single stroke. His forger used three separate strokes.

But such information would come later, and while each instance would raise more questions or doubts, no one single discovery would be sufficient to arouse the media or the public from its lethargy. If something sinister had happened, no one wanted to know.

Lisa Foster, the dead man's wife, was finally interviewed ten days after her husband's death. She was shown a silver gun and asked if it belonged to her husband. She admitted that it looked like the silver revolver she had sometimes seen around the house. Yet later, when ABC television obtained one of the photographs of the death scene, it clearly showed that the gun in Foster's hand was black, not silver. This was confirmed by the first Senate investigation, which also revealed that the gun was assembled from two different Colt revolvers with two separate serial numbers stamped on their pieces.[18]

The controversy over the gun would continue to fester. Neither the FBI nor the police could confirm that the silver gun shown to Lisa Foster did, in fact, belong to her husband. Only two bullets were found in the weapon and, remember, the first two persons to find the body said there was no gun at all. No matching bullets were ever found in the Foster home, the Foster automobiles, or at the crime scene. Nor was any proof forthcoming that the gun found with the victim actually fired the fatal shot.[19]

There would also be little chance for leaks of photos or any other evidence. First, most of the Polaroid photos of the crime scene vanished. Then it was learned that all 35 mm film of the crime scene was "overexposed" or had disappeared and Dr. Beyer's X rays were "misplaced" and never recovered. Meanwhile, all police and paramedics at the scene were ordered not to discuss the case.[20]

Independent prosecutor Robert Fiske eventually completed a report determining that Vince Foster had indeed committed suicide, but the report was so riddled with inaccuracies, it only contributed to the controversy. Dr. Haut was now changing his testimony to fit the new scenario. Leads were not followed. Questions were left up in the air. Robert Fiske's hard-driving staffer, assistant U.S. attorney Miguel Rodriquez, resigned in disgust, not wanting to be part of a cover-up.

Part of the criticism was directed toward the weak motive for the alleged suicide. Foster had eaten a full lunch, joked with his staff, and promised to be right back when he drove off to his rendezvous in Fort Marcy Park. Foster's friend and attorney Jim Lyons was coming from Colorado to meet with him the next day, and Foster had expressed eagerness to show him around. Likewise, he had double checked to make sure he would be free to take his sister on a personal White House tour the next morning. His appointment book, critical to the running of his office and, incidentally, critical to the investigation, was never found. As in the case of the police pictures and the X rays taken at the autopsy, it disappeared into the firmament.

Eventually, Congress enlisted Kenneth Starr as a more forceful independent prosecutor. Robert Fiske was gone. Starr was viewed as less likely to be influenced by his partisan Democrat superior, Mark Tuohey IV. Likewise, two journalists picked up the trail of the Foster death, giving some public exposure to controversial facts that the rest of the media were ignoring.

The Media to the Rescue

Once more, the CBS television production *60 Minutes* came to the rescue of Bill and Hillary Clinton. During the campaign of 1992, when the story of Clinton's promiscuity had reached its most critical stage, *60 Minutes* gave the Clintons a national audience. Mr. Hewlett, producer of the show, had been quoted as saying he could have buried Bill Clinton's presidential chances in the snows of New Hampshire if he had been so inclined.[21] He was not. And this time his program sought to answer the growing questions regarding the Vince Foster affair.

The paramedics and their reports were ignored by *60 Minutes*. None of them were interviewed. The show even ignored the confidential witness, telling its national audience that a park policeman was the first person to discover the body. It was absolutely false. A bold misrepresentation. But then, who reads or pays attention? When CBS did interview someone, the testimony was very selective. Park policeman Kevin Fornshill was given a chance to say that the ground around the body was not trampled, lending credence to the theory that there was no struggle at the scene of the crime; but Fornshill was not asked about his report that there had been no gun in the victim's hand.

Later, the FBI revisited C.W., the confidential witness who had first found the body. He had told them that the vegetation under Foster's feet and on the path nearby was trampled. This was now a public issue. Was he sure about his facts? C.W. insisted that he was. He offered some helpful speculation. If it were a suicide, the dead man may have been pacing before he shot himself. But it was definitely trampled. And it would have taken a lot to flatten the vegetation. C.W. was actually taken to the crime scene twice by the FBI, each time answering the same way.

Ignoring altogether any critical questions about the gun, the lack of fingerprints, and the so-called suicide note, *60 Minutes* focused most of its attention on the differing testimony about the blood at the scene. Dr. Haut's testimony to the FBI was never mentioned, while the new version of his testimony was featured. Viewers were not told of the discrepancy.

The coup de grâce was a clever straw man built out of the fact that critics were suggesting Foster was left-handed when the gun was found in his right hand. CBS triumphantly informed the nation that this was all bogus. Foster was indeed right-handed. But this was not an issue of serious critics who already knew Foster was right-handed. The point was that the first official and nonofficial persons to arrive at the scene were insistent that there was no gun at all, in either hand. Such testimony was ignored.

The program had its intended impact. Much of the public furor driving the independent prosecutor's investigation into Foster's death was deflated. But the most powerful revelation concerning Vince Foster was yet to come.

Two journalists, Chris Ruddy of the *Tribune-Review* in Pittsburgh and Ambrose Evans-Pritchard of the *London*

Sunday Telegraph, had been snooping around the far edges of the Foster scandal for months. Evans-Pritchard was able to determine that Vince Foster had made at least two secret, unofficial trips to Switzerland. He had canceled a third visit only twelve days before his death. His wife, Lisa Foster, had no knowledge of the trips. This was remarkable, almost unbelievable, news. But the story was soon confirmed and published in the *Telegraph*. What was Foster doing in Switzerland?[22] Still, for the most part, a strangely silent media looked on with disinterest.

Meanwhile, key witnesses, whose testimony raised doubts about the favored suicide theory, found themselves the target of harassment. These people had only done their duty as citizens. In no case had any of them written books or demanded money from tabloids or commercialized their information in any manner. C.W. was still anonymous. The others usually refused any requests for interviews. None were deemed partisan or critics of the administration.

Patrick Knowlton, the man who had witnessed suspicious people in the park just before the body was found, was followed around the streets of Washington, D.C. Sometimes his antagonists would openly harass him or glare at him. Knowlton contacted a lawyer who made a careful record of each instance, which constituted clear violations of federal law prohibiting "tampering with a witness, obstruction of justice, or any intimidation of a witness." The lawyer wrote that the number of persons used in the surveillance of Mr. Knowlton and their expert knowledge of his daily routine suggested enormous resources at work.

Suicide or Murder?

What happened in Fort Marcy Park that summer of 1993? Was Vincent Foster murdered? Was he advocating a course of action that would have been embarrassing to powerful people? Or did he really commit suicide? Do all of the incriminating circumstances relate only to the crimes of Whitewater or are there other embarrassments that powerful people feared might have come tumbling out of the closet if the police had looked too closely? Either explanation, of course, points to a crime.

And what has happened to the country whose sensibilities were once aroused over Watergate and the "bugging" of the offices of one political party by activists working to promote the cause of the other? You will remember that President Richard Nixon was driven from office, not because he authorized or even knew about the action, but because he covered up a crime committed by others.

Today, we openly talk about the cover-up of Whitewater. No one seems to care. Not the press, not the church, not the public. To criticize the sexual infidelities of public officials is viewed as judgmental and intolerant. And the number three man at the White House just may have been murdered. Webster Hubbell, the former deputy attorney general of the United States and a close friend of both Hillary Clinton and Vincent Foster says, "One thing for sure, Vince Foster did not kill himself."[23] But we are all into self-denial. A series of coincidences and accidents, we tell ourselves. We don't want to face the responsibility of knowing the details or the facts, so we hide behind the comforting thought that it is just too incredible to be true. We know that teenagers are murdered for their designer tennis shoes on the streets outside our door, but surely not Vince Foster. We are deceived.

David speaks of a time when "the wicked in his pride persecutes the poor; . . . In the secret places he murders the innocent; . . . Arise, O LORD! / O God, lift up Your hand! / Do not forget the humble."[24]

At the Rose Law Firm in Little Rock, Arkansas, they were three peas in a pod. Webster Hubbell, Vincent Foster, and Hillary Rodham Clinton. Today, Webster Hubbell is peeling potatoes in a federal penitentiary, Vince Foster is dead, and Hillary Clinton is ruling her kingdom from the

White House. But all three will one day bow before the Lord, who is judge above all. And each will answer for every word and deed. Until that day, do not be deceived; God is not asleep. He is watching and listening. Though "what is vile is honored among men" and the "wicked freely strut about," He will rise to action in these latter days. He always has. He always will. God is faithful to keep His Word!

Chapter Three

Who Controls America?

I n the early 1990s President George Bush and Secretary of State James Baker seemed to be in a political footrace to see who could use the latest and most trendy political phrase: New World Order. President Clinton, sensitive to the criticism of millions of Americans, has cleverly avoided the expression, but the policies they represent remain on the fast track with no interruption or challenge in sight.

The concept of a New World Order is nothing new. It was the driving principle on the plains of Shinar where Nimrod proposed to build the tower of Babel almost four thousand years ago. The purpose of the tower of Babel was to defy the authority of God and to drive Him out of the affairs of men. It was satanic and demonic, manifesting itself by the occult symbols that were attached to its side.

In the twelfth century B.C., the Babylonian kingdom became the first of several great empires to rule the civilized world. From a purely historical standpoint, the Babylonian era was the most glorious and most evil of any that followed. In the sixth century B.C., the Jews, God's chosen people, were once more dragged off into slavery.

The Medes and the Persians were the next great empire to achieve world domination. Their kingdom, steeped in idolatry, stretched from middle Europe to India.

According to revisionist historians, the most progressive one world order was established by the Greeks. Today's schoolchildren are taught that the glorious Greece of antiquity practiced the purest form of democracy. In fact, the Greek experiment with freedom was brief and limited. More than half of the population of ancient Greece were slaves. And of those who were "free," half were women who could not vote, own property, or testify in court; they were not even counted in the official census. The famous pure Greek democracy, praised by modern educators, was fine if you were one of the lucky 25 percent.

For years the government and social life of the Greek empire and its one world order was dictated by the Pythia, the mysterious Oracle of Delphi. Priests would take an ordinary peasant woman, invoke "the spirits," and when she finally fell into a trance they would submit their list of questions to her. Through the peasant woman, the Pythia for the day, the spirits would miraculously speak back, sometimes in various languages.[1]

The Roman empire, the last successful "world order," was virulently anti-Semitic and anti-Christian. Under the emperor Nero, Christians were fed to the lions in Rome and hung as grotesque human torches for his garden parties. In A.D. 70, the Romans, under General Titus, finally destroyed Jerusalem.

In the great temptation of Jesus, Satan himself proposed a New World Order. "All these things I will give You," he says, "if You will fall down and worship me."[2] And understand, they were Satan's to give. Today, he is still offering that promise. Through seemingly benign and benevolent world statesmen, he is promising a world without war and an end to hunger—heaven on earth. But the Bible says the world will soon turn into a living hell.

The Illuminati

In more recent centuries there has been the confusing and mysterious story of the Illuminati. There have been so many exaggerated and unfounded theories written about this organization and its history that it can be a chore to separate fact from fiction. What we know is this: The Illuminati did exist. It was a supersecret European organization of international financial power brokers whose initial goal was to bring about worldwide economic stability but whose quick success, and sometimes very hostile resistance, prompted the more grandiose goal of worldwide dominion. Born at a time of great rebellion against the corrupt, organized church and influenced by the radicalism of the French Revolution, their leadership was exclusively atheistic, with the notable exception of several committed, practicing satanists.[3]

At various times in recent centuries, the power and reach of this organization within world financial and governmental circles has been astounding—a virtual banking-governmental mafia. Look on the backside of an American dollar bill and you will see three Latin words, *Novus Ordo Seclorum,* "New World Order." These words are carried on a waving banner just under a pyramid and topped by an all-seeing eye. Some say this all-seeing eye represents providence. Others say it represents the eye of the ancient Egyptian deity, Osiris. This remarkable seal, approved by Congress in 1782, was designed by Charles Thompson, a member of the Masonic order, who served as the secretary of the Continental Congress.[4]

Hitler's Attempt

In his 1932 election bid, Adolf Hitler told the people of Germany, "If you will elect me as the Führer of this nation, I will introduce a New World Order that will last a thousand years." A compilation of Hitler's speeches, published in English, was appropriately entitled *My New Order.*

Only in the decade after the Nuremberg Trials did researchers begin to understand how deep-seated and mystical was the pagan and satanic ritual embraced by many of the Nazi leaders. Heinrich Himmler, leader of Hitler's *Schutzstaffel*, the infamous SS, and the man entrusted with the diabolical orders to exterminate the Jews, embraced a wide range of pagan and satanic beliefs that would be considered "New Age" by the naive of today. For Himmler and his SS, Christian rites of christening, marriage, and death were replaced by neopagan ones. Christmas was replaced by Julfest, a celebration of the winter solstice on December 21. Initiation rites for highest SS officer recruits included taking an oath before sixteen blazing altars towering three stories tall, the obelisks of the Feldherrnhalle, the Nazi Temple of Honor in Munich. The names of sixteen martyred Nazis were intoned by a voice-over and the new officers would shout, "Present." Himmler himself believed in reincarnation, telling people that he was really a new manifestation of King Heinrich of the Saxons. In 1937 he had the bones of the ancient king interred at Quedlinburg Cathedral.[5]

The eminent historian Francis Miller suggests that twenty million people died because of Hitler's "new order," including six million innocent Jewish men, women, and children.[6]

The Communist Deception

Even before Hitler and his gang were buried, Stalin and a small criminal society controlling the Soviet Union began secretly planning their own New World Order. Stalin's eventual successor, Nikita Khrushchev, once announced to Richard Nixon, "We will bury you."

By the mid-1960s the sheer volume of Soviet horrors was hard to deny. Eyewitnesses spoke of millions of innocent people consigned to virtual slave labor in Siberia, and others spoke of millions dying in the prison camps in the Gulags. In 1963, in an audacious attempt to regain international credibility, Khrushchev blew the lid off many of those state secrets, admitting that Stalin was a criminal who had consigned millions of innocent people to their deaths but that the Soviet Union had now abandoned its insane ideas of conquering the world and was seeking to make the ideal of communism and humanism really work.[7]

Communism was a powerful and intellectually seductive concept, so brilliant and sincere that people were drawn into its vortex. But behind its benevolent, humanitarian promises was a violent and hideous reality. Both Jews and Christians were murdered and persecuted for their beliefs. During the malevolent reign of Pol Pot's Khmer Rouge in Cambodia, the nation was turned into "killing fields." Pol Pot marked for execution all doctors, nurses, teachers, and government workers. All members of the media and clergy and anyone associated with the arts, the theater, and the ballet were also marked for execution. If you wore eyeglasses you were put on the list, because if you wore eyeglasses you could probably read, and if you could read they would have to kill you. Incredibly, Pol Pot is still alive. Though he and his armies have been driven into the jungles, no one is calling him to accountability—not the United Nations, not the United States, no one. No one is calling for a modern Nuremberg Trial for this ruthless Oriental Hitler of our generation.

In the late 1980s, Mikhail Gorbachev tried to do again what Nikita Khrushchev had done twenty years before. Once more the lid was blown off communism and a new Soviet leader admitted to the crimes of his predecessors, including not only Leonid Brezhnev, but the phony reformer Nikita Khrushchev himself. But this time it didn't work, and the Soviet empire collapsed like a house of cards.

The United Nations

After World War I, President Woodrow Wilson became the most famous public voice calling for a one world order.

The League of Nations failed, but the idea surfaced again after Hitler. In 1946, the United Nations was born.

On January 29, 1991, then-President George Bush proclaimed a New World Order in a speech to Congress during the Persian Gulf War. "What is at stake is more than one small country," he said, referring to Kuwait. "It is a big idea—a new world order."[8]

To the surprise of the Bush administration, most evangelical Christians recoiled at those words. Some associated them with secret societies (almost always anti-Semitic and anti-Christian), with Hitler's famous public boasts, or with the communist promises that turned to nightmares unless you were on the right side of the gun barrel. But most Christians associated the words with the coming holocaust prophesied in Scriptures: the great promise of a peaceful one world government that will, instead, turn this planet into a living hell.

Today, with the encouragement of the Clinton administration, the United Nations is saying they will produce this New World Order. What does it mean? When you hear it, what does it say to you? Read the words of Brock Chisolm, the director of the United Nations World Health Organization. "To achieve world government, it is necessary to remove from the minds of men their individualism, loyalty to family traditions, national patriotism, and religious dogmas."[9]

During the last twenty-five years the United Nations has been transformed into a propaganda platform for the enemies of the United States and Israel. Time after time in that world body, America and Israel have stood all alone against every other member nation in the world. And sometimes we have simply been voting for Israel's right to exist.

For example, in 1974 PLO terrorist Yasser Arafat was invited to address the United Nations General Assembly. The PLO had just implemented a "plan of phases" that called for the destruction of Israel in stages, since it appeared they would be unable to eliminate Israel all at once.

Then in 1975, the barbaric Idi Amin, dictator of Uganda and at that time chairman of the Organization for African Unity, addressed the General Assembly. Posing as a diplomat, this bloodthirsty barbarian also called for Israel's destruction and accused the U.S. of being in a conspiracy with the Zionists.[10] Both Arafat and Amin received standing ovations and were honored at public receptions and dinners after their UN appearances.

"Well," you say, "from an economic and peacekeeping perspective, the United Nations has been an international joke, a fiasco, an international nothing. How can powerful people now talk seriously about this organization running things? It isn't logical. It will never happen." You're wrong! This isn't about logic. It isn't about peace. It isn't about feeding hungry people. This is about power, worldwide power. It's about a one-world government; it's about a one-world economy; it's about absolute dictatorial control over every American citizen and the citizens of any democracy on earth.

For the Christian, the biblical account and man's own recorded history clearly show the same syndrome. The need for world domination, whether out of benevolence or greed, has ultimately been corrupted. It is almost always idolatrous, satanic, or atheistic. It is usually anti-Semitic and anti-Christian. Look at the record. Look at Babylon. Look at ancient Greece. Look at Rome, at Hitler, at Stalin and his successors. It is a demon spirit anointed in the bowels of hell to rob, to kill, and to utterly destroy.

Randall Baer, whose bestselling Harper and Row books once made him the world's New Age authority on crystals, tells about how "the cosmic gods were paving the way for me to do important work in bringing about a revolutionary *New Age, One World Order*."[11]

Curiously, Baer, who claimed that "spirit guides" dictated his books, frequently invoked that ancient symbol associated with the Illuminati and boldly planted on the American dollar. "The spirit guides told me to take twelve quartz crystals and lay them out in a circle, to tape another one to the occult 'third eye,' and to suspend a large pyramid overhead."[12]

Jean Houston, the first lady's famous self-described "spiritual psychic" whose visits to the White House have included several lengthy stays, calls herself "a global midwife." Houston says that she works "with heads of state all over the world."[13] But if she is a "global midwife," just what do the New Agers want to be born?

The Antichrist

There is going to be a New World Order in these latter days. From ages past, the prophets have said it would happen. Jesus spoke of it in great detail. It will be led by Satan's messiah, whom the Bible calls the Antichrist. When the world rejects truth, all that's left is a lie. When the world rejects light, all that's left is darkness. When the world rejects Jesus Christ, all that's left is Satan's messiah, the Antichrist. And God the Father is saying from the plains of Shinar and the tower of Babel to the United Nations, "Men have been trying to get rid of Me, they have been trying to get rid of My Son Jesus Christ, and they have been trying to escape the Word of God. All right, I'm going to let you have a New World Order. I'm going to turn Satan's messiah, the Antichrist, loose to rule the earth with an iron fist, producing the New World Order."

He's going to turn the streets of the world into a bloodbath. According to the prophets, one-third of all humanity is going to be massacred under this monster who is going to make Adolf Hitler look like a choirboy.

The apostle John described it two thousand years ago, long before bank wire transfers or even banks. Long before there was a social security system requiring you to have a number. Long before computer technology made such feats possible, John described how the Antichrist will control world commerce. Every person alive will receive a mark on the back of his right hand or between his eyes. Without it, you won't be able to buy or sell a shoelace. The Antichrist will set himself up as the all-powerful currency controller as he institutes a one-world government and a one-world currency. Jesus warned that, eventually, he will try to set himself up as God.

Revelation 13:16–17 says, "He causes all, both small and great, rich and poor, free and slave, to receive a mark on their right hand or on their foreheads, and that no one may buy or sell except one who has the mark or the name of the beast, or the number of his name."

This will be the long anticipated New World Order. But according to the prophets, Brock Chisolm of the World Health Organization is at least partially correct. Five things will have to happen first.

The Destruction of Money

First, there must be the destruction of the monetary system, your currency. I believe America's economic problems were not created by market conditions but were planned and orchestrated to devalue and destroy the American dollar. This was done by that unseen government Dwight D. Eisenhower called the "Eastern Establishment."[14]

Consider the following. Our government deliberately went off the gold standard to which it was attached and on which it was founded. From the day that the dollar was removed from the gold standard it has floundered. If anyone tells you that you look as sound as a dollar, start looking for a casket. You're in big trouble.

The major banks of America poured billions of dollars into communist governments and into third-world nations, knowing full well that those governments had no ability or willingness to pay the money back. Why would they do that? Go to your banker tomorrow and say, "I don't have the ability to pay you back, and I don't even want to pay you back. I'd like to borrow ten billion dollars, please." See what the response would be.

Yet our banks, backed by our own government, gave away hundreds of billions of dollars. Why? Because what few Americans know is that the Monetary Control Act of 1980 gives the Federal Reserve Board the power to exchange U.S. dollars for third-world debt. That simply means that the banks in New York and the major banks of America controlled by the Eastern Establishment will not lose a dime but that you, America's taxpayers, are going to pay the bill.

According to Stanford University, the final bill on the failed savings and loan crisis will cost the taxpayers of America $1.3 trillion. Now get a picture of this in your mind. If you start making a stack of crisp, new $1,000 bills your stack will go four inches high to equal $1 million. So how high will the stack have to get to equal $1 trillion? Remember, we are talking about $1,000 bills. The answer? A stack over sixty-three miles high will equal $1 trillion. The savings and loan fiasco all by itself will cost even more.

Bankruptcies in America are at an all-time high. Mergers and hostile takeovers are putting more and more wealth into the hands of fewer and fewer people, which is exactly the cause of the crash of 1929. New bank failures are mounting. Twelve hundred fifty-six banks are now on the Federal Regulator's problem list. If the banks follow the pattern of the savings and loans, the FDIC is going to be wiped out. Currently, there are about 1.5 pennies backing up every dollar that you have in savings.[15]

Some people have built their life around the dollar, but God is saying, "You had better build your life around Me, because I'm the only thing that's going to endure." The currencies of this world are not going to endure. The kingdoms of this world are going to collapse. The only kingdom that is going to endure is the kingdom of the Lord Jesus Christ, and of His kingdom, thank God, there shall be no end.

Logical people would say, "Why can't the Congress of the United States stop the death of the dollar?" Congress does not control America's economic destiny. Our economic destiny is controlled by the Federal Reserve System. This system sets the rate of interest on the money in your pocket. When they determine this rate of interest, they determine the value of your dollars.

The Federal Reserve has no elected officials. Not one United States senator or representative sits on its board. Neither does the president of the United States or the vice president. The Federal Reserve has never been audited, and yet it totally controls the value of money in this country. It was formally authorized on December 23, 1913, over a Christmas holiday, when most of the U.S. Congress was gone. It is controlled by Class A stockholders. The major stockholder in America is David Rockefeller. While most of the stockholders are members of the so-called Eastern Establishment, allegedly the four largest stockholders are not even Americans but members of the Rothschild family of Europe.

Thomas Jefferson once said, "A private central bank issuing public currency is a greater menace to the liberties of the people than a standing army."[16]

Am I worried about that? If my faith were centered around the American dollar and if all my hopes were pegged to the United States government, I'd give birth to peptic ulcers before I finished writing this book. But I am not worried because my hope is in the Lord Jesus Christ and in the authority of the Word of God. God is in charge and God is in control.

Have you ever heard of the golden rule? "Those who have the gold make the rules." God says in the book of Haggai, "The silver is Mine, and the gold is Mine."[17] He's not controlled by the Eastern Establishment, He's not controlled by the Rothschilds, He's not controlled by the Federal Reserve. He is sovereign God. He says in James 5:1,3, "Come now, you rich, weep and howl for your miseries that are coming upon you! . . . Your gold and silver are corroded, and their corrosion . . . will eat your flesh like fire. You have heaped up treasure in the last days."

People ask, "Why would God allow a financial collapse in America?" I'll tell you why. Because the First Commandment says, "You shall have no other gods before Me." And in America, money is a god. Money has replaced our love for each other. Money has replaced our love of the family. Money has enthroned itself as lord of all. We are the generation of instantaneous gratification. We want what we want and we want it NOW! It makes no difference what it takes to get it.

America's materialism, greed, and demand for instantaneous gratification have produced a nation of drug addicts, a nation of alcoholics, a nation that's addicted to pornography, and a condom culture for "safe sex." It has taken fathers away from their children. It has destroyed marriages. We have squandered our health in the pursuit of money. We have built cathedrals of worship to the gods of money. They're called banks. When you go there tomorrow and talk to your banker, be sure and hold your hat in your hand and tuck your head in reverence, or you won't get what you want.

God is saying to America, "You shall have no other gods before Me." The gods of America are falling. The banks are falling. The savings and loans are falling. Eventually Wall Street will utterly collapse. I've got good news for you. God is not falling. He is on the throne and is all-powerful. "For Yours is the kingdom and the power and the glory forever."

The Death of Patriotism

The second thing that has to happen before the New World Order can take place is the destruction of nationalism and patriotism.

The unseen government—those who are pushing the one world government and the New World Order, those professional politicians whose only objective is to get reelected—are searching for ways to destroy patriotism in America, and they have been long at it.

The Korean War was a United Nations war; it was called a police action. For the first time in America's history we went to war without the objective of winning. It wasn't even in the equation. General Douglas MacArthur resigned in disgust. The old soldier from the long gray line stood before the Congress of the United States and said, "There is no substitute for victory."

History has proven General Douglas MacArthur right and the Congress of the United States wrong. There is no substitute for victory, and any time we commit American lives to the battlefield it ought to be for the purpose of victory and victory alone. It should not be as an instrument of the United Nations and its objectives or as the pawn of the military-industrial complex that grows rich in a time of war.

Vietnam was a controlled war. We could not attack the enemy sanctuaries. We could not mine the harbors. As a result, America was portrayed to the world as a loser. For twelve years our sons bled and died, and we couldn't whip a nation the size of Vermont, a nation that employed medieval military techniques. Patriotism in America reached an all-time low. U.S. soldiers came home and were literally spit on by the American public. America's leaders owe the Vietnam veterans a public apology for sending them into a war where victory over the enemy was not our objective.

Why all the flag-waving over the war in the Persian Gulf? To sell the American people on the idea that the United Nations is a better way of government for the community of nations. To sell the idea that the New World Order is indeed the best way to bring balance and justice to a world in chaos.

Understand that 85 percent of the membership of the United Nations consists of third-world representatives who hate America. Around the world we are called "The Great

Satan." It is an economic fact that you, the taxpayers of America, pay 90 percent of the annual budget of the United Nations. The rest of the world pays 10 percent.

Here's what the New World Order will mean to you nationally and spiritually as Americans and as Christians and Jews. The United Nations traditionally votes against Israel. Zionism has already been labeled by the United Nations as racism. Are you willing to send United States troops to fight Israel? That's what could very well happen if the United Nations's New World Order comes to power.

Are you willing to see the United Nations vote to redistribute the wealth of America to third-world nations? That legislation is already in place. Welcome to the New World Order. If we submit our national will to the will of a clique of international power brokers using the United Nations, they could simply vote the wealth of this nation away to any other nation they desired while our Congress sat by and watched.

Are you willing for United Nations troops to appear on the streets of America and shut down every synagogue and every Bible-believing church in the country? "Preposterous," you say. And yet most delegates to the United Nations come from third-world countries, most of which are Islamic. In 1981, the General Assembly of the United Nations adopted what was called "The Declaration of the Elimination of All Forms of Intolerance and Discrimination Based on Religious Beliefs."[18] Sounds good, but it was only a new device for propagating anti-Semitism. According to fundamentalist Islamic teaching, a Christian or a Jew has one alternative: He can convert to Islam or have his head cut off. It's in their bible. Welcome to the New World Order. It would also terminate Christian evangelism because evangelicals are intolerant of pagan religions and their doctrines. Unity, at the expense of truth, is the gospel of the New World Order.

An Attack on the Church

The third thing that has to happen before the New World Order can assume power is the destruction of the evangelical faith.

Now there is debate within the evangelical church over just when and how this will take place, but there is little debate about the fact that the prophets warned that a great persecution of believers would come.

Why? Because as long as you believe in the Word of God, you are loyal to the kingdom of God. You represent a government within a government and you are a hindrance to the New World Order. Your credibility and your confidence must be shaken. Your confidence must be shaken in your leaders, it must be shaken in your cause, and finally it must be shaken in yourselves. Evangelicals can expect to be attacked through the law, through the media, through Hollywood, and through the educational system under the control of the National Education Association (NEA).

Only a few years ago, when the American Bar Association, the foremost legal fraternity of America, met in San Francisco, their plenary session focused on attacking the church through tort law.

In California, a young lady answered an altar call and came down the aisle to receive Jesus Christ. Her relatives later said that the preacher used an emotional appeal to bring her to the altar, and she was psychologically damaged by being brainwashed into receiving Jesus Christ. Her parents sued the church for damages and they won.

This is where many in the legal fraternity now have their mind-set. Churches are seen as a source of money and are being sued for doing what they were organized to do, preach the gospel of Jesus Christ. Parishioners and pastors are having to spend their time and money to defend their right to worship according to their beliefs. This is not something that is coming to America. It's here!

In 1990, the U.S. Congress passed into law the Hate Crime Bill. Police agencies are now being directed to track crimes of hate. It sounds wonderful. A blow against intolerance. But the devil is in the details. Tacked onto the end of one clause was the remarkable phrase forbidding speech "in any negative manner about a person's sexual preference."

According to some interpretations, a pastor standing in his own church reading aloud the Bible verses describing homosexuality as an abomination to God is now breaking federal law. He could be fined or put in prison. This is not something that is coming. It is here—in America in these latter days.

Likewise, attacks against the church in the national media are well under way. Sadly some major ministries in America have given the media plenty to attack. When the media expose an evangelist who sleeps with prostitutes or defrauds his own followers of millions of dollars, they are not only doing a favor to society, they are doing a favor to the church, as well. But don't be deceived by media smear campaigns. Remember, much of the Bible was written from prison. But you say, "They wouldn't be in trouble if they were really innocent." Remember, Jesus was crucified by an angry mob who saw him as a blasphemer, and He was innocent. Rome saw Him as an insurrectionist too dangerous to live. The apostle Paul was innocent, yet he went to jail. The founding fathers of the church were innocent, yet martyred.

In one national case the minister's attorneys went to court and obtained from the national television network the actual raw video footage taken during their coverage of the ministry. After videotaping an interview, one of the most popular television reporters in America got in her car to leave, but unbeknownst to her and the camera crew, the videotape was still going. The video itself only showed the dashboard and floorboard of the automobile, but the audio records a remarkable conversation. America's sweetheart reporter curses and allegedly announces, "Well, he's innocent but we can destroy him anyway."

Christian bashing is now an art form in America. According to the Gallup organization more than 42 percent of the American public claim to be born-again Christians, but you seldom read a positive story about them.[19] They are now blasted by the media as right wing, fundamentalist, homophobic hate mongers! Jesus said, "You will be hated by all for My name's sake."[20]

What is the driving force behind the attack? Why don't they attack all churches? Why just the Bible-preaching churches? Is it the New World Order that sees you as the government within the government? Again, the Eastern Establishment controls the major New York banks, who have taken their huge multibillion-dollar trust resources and bought the stocks of ABC, NBC, CBS, *Time*, and *Newsweek*. You will never read a bad word about David Rockefeller. You will never read a good word about evangelicals, because we are seen as "dangerous and intolerant" by the national media.

One remarkable survey found that fewer than 30 percent of American journalists believed in a personal God, while 95 percent of the American public said they did believe in a personal God. Not even 3 percent of American journalists said that they attend a church or synagogue. *Time* magazine, whose masthead carries the names of its 120 editors, reporters, and staff, can name only two born-again journalists. *Newsweek* can only name three. Obviously, when the American media talk about "inclusiveness," they are not referring to the 42 percent of the American population who claim to be born again.

An Attack on Education

Fourth, evangelicals can expect to be attacked through the American educational system.

It is now the modus operandi of the public school system to attack God. Understand that the Supreme Court of the United States has already ruled it unconstitutional for the Ten

Commandments to be posted on a classroom wall. Why? Because it might affect the moral judgments of students who read it and hence violate the separation of church and state.

You say, "This doesn't make sense. We need to have someone who can do a better job articulating what we believe. We need to explain why we should have a chance to practice our faith without having that undermined. Is this some new twisted logic? What's wrong? Why can't they understand?"

The answer is this. They do understand. If someone has determined that it is against the law to publicly post the Ten Commandments in a classroom, a document whose historical and cultural impact on the world alone makes its words some of the most important words in history, then no amount of patient explanation will prevail. This isn't about logic. This is about power, power to control the world, power to control America, and power to control you!

When my son Matthew was in the second grade, he was asked by his teacher to turn in a two-paragraph story on Christmas in Mexico. He wrote about the wise men pursuing the Christ child. The teacher rejected his paper because the word *Christ* was mentioned. You can be sure Matthew's father went to the schoolhouse and got that ludicrous decision rescinded.

The National Education Association, which controls education in America, was funded by the Rockefeller Foundation, and the NEA has made it pretty clear that one of its objectives for education in America is to get God out of the schools. This is not something that is coming. This is here. You can read *The Satanic Bible* in public school but not the Ten Commandments. This is America in these latter days.

There is a strange irony here. Former communist leaders are now coming to America and inviting Christians to go to the Soviet Union to put together Christian education blocks because they're trying to repair the massive moral damage brought about by atheism. Meanwhile the Supreme

Court of the United States and the ACLU are insisting that a new generation of young Americans must now try what has already failed in the former Soviet Union. Freedom *of* religion versus freedom *from* religion is the difference between democracy and dictatorship. Which rules America?

You don't have to be a rocket scientist to know that when the Ten Commandments are thrown out and condoms are brought in, schools are going the wrong way. Isn't it strange that a teacher cannot by law give your daughter an aspirin for a headache without a written letter of permission from you, her parents, but can counsel an abortion and even provide transportation to the clinic without ever telling you or giving you the right to talk to your own daughter.

Margaret Sanger, who founded Planned Parenthood—which, not surprisingly, was also funded by the Rockefeller and Ford foundations—has been called the author of abortion. Sanger advocated unrestrained sexuality for teenagers, and called for the sterilization of blacks, Jews, fundamentalist Christians, and mental defectives.[21]

If you want to know what the world thinks about you, read Sanger's 1920 monograph, *Breeding the Thoroughbred*. She was an advocate of eugenics, the use of genetics to breed a superior race. Adolf Hitler was demonized (and rightly so) for his eugenics program. Yet Margaret Sanger is lionized by the same media that call you a bigot because you believe in the Bible.

Those new bywords on American campuses and in American newsrooms, *politically correct*, were coined fifty years ago. They translate simply as anti-God, anti-American, and pro-New World Order. It is nothing other than intellectual Nazism. Youngsters sent to secular universities are going to go through four years of intensive brainwashing and become secular humanists unless they are rooted in the sustaining power of the Word of God.

This is why Christian colleges and Christian universities have to stay open in America. They help give this nation a chance to preserve its heritage and its faith.

The Attack on the Family

Fifth, before the rise of the New World Order in America, there must be the destruction of the traditional family.

This process is also already upon us. The traditional family in America is coming unraveled. Increasingly, the objective of the state is to remove the authority of the parent over the child. If you've ever read the objectives of the United Nations's International Year of the Child, you will have no doubt of their intentions.

Consider this: The same system that will allow a young lady injured in an automobile accident to suffer and bleed in a waiting room without anesthetic or treatment until parents are notified and have physically signed for a life-saving operation, will fearlessly and quickly kill her baby without any advice or input, or even without her parents knowing. All of this is justified, they say, because of the increase in teenage pregnancies. The parents haven't been able to solve the problem, so "We, the state, will do it for you."

You say, "Well, it hasn't worked. Teenage pregnancies are rising with the added bonus of epidemic venereal disease. Bring the parents back into the equation. Let us share our values with our children without undermining us by issuing programs and policies that contradict what we believe and are trying to teach to our children at home."

Our children belong to us, not the government! You are perplexed and you wonder why the school boards and the teachers unions can't see the obvious. That's because you are still under a delusion. You think that you are part of a great public debate about what is best for your children. You imagine that the right argument will work; they will see the logic and change their minds. You are deceived. This isn't about logic. It isn't about what is best for your children. It's about power, power to train your child to abandon Judeo-Christian beliefs and become a submissive dupe to the New World Order.

How valuable is a high school diploma today? Boston University President John Silber states, "What a high school diploma tells you is that a student was *institutionalized* for about twelve years. You wouldn't know whether the student had been in a prison colony, a reform school, or a place for mental defectives."[22]

A Boston radio talk-show host saw his ratings soar when he conducted an on-air, no-holds-barred sex survey for women. Callers fought for the opportunity to do a psychic striptease by describing their favorite locations for intercourse, preferred positions, homosexual encounters, and the date when they lost their virginity.

The soul of America is sick. Recently in New York City, dozens of motorists stopped to gawk, but made no move to intervene, while a man allegedly raped his three-year-old niece. Perhaps they thought they were watching the live production of a soap opera?

In the past thirty years, the minds of our children have been vacuumed and sanitized. They have been poisoned against God. They have been poisoned against America. And the founding fathers of our nation are now being presented as lust-driven lunatics and as opportunists and non-patriots. In some classes more time is spent speculating on unproved, revisionist theories of Thomas Jefferson's alleged mistress than on the very lofty Jeffersonian principles that form the basis of our Bill of Rights. Seventy-five percent of America's high school graduates cannot give you the names of the last three presidents of these United States.

Woodrow Wilson said, "There is a power somewhere so organized, so subtle, so watchful, so interlocked, so complete, so pervasive, that they better not speak above their breath when they speak in condemnation of it"[23] The president of the United States was speaking of the clique of financiers and bankers who controlled America in his day.

During our generation they rule from the Council on Foreign Relations.

During the last fifty years the Council on Foreign Relations has subtly co-opted or seized control of the U.S. State Department, the Treasury, the Federal Reserve, the Rockefeller, Ford, and Carnegie foundations, Harvard, Columbia, Yale, scores of international corporations, and every major media outlet in America. Since 1940, every secretary of state except one has come from this exclusive club. Is the picture beginning to focus for you?

This clique is trying to produce a one-world government that will kick God out. They see you as a nuisance, and the only way they can neutralize you is to attack and reshape your image into one seen as totally counterproductive to progress in these United States.

The Last Warning

If one accepts the biblical timetable, someday soon Satan's messiah will present himself. Most Bible scholars expect him to emerge somewhere out of the European Economic Community. The ancient prophet Daniel gives a very clear description of a last days European Union reconstructed out of the nations of the Roman Empire of long ago. Daniel describes ten nations coming together in this union, with three of the smaller nations actually merging into one state.[24] Even as you read this book such an idea is being pushed by politicians and bankers in the nations of Belgium, the Netherlands, and Luxembourg. Many Europeans are already calling this union Benelux.

The rise of the Antichrist will be sudden. In one single hour this new European Union will do its deed, signing over their legislative and bureaucratic powers to this new dictator who will be universally acclaimed as the world's best hope. The Bible says that in that hour the whole world will marvel and follow after him.[25]

People have told me, "Well that's impossible. It will not fall into place that quickly." Only a few years ago, learned history professors were teaching that this was the age of communism. Former Secretary of State Henry Kissinger caused a scandal when a Canadian journalist overheard him whisper to a dinner guest that the Soviet Union was in the ascendancy and the American era was over. Political science teachers were telling students that it would take a hundred years for the Berlin Wall to come down. But when God gave it a swift kick, it came tumbling down in one evening. And understand, God Himself is going to allow these events to take place.

The Bible offers a detailed description of Satan's messiah. He will appear on the world's stage as a man of peace. "He shall cause craft to prosper."[26] After a collapse of the world's monetary system, he will assume control and usher in a few years of unprecedented and spectacular prosperity and peace.

Eventually, he will have a mystical or spiritual following. The Bible says that he will be "wounded in the head" and yet he will miraculously recover. He will have a New Age following. A great religious leader, described in the Bible as the false prophet, will influence all organized religion to unite. "Why do we need Christ?" people will ask. "Haven't millions of people died fighting over Christ? Here is a man of peace. We have it all right here. He has even been assassinated and come back from the dead. What more could you ask?"

The Antichrist will even tackle the centuries-old problems of the Middle East. His solutions will appear miraculous and cause the world to "wonder after him." It will please the Arabs and, at the same time, guarantee the security of Israel by a seven-year peace treaty. But don't be deceived. The same prophets who say he will parade publicly as a man of peace, warn privately that he is, in fact, a beast, the Son of Perdition, meaning the "Chief Son of Satan."

The prophets declare that in the last days, Solomon's Temple will be rebuilt. In the middle of his treaty with Israel, after three-and-a-half years of peace, the Antichrist will go to Jerusalem and walk into the Temple and formally announce to the people of the world what so many of them had already been saying. "You want God? All right, you've got him. I am God."

This is the climactic moment of the ages. Daniel writes about it. John writes about it. The Bible calls it "the abomination of desolation." Jesus said to those who see it happen, "Run to the mountains."[27] Don't even pack your bags. Run. It will be the last sign. There will be no other warning. And you will have very little time. It will trigger a period of unprecedented horrors. Even as the Antichrist is appearing as the man of peace—the fulfillment of John Lennon's famous song, uniting the world's religions, ending all wars—he will be betraying Israel, offering her up to her enemies for slaughter and extermination.

The Bible describes a two-hundred-million-man army from "the East" that will close in on Jerusalem. Consider this, these remarkable words were prophesied at a time when the entire population of the world was only 250 million. Only today, in our lifetime, has any nation ever been able to claim a two-hundred-million-man army. That is the exact number of the combined standing army and militia of the People's Republic of China. John Barron in his remarkable book *Operation Solo* writes about how the Chinese leaders often expressed the advantages of a nuclear war. "China would emerge the winner," they said, "because China has people in abundance. It is our one advantage."[28] They may get their wish.

War will break out upon the earth. It will not be just any war. It will be the ultimate expression of man's violence to man, ironically occurring just as mankind thought it had solved its problems. One prophet calls it "The Great Tribulation." The Bible's vivid descriptions are horrific. It is hard to imagine it as anything other than a nuclear holocaust. One-third of the earth's living creatures and plants will be destroyed. One-third of all life in the seas will be contaminated.

Whatever the Jewish people may think of Jesus, at that moment, many will take His advice. They will run to the mountains, hiding in a place among the cliffs called Petra. There, in horror, they will await their messiah, their deliverer. The Antichrist will finally set himself up as the object of worship in the city of Jerusalem. The Bible says, "He opened his mouth to blaspheme God."[29]

Literally, the Antichrist, Satan's messiah, is going to look into the heavens and say to the angels, "Had you followed me, had you followed my master, lord Satan, when he was kicked out of the heavens, you would have controlled these kingdoms of the world with me."

The Second Coming

That blasphemy, that ultimate challenge mixed with the cries of God's chosen people trembling with terror in the rocks of Petra, is the defining moment of the ages. Jesus will return to the Mount of Olives in Jerusalem. It will be the same spot from which he ascended into heaven two thousand years ago. And this time he will be back with an army of angels and the raptured, resurrected church of the Lord Jesus Christ.

John describes it best in Revelation 19:11–20:

Now I saw heaven opened, and behold, a white horse. And He who sat on him was called Faithful and True, and in righteousness He judges and makes war. His eyes were like a flame of fire, and on His head were many crowns. He had a name written that no one knew except Himself. He was clothed with a robe dipped in blood, and His name is called The Word of God. And the armies in heaven, clothed in fine linen, white and clean, followed Him on white horses . . . And He has on His robe and on His thigh a name written: KING OF KINGS AND LORD Of LORDS . . . Then the beast was captured, and with him the false prophet who worked signs in his presence ... These two were cast alive into the lake of fire burning with brimstone.

So there are two world orders just ahead. One is led by Satan's messiah. The other is led by the true Messiah, Jesus Christ. You are likely to be a part of one of these two world orders. Paul said you're either servant to the Lord Jesus Christ or a slave to sin and Satan.

Some who actually read this book may very well receive that famous "mark of the beast," the number stamped on their forehead or right hand. They will be deceived. They have rejected the Word of God. They have rejected Jesus Christ. God has no place in their families. They are literally awaiting the messiah who will come out of Europe to destroy their families and their souls. They will say to themselves, "I have no choice. I cannot buy or sell without it." And when they receive the mark they will lose their souls for eternity.

Some who read this book will see the return of Jesus Christ. He will set up His throne in the city of Jerusalem. The first time, He came as a baby wrapped in swaddling clothes, lying in a manger. The next time He comes, He'll be wearing a crown and He shall be called the King of Kings and the Lord of Lords, "and of His kingdom, there shall be no end!"

The first time He came into Jerusalem, He was riding on a donkey. The next time He will come in the final world order. He'll be riding a white horse followed by the armies of heaven. It will be the greatest mounted posse ever to split the clouds.

The first time He came into Jerusalem, He was dragged before Pilot and Herod. Soldiers whipped Him and spit on Him. The next time He comes, Herod and Pilot will be dragged before Him. Adolf Hitler will be dragged before Him. Joseph Stalin will bow. Nikita Khrushchev will bow. Jean-Paul Sartre, who long ago predicted the Bible would soon be found only in museums, will bow. Professor Thomas Altizer, the father of "Christian atheism," will bow. Doctor Death, Jack Kevorkian, will bow. Scientist Carl Sagan will bow. David Rockefeller will bow. The Bible says that "Every knee shall bow and every tongue shall confess that He is Lord."

The first time He came, He was crucified at Calvary. The next time He comes, He's going to reign on the throne of His father David. You've heard of New Delhi, of New Brunswick, of New York. Well, according to the prophets of long ago, Jesus will reign in a "New Jerusalem." The governors and rulers of His kingdom will come and go from there. The truth of the Word of God that Jesus is the Lord to the glory of God the Father will be proclaimed from Zion's hill.

Don't be deceived by what is happening in America. Don't be perplexed by the outrageous actions of your government, by the injustice of the media, by the confusing economic signals. Jesus once gave this warning and this promise: "In the world, you will have tribulation, but be of good cheer, I have overcome the world."

Chapter Four

Land of the Free?

Most Americans have a vague, uncomfortable feeling that the freedom and justice we once took for granted in this country is slowly slipping away, but few are aware of how quickly that slippage has taken on landslide proportions. If you still think you live in an America where the people have the power, their vote determines their destiny, and the right to own property is inviolable, then you have missed a few key episodes of the evening news. You are deceived.

Consider, for example, the rise of the homosexual lobby and its power to impose its agenda against popular opinion and the will of the people. Students at public schools in Massachusetts were ordered to perform in a "gay skit." Girls were directed to hold hands and act out the parts of lesbians. One boy had the line, "It's natural to be attracted to the same sex." In Boston a first grader came home telling his father that boys could become girls if they wanted to. The school had invited a transsexual to give the first graders a little education into life.

In Newton, Massachusetts, a parent decided to get involved. Teachers in the seventh grade were giving their classes graphic illustrations of oral and anal sex, but when Brian Camenker showed up at the school office asking to see the curriculum he was met by the principal and given a flat, "No."

"But statutory law gives parents the right to view curricula."

"Tough luck," he was told. "If you don't like it, take your kids to a private school."

Which is exactly what many parents in Massachusetts have done. Private school districts in Boston comprise some of the largest in the country and rival the public school system in the city. Parents who pay tuition at the private schools and pay property taxes supporting the public schools get hit twice. But poorer families don't have that option. The withdrawal of thousands of caring parents from the public school system has only accelerated the move toward the new gay agenda. Those left behind often feel abandoned and are left to deal with the outrageous co-opting of the public educational system by a political lobby born in the bowels of hell.

In 1990 thousands of people in Colorado became alarmed by the growing homosexual lobby in their state. The lobby was pressuring local school boards to distribute pro-homosexual materials in classrooms and convincing state legislators to jump on the gay legislative bandwagon. Not wanting to see a repeat of the Massachusetts mess in their own state, delegations of citizens visited their representatives. One of the entrenched, liberal, incumbent congressmen openly laughed at them. Meanwhile, some local state legislators privately encouraged citizens groups to get organized and warned them that if there was no opposition to the gay lobby the state would be steamrolled.

At the same time several Colorado municipalities were pressured into passing pro-gay ordinances, which granted homosexuals minority status. The door was open for gays to claim bias if they were denied employment, housing, health, and welfare services. Christian schools were now fearful that they would be required to hire gay teachers and be taken to court if they didn't. Christian landlords faced the same dilemma. Businesses could be sued if they could not show that they had hired their quota of gay workers.

Opposition leaders argued that minority status was granted to blacks and other groups for unique reasons that had no application in the gay community. Minorities were defined by the courts as having experienced economic disadvantages because of their race. For 150 years many American blacks had been slaves. Gays, on the other hand, earned far more than the average American, were three times more likely to be an airline frequent flyer, and had, on average, much more education than the norm. Why should minority status be granted to someone based on his or her choice of behavior? How could minority status be granted when the very same group was still outlawed by many state laws?

In 1992 groups of Colorado citizens set out to legally amend their state constitution. In spite of what you may have read in the press, no citizen of Colorado was advocating that homosexuals be denied the same freedoms any other American enjoys. The referendum simply stated that homosexuality and bisexuality could not be the basis to claim minority status or quota preferences. It was a very benign initiative, and purposely so. If this wouldn't pass, the homosexual lobby would own the state.

Thousands of citizens obtained the petitions, verified the signatures, overcame purposely misleading news stories spread by hostile media, and successfully placed their initiative on the ballot. Now it was in the hands of the voters, or so they naively assumed.

Of course, Colorado voters overwhelmingly passed the initiative. In spite of daily newspaper attacks, it was never in doubt. National independent polling shows that six out of ten Americans disapprove of gay marriages and gay adoptions, even if it does buck the trends of Hollywood policy and American newsrooms.

The national media were outraged. This wasn't politically correct. Hollywood magnates and gay activist leaders called for a Colorado boycott to punish the voters. Attempts to explain what was really going on in the state were panned.

And then, it happened. Judicial reversal. The Supreme Court of the United States, which in 1986 had upheld state laws making homosexual acts criminal offenses, now told the people of Colorado they could not even amend their own state constitution. Their votes didn't count. Their concerns for their children and their beliefs didn't count. The same Supreme Court that outlawed the posting of the Ten Commandments in a public classroom in Tennessee and ordered a manger scene pulled off the lawn of a city courthouse in Connecticut was now telling the people of Colorado that the laws they passed, even the constitutional changes they made, would have to fit the dictates of a politically correct, Satan-inspired, homosexual agenda. Don't be deceived. America is no longer a free country whose destiny is determined by citizens voting their beliefs. America's destiny is being determined by activist federal judges who are beyond the reach of the election process. It is a government by fiat! It's time for federal judges to face the ballot box. To believe activist federal judges will allow the citizens of America to live by any conviction they don't condone is deception.

But the assault didn't end there.

A Godless Government

In 1993 a new American president legitimized homosexuality by demanding that gays be accepted into the military. God calls it sodomy, an abomination. Sodomy is a sin. One is not born that way. It is a choice. In his first week in office the new president made it clear that the abortion mills would continue the killing of millions of babies. Within days he had announced a new surgeon general of the United States who, among other things, encouraged the idea that grade-school children be taught how to masturbate as a form of "sex control." Yet millions of born-again Christians continue to support this president and other politicians because "the economy is strong." Mammon wins over morality.

Carrying a Bible before crowds and television cameras does not make a godly man. Attending church once a week does not make a godly man. A politician who goes to the White House and is sworn in with his right hand on the Bible while his left hand is signing documents that federally fund partial-birth abortions is not a godly man. God does not judge mankind on style, only on substance. As a people, we have been deceived by symbolism over substance.

Today, as a direct result of that loss of discernment, America has its most wicked, evil, and dangerous leadership in its more than 220-year history. It is a leadership saturated with socialist, Marxist, gay, and lesbian ideals. America's new elitists seek to destroy America's Constitution. They lead a constant assault against traditional family values, the religious heritage of our nation, and a free-enterprise economy. They are a self-serving, politically correct crowd, using the politics of hate and class warfare to undermine our basic principles.

The result?

The process begun by activist judges in the 1960s has become an avalanche. America is a sick society! Our children are deluged with daily messages of "safe sex," which have only encouraged promiscuity. Children in fifth-grade classrooms are passed a banana and shown how to put on a condom. America has one million teenage pregnancies each year. Half of teenage females between the ages of fifteen and nineteen are sexually active. Sixty percent of black children are born out of wedlock. By the year 2000, if the present rate of illegitimacy continues, the government projects that 60 percent of all children born will be illegitimate.

Abortion has only accelerated the idea that life is cheap. We read daily headlines of drive-by shootings and recreational murders. Women are being raped at a rate of one every forty-eight seconds. Prime-time television now glorifies profanity and nudity.

"Professing to be wise, they became fools." Meanwhile, America's educational system is in disarray. Thousands of children carry guns to public schools. Teachers are assaulted by students on a daily basis. The classroom, once a center for learning, has become a center for governmental mind control. Secular humanist educators continue to poison the minds of our innocent children.

The Village Wants Your Children

Hillary Clinton has written her book, *It Takes a Village*. The idea is that none of us can make it alone. We need the village, with its various talents and protections. Sounds good, doesn't it? And according to Hillary Clinton, it is impossible to raise a child without the help of the village. Insert the words *big government* for *village* and you have Hillary's concept.

Childrearing is a tough business, especially if the mother is off doing something truly fulfilling with her life, like becoming a lawyer and promoting liberal causes to advance humanity.

Oh, yes, children have rights too. That's part of the formula. In fact, children should have the same rights as parents. A child should be able to divorce his or her parents. Children do not belong to parents, they belong to the village, and sometimes the village has to take them away. Sometimes their needs supersede the needs of the parents. Hillary Clinton calls such a society "a village," but the trend is not new; it has been underway in this country for thirty years. And it is not a village. It is an all-powerful government dictating to parents what they can and cannot do with their own children.

A third-grade teacher in East Lansing, Michigan, decided on her own that a young male student was too shy. He needed "a friend." Without the parents' knowledge or permission, she ordered him into psychological therapy sessions with a counselor. When the parents learned of the action and objected, a negotiation ensued. The parents finally agreed that their son could "play games" and chat with the counselor. They imagined a friendly conversation over a game of Chinese checkers. They assumed the counselor was a professional. Surely, the village is that competent.

Within a week the boy began to show signs of severe emotional problems. The parents became alarmed and started asking questions about the school therapy sessions. They were told in no uncertain terms to "butt out." Such sessions are "confidential." The boy was given strict instructions not to tell his parents what the sessions were all about. Understand, you don't own your child. The village owns your child.

When the boy's problems became worse, they took him to a psychiatric doctor of their own choosing. He concluded that the boy had "separation anxiety disorder and panic attacks." Something at school was only aggravating a serious problem. The parents, unable to get the school to respond or even to reveal what was going on in the secret sessions with their child, took the school to court. In fact, it went all the way to the Supreme Court. In the process they learned that the boy's counselor was not a professional, he had only taken a few undergraduate psychology courses. The game he was playing with the boy was called the "Talking, Feeling, and Doing Game." It had been recommended by the music teacher. I'll leave it to your imagination to figure out what was going on. The parents charged that they had been deprived of their parental rights to raise their child and properly watch over his medical well-being.[1]

Of course, going to court in these United States is the last place one will find justice. The U.S. District Court naturally sided with the school, and the Supreme Court refused to hear it. In a related case, Texas judge Melinda Harmon ruled that "parents give up their rights when they drop the children off at public school."

And that's only one case. Believe me there are others as disturbing. In March 1996 fifty young girls in an East

Stroudsburg, Pennsylvania, intermediate school were given genital examinations. The girls were forced to disrobe and stand in line while a female pediatrician gave the exams. She said she was looking for genital warts.

Mrs. Kate Tucker, mother of one of the eleven-year-old girls, said that the pediatrician had them "lie down on a table, spread-eagled, with nothing covering them." The daughter said the exam was given despite her pleas to call her parents. Many of the girls were crying and trying to get out the door, which was barred by a nurse. It takes a village, folks.

"My mother wouldn't like this," one of the girls said. "I'd like to call her." She was told, "No." The girl then calmly said that she didn't want the test done. "Too bad," the nurse responded. The doctor refused to talk to the girls or offer any explanation for the examinations.

Parents felt helpless and then enraged. They learned that Pennsylvania state health guidelines require public schools to notify parents and urge them to attend medical exams. Still, nothing was done; no apology was given. The school district investigated and decided that there were no improprieties.[2] After all, the children don't belong to the parents. They belong to the village, and if the village wants to take a look, they can do it. Remember what the court says, "Parents give up their rights when they drop the children off at public school."

One thing is for sure, we may no longer be the land of the free, but we still are very much the home of the brave. It takes courage for parents and children to survive in this jungle they call "a village" in these latter days.

The NEA Takeover

Some villagers are more favored than others in the New America, and no one is more favored than the National Education Association. The NEA is the nation's largest teacher's union with more than 2.2 million members. While the organization is highly political and partisan, it has been given a special "national charter" by Congress, exempting it from more than $16 million in real estate taxes, money which would normally go to help the local public schools. This "national charter" is the same status given to the Red Cross, but I guarantee you the NEA is not in the business of educating your children. They are nothing but a tax-funded, liberal, political lobby that could care less about educational excellence in America.

In the past decade, the NEA has taken up the fight to separate children from their parents. You could call it "Village Empowerment." Former NEA president Keith Geiger and both candidates seeking to replace him think parent involvement takes away from a teacher's authority and, thus, schools must be "protected."

While the NEA led the fight to strip the Christian Coalition of its nonprofit status for engaging in "partisan politics," the NEA has hypocritically and blatantly displayed its power by its open partisan agenda. In the 1996 election cycle, the NEA spent $5.5 million in political action committee (PAC) funds to elect liberal politicians and defend the liberal agenda, plus another $20.7 million on training members for political campaign work and lobbying. Out of 235 candidates endorsed by them in the 1996 election, only one Republican was given any money.[3] The NEA is openly using compulsory union dues and millions of dollars in federal grants to support a liberal political agenda.

In seeking to eliminate stereotyping and discrimination, NEA resolution B-7 decided that homosexuality should be listed in the same category with race, gender, immigration status, physical disabilities, and ethnic origins. The idea is that people are born gay and lesbian; they have no choice in the matter, and so their practices and behavior must be accepted. It doesn't matter what the Bible says. Incidentally, there is no mention or concern about religious stereotyping or discrimination.

Resolution B-7 is a follow-up to resolution B-9, passed at the 1995 NEA convention. B-9 requires positive plans and ongoing training programs to teach about "homosexuals throughout history," to promote acceptance of "diverse sexual orientations," and to celebrate "Lesbian and Gay History Month."

Now, let me give you a little bit of good news in the midst of this thunderstorm of decadence. Resolution B-9 was rendered ineffective after an outcry from Christian parents. Twelve NEA state affiliates condemned it, and numerous teachers around the country resigned from the NEA in protest. The vast majority of teachers refused to participate in "Lesbian and Gay History Month." Don't be deceived. Things are bad, but they would be even worse if godly influence was totally withdrawn from this country. The answer is not to run off and hide in a cave somewhere. The answer is to stand up and expose the darkness. The answer is to be salt and light in these days of decadence and deception.

Even so, the new resolution B-7 is even more dangerous than its predecessor. The same objectives of promoting the gay and lesbian lifestyle are all there, but now they are hidden amid honorable programs for minorities and the handicapped. Those who speak out are labeled racist, insensitive, intolerant, homophobic, right-wing, Bible-believing hate mongers.

There is nothing that the NEA fears more than a voucher system, a tax credit that would allow parents to enroll their children in a school of their choice. They know what would happen. Many parents would take their vouchers to Christian schools. And if that was prohibited by the courts, as it most surely would be, they would at least enroll their children in schools that teach more educational basics and less liberal political dogma.

In recent years the public clamor for a voucher system has reached a crescendo. The NEA and Bill Clinton have suddenly teamed up, declaring themselves as born-again proponents of the popular idea. Again, don't be deceived. The new charter schools of Clinton and the NEA will be exclusively nonreligious and far more liberal and experimental than anything ever seen in a public school that has had some measure of accountability.

One part of the new look of education is "outcome-based" education.

Outcome-Based Education

In recent years, our educational leaders have seized on a new system called outcome-based education, commonly called OBE. Its mission is to eliminate academic competition from the classroom. There will be no grades. There will be no year-end accomplishments. No one will fail. And no one will succeed or receive honors. To receive an honor might offend those who received no honor . . . unthinkable! All superachievers must be dumbed down so mainstream students can feel better about themselves. This will supposedly restore self-esteem and encourage a community spirit. OBE will not teach subjects such as reading, writing, and arithmetic; instead it will teach attitudes, environmentalism, global citizenship, and multiculturalism.

The rest of the world is teaching their students math and science while in America we're teaching our children to get in touch with their inner selves. Moreover, the student's "attitude" will be evaluated by the teacher, and if a child has a "politically incorrect" attitude, he or she will be denied a diploma. Ironically, the only failure allowed will be ideological. They even propose that all businesses contact the school before hiring a graduate to be sure the student has a "politically correct" attitude before getting a job. Hello, New World Order!

So far, America's new secular, anti-Christian campaign has not led to the intellectualism some anticipated. No government or laws can inhibit man's intuitive search for the spiritual world beyond. But instead of seeking God's wisdom, the New Age religions search for spiritual answers from alien beings, fortune-tellers, and demons. Environmental pagans are now worshiping Mother Earth. Increasingly they call on Gaia, the ancient earth goddess who is only a recycled version of Baal, the pagan god of biblical history.

A little-known fact about these fanatical environmentalists is that they consider Christians to be the enemy. Environmentalist Lynn White Jr. advocated that a worsening ecological crisis would continue until Americans rejected the Christian axiom that nature has no reason for existence except to serve man.

God said, "Let Us make man in Our image, according to Our likeness; let them have dominion over the fish of the sea, over the birds of the air, and over the cattle, over all the earth and over every creeping thing that creeps on the earth."[4] This paragraph offers God's perspective of exactly why the physical world was created. It was created for the benefit of all mankind. And as the benefactors of the earth, mankind has a very real responsibility for nurturing this great gift from God; but God is above nature and the earth is the Lord's.

The Collapse of Moral Law

The book of Isaiah speaks about a time when people will seek for justice and not find it. That time is here for America. Our courts, once held up to the world as examples of justice and fairness, are now the object of scorn and mistrust. Right and wrong no longer matter.

In America, celebrities commit murder and walk, while first graders are expelled for kissing. Our priorities are sick! God has been abandoned in American public life and with Him any belief in absolutes of right and wrong. Wrong is only what the state says is wrong; it does not exist on its own. Thus the question no longer is, "Did this man rape and murder the little girl?" Even if we know the answer to that question—even if the jury knows the answer—it isn't enough. The important questions are now, "Was the accused apprised of his rights? Was the police paperwork done correctly?" If not, he can go. In the absence of moral law we are only left with procedure.

The government's own statistics show that 6 percent of all violent criminals commit more than 70 percent of all violent crimes. The same people are committing their crimes over and over as liberal judges release them to attack taxpaying citizens over and over like packs of ravenous wolves. In fact, half of all suspects charged with a violent crime will be returned to the streets even before their trial begins. During this time, 20 percent of them will escape and 16 percent will commit another crime, even before they have been tried for the first one. Justice delayed is justice denied!

Even more shocking is the vast number of criminals caught in the act who are simply let loose without a trial. For every one hundred serious crimes committed in this country, only five criminals will go to jail.

Typical was the experience of New York police officers in a celebrated drug bust that happened in broad daylight on the streets of the city. The officers were cruising a well-known drug area at five in the morning when they became suspicious of a slow-moving automobile with out-of-state license plates. The car stopped and four men appeared with two large duffel bags that were thrown into the trunk of the vehicle. When the police approached the car, the men fled in opposite directions.

Some of the men and the driver, a woman, were apprehended. Inside the open trunk police found eighty pounds of cocaine. Now, these were not novice policemen. They had already experienced their fair share of cases thrown out of court on technicalities. The officers were very careful to advise the suspects of their rights under the Miranda ruling of the Supreme Court. Even so, the driver openly confessed on videotape saying that this was just one of a number of drug buys made that very day in the city.

The prosecutor's office was ecstatic. This time the police officers had done everything right. Their pursuit was warranted; after all, the suspects had fled. Their search passed the stringent "probable cause" requirement, which prohibits a policeman from searching you or your vehicle without a reason. They had witnessed the men throwing duffel bags in the trunk of their car; in fact, that action had precipitated their flight. The trunk was open. Best of all they had read the suspects their Miranda rights, the suspects had confessed anyway, and all of it had been captured on videotape.

The predictable happened. Federal judge Harold Baer, a Clinton appointee, dismissed the case, announcing to a shocked courtroom that the police search was unreasonable after all. Since policemen in the neighborhood were generally regarded as corrupt, it was a natural reaction for the men to flee and thus it was unreasonable for the police to be suspicious. As columnist John Leo said, the criminals had the right to suspect the police but the police didn't have the right to suspect the criminals!

I love America. I believe God has blessed her for her original covenant with Him. It is my prayer and hope that America will awaken to the Word of God and turn back to Him. But if you still operate under the illusion that this is the land of "liberty and justice for all," you are deceived.

If you need more evidence, consider these cases:

- A three-judge panel on a U.S. Circuit Court reversed a conviction against a would-be bomber trying to kill the U.S. attorney who had once prosecuted him. The court determined that the bomb had been badly built and could not, therefore, be considered deadly or dangerous. Case dismissed.

- A young woman, seeking protection from an abusive ex-boyfriend, was unlucky enough to find herself in the New York courtroom of judge Lorin Duckman. The ex-boyfriend, a convicted rapist, had already attacked the young lady three times. After commenting that the woman was bruised but not actually disfigured, the judge lowered bail for the man. He advised the woman that her former boyfriend would probably stop beating her if she would just give him back his dog. Before the end of the month the former boyfriend had shot the woman to death.

- Judge Rosemary Barkett, a typical Clinton appointee, opposed Georgia state laws requiring candidates to be tested for drugs. She said it was unfair. It would be prejudicial to candidates who favored legalizing drugs. While a member of the Florida Supreme Court, she insisted that police be stopped from searching for drugs on public buses, even with permission from the passengers. She now sits on the U.S. Court of Appeals.

Without God, without absolutes, without a belief in right or wrong, justice in these United States has been reduced to a game of regulations. Morality does not exist outside of the law. Guilt and innocence do not exist outside the law. And the law is no longer in the hands of the citizens. Corrupt, activist judges now hold the power. The law is what they decide it will be, and that can change by the hour.

In Cleveland, Ohio, a nineteen-year-old woman was ready to plead guilty to credit card abuse before judge Shirley Strickland Saffold. Before accepting the plea, Saffold began a lengthy lecture. "Men are easy," she said. "You can go sit in the bus stop, put on a skirt, cross your legs, and pick up twenty-five. Ten of them will give you money. If you don't pick up the first ten," the judge solemnly advised, "then all you got [sic] to do is open your legs a little bit and cross them at the bottom, and then they'll stop." The judge suggested that the young woman find a doctor and marry him. This would solve her financial problems.[5] Welcome to justice in America. Welcome to America without God.

The prophet Isaiah wrote, "He brings the princes to nothing; / He makes the judges of the earth useless."[6]

Agencies of Injustice

In the Bible, David talked about justice turned upside-down, when right is wrong and wrong is right. Sound familiar? While the guilty freely walk the streets of America, the innocent are often successfully prosecuted and harassed by a government that has lost a belief in right and wrong and is solely driven by rules and regulations.

A man living in Knoxville, Tennessee, saved $3.33 by mailing his tax form to the IRS by regular mail. The small savings, however, turned into a tragic loss. James Carroll mailed his tax document to the Internal Revenue Service on January 21, 1987. It was due in March of the same year. Somehow the IRS did not receive the document, and although Mr. Carroll could prove he had sent it, he could not prove that the IRS had received it.

A 1916 common law, amended by Congress in 1954, seemed to support Mr. Carroll. The law stated that proof of a letter mailed, "creates a presumption that it reached its destination and was actually received." An updated 1954 amendment added that a record showing that a document sent by registered mail would constitute "prima facie evidence of delivery to the IRS."

It was now up to the Circuit Court of Appeals to interpret the amendment. What was the intent? Was it only adding the idea that the use of the new registered mail service would also be proof or was it actually negating the original law applying to regular mail? The Eighth and Ninth Circuit Courts, as well as the Tennessee Tax Court, had already sided with the original common law, "proof that the letter was mailed creates a presumption that it reached its destination and was actually received." But Mr. Carroll lived in the Second Circuit Court's district. It was their call.

What was lost in this whole discussion was the fact that Mr. Carroll was innocent. No one, not even the IRS, denied that. The question was purely technical. The Second Circuit Court decided that the old common law of presumption no longer applied and that Mr. Carroll was at fault for not having sent the tax information through the registered mail. An innocent man was fined $22,000 in late fees and court costs. That will teach you to use the U.S. mail. Welcome to the new style of justice in America in these latter days.

In 1988 Nobel peace prize recipient Mother Teresa and her Missionaries of Charity were given two abandoned buildings from the City of New York for a dollar bill. The sisters proposed to convert these buildings into homeless shelters. A year-and-a-half later, the city finally approved the plan and restoration began. But soon after efforts were underway, the Missionaries of Charity came face-to-face with the reality of trying to do something in the new America. The sisters were told that under New York's building code, all new or renovated multiple-story buildings were required to have, or install, an elevator. The Missionaries of Charity explained that because of their oath of poverty, they would never use the elevators and, in any case, they didn't have the extra money to put the elevators in.

Although there were thousands of buildings in New York City without elevators, the buildings given to the sisters were abandoned and unused, and the missionaries simply wanted to provide food and shelter to the homeless, they were denied any waiver. The city took back its buildings. They are empty to this day! Better to have homeless people sleeping in the streets in snow than sleeping in a nice, warm bed in a building without elevators.

The Government and Your Property

Few Americans understand how important faith was to the founding of our country. The Mayflower Compact was a covenant with God. Most of our Constitution and early amendments are rooted in Scripture. The Fifth Amendment, which clearly prohibits government from taking property without just compensation, is no exception. The Bible teaches that a man's property is sacred: "Do not remove the ancient landmark / Which your fathers have set."[7]

In 1964 Gaston and Monique Roberge began looking for a secure retirement investment, not an easy chore in an economy periodically given to bouts of rampaging inflation. They finally decided to invest in real estate, and their search led them to a small, 2.8-acre plot near the banks of the Atlantic Ocean in Orchard Beach, Maine.

There they dreamed of a day when increased tourism and nearby development would increase the value of their land. By 1976 the area was indeed experiencing rapid growth. With development soaring, the city government asked the Roberges if one of their sewer contractors could dump excess dirt onto part of their land. It seemed to be a good idea. The Roberges wanted to be cooperative. The city would provide the permits, and some of their marshy land would receive a much-needed land fill.

By 1986, with Orchard Beach thriving, Mr. Roberge's health was now in full decline. There had been two heart attacks, and doctors were informing him that he was going to lose his sight. The Roberges decided it was time to sell. A developer quickly offered them top dollar for their property, planning to build condominiums on the area that had been filled ten years earlier. Orchard Beach officials approved the zoning. Mr. and Mrs. Roberge could finally cash in on their investment and start their long-awaited retirement.

But life is seldom that simple in these United States in these latter days. There was one more step. The federal government. And what did the federal government have to do with a small real estate transaction in the state of Maine, you may ask? The developer, sensitive to the growing regulatory role of the Environmental Protection Agency and the U.S. Army Corps of Engineers, wanted to make sure that everything was okay with them—just in case.

Sure enough, the Army Corps of Engineers decided that the small property could be technically categorized as "wetlands." An investigation ensued. The sale was postponed, and after five months of waiting the developer was finally denied permits to build. Investigators concluded that the land filled in by the sewer contractor ten years before was part of a marsh extending beyond the Roberges' property. The Corps insisted that federal permits should have been obtained before the land had been filled in. The city, of course, had initiated the project and had issued permits allowing the land to be filled. Everything was legal at the time, but now, retroactively, the Corps decided to hold the Roberges accountable. To add to the absurdity of this tale, no federal agency had even issued such permits ten years before. Preservation of wetlands was a political issue not yet born. At the time, the Roberges could not have obeyed such a regulation even if God Himself had shown them the future.

Now, belatedly, the Roberges filed for a federal permit. They were denied. They hired experts to assist in obtaining technical information for an "after the fact" permit, but that costly process was also in vain. New applications from the Roberges only prompted a continuous cycle of requests from the agency for additional information.

Eventually the Roberges found an attorney to work on contingency and a five-year legal battle began. Among other things, the attorneys discovered an existing internal policy that prohibited the pursuit of alleged violations more than five years old. This was something the agency understood—a regulation. The government finally issued the permits that should have been issued so many years before.

Then came the shocker. Further investigation revealed that the Corps had had all the necessary information from the Roberges all along. Its refusal to issue the permits was inconsistent with standard practices. Additionally, they discovered that one man in the Corps had been responsible for the continued hassles and delays. He had been bored with his position and had been trying to "squash" the Roberges to set an example of the agency's power. Even so, no apologies were given, and no one in the agency was disciplined. Welcome to the land of the free!

When the government fears its citizens you have democracy. When the citizens fear the government, you have tyranny. After Waco, Ruby Ridge, and Travelgate, Americans fear the government, and justly so.

Americans, beware. Look to history as your warning. The psychic gods of Nazi Germany led to unspeakable horrors across Europe. It happened once; it can happen again! America's new atheistic, secular state is not unprecedented. It was performed with precision by the Soviet Communists and led to an amoral, unproductive, cynical, and atheistic population that destroyed its own economy and is only now having to learn how to think and live freely. Even so, against all logic, America's leaders try to force upon us a system of government that has repeatedly failed in Europe and Russia. Why? There is no logical answer.

But, remember, this is not about logic. Logical people do not reject a political system that has given them freedom and prosperity. Logical people do not regress to the centuries-old worship of Baal. This is not about what is right or wrong for America. The other side doesn't even believe in right or wrong. This is about principalities, powers, and the rulers of darkness. America is in a spiritual crisis. This is a battle for America's soul, and while you may not be around to experience it at its climactic worst, your children and grandchildren will be there. The antichrist system is taking shape. America's future hangs in the balance in these latter days.

How to Fight Back Spiritually

There is good news in the midst of this depressing recital of America's woes. All power is from God. The Bible says, "Let every soul be subject to the governing authorities. For there is no authority except from God, and the authorities that exist are appointed by God."[8] Every politician, every judge, every policeman and king are servants of God. America's leaders are controlled by God.

Consider Daniel and King Nebuchadnezzar of Babylon. The king had a terrifying dream but had forgotten it. He commanded his witchcraft corps to tell him what he had dreamed or he would rip them limb from limb. Daniel, an Israelite captive trained as a wise man in the court, asked for time to pray about it. "The God whom we serve will give us the answer," he said. When God revealed the dream and the interpretation, Daniel announced, "Blessed be the name of God forever and ever, / For wisdom and might are His."[9] God has all the might and all the power. "The king's heart is in the hand of the LORD, / Like the rivers of water; / He turns it wherever He wishes."[10]

Now here is the irony: Who controls the president's heart like water? God! Who controls the senators' hearts like water? God! And ultimately, the only Supreme Court that makes a difference is God. "For exaltation comes neither from the east / Nor from the west nor from the south. / But God is the Judge: / He puts down one, / And exalts another."[11] America is not in the hands of politicians; the politicians are in the hands of God.

King Belshazzar of Babylon was having a massive government gala with a thousand of his lords, and they were mocking God. "They drank wine, and praised the gods of gold and silver, bronze and iron, wood and stone. In the same hour the fingers of a man's hand appeared and wrote opposite the lampstand on the plaster of the wall of the king's palace; and the king saw the part of the hand that wrote." The Bible says that his countenance changed. His thoughts troubled him, so that "the joints of his hips were loosened and his knees knocked against each other."[12] The king was terrified. God scared the devil out of him.

The queen called for Daniel, and when he arrived he gave the interpretation. He told them God was saying that the kingdom was finished; they had been weighed in the balances and found wanting. This great world empire would be divided between the Medes and the Persians.

That very night the Persians reversed the flow of a key tributary of the great Euphrates river and came in under the massive walls of Babylon. The king of Babylon was killed, and by morning the world had a new Persian ruler.

"All power is from God."

"If God is in charge, why doesn't He do a better job of picking his leaders?" you might ask.

The answer is simple. God has given to men the gift of free will. The choice is ours, not God's. The crisis that America is experiencing today is one that we ourselves have brought on our own heads. The elections are more about the character of the people than the candidates for office. When Israel journeyed through the desert, God sent them manna from heaven. No one cooked meals. No one did dishes. No one even had to pack up the leftovers in Tupperware. Manna was nutritious, and God always sent enough for each day's need. Even so, the Israelites complained. They knew better than God. They wanted meat.

So God gave them their desire and sent the fowls to the Israelites, and Numbers records that "while the meat was still between their teeth, before it was chewed," God killed them.[13] One of the worst things that can happen to you is to get what you want. I believe God is saying to America,

"How much corruption will you endure before you say 'Enough is enough'? How long will you endure evil under the banner of 'tolerance'? How long before you cry out for a revival of righteousness?"

The Israelites' story is the story of America. Our founding pilgrim fathers prayed for God's blessing. They stamped "In God We Trust" on their money. They declared a day of Thanksgiving as a national holiday so their children and grandchildren for generations would know what God had done for them. Harvard University was built by Puritans to educate their ministers to preach the gospel. Every school day began with a moment of prayer. Every session of Congress began with a prayer. And God blessed America with unprecedented prosperity and freedom. American cars filled the highways of Europe, Asia, and South America. Students came from every country to gain the prestige of a diploma from an American university. American medicine was the envy of the world. Our industrial power reached a crescendo during World War II, burying Hitler's Nazis. Our farms prospered. America was feeding the world with its leftovers.

But in our power, in our strength, we grew proud and godless. We chose hedonism, humanism, and paganism as our new gods. It was not just a calculated decision of Hollywood. Born-again Christians voted by marching off to every *Friday the 13th* movie that came out. Our habits and tastes drove the machine. We chose pornography and promiscuity. We chose materialism and greed and selfishness that led to abortion and incest. In our permissiveness we created the vacuum for an aggressive, man-hating, lesbian-run, feminist movement. We wanted our children to like us, so we abandoned God's plan for the family and gave them what they wanted, and a savage, virulent form of teenage violence resulted.

The Bible is very clear. The Bible reminds us that we are not a part of this world. 1 John 2:15 warns "Do not love the world or the things in the world." Even so, we sought the world's opinion and favor more than the favor of our own Creator. We tried to please the trendy appetites of a jaded and corrupt crowd of journalists. We sought the favor of an arrogant, godless, new breed of academia. Just as Satan used God's words to tempt Eve and to tempt Jesus, we used God's words to justify our compromises with a growing secular society. After all, the Bible says to live in peace. We showed the world that we weren't intolerant, Neanderthal, Christian cavemen. We could be "liberal." We voted in the governments that appointed anti-God judges. We voted in anti-God school boards and sat at home when they held their meetings. We fed the monster, and today we are its prisoner!

God responds to our choice—not His choice, our choice. Do you want to know what God is doing in heaven right now? He's looking down at us asking, "I wonder just how much filth they'll accept before they answer the wake-up call?"

Before pleading with God for intervention we must ask ourselves what we are doing to change things. We can fight back. We can make a difference. As good stewards do we exercise our right to vote? Do we petition government? How can we criticize if we have not confronted? You say, "Well, what good will writing a letter do?" But our responsibility is to do our part, and the Bible teaches confrontation. The government is responsible before God for its reaction.

Our church members in San Antonio and ministry partners across the nation have taken the lead on many issues. In early 1994 we issued a call to block proposed EEOC guidelines that would have prohibited workers from wearing religious jewelry or having a Bible on their desks. Within weeks we had delivered over 83,500 "Petitions of Outrage" to Senators Bob Dole (Republican) and Howell Heflin (Democrat) on Capitol Hill. As a result of our Washington meetings, Congress passed a "Sense of the Senate" resolution telling the federal bureaucrats to remove religion as a category covered by the proposed regulations.

The godless legislation died in the birth canal because the righteous stood up and spoke up. The Bible says: "Let the redeemed of the LORD say so"![14]

We are Americans! Heirs to pilgrim pioneers who looked to this land as a haven for freedom of worship. Heirs to founding fathers whose dreams will die if we give up. We must participate! And we must vote for the things that matter most, the character and integrity of the candidates. "Those who forsake the law praise the wicked, / But such as keep the law contend with them."[15] We are in a war for the soul of this nation. Don't expect to be liked. Jesus said, "You will be despised by all men for my sake." Don't expect to get justice in the enemy's court. Don't expect to be praised in the enemy's newspapers. The future of America, of our children and grandchildren, is at stake and the price is freedom. It is time for God's people to stand up. It is time for God's people to speak up, to "contend" with the wicked. But be warned, the clock is ticking. It is late in the battle. This one will never be won by ballots alone. It will take a miracle.

Can we take America back? The answer is yes!

How? Through the power of prayer that God will send a mighty revival of righteousness to America—a revival of evangelism, traditional family values, morality, integrity, work ethic, and individual responsibility.

Take Our Country Back

I recently met with a born-again Christian who served two presidents of the United States. He worked on the White House senior staff, saw the president almost daily, and sometimes sat in on meetings with heads of state. "At first I saw Christian activism as the only solution," he told me. "But after watching how things work, I quickly realized that running a government was not that much different from running a family. Prayer is often more powerful than anything you can say or do."

The Bible echoes the wisdom of this statement:

- "Call to Me, and I will answer you, and show you great and mighty things, which you do not know."[16]
- "You do not have because you do not ask."[17]

The initiative rests with us, not with God. "Whatever you bind on earth will be bound in heaven, and whatever you loose on earth will be loosed in heaven."[18] I repeat, the initiative rests with us. Our prayers on earth determine what God will do in heaven. Authority is given to be used, and the church has the power of His name, His blood, and His Word. Jesus said to his disciples, "Behold, I give you the authority to trample on serpents and scorpions, and over all the power of the enemy, and nothing shall by any means hurt you."[19] We are told by the prophets and by Jesus that we have the power to go directly to Almighty God and that He will give us the desires of our hearts. Now that's power! But we must use it.

America's future is not in the hands of the ungodly, it is in the hands of God's children. It is up to us to seek God's help. "And you shall be to Me a kingdom of priests and a holy nation.' These are the words which you shall speak to the children of Israel."[20]

When Nehemiah, cupbearer to King Xerxes, heard about the destruction of Jerusalem, he fell on his face before God and wept. He didn't apply for a government grant. He didn't seek an audience with the king. He understood how spiritual power works. He placed his need before the One who has all power in heaven and in earth and cried out to God for Jerusalem.

The king asked Nehemiah, "How are you? You look sick." Nehemiah told the king his burden for Jerusalem and the king said, "I'll give you the timber, the money, and the time to go and rebuild the walls." One man, one prayer, and God moved a king's heart like water. That one prayer reshaped history.

When Israel was besieged by the vast Assyrian armies, the prayer of Hezekiah changed the course of battle. The angel of the Lord walked through the Assyrian camp and slew the thousands of men who the day before had openly mocked the God of Israel. He smote the sentries at their posts. He smote the officers as they rehearsed their battle plans and the rank and file as they slept in their tents. Suddenly and swiftly, the angel of the Lord moved through that camp leaving 185,000 dead Assyrians in his wake, and Israel was delivered from certain annihilation. Why? Because one man prayed one prayer and God answered him. One man's prayer shaped history. Now that's power!

And modern church history is filled with the same kinds of stories. Just after World War II, Joseph Stalin revealed to a few trusted staffers that he was going to execute the Jews of Russia. When word eventually leaked out of the country, the believers in England began to fast and pray for God to save the Jews. At the end of the twelfth day, Stalin had a brain hemorrhage. Sixteen doctors worked to no avail; he died and the Jews were saved. There is the power of prayer!

Ask yourself, if the prayer of one man like Hezekiah or Nehemiah can make a difference, what would happen if thousands of American Christians began praying for a revival of righteousness in our country? Prayer is the most powerful tool we have; it is our direct link to God. It is "access." Understand, God is not a genie in a bottle. He cannot be sent forth to run our errands or make our fantasies come true. But prayer does release His power on our enemies, our accusers, our sick bodies, or on the Prince of Darkness. But as powerful as God is, He cannot answer prayers that are not prayed.

Do you love America? Pray! Do you love your children? Pray! We must accept this responsibility or we will suffer the consequences.

When the crisis was upon us in the 1960s, thousands of

Christians prayed and fasted and for a brief time the drift away from God was stemmed. God is waiting for the church of the twenty-first century to answer His wake-up call. He is waiting for us once more to take a stand against evil with prayer and fasting. He has given us the awesome opportunity to talk to Him face-to-face. The veil in the temple has been ripped from top to bottom. We have the power to take America back to God and to goodness in these latter days.

Let's do it! If not now, when? If not you, who?

Chapter Five

America
Under a Curse

For years, preachers have warned from their pulpits that America is heading toward the judgment of God. According to the Bible it is already here, and I am going to show you why that's true and how that judgment is already at work in this country.

With God there are only two choices. Either we live under His blessing or we live under His curse. Incidentally, that choice is ours. God's blessings come from obedience to His Word. His curse comes from disobedience.

The Bible teaches that curses are very real. They can follow a person or a nation for generations, finally breaking them spiritually. Proverbs 26:2 says, "Like a flitting sparrow, like a flying swallow, / So a curse without cause shall not alight." When someone speaks a curse against you and you are not protected by the blood of Christ, that curse will stick. It can follow you and your family for generations.

The "Genesis curse" is an example of a curse that plagues all mankind. When Adam and Eve sinned by partaking of the forbidden fruit, God spoke the curse into existence. God cursed the ground, the woman, the man, the serpent, and Satan. It was a curse that changed mankind forever.

The ground was cursed so that it produced thorns and thistles, weeds and crabgrass—and that curse exists to this day. In spite of our ability to attack weeds with powerful chemicals and John Deere tractors, the tares are still with us because of the Genesis curse.

The woman was cursed with the pain of childbearing and monthly menstruation. And she still is.

The man was cursed so that he had to earn his living by the sweat of his brow. And he still has to. All because Adam ate that wretched apple. I'm going to kick his shins the first thing I do when I get to heaven.

The serpent was cursed in that it had to crawl on its belly in the dust from that day forward. When weeds no longer grow, when women no longer have pain in childbirth, when men no longer work to make a living, and when snakes stop crawling, the curse will cease. Until then curses are very real!

Christians who believe that such curses cannot be personalized should consider the biblical account of Jacob, who unknowingly destroyed his own wife Rachel. Jacob informed his wives Rachel and Leah that they were leaving to go to the Promised Land. Unknown to Jacob, Rachel took the idols of her pagan father, Laban, with her. When Laban discovered they were missing, he pursued them, catching up to them in three days.

Laban accused Jacob, saying, "You have stolen my idols!"

Jacob, believing Laban was tricking him to get him to return, spoke a curse: "If any one of my servants has taken your idols, let him or her die."[1] One year later, his own young wife Rachel died in childbirth.

And that's far from the only illustration of curses in the Bible. Joshua also invoked a curse. After destroying the city of Jericho, Joshua made a bold announcement. "Cursed be the man before the LORD who rises up and builds this city Jericho; he shall lay its foundation with his firstborn, and with his youngest he shall set up its gates."[2] Hundreds of years later, as recorded in 1 Kings 16:34, a man by the name of Hiel attempted to rebuild the city of Jericho. Just as Joshua had prophesied, the man's oldest and youngest sons died. Has it happened since? Yes. When I visited Israel a few years ago, the guide told our group that in the 1960s a man tried to rebuild Jericho as a tourist attraction. When he started, his oldest son died instantly and mysteriously. According to the guide, the man immediately stopped work on the cursed city. Had he continued, his youngest son would have also died. I repeat, curses are very real!

Behind every curse is a cause. Anti-Semitism is an example. In Genesis 12:3, God says to Abraham, "I will bless those who bless you, / And I will curse him who curses you; / And in you all the families of the earth shall be blessed."

It is a historical fact that the nations of the world have been blessed through the Jewish people. Jesus said, "Salvation is of the Jews."[3] The Jewish people gave Christianity the patriarchs—Abraham, Isaac, and Jacob. The Jewish people gave us the prophets—Daniel, Ezekiel, Jeremiah, and Isaiah. There is not a Baptist in the bunch. Contrary to what most Renaissance artists depict, Mary, the mother of Jesus, is not an Italian. Mary, Joseph, Jesus, the first family, they are all Jewish. Almost every word in the Bible was written by Jewish hands. I believe that is why Satan hates the Jewish people so intently. They produced the Word of God, and they produced the Son of God that broke Satan's hold over humanity. I believe that anti-Semitism is a demonic spirit born in the bowels of hell to retaliate against the Jewish people for the good things they have done to bring the light of God to humanity.

It's time for Christians to stop praising the dead Jews of the past, such as Abraham, Isaac, and Jacob, while hating the Goldbergs across the street. The Jews are the seed of Abraham, and God loves them. They are the apple of God's eye, and they are the family of God. If you bless them, God will bless you. And if you curse them, the judgment of God will come upon you.

The simple fact is, what you do to others, God will do exactly to you. Pharaoh, who drowned the Jewish babies at the time of Moses' birth, was later drowned by the hand of God. Haman, who long before Hitler planned the genocide of the Jewish people and built the special gallows to execute the Jewish leader Mordecai, later met his own fate on those very gallows—and so did his family. Exactly what he had intended for the Jewish people happened to him!

The Judgment of God on an Individual

A litany of curses plague individual Americans. A father may place his family under a curse by his dishonest business deals. Proverbs warns: "Whoever rewards evil for good, / Evil will not depart from his house."[4]

We have seen that curse at work right before our eyes in American history, where several very rich and powerful tycoons made their fortunes illicitly or by grinding the faces of the poor, only to see bizarre accidents cut short the lives of their famous and powerful children. The Bible teaches that such curses follow four generations—160 years. We have seen the troubles spill over to the third generation of some of these great families. Father, if you are making your living by misrepresentation, inside deals, or cheating the public, stop it! You are placing your family under a curse from God. It will stay there for 160 years! Nothing can remove that curse—other than repentance and restitution.

A curse also comes with dishonoring your father and mother. Let me tell you flatly and emphatically that millions of American young people are under this curse of God for their rebellion against their parents. The Bible clearly states that you shall honor your father and your mother "that your days may be long upon the land which the LORD your God is giving you."[5] Some earthly parents seem to tolerate, even invite, abuse and neglect, but your heavenly Father is watching, and He is not amused. He will not allow it. Understand this, He will have the last word.

He controls your breath and your heartbeat, and He has the muscle to control you.

The Bible teaches that there is a curse on anyone who commits incest. Deuteronomy states, "Cursed is the one who lies with his father's wife."[6] Incest brings God's judgment on an individual. And, because about 25 percent of all American girls are victims of incest, many of America's fathers are under the curse of God. Father, if you are sexually abusing your daughter, you may have your wife intimidated, and you may have your daughter terrorized, but God is not shaking. Don't look back. The judgment of God is right behind you. The only reason He hasn't smashed you like a peanut under the hoof of an elephant is because of His mercy. Do not overstep the bounds of His mercy. God has the power to take you out!

The prophet Zechariah speaks about a curse that afflicts millions of people all over the earth. "Every thief shall be expelled."[7] Do you steal from your employer? God has cut you off. Do you steal from the department store? God has cut you off. When you watch riots unfold on the evening news and you see streams of people hauling merchandise out of stores, remember, God has cut off each and every one of those people. And until those people take it back or make it right, the judgment of God will follow their families for 160 years. If you have stolen, take it back. Make it right.

Perhaps the most common curse on man comes from violating the first commandment: "You shall have no other gods before Me." Many people can quote this Scripture, but most are unaware of its companion text. Carefully read the words. "You shall not make for yourself a carved image—any likeness of anything that is in heaven above, or that is in the earth beneath, or that is in the water under the earth; you shall not bow down to them nor serve them. For I, the LORD your God, am a jealous God, visiting the iniquity of the fathers upon the children to the third and fourth generations of those who hate Me."[8] That's 160 years. God is saying, if you have a statue of any other god in your home, then you hate Me. Jesus said the same thing when he told the disciples, "He who is not with Me is against Me."[9] You cannot be on both sides of this issue.

The fact is this: False gods empower curses. Statues, crystals, horoscopes, satanism, witchcraft, mind control, and Eastern philosophies are all among the spiritual adulteries that bring the wrath and judgment of God. And if you put that statue on the dashboard of your car or on your charm bracelet or around your neck, then you are living in what the Bible calls spiritual adultery. And it brings the wrath of God instantly and permanently, until it is repented of and broken in the supernatural. This doesn't just happen sometimes. It happens every time. In their search for truth, the misguided have turned toward evil and they are, by their own hands, falling subject to the curse of God. Sadly, it subjects not only themselves but their loved ones, the future generations of their family, and their nation as well.

There was a woman in my church years ago who was experiencing a living nightmare. Everything she attempted to achieve would suddenly collapse. She said to me, "I think I'm jinxed. Would you come to my house and see what the Lord would tell you?"

I visited the woman at home one day and saw that the entire inside of the home was filled with statues of dragons. The Bible says that Satan is "that old dragon, the devil." I told her, "Lady, it is my belief that if you recognize Satan in any way, with statues, with the occult, with witchcraft, with mind control, with Eastern philosophies, then Satan has a legal right for his demon powers to live in your house. He has a legal right to claim your life, your soul, and your children. And I recommend that you throw them out, and do it now."

She did, and I can tell you that her life turned around immediately and permanently, because she obeyed the Word of God. It is not good enough to recognize God as the first and greatest God. You must recognize Him as the only God. Isaiah 45:21 says, "There is no other God besides Me." Jesus cannot be placed on your mantel among your idols. Jesus is either the Lord of all or He's not Lord at all.

Remember, God plays hardball. He doesn't sit up in heaven saying, "Oh, my goodness, they're not obeying Me." He controls your breath. He controls your heartbeat. God says, "Hey, I can't get his attention." So He shuts off your business; He sees to it that your new car breaks down once a week; He has your mother-in-law move in with you; He has the IRS call and say, "We'd like to inspect your tax records all the way back to the Civil War."

He puts you in the hospital in a full body cast with your feet and arms suspended in all four directions and you ask, "I wonder if God is trying to speak to me?" Why yes, Bubba, He is.

The Curse on America

As a nation, America is under the curse of God, even now. Look at the Scriptures and decide for yourself. The stand we have taken on abortion, the stand we have taken against God in our classrooms, just may have sealed our doom. Deuteronomy 30:19 says, "I call heaven and earth as witnesses today against you, that I have set before you life and death, blessing and cursing; therefore choose life, that both you and your descendants may live." Only through God's power and anointing touch can America be saved.

A couple of years ago, *USA Today* printed a front-page picture of five young men, all of them carrying high-powered rifles, pistols, and bullet belts. The accompanying article described how those young men were going to burn down the city of Los Angeles if a high-profile court case didn't turn out the way they wanted. City officials were aghast. Newspaper columnists speculated about the social conditions that spawn such violence.

The fact is that those young men came from America's public schools where secular humanism has taught them there is no such thing as right and wrong. It has taught that there are no moral absolutes. It has taught young people to do their own thing. And what is the practical expression of this philosophy? If it feels good, do it. If you want it, steal it. If someone resists you, shoot them.

America's youth are in schools where they get grades they do not work for from teachers who are afraid to discipline them or simply do not care. This is a blackboard jungle ruled by guns, knives, and fear, an environment of absolute rebellion against authority. Our students are America's new, young barbarians. And this is the generation of the future.

David wrote in Psalm 50:22, "Now consider this, you who forget God, / Lest I tear you in pieces, / And there be none to deliver." I assure you, that stands for America today.

The spirit of this new generation is born in the movie and television studios of Hollywood where macho violence is romanticized, Satan is lord, and witchcraft is the source of power. America's new generation has seen Jesus Christ portrayed as a demonized, lust-driven, spineless buffoon in such movies as *The Last Temptation of Christ*. Hollywood continues to show its hatred toward God, because Hollywood hates Christianity. It is an industry of gluttony motivated by money and pride, a cancer that eats at the soul of the country.

During the release of *The Last Temptation of Christ*, 25,000 Christians gathered in front of Universal Studios to protest the sacrilege. The movie moguls of America and their media stooges categorized these Bible-carrying demonstrators as "the lunatic fringe of religious fanaticism" or "right-wing extremists."

The *Detroit Free Press* called these Christians "the

American ignoramus faction, fun-loathing people full of self-righteous bile."

In contrast, consider how Hollywood and the secular media responded to concerns by animal rights activists. In 1990, such activists demanded that Disney Studios eliminate a scene from the movie *White Fang*. They considered the movie to have an antiwolf theme. The film showed a man being attacked by an unprovoked wolf. Activists claimed that this would never happen, that there was no scientific evidence to support that a wolf would behave in such a way. It is much more popular in America to be anti-Christ, than to be antiwolf.

In the movie *Cape Fear*, a vicious rapist-murderer is portrayed as a Pentecostal Christian. He has tattoos of the cross on his body and Scripture verses on his arm. As he rapes his victims, he asks them, "Are you ready to be born again and speak in tongues?" What do you think would happen if any other minority group in America was so reviled and miscast? The makers of such a movie would be swimming in lawsuits and making mountains of apologies and settlements. Christianity bashing, however, is considered an art form in Hollywood.

Christianity and morality are not only losing in the movie theaters, the same theme is now running through American popular music. The young "gangstas" who have taken over America's streets use violent rap music for their inspiration. Time-Warner produced the hit song "Cop Killer," which encouraged a New York youth to murder a policeman in cold blood. Rock music, in general, often promotes drug abuse, satanism, rape, murder, and suicide.

In his insightful book *Cults That Kill*, Larry Kahaner tells the story of a sixteen-year-old boy who attended a rock concert, received a message from Satan, and took an oath to carry it out. When he returned home, he murdered his father and mother, and with their blood wrote "Hail Satan" on the wall.[10] This is today's America. "The wicked shall be turned into hell, / And all the nations that forget God."[11]

Murders have now surpassed automobile accidents as the number one cause of death among young blacks. The majority of these murders are black on black. Most of these new killers are the products of fatherless homes. Twenty-five percent of America's adult black male population is in prison or on parole. And of all the fathers, both black and white, who are present in their homes, they will average only forty-five seconds a day talking with their children.

Many parents who don't have time for their children simply place them in front of the television set. The average child will spend more than forty-eight hours a week watching television. It has become the great baby-sitter, teacher, and brainwasher. The outcome is a generation filled with violence, lust, greed, witchcraft, and fear. Meanwhile, American parents ignorantly sit by and let strangers teach and control their children, every single day, through the medium of television. The time has come for Christian parents to become the stewards and the watchdogs of their children. If a television program does not glorify God and the purity of His holiness, turn it off. At least for now, we have that much power over our enemies.

The Curse on the Home

In the remarkable twenty-eighth chapter of Deuteronomy, Moses outlines the curses God will place on a people or nation disobedient to Him. It is a frightening litany of evil that begins in the home, moves to the city, and eventually affects the economy of a whole nation.

First, Moses warns, "You shall betroth a wife, but another man will lie with her; you shall build a house, but you shall not dwell in it." This speaks of the destruction of the traditional family. "Another man shall lie with her" speaks of rampant adultery followed by divorce. Children are scarred and scattered like straw in a tornado.

The future of America is not going to be determined by

politicians in Washington, D.C., but by godly parents teaching their children the precepts of the Word of God. Our children must know the teachings of righteousness, truth, and integrity before they can apply these principles to their lives and country. This is the foundation upon which America can stand.

The Curse Against People

Second, in describing God's curse against a disobedient people, Moses warns, "Your sons and your daughters shall be given to another people, and your eyes shall look and fail with longing for them all day long."

Does America enjoy her children? With few exceptions, the answer is no. Four thousand of them are murdered every day in America's abortion mills. *Home Alone* is not just a movie, it is a subconscious parody of a national tragedy. Child abuse is a national shame. Vile, tear-jerking, child pornography is a vicious, multibillion-dollar industry in our country. Meanwhile, nude pictures of children in various adult poses are subsidized by grants offered by our government and labeled by the media as "art." Your tax dollars at work!

Do we enjoy our children? Ask the thousands of missing children whose faces appear on milk cartons that question. It seems that if a child escapes the abortionist's knife, a host of other evils are anxiously awaiting him or her: drug pushers, molesters, satanists, homosexuals, feminists. Even our government awaits them, dictating the humanistic teachings in our schools. Forty years ago people did not believe in a real devil. Today, hundreds of thousands openly worship Satan, murdering children in the sacrificial honor of his name. Do we love our children? I think the answer is clear. We will explore the curse on the home more fully in Chapter 6, "Witchcraft in Your House."

The Curses of the Cities

Third, in describing God's curse against a disobedient people, Moses declared, "Cursed shall you be in the city."

Take a good look at the cities of America. Riot-stricken Los Angeles is a time bomb waiting to explode. Gangs rule the inner city. New York's boroughs are still controlled by organized crime, either the mafia or the new Chinese syndicates. San Francisco is governed by homosexuals. Las Vegas is controlled by the lords of casinos. And, in New Orleans, prostitution rackets have taken over the city. America's cities are suffering under the load of lawlessness. The jails are flooded with criminals. Murderers and rapists roam free because of early paroles. You know that justice has been turned upside-down when a mugger can hit you in the head with a pipe and be out of jail before you are out of the hospital.

We sing about an America that is "the land of the free and the home of the brave"; meanwhile, we live behind locked doors and barred windows. Our homes are equipped with state-of-the-art burglar alarm systems. Attack dogs are straining at their leashes. Ladies carry mace on their key chains. Doors have multiple locks. Guns are cocked and loaded. Burglar bars are over our windows. We, the tax-paying citizens of America, are prisoners in our own homes and victims on our own streets. It you think America is free, you are deceived.

The Economic Curse

Fourth, Moses warns, "Cursed shall be your basket and your kneading bowl." He is, of course, referring to the economy.

And exactly how is America's economy doing?

- The United States of America is nearly $5 trillion in

debt, and that debt continues to race out of sight at a rate of about $1 billion a day.

- Just to pay the interest, the national debt needs all of the taxes collected from every citizen west of the Mississippi.
- The federal debt currently stands close to $18,000 for every man, woman, and child in America.
- One leading economist has warned that "we are racing toward a bankruptcy that will place our children and our grandchildren in an economic slavery to foreign countries. America is blindly moving toward becoming a third-world economy, and there will be no recovery simply because we have spent beyond our means for forty years."
- In the insightful book *Banking on the Brink*, one leading economist has predicted that more than two thousand banks in America will soon take a dive.[12] Banks don't fail, they merge. Notice how we now have more megabanks and fewer smaller ones? This means there is more wealth in the hands of fewer people, which was a major cause of the crash of 1929.
- The savings and loan crashes will eventually cost the coming generation $1.3 trillion plus interest.
- A pension crisis is now hanging over the heads of American workers, the result of greedy, get-rich-quick, junk-bond investments in the market. Most of it is paper and now worthless.

Just on the horizon is the greatest economic crisis we have faced since independence. For years, the federal government has been raiding the social security fund. They have taken billions of dollars from this trust, replacing it with IOUs worth only what the government is willing and able to pay. In the past decade, that great resource has been bled dry, and no one knows how to put it back in order.

One so-called solution is to extend the retirement age to seventy and pocket the money that should go to retirees. Another is to demand a forfeit of benefits to all who are entitled to social security but have enough money to live on. The government, of course, will decide what constitutes enough.

The result is that the richest country in the world now faces an uncertain financial future simply because our government couldn't control its own spending. During the Reagan administration the Grace Commission conducted an in-depth study to show how America spends its money. It found that for every dollar in new taxes, the government spends $1.80.

The economic options for America are few. Someday in the near future, an American president will be faced with just two choices: Either he will declare America bankrupt, or he will instruct the Treasury Department to print more money, launching a round of hyperinflation that will destroy our economy.

The Curse of the Plagues

Fifth, in describing God's curse against a disobedient nation, Moses warns, "The Lord will make the plague cling to you until He has consumed you."

AIDS is one such incurable plague. No matter what new medical breakthroughs come forth, AIDS is still as deadly as ever. Everyone who contracts AIDS dies. And the fact is, there are tens of thousands of silent carriers of the disease in America.

But there is good news. Every born-again believer who has been washed in the blood of Jesus Christ has a life insurance policy that no one can take away. Psalm 91:10 states, "No evil shall befall you, / Nor shall any plague come near your dwelling." There is hope. AIDS is no match for the power of Almighty God.

Just as huge portions of the population have succumbed to AIDS, many more have died on the battlefields fighting for America. Examine what Moses said in Deuteronomy 28:25, "The LORD will cause you to be defeated before your enemies; you shall go out one way against them and flee seven ways before them." God judges and destroys a nation for its sin. Israel lost the battle at Ai because of the sin of one of its sons. In our lifetime we have seen weak enemies, without international diplomatic clout, without great financial resources, without advanced weapons, defeat America. We lost in Korea. We lost in Vietnam.

Victory even eluded America in Desert Storm. Even after the triumphant destruction of our enemy with overwhelming weapons and overwhelming odds, he has crawled right out from underneath a rock to snub us again. What changed with the billions of dollars spent on Desert Storm? Saddam Hussein is still in power. He still works toward nuclear capability. He still threatens Israel. He still intends to conquer Jerusalem. And the people we went to help, the Kuwaitis, see us as such an unreliable partner they are limiting our ground troops in their country lest they provoke Hussein.

The Curse of Servitude

Sixth, Moses warns the disobedient nation that "the alien who is among you shall rise higher and higher above you, and you shall come down lower and lower." Hosea wrote, "Aliens have devoured his strength, / But he does not know it."[13]

Foreign countries are currently buying our land, businesses, real estate, and industry out from under our feet. The foreigners are not to blame, but whose financial interest do you think they are going to protect? Our national leaders tell us that economic time bombs have been planted on Wall Street. Other nations have so much interest in stocks and bonds, they hold America hostage. If Congress does not vote the way these nations want, they threaten to pull out. The result could be disastrous. Our economy would literally plunge and collapse overnight. We are not in control of America's economic destiny. Other countries are.

Solutions do not rest with our Congress or national leaders; they rest solely with the church of Jesus Christ. The Bible tells us in 2 Chronicles 7:14, "If My people who are called by My name will humble themselves, and pray and seek My face, and turn from their wicked ways, then I will hear from heaven, and will forgive their sin and heal their land." This is our call to return to absolute loyalty to the Word of God. It is our only hope to take our country out of the hands of the foreign powers holding us hostage.

In our calling to absolute loyalty to God, we must, as a nation, stand up for that which is right and clearly oppose the wrong. Remember, God is watching. He is the only one to fear.

When the president stands before the nation and calls for homosexuals to be legally acknowledged by allowing them into the military, we as a nation must rise up and let him hear our voices: "No! While we have great love for every single human being, that behavior is an abomination under the Word of God. We will not accept it!"

When Hillary Clinton calls for children to have the right to sue their parents for divorce, we must let her hear our voices: "No! Children, honor your father and your mother, that your days may be long upon the earth."

If the welfare department continues to tax men who work and then give money to men who can work but will not work, we must take a stand against it and let the nation's leaders hear our voices: "No! The man who does not work will not eat."

We must make the Word of God known to our children, known to our neighbors, and known to our politicians; it is our only hope. If we are ridiculed and demeaned, so what? Jesus was ridiculed and demeaned. If we are outlawed and imprisoned, so what? David was an outlaw. Peter and Paul were both imprisoned.

Remember, the basis of either a blessing or a curse is obedience to God's Word. Has America been obedient? The answer is obvious. America's number one problem is not the economy, it is not the crime rate, it is not our corrupt politicians. America's number one problem is the judgment of God, because God hates sin and America is saturated with it.

The solution is not in the hands of our politicians, our Congress, our government. The only solution is in the hands of every believing Christian who has the faith to pray and believe that once again God will bless America and raise her up as a testimony to the world. God is the only one who can save us. In Genesis, He scooped up a handful of dirt and breathed into it, and man became a living soul. The God that we serve is the Creator, our Lord, and our Master. He is the only God, and He is our only salvation.

Deception in the Home

Chapter Six

Witchcraft in Your House

Deception in government and public life cannot hold a candle to the witchcraft that has invaded the homes of America in these latter days. Divorce is now epidemic and seen as a cure-all to any marital conflict. Some new state laws make it easier to get a divorce than a driver's license. Feminists are trying to tell us that there is little difference between the sexes. Fashion designers encourage boys to carry purses and girls to carry footballs. Biblical teaching about marriage and the home, which has been an essential part of Western civilization since Constantine, has been unceremoniously dropped.

The spin-off has been catastrophic. America is engulfed in a tidal wave of venereal disease, juvenile crime, and a new category of poverty: single-parent homes. For the last thirty years, America has been in a moral free fall.

Here is the irony. While screamers in Hollywood complain that Christian political activists are trying to ram their theology down the throats of society by legislating morality, they, themselves, have rammed their godless philosophy down the throats of American youth. Seeking to justify their own perverse lifestyle, the entertainment industry has glamorized and promoted the downfall of the American marriage. In motion pictures and television sitcoms, promiscuity and sex outside of marriage are romanticized with only token acknowledgment to the pain and consequences. Venereal disease is given a new designer name, STD, sexually transmitted disease. One young teenager said, "I think herpes is sexy." So rampant is America's abandonment of the monogamous relationship that new strains of incurable genital warts have started appearing.

I've got news for you. Divorce is not the solution. Sociologist Lenore Whitesman states that the average woman's standard of living will decline 73 percent within the first year of her divorce. Contrary to what you've seen from Hollywood, it is not a passport to paradise. It is a ticket to a living hell. The survival rate of second marriages is a mere 30 percent. The survival rate of a third marriage is 15 percent, and it goes downhill from there.

Diane Medved, author of *The Case Against Divorce*, offers clear and convincing evidence that the aftereffects of divorce are almost always worse than the original problem. Former marriage partners and children are often damaged physically as well as emotionally. The pain lingers for years. Most counselors have learned that the initial, conscious level of pain will last at least half the time of the relationship, which means that the breakup of a twenty-year marriage will require at least ten years to heal. But even then, some scars will linger.[1]

Make no mistake about it, your marriage, your children, and family life in America are under attack in these latter days. Values and principles that have guided civilized man for centuries are coming unraveled by the minute. You can't hide from it. You can't wish it away. And you certainly can't afford to be lulled into a catatonic, self-deceived state of ignorance. Survival is dependent on knowing and understanding the events swirling around you and then acting according to the emergency plan laid out in Scripture.

The American Family

What is a family? The word has been used by so many groups to mean so many things that it has lost the essence of its meaning. In the movie *The Godfather,* Vito Corleone describes his band of cold-blooded Mafia murderers as "family." When Charles Manson was on his murdering spree through southern California, leaving the blood of movie stars splattered on the walls with gory graffiti, he called the mindless group of riffraff who followed him his "family." The Atlanta Braves call themselves a "family." In churches across the world we sing songs about "the family of God."

Today, social revisionists in America are trying to redefine the word *family* to mean "two consenting adults and their children." There is a massive lobby with millions of dollars behind it. The reason? So homosexuals can live together, adopt children, earn same-sex benefits, and be socially acceptable. With superior earning power and no family to support, they can form political action committees, pass laws, control government, and throw preachers in jail for preaching the Word of God. But they are still not a family and never will be a family according to God's Word.

A family is not a house with a prestigious address. A roof will keep out the rain. Four walls will keep out the cold night wind. A floor will support the tottering steps of the infant or the aged. A door will welcome friends and keep out enemies. A fireplace will warm those who nestle close on a cold winter's night, but this is not a family.

A family is the picture of a mother cooking dinner for people she loves. A family is the laugh of a baby. It is the strength of the presence of the father. A family is the loving warmth of hearts, light from happy eyes, kindness, loyalty, and covenant love and demonstration. A family home should be the first school and the first church that a child ever attends. It is there that a child should learn to pray. It is there that a child should see from the father how to treat the mother. It is there a child should see from the mother how women relate to men. It is there, long before school begins, that a child should learn from his parents what is right and what is wrong.

Families are where you go for comfort when you are hungry or sick or when you have been battered and bruised by the world. Families open the very doors of heaven and heal you. They anoint your wounds with the oil of gladness and wrap their loving arms about you.

Families are where joy is shared. Your family will be delighted with your promotion on the job. They will be proud of you for making the honor roll in the public school. They will buy every newspaper on the rack when your name is in it as the high school football hero, debate star, cheerleader, or valedictorian.

Families are where children respect fathers and mothers. They're never called "old man" or "old lady." In advancing years, they're not shuffled to the sidelines to be ignored. Whether they are in wheelchairs or reclining on a couch too feeble to sit erectly, they are there because they belong.

Families are where children are considered the blessings of the Lord and not looked upon as an inconvenience to a precious career. Children are not considered detestable because they might destroy the high-school figure of the mother. They are angels unaware that God has sent into the care of a husband and wife for a very few days until they go into society to make their own contributions. Families are where the simplest food is good enough for kings because it has been earned with the sweat of an honest day's labor. That's family, and may God bless it and preserve it in these United States of America. Yet what occurred in the beginning, still occurs now.

What Occurred in the Beginning, Still Occurs

Genesis is called the book of beginnings. Everything God wanted to begin began in Genesis. The plan of salvation itself begins in Genesis. Satan also began his plan to destroy your home in Genesis. The book begins with a crisis between man and woman.

- In Genesis 1, the heavens and earth were created by the spoken Word of Almighty God.
- In Genesis 3, man rebelled against God's spoken Word. Satan deceived Adam and Eve, saying "Has God indeed said . . . ?"
- In Genesis 4, there is murder as Cain killed Abel.
- In Genesis 9, there is pornography.
- In Genesis 15, God gave Abraham a blood covenant for the Promised Land.
- In Genesis 16, there is adultery.
- In Genesis 19, there is homosexuality.
- In Genesis 34, there is fornication.
- In Genesis 38, there is incest and prostitution.
- In Genesis 39, there is the seduction of Joseph by Potiphar's wife.

Why is there such a conflict in the American home? Because Satan has been busy laying his plan to destroy you. Now, thousands of years after the experiences of Genesis, you go home, turn on the television, and the very same temptations come into your living room. There is the theme of man versus woman, of polygamy and pornography. There is adultery, fornication, homosexuality, incest, prostitution, and seduction. And you sit there and suck it all in. Dad, do you think that some lines written by Norman Lear, a man who is single-handedly trying to bring down family values in America, are going to edify your children? Mom, when you hear some television star rail against her husband with the most vindictive and vicious words imaginable, do you think that you are influenced?

You say, "Not me. I can censor all those thing in my mind. I know what I believe."

Let me tell you something. Big business doesn't pay a million dollars a minute to advertise if it doesn't have influence. Everything you and your family sees goes right into your little Univac. Click. It's in there. Jesus says that "a good man out of the good treasure of his heart brings forth good things."[2] How many abundant hours of television are in your subconscious? Compare it to the number of hours you spend reading the Bible with your family. Who is Lord of your home: the Holy Spirit or Hollywood?

The reason most American homes are breaking apart is because we have allowed our intellects, our emotions, and our spirits to be pickled and duped by a secular society that is doing nothing more than taking the seduction plan of Genesis, putting it into a Hollywood script, and pouring it out for America.

This book is a warning. Satan's desire is to destroy your family, your marriage, and your children. If you can't see it, then you are deceived. God's desire is that you be in health and prosper, spiritually and materially, and that you be filled with His Spirit.

I'm saying to you, in Jesus' name, generally the best thing on secular television is the knob that turns it off. Instead, turn on the Word of God and be filled with the Spirit. Drink in Living Water, not Hollywood's toxic waste.

And God Created Woman

The American church has done a disservice to the women of this nation because it has failed to portray the successful woman as a mother. Nothing on this earth is more honorable than being a godly mother. Though the press and the media applaud women who become bankers or judges or politicians, God's Word paints the portrait of a mother as the ultimate success story. Nothing is more praiseworthy. Nothing is more holy. Nothing is more lofty. God's top priority for women is to be mothers.

CEO of the Home

A mother is a chauffeur, a chef, a social director, a banker, a boss, and a zookeeper. In motherhood, a woman is fulfilling one of her God-given reasons for existence.

God's command is to be fruitful and multiply.[3] When you reject God's plan, you reject truth. And when you reject truth, all that is left is a lie. God's Word is very clear: If you obey the Lord, you prosper. If you rebel against God, the judgment of God comes against you. I am telling you, the judgment of God is not coming to America; the judgment of God is on America right now. And it is manifest in this single command: Be fruitful and multiply.

I hear ladies saying, "Well, I'd like to have a baby, but you know this is a very troubled time to bring a new child into the world." When Moses was born, the government was drowning all male Hebrew babies in the Nile River. When Jesus Christ was born, King Herod was sending out his elite palace guard to butcher every child within a ten-mile radius of his birthplace. For a sinful world in rebellion against God, it is always a dangerous and troubled time to give birth to an innocent and vulnerable child. Quit worrying about Washington's policies and start thinking about God's policies. Live according to God's policies, and you shall "prosper and be in health."

Motherhood

What does God expect from the mother? Proverbs 31 paints the portrait.

She is virtuous. Proverbs asks, "Who can find a virtuous wife. For her worth is far above rubies." Ladies, teenage daughters, your virtue makes you priceless. Teenage girl, if you're dating some hormone hurricane who has the urge to merge, and if he says something stupid like, "Honey, to prove your love to me, let's go all the way," you slap his face until his ears ring like chapel bells on a cold Christmas morning. Then get out of his car and take a cab home.

There's a difference between love and lust, and many people don't know the difference, so let me give you three quick lessons:

1. Love gives. Lust takes.
2. Love gives a ring. Lust gives a condom.
3. Love is patient, kind, and understanding. Lust is rude, crude, and very demanding.

You ought to write that down somewhere until you can say it in your sleep.

She provides food. She "rises while it is yet night, / And provides food for her household." She knows how to make something for supper other than reservations.

She is a worker. "Her lamp does not go out by night." She gets up early. She stays up late. She's not sitting on a couch eating bonbons and watching Sally Jesse Raphael.

She is discreet. "On her tongue is the law of kindness." She's not some party girl from an Ivy League school who can outcuss a Marine drill sergeant. Some people make you glad when they come. Other people make you glad when they go. You're always glad to meet the woman of Proverbs 31. She is married and a mother, in that order, something America's young people need to get in their minds.

She is submitted to her own husband. It's taught in the Old Testament. It's taught in the New Testament. It's taught by Paul. It's taught by Peter. It isn't popular, but it is everywhere in the Bible—that submission thing.

That Submission Thing

Compare those famous verses in Ephesians 5:22–24 to what the Bible says in Colossians 3:18. "Wives, submit to your own husbands, as is fitting in the Lord." Look at the Bible record of trouble that started when a man submitted to the lead of his wife. Not to the need of his wife, but to the lead of his wife.

Adam listened to Eve, and God kicked them out of the Garden of Eden because he ate the forbidden fruit. It was God's intention for his human creation to enjoy the pleasures of the Garden of Eden. And no mosquitoes. But Adam took the fruit, and between the two of them they ate us out of house and home.

I came home one day after work and Diane was fixing dinner in the kitchen; so I just stood by talking about my day. "Here," she said, and she brought some food up to my mouth. "Eat this." Like some obedient beast, I ate it. "Now," she said, "see how easy that was?" All right, but I'm still going to kick Adam in the shins when I get to heaven.

Abraham also listened to his wife, Sarah. They had been trying to have children for years but Sarah was barren, so she said, "Go to my maid, Hagar, and have a baby with her."

Abraham said, "Sounds like the will of God to me." Zip . . . off to Hagar's tent. And pretty soon a bouncing baby boy arrives. The surrogate mother plan, however, doesn't make Sarah happy. Hagar gets haughty and flaunts her new status as mother of the heir, making Sarah's barrenness more painful than ever. But finally, a few years later, Sarah's dream comes true and she also has a son. Then Sarah decides that Hagar and her son should go away and that Abraham should be the one to kick them out. Abraham obeys. Hagar and her son, Abraham's firstborn, are ordered out into the wilderness.

Hagar almost died, but God was watching and always protects the innocent. The problem is, the boy Ishmael grew up to be the father of the Arabs. Sarah's baby was Isaac, the father of the Jews. What started out as a family feud six thousand years ago is now an international crisis in the Middle East. It happened because a man listened to his wife's command—not God's!

Women's liberation is not about equal pay for equal work. Women's liberation is about authority. It's about who is going to lead in the home and who is going to lead in the workplace. The greatest battle in the American home is the battle for authority. Who is the head of the house? One body with two heads is a freak. One family with two heads is a war zone.

Righteous authority is given by God to men to lead the home lovingly and for kings and all who are in authority to rule in government. God says, "I have given that righteous authority to Adam. It is his. He is the head of the house." Anyone who attacks the husband's authority is literally attacking God's plan. God operates through delegated authority, which is a righteous authority. In the home, God operates through the authority of the father. In the nation, He operates through governments, as outlined in the thirteenth chapter of Romans.

Unrighteous authority is given by Satan to rebel against God's plan for man. Everything Satan does is through unrighteous authority, and it is diametrically opposed to God's rule. Witchcraft is the method used to carry out Satan's unrighteous authority. The three manifestations of witchcraft are manipulation, intimidation, and domination.

Let me give you an example. The little lady of the house lets the man know that if he will do what she wants him to do, or if he will buy what she wants him to buy, the bedroom will come alive tonight. But if he doesn't, it will be as cold as an iceberg.

That's witchcraft, pure and simple. The Bible says, "The wife does not have authority over her own body, but the husband does."[4]

Women who control their house with bad moods are practicing witchcraft. Jezebel controlled Israel by manipulating Ahab through her moods. The Bible says there was never a woman on the face of the earth like Jezebel. I have heard husbands say, "I have to give in to my wife or she'll be angry for days." I want you to understand something. When you give in to that, you only feed it. It grows. It multiplies. You are not doing your wife a favor. In the long run you are only going to make her miserable. She is exhibiting a spirit of witchcraft, and if it works, she'll keep using it to dominate you. Stand up. You are the head of that house. Get out from under the bed and take charge.

Guilt is also the chief weapon of the manipulator. The wife says to the husband, "I just want to remind you that I almost died giving birth to your son." Of course the husband is now sixty-two years old, but she wants to remind him of that pain. "I married you when my mother said I shouldn't, bless her sacred memory. And ten years ago, you were late for supper, and don't you forget it." That is manipulation through guilt. That's witchcraft.

How do you break that cycle? It is not by evasion; witchcraft seeks to control without confrontation. The Bible says to confront, "speaking the truth in love."[5] So when you have a problem with your spouse, don't run away; look at the problem eyeball to eyeball and lovingly, with spiritual principles, resolve it.

Some wives will complain, "But I can't trust my husband's leadership. He doesn't make good decisions." He decided to marry you, didn't he?

Women and the Church

The Bible says in 1 Timothy 2:9 that women should "adorn themselves in modest apparel." What you wear says a lot about you. There have been books written on the subject. I have a psychology text in my office that says bizarre dress is a sign of being mentally disturbed. If that's true, half of America must be having a nervous breakdown!

Wife, according to the Word of God, your dress is to be modest. If you want people to treat you maturely as a human being with sensitivities, dreams, and hopes like anybody else, then dress like it. Modest apparel is more than good taste, it shows that you have some self-respect.

Likewise, in his letter to Timothy, Paul says that a woman should not be a showcase for her husband's wealth. She should not be a walking boutique of gold, pearls, and designer dresses. God is not crass. He has good taste. And

He is not nouveau riche. His wealth has been around for years. He wants to be proud of us, so He cares enough to teach us what to wear.

Paul's letter is very clear. The woman is not to have spiritual authority over a man. A pastor is someone with spiritual authority. To ordain a woman as a pastor over a man violates the very clear teaching of the apostle Paul. Ordaining women is not progress, it is contrary to the teaching and the preaching of God's Word. Yes, the lady can have a healing ministry. Yes, the lady can have a teaching ministry. Yes, the lady can work under her husband's authority. But she is not to be the pastor of the church. That is the teaching of the Word of God.

But why so strict? Why does Paul say that women must even be "silent in the church"?

In an orthodox synagogue, the men and women were separated. When Paul or anyone else was teaching, an aggressive woman would call over to her husband, "Hey Abe, what's he saying? Do you agree with that?"

Paul said, "Talk it over at home. I don't want the whole church service torn up by a family discussion."

In 1 Timothy the Bible gives clear instructions for widows. The Bible says that widows are to be honored, to be cared for, to be supported. But the Bible has some clear qualifiers. The widow must be sixty years of age. She must have been faithful to her husband. She must have trained her children well. She must have shown hospitality to the saints, helping those in trouble and devoting her life to good deeds. That's what constitutes a biblical widow. Somebody who lived her life down at the Crystal Pistol and now comes walking down the aisle to get saved and says "Take care of me" is not a biblical widow. That's not how it works. You invest your life in the kingdom of God, and then the kingdom of God takes care of you. That's how it works.

There's more. If a widow has children or grandchildren, those children should support her. Remember, the Bible says that anyone who does not provide for his own has abandoned the faith and is worse than an unbeliever.[6] It does not apply exclusively to men.

Chapters two and three of the book of Titus say that older women are to teach younger women "how to be sober, how to love their husbands, how to love their children, and how to be keepers of the home." Is that what young people are being taught in Christian homes today? No. Generally, the older women in the American home are saying, "Honey, if old meathead opens his mouth, you tell him, 'It's my way or the highway. Hit it.'"

We have a new generation of parents who were raised without discipline. They got anything they wanted when they wanted it. And when they got married and had to work with a marriage partner instead of pliable old Mom and Pop, they were shocked.

Do you know why McDonald's is hiring older people right now? Because they know how to work. There is a generation of young people who don't know how to do anything but toast Pop-Tarts and push buttons on television remote controls. And the generation right behind them is in worse trouble. Social workers can tell you who is raising the children of America today. Either the jailhouse, a day care, or grandparents. At least the grandparents know how to take care of children. This "me first" generation doesn't know. It wasn't taught.

Children of today can say, "If I want it, give it to me now. If you don't, I'll throw a fit and embarrass you. If you spank me in public, you can get arrested."

I want you to understand that when you accept God's portrait of the family, that nonsense stops. The father leads, the wife submits to that lead, and their children honor them as the authority in their lives, if they don't, their backsides burn.

In the past thirty years, the parents of America have relinquished their children and turned them over to the state. I want to tell you something. There's not a verse in the Book that says your children belong to the state of Texas, or your children belong to Washington, D.C. Mother, the children in your house were given to you by God Himself. They are your children, and you need to act like it and you need to fight for their spiritual survival.

The Word of God is calling for pure, chaste, honorable women who love their children, care for their parents, and show hospitality to all. That's the portrait of God's perfect woman. And that's as far away from the stereotypical "babe" in the cigarette commercials as it is from "the church lady" on *Saturday Night Live*.

Chapter Seven

Dads of Deception

Before God was Judge, He was Father. Before He was Creator, He was Father. And as Father, He has established the biblical pattern of family government. He understands our psychological needs. He knows all about our desires, and He has taken the time to tell us what He expects from each member of the family.

In the Word of God, the father is provider, priest, prophet, and king. As provider, he works. As priest, he guides. As prophet, he protects. And as king, he governs.

The Man as Provider

The Bible's caution, "If any provide not for his own . . . he hath denied the faith, and is worse than an infidel,"[1] applies especially to the head of the house, the father. These are powerful words, and America needs to hear them. While the rest of the world has abandoned their experimentation with socialism and declared it dead, we are being led by a brainless cadre of wealthy media elitists who want to salve their guilty consciences by forcing it down our throats. The media tell us that the government has a responsibility to bail us out. But God expects dads to get up and go to work and provide for their families. If you are physically ill or handicapped and can't work, that's another story. If you are physically able and don't work, you are worse than an infidel in the eyes of God.

You say, "Well, doesn't God provide?" Yes, He does. He provides worms for the birds, but he doesn't throw them down their throats. You get up and go get it. As long as you do your part, God will do His part. Every miracle has two parts: your part and God's part. The old saying "Work like everything depends on you, pray like everything depends on God" is all too true. Remember, the Bible says, "If anyone will not work, neither shall he eat."[2]

God Himself is a provider. He is *Jehovah-Jireh*, and He expects earthly fathers to provide for their own. America is now saturated with a growing subculture called "deadbeat dads": men who sire children with their live-in lover or wife-of-the-week and then leave the mother stranded and alone to care for the baby. That is not sexual independence; it is moral insanity. Citizens of America, we need to send a very clear message to these deadbeat dads, "Provide for the needs of that mother and that child or go to jail and stay there."

Hollywood public relations people fawn over movie stars who raise and support illegitimate children. Meanwhile, the father is off in another relationship in search of himself. The television sitcom *Murphy Brown* tried to cloak the whole experience with respectability. Madonna gave birth out of wedlock and Hollywood applauded. But it isn't a laughing matter to a sixteen-year-old girl in the projects whose life is ruined, who can't support herself or her baby, and who is now headed for generations of welfare dependence. Sexual freedom is not the right to do as you please. Freedom is the right to do as you ought, and the Bible, God's instruction manual, will show the way. Winston Churchill said, "Responsibility is the price of greatness."

God the Father is also *Jehovah-Shammah*, which simply means "the Lord is there." Make no mistake about it, God expects the earthly father "to be there." Many fathers are gone. They simply abandon the home. Some are gone even when they're home. They are more committed to their work and their careers than to their wives and children. Some provide rooms full of toys and yards full of plastic playhouses and cars but provide no emotional, spiritual, or intellectual support. In that sense, they are gone.

Sociologists now have a name for these people. They are called "phantom fathers." Where are they? One study showed that "69 percent of rapists, 72 percent of adolescent murderers, and 70 percent of long-term prison inmates once lived in a fatherless home."[3]

Forty percent of America's children now live in homes without their biological fathers. By the year 2000, our government says, 60 percent of all children born in the United States will be illegitimate. We are watching the death and destruction of America.

What does God think about it? Malachi 4:6 says, "And he will turn / The hearts of the fathers to the children / . . . Lest I come and strike the earth with a curse." Have you ever had a father or a mother who took that seriously? Mine did.

Bill Bennett, former secretary of education and drug czar, marshaled the data on what has happened to the fatherless American home during the past thirty years. Those stats? A 560 percent increase in violent crime; a 400 percent increase in juvenile arrests; a 200 percent increase in teenage suicide.[4] All this while the American people were spending billions of dollars to conquer the problem.

I said in Chapter 5 that America's major problem is not poverty, crime, or the government. America's number one problem is the judgment of God, and God is judging this country for fathers missing from the home. We need a program to get fathers back in the house to raise the children they have fathered. God has that program.

The Man as Priest of His Family

As priest, the father represents his family to God. In Exodus you will read the story of the Passover. In spite of a series of plagues that ravaged the land, the stubborn government of Pharaoh would not release the Israelite slaves. So God sent his death angel to pass over the city. The angel would take the firstborn son of every Egyptian family. Each Israelite family was warned to sacrifice a lamb and sprinkle its blood over the doorposts. This was the father's responsibility.[5] Without that blood, the family would be visited with death. The safety of the family depended on what each father did. If the father failed, the oldest son died.

In our generation, the death angel is passing over the United States of America, and he's coming with drugs and sexual diseases and rebellion. Dad, if you don't take the blood of the cross and place it over the doors of your soul and the souls of your children, your family doesn't have a chance of survival.

In the first chapter of Job, the father offered a burnt sacrifice for each son and each daughter by name to protect them from the judgment of God. He knew that if he failed to do that, if he failed to represent his children to God by name, his children would be destroyed. Dad, do you represent your children to God? If not you, who? And if not now, when are you going to do it? America's children are being destroyed by fathers who refuse to be the priests of their homes.

The priest leads his family in worship. I am not concerned about the schoolhouse nearly as much as I am concerned about your house, because it's not the schoolteacher's responsibility to teach your child to pray, and it's not the schoolteacher's responsibility to teach your child the principles of God's Word. It's your responsibility.

Let me tell you a little secret learned from years of marriage counseling. Prayer produces intimacy, and with spiritual intimacy, there can be truly fulfilling sexual intimacy. Marriage is spiritual and nothing accentuates the intimacy of your marriage more than prayer.

When Moses went to Mount Sinai, it was the place of prayer. He stayed so long that the Bible says, "The LORD spoke to Moses face to face, as a man speaks to his friend."[6] In other words, God Himself became intimate through prayer. On the day of Pentecost, the disciples prayed until they were in one accord. They became so intimate in that ten days of prayer that they went out and sold everything they had to help one another. When you pass the offering plate in the average church today, you're lucky to get the plates back!

The Man as Prophet in His Home

As a priest, man represents the family to God; as a prophet he reverses the flow. Man, the prophet, represents God to his family.

The Bible says in Genesis 6:8 that "Noah found grace in the eyes of the LORD."And the Lord said to Noah, "Come into the ark, you and all your household."[7] God spoke to Noah, the father, and told him what to do. God described the coming flood. He told the father how to escape, and in the end "Only Noah and those who were with him in the ark remained alive."

Hebrews 11:7 says, "By faith Noah, being divinely warned of things not yet seen, moved with godly fear, prepared an ark for the saving of his household." Hear me, Dad. There will come a time in America when your family will be saved depending on what you hear from God. There will come a time in the life of your family when they will live or die spiritually based on what you hear from God. You are the priest and you are the prophet.

As Prophet the Father Is On Guard

The Bible says Satan is going about like a roaring lion seeking to devour, and he seeks to devour your family. He seeks to devour your wife and your children. You guard them by teaching them the Word of God. Satan is not impressed by the peppy, motivational slogans that you bring home from the chamber of commerce. He's not diminished by the Boy Scouts or the Girl Scouts or the Little League, but the devil is destroyed by the Word of God. He knows its power.

In one parable, Jesus described a rich man and a beggar named Lazarus. The rich man died and went to hell. Lazarus died and was "carried by the angels to Abraham's bosom." From hell the rich man called out to Abraham to send Lazarus to talk to his family still on earth. But Abraham rebuked him, saying, "If they do not hear Moses and the prophets, neither will they be persuaded though one rise from the dead."[8]

The Psalmist says, "Your word I have hidden in my heart, / That I might not sin against You."[9] The Word of God is a light in a dark world. It is bread, it is living water. The Word is the sword of truth. Paul calls it milk for infants and meat for men. The Word is a book of love, a book of mystery, of revelation, of hope, of prophecy. Do you want to know the future? Read the Word of God. The Bible is the greatest sex manual in existence. Sex is wonderful! Most of you are here because of it. The Word of God is a book of family planning. Most important of all, this book introduces your children to the living God.

Understand this, God is not a cosmic bellhop standing in heaven waiting for your religious tip on Sunday morning. He is not a doting grandfather sitting benignly in heaven approving of your godless life. God is a sovereign monarch of might and majesty. He rules from a throne. He has billions of agents coming and going, carrying out His orders. He is a monarch of judgment and wrath as well as of compassion and love. He is a God who expects you to do what He tells you to do in His Word. Jesus said, "And why call ye me Lord, Lord, and do not the things which I say?"[10]

Your children are not going to meet God in a Nintendo game. They are not going to meet Him on ESPN. You, father, are responsible for introducing your children to God. He gave you the assignment. It's called leadership. It's called being the head of the house. It's called being the prophet in your family. And someday He will demand a report on how things went.

As Prophet the Father Blesses His Family

In the Bible the blessing of the father determined the success or the failure of the family. The father is the spiritual authority. Father, what you say to your wife or children literally predestines their intellectual, emotional, and perhaps even their physical development.

- Proverbs 15:4 says, "A wholesome tongue is a tree of life."
- Proverbs 18:21 says, "Death and life are in the power of the tongue."
- James 3:6 says, "The tongue . . . defiles the whole body" and is "set on fire by hell."

That's the kind of power the Bible says you have through your words.

When Isaac was old, his eyes were so weak he could not distinguish his sons without feeling their skin (Jacob was smooth-skinned, and Esau was hairy). Jacob and his mother, Rebekah, conspired to steal the birthright, the father's blessing, from Esau. You know the story of Genesis 27, and how absolutely successful was Jacob's plot. Isaac, the aging father, blessed Jacob in Genesis 27:27, and every word of that blessing came to pass. Jacob was no sooner out of Isaac's tent than Esau entered with a mess of pottage, seeking his father's blessing.

Isaac trembled with rage at Jacob's deception. But note this: The blessing he spoke upon Jacob could not be rescinded. Isaac said, "I have blessed him [Jacob]—and indeed he shall be blessed."[11]

Esau begged his father for a blessing, and Isaac spoke a blessing that was more of a curse: Esau would live in the desert. He would live by the sword and would serve his younger brother, Jacob. Those three things came to pass exactly as Isaac said.

Years later Jacob, the spiritual authority of his house, blessed his twelve sons when he was dying and everything he spoke into their lives also came to pass. He was not just close; his patriarchal blessing was fulfilled in *every* detail. Father, your words have power—power to shape the lives and destinies of your children.

Every Friday night Jewish mothers and fathers bless their children. At the bar mitzvah they put their hands on them in front of the congregation and bless them. What do they say? They often use the blessings of Numbers 16, and they may add other blessings they want to come to pass in the life of that child. And with the power of the blessing of their parents, these children go right out into life and do these great things. They were given spiritual authority to accomplish it, through the power of the blessing.

How many fathers look at their children and shout obscenities? How many actually use God's name to damn them? How many call them stupid, cursing their intellectual potential? How many shout, "You'll never amount to anything," which is a curse upon their economic potential.

You are the prophet in your home. You are the spiritual authority over your wife and over your children. When you speak to your wife, bless her in the name of the Lord. When you speak to your children, bless them in the name of the Lord. What you speak will come into existence. Your blessing or your curse will follow your children and your grandchildren to their graves.

Dad as King

And finally, according to Scripture, the man is the governor of his home. He is king. Some men imagine that it is God's scriptural plan for them to sit in an easy chair and watch ESPN while their wives serve them lemonade, but that is not what a king is all about. A king is a ruler. Not a couch potato.

Why did God select Abraham to be the father of all who believe? Genesis 18:19 says, "For I have chosen him, so that he will direct his children and his household after him to keep the way of the Lord" (NIV).

That means you tell your children how much they're going to watch TV and how much they're not going to watch TV. You decide. You tell them whom they're going to date, when they're going to date, and when they're going to be home. You do that. You don't hand them the keys and say, "When are you coming home?" You hand them the keys and say, "Be home at eleven, or you're not going out."

You determine what they do, when they do it, how long they do it, and if they do it. Quit acting like the wagon is dragging you. You're the leader.

Before you pick up the Bible as your textbook let me warn you, Dr. Spock didn't get to edit this one. The Bible calls sin by its name. The Bible tells it like it is!

American young people say, "I have a problem." If you have "a problem" in this country, you can get infinite sympathy. You can get counseling, you can get endless attention, and you can find a support group. But when you say, "I have sinned," all you can do is confess and repent. This is the Spock generation, and our jailhouses prove it. They are packed to overflowing with people who want their sins explained—not forgiven.

One of America's biggest problems right now is gangs. Some areas of metropolitan Los Angeles and New York are controlled by gangs. Police cruisers patrol like an invading military occupation force in a hostile enemy city. Who are the members of these gangs? Rebellious little boys who never learned to mind. Sons who were abandoned by their fathers. Daughters who were sexually abused and joined a gang where they have sexual intercourse with every male gang member to join. Their slogan, "Blood in and blood out!" The only way out of the gang is death.

The astonishing thing is that many of them, like the Menendez brothers, have fathers from well-to-do homes. I assure you that the only thing my father had to do to get my attention was to point at me. Just point. I tried to read his mind while his hand was coming down. I learned very early that there is a definite physiological connection between your cerebral cortex and your gluteus maximus. When you stimulate the gluteus maximus, your children will get a new revelation about who you are.

Father, you need to go home, turn off the television, and introduce yourself to your children. "Hello, children, I'm Dad. This is Mom. We're taking over this house. I haven't been very fair to you, children, but that is going to change. There are going to be some rules. At first, it may seem kind of awkward, even hard. But eventually, when you are thirty-five, you are going to love me for it."

Proverbs 13:24 says, "He who spares his rod"—and that is not referring to the family car—"hates his son, / But he who loves him disciplines him promptly."

Proverbs 23:13–14 agrees: "Do not withhold correction from a child, / For if you beat him with a rod, he will not die. / You shall beat him with a rod, / And deliver his soul from hell."

A Milquetoast father once said to me, "I can't spank my boy; I cry when I discipline him."

Then go home, spank him, and cry. Cry now or cry when he goes to jail.

I'm tired of people telling me, "I have a strong-willed child, and I just can't teach him anything." Wrong! I have been to Sea World, where they can teach a porpoise how to play basketball. Surely you can teach your child to clean up his or her room, carry out the trash, and wash the supper dishes.

When your child comes up to you and says, "Will you buy me a little red truck if I'm good in church?" Tell him, "I'll give you a little red rear if you're not."

American fathers are saying, "My son's on drugs." That's

a serious problem, but it's not an excuse for shirking your responsibility as a father.

I had a drug problem when I was a teenager. I was "drug" to church on Sunday morning, "drug" to church on Sunday night, and "drug" to church for the midweek service. I was "drug" to Vacation Bible School when I was old enough to teach it. I was "drug" to four revivals every year that lasted three weeks, sometimes four, and we went every night. I was "drug" to the family altar every night where my father read the Word. I was "drug" to the woodshed when I disobeyed. Those "drugs" are still in my veins. They affect my behavior. They're stronger than cocaine, crack, or heroin. Fathers, I say go home and give that "drug" problem to your sons and to your daughters, and America will be a better place to live.

Remember, Dad, discipline without love is abuse. Never fail to put your arms around your children and let them know you love them more than life itself. As a father I make it a point to hug and kiss my children every day.

One day my son Chris got out the door for school before I could kiss him. I walked to where the children of our neighborhood were gathering to catch the bus. Chris saw me coming and started screaming as he ran from me, "No, no, no!" He knew I was going to kiss him, and it was unthinkable in the presence of other teenagers. But I had to catch him once he screamed since several mothers were now on their front porches, hands on hips, ready to call the cops. Fortunately I was able to catch Chris quickly, kiss him, and get into my car for a quick getaway!

In the sixteenth chapter of Acts, Paul and Silas were in jail. God sent an earthquake, and they walked out with the jailhouse keys in one hand and a convert in the other. The guard, who by Roman law had to serve the sentence of anyone that escaped, shouted in terror, "What must I do to be saved?"

Paul said, "Believe on the Lord Jesus Christ, and you shall be saved, and your household." And your household?

Why? Because that answer was given to a father, and it's the father's responsibility to lead his household to God.

Don't send your children to Sunday school. Take them to Sunday school. They ought to hear more about God out of your mouth Monday through Saturday than they ever hear in the Sunday school or from the pulpit. If they don't, you're failing as a father.

Ephesians 6:4 says, "Fathers . . . bring [your children] up in the training and admonition of the Lord." The word *train* is the Greek word *gymnot* from which we get *gymnasium*. God expects the father to show his sons and daughters how to live righteous lives. Just like a baseball coach would instruct someone on how to hit a baseball or a football coach would instruct someone on how to kick a football, God expects the father to teach and show his children over and over and over again how to serve God through their lives.

In the Old Testament, Lot led his family into Sodom and lost them. He did not command them. And because of his godless leadership, they perished. Compare that to Joshua's statement in 24:15, "As for me and my house, we will serve the LORD." That was a command. Joshua didn't look over to his wife and say "Is that all right with you?" It was not a request. It was a command performance. Every father and every husband should look in the mirror every morning and repeat those words. "As for me and my house, we will serve the Lord."

Which brings up a very unpopular scriptural principle. The Bible teaches that the man is not only the leader of his children, he is the leader of his wife. 1 Corinthians 11:3 says, "But I want you to know that the head of every man is Christ, the head of woman is man."

We talked about women submitting to their husbands in Chapter 6, now let's turn the nickel over.

A Man and His Remote Control

Some wives have a real problem. They married a Caspar Milquetoast who won't lead. A wife can't follow a parked car. Some men haven't had a new idea in twenty years. They need to give the family some leadership.

The number one addiction in this country is not marijuana; it is not crack cocaine. It is television, and it is systematically brainwashing each subsequent generation. Television has become the nation's new guru. It is our religion. It is an idol before which every person bows. Today's new fathers were raised on a fictional television character named Archie Bunker. This supposed personification of fatherhood was a loudmouthed, arrogant, ignorant, sloppy racist. He was held up as the stereotypical father figure. Funny, but at whose expense?

In the program *Soap*, the father was a weak-willed, vacillating stooge. The family received all of its direction from the homosexual son. That is the father image that is burned into the minds of America's young people. That is the look and feel of a "Dad."

Dinner used to be a great time for the family to be together. The problem is that in today's America, children gather around the television and watch murderers, rapists, drug addicts, and child abusers while the delinquent father reads the *Wall Street Journal* or the sports page. I want to give you a divine command from the throne of God: "Turn off your TV at supper and talk to every member of your family." You need to get involved in the lives of your children and the life of your wife. Your kids may be little people, but they are people with feelings and they are people with a future. If you don't get involved now, somebody will, and if that somebody is not a godly influence, you will lose your children and your home because of your own negligence.

David says in Psalm 101 that he watches carefully who comes into his house. They must not practice deceit. They must be, in David's word, "blameless." Yet, through the screen door of television you allow people to enter your home that you wouldn't let stand on your front porch without a shotgun in their faces. These media invaders teach your children murder and rape and social violence.

This intellectual cancer mocks your values and your faith. Take action. Turn off secular TV programs! Expel the evil invaders. Hear King David's admonition: "I will set nothing wicked before my eyes."[12]

If fathers are going to assume the role that God has ordained for them, they are going to have to have the discipline to turn off the television and get into His Word. If fathers refuse to lead their families, the American dream will become a nightmare and the nation will collapse from within.

The Woman's Need

The Bible also clearly teaches the husband to submit to the need of his wife. He doesn't submit to her lead, rather, he submits to her need. The lead is his.

The Bible tells husbands to "love your wives, just as Christ also loved the church."[13] And how did Christ love the church? Look at the record. Christ cooked breakfast for His disciples one morning because that was their need. Have you ever cooked breakfast for your wife? I mean, she doesn't have to have a 104-degree fever and be shaking with convulsions before the idea comes to mind. It doesn't have to be your silver or golden anniversary. Sometimes she just needs a break.

Jesus washed the feet of His disciples. Why? Because that was their need. It was a dirty job. What does your wife need? Does she need someone to help her with the dishes? "Boy, I'd never wash the dishes. I'm a man." Look, John Wayne, if soap and water will wash away your manliness, you need a hormone shot.

What does your wife need? Does she need you to go to the opera with her? "Opera! Maybe George Strait, but opera? Who wants to hear some fat Italian sing love songs in a language you can't understand?" But if that is her need, go. And I mean without dragging your heels in the carpet like a boat anchor. Does she need someone to talk to in the middle of the Dallas Cowboys–Washington Redskins football game? Then turn it off and talk to her.

I repeat: Don't follow her lead, but do everything in your power to meet her need.

Now I've talked to you about the role of the father and husband as priest, as provider, as prophet, as king of the house; but he is also something more. He is not only the leader, he is the lover. Don't laugh. They say that men who are bald in front are thinkers. Men who are bald in the back are lovers. Men who are bald from front to back just think they're lovers.

The Husband as Lover

Now, here's what I mean by lover. Moses was the first king in Israel.[14] Israel had rebelled against God saying, "If only we had died in Egypt! Or in the desert! Why did God bring us into the wilderness to let us fall by the edge of the sword?" The whole assembly talked about stoning Moses. Then God spoke from heaven saying: "How long will these people treat me with contempt?. . . I will strike them down with a plague and destroy them, but I will make you [Moses] into a nation greater and stronger than they."[15]

Moses could have become the father of a nation greater than Israel. Instead he pled with God to forgive the people of Israel. That's leadership! That's being a lover.[16]

Jesus Christ was the King of kings. He went to the cross and allowed himself to be crucified for you. When you love your wife and your children as Christ loved the church, when they know you are willing to lay down your life for them and submit to their needs without question, it will be a lot easier for them to submit to your leadership. It is not possible for an intelligent woman to submit to a macho Hitler in the house. You are equal partners, mutually submissive to each other for the glory of God so that your home can be "like the days of the heavens above the earth."[17] That is God's will.

Paul said in Ephesians 5:28, "So husbands ought to love their own wives as their own bodies." Go to the nearest health club and look at the men lifting weights. Watch them as they pass the wall of mirrors, looking at themselves with adoration in their eyes. When you look at your wife, she doesn't need to see acceptance, she needs to see adoration.

Whatever happened to romance in marriage? I read an article years ago that described attitude transitions in marriage over a seven-year period, using the common cold as the basis of satire.[18] It went something like this:

What happens when your married partner catches a cold?

The first year of marriage, the husband says to the wife, "Sugar Dumpling, I'm worried about my baby girl. I'm putting you in the hospital for a rest. I know the food is lousy, so every night I'll bring you food from our favorite restaurants."

The second year he says, "Listen, Darling, I don't like the sound of that cough. I've called the doctor and he's coming over. Go to bed."

The third year: "Maybe you'd better lie down a bit."

The fourth year: "Look, be sensible. After you've fixed supper and washed the dishes, go to bed."

The fifth year: "Why don't you take a few aspirin for heaven's sake?"

The sixth year: "Can't you gargle? Do something. Don't just sit around the house barking like a seal all night."

The seventh year: "Stop sneezing for heaven's sake! You'll give us all pneumonia!"

Whatever happened to romance in marriage? I'll tell you. Paul gives the answer in 2 Timothy 3:1–2 when he says, "But know this, that in the last days perilous times will come: For men will be lovers of themselves." Not lovers of their wives, not lovers of their children, but lovers of themselves.

146

I saw a cartoon the other day about a guy sitting in his easy chair in front of the TV. A football game was on the screen. Surrounding him were three cases of beer and 400 pounds of food. The calendar behind him read "September." Looking at his wife he said, "Is there anything you want to say to me between now and January?"

The most important thing a father can do for his children is to love their mother. Self-love destroys submitted love. Self-love is idolatry. It is spiritual adultery. Self-love says to the wife, "What can you do for me? You can cook, you can clean the house, you can bear the children, and you can satisfy my sex drive." That's not a marriage. That's not a relationship. That's not love. That's slavery, and it has no place in your family.

The Bible instructs the husband to love his wife as Christ loved the church. Love is not an emotion; it is an act of the will.

Husbands say, "I can't love my wife as Christ loved the church. I can't give up my self-centered life. I can't give up my pornography or my X-rated movies or my business career or . . ."

The truth is, you can, but you won't because you're self-centered. You won't give up what you want, not for your wife, not for God, not for anybody else, because you love *you* the most. That same cancerous idea is being planted in the mind of every child who watches television for more than thirty minutes.

A very meticulous man who demanded that his wife be an excellent, fastidious housekeeper, passed the piano one day and found it covered with dust. In the dust he printed, and underlined, "This needs to be cleaned." When he came home from work the next day, he found that his wife had placed a dust cloth on the piano. Good for her!

Effective leadership is not leading her your way. Effective leadership is leading her God's way. Submitted love means you meet the need of the other person whether they deserve it or not. Listen to that. Whether they deserve it or not. The Bible says: "But God demonstrates His own love toward us, in that while we were still sinners, Christ died for us."[19] Those who need love most, deserve it least!

A major problem is this. The husband sees the need of the wife, but his macho mentality says, "I'll hang on until she caves in." The problem with that modus operandi is that the little lady has a lot of spunk herself. She can get as mean as a junkyard dog. And then she eats his lunch. Soon, they are on the way to see the lawyer.

Rather than submitting to each other, they have demanded their rights. I have seen it flare up a hundred times in a marriage counseling session. I call it a "rights fight." No family can survive a "rights fight." If you start saying, "my rights" and "her rights," it's over. Call the attorney and get ready to divide everything you have. Let me ask you a question: Do you want to be right or be reconciled?

When you come to the Lord Jesus Christ, He says, "I see both of you, or I see neither of you. You are submitted to each other. Lady, you follow his lead; husband, you meet her need. Love each other as I loved the Church. Be willing to give yourself for her, unreservedly, with love that is extravagant."

Much has been written about wives who marry men with the intention of changing them, but it really works both ways. Many men think the same way. "I will marry her, then I'll change her." Read my lips, Leroy, it won't happen. There is not a verse in the Scriptures that says, "Husbands, change your wives;" nor is there a verse that says, "Treat your wife like your oldest child."

Now, let's review what we've said here. The God-ordained role of the father is that of provider, prophet, king, and priest. Wives, submit to the lead of your husbands. Husbands, submit to the need of your wives. That's God's divine order for our lives. And husbands, love your wives, just as Christ loved. There is only one way to handle a woman. Richard Burton sang about it in the

Broadway version of *Camelot*. "How to handle a woman? Simply love her, love her, love her."

Make no mistake about it, if the traditional family falls in America, the nation will fall. If you cannot love and support your family, you cannot love and support the nation. If you cannot be loyal to your wife and children, you cannot be loyal to your government or to God. The fabric of the traditional family in America is being ripped to shreds by divorce, abortion, alcohol, drugs, child abuse, pornography, homosexuality, greed, and materialism. Men are more given to profits, power, and pleasure than they are the purposes of God and their family. The solution is God-inspired manhood. America needs men who will assume the role God has ordained for them. God is the creator. God understands us. And He can bring harmony to our lives if we have the courage and discipline to do what He says.

Chapter Eight

Deception in Communication

Talking is not communication. You can talk all day without meaningful communication. Differences in marriages will never be solved until you have the courage to open up emotionally. Some couples reading this book have deep-seated problems in their relationships, problems that have never been addressed. Some are sexual, some are financial, some are emotional; but these couples cannot, or will not, open up about them. A crisis is in the making because there is no communication.

Other couples may communicate volumes without saying a word. They are sitting alone in front of a fireplace holding hands. The lights are out. No one is speaking a word, but the electricity is flowing and the sparks are bouncing off the wall. Talking is not communication. The best communication possible sometimes occurs without words.

Have you noticed that young lovers rarely lack communication skills? That's something that develops after marriage. Usually, it is not the lack of communication but wrong communication that is at the root of the problem.

Communication problems in marriage date back to Adam and Eve, who had the only ideal marriage. He didn't have to hear about all the men she could have married. She didn't have to hear about what a great cook his mother was. When she asked Adam, "Do you really love me?" Adam could honestly say, "Who else, Eve? Who else?"

We have developed communication systems by which men can talk to people walking on the moon, yet very often husbands and wives cannot talk to each other across the kitchen table. Problems and differences in marriage are not dangerous. But not being able to talk about those problems and differences is very dangerous.

In general, women have greater verbal skills than men. They express themselves by what they say while men express themselves by what they do. There is no doubt that when God passed out the gifts of communication, men got short-changed, at least when it comes to communicating with their wives. Now, talking with another man is a different story. The only way some women can find out what's going on in their husband's life is to listen while he talks to another man on the phone.

The really verbal husband has developed a few words in his husband-to-wife vocabulary. The most popular one is, "Nothing," which he pronounces, "Nuthun."

"What happened at work today?"

"Nuthun."

"What are you watching on television?"

"Nuthun."

"What's bothering you? You look troubled."

"Nuthun."

Husbands who are riddled with doubts and fears are always dogmatic, and a dogmatic husband is usually an insecure husband. He can never afford to be wrong because he is emotionally weak. He has to dominate his wife.

If we husbands demand that our wives accept our viewpoint all the time, we are incapable of a vital marriage relationship. Understand, we don't have to be right all of the time. Someone else can be right part of the time. We are not omnipotent. We are not the general managers of the universe. We are not angels, even though we may be up in the air, harping about something all of the time.

When we demand that our wives (or husbands) agree with us absolutely, in every situation, we are denying them the emotional and intellectual lives they must have to be people. No one can survive psychologically and be so dominated. That person will get a divorce to get away from you or find someone else to communicate with just to preserve sanity. In the final analysis, wives and husbands must have the opportunity to express their own opinions and deepest feelings.

Men say to their wives, "I don't want to talk about it. This conversation is over."

Read my lips, Bubba. It's not over. You'd better let her have her say right now, because if you keep it blocked it will someday all come out in a rush, and you're going to wish you had given her a chance to talk.

After years of counseling I have identified five levels of communication. All of us resort to these levels at different times in our lives. Sometimes the occasion or the person demands it. Understanding and identifying these levels may help us move onto a deeper and more intimate communication with the people we love.

Five Levels of Communication

Level One: Communication by Cliché

Level one is a very shallow dimension. Everyone remains in isolation. Everything is pretense. Everything is sham. We dare not reveal our emotional selves.

Someone asks, "How are you?"

Of course, the answer is, "Fine."

They weren't really asking and you weren't really answering. The truth may be that you may have a 104° fever, and you are on the verge of convulsions. You are still going to say, "Fine." Why? Because you're not really communicating truth. You are only saying words.

Someone asks, "How is the family?"

You know the answer. You've given it ten thousand times. Now, the truth may be that your wife hasn't spoken to you in two weeks. She's pouting. You have three kids, two of them are in jail, the other's out on bail. But you say, "Fine."

Liar.

On the other hand, if someone asked how you were doing and you actually told them, they would pass out. They would be thinking, "Hey, I didn't ask for your medical history, I was just talking. I didn't really want to know. I have my own problems." That's not real communication. The first level, communication by cliché, is simply pretense. It's deception.

Our society places a great deal of emphasis upon being authentic. But the truth is, most of us are liars. We place a mask over our real face, and we begin to play a role. Some of the greatest theatrical performances of all time were not played out on a Broadway stage in New York or on the West End of London. They were played out in the bedrooms of America. Many of us wear masks.

There's the John Wayne mask. I'm big. I'm strong, invincible, a man of iron. "I really don't need all this mushy stuff, Miss Ellie. I don't need all this huggin' and kissin'. I told you back in 1942 I loved you, and if something changes, I'll tell you." So she stops telling him she loves him. And six months later he is crying out. "She doesn't love me like she used to!" She didn't know he was lying. She thought he was telling the truth. I know a man who didn't kiss his wife for ten years, and then shot somebody else who did.

There's the messiah mask. Meet God's little helpers, the saviors of the universe, general managers of earth and all nearby planets. They are spread so thin doing so many good things, they have nothing left to give their marriages when they get home. They're so heavenly minded they're no earthly good. Be real! Be natural and let God be supernatural. Stay home and take care of your family and your children. Let me tell you something. Kissing wears out. Cooking never does.

There's the religious mask. You're so full of religious buzzwords, you're like a windup doll.

"I hear you're having family problems."

"Yes. The husband's left, but God's grace is sufficient."

"Your son is in jail?"

"Yes. But all things work together for good to them that love the Lord."

Hey, it's all right to say, "Things are not going right. We're in trouble." It's all right to say, "I'm hurting." It's all right to say, "I'm a Christian but I still need somebody to pray with me or I'm going to lose control." Quit running around trying to act like the apostle Paul when you can't find the book of Ephesians with a seeing-eye dog.

What game are you playing? What mask are you wearing? Take it off and introduce yourself to your wife, to your husband, to your children, and to the body of Christ. Role-playing is dangerous. It's emotional suicide. Why? When your marriage partner and friends change their minds about what role they want you to play, you won't know whom you're supposed to be. In the process, you will lose contact with someone who's very important to you. Yourself! You will be lost! You will wake up someday saying, "Who am I?" And you won't know. You've worn so many different masks, pretending to be so many different people, you won't know who you are. The only guy who needs a mask is the Lone Ranger, and they've even given his mask to somebody else.

This special note to singles who are dating. People always wear a mask on a date. They have their best foot forward. Any nut, any moron, any orangutan can look good for three hours on Saturday night. Just remember, the real person is home in a cage waiting to get out. Date long enough to find out who this "perfect person" really is.

Level Two: "Just the Facts, Ma'am."

Most baby boomers will remember Sergeant Friday on the television series *Dragnet*. He was usually interviewing a witness when he would give his trademark line, "Just the facts, ma'am." On the second level we start reporting facts about other people and what they are doing.

A wife said to her husband, "Did you see Mrs. Jones's new dress at church today?"

"No."

"Did you notice the Smiths didn't get the first row. Someone took their seats."

"No."

"Did you see Mrs. Garcia's new car today at church?"

"No."

"Well," she said, "a lot of good it does for you to go to church."

There are four questions Christians should ask themselves before talking about someone else, especially if the information is negative. First, is it true? Second, is it information the other person needs to know? Third, what is your motive in telling your story? Remember, the Bible says that in all you do, glorify God. Fourth, when you're telling a story about a fellow believer, ask yourself if it edifies the kingdom of God and blesses everyone involved. If the answer to any of these questions is no, then be quiet. It's deception.

"But I said it without thinking."

Let me tell you something about your anatomy. It is not possible for your tongue to begin to speak of its own volition. It does not operate by involuntary reflex. It has to have clearance from your cerebral cortex. You say "sic 'em" and the thing starts rattling. Don't tell me, "I just didn't think." You didn't think long, but you thought.

Level two is not self-revealing. We ask nothing of the other person. We give nothing of ourselves. It's empty, it's meaningless, and the sad thing is that the communication in many marriages stays right on level two, an empty reporting of the facts of other people. If it weren't for *As the World Turns*, the *National Enquirer*, and the sports page of the local newspaper, there wouldn't be anything to talk about.

Level Three: The Sharing of Ideas

On level three a couple begins to share some of the things they are thinking with each other. They talk about some of their decisions and how they were made. They may even touch on some of their material goals or dreams.

They are saying, "I will give you just a little peek at the real me, but as I communicate I will carefully watch your every move. If you raise your eyebrows or if you narrow your eyes, if you start yawning or looking at your watch or shaking the newspaper, I will retreat. I'll go back to levels one or two, reporting trivia. I will change the subject. I may continue talking, but I'm not going to step any further toward revealing who I am or what I honestly feel. Not now. Maybe never."

Those who communicate on this level need to be wary of two communication killers: tears and silence or pouting. Tears are used most effectively by women, but some men use them too. What are you saying? You're saying, "Don't tell me my shortcomings or I'll cry." In those first marriage spats, she will usually turn on the waterworks. She's communicating. She's saying, "This is the line in the sand, Sweetie. You cross over and I'll drown you!"

Many Christians have also mastered the technique of silence or pouting. They realize that it's not spiritual to explode all over the place, so they pout, which is only another type of anger. Pouting just may be the leading cause of high blood pressure, ulcers, and other diseases. And, incidentally, it is a leading cause of divorce as well.

Level three isn't deception. It's just cowardice.

Level Four: The Revealing of Emotions

Jesus finally said to His disciples, "Who do you say that I am? I really don't care what they're saying on the street, but who do you say that I am?" This is gut-level conversation. At this level I am communicating the real me, what I feel way down deep in my spirit. I'm getting ready to open my emotional nakedness and show you who I really am. There's no mask here. There's no deception.

Communication in marriage begins on this level, without a fear of blowup, without a fear of pouting, without a fear of resentment, without a fear of being manipulated by the other person.

Level Five: *Symphono*

And finally, there is the absolute peak of communication, the symphony of the soul. This occurs when two human hearts begin to share their deepest and most sensitive feelings, like two violins playing in an exact harmonic tone. Jesus spoke from this level at the Last Supper when He explained His death to His disciples.

The Bible often talks about the power that comes when any two persons can agree about something. In these Scriptures, the Greek word for agree is *symphono*, two human hearts beginning to share a pure and exact level of communication. There is no room for pretense in such communication.

The relationship with *symphono* has a beautiful sense of the presence of God. In that home, the angels leave the balconies of heaven and come to watch how a man and woman can be spiritually one. Here they can share the deepest feelings of their hearts without being crucified or belittled by their partner. Do you have that? Well, let me tell you that ought to be your goal, because that's where real living begins.

The first step to *symphono* begins with a greater understanding of the feelings, hopes, and fears of your partner. I call it the "Ezekiel Method."

The Ezekiel Method

In the third chapter of Ezekiel, the prophet describes his journey to an Israelite refugee camp near Tel Abib. Now, God has already given Ezekiel a message to deliver to these people—a message that is burning inside him. But Ezekiel travels to the community where he "sat where they sat, and remained there astonished among them for seven days."

This is the key to effective communication, to communication without deception. Sit where they sit.

Ezekiel was a prophet in a concentration camp for Jews exiled in Babylon. They were slaves and refugees who had lost their homes. There was no freedom, there was no hope. The Bible says they sat down and wept when they remembered Zion. Ezekiel wanted to communicate to these refugees, so for seven days he ate their crusty, worm-filled bread and drank their dirty water. He slept with their lice and listened to their mournful songs. He sat where they sat.

Ezekiel became a captive, he went to live with them, he let the blows of humiliation fall on his back, he looked at the world through their eyes. He saw a hopeless world where everything a man possessed was on his back. He sat where they sat. He felt what they felt. It changed his viewpoint. In his own words, he was astonished.

Husbands and wives can communicate in this powerful way. One of the most dramatic marriage encounters I ever conducted included the Ezekiel Method. Some of the husbands were not very appreciative of the duties of their wives. One of these men was a macho orangutan who was totally unimpressed with his wife's role as homemaker.

"I'll tell you what you need to do," I said. "You pick a day, any day you want, and you stay home all day with your three small children. I want you to clean the house while they mess it up right behind you. I want you to wash all the dishes, cook all the meals, and mop the floors. I want you to wash and iron the clothes. I want you to change the diapers. I want you to potty-train this little character right here. I want you to answer the phone pleasantly every time it rings. You get any groceries that are needed, and when your wife comes home at 5:30, I want you to be dressed fit to kill with a rose in your mouth and supper on the table."

He looked at me and said, "You're crazy!"

I said, "Hey, John Wayne, you got worn out just listening to it all. But think about it."

Sit where they sit.

And husbands and wives are not the only individuals who need to adopt the Ezekiel Method.

Doctors are wonderful people; a number of them are in my family. But I think every doctor needs to get sick once a year and be admitted to his own hospital as a John Doe in order to escape the messiah complex that most of them have when they walk into that hospital. They need to feel what it's like to be kept in the dark while their colleagues confer. They need to be asked for their insurance card while holding their convulsing child in their arms, as I once was.

They need to experience the joy of some female "Ironsides" invading their room at 5:30 in the morning, cheerfully asking them if they are resting well while she sticks them in the rump with a needle about a foot long.

Every highway patrolman needs to receive a speeding ticket by some Kojak with a Kodak, who's been hiding behind a billboard all day with a radar gun while people are being raped and robbed all over town.

Every preacher should have to sit in a pew and listen to some of the dry, meaningless, long-winded sermons he cranks out when he doesn't study.

Every church member should have to sit in the pastor's office one week out of the year and prepare three original, life-changing, entertaining, yet theologically profound sermons—and do that while juggling life-and-death counseling sessions with at least twenty neurotics—run a day school, visit the sick, kiss the babies, marry the living, bury the dead, be out of the house twenty-eight nights out of thirty, throw banquets and a couple of formal dinners that week, write best-selling books, magazine articles, manage 480 employees, deal with the press, and juggle lawsuits—and still keep up with everything else. To this day some moron will periodically ask my wife, "What does your husband do between Sundays?" Such people need to try to study thirty hours for a sermon while the phone is ringing off the wall. I've often said, "If I wake up in eternity and hear the phone ring, I'll know I died and went to hell."

Sit where they sit.

Children have a marvelous capacity to enter each other's world through imagination. I was a youngster at a time when every child didn't have two hundred different toys. There was no Toys R Us. We put a stick between our legs and a straw hat on our head and announced, "Hi ho, Silver, away!" Make no mistake about it, law and order had come to ride in the West. All crooks were in jeopardy. We had become justice. Children can imagine great things. This is also the key to understanding in marriage—to imagine the times and trials of your partner. Think it through and you will discover the words and the keys to healing and binding up that relationship.

One of the most insensitive things you can say to a person in the hour of crisis is, "I know how you feel." You can't possibly know how a person feels unless you've experienced the same thing. You have to sit where they sit before you can begin to grasp the magnitude of what they feel.

Laura Hobson wrote a remarkable book, *Gentlemen's Agreement*, about a Gentile newspaperman assigned to write an article on anti-Semitism, the hatred of Jews in our society. And so he took the name of a Jewish person and moved to another side of town where he could live as a Jewish man. Suddenly he found himself snubbed at all of the proper clubs because his name was not the right name. Once he was refused a hotel room. In one experience after another he was ostracized and shut out. He then wrote his article on anti-Semitism in America.[1]

Right now in our nation we have what many people call a problem with undocumented labor. On a weekly basis I hear snide remarks about Mexican men who come across the Rio Grande to work in this country. Put yourself in their place. If I were a father in Mexico and my mother and wife and children were starving, you couldn't build a fence high enough or a ditch deep enough to keep me out of this country! I would be over here working any way I could. And if it's a problem, it's only because American men aren't willing to work as hard as many of those people.

On a recent trip to an Eastern city I drove through a ghetto where children were playing in the streets. In some cases, their parents didn't know where they were and probably didn't care. My heart was broken. Here were children growing up with a distorted view about what life can really be. It's deception.

If you want your marriage partner to have a change of mind, you must first understand what he or she wants and thinks, and why. You can't change an opinion if you don't even know what it is. Understanding is the first step. Then the tools will be available to make an adjustment. You may be surprised; you may be the one making the adjustment.

Adopt the Ezekiel Method. You must communicate through compassion. To arrive at symphono you must not only understand what your partner has experienced in life, you must feel it.

Compassionate Communication

Ezekiel already knew what was going on when he went to Tel Abib. He even had God's answer for the captives. But what he felt in those seven days astonished him nonetheless.

There are times when words are too feeble to express the pain of the heart. There are times when you go into a home and someone has suddenly and tragically died. The most genuinely communicative thing you can do is to wrap your arms around your friends and hold them. Let them know by your presence that you love them.

There are times in every relationship when the only language that can carry the message is the language of tears. When sorrow knows no limit, it can only be contained through compassion. Of all the music on the earth, none is nearly as beautiful as the music created by the symphony of two loving hearts in perfect communication.

Some who read this book will say to themselves, "I could have had a happy life and I could have had a meaningful life if I hadn't experienced such trauma as a child." Others will say to themselves, "I could be happy if I weren't a member of a minority." Such rationalization is self-deception. Jesus was a member of a minority and He lived a successful life, and you can as well, if you get the chip off your shoulder and start taking advantage of the opportunities that are available to you now.

Jesus, the crown Prince of glory, came from heaven to sit where you sit. He was born into poverty. There wasn't even a bed or fresh sheets, just manure and flies in that manger. Jesus worked His early years as a carpenter's assistant for minimum wage.

Has someone accused you of being illegitimate? Every day Jesus lived, people said, "He's illegitimate."

Have you ever been rejected? Jesus Christ was rejected by His own people. The Bible says, "He came to His own and His own did not receive Him."[2]

Have you ever been betrayed by a dear friend—not just betrayed, but delivered over to be killed? That happened to Jesus. Judas sold Him to be crucified like a common criminal.

Have you been falsely accused, set up by a rigged bureaucracy? Jesus Christ went through that charade. He was brought into a court and confronted with charges that were trumped up by the state.

Have you been falsely convicted in a fraudulent scheme? Jesus was falsely convicted. Pilate said, "I find no fault in this Man,"[3] and, according to Roman law, the trial should have ended. But because he was such a cowardly legal barrister and judge, Pilate allowed public opinion to rape justice. And Jesus was crucified.

Have you been tortured for your faith? Jesus was. They spit on Him and put a crown of thorns on His head. They nailed Him to a cross and suspended Him between heaven and earth. Finally, they buried Him in a borrowed grave.

How did it affect Him? Jesus forgave them everything. Even while He was still on the cross, He forgave them. And He came out of the grave triumphant. Jesus did not say to His disciples, "Run for your lives. I never dreamed it was going to be this bad." Jesus said, "Be of good cheer, I have overcome the world."[4]

Whatever your plight, Jesus came from glory to sit where you sit, to know what you feel. That's why we pray to the Father, in Jesus' name. Jesus knows the pain you're going through. He has sat where you sit. This is the key to pure, effective communication. There must be understanding. There must be compassion.

Finally, I always recommend six steps to effective communication to those couples I counsel. This is the final way to beat deception in communication.

Six Steps to Effective Communication

1. Speak the truth in love. The Bible says, "Speaking the truth in love."[5] Repeat that to yourself—aloud. "Speaking the truth in love." Just keep this in mind: Truth is a two-edged sword. Be very careful when you approach your wife or your husband with it. The more truth you speak, the more love you should convey. Nothing improves your marriage partner's hearing like the sound of praise.

2. Plan a regular time for communication with your partner. I wake up in the morning bright eyed and ready to go. I almost hurt myself rushing to the shower. My wife, Diana, doesn't warm up until 10 A.M. We do not talk in the morning.

Ladies, when your husband comes home from work looking like the matador who just got gored and run over by the thundering herd, don't tell him, "The washing machine broke today," or "The IRS called and wants to investigate you for the last seven years," or "I wrecked your new Mercedes this afternoon," or "I ran over your new golf clubs backing out of the garage." There is a right and a wrong time to break bad news.

3. Don't raise your voice. Proverbs 15:1 says, "A soft answer turns away wrath." Here's the formula: kindly, calmly state your objection in love, and state it only once. That's right, only once. Then trust the Holy Spirit to produce a positive result. You will never get anything changed by nagging. Be calm and gracious, and then be quiet!

4. Allow time for reaction. Remember, you've had the advantage of thinking about what you're going to say. You've prepared your speech. You've pondered his reaction. You have mentally rehearsed your encounter. You have said, "If he says this, I'm going to say that. And if he says this, I'm going to come back with something else."

He is coming to this moment unprepared. He doesn't know that it is all predestined, that you've written the script, that he is already in the corral, and that the gate is locked. It doesn't dawn on him. But the next day he can see it clearly. "I have been had." When he comes home from work, he comes through the door saying, "Let's talk!" What happened? You're hurt. He has changed his mind. He promised. No, he just caught on. It finally hit him. He's had time to think about it.

5. Pray together. When you start praying with each other and for each other wonderful things happen. You start seeing your spouse through the eyes of God. You begin to understand him or her. And it is hard to pray with each other while holding a grudge.

6. Share the details. Men hate details. Women love details. It's been estimated that in a twenty-four-hour day, the average woman speaks twenty-five thousand words and the average man speaks about ten thousand words. It has been calculated that the average working man and woman use about nine thousand words. If that's true, when the man and the woman get home in the evening, he has one thousand words left and she is just warming up. A successful marriage will close that gap!

Deception in Spiritual Beliefs

America and the Occult

My knowledge of the occult and satanism wasn't forged in a library. It didn't come from newspapers or books. It came from firsthand experiences that occurred over a period of a few weeks in 1971. My knowledge of satanism came from a literal invasion of supernatural powers that hit my hometown of San Antonio, Texas. It was like a chapter out of a Frank Peretti book.

Twenty-five years ago the *San Antonio Light*, my hometown newspaper, published a remarkable story about the rise of the occult in our city. Robert Pugh, Bexar County director of mental health, was quoted in the article as saying that more than 55,000 citizens of San Antonio openly practiced witchcraft. Readers were told that satanic cult members were systematically performing torture murders, supposedly on orders from the devil. Pugh himself referred to three recent, separate accounts of murders accompanied by bizarre rituals. In one case a man had been ordered to castrate himself. And he did! Another cult member had been ordered to put someone's eyes out. When he grew squeamish and failed the assignment, he was driven to despair. Finally, as proof of his commitment to Satan, he put his own eyes out.

Only days after this article in the newspaper a very attractive, well-dressed, well-educated woman came to my office for counseling. Her family had sent her. They wanted to find out why this woman seemed to have such uncanny ability to control other people. As she sat down, she looked me straight in the eye and started talking. "I worship Satan. Satan is god. His presence is more powerful than Jesus Christ. You Christians kneel and beg God for what you want. But I ask the devil and he delivers, whether it's power or money or sex or curses or spells on my enemies. I can control people at my will with just pins and dolls." As she looked deep into me, her eyes seemed to glow.

I grabbed my Bible and began to read, but before I could get started she slapped at the book like a cat that was cornered.

"That book is a lie!" she screamed. "Nothing more than a pack of lies. Put it down."

You didn't have to be a Phi Beta Kappa in theology to know that she was demon possessed.

I looked her in the eyes and said, "Jesus is Lord and Satan is defeated, and don't you ever forget it. You and all of your pins and voodoo dolls can't begin to touch one of God's anointed children covered by the blood of the cross.

"You hate this book because it is life and it is truth, and you represent a lie. The Bible says that Satan is a liar and the father of lies. He has been from the beginning of time. He has no power in an environment of truth."

She looked back at me and screamed, "Shut up!" She just kept repeating it: "Shut up! Shut up!" She stormed out of my office still repeating the words.

I sat there for a long moment and finally said to myself, *They don't really get into this in much detail in Abnormal Psychology Class 101, but what you have just experienced, John Hagee, is certainly in the Bible. It's on every other page of the Gospels.* At the university I was taught to believe that such experiences were based entirely on ignorance and superstition, but that was not what I had just seen in the woman in my office. She was deceived but not ignorant— a child of the devil who was obviously anointed by demonic power.

I had often wondered why demonic spiritual activity was so prevalent in every other continent except North America—Asia, Africa, South America, and even parts of sophisticated Europe, such as France. Accounts of such activity were clearly in the Scriptures and yet so absent from modern American public life. I often wondered why the devil and his demons couldn't seem to get across the Rio Grande River.

Spiritual Deception in America

One of the most succinct fulfillments of Bible prophecy in recent years has been the rise of the occult in America. What began in the 1960s as an amused flirtation with the horoscope has now grown into a full-fledged popular movement with its own books and rock music. At night, psychics rule the television airwaves. Parapsychology has been declared a legitimate arm of science while most state laws prohibit the teaching of Creation, even in private, church-run universities. Major news stories reveal that American defense industries have been spending millions of your tax dollars every year researching the occult. The CIA even hired psychics to tell them where Saddam Hussein was hiding and what the Russians were doing. Police detectives routinely seek the counsel of psychics to solve difficult murder cases. The number one, best-selling books in the country describe out-of-body experiences and visits from the grave. Former First Lady Nancy Reagan planned the White House calendar with the advice of her astrologer. During his term as governor of Massachusetts, presidential candidate Michael Dukakis was featured in *National Geographic* as honoring the state's leading witch. As I mentioned in Chapter 1, Hillary Clinton talks to the dead with the assistance of New Age psychic Jean Houston.

How did it happen so quickly? Wasn't America founded on the promise of religious liberty? Wasn't the Mayflower

Compact a commitment to God? Don't we mint our coins with the slogan, "In God We Trust"? How could a country as sophisticated as America reject the God who blessed her and prospered her, only to embrace a renewal of pagan worship and occult ritual long since discredited and abandoned by modern man?

The generation before ours couldn't count ten books on the occult in the public library. Occasional publications on the subject were privately printed, but no reputable book company would touch such a manuscript. Palm readers lived in house trailers or shacks in the slums.

Then came the government's war on the churches. Prayer in school was outlawed. The Ten Commandments were ripped off the walls of America's classrooms. School Bible clubs were shut down. America proclaimed itself a new, secular society. The ACLU has aggressively fought for freedom from religion, not freedom of religion, under the shroud of "separation of church and state."

Into the vacuum stepped the followers of Jeanne Dixon, Edgar Cayce, and a whole new generation of psychics. Americans were amused. "It's only a game," they said. Horoscopes were published in the newspapers. But amusement soon gave way to fascination. "It's all in the mind," they explained. "Autosuggestion. But, hey, it works." Bookstores across the country began devoting entire shelves to the occult. Today such publications take up prominent sections of major bookstore chains. Excluding the Bible, they outsell Christian books two to one. Year after year the psychic hot lines outperform all other infomercials on television. Make no mistake about it. Those numbers are driven by public interest and demand. Nielsen ratings of these satanic infomercials reveal television audiences many times larger than the leading religious programs in the country. The New Age is fascinated by "angels," who are nothing less than demonic spirit guides leading their captives deeper into deception.[1]

The Rise of Satanism

While most Americans involved in the occult naively play on its fringes, some have taken it to its ultimate conclusion and embraced its most extreme rituals and manifestations. In 1966 Anton LaVey founded the Church of Satan. Two years later he wrote *The Satanic Bible*, and scores of spiritually hungry Americans, mostly young people, began to flood into the new "church." From this cauldron was born a new form of acid rock music with lyrics of adoration to the devil. The Rolling Stones recorded songs like "Sympathy for the Devil," "Their Satanic Majesties Request," and "Goat's Head Soup." (A goat's head is used in satanic worship. This is acknowledged in Scripture where followers of Christ are "sheep" and Satan's followers are "goats."[2])

Satanic Acid Rock

Let me tell you something. Most acid rock concerts are nothing more than satanic worship services. I've gone. I've seen for myself. When the mayor of San Antonio asked a blue-ribbon committee of clergymen to stand with him against the demonic influence of rock music, I went to a rock concert to see for myself. If we as clergymen were going to have a press conference to condemn it, I wanted to know firsthand what we were fighting. I was shocked and sickened!

I watched the leaders stamp the floor with the satanic salute and scream their oaths and sing songs that glorify drug use, rape, and murder.

"Oh, they are just performers," young people will naively say. "They don't really believe any of it."

Not so. Some famous members of rock groups are on record that they have sold their souls to the devil for public popularity. They wanted to be as gods, receiving the worship and adulation of the masses. They wanted it, and they have it.

Former Black Sabbath lead singer Ozzy Osbourne sang openly of demons in "The Devil's Daughter." Osbourne argues, "I'm not a maniac devil worshiper. I'm just playing a role and having fun with it."

Richard Ramirez, the Night Stalker, was obsessed with the satanic themes in the album *Highway to Hell* by the heavy metal band AC/DC. His favorite song, "Night Prowler," was about slipping into the rooms of unsuspecting women. It is no coincidence that Ramirez slipped into the rooms· of his female victims, killed them, and then painted satanic pentagrams on the walls.

Dea Lucás, a high priestess in the Church of Satan in Van Nuys, California, claims that heavy metal is a prime recruiting tool for their church. "Heavy metal groups are influencing the kids to come to Satan . . . The groups are into satanism even though they deny it. Just by listening to the lyrics, being a satanist myself, I can read between the lines."[3]

The lyrics of current heavy metal and black metal bands are even more perverse and satanic, dealing with such topics as the death of God, sitting at Satan's left hand, sex with corpses, calling Jesus Christ the deceiver, glorifying human sacrifice, and the names of Satan.

You say, "Well, our children are just listening to music." Wrong. They cannot live on a musical diet of drugs, murder, rape, suicide, satanism, and doctrines of devils without damaging their eternal souls; and if you are allowing it in your house, you are liable for what happens.

Satanic Role-Playing Games

In the late 1970s new "role-playing" games popularized by Dungeons and Dragons began to appear in toy stores across the country. By the 1990s even Christian parents naively allowed their children to play along. This new generation of "games for the mind" could be played with a crowd or alone. The more advanced the games, the more elaborate the satanic rituals.

"It is only play, it is only play," parents protested. "After all, there are wizards, witches, and devils in kids' literature and the Bible." But these games were a far cry from the children's fairy tales passed down from Charles Perrault and the brothers Grimm. These were full-blown, illustrated textbooks on sorcery and witchcraft, including human sacrifice, ritual suicides, and sadomasochism.

Some young people couldn't get the scenes out of their minds. Several years ago, while conducting my own research on the occult, several deaths occurred, most of them within a few days of one another. In September of that year the body of a bright, seventeen-year-old California boy washed up on a San Francisco beach. He was a suicide victim. Days later, a twelve-year-old Colorado boy fatally shot his sixteen-year-old brother and then killed himself. Two days later in a suburb of Chicago a boy and a girl, both seventeen, committed suicide by running the family car in a closed garage. In Arlington, Texas, a teenager walked into a classroom with a sawed-off shotgun, put the gun to his head, and fired. Finally, in Goddard, Kansas, James Kirby, a fourteen-year-old Eagle Scout, opened fire with a hunting rifle at his local junior high school. The principal was among the dead. Each incident had in common the complex, role-playing game called Dungeons and Dragons.

Satanic Ritual Murders

Only a few years ago, news reporters were debunking public fears of the rise of satanism. Reports of missing children were ridiculed as sensationalistic and hysterical. It was all reminiscent of the witch trials of Salem, Massachusetts, we were told. Today, one account after another appears in our daily newspapers. The satanic ritual murder of Mike Kilroy shook many Christians from their lethargy. Kilroy was a young medical student, kidnapped off the streets of Matamoros by members of what the press called the "Ranch of the Devil." In a ritual satanic ceremony his legs were chopped off, his spinal cord was cut out, and his brains were extracted with a machete.

On July 4, 1984, police found Gary Lauwers's body in a wooded area of Northport in New York's Long Island. According to a statement by police, Ricky Kasso, seventeen, admitted to killing Lauwers by stabbing him in the face and cutting out his eyes. Kasso said he screamed at Lauwers, "Say you love Satan," before the boy was killed in a satanic ritual that lasted for a period of four hours. Finally, mercifully, they burned him alive. As he was dying, Lauwers screamed, "I love you, Mother."

For several years Kasso and at least twenty others had belonged to a satanic cult called "Knights of the Black Circle." Kasso had an inverted cross tattooed on his arm and had been arrested the previous April for digging up bodies for use in rituals. He had stolen a left hand from a corpse. (The left hand is a choice portion of the anatomy of a corpse because satanists are children of the devil who will, on Judgment Day, be forced by God Almighty to stand at His left hand.[4]) My own research reveals story after story, too gruesome to print.

Some people say, "Oh, that's a rare occasion. It only happens once in a while." Wrong. It's happening all over America, all of the time.

Today's crime wave of satanic murders or "sacrifices" is well-documented. Larry Kahaner, an award-winning investigative reporter who has written for the *Washington Post* and a long list of the nation's most prestigious newspapers, has authored the shocking book, *Cults That Kill*. (As you probably know, the *Washington Post* is not an evangelical Christian publication.) Kahaner traveled America from coast to coast, interviewing police detectives who specialize in occult crimes. The results were astounding. The problem is epidemic.

Kahaner learned that the moment of supreme power for a satanist is in the defilement of an innocent child, both through sexual abuse and, ultimately, sacrificial murder.

The sacrificial offering is considered the ultimate expression of loyalty to the devil. And where do they get these children for ritual slaughter? They kidnap them off the streets. (Their pictures adorn the milk cartons on your breakfast table.) They steal them from their hospital beds. They buy them from drug-addicted mothers. In some satanic cults, mothers are required to give up their own children. An Associated Press story told of an El Paso woman who handed over her five children for satanic slaughter. She said it was an honor. Many missing children are tragic victims of satanism and will never be found. (It is no coincidence that the numbers drastically increase the week of Halloween.)

According to retired police Captain Dale Griffis of Tiffin, Ohio, babies make the best sacrifices. "Satanists believe babies are best because babies are pure. They haven't sinned or been corrupted yet. They possess a higher power than adults. When you sacrifice a baby, you get greater power than if you sacrificed an adult. One of the most prized possessions of a satanist is a candle made from the fat of an unbaptized baby."

Female satanists breed themselves to give birth to children for the ritual offerings. Doctors in the satanic groups deliver the baby, filing no birth certificate. As far as the state is concerned, the person never existed. But then, the state is not big on protecting children anyway—in the womb or out of the womb. The baby is ritually slaughtered, cremated, and the fat is used to make candles for satanic worship at a later date.

Police report that most bodies used in such slayings are never found. Children of satanists convicted of murder told police that most bodies were simply buried in graveyards, right under the noses of authorities. According to the testimony, cult members find a new grave ready for burial the next day. They dig another few feet deeper, bury the body, pack the dirt, and the next day the planned burial takes place with a casket lowered down on top of the murdered victim. Once the official body is buried there is little chance of it being dug up again to search for a second body. Family members owning the official burial place will not want their loved one's remains disturbed. The murdered victim is never found.[5]

The second favorite method is cremation. Each cult member takes some of the ashes home where they are scattered in fifty directions.

And why don't we hear more about this in the press? Kahaner says that police departments themselves carefully squash the stories. Kahaner was told by policemen all across the country that if the words *Satan* or *satanist* appear in an official police report, the attorney representing the accused immediately pleads diminished capacity or insanity, and the criminal walks scot-free. After all, we all know there is no devil! Police are careful to keep that word out of any official reports and any leaks to the press.

There is another cynical reason why police squash such stories. Sometimes city politicians and police chiefs clamp a lid on the information for fear of diminished real estate values. Remarkably enough, some of the gruesome crimes occur in affluent neighborhoods.

The most disturbing reason why you don't read more about the epidemic in your local newspaper is because some publishers, city fathers, and even police officers are occasionally involved in occult practices themselves. They usually fear such horror stories will give what they believe to be "responsible occult activities" a black eye. But other times they are involved in the crimes and don't want an investigation. Journalist Kahaner was tipped off by numerous policemen that their profession was the profession of choice for a small, but deadly, number of satanists.

Who Is He and How Did He Get Here?

Students of comparative religion can tell you that the concept of Satan, or a "great evil spirit," is as old as mankind. Even the most remote, isolated regions of the world have had their encounters with the personality the Bible calls the devil. They may have had different names for him, but he was always there. Pagan worship included self-mutilation, and there was always that horrible concept of human sacrifice. The Aztecs murdered tens of thousands to avenge their god. Revelation 12:9 refers to "that serpent of old, called the Devil." Old, because he's been around since before the Garden of Eden.

From the teachings of Jesus and the prophets, we have six descriptions of Satan.

Satan, the Rebel

First, Satan is a rebel. By definition, a *rebel* is one who always finds fault with delegated authority.

The Old Testament describes Satan as an archangel created by God. He was one of the three highest supernatural beings in the genesis of time. He was beautiful. He had great knowledge and great power. And because of it, he became proud and led a great rebellion against God, taking a third of the heavenly angels with him.

The history of this rebellion was recorded by the prophet Isaiah. "I will ascend into heaven," Lucifer proclaimed. "I will exalt my throne above the stars of God; / I will also sit on the mount of the congregation / On the farthest sides of the north; / I will ascend above the heights of the clouds, / I will be like the Most High."[6]

Satan wanted God's authority, and he still wants it. He hates all authority. Even now, he is inspiring people to undermine God's delegated authority on earth, to undermine that authority in the home, as well as the church. Satan found fault with God's leadership in the Garden of Eden, and suggested to Eve that God was only being selfish by warning her against eating from the tree of the knowledge of good and evil. He was the inspiration behind Miriam's criticism and rebellion against Moses in the wilderness, until God gave her leprosy. Then she finally stopped talking. And he was the inspiration behind Absalom's rebellion against King David saying, "If I were king in Israel, we wouldn't allow this injustice to continue."

The teenager finding fault with his or her parents is in rebellion, and that rebellious spirit does not come from God. The wife who berates her husband is in rebellion to God's delegated authority. The church member who constantly finds fault with church leadership is often influenced by demonic spirits for the purpose of bringing discord to the body of Christ.

You are either under God's delegated authority or you are acting under the authority of the Prince of Darkness, Satan himself. You're either a slave to Satan or a servant of Christ.

Satan, the Master of Deception

Second, Satan is not only a rebel, he is a master of deception.

Satan is exposed in Scripture as a "wolf" in "sheep's clothing."[7] The Bible also warns us that Satan is "more cunning than any beast of the field."[8] He is often likened to a serpent. He sneaks his way into your life. He is suddenly upon you and attacks furiously and relentlessly at your weakest point in your weakest moment. When he tempted Jesus, he tempted Him with bread when He was hungry from a forty-day fast. He then tempted Him to prove He was truly the Son of God. Each time Jesus answered Satan with, "It is written"![9]

Listen to this! Satan did not deny that the Word of God was true. Secular universities may deny the Bible is true, but even the devil knows God's Word is true.

Satan also quoted Scripture to Jesus but twisted it in an attempt to get Jesus to jump from the highest point of the temple. If Satan twisted Scripture with the Son of God in an effort to destroy Him, he will twist it with you to destroy you. Distorted truth leads to deception, producing false doctrines, division in the church, and distrust in the absolute truth of the Word of God.

Over and over throughout the years I've had distraught mothers and teenagers sit in my office explaining how it all began so innocently by opening their minds to parapsychology and to the world of the occult. Millions of people were seduced by the teachings of Jeanne Dixon. "It's only mind over matter," they would say. But in her own autobiography Dixon describes the day that she lay on a bed and watched the serpent crawl up on the bed with her, look her in the eyes, and give her the strange power.

Satan is a spirit, and when you open the door, he will come in like a roaring lion and possess you. Satanism is not a fad you can forget. Once you open the door, it takes you over.

Jim Hardy of Carl Junction, Missouri, began experimenting with drugs as a sixth grader and was hooked by the age of thirteen. He and two friends forged a bloodbrother relationship around drugs, heavy metal music, gory movies, witchcraft, and satanism. At age seventeen they committed a human sacrifice. Jim later explained, "I would kind of just pray to God and Satan at the same time to see who was more powerful, and little by little I fell out of God and started falling into Satan . . . You can't just dabble. It sucks you in real quick."[10]

You can't get rid of Satan with a psychiatrist or meditation. You do it through the name and the power, the blood and the authority of Jesus Christ.

According to Larry Kahaner, people join satanist organizations primarily for one purpose: to obtain power—power over other people, power over circumstances, power to make more money, sexual power, some kind of power. The satanists in Matamoros who murdered the young Kilroy boy wanted power to sell drugs and power to escape detection by the police.

The Bible teaches that Satan does have power, and he will give you that power—for a short period of time. All it costs you is your eternal soul!

Those famous members of rock groups who sold their souls to the devil have paid the price of their eternal souls. "He who believes in Him is not condemned; but he who does not believe is condemned already."[11] So when you are channel surfing through the stations featured by your cable television carrier and you see one of these famous acid rock, satanic high priests spouting his lyrics of praise to Lucifer, just remember you are looking at a poor, lost soul who is only a heartbeat from eternal hell—not some god strutting his stuff like a peacock, but an absolute idiot who has sold his soul to the devil.

Satan, the Angel of Light

Third, Satan masquerades as "an angel of light."

Even while the Bible speaks of Satan's subtlety as the "angel of light," it warns that he can change his guise, in a moment, into a terrible creature. Peter describes him as intimidating and fearful, "a roaring lion, seeking whom he may devour."[12] Satan will use fear to paralyze and control people's lives.

I saw how Satan changes his guise from an angel of light to a lion who seeks to devour that day in 1971 when the woman came into my office and announced, "I worship Satan." After she left, I sat there and quietly prayed. "Lord, You said that if any man lacked wisdom he should pray and ask for it and You would give it. And that You would give it freely. Well, I'm asking. Teach me the truth. Show me what You know that I don't know."

Then I opened the Bible and read the story in Luke 8 of the demoniac of Gadara who had been possessed by demonic spirits. He was in chains, the asylum of his day. He had supernatural strength. People were afraid of him. He had power. I read the story several times, not knowing that in less than twenty-four hours it was going to change my life forever.

The next morning I arrived at the office at eight. The

telephone was ringing. A female voice on the other end asked, "Is this Pastor Hagee?"

"Yes."

"Pastor Hagee," she said. "I believe I have a demon spirit in me."

This was just too coincidental. I said, "Is that so?" Suspicion and doubt were apparent in the tone of my voice. Was my friend from the day before trying to set me up? I asked for her name but didn't recognize it. "You don't go to my church, do you?"

"No, I don't."

"Then why did you call me?"

"Because I pass your church every day going to work," she said. "I saw your name, I saw your phone number, and I just thought you might be able to help." She told me her story, gave me her address, and I reluctantly agreed to stop by and pray for her.

The woman lived in a very exclusive subdivision—not what I was expecting. I rang the doorbell, planning to leave if she didn't open the door immediately. She was breathless. "Thank you, thank you," she said. "I was afraid you weren't going to come." She reads minds, too, I thought.

We went into the den. She sat down; I remained standing. She said that her husband was a very powerful and important businessman who worked mostly in New York. She had dabbled very lightly in the occult, mostly tarot cards. It relieved the boredom and loneliness. It appeared harmless (Satan masquerades as an angel of light, remember). Nothing bad had ever happened until last Thursday.

"I was alone in the house, at about midnight, sitting on this very couch," she said. "I heard the front door of my home open. I could hear the footsteps of something walking down the hall, down the marble floor."

"Something? Or someone?" I asked, wanting to get that clear.

She said, "It was something. It didn't sound human, but it was certainly not a dog or other four-legged animal either.

I called out, 'Who's there?' It kept walking down the hall very slowly. I could hear every footstep. Then it entered this room. I could see nothing, and yet at the same time I could feel its presence beside me. And then it entered me."

I said, "It what?"

She said, "It entered me."

"And what makes you think that it's still there?"

"I know it," she said. "My life has dramatically changed. My mind is filled with the most terrible and vulgar sex scenes. I have thoughts of violence. I find myself violently cursing people in public, people that I don't even know and have no reason to harm. Understand, I have never cursed in my life. This isn't me. I have thoughts of murder. Something is very wrong. Can you help me?"

Satan was showing his true colors to this woman.

The Lord seemed to be whispering in my ear, "John, remember that story you read the other day, the one in Luke 8? Well, whip it out."

As I began reading the story of the demoniac of Gadara from the Bible, I instantly noticed a change in the woman. Her eyes glazed over. They had the vacant look of a cat; there was no humanity there. I knew I was facing something that the professor had failed to mention in abnormal psychology. I plowed right ahead, acting as if everything were normal.

"You'll notice that Jesus commanded the demons to identify themselves," I said, "and then He commanded them to leave. They had to obey. Are you ready for this to happen?" My voice was very calm, very clinical. But it was as if she were no longer there. "In the name of Jesus," I said very calmly, with no emotion, "by the power of His shed blood, through the authority of His word, I command this evil spirit to come out of this woman."

What happened next made the hair on my head stand straight up. The lady began to contort. She was a tall woman, probably six feet, and very slender. She was sitting on the couch but she reached down, grabbed her ankles by her hands, and pumped her knees up into the air above her head. Her head was now beneath her feet. She was literally bent double. Ten surgeons couldn't get me in that position. And as she went down, she was looking at me with those glassy, catlike eyes and exhaling a long, gutteral, chilling growl.

I thought to myself, *Lady, where would you like the new door in your house, because I am getting ready to make you one! It will be about five feet, eight inches high and about four feet wide.* I had never seen anything like that in my life. She slowly lifted her head, hissing at me like a snake, pure hatred in her eyes; then she spoke in a deep, baritone, masculine voice. "I hate you, John Hagee."

I thought, *Hey, you know, we just met. It usually takes people a day or two to hate me.* Of course, I knew that the demon spirit was speaking through the woman. This was spiritual warfare, and in any confrontation every fiber of my being says, "Attack, attack, attack!" So I turned up the volume and looked her straight in the eye and said, "Come out of her in Jesus' mighty name!"

Throughout all of this I did not once touch the woman. But if I had hit her in the face, she wouldn't have jumped any quicker than she did at those words.

The demon's deep baritone voice answered back, "I won't leave her alone."

I started quoting Scriptures. "Whoever calls on the name of the LORD / Shall be saved."[13] "Therefore if the Son makes you free, you shall be free indeed."[14]

After forty-five minutes of intense spiritual warfare, the lady let out a bloodcurdling scream and fell to the floor like she was dead. Moments later she sat up with a radiant smile on her face. The catlike countenance was now the portrait of peace. "I'm free," she said. "It's gone. It's gone. It's gone. I'm changed. Thank God. Thank God."

There was no doubt in my mind that Satan had possessed this woman. He had entered her life through what seemed a harmless pastime—reading tarot cards—and then tried to destroy her mind, body, and, finally, her soul.

Satan, the Accuser of the Brethren

Satan is a rebel, Satan is a master of deception, Satan masquerades as an angel of light, and, fourth, Satan is an accuser of the brethren.

The Bible teaches that Satan is the accuser of the brethren.[15] When you make accusations against a fellow believer, you are doing the work of the devil. Yes, stand up to evil. Expose the darkness. But God expects us to be forgiving and accommodating to the brothers and sisters of the faith. He expects us to get along.

James said that the tongue is set on fire from hell itself. You can murder another person with your toxic tongue. You can murder their reputation. You can murder their character and their influence. You can murder their marriage relationships by planting words of doubt and suspicion. You can murder their hopes and dreams. This is the work of Satan.

Satan, the Tempter

Satan is an accuser of the brethren and, fifth, Satan is also a tempter.

Matthew's Gospel teaches that Satan entices men to sin. I remember talking with a young drug addict. "And what do you call the stuff you're using?" I asked.

"It's angel dust," he said.

That aroused my curiosity so I learned a little bit more. There is a drug called "ecstasy." There is even one called "heaven." But of course, when you get hooked, it's hell.

Satan, the Killer

Sixth, Satan is a killer.

John 8:44 says that Satan "was a murderer from the beginning." This is why he demands sacrifices. This is why he likes innocent blood, the young girls, the virgins sacrificed by the thousands by the Aztecs, and the babies sacrificed by the millions on the altars of Molech. His delight is the damage done to the soul of the murderer.

The respected historian Gitta Sereny, seeking to solve the puzzle of the monstrous crimes of the Hitler regime, writes about an interview with one of the secretaries close to Hitler who saw it all unfolding. After many interviews, when Sereny had finally gained the woman's trust, she reluctantly explained that she had finally resolved in her own mind what had happened. It may not sound very intellectual, she admitted, but she firmly believed that Hitler had become demon possessed.

Detective Chip Wilson of the Denver police department told Larry Kahaner, "Where all these cults go bad is when people aren't satisfied to live within the environment they have created. It's not enough to have power over themselves. They want to control the heavens and each other. As the need for power grows, occult crime increases."[16]

Lieutenant Mike Davison, chief investigator for the Monroe County sheriff's special investigation unit in Michigan, reports other evidence of Satan as a killer—the cold-blooded murder of Lloyd Gamble, age seventeen, by his fifteen-year-old brother.

The fifteen year old called the police department and calmly reported that he had just shot his brother twice in the head at point-blank range.

He said his parents were due home at any minute, and if the police didn't stop him he would shoot them when they got home.

When the police arrived at his home, he calmly gave himself up. The police found his brother's body downstairs, shot twice in the head as reported.

Three days later, the parents called police and asked them to return to the house. When the police arrived the parents brought out a green vinyl bag that had been hidden in a closet. It contained a hood, a long black robe, a silver chalice, a dark blue candle, a glass bottle filled with red liquid, and eleven cassette tapes of Mötley Crüe, Black

Sabbath, and other heavy metal groups. There was a book titled *The Power of Satan*, a paper pentagram, a sword, and an upside-down cross.

The book, *The Power of Satan*, came from a satanic group in Canada. The parents believed their son got the information about the group when he attended a Mötley Crüe concert. The book gave step-by-step instructions on how to perform a satanic ritual.[17]

Let me warn you. Satan is a killer. He doesn't like you.

"Well," you say, "what if I'm on his side?" There is no "Satan's side." If you let him, he will use you, possess you, and, if he can, he will then get you to commit suicide. There are not two sides. There is only one side, God's side; and you are either on God's side or you are lost, vulnerable, and in danger.

I am writing this book to serve notice that Satan is real. It was a very real Satan who appeared in the Garden of Eden. A very real Satan attacked Job. A very real Satan tempted Jesus, and a very real Satan has deceived the United States of America and most of its people. Some parents are fighting a very real Satan in their own homes because their children are involved with occult practices.

How to Fight Satanism in the Home

Most parents shudder at the thought that their children might be involved in satanism. And I don't blame them. Some parents even deny the possibility until it is much too late. Instead I suggest that all parents be aware of the signs of occult involvement. Here are a few telltale signs from *Satanism: The Seduction of America's Youth* by Bob Larson, a man who has worked with young people for years:

- An unhealthy preoccupation with fantasy role-playing games like Dungeons and Dragons. You will remember that the twelve-year-old Colorado boy who fatally shot his sixteen-year-old brother and then killed himself, the Chicago boy and girl who committed suicide, the Arlington, Texas, teenager who shot himself in school, and the fourteen-year-old Eagle Scout who opened fire in a local junior high school were all heavily involved with Dungeons and Dragons.

- An interest in tarot cards, Ouija boards, and other occult games. The woman who called me so desperate that day in 1971 had dabbled in tarot cards before she came under satanic oppression.

- An addiction to horror movies like *Friday the 13th* and *Nightmare on Elm Street*, whose main characters kill and maim.

- An obsession with heavy metal music, particularly black metal bands like Slayer, Venom, Ozzy Osbourne, Metallica, Megadeath, King Diamond, Iron Maiden, and other groups that evoke satanic symbolism.

- Withdrawal from church and a drop in grades. The child may begin to show a hostile attitude toward Christianity and previous Christian friends.

- An attraction to satanic literature and such books as *The Satanic Bible* and the *Necronomicon*, the writings of Aleister Crowley.

- An involvement with friends who dress in black, greet each other with the satanic salute (index and pinkie finger extended, with palm facing inward), speak and write backwards, or organize secret meetings.

- Drug and/or alcohol use.[18]

These are the initial signs of involvement with the occult. If you see such signs, you should be watchful, but as Larson says, "Beware of the temptation to search a child's room or screen his mail, which would breach his trust in you. Don't suddenly demand that every offensive poster come off his wall and every distasteful record album go to the garbage. Precipitous action will instill further anger and rebellion. Instead, be alert for additional clues of satanic involvement."[19]

Signs of deeper satanic involvement are:

- A preoccupation with psychic phenomena like telepathy, astral projection, I Ching, and parapsychology.

- An affinity for satanic paraphernalia, including skulls, knives, chalices, black candles, and robes.

- An inclination to write poems or letters about satanism or to sketch designs of upside-down crosses, pentagrams, the number 666, names of the devil, or skulls and other symbols of death.

- Keeping a private journal such as a Book of Shadows (a self-designed secret chronicle of satanic activities and ideas).

- An obsession with death and suicide.

Larson warns parents, "If your child shows any interest in the occult, don't wait until there is a fire to set off an alarm. At the first sign of smoke, get help quickly. Contact a minister, counselor, or police expert familiar with satanism." Larson suggests that many public and private mental health treatment centers recognize the problems of youthful involvement in the occult and have excellent cult treatment programs. Their phone numbers are generally listed in the Yellow Pages.[20]

Every Christian needs to be alert to the possibilities of satanic involvement so that we will be prepared. Certainly I will never forget the last incidents in that couple of weeks in 1971.

Satanic Symbols[21]

HORNED HAND
The HORNED HAND is a sign of recognition between those in the occult. It is also used by those at heavy metal concerts to affirm their allegiance to the music's message of negativism.

ANARCHY
The symbol of ANARCHY represents abolition of all law. First used in "punk" music, it's now widely used by heavy metal music fans.

ANKH
The ANKH is an ancient Egyptian symbol for life and fertility. The top portion represents the female, the lower portion the male. This symbol supposedly has magical sexual significance.

CROSS OF CONFUSION
The CROSS OF CONFUSION is an old Roman symbol that questions the validity of Christianity. It is used on albums by the rock group Blue Oyster Cult.

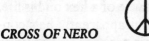

CROSS OF NERO
This symbol represented peace in the early '60s. Among today's heavy metal and occult groups, it signifies the CROSS OF NERO. It shows an inverted cross with a cross anchor broken downward, signifying defeat of Christianity.

PENTAGRAM
The PENTAGRAM (without the circle, the PENTACLE) is used in both Black and White Magic. The top point represents the spirit. The other points represent wind, fire, earth, and water. It is believed to have power to conjure good spirits and ward off evil.

ANTIJUSTICE
The Roman symbol of justice was an upright double-bladed ax. The representation of ANTIJUSTICE inverts the double-bladed ax.

BAPHOMET
The upside-down pentagram, often called the BAPHOMET, is satanic and represents the goat's head.

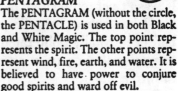

SWASTIKA
The SWASTIKA or BROKEN CROSS originally represented the four winds, four seasons, and four compass points. Its arms were at 90° angles turned the opposite way, as depicted here, and turned clockwise, showing harmony with nature. The SWASTIKA shows the elements or forces turning against nature and out of harmony.

191

One Final Round with the Devil

By the time I got back to the office after my visit with the woman in that exclusive subdivision, I was exhausted. It wasn't yet ten o'clock in the morning and I already felt like I had run a five-mile race. In one hour my theology had been totally obliterated. I thought, *I'll never see anything like that again in all my life. I'd better learn what I can from it.*

But the day wasn't over. I was in God's classroom. I had asked for His wisdom on the subject, and He was giving me a heavy dose of spiritual reality.

That night a church member phoned with a bizarre story. "Pastor," he said, "I just hung up the phone after talking with a man who said he is going to murder me tomorrow."

I almost laughed aloud. Did you ever have one of those days? You had just a little bit more excitement than you knew what to do with? (And in the middle of the day, a couple, God's little helpers, called all offended because their name was misspelled in the church newspaper for bringing color toothpicks to the church barbecue. They didn't understand why I couldn't appreciate the pain of such a slight.)

I asked the man, "Well, what did you do to him? What's the problem all about?"

He said, "Pastor, I haven't seen this man for twenty years. Look, I know this sounds crazy, but he's gotten involved in witchcraft. Every day he's in touch with some so-called witch in California who passes on her instructions to him. She told him that I am the cause of a hex on his life. I don't even know what a hex is, but apparently he's convinced that I'm to blame for all of his problems." The voice on the other end of the line was sometimes panic-stricken, sometimes apologetic. "Can you believe me, Pastor?"

You caught me on a good day, I thought to myself. *Yesterday, I wouldn't have believed you. Today? I can believe anything.* "Get the man to meet me tomorrow in my office. You come too. Tell him that I can solve his problem with the hex."

The voice on the other end of the line was hesitant. "I don't know if I can pull that off, Pastor, but I'll try."

The next morning the two men walked into my office. The man who had called me on the phone looked terrified. I immediately opened Pandora's box. Why waste time? I looked his tormentor straight in the eye and said, "You think there's power in witchcraft? The blood of Jesus Christ gives every believer absolute authority over all the demons of hell."

He jumped like I had stuck him in the behind with a pitchfork. For a moment he was dumbfounded. When he recovered, he started in right where the lady had left off the previous morning.

"I know there is power in witchcraft," he said. "I can work a hex on any person I choose with voodoo dolls and powders. I can make bad things happen to people who make me mad." He was obviously threatening me.

I picked up the Bible, where the fight ended the last time, and said, "Satan is liar, and according to this Book, he is a deceiver and a murderer. Anyone who follows him is going to spend eternity in hell, including you. Does that make you mad?"

It certainly did. He jumped to his feet, ran out, and slammed the door, saying very ugly things about my personhood.

The next Wednesday night I began teaching my congregation from Luke 8. I thought they needed to know what I was discovering. Of course, some didn't want to know. One lady told me, "Pastor, stop teaching us about the devil. I don't bother the devil, and the devil doesn't bother me."

Let me tell you something. That's a joke. The Bible teaches that Satan has come to kill and to destroy. You are in this fight, like it or not, and it's a fight to the finish. You will either defeat Satan and his demonic hordes through the power of the blood or you will be destroyed. Paul commanded the church to "fight the good fight."[22]

Fight to win! Fight with confidence! Fight with the spiritual weapons of Ephesians 6.

While I was teaching the congregation on this particular chapter of the Bible at the Wednesday evening service, the man who played with voodoo dolls walked into the church. He was carrying a gun, cocked and loaded, cursing God's holy name as he walked right up the aisle. He stopped at the pew where the man he had threatened to murder was sitting, put the gun behind this man's head, and roared like an animal. He took his hostage and walked him up the aisle at point-blank range and made him stand beside me at the pulpit.

"Now both of you," he shouted, "get down on your knees and beg for your lives. I am going to kill you right here."

I said, "This is the house of God. We are under the authority of Jesus Christ, and you have no power here. The Word of God says, 'No weapon formed against [us] shall prosper.'[23] We're in charge here. You are not."

He started counting, "One, two, . . ." and then he opened fire. It was surreal. He was pointing a loaded gun at us and firing away. We actually have a tape recording of that service. People in the congregation will sometimes play it. It will send chills down your spine. I promise you this, it was not a dull Wednesday-night prayer service, and it was all on the front pages of the newspaper the next day. Not one bullet hit either of us.

That was twenty-five years ago. It was only the beginning of my new education about the spirit world. Forget all the ridiculous concepts of childhood, but believe this: There is a very real devil. He is a demonic spiritual being who can use people in an effort to control the physical world. His object is to destroy your heart, soul, mind, and body; to destroy everything that you love, everything you hope for, and everything you dream about. The Bible says that Satan comes "to steal, and to kill, and to destroy."[24]

Every person who reads this book is either saved or lost. You are in one of those groups. There is no in-between. You are either sheep or goats, wheat or tares. You've either publicly confessed and received Christ, or you are the property of Satan. You say, "Preacher, I would never join the occult." Let me tell you something: Without Jesus Christ you are as much in the occult as those people who murdered Mike Kilroy in Matamoros. You are his property right now. He owns you. The first step away from Jesus Christ is your first step toward the Prince of Darkness. When you reject the truth, all that's left is a lie and deception.

James 1:14–15 says, "But each one is tempted when he is drawn away by his own desires and enticed. Then, when desire has conceived, it gives birth to sin; and sin, when it is full-grown, brings forth death." Romans 6:23 says, "The wages of sin is death."

What is sin?

James 4:17, "To him who knows to do good and does not do it, to him it is sin." Romans 14:23 says, "Whatever is not from faith is sin."

Is there unconfessed sin in your life? If so, Satan has his fangs in your soul. No one ever recovers from sin without the blood of Jesus Christ. Hebrews 9:22 says, "Without shedding of blood there is no remission [of sin]."

Jesus said, "He who is not with Me is against Me, and he who does not gather with Me scatters abroad."[25] You can't be both things. You are either the property of Jesus Christ or a slave to sin and Satan. There are two lords: Lord Jesus and lord Satan. There are two families: the family of God and the family of Satan. There are two destinations: heaven and hell.

The Good News

Now for the good news. If you are a Christian, if you have committed your life to Him and been born again, Satan is a defeated foe. When Jesus Christ climbed Calvary's hill, He defeated the forces of hell. He became the sacrifice, the only sacrifice that is necessary to atone for your sins. Satan's power was broken forever. I thank the Lord for His shed blood. I thank the Lord for the blood of the cross, because through that blood we have victory and deliverance; we have freedom from sin and its dominion. Every shackle has been broken. If you are addicted to drugs, you can be free today. If you are a servant to alcohol or pornography, you can be free today. If you are controlled by the wild emotions of anger, fear, resentment, or depression, you can be free. We have been made kings and priests, sons and daughters in the kingdom of God by the blood of Jesus Christ.

The name of Jesus Christ is *El Shaddhai*, the Almighty One. He alone has all power, and He has given it to us. Before He went to His father, He said, "All authority has been given to Me in heaven and on earth . . . and lo, I am with you always, even to the end of the age."[26] When Satan roars against you like a lion, fight back in the name of Jesus and the power of His precious blood. The Bible says that even the demons tremble in fear. The victory is ours. The Bible says, "Resist the devil and he will flee from you."[27]

There is deliverance from Satan's deceptions.

Chapter Ten

Witchcraft in the Church House

Witchcraft in the church house!? Now you've gone too far, Hagee," you may be thinking. "Are you really sure the devil can operate within the walls of the church? Can he use churchmen, preachers, and laymen?"

Yes, the devil can. He does now—and he has for centuries. Remember what Jesus said to some of the religious leaders of his day: "You are of your father the devil."[1]

Jesus made it very clear that at the end of the age the most subtle of Satan's deceptions would hit the church itself. He warned that his own believers were in danger.[2]

Let me give you some very concrete examples: the goddess movement within many denominations, clergy homosexual involvement, and errant philosophy and unusual manifestations of the spirit in the evangelical church.

The Goddess Movement

Perhaps the most stunning heresy ever to appear in the Christian church is the growing worship of the goddess Sophia. One United Methodist minister was surprised to encounter Sophia at his local church.

In 1993, Thomas Oden, a professor at an American theological school, attended a regular Thursday Holy Communion service at this school.

The first hymn, "Sophia," sang the praise of the goddess Sophia, who *ordains* what God will do." "She's the teacher we esteem, and the subject of life's theme."

Oden began to feel uneasy. *Am I in a place where some Lord other than Jesus Christ is being worshiped?* he wondered.

It didn't take long for him to realize this was true.

The sermon didn't focus on a Scripture text, but on an event in the woman's experience as a feminist preacher. She told a "victory" story, in which a "pious" Methodist lay leader and other members were forced to join another church after they challenged her authority to offer the Lord's Supper in the name of the goddess Sophia. She proudly described a sermon she preached to recount their disapproval, in which she invited all members who did not agree with her to look for another church.

The Scripture for this service was chiefly from the Apocrypha, Proverbs, and Psalms—mainly passages that deified wisdom. Then, incredibly, this minister likened the yoke of discipleship to sadistic and masochistic sex.

Thomas Oden wondered, *Can I in good conscience receive Holy Communion under these circumstances?*

The question was answered for him when the preacher offered the invitation to come to the Lord's Table, not in the Lord's name, but in the name of the goddess who was speaking through Christ. The congregation was invited to Christ's table, but in Sophia's name.[3]

Thomas Oden's experience is not unique. The goddess movement within the church finally catapulted into public debate after an international, ecumenical conference held November 4-7, 1993, in Minneapolis, Minnesota. Inspired by the decade-long World Council of Churches celebration of "Solidarity with Women," the event drew thousands of participants from fifty states, twenty-eight countries, and dozens of Christian denominations. Twenty religious organizations funded the conference, including the Presbyterian Church, the United Methodist Church, the Evangelical Lutherans, the American Baptist Convention, the United Church of Christ, and four religious communities of the Roman Catholic Church. The Presbyterians drew $66,000 from their "Missions Fund" to help sponsor the event.[4]

Not only was the goddess Sophia celebrated in open worship, but Jesus was roundly denigrated. Theologian Delores Williams, speaking about the doctrine of atonement, declared, "I don't think we need folks hanging on crosses and blood dripping and weird stuff."[5] A female professor from William Patterson College declared that the cross symbolized God as an abusive parent. The atonement was said to be a "wild doctrine that encourages the violence of our streets."[6] Two thousand delegates opened the evening chanting, "Bless Sophia. Dream the vision. Share the wisdom dwelling deep within."

Speakers encouraged participants to search their souls and identify their own "goddess" and not be inhibited by past restrictive traditions. Above all, delegates were told to "be inclusive." Participants named dozens of goddesses: "fire of love, she who is eternal, earth mother, spirit woman, yin and yang." A delegate from Union Theological Seminary introduced the conference to Kali, the Hindu goddess; Quani, the Buddhist goddess; and Enna, the Animist goddess of the Philippines.

"Buddha died in his eighties," the speaker said. "Jesus died at thirty-three. Maybe Jesus should be called too young to understand."[7]

Participants laughed and roared their approval.

A feminist from India anointed delegates' foreheads with red dots to celebrate "the divine in each other" and to protest the oppression brought to India by Christian missionaries. Chung Hyun Kyung, a Korean theologian, told the conference that "my bowel is Shamanist, my heart is Buddhist, my right brain is Confucianist, and my left brain is Christian. I call it a family of gods, and they are all together."[8]

Sometimes the conference was not only anti-Christian, it

was anti-God. Chung Hyun Kyung took a bite from an apple, symbolizing Adam and Eve's sin and demonstrating defiance of God the Father, and asked the audience, "What taboo have you broken today?"[9]

Speakers also discussed the new sexuality. Roman Catholic leader Mary Hunt of Maryland reminded the audience of feminist theologian Virginia Mollenkott's popular quote, "Grace is a lesbian." In encouraging the delegates to become champions of the gay and lesbian agenda, she said, "Whether it is Christian or not is frankly, darling, something about which I no longer give a pope."[10]

In another session, Melanie Morrison conducted a "Lesbian altar call" while a choir sang in the background, "Keep on moving forward . . . Never turning back."[11] Hunt encouraged delegates to "imagine sex among friends as the norm. Imagine valuable genital sexual interaction in terms of whether or how it fosters friendship and pleasure."[12]

The most remarkable sacrilege of the conference was the concluding "communion service," listed in the program as a "Blessing over Milk and Honey." The worship leader led the audience in a liturgical response, "With the hot blood of our wombs we give form to new life . . . With the milk of our breasts we suckle the children . . . With nectar between our thighs we invite a lover. . . we birth a child; with our warm body fluids we remind the world of its pleasure and sensations."[13]

How could it happen? How could leaders in major denominations be swept into such doctrines? How could some evangelical writers and ministers be seduced?

Sophia is the Greek form of the Hebrew word *Chokmah*, used 141 times in the Old Testament. As in many languages, all Hebrew words are either masculine or feminine. *Chokmah* is of the feminine gender. In Proverbs, in a poetic sense, the writer personifies wisdom, saying she was present at the very creation.[14] Feminists declare that this wisdom—the Chokmah—present at creation, is the goddess Sophia.

None of this comes as a great surprise to students of the

Bible. Satan has always used God's own words to tempt and subvert His people. In the Garden of Eden he subtly misquoted God's warning to Eve, suggesting that God had put everything off limits. "Has God indeed said, 'You shall not eat of *every* tree of the garden'?"[15] Of course, God had said no such thing. He had placed his prohibition on only *one* tree and Satan knew it; the thousands of others were available to Adam and Eve. Satan twisted God's words to discourage Job. He twisted God's words to tempt Jesus. And he is twisting God's words today to corrupt and deceive the church.

Of course defenders of the faith are in every denomination, people who have experienced God's power and who are committed to His Word, but more and more they are routinely ridiculed or dismissed. When a great host of Presbyterians objected to the Sophia movement, Mary Ann Lundy, a feminist theologian, countered with the charge that there is a "battle for the soul of the Presbyterian church launched by political forces led by the far or radical right."[16] Many opponents, not wanting to appear intolerant, backed down.

In the last three years the movement has only picked up more steam. In June 1994 hundreds of women attended the Renaissance of the Sacred Feminine Conference at San Francisco's Grace Episcopal Cathedral. Again women chanted to Sophia: "We bow to your sacred power, the holy wisdom of Sophia, our beloved mother who is in heaven and earth."

A paragraph in the program said, "This participatory event celebrates and honors the presence of the Divine Mother at the heart of the emerging global civilization. The Sacred Feminine has a central role in the healing of our divided minds and endangered planet . . . Without spiritual transformation on a massive and unprecedented scale, humankind will not survive."

It doesn't take a rocket scientist to see where "Sophia" is taking her followers.

One of the many deceptions in the goddess movement—lesbianism and homosexuality—is also found in other areas of the church.

Homosexuality in the Church House

In many denominations, traditional Christian doctrine has collapsed in the face of the popular immorality of our day. The Bible refers to this kind of deception:

> Professing to be wise, they became fools, and changed the glory of the incorruptible God . . . Therefore God also gave them up to uncleanness, in the lusts of their hearts, to dishonor their bodies among themselves . . . For even their women exchanged the natural use for what is against nature. Likewise also the men, leaving the natural use of the woman, burned in their lust for one another.[17]

As recently as 1979 the Episcopal church went on record condemning sex outside of marriage. At its annual convention it passed a resolution stating that "it is not appropriate" for the church to ordain practicing homosexuals or adulterers. But only a decade later, influenced by the cultural changes sweeping the nation, the church changed its mind. In 1990, Episcopal Bishop Walter Righter ordained a noncelibate homosexual man for ministry in the church. When the action was challenged, Bishop John Spong of the Diocese of Newark announced, "This church of ours has done an audacious thing. We will not now tremble at our audacity. Rather we will step boldly into the future that we have helped to build."[18]

Then only four years later, in 1994, at the General Convention of the Episcopal Church, seventy-one bishops signed a "Statement of Koinonia," saying that "homosexuality and heterosexuality are morally neutral."[19] When conservative Episcopalians attempted to reaffirm biblical morality, they were answered by Bishop Orris Walker of the Long Island diocese who pointed out that many of his parishioners were single. "Is this church going to say to them that sexual intimacy for them is abnormal if it does not occur within marriage? If this church expects me to go back to the streets of Brooklyn and Queens with that one, it ain't going to fly."[20]

Conservatives were defeated.

In 1996, by a vote of seven to one, an Episcopal council of bishops in Wilmington, Delaware, dismissed the whole controversy with the remarkable statement that there was no "core doctrine prohibiting the ordination of a noncelibate, homosexual person living in a faithful and committed sexual relationship with a person of the same sex."[21] That same month, two gay men stood before the altar of St. Mark's Cathedral in Seattle to exchange vows and receive the blessing of the church on their homosexual union. The presiding minister announced, "Let their love be without shame, a sign of a new world of justice and peace."[22]

One of the great weapons of people in deception is the word love. The premise is "God is love," therefore anything under the banner of love must be accepted. That's wrong. Any kind of love that does not result in the absolute obedience to the Word of God is unscriptural and a deception.

In John 14:15, Jesus said to His disciples, "If you love Me, keep My commandments." His words in verse 21 are very clear. "He who has My commandments and keeps them, it is he who loves Me." Hebrews 12:5-8 is addressed to Christians:

> "My son, do not despise the chastening of the LORD,
> Nor be discouraged when you are rebuked by Him;
> For whom the LORD loves He chastens,
> And scourges every son whom He receives."

If you endure chastening, God deals with you as with sons . . . But if you are without chastening . . . then you are illegitimate and not sons.

The apostle Paul tells Christians not to despise the chastening of the Lord. It is proof positive of His eternal love in shaping our lives and destinies. God never stops disciplining His children.

Look at Moses, at age eighty, chosen of God and commissioned to deliver the children of Israel from Egypt. God sent him back to Egypt and on the way the Lord met him and tried to kill him.[23] Why? He had not circumcised his son, which means that he had disobeyed the sign of the covenant God made with Abraham and his descendants. God would rather have seen Moses die than go through his ministry in disobedience.

Make no mistake, anyone who teaches "love" without "discipline" is teaching a lie. Love demands discipline. Anyone who tells you that you can have peace without God's price of repentance is teaching you a lie. It is the doctrine of demons pure and simple. Timothy warned that in the last days men would be "lovers of pleasure rather than lovers of God, having a form of godliness but denying its power."[24]

It finally took a pornographer to put the whole Episcopal controversy in perspective. In its December 1996 issue, *Penthouse* magazine published an exposé of a "sex-boy service" allegedly operated by priests of a Long Island, New York, church. In an ironic bit of sermonizing, the magazine warned readers that its story "may well shatter any trust you have left in our religious institutions."[25]

According to participants, young men from Brazil were brought into the United States by clerics to serve as their personal "sex toys." The young men were invariably shocked to learn the real purpose behind their exciting opportunity to visit the States. According to one source, sex acts took place before the altar, with priests wearing their vestments and others dressed as women. The apostle

Paul warned the Ephesians that some "have lost all sensitivity and have abandoned themselves to licentiousness, greedy to practice every kind of impurity."[26] Paul wrote that their activities were too shameful to mention.[27] I know the feeling. But *Penthouse*, which has no shame, spelled it out in lurid detail, complete with pictures of naked priests and boys in bed together and stories of priests defecating on each other in orgies.[28]

If the Episcopalians seem to be leading the way down the slippery path to destruction, plenty of others are lined up to follow. In 1996, seventy-five Presbyterian congregations declared themselves "willing to ordain gay and lesbian persons."[29] Meanwhile, the legislative committee of the United Methodist Church has recommended that the church open the door to homosexual practice by stating it is "unable to arrive at a common mind" on the subject.[30]

The Word of God is not running for reelection. It needs no reconfirmation. It is a fact. No committee vote, no national convention, no trend, no compromise can negate it. Bishop Spong cannot save you on Judgment Day. Those seventy-five Presbyterian congregations will have no power on Judgment Day. The legislative committee of the United Methodist Church will not prevail on Judgment Day. Ten thousand bishops telling you that you are okay will not save your soul. Let no man deceive you. You and you alone will answer for your actions. And you will be judged according to God's Word, not man's word, not the trend of the time, but the eternal Word of God that never changes.

Finally, errant philosophies and unusual manifestations of the spirit are creeping into the church during these latter days.

Errant Philosophies and Unusual Manifestations of the Spirit

Satan's tactics are often a mirror of his own rebellion. He came to Eve in Genesis, saying, "You can be like God."

This temptation prompted his own downfall and he knows its allure. Such teaching is rampant in the traditional Christian church where writers and teachers are invoking New Age philosophies. "We are all gods," they suggest. Like the acceptance of homosexuality within the church, people promote this errant belief in the name of love and of helping discouraged people find self-worth. And extremist teaching in the evangelical Christian church is a frightening parallel to this same dangerous philosophy.

Right now, in the evangelical Christian church, teachers and writers suggest: "You can be like God." After all, didn't Jesus say, "greater things than these shall you do"? Such teaching suggests that all elements of nature are subject to you. Even God Himself must respond if the formula is right. (He cannot resist your power because He has committed Himself to those same laws of faith.) The result is that God is reduced to a genie in a bottle, obligated to our three wishes, no longer Father God with a sovereign will. If God is not sovereign, He is not God!

And that's not all. Other errant philosophies are also creeping into the evangelical church.

The Bible says very plainly not to consort with the dead.[31] But right now, in the evangelical Christian church teachers and writers are proclaiming, "I was inspired to write this book because I talked to my dead brother or my dead sister." It is often proclaimed from the pulpit. You can hear them on America's major religious networks preaching their gospel.

How did it happen? It is deception. It comes from an ignorance and a blindness to the word of God. It happens when we fall in love with the message of another man—not the Son of Man, Jesus. It comes from pride of authorship, when a teacher finds his unique niche and an audience approves. And it comes when experience is elevated above God's own Word. Some of Satan's most effective deceptions come from good experiences. When Satan can't stop you face to face with his "roaring lion" act, he will come forth as "an angel of light" and inspire you to take a doctrine or experience to extreme. You destroy yourself with your own energy and enthusiasm.

Errant philosophies have crept into the evangelical church and so have unusual spiritual manifestations.

The Toronto Blessing and the Discerning of Spirits

Today the evangelical church is filled with questions about the "Toronto Blessing," a spiritual awakening that hit a small congregation of believers calling themselves the Toronto Airport Vineyard Christian Fellowship. It happened in January 1994 and spread across the world.[32]

Laurence J. Barber, senior pastor of Kingsway Baptist Church in Etobicoke, Ontario, went to see for himself.

> At one evening service, I began to feel a heaviness in my body, particularly in my hands and forearms, as though I'd just spent hours sculpting my father's garden hedge with old, manual trimmers . . . As I stood to receive prayer, I was determined not to fall down as some did, wanting to worship Jesus and invite his presence in my own way. But then my legs completely melted, and I fell backwards to the carpet for several minutes. My mind was still alert, wondering, until convulsions started in my stomach, and I began heaving sobs from the pit of my being.
>
> A sense of peace followed my crying in which I knew that I was deeply known, forgiven, and loved in the presence of God . . . Through my experiences at the Toronto Blessing, God has moved me beyond my normal comfort zones. Scripture speaks of many manifestations, like physical stirrings and shakings, that discomfit. Even though I was averse to them at the start, God has used them to humble me, reveal himself, and get my attention.[33]

Audiences were sometimes swept by waves of laughter. Participants defended the experiences, reporting that they were overwhelmed with God's joy, and laughter was only the result. There were thousands of conversions and claims of deliverance from former drug addicts. But soon, even more strange aberrations began to pop up.

Some participants began to bark like dogs, claiming they were under the influence of the Holy Spirit. Some crowed like a rooster, justifying their action by saying, "It's the dawning of a new day!" Toronto church leaders defended the activity, saying that the practice was rare and that it usually involved committed Christians who reported the incidents as very meaningful.

There is a cult of laughter in Japan where worshipers flagellate themselves with long-stemmed roses with thorns and roar with laughter. Take away the roses, and you can't tell the difference between this cult and some charismatic services I've attended.

Critics question the Toronto Blessing, saying it is unscriptural. Some even say it is demonic. Hank Hanegraaff, author of *Christianity in Crisis*, says that the Airport Vineyard represents something "extremely dangerous that could be a road to the occult" because of the focus on subjective and chaotic religious experience."[34] Ultimately, the church in Toronto was disfellowshiped by its own small denomination.[35]

George Byron Koch, pastor of the Church of the Resurrection in West Chicago, Illinois, also went to the Toronto Blessing to see what was occurring. His experience was different from Laurence Barber's.

After a time of praise and worship choruses, announcements, and preaching, an invitation to receive prayer and the Blessing was given, and authorized prayer ministers moved through the crowd, using trademark gestures:

One minister stood behind a couple who wanted prayer for their struggle with infertility. He held his hands above their heads, palms downward, and began pumping vigorously up and down, as if pushing something into them.

Another minister stood in front of a man desiring prayer, resting his left hand on the man while scooping the air in a sideways motion with his right hand, as if pulling something out of the air and into the man's body.

Eventually, this man and others fell to the floor to "rest in the Spirit." As the minister moved on, he occasionally looked back at those on the floor and scooped his hand through the air again, lightly throwing "something" toward them.

Other ministers blew on those being prayed for with a series of quick breaths."[36]

George Koch is an evangelical charismatic who accepts phenomenal gifts of the Holy Spirit, yet he says, "What I found at the Airport Vineyard is an apparent theology of the Holy Spirit, on the part of some ministers and others involved in the worship, that is both unorthodox and potentially much more serious than the phenomena on the fringe of the worship."[37]

Koch says that the churches to which the Blessing has spread "should move quickly to give clear, regular, and thorough teaching on the person of the Holy Spirit to ministers and congregations. It may even be that some of the more bizarre phenomena will flee when those involved acknowledge the person and sovereignty of the Holy Spirit, invite him in, and rebuke and renounce any other 'power' that any individual might personally control."[38]

In these latter days, each Christian needs to ask himself: What is of God? What is a deception? How can I discern the difference? Hear this! If you laugh because you are happy, it can be a manifestation of the Holy Spirit because "the fruit of the Spirit is . . . joy."[39] If you are laughing to become happy, this is a manipulation of emotion, which is witchcraft.

Testing Spiritual Experiences

The first question that must be asked when a supernatural manifestation happens in the church or in the life of a believer is this: "Is the manifestation of the Holy Spirit sensual or ego driven or is it demonic?" Every manifestation comes from one of these three sources.

Many readers may be shocked by the concept that a demon spirit could manifest itself in a church worship environment. Yet some of the most powerful demon manifestations I have ever seen happened while I was preaching the Word of God. In the last chapter I described a man, claiming to be under the influence of a witch, who strode into our church with a loaded pistol, intending to shoot me before the congregation.

I am alive today because of the supernatural power of God to protect and defend the righteous. Satan hates the Word of God! It has the ability to expose him and the power to cast him out of people and out of the church. But make no mistake, Satan can operate in a church worship setting. The Bible says we must "test the spirits."[40]

Some Christians who are caught up in supernatural manifestations will teach that it is a sign of ungratefulness or a lack of faith to question or test what is happening. "Just open up to it," they will urge. "Just receive it."

Hold on. That is plainly contrary to the Word of God. Paul warns the early Christians: "Test all things; hold fast what is good."[41] Discouraging the testing of doctrines and experiences is in violation of Scripture.

Unfortunately when some people don't receive these manifestations, those who do label those who don't "hard to receive." The message? "You're not as spiritual as we are." That is Pharisaism!

Our hearts and emotions are not a valid basis of truth. Proverbs 28:26 states, "He who trusts in his own heart is a fool." Do not rely on what your heart tells you, because it is not reliable. Jeremiah writes in 17:9: "The heart is deceitful above all things, / And desperately wicked; / Who can know it?" I have heard many people justify manifestations based on their emotions, their feelings, or their experiences. This is quicksand. Only the Word of God is a valid foundation for what you believe.

The difficulty with supernatural manifestations in the church is the ability of believers to discern between manifestations. I have been in church services where a bona fide manifestation of the Holy Spirit was occurring in one person's life and on the same pew another person was manifesting a demon spirit.

King Saul is the perfect illustration of this mixture. Saul ruled Israel for forty years. He was a successful military commander. But his life was destroyed because he allowed a mixture of spirits to rule his life. The Bible records the same man prophesying under the influence of the Holy Spirit and later prophesying under the influence of a demon. On the last night of his life, he went to consult the witch in the cave of Endor. The next day he committed suicide on the battlefield.

A mixture of spirits will destroy a man and any church where it's permitted.

Such a mixture will produce two things: confusion and then division. A woman came into my church who had visited one of the highly publicized revivals where manifestations are apparently rampant. Her first Sunday back at Cornerstone Church, she sat in the pew during the song service and shook both hands in the air violently as though swatting at a horde of invisible bees. Although she was in the balcony, I had the ushers escort her out of the service. She was out of order.

Every pastor in every church in America should escort anyone out of the service whose bizarre behavior or manifestations attract attention so exclusively to them that other people are distracted and worship is disrupted. For a pastor to allow anyone's personal manifestation to destroy a worship service is a dereliction of duty.

Because I had the woman ushered out, some who thought of the woman as deeply spiritual were now confused. Others rejected her personally, which is division. I repeat, a mixture of spirits produces confusion and division.

The Bible gives us no liberty to tolerate the intrusion of evil into the church. We are not to be passive; we are not to be neutral. Proverbs 8:13 says, "The fear of the LORD is to hate evil." It is sinful to be neutral toward evil. Jesus said in Matthew 12:30, "He who is not with Me is against Me." There is no room for neutrality.

I have this word of warning for the church: Any "manifestation of the spirit" that prohibits the preaching of the Word of God on a regular basis is not from God. Satan hates the Word. If he can fill the House of God with confusion, created by an aberrant supernatural manifestation, and stop the preaching of the Word of God, he will do it!

George Koch was right when he said churches "should move to give clear, regular, and thorough teaching on the person of the Holy Spirit." A public manifestation is either from the Holy Spirit, which is acceptable, from the person himself—a human, sensual act—or from a demon spirit. The latter two are unacceptable.

Recognizing the Holy Spirit

How then do we recognize the Holy Spirit? There are three clues.

1. If a spirit is used for control or manipulation, **even of a congregation, it is not the Holy Spirit**. The Holy Spirit is God, and no one uses God. One of the great dangers of those who minister in the supernatural realm is the temptation to use spiritual gifts to dominate people. This is the spirit of witchcraft, not the Holy Spirit.

2. **The Holy Spirit is the servant of God the Father and God the Son.** This is an exciting revelation because it gives

such a high value to servanthood. Think of it, one aspect of God Himself is that of a servant. Unfortunately many people today despise the idea of servanthood.

In John 16:13-14 Jesus gives us a glimpse of the Holy Spirit's ministry and activity: "However, when He, the Spirit of truth, has come, He will guide you into all truth; for He will not speak on His own authority, but whatever He hears He will speak; and He will tell you things to come. He will glorify Me, for He will take of what is Mine and declare it to you."

The Holy Spirit does not speak for Himself. He has no message of His own. He only reports to us what He is hearing from God the Father and God the Son. His aim is not to glorify Himself but to bring glory to Jesus Christ. Anything that brings glory to a man will eventually lead to deception. When you hear a soloist sing a mighty song of the church do you say, "What a great singer" or "What a great Savior"? It is proper to "give honor to whom honor is due," but glory alone belongs to God.

3. By His very name, He is holy. In Hebrew, He is the *Spirit of Holiness.* Most "cafeteria Christians," those Christians who pick and chose the doctrines they want, consider holiness optional. It is not!

In Hebrews 12:14 the writer says, "Pursue peace with all people, and holiness, without which no one will see the Lord."

Ministers who manipulate audiences with hype or psychic powers, pretending to do so under the auspices of the Holy Spirit, are in grave danger. Jesus warns in Matthew 12:31–32, "Therefore I say to you, every sin and blasphemy will be forgiven men, but the blasphemy against the Spirit will not be forgiven men. Anyone who speaks a word against the Son of Man, it will be forgiven him; but whoever speaks against the Holy Spirit, it will not be forgiven him, either in this age or in the age to come."

Jesus gives this frightening warning Himself. Beware how we speak about the Holy Spirit and how we represent the Holy Spirit. Jesus uses the word *blasphemy*, the primary meaning of which is "to speak lightly or amiss of sacred things." When you speak lightly or amiss of the Holy Spirit you are by definition practicing blasphemy.

Today, many Christians are far more interested in signs and wonders than they are the preaching of the Cross. Hear this! Signs and wonders do not determine truth! Truth is determined by the Word of God. In John 17:17, Jesus is praying to the Father, and He says, "Your Word is truth." It's not trying to be truth, it is truth.

Signs and wonders will be the forte of the Antichrist. The apostle Paul warns the Thessalonians:

> The coming of the lawless one [the Antichrist] is according to the working of Satan, with all power, signs, and lying wonders, and with all unrighteous deception among those who perish, because they did not receive the love of the truth, that they might be saved. And for this reason God will send them strong delusion, that they should believe the lie, that they all may be condemned who did not believe the truth but had pleasure in unrighteousness.[42]

What happens to the man, the church, or the denomination that will not receive "the love of the truth"? Paul states that God sends them strong delusion. This severe judgment will happen to any person who allows his relationship with God to be controlled by his opinions (which is intellectual idolatry), by his emotions, or by experiences that are not in harmony with the Word of God.

Besides a true knowledge of the Holy Spirit, we have another scriptural antidote to deception in the church in these latter days.

The Antidote to Deception

Christians must maintain an eternal perspective, rather than an earthly one in which our vision is completely limited to the here and now. If all we are expecting from God through salvation are things that belong to this life—prosperity, healing, success, and power—we will never reach our spiritual destiny.

Abraham is the prime example of a believer who maintained an eternal perspective and was not limited to an earthly perspective. In Hebrews 11:9–10, speaking about Abraham, the Bible says:

> By faith he dwelt in the land of promise as in a foreign country, dwelling in tents with Isaac and Jacob, the heirs with him of the same promise; for he waited for the city which has foundations, whose builder and maker is God.

Abraham was in the Promised Land. It was promised to him and given to him by God through a blood covenant, but he never lived there as if he owned it. He always lived in a tent. He never bought a house. Abraham had a vision that extended beyond time into eternity. I believe this is how God expects Christians to be. We are not at home in this world. Our citizenship is in heaven. When we become at home in this world, we become soulless. "Do not love the world or the things in the world. If anyone loves the world, the love of the Father is not in him."[43]

Compare Lot to Abraham. Lot looked toward Sodom, and the next thing we read is that he is not just looking toward Sodom, he is in Sodom; he is living in a house, no longer a tent. He is the type of earthly man of God who ceased to see the eternal and almost lost his soul.

Moses never lost sight of the eternal. Hebrews 11:27 states: "By faith he forsook Egypt, not fearing the wrath of the king; for he endured as seeing Him who is invisible."

The key for victorious Christian living is never to lose sight of the eternal. Look beyond time. Look beyond the burden you carry. Look beyond the present into God's tomorrow. Test the spirits to see if they are of God. Stay rooted in the Scriptures. Work out your own salvation as the Bible says, "in fear and trembling."

PART FOUR

Truth over Deception

Chapter Eleven

Deliverance from Deception

"A ll right," you say. "I give up. Compared to the strict standard of God's Word, America is indeed living in deception." Our government pretends to be democratic but has been co-opted by a clique of willful, anti-Christian bigots, bent on discrediting God's Word and God's people, only to justify their own immorality. Some are bureaucrats. Most are judges, ruling America by fiat.

Think about this! When one branch of the federal government makes the laws, enforces the laws, and interprets the laws, you have a dictatorship.

When Hitler did this in Germany, it was called Nazism. When the Bolsheviks in Russia did this, it was called communism. When America's activist judges do this, it's called "compassion" for a people too incompetent for self-rule.

- When the people of California voted against Proposition 209, stating there would be no more affirmative action, a federal judge overturned the will of the people, calling it unconstitutional.

- As this book goes to print, the Hawaiian Circuit Court has ignored a mountain of evidence that homosexuality is destructive to individuals, families, and societies by striking down a Hawaii state law that preserves marriage as a union between one man and one woman. Once again, the liberal court has ignored the will of the people who voted overwhelmingly in recent elections to support marriage.

The vote of the people no longer matters. Politicians wonder why more American people don't vote. The simple answer is, if the will of the people differs with a federal judge, the will of the people means nothing.

The Battle Against Deception

Three God-given weapons can bring deliverance from deception. Three weapons can cut through the fog. One is praise, one is faith, and the last is action.

It isn't good enough to believe in God's Word and agree that the philosophy of this age has been corrupted. The demons themselves tremble and believe.[1] The Bible says that "faith without works is dead."[2] In His challenging Sermon on the Mount, Jesus didn't call for believers. He didn't say that the wise man would believe Him. He said that the wise man, the man who built his house on a rock, would do what Jesus had commanded. It is what we do that will break Satan's hold on our life and our nation. It is time to go to work.

"But what can I do?" people ask me. "I am one person. How can I stem the tide of corruption in Washington? What can I do to restore marriage values to American homes? I'm not even a preacher, so how am I supposed to influence the direction of my church?"

God does not demand results, He demands obedience and action. He expects us to be faithful. When the angel of the Lord appeared to Gideon he came with this solemn charge, "Go in this might of yours, and you shall save Israel."[3] Gideon was flabbergasted. This angel apparently didn't know who he was talking to.

Gideon was thinking, *If I could do something I would have done it a long time ago. I am too weak. I can't. Our enemies have oppressed us for years. Only God can change that . . . What is this? Why are you telling me to go save my country?* Gideon told the angel that he was the least family member, in the least family, in the least tribe, in all of Israel.

But God said go. And He did not just say go. He said, "Go in your power."

All of us have power. It may not be much. But God wants it. He wants us to use it, to exercise it. He wants us to give it to Him so He can bless it and put it to work. The Bible says that God will judge the nations. We will be judged as Americans. We will have to give account for what happened to our country on our watch. On our watch. What will we say to Him? "We couldn't do anything, so we did nothing"?

He will say, "You had the freedom to petition government. Did you write your senator, your congressman, your judges, your president? You had freedom of the press. What did you publish? You had freedom to speak. There were people dying all around you. What did you say?"

And we will say, "But I didn't think that my letter would make a difference."

God does not expect us to change the world. He does, however, expect us to be obedient.

"I agree," you say. "The American family has been hijacked by a selfish, do-what-makes-you-feel-good, hedonistic philosophy that has already proven its destructiveness by unleashing a wave of venereal disease, unwanted pregnancies, and tragic divorces, poisoning a second and third generation to come. No one even questions that philosophy. As bankrupt as it may be, it is considered the gospel to this end-times generation. To challenge it is to be considered ignorant or reactionary.

"And yes," you say, "even the Christian church has fallen prey to Satan's deceptions. As preposterous as it sounds to people about to enter the twenty-first century, church leaders are reviving ancient forms of idol worship and worship of nature and bringing into the sanctuary rituals and sorcery that God punished Israel for thousands of years ago.

"Yes, America is deceived. But so what? What can I do about it? What can anyone do about it? Anyway, didn't Jesus say something exactly like this would happen?"

There are biblical answers to all of those questions, but first listen closely to the warning Jesus gave that peaceful afternoon on the Mount of Olives two thousand years ago. "Let no man deceive you. Let no man deceive you." Don't let it happen. Stop it!

"Yes," you say, "but how?"

Let's look again at those three areas of deception—in government and public education, in marriages, and in spiritual beliefs—to sum up the situation and find some answers.

Deception in Government

The Declaration of Independence pledges "life, liberty and the pursuit of happiness," yet the Supreme Court defends *Roe v. Wade*. The president of the United States promotes D & X abortion procedures, known as partial birth abortions, where all but the head of a child has exited the mother's body.

The doctor inserts scissors at the base of the skull and literally sucks the brains of the child out with a syringe. The skull collapses and the child dies instantly.

The Clinton Administration says that the D & X procedure is "rare." The subservient liberal media parrot the word *rare* and the American people are deceived. How rare is it?

Recently a defender of this dreadful practice said flat out that it happens in only 1 percent of all abortions.[4] That means it happens 15,000 times a year or forty times every day. That's like a major plane crash, like the recent ValuJet or TWA crashes, every three to five days.

What's your definition of a really rare event? If a ValuJet went down every three days with 120 people on board each time, would you call it rare? Do you think the Federal Aviation Administration would be concerned? Remember, I am using the statistics of the defenders of the practice. It's really a lot worse. America has been deceived!

Abortions are dangerous. Most assume that a visit to an abortion clinic is a routine medical procedure. Wrong! Some women come out of abortion clinics sterile, with a perforated uterus or a permanent colostomy. Some die!

The question for Christians is, What can we do about this?

We have petitioned Congress to no avail. We have stood outside clinics across the nation in quiet protest, holding posters saying, "Abortion Kills Babies" to no avail. The slaughter of the unborn continues.

Politicians live to get reelected. They get reelected with money, and Planned Parenthood gives millions to liberal politicians for radio, TV, and newspaper ads guaranteeing political victory. A picture on the evening news of you standing in silent protest may get your congressman's ear—but not his vote.

I have a solution that will bring the abortion industry to a screeching halt. It cuts to the chase and gets to the bottom line instantly. It stops the flow of money into the abortion mills. Here's the plan.

We are constantly looking for any woman who has been medically injured in an abortion clinic: someone who has been rendered sterile, or someone whose abortion resulted in a punctured uterus or a permanent colostomy.

First, when you find a woman who is willing, and emotionally capable of enduring a lawsuit, file one against every doctor, nurse, and property owner of that abortion clinic.

Here is how it financially guts the abortion industry. First, each person sued has to find an attorney that will be paid by the abortion clinic. Every dollar you force Planned Parenthood or any other pro-abortion agency to spend paying an attorney is one dollar less they will have to use in the slaughter of the unborn. One attorney on our side can cause many expensive attorneys to be necessary for the pro-abortion side.

Second, the defense of any personal injury case in an abortion clinic can easily cost $100,000. Hit them in the wallet!

Third, if you win the case with the right plaintiff the advantage is yours, you can win a personal injury settlement in the millions of dollars. Remember, it took only one case in court to prove R. J. Reynolds Tobacco Company was liable for the cancer of cigarette smokers, which turned that whole industry upside down.

When aggressive Christians begin to file lawsuits by the dozens across America against abortion clinics, the insurance companies will see the danger of this exposure and dramatically raise insurance rates, which will drive many abortion clinics out of business.

Fourth, there is the fear factor. Right now doctors and nurses in abortion clinics use their medical skills to crush the skulls of America's unborn babies and pull their mutilated bodies out in shreds with absolutely no fear of any consequence.

If the righteous will be "as bold as a lion" and cause these doctors, nurses, and property owners to be sued in the courts from coast to coast, the fear of financial ruin will force them to cease and desist.

Deception in Public Education

Then there's deception in public education.

Parents in America believe their children go to school to be educated in the disciplines of reading, writing, and arithmetic. Not so! Other countries are teaching their children this core curriculum; in America our children are being taught how to get in touch with their inner selves and to become subservient pawns of a global society.

As I mentioned in Chapter 4, the NEA has a special "National Charter," granted by Congress, allowing exemption from $1.6 million in real estate taxes on two Washington, D.C., office buildings with an estimated value of $65 million. I repeat, the NEA is a union with a political agenda.

Petition your congressman to strip the NEA of its "National Charter" and force it to pay taxes and to curb its lobbying activities and political campaigning. Get involved in your child's academic life. Go to PTA and school board meetings. Demand to know what your child is being taught. God gave you your children; they do not belong to the state or to the NEA. Do not live like a second-class citizen begging for crumbs. Get informed and demand to be heard!

Another important educational issue is prayer in schools. Every believer in America must realize he or she has a constitutional right to pray in public schools *right now*! It's not necessary for Congress to pass any additional legislation.

I tell the children of my congregation, "If you want to pray in school, do it! If you want to pray over a test, before you get on the bus, at the flagpole, or over your meal, don't let anyone stop you. If a teacher or principal tries to stop you, call the church. We will file a lawsuit that day against that principal, that teacher, and that school district."

You may be thinking, *That's okay for you, pastor. Your church is a megachurch. Our church doesn't have that kind of money.*

Maybe not. Still that needn't stop you. Two excellent organizations—The American Center for Law and Justice and The Rutherford Institute[5]—are willing to aid Christians who have justifiable grievances. We are not alone in this battle.

Always remember, those who do not use their freedoms to defend their freedoms will lose their freedoms.

What can we do about all this deception in government?

Here are seven steps you can take to expose deception in government:

1. Get informed and stay informed! Read your Bible and your newspaper and decide to take action.

2. Stop voting for liberal politicians whose "tax and spend" philosophy has America on the verge of bankruptcy. Stop listening to what politicians say and watch how they vote. Stop being deceived by symbolism over substance. Go into the voting booth and send righteous men and women to represent you locally, in your state, and in Washington, D.C.

3. Write and call your representatives and protest laws that infringe on your freedom to worship and teach your children godly principles.

4. Write and call your representatives and demand impeachment proceedings against federal judges who have hijacked the American Constitution and have taken power from the people to impose their own godless, antireligious agenda. It's time to advance the idea that the judge who violates the Constitution and violates the will of the people has committed a crime as great as that of any bank robber or rapist.

5. Call in and speak out on radio talk shows. Write letters to the editor when a newspaper editorial or column violates Christian beliefs.

6. After tithing to your church, give offerings to ministries that are speaking out "against principalities, against powers, against the rulers of the darkness"[6]—minstries that are taking the lead in fighting for your religious freedom.

7. Consider running for a local position—on your school board or local government—yourself. Or back a friend who will represent your values.

These are all legal, peaceful steps, which we can take to protect our rights. We are in no way disobeying those in authority in this country.

"Okay, pastor, I agree with these steps," you say. "But sometimes things still don't change. Is it ever right to disobey the government with God's blessing?"

Yes—but *always peacefully. There is no room for violence.*

Three Bible illustrations support *peaceful opposition.*

When Pharaoh commanded Egyptian midwives to drown male Hebrew children born to the Israelites, they refused to obey his order and God blessed them for their action.

Pharaoh was the civil authority. What he commanded, God condemned. The midwives disobeyed the Egyptian government with God's blessings.[7]

The second illustration is that of the wise men who went to worship Jesus Christ in Bethlehem's manger. They called on Herod and asked where the infant king was born.

Herod, a murderous, paranoid monster, told them, "When you have found Him, bring back word to me, that I may come and worship Him also." The Bible says the wise men "departed for their own country another way."[8]

Herod was the civil authority. He commanded the wise men to tell him where he might find Jesus. Divinely informed that Herod would kill the infant, they disobeyed the order of civil authority with heaven's blessing.[9]

The third illustration is found in the book of Acts where the apostles were commanded to stop preaching in the name of Christ. They instantly disobeyed civil authority because the government commanded what God condemned.[10]

How does this apply to our society? When the president of the United States gives his support for homosexuals in the military, we stand with the Word of God—not the president.

When the government demands that our children go to public schools where they learn about putting condoms on bananas, lifeboat ethics, and the Rainbow Curriculum, which shows nine year olds how to have anal intercourse, it's time to remind the government that these children belong to us—not them. It's time to force the government to return the public schools to local control.

We can defeat deception in government. We can also defeat deception in our own marriages.

Deception in Marriage

Getting married is easy. Staying married is tough. A boob-tube generation of Americans has been brainwashed by Hollywood's version of the successful marriage. It appears effortless, and if asked to sacrifice, the instant answer is divorce. This is deception!

Marriage is a covenant. In the Bible, a covenant demands that the will of two people die and a sovereign unified will be born. Every marriage conflict comes because one or both in the marriage relationship refuses the crucified life. One or both wants his or her will at all costs. It becomes a rights fight.

We send our children to universities where they study for years to become teachers, doctors, and lawyers. Yet we allow them to leap into marriage, a relationship that creates life, that determines their happiness and well-being, with little or no instruction in how to be a successful wife or husband.

We Are Deceived about Sex in Marriage

Paul's first command to men was "Let each man have his own wife."[11] Sex outside of marriage is absolutely forbidden. There are no excuses. God has zero tolerance. Safe sex is sex with a marriage license.

Paul's second command to man was "Let the husband render to his wife the affection due her."[12] He was referring to sex. Sex is not just for procreation. It's the symphony of the soul for married couples. It's joy. It's giving and sharing. It's tender and holy.

"The affection due her" means the payment of what is due. When you rent a house, the rent is payment of what is due. When you buy a car, the car note is payment of what is due. When you get married, sex is payment of what is due.

Men and women are deceived in marriage about what each other desires. Here are seven steps you can take to combat deception in your marriage:

1. Husbands, love your wives completely, passionately, and romantically. The Bible says, "Husbands, love your wives, just as Christ also loved the church and gave Himself for her."[13] In short, your wife wants a lover.
2. Remain faithful to each other. Women do not want a playboy husband. Playboy husbands will sooner or later come home with AIDS. Men don't want unfaithfulness either. God does not demand that any woman or man stay in a relationship that is repeatedly unfaithful.
3. Husbands, give your wives nonsexual affection. In counseling sessions, I have asked men and women this question. "How would you feel if you knew you could never have sex again with your mate?" Almost all women said, "It's really no big deal if I never have sex again with my husband. But it would be a big deal if we never touched or kissed or romanced again." That's nonsexual affection. Now when I ask men the same question, their eyes bulge, nostrils flare, and sweat pops out on their forehead. "Give up sex? Not in this lifetime!" To ask a man to give up sex is like asking him to give up breathing.
4. Diana and I have something we call O.W.E.D. It means one way every day. Every day both of us do something to remind the other of our love and fidelity one for the other. Try it, you'll like it.
5. If you are both believers, read the Bible together. Do it early in the day.
6. Pray together. The Bible says, "A threefold cord is not quickly broken."[14] A man and his wife, bound together with God in prayer, is an unbreakable union.

7. Pray for each other. It's hard to treat someone unfairly if you are praying for them.

We can overcome deception in marriage. And we can overcome deception in spiritual beliefs.

Deception in Spiritual Beliefs

I mentioned four major areas of spiritual deception in America in chapters 9 and 10: satanism, the goddess movement, clergy homosexuality, and errant philosophy and unusual manifestations of the spirit.

Let me add two others here briefly: denominationalism and racism.

Denominationalism is to approve of a person because he belongs to your brand of church. Denominationalism is idolatry. It's love for who you are, not what you are.

When I hold crusades in the metropolitan areas of America, denominationalism is ever present. If you invite the Baptists, the Pentecostals don't want to come, fearing it will be too formal. If you invite the Pentecostals, the Baptists don't want to come, fearing it will be too emotional. If you invite the Catholics, both Baptists and Pentecostals start quoting Scripture from Revelation 17.

The devil's crowd can come together in absolute unity over anything. God's crowd looks for a reason to reject anything spiritual not born by our respective denominations. The concept seems to be, "If we didn't think of it, neither has God!"

It's time to remove denominational barriers. As long as we agree on the inerrancy of the Word and blood atonement of the Cross, we should stand together in love.

A second area of spiritual deception is racism. Racism is very real in the church. Yet when you read the Word of God there is no white church, black church, brown church, red church, or yellow church. There is only the blood-bought church of Jesus Christ.

Too many churches are looking for members with the "right stuff." We need to open our doors to "whosoever will" with love and compassion. We are saving souls, not skins.

A black man tried to join a very proper all-white church in the deep South. His application for church membership was turned down six times. He stopped applying. After several months, he bumped into the pastor at the local supermarket. The pastor asked him, "Why did you stop applying for church membership?"

The black man responded, "It hurt my feelings at first, but I prayed about it and God said, 'Don't worry about it, I've been trying to get in that church for fifty years and they won't let me in either.'"

Racial barriers must also come down. All Christians are brothers and sisters of the King.

If I could summarize the doctrinal deception within the church in one sentence, it would be this: We have lost the centrality of the Cross of Jesus Christ in our preaching and teaching.

The apostle Paul wrote, "But God forbid that I should boast except in the cross of our Lord Jesus Christ."[15] The church has permission to boast in one thing: the Cross. Not stained glass windows. Not buildings. Not budgets and baptisms. Not pipe organs and prestigious memberships. Just the Cross.

What is the difference between the atheist who hates the church and the church member who says, "I love the church" but won't go to church. There is no difference. The end result is the same, neither goes to church.

What is the difference between the atheist who disbelieves the Bible and the man who says, "I believe the Bible," but he doesn't read the Bible? There is no difference.

The point is this: It isn't what you know, it's how you apply what you know. You can intellectually know the Sermon on the Mount. You can applaud it, but without the Cross you can never apply it.

The Cross is the source, the origin, and the center of every blessing. I am saved through the blood of the Cross of Christ. I am healed by the stripes on His back. The Cross guarantees a peace that surpasses understanding. Without the Cross even the act of prayer is an absolute waste of time.

Without the Cross we have ritual without righteousness, ceremony without change and hype without holiness.

How do you see the Cross?

Most go to the Cross for forgiveness of sin, but we refuse to go to the Cross and accept the crucified life. We do not want to die to self. We do not want to surrender our wills for His will. We are willing for Christ to forgive our sins but won't crucify our flesh.

Do you see the suffering Son of God on the Cross? Who put Him there? God the Father! Why? Because His Son took upon Himself the sin of the world and it pleased God to pour out His wrath upon His own Son.

If it pleased God to pour out His wrath on His own Son because of sin, do you think for one instant God will excuse the sin in your life?

God could care less about your religious activity and your social standing. He is only interested in your relationship to His Son through the Cross. If there is no relationship, He will judge the sin in your life just as He did His own Son. The angels of God will escort you into the fires of an eternal hell.

If praise can puff you up, you are not dead to the flesh. If criticism can hurt you, you are not dead to the flesh. If persecution can stop you, you are not dead to the flesh.

Here are four action points for combating spiritual deception in the church:

1. Read the Bible every day. Underline passages that you fear are neglected or violated in your life.
2. If your church does not teach biblical truth, make an appointment with your pastor and share with him the

verses you have read. If he and the elders don't listen, leave that church. Your commitment is to God, not that church. The apostle Paul commands, "From such turn away."

3. Pay your tithes and offerings. This is obedience to God's Word. If good teaching is supported, it will prosper and grow. If it is not, it will wither and die.

4. If you are a member of a denomination where biblical values are being questioned, voice your opinions at national conventions. If you are not heard, then you must leave that denomination.

We must have an American reformation. Every Bible-believing Christian must make an absolute commitment to live by the standards of righteousness as prescribed in the Word of God.

There must be a new and fresh commitment to personal evangelism that burns like fire in our bones. America cannot be changed from the top down. Giving our money to elect a presidential candidate has proven an absolute fiasco. As soon as they win the nomination, they ignore the moral and spiritual values Christians cherish.

We can take America back one heart at a time, one home at a time, one church at a time, with a grassroots spiritual revolution created by winning the lost to Christ.

When a person gets saved, he becomes a member of an alternative society whose constitution and bylaws are written in the Word of God. We are not just citizens of America. We are citizens of the kingdom of God.

As citizens of the kingdom, we do not condone in our government what God condemns. When the government condones what God condemns, our loyalty is with the Word of God.

Action is one of the weapons God has given us. He expects us to be obedient "doers of the word, and not hearers only."[16] But without faith, all of our works will amount to nothing. With faith, He can use even the little bit we give Him.

Faith Is the Key

With faith Jesus fed five thousand with a handful of loaves and fishes. With faith God kept a prophet, an old woman, and her son alive for months with a handful of oil. It doesn't take much if God is in it. Your letter to the congressman isn't much, but if you will pray, anoint it, and send it with faith, God will multiply its power and use it.

When Gideon told the angel that he was "the least," that God had obviously made a mistake, that he, Gideon, wasn't qualified, the angel answered back, "But God will be with you."

That's the difference. Out of the Holocaust God gave birth to the modern state of Israel. Out of the darkness of an iron curtain, He is bringing revival and healing to many thousands who no one ever thought had a chance.

"Let no man deceive you." Don't let it happen. Believe. Have faith.

Sunshine Through the Fog

Finally, there is one last weapon God has given us to defeat the enemy. It is a spiritual weapon that can only be appreciated by those who have felt its power in time of crisis. When there is darkness, confusion, defeat, and deception, the Bible teaches God's people to praise Him, literally to rejoice.

Jesus said, "Blessed are you when they revile and persecute you, and say all kinds of evil against you falsely for My sake. Rejoice and be exceedingly glad, for great is your reward in heaven, for so persecuted they the prophets who were before you."[17]

The Israelites once experienced a time of great decep-

DELIVERANCE FROM DECEPTION

tion, parallel to what America is experiencing today. Their government became corrupted. Their youth intermarried with other tribes and violated all of God's many tender and merciful instructions for having a happy home. Their worship turned into idolatry and satanism.

Then someone rediscovered God's Word and began to read it. Soon the whole nation began to publicly read what the prophets had written. Great fear swept the nation as they realized their deception and the extent of their sin against God.

"What can we do?" they asked. "Should we divorce our heathen wives and find new ones? What a mess we are in."

The prophet Nehemiah stood up and called for attention. "This is no time for despair," he said. "This is a time to rejoice. We are rediscovering God's Word. We can't solve everything in one day. But we have begun the journey out of deception. Go home, prepare a feast. No one should work. It is a holiday. And *may the joy of the LORD be your strength!*"[18]

I don't know your situation. I don't know what is happening in your marriage, what is happening to your children, or what is happening in your church. I don't know what will happen to America, whether she will once again find her way or whether she will soon slip into the abyss that has engulfed so many great civilizations and poisoned so many noble ideals.

But I do know my Redeemer. He said He would be with you to the end of the world. He said He would never forsake you. If you have found Him, if you have given your life to Him, you and your family can be saved from the destruction to come.

The Bible makes it very clear that warnings of the end times are meant to give God's people an advantage, an edge. "Therefore comfort one another with these words."[19] Do what you can, be obedient to His Word. He may yet spare our nation. But even if He does not, even if we as a people are engulfed by our own sins and destroyed

235

by the spirit of our days of deception, rejoice in God, in His salvation, in His protection.

"Look up and lift up your heads, because your redemption draws near."[20]

Notes

Chapter 1

1. 1 Kings 18:13.
2. 1 Kings 19:4.
3. Rush Limbaugh, *The Limbaugh Letter*, (New York: EFM, February 1996), 5.
4. Tom Squitieri, *USA Today*, 27 November 1996, A1.
5. Report of the 1994 Senate Hearings.
6. This information came to me from a former senior White House staffer who had studied this issue for five years. According to the staffer, since 1986 the IRS has been recommending to the White House that all religious organizations lose their tax-exempt status with the exception of churches and religious orders as defined by the IRS themselves. Billy Graham's evangelistic organization, for example, would be out of business. Curiously, only days after this conversation, a government agency called for the revocation of the tax-exempt status of the Christian Coalition.
7. H. B. London Jr., "The Pastor's Weekly Briefing," *Focus on the Family*, 4, no. 26, 28 June 1996.
8. Bob Woodward, *The Choice*, (New York: Simon and Schuster, 1996), 131.
9. "The Pastor's Weekly Briefing," 2.
10. "The Case Against Clinton," *Human Events*, 16 August 1996, 23.
11. Ibid. This quote was taken from a transcript of the telephone conversations between Gennifer Flowers and Bill Clinton as released to the *Star* in a New York press conference in January 1992.
12. Jack W. Germond and Jules Whitcover, *Mad as Hell: Revolt at the Ballot Box 1992* (New York: Warner Books, 1993), 420-421.
13. Taken from a personal interview with the White House aide.
14. "Stumbling into a Combat Zone," *Time*, 3 June 1996, 26.
15. Center for America Values, Box 91180, Washington D.C., 20090-1180, *The Clinton Record*.
16. Matt. 10:25-26.
17. See Matt. 14.
18. Luke 13:32.
19. Ps. 97:10.
20. Matt. 12:30.
21. James 4:4.
22. Anthony Read and David Fisher. *The Fall of Berlin* (New York: Da Capo Press, 1992), 7.
23. Ibid.
24. Gitta Sereny, *Albert Speer: His Battle with the Truth*. (London: MacMillan, 1995), 27.
25. Read and Fisher, 32.
26. Ibid, 294.
27. Eph. 5:6-13.

28. Cal Thomas, syndicated column, "Whitewater verdict reveals crime cover-up," *The Conservative Chronicle*, 3 June 1996.
29. Ibid.
30. Limbaugh, 4.
31. Thomas.
32. White House Press Conference, 22 April 1994.
33. Limbaugh, 5.
34. Ibid, 4.
35. Ibid, 5.
36. Ibid, 5.
37. Taken from an interview with a former White House staffer.
38. The House Government Reform and Oversight Committee issued their finding that President Clinton "engaged in an unprecedented misuse of the executive power, abuse of executive privilege and obstruction of numerous investigations into the travel office." The Committee said travel director Billy Ray Dale and his colleagues were dismissed so that Harry Thomason, a Hollywood producer friend of the Clintons, and Catherine Cornelius, a distant cousin of the president, could seek a share of the government's travel business. ("Clinton accused of leading wide travel-office cover-up" *Arizona Republic*, 19 September 1996, A3.)
39. Doug Bandow, *The Conservative Chronicle*, 26 June 1996, 4.
40. James B. Stewart, *Bloodsport* (New York: Simon Schuster, 1996), 260.
41. Limbaugh, 15.
42. Ibid, 5.
43. Ibid, 5.
44. Ibid, 5.
45. Ibid, 5.
46. Bandow, 5.
47. Limbaugh, 15.
48. Bandow, 4.
49. Jer. 3:9.
50. Ps. 12:8
51. Rev. 22:15.

Chapter 2
1. Stewart, 260.
2. Ibid. (James Stewart, a journalist who was in contact with Hillary Clinton and originally encouraged by her to write a book, makes a rather remarkable statement in his book *Bloodsport*. Instead of saying that no one can prove they were, in fact, having an affair, Stewart writes the opposite, saying that no one could prove that they weren't. Stewart adds that both Vince and Hillary's friends say they "weren't the type.")
3. Gary Aldrich, *Unlimited Access* (Washington: Regnery, 1996), 70.
4. "Inaccuracies Regarding Foster's Death," Microsoft Internet Explorer, 18 June 1996, 3.

5. "*60 Minutes*' Report on the Death of Vince Foster," House of Representatives, 26 October 1995, H11373.
6. Testimony of Mr. Burton, congressman from Indiana. House of Representatives, 26 October 1995, 3.
7. "Inaccuracies Regarding Foster's Death," Microsoft Internet Explorer, 1.
8. Chris Ruddy, *Tribune-Review*, Pittsburgh, 16 June 1995. (Gonzalez, interviewed long after the event, told a reporter that he thought the second wound was in the forehead. But after examining photos, Gonzalez told investigators for the independent counsel that trauma to the neck would be consistent with what he saw.)
9. "Inaccuracies Regarding Foster's Death," Microsoft Internet Explorer, 5.
10. "Inaccuracies Regarding Foster's Death," Microsoft Internet Explorer, 1.
11. Stewart, 260.
12. Aldrich, 77.
13. Testimony of Mr. Burton, congressman from Indiana, 4, and Microsoft Internet Explorer, 4.
14. Chris Ruddy, *Tribune-Review*, Pittsburgh, 10 December 1995.
15. Aldrich, 77.
16. "Witness Tampering," Microsoft Internet Explorer, 18 June 1996.
17. *New York Times*, as reported in the *Arizona Republic*, 28 August 1996, A6.
18. The obvious question was, How had Foster gotten such a gun? Serial numbers showed that one part of the gun was purchased in Seattle, the other in Indianapolis. Was this a professional hit?
19. "*60 Minutes*' Report on the Death of Vince Foster," House of Representatives, 26 October 1995, H11373.
20. "Inaccuracies Regarding Foster's Death," Microsoft Internet Explorer, 3.
21. Testimony of Mr. Burton, congressman from Indiana.
22. According to one account, Foster had a Swiss bank account that "was emptied of $2.7 million a week before he died." Microsoft Internet Explorer, "Inaccuracies Regarding Foster's Death," 2.
23. *Esquire* magazine interview.
24. Ps. 10:2,8,12.

Chapter 3
1. Jerome Burn, editor, *Chronicles of the World* (London: Longman Group UK Ltd., 1989), 87.
2. Matt. 4:9.
3. Pat Robertson, *The New World Order* (Dallas: Word Publishers, 1991), 115.
4. Ibid, 35.
5. Peter Padfield, *Himmler* (New York: Henry Holt & Co., 1990), 148.

6. Francis Miller, *The Complete History of World War Two* (Chicago: Readers Service Bureau, 1945), 5.
7. John Barron, *Operation Solo* (Washington: Regnery, 1996), 54.
8. Robertson, 14.
9. Ibid, 7.
10. Ibid, 53-54.
11. Randall Baer, *Inside the New Age Nightmare* (Lafayette, La.: Huntington House, 1992), 13.
12. Ibid, 17.
13. London, "The Pastor's Weekly Briefing," 1-2.
14. Robertson, 112
15. Willard Cantelon, *The Day the Dollar Dies* (Jacksonville, Fla.: Logos International, 1973).
16. Robertson, 119–120.
17. Hag. 2:8.
18. Robertson, 177.
19. Gallup GO 84148, September 1992.
20. Matt. 10:22.
21. Robertson, 221.
22. John Feder, *Pagan America* (Lafayette, La.: Huntington House, 1993), 228.
23. Robertson, 95.
24. Dan. 7:7-8, 19-20.
25. Rev. 13:3.
26. Dan. 8:25 KJV.
27. See Matt. 24:15-19.
28. Barron, 54.
29. Rev. 13:6 NIV.

Chapter 4

1. James J. Kilpatrick, syndicated column, 27 December 1995.
2. Christian Coalition Special Action Alert, 10 May 1996 (taken from the *Washington Times*, 27 April 1996), 1.
3 *Conservative Chronicle*, vol. 11, 10 January 1996, 4.
4. Gen. 1:26.
5. "'Men Are Easy,' Judge says." *Arizona Republic*, 16 August 1996, A13.
6. Isa. 40:23.
7. Prov. 22:28.
8. Rom. 13:1.
9. Dan. 2:20.
10. Prov. 21:1.
11. Ps. 75:6–7.
12. Dan. 5:4–6.
13. Num. 11:33.
14. Ps. 107:2.
15. Prov. 28:4.
16. Jer. 33:3.

17. James 4:2.
18. Matt. 16:19.
19. Luke 10:19.
20. Ex. 19:6.

Chapter 5
1. See Gen. 31:1-32.
2. Josh. 6:26.
3. John 4:22.
4. Prov. 17:13.
5. Ex. 20:12, see also Eph. 6:2.
6. Deut. 27:20.
7. Zech. 5:3.
8. Ex. 20:4–5.
9. Matt. 12:30.
10. Larry Kahaner, *Cults That Kill* (New York: Warner Books, 1988).
11. Ps. 9:17.
12. Roger J. Vaughan and Edward W. Hill, ed. by Michael Barker, *Banking on the Brink* (Washington: Washington Post Co. Briefing Books, 1992).
13. Hos. 7:9.

Chapter 6
1. Feder, 21.
2. Matt. 12:35.
3. Gen. 1:28.
4. 1 Cor. 7:4.
5. Eph. 4:15.
6. See 1 Tim. 5:8.

Chapter 7
1. 1 Tim. 5:8 KJV.
2. 2 Thess. 3:10.
3. *Conservative Chronicle*, vol. 11, 13 March 1996, 23.
4. Rush Limbaugh, The Limbaugh Letter, (New York: EFM, May 1993), 11.
5. Ex. 12:3.
6. Ex. 33:11.
7. Gen. 7:1.
8. Luke 16:19–31.
9. Ps. 119:11.
10. Luke 6:46 KJV.
11. Gen. 27:33.
12. Ps. 101:3.
13. Eph. 5:25.
14. Deut. 33:4–5.
15. Num. 14:11–12 NIV.
16. See Num. 14:13-19.
17. Deut. 11:21.

18. "Seven-Year Cold," *Life*, 1982.
19. Rom. 5:8.

Chapter 8

1. J. Hamilton, *Where Now Is Thy God?* (Grand Rapids, Mich.: Revell, 1969), 67.
2. John 1:11.
3. Luke 23:4, 14; John 18:38.
4. John 16:33.
5. Eph. 4:15.

Chapter 9

1. 2 Cor. 11:14.
2. See Matt. 25:32–46.
3. Johanna Michaelson, *Like Lambs to the Slaughter* (Eugene, Ore.: Harvest House Publishers), 267.
4. Matt. 25:41.
5. Kahaner, 218.
6. Isa. 14:13.
7. Matt. 7:15.
8. Gen. 3:1.
9. Luke 4.
10. *Los Angeles Times*, 19 October 1988, 21.
11. John 3:18.
12. 1 Peter 5:8.
13. Acts 2:21.
14. John 8:36.
15. Rev. 12:10.
16. Kahaner, back jacket of book.
17. Ibid, 183–185.
18. Bob Larson, *Satanism: The Seduction of America's Youth* (Nashville, Tenn.: Thomas Nelson Publishers, 1989), 29.
19. Ibid, 29.
20. Ibid, 30.
21. Ibid, 109. Used by permission.
22. 1 Tim. 6:12.
23. Isa. 54:17.
24. John 10:10.
25. Matt. 12:30.
26. Matt. 28:18–20.
27. James 4:7.

Chapter 10

1. John 8:44.
2. Matt. 24:4.
3. Thomas Oden, "Encountering the Goddess at Church." *Christianity Today*, 16 August 1993, 18.

4. Timothy Morgan, "Re-Imaging Labeled 'Reckless.'" *Christianity Today*, 18 July 1994, 49.
5. Susan Cyre, "Fallout Escalates Over 'Goddess' Sophia Worship." *Christianity Today*, 4 April 1994, 74.
6. James R. Edwards, "Earthquake in the Mainline." *Christianity Today*, 14 November 1994, 42.
7. "Re-Imagining God," Friday Plenary, Tape 2-2, Side A.
8. Ibid.
9. Edwards, 39.
10. Edwards, 43.
11. Edwards, 40.
12. Edwards, 43.
13. Edwards, 42.
14. Prov. 8:23.
15. Gen. 3:1, emphasis mine.
16. Morgan, 49.
17. Rom. 1:22-27.
18. ENI, "US Methodists reaffirm ban on promoting homosexuality," *The Episcopal News Service*, 23 May 1996, 13-14.
19. James Solheim, "Preliminary hearing held in trial," *The Episcopal News Service*, 12 December 1995, 10.
20. The General Convention Edition of United Voice, 25 August 1994.
21. ENI, "US Methodists reaffirm ban on promoting homosexuality," 8.
22. James Solheim, "Seattle dean blesses relationship of gay couple." *The Episcopal News Service*, 23 May 1996, 15-16.
23. Ex. 4:24-26.
24. 2 Tim. 3:4-5.
25. "The Boys From Brazil," *Penthouse*, December 1996, 6.
26. Eph. 4:19, paraphrased.
27. Eph. 5:12.
28. *Penthouse*, 74.
29. ENI, "Homosexuality issue to dominate Presbyterian agenda," *The Episcopal News Service*, 25 June 1996, 41.
30. ENI, "US Methodists reaffirm ban on promoting homosexuality."
31. Deut. 18:11.
32. Actually, the phenomena began in Lakeland, Florida, almost a year earlier. *Charisma* magazine chose to publicize the Toronto experience and so it was dubbed by their writers as the "Toronto Blessing." The name stuck.
33. Laurence J. Barber, "How I Was Blessed," *Christianity Today*, 11 September 1995, 26.
34. James A. Beverly, "Toronto's Mixed Blessing," *Christianity Today*, 11 September 1995, 24.
35. "Toronto Church Ousted From Vineyard," *Charisma*, February 1996, 12.
36. George Byron Koch, "Pumped and Scooped," *Christianity Today*, 11 September 1995, 25, adapted from the Spiritual Counterfeits Project Newsletter, Berkeley, California, Spring 1995.

37. Ibid.
38. Ibid.
39. Gal. 5:22.
40. 1 John 4:1.
41. 1 Thess. 5:21.
42. 2 Thess. 2:9–12.
43. 1 John 2:15.

Chapter 11
1. James 2:19.
2. James 2:20.
3. Judg. 6:14.
4. "The Pastor's Weekly Briefing," *Focus on the Family,* 4, no. 48, 29 November 1996, 2.
5. If you want to report a violation of your religious rights or are seeking information about legal issues pertaining to religion, you can write to the American Center for Law and Justice, P.O. Box 64429, Virginia Beach, VA 23467, (757) 226-2489, or The Rutherford Institute, P.O. Box 7482, Charlottesville, VA 22906, (804) 978-3888 to report an incident or (800) 441-3473 to request information from the institute's radio show, *Freedom Under Fire,* about a particular legal issue. The Rutherford Institute can also be reached by e-mail—tristaff@rutherford.org—or check out its Web site at http//www.rutherford.org.
6. Eph. 6:12.
7. See Ex. 2.
8. Matt. 2:8, 12.
9. Matt. 2:12.
10. Acts 4:18–31.
11. 1 Cor. 7:2.
12. 1 Cor. 7:3.
13. Eph. 5:25.
14. Eccl. 4:12.
15. Gal. 6:14.
16. James 1:22.
17. Matt. 5:11–12.
18. Neh. 8:9–10, paraphrased.
19. 1 Thess. 4:18.
20. Luke 21:28.

ABOUT THE AUTHOR

Dr. John Hagee, author of the best-sellers *From Daniel to Doomsday, His Glory Revealed, Beginning of the End, Day of Deception,* and *Final Dawn Over Jerusalem,* is the founder and senior pastor of the seventeen-thousand member Cornerstone Church in San Antonio, Texas. He is also the president of Global Evangelism Television, which broadcasts Pastor Hagee's daily and weekly television and radio programs throughout the United States and around the world. John and his wife, Diana, have five children: Tish, Christopher, Christina, Matthew, and Sandy.

OTHER TITLES BY JOHN HAGEE

The Revelation of Truth

"There were no cameras in Jesus' day," writes Dr. John Hagee, "and though artists and sculptors abounded in Roman culture, we have no definite record of His earthly image. But as we look at God's revelations of truth in Genesis, you will see Jesus."

In this study of the myriad portraits contained in the first book of the Bible, you will come to know the Savior far better than you could know Him from studying His image in a photograph or video. Just as the mosaic image on the cover of this book is composed of scores of individual pictures, so the pictures within Scripture combine to create a living, loving portrait of the Savior. As Pastor John Hagee guides you through each epoch of history, you will be thrilled to know that one thing has remained constant throughout the ages: God loves mankind, and He yearns to redeem men and women.

ISBN 0-7852-6967-3 • Hardcover • 320 pages

From Daniel to Doomsday

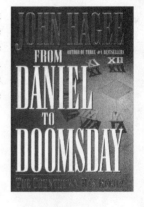

In his most provocative and comprehensive book about end times, Dr. John Hagee counts down the prophetic minutes from the time of Daniel through the twentieth century. While Wall Street revels in economic euphoria and proclaims that all is well, *From Daniel to Doomsday* reports on the rumblings of the coming Rapture in such current world events as:

- The collapse of the Asian and Pacific Rim economies
- The expanding threat of cyber terrorism and germ warfare
- The continuing moral decay among national leaders
- The devaluing of human life through the practice of abortion

The Day of Apocalypse. The End of the World. Call it what you will, but with the new millennium, people's thoughts have turned toward Christ's final reckoning. *From Daniel to Doomsday* not only interprets the times but also unveils what has yet to occur before that fateful moment when every unredeemed individual must face God on Judgment Day.

ISBN 0-7852-6966-5 • Hardcover • 320 pages
ISBN 0-7852-6818-9 • Paperback • 320 pages

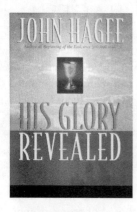

His Glory Revealed

This unique and stirring seven-week devotional explores the feasts of Israel: The Feast of Passover, The Feast of Unleavened Bread, The Feast of Firstfruits, The Feast of Pentecost, The Feast of Trumpets (Rosh Hashanah), The Feast of Atonement (Yom Kippur), and The Feast of Tabernacles. In *His Glory Revealed*, Dr. Hagee helps you understand not only the meaning of these seven feasts but also the prophetic significance of each festival. These daily readings will also give you a better appreciation for the incredible complexity and majestic simplicity of God's divine seven-thousand-year plan for mankind.
ISBN 0-7852-6965-7 • Hardcover • 192 pages